D0874394

GEORGES VAN VREKHEM

THE MOTHER

THE STORY OF HER LIFE

The Mother

The Story of Her Life

Georges Van Vrekhem

Acknowledgements

The author sincerely thanks R.Y. Deshpande (India), Alan Herbert (UK), Lynda Lester (USA), Jyoti Sobel (France) and Carel Thieme (The Netherlands) for the care with which they read the manuscript and for their corrections and suggestions.

Original English edition published in India by Rupa & Co. in 2000

ISBN 978-1478197249

This story of the Mother's life is dedicated to Akash, now eight years old, for when he will be able to read and understand it.

George Uncle

Contents

List of Illustrations

The world unknowing, for the world she stood …

Sri Aurobindo, *Savitri*, p. 13

One shall descend and break the iron Law,
Change Nature's doom by the lone spirit's power.
A limitless Mind that can contain the world,
A sweet and violent heart of ardent calms
Moved by the passions of the gods shall come.
All mights and greatnesses shall join in her;
Beauty shall walk celestial on the earth,
Delight shall sleep in the cloud-net of her hair,
And in her body as on his homing tree
Immortal Love shall beat his glorious wings …
She shall bear Wisdom in her voiceless bosom, Strength shall be
with her like a conqueror's sword And from her eyes the Eternal's
bliss shall gaze.
A seed shall be sown in Death's tremendous hour,
A branch of heaven transplant to human soil;
Nature shall overleap her mortal step;
Fate shall be changed by an unchanging will.

Sri Aurobindo, *Savitri*, p. 346

Author's Notes

1. The quotations from works of the Mother are from the Centenary Edition of the Collected Works of the Mother (CWM). The quotations from the works of Sri Aurobindo are from the Sri Aurobindo Birth Centenary Library (SBCL), except for those from his epic *Savitri*, which are from the revised edition of 1993 (CWSA), or where otherwise indicated.
2. The -ize and -ization spelling has been used throughout.
3. The English translations of texts originally spoken or written in French were checked and corrected where it was found to be necessary.

Part One:

Convergent Roads

Mirra Alfassa at the age of 11

1.

Growing Up in Paris

When I was a child and happened to complain to my mother ...
she would ask me if I was under the illusion that I was born for
my own satisfaction. 'You are born to realize the highest ideal,' she
would say and send me packing.[1]

– The Mother

Daughter of the Middle East

Paris in the 1870s, and for some decades to come, was the vibrant cultural and political capital of the world. All countries looked up to its celebrities and its trend-setting creations on canvas, on the stage and in music. Everybody dreamed of visiting, if only once in a lifetime, its exhibitions and museums, its monuments, boulevards and picturesque neighborhoods, its cafés, and the crowded nightlife with the café-concerts, theatres and dancing halls.

The creations of the Parisian *haute couture*, then of quite recent origin, and of the new Parisian department stores such as *La Samaritaine* and *Au Bon Marché*, were worn and imitated wherever men, and especially women, dressed in the Western way. The French language was spoken in the upper circles of all European countries and used as the global diplomatic language. And although France had suffered a traumatic defeat at the hands of the new and threateningly ambitious Germany in 1870, its capital remained a hotbed and testing ground for all kinds of political theories and convictions, from some of the crankiest to many that would help shape history.

Such was the metropolis where she, who would become known as 'the Mother,' was born on 21 February 1878 as Blanche Rachel Mirra Alfassa.* The propitious event took place in the parental house at 41, Boulevard Haussmann, named after Georges, baron Haussmann, who had recently given Paris its now world-famous new look. The house still exists, just opposite the department store *Au Printemps* and close to the *Opéra*.

Mirra, as the girl would be called, was not French at the time of her birth. Her father was Turkish and her mother Egyptian, and there are indications that both were also of Jewish descent. They had emigrated to France a few months before Mirra's birth and would become French citizens only in 1890, when the head of the family would become naturalized through a presidential decree.

Her father, Maurice Moise Alfassa, was born in 1843 in the Turkish city of Adrianople, now Edirne; he was a banker by profession. Her mother, Mathilde Alfassa née Ismalun, was born in 1857 in the Egyptian city of Alexandria; she too stemmed from a family of bankers. 'The Mother's mother said that she had wanted to marry that gentleman because he had a lot of books! She thought that with a library that big in the house she would never get bored.'[2] They married in 1874 and went to live in Maurice's home town. There their first child, a boy, died from a vaccination against smallpox. A second boy, Mattéo, was born in Alexandria in 1876; he probably got his name from the Italian family into which Mathilde's sister, Elvire, had married. (This was decidedly a family with international ramifications.) Mirra was the third child. There would be no other.

In later years the Mother sometimes reminisced about her parents. Her father seems to have been a rather easy-going man with wonderful health and an unusual stability of character, more interested in practical things than in philosophical or religious abstractions. He was so strong, the Mother once said, that he could bring a horse to its knees simply by pressing his legs into its sides. He had studied in Austria and knew French, German, English, Italian, Turkish and Egyptian. He had, moreover, an uncommon gift for numbers.

Mirra's mother was an intelligent but very strong-minded woman

---

* At 10:15 a.m. according to the birth certificate.

– at one time compared by her daughter to 'an iron rod' – thoroughly influenced by the spirit of the nineteenth century and by the ideals of the Enlightenment and the French Revolution. She was a confirmed materialist and atheist to whom only what one touches and sees was important, but she believed in unending progress and self-perfection. After her first baby had died, the aspiration had grown in her that her children, whom she loved with a kind of stoical love, would become the best in the world.

Why did Maurice and Mathilde leave Egypt and emigrate to France? Some say that Mathilde refused to curtsy before the Khedive, the Egyptian Viceroy of the Ottoman Empire, to which Egypt had belonged since 1517 (and would belong only for a few more years to come). If true, there must surely have been a very strong motive for such behavior towards the highest authority in the land, even from strong-minded Mathilde. The late 1870s were troubled years in Egypt, where the nationalist movement had gained ground since the opening of the Suez Canal in 1869, and there were signs of revolt against foreigners and the Anglophile Khedive, Tewfik Pasha. Whether this explosive political situation was related to the facts that forced Maurice and Mathilde out of the country, remains unknown.

Their settling down in Paris was prepared by a remarkable woman, namely Mira Ismalun née Pinto,[3] Mathilde's mother. She was one of the very first emancipated Egyptian women and dared to travel abroad unaccompanied. She became a kind of celebrity at all the West European 'in' places of the period and befriended countless famous people, charming them with her wit and her glamorous exotic attire. She was unusually broad-minded, so much so that she let her daughters choose their husband; nationality and religion were no bar. And she had a keen eye for business, for she provided the Egyptian princesses in their harem and other secluded ladies with jewels and dresses from Europe, and had their portraits painted by the best French artists. Mirra would grow very close to this grandmother and always remember her with affection.

However, an interesting library does not seem to be a guarantee of a happy marriage. Maurice and Mathilde grew apart and lived practically separate lives in their *hôtel** at 62 Boulevard Haussmann, where they had moved after Mirra's birth. (Grandmother Mira was their neighbor.) The children remained attached to their father. He told them thrilling adventure stories – always with himself in the role of the hero – and he let his birds fly freely about the room which had become his private domain. He also took Mattéo and Mirra for walks in the gardens of the Tuileries, in the Bois de Boulogne or the Botanical Garden, or on a visit to an interesting museum such as the Louvre or the Guimet Museum.

And he took them to the circus, which he loved. At the time there were no less than five permanent circuses in Paris – *Cirque Raney, Grand Cirque Sidoli, Cirque d'Hiver, Cirque Fernando* ... and some of the performers were known by the young and the old alike. There was Miss La-La, twirling high above the heads of the anxious spectators hanging by her teeth; there were the bareback riders, trapeze artists and jugglers; and there were the clowns, Footit and Chocolat, and the famous Boum-Boum. Many of them have been immortalized in the paintings of Degas, Renoir, Toulouse-Lautrec, Seurat, Picasso, and other masters.

Mirra grew up in that bourgeois family, so typical of the nineteenth century. 'The Mother's parents lived the life of the rich, with horses and carriages.'[4] She had an English nanny, Miss Gatliffe, who made Mirra scream in protest against the cold baths that she forced her to take. There were family visits and luncheons for which one had to dress up and to behave in style. The house, on one of the chic boulevards, had a salon with that piece of furniture indispensable to every bourgeois family, a piano. The family members belonged to the banking world and other respectable branches of society. One cousin would become Director of the Louvre, and Mattéo himself became Governor-General of French Equatorial Africa.

But then the Panama Scandal erupted, 'the greatest financial disaster in France for 200 years,' rocking the country's financial institutions and galvanizing public opinion. Ferdinand, Count de Lesseps, having successfully completed the Suez Canal in 1869, wanted to create a passage through the land mass of the Americas by digging a canal through the Panama isthmus. This would again make the globe a smaller place and

---

* The French word *hôtel* also means a palatial building, mostly on a large boulevard.

forever leave the already famous engineer's imprint on it. Yet things went wrong financially: there was mishandling of funds, fraud and a whole series of cover-ups by the governmental authorities and the press. Count de Lesseps and other prominent persons, among them Gustave Eiffel, the builder of the famous tower named after him, were brought to justice. And the customers of Maurice Alfassa's *Banque Ottomana* lost all the money they had invested in the project, as did thousands of other small savers.

'The Mother's papa did bad business and all of a sudden went completely bankrupt ... Then life became difficult of course. And as he was a very honest man, instead of making himself scarce, as did many others, he sold everything he owned to pay off the debts of his bank, and the family situation changed considerably for the worse ... Now that her father was ruined, they no longer had horse and carriage, and when the family went to visit friends, they had to go on foot instead of in a carriage. And the Mother would arrive there with dirty shoes, there was dirt on her little ankle-boots, and the other children mocked at her because her ankle-boots were dirty as she had to go on foot.'[5] It must have been at this time that the enterprising Mathilde kept chickens to sell the eggs, and got in trouble with the revenue office because of non-payment of taxes.

On the whole, however, Mirra seems to have had a sheltered childhood. Her mother would often say that she was a rather taciturn girl, and she herself would later concede that she was not an easy character. Although Mathilde wanted her children to be the best of the best and to realize the highest ideals, she was intelligent enough not to force them and by forcing them to thwart their mental growth. Mirra learned to read only when she was seven years old and after her brother had put her to shame because of her ignorance, and she agreed to go to school only at the age of nine. In the meantime her interests proved to be many-sided. 'I remember having learnt to play tennis when I was eight. It was a passion.'[6] She started drawing and painting at that age, and learned to play the piano and to sing. She also played with one of the Navajo Indians brought to France by Buffalo Bill for his Wild West Show in 1889, the year of the great Paris Exhibition and the completion of, at that time, the still highly controversial Eiffel Tower. From this

Red Indian friend she learned, among other things, how to tell the distance of footsteps and carriages by putting her ear to the ground.

So many were her interests that she was scolded by her severe mother for her apparent lack of deeper, permanent concerns; she never would be good at anything, said Mathilde. Thus Mirra was promoted to the legion of the youthful good-for-nothings who, in adulthood, changed the world.

Mathilde sent her daughter to a private school for the children of the better-off class, deeming the public schools not suitable for a daughter of hers. The school enjoyed a high reputation and had a staff of excellent teachers. Mirra was always among the first in her class, simply because she wanted to understand the knowledge taught her instead of passively receiving it and memorizing it by rote. It was in that school that she wrote, in 1893, the first preserved text from her hand, a short essay entitled *Le sentier de Tout-à-l'heure* (The path of later on). It contains the prophetic exhortation: 'Come … to the beautiful, the good, the true; do not be misled by indolence and weakness; don't fall asleep in the present: come to the future.'[7] She studied at that school from 1887 to 1895.

In the meantime her brother Mattéo was preparing for his entrance examination to the *École Polytechnique,* one of the Parisian super schools that gave France its best civil and military mathematicians and engineers. In addition to his successful studies at that institution, Mattéo would also graduate in arts from the not less prestigious *École Normale Supérieure.* Mirra was very close to her brother, who was eighteen months older. When once their father put him across his knee to slap his bottom, she stood up for him and said, with all the dignity she could muster: 'Papa, if you ever do this again, I'll leave this house at once!' But she could also tease Mattéo, well aware that he had a terrible temper and would get furious at the slightest provocation. 'My brother … was extremely excitable in his boyhood. I was an expert in making him angry. Both of us were fond of each other, but when he was angry he lost all control of himself,'[8] almost killing her on three occasions. When he was warned by his mother, who adored him, that the next time he might really kill Mirra, he exerted his strong self-control and never did it again.

When Mattéo was preparing for that formidable entrance examination, Mirra studied together with him, for she was that exception who found numbers and mathematics fascinating. When she came up with the solution of a problem Mattéo was unable to solve, his astonished tutor exclaimed that it was the girl who should sit for the examination. Later, when talking about her youth, the Mother said that at the age of thirteen or fourteen she read all the books in her father's library, some eight hundred or so. In that way her keen intelligence, so necessary for the great task awaiting her, developed and sharpened, and she acquired the stylistic mastery over the French language that she would show all through her life.

The Early Sadhana*

All this was part of Mirra's life on the surface – verifiable facts of what people call the everyday life, there for anyone to see. But all along she lived an intense parallel life nobody knew about – and nobody wanted to know about. Her father, externally a commonsense man-about-town while having internally withdrawn into a private kind of dream-world, showed no interest in the fancies or secret life of others, not even that of his daughter. (She may not have tried to confide in him very often.) And to her positivist mother all unusual inner experiences were 'brain disorders,' to be treated without further ado by the family physician.

Her conscious inner life began when she was five years old. 'I started at the age of five … I was five or six years old; at the age of seven it became very serious.'[9] 'She went and sat in a small armchair, specially made for her. It was a very small padded armchair like they made them at the time, covered with grey-blue cloth and [patterned with] flowers … She sat down and always felt that Consciousness above the head.'[10] There is a photo of Mirra at that age, standing next to her small chair to which she withdrew when life was lashing out at her, in order to feel the

---

* Spiritual practice or discipline.

very pleasant sensation of the light of that Consciousness – so pleasant and so interesting that at times she preferred it to going to the circus with her father.

The Mother also said that her *sadhana* actually started in the womb: 'When I was five, even three years old, I was conscious. The beginning was made in the womb.'[11] And she said several times that she had chosen her parents before her conception. To understand this one must accept reincarnation. 'Rebirth is an indispensable machinery for the working out of a spiritual evolution; it is the only possible effective condition, the obvious dynamic process of such a manifestation in the material universe ... Rebirth is not a constant reiteration but a progression, it is the machinery of an evolutionary process.'[12] (Sri Aurobindo)

When the soul has gone through all the necessary experiences in a given life, it withdraws by a process we call death and goes to rest in a world where it assimilates the essence of the life just ended. When in the course of their evolution certain souls have reached a level of maturity, or when certain souls descend with a special mission, they are able to choose the circumstances of their rebirth – in the first place their parents, and more specifically the mother, for the simple and obvious reason that the body of the reincarnating soul will be formed within the mother's physical and psychological being. It is as if from its soul-world the soul spots a kind of beacon on the Earth, lit by the aspiration of the mother and calling for its descent. We remember Mathilde's strong aspiration that her children would be the best in the world. Considering this, and the solidly practical, positivist family environment in addition to the physical robustness of Maurice, we can guess some of the reasons why the Mother chose these parents as her instruments of reincarnation. The practical importance of the choice will become clearer as our story unfolds.

Young Mirra had many strange experiences and sometimes went into trance in the middle of a sentence or a gesture. She was supposed to have fallen asleep. At the time she herself had no explanation for this kind of occult experience, 'but the faculties were already present.' Thus it happened, during a ceremonious family luncheon at her parents' house, that she perceived 'something quite interesting' in the atmosphere of a cousin, the one who would become Director of the Louvre. She had brought her fork halfway to her mouth and remained sitting like that as if she had been changed into a statue! She was severely scolded, of course, and told that she should not be present at such events if she did not know how to behave properly.

At one time she started sleepwalking and writing poems during her nightly perambulations. Sometimes when she read history books, the text would suddenly become transparent as it were, and she would see other words or pictures telling her the true historical facts behind the fiction. Once, in the spacious *salon* (drawing room) of the house on the Square du Roule, where the family had moved in 1886, she wanted to show her friends how to dance. A running start being out of the question, she pushed off into the air, touched the floor once in the middle of the *salon* and came gracefully down, as if she had been carried, near the opposite wall some twelve metres away. On a visit to the Forest of Fontainebleau, where Mathilde had rented a cottage, she was pursued by her playmates and fell from a high bank onto a road covered with nasty cobblestones; everyone thought she must have broken a limb at least, but she had fallen 'very slowly, as if carried.' That was how she always felt: as if carried.

'Interestingly there was nothing mental about it, I didn't know the existence of these [occult] things. I didn't know what meditation was, I meditated without having the least idea of what it was. I knew nothing, absolutely nothing. My mother had kept it all completely taboo: those subjects were not to be broached, they drive you crazy.'[13] 'I practised occultism when I was twelve. But I must say I was never afraid. I was afraid of nothing.'[14] Fear, as she would later warn time and time again, has no place in occultism; it is even extremely dangerous, for it attracts precisely that which is being feared.

Gradually Mirra's experiences grew in scope and importance. At the age of thirteen, for nearly a year, she used to go out of the body every night. 'As soon as I had gone to bed, it seemed to me that I went out of my body and rose straight up above the house, then above the city [Paris], very high above. On those occasions I used to see myself clad in a magnificent golden robe, much longer than myself; and as I rose higher, the robe would grow longer and spread out in a circle around me to form something like an immense cupola over the city. Then I would see men, women, children, old men, sick and unfortunate people coming out from everywhere; they would gather under the outspread robe, begging for help, telling of their miseries, their suffering, their hardships. In reply the robe, supple and alive, would extend towards each of them individually, and as soon as they touched it, they were comforted and healed, and went back into their bodies happier and stronger than they had come out of them. Nothing seemed more beautiful to me, nothing could make me happier; and all the activities of the day seemed dull and colourless and without any real life compared to this nightly activity which was the true life to me.'[15]

'When and how did I become conscious of a mission which I was to fulfil on Earth? ... It is difficult to say when it came to me. It is as though I was born with it, and together with the growth of the mind and brain, the precision and completeness of this consciousness grew also. Between eleven and thirteen a series of psychic and spiritual experiences revealed to me not only the existence of God but man's possibility of uniting with Him, of realizing Him integrally in consciousness and action, of manifesting Him upon Earth in a life divine. This, along with a practical discipline for its fulfilment, was given to me during my body's sleep by several teachers, some of whom I met afterwards on the physical plane.

'Later on, as the interior and exterior development proceeded, the spiritual and psychic relation with one of these beings became more and more clear and frequent; and although I knew little of the Indian philosophies and religions at that time I was led to call him Krishna, and henceforth I was aware that it was with him (whom I knew I would meet on earth one day) that the divine work was to be done.'[16] We will see later on how Mirra met this 'Krishna.'

And so she grew up, that quiet, well-behaved, intelligent and talented girl *de bonne famille*, and nobody knew about the crowded experiences she was involved in day and night – as nobody anticipated the drastic step in life she would soon take.

2.

Artist among the Artists

It was not becoming for a girl of the better classes to take up art as a career. It would have been tolerated that she did water colours or painted fans and screens, but not paintings on canvas! This was not included in the catalogue of the conventions of the higher bourgeoisie.[1]

– Jean-Paul Crespelle

The Julian Academy

In 1893, when she was fifteen, Mirra passed her final school examinations and joined an art studio, the Académie Julian, one of the many private art schools in Paris. She would attend its courses for four years. 'The name of the institution to which the studio belonged is not mentioned in her [the Mother's] recorded talks or in any available documents. However, it can be inferred with reasonable certainty from several facts.'[2] This important, self-chosen step in her life, had no doubt repercussions in the family. Her father may not have cared much, but her mother surely did; for Mathilde, as for any respectable member of the bourgeoisie, art and artists belonged to a shadowy, suspect social subgroup on the margins of society. Artists belonged to la bohême, the 'bohemian life,' a term made popular by Giacomo Puccini when he chose it as the title of one of his operas (1896), and meaning a world where society's moral code was not observed.

There are no published texts documenting this turn in Mirra's life, except a passage in a play she would write many years later. 'Born in a thoroughly respectable bourgeois family where art was considered as a pastime rather than a career and artists as rather unreliable people, prone to debauchery and with a dangerous disregard for money, I felt, perhaps out of contrariness, a compelling need to become a painter.'[3] This certainly points back to her own experience.

Not only did Mirra feel attracted to an art she had practised since an early age,* she also distanced herself in a dramatic way, 'out of contrariness,' from the drab, shallow and hypocritical bourgeois world in which she was brought up, in 'that age of extreme and practical philistinism, the Victorian age [in England] and in France the Second Empire.'[4] One can only guess at the reactions of her parents, but it was probably in the following couple of years that she had to varnish her fashionable boots because they were cracked and she did not have money to buy a new pair.

The most important painting school in Paris was the prestigious École des Beaux-Arts. Successful study at that institution was a prerequisite for anybody who wanted to pursue a career in the arts world. Yet it seems that in spite of all the laurels bestowed on it by officialdom, the Beaux-Arts was not the first-rate place it is supposed to have been in matters of teaching, and of art itself. Its professors, highly esteemed and officially rewarded painters, did not always show up to teach their courses, for they were too busy with their own pursuits and with the private schools they were running. The result was that the Beaux-Arts had become a place where rough camaraderie and practical jokes often took precedence over the study and contemplation of harmony and beauty. It was also notorious for its *bizutage*, the French word for 'ragging,' 'badgering' or 'hazing'; this was the abusive and humiliating ritual of bullying and ridicule all newcomers were subjected to.[5] However, women were not admitted at the Beaux-Arts before 1897 – and Mirra was not interested in an artistic career, but in the practice, mastery and enjoyment of art itself.

The Julian Academy, 'the only serious art school for women,' was founded by the painter Rodolphe Julian in 1868 and had several branches in Paris. Like the Académie Suisse and other Parisian schools

---

* A charcoal drawing of hers, 'Le Pont de la Divonne (Ain),' was shown at the International 'Blanc et Noir' Exhibition of 1892.

of the kind, it was a place of great freedom. There were no entrance examinations, one did not necessarily have to submit one's work for approval or corrections, and the teachers never imposed their view or their authority. (And the fees were not very high.) Rather it was the general atmosphere of the place, which was totally devoted to painting, that acted as the instructor. One worked, one discussed, one compared, one frequented the same cafés and restaurants, one became a member of the profession known to co-disciples and would-be artists from other institutions. And there were the models, too expensive to be hired in private – probably on the usual basis as at the Académie Suisse: for three weeks (older) men would pose as mythological and biblical figures, for one week women as Venuses and Virgins.

How did Mirra come to meet Henri Morisset, who was eight years older than she? It was grandmother Mira, who had known Henri's father, Edouard Morisset, for many years, who introduced the two. Edouard was one of the artists from whom in former years Mira, the grandmother, had ordered portraits of the Egyptian princesses 'to be done from photographs.' Mirra may also have met Henri, already a painter of established reputation, in one of the many places where the artists' crowd met. He had actually visited the Julian Academy while he was a student of the famous Gustave Moreau at the Beaux-Arts.

Henri and Mirra married on 13 October 1897 in a civil ceremony in the town hall of the VIIIth Arrondissement. They went to live at 15 Rue Lemercier, behind the Porte de Clichy, i.e. near Montmartre and in the heart of artistic life of Paris. As one can see in many paintings of that time, the *quartier* looked quite different then.

Impressionism

> *Modern art is an effort, still very awkward, to express something other than the simple physical appearance.*[6]

> – The Mother

Together with Mirra we have landed in the middle of an upheaval in the artistic world, of which the consequences are still very much with us today, although its real scope and significance are not sufficiently realized. We are talking about the revolutionary artistic movement called Impressionism.

In the early 1860s a group of painters, for reasons they were mostly still unable to formulate, started working in a way that ran counter to all the standardized, academic rules of the day. Instead of painting scenes from the Bible, from Greek or Roman history, or from traditional European history, they chose as their subjects everyday life – as they saw it. They painted scenes from Paris, its streets, churches and monuments, its cafés and dancing halls and their customers, its circus and theatre life, its folksy types; and they went out into the countryside, as Mirra Alfassa would do,* and painted – rapturously – the unending and ever-varying wealth of landscapes, river views, and everything else that struck their eye as beautiful and worth painting.

A dam had burst; the artificial bourgeois world was being discredited and discarded, and the plunge was taken into reality as it is directly, genuinely experienced, in this case by the artist's eye. The bourgeois society of the nineteenth century was the successor of a European caste society, which was as sharply divided as that in India. During the *Ancien Régime,* with its roots in the Middle Ages, society had consisted of the classes of the clergy *(brahmin),* the nobility *(kshatriya),* the merchants *(vaishya)* and the common workers *(shudra),* most of whom had been serfs, in other words, slaves. Thanks to the philosophical evolution of the European mind during the Renaissance, the Enlightenment and the French Revolution, the dominant classes of the clergy and the nobility had lost most of their privileges and the bourgeois class had taken over. (A look at the environment in which young Mirra grew up has given us an idea of the life of the bourgeoisie at the end of the nineteenth century.)

This new dominant class, however, had no history of its own, for European history had been made, at least in the opinion of the premodern historians, by the Church and by the blue-blooded families of kings, counts and barons. The bourgeoisie had no historical or mythological

---

* She used her maiden name even after her marriage.

roots; they were upstarts who had to borrow their past from the previous classes in power. This borrowing smelled strongly of imitation, plagiarizing and unnaturalness, and led to a set of public morals that were felt to be artificial and hypocritical by sincere people: 'Everything was permitted on condition that a façade of conventional dignity remained in place.'[7] This lack of sincerity, of authenticity in social mores, was what Mirra revolted against, and the lack of the same qualities in the artistic experience was what Impressionism revolted against; both attitudes were closely connected in her person as well as in the great painters known as the Impressionists.

At the end of all myths and stories, humanity stood confronted with itself. Mirra was born at a time when the human being turned inwards and subjected to close scrutiny all that had gone before. This happened in literature (Proust, Rimbaud, Mallarmé), philosophy (Nietzsche and Bergson), psychology (Freud and Jung), biology (Darwin, Pasteur) and physical science (the Curies, Planck, Lorentz, Einstein). The incredible twentieth century, the greatest show in all history, was being prepared. And Impressionism – thanks to the passion for perceptual honesty in that group of diverse characters, who all possessed a stroke of genius – was the first movement leading to an era of profound change, the end of which is not yet in sight.

The Mother said more than once that all the great cultural periods in history have been brought about by 'families of souls' incarnated to that end. 'There are large families of beings who work at the same task, who have gathered in a certain number and who come in groups as it were.'[8] 'From an occult point of view it is almost always the same forces and the same beings who incarnate during all the ages of artistic beauty upon earth … It is the same forces which are at work, and they are grouped according to their affinities … They reunite at a certain place, and in this place there develops a new civilization, or a special progress in a civilization, or a kind of effervescence, a blossoming, a flowering of beauty, like in the great ages in Greece, Egypt, India, Italy, Spain …'[9] There is little doubt that the Impressionists were such a group. One finds this indirectly confirmed by a neutral witness like Jean-Paul Crespelle, who writes: 'One of the aspects of the life of the Impressionists is their liking, not to say their need to work together, even to live together in spite of their differences ... All felt the need to know what the others were doing, to compare their work and to exchange their ideas.'[10]

The Artist's Life

For ten years Mirra would live as an artist among artists. 'I knew all the greatest artists of [the end of] the last century and of the beginning of this century.'[10a] 'All the artists I knew at that time were truly artists, they were serious and made admirable things which have remained admirable. It was the period of the Impressionists, it was the period of Manet. It was a beautiful period, they made beautiful things.'[10b]

Henri and Mirra seem to have been rather well-off, maybe with some help from father Edouard. In Rue Lemercier they rented an apartment on the first floor, connected by a footbridge with their glass-topped studio in the 'fairly large' garden.

'When [Mirra] was married to that painter, she went on holiday to Beaugency, on the river Loire, where they had a country house. It's a very beautiful place and they made some paintings there. It's a region in France where, during the Renaissance, the kings had their chateaux, and those chateaux are visited as historical monuments. One day, she was in one of those chateaux. I think it was the one at Blois where there was a series of portraits of a royal family done by the painter [François] Clouet. She was stopped in her tracks before one of those portraits and said [aloud]: But why has he given me that kind of hairdo? Then she saw that people were staring at her and she stopped talking. But she had been that lady in a past existence, and in front of that painting the whole memory come alive again, and she remembered that she had not been wearing that dress, that her hair had not been done like that. And [when later telling this story] she added: "I stopped talking aloud, for the people would have thought that I was mad!"'[11] That lady in a past existence was Marguerite de Valois (1553-1615), the highly cultured queen of France and Navarre. 'It was positively me. That was my portrait, that was me!'[12] The portrait is now at the National Library in Paris.

Mirra Morrisset in Paris, ca. 1985

Then we find Mirra in Pau, a town in the south of France with a magnificent view of the Pyrenees, the mountain range that separates France from Spain. Henri had been invited there to paint a series of murals in the Church of Saint James the Great. He did four: *The Vocation of James the Fisherman, Saint James Preaching to the Masses, The Martyrdom of Saint James* and *The Apotheosis of Saint James.* All are still there (though somewhat 'faded by time,' according to a recent visitor) bearing Henri Morisset's signature and the date 1898. In the *Bénézit,* a French dictionary of artists, Henri Morisset will be mentioned mainly because of these murals.

The principal place of veneration of St James the Great was Santiago de Compostela, like Rome and Jerusalem the goal of a famous religious pilgrimage in the Middle Ages. Santiago de Compostella is a town near the northwest coast of Spain, and legend has it that the body of St James the Great, brother of St John the Evangelist and a major apostle of Christ, had arrived on that coast in a miraculous way. Many thousands of pilgrims still flock there on foot from all over Europe as penitents or to ask favours from Santiago. In the former unsafe times the pilgrims followed fixed and partly protected routes, and Pau sat on one of those routes which went across the Somport Pass through the mountains; this was called the *Camino Frances* or French Road.

Mirra collaborated with her husband on the panel called *The Apotheosis of Saint James.* It represents a scene from the Battle of Clavijo fought in 844 between the Spanish Christians and the Muslim Moors, who occupied a large part of the peninsula. The battle was fought because one hundred promised virgins had not been delivered to the Caliph of Cordoba. At the crucial moment St James, wearing shining armor and 'in golden light on a white horse, almost like Kalki,'* appeared on the side of the Christians and attacked the Infidels, thus carrying the day for the Christians. Since then Santiago Matamoro (Saint James killer of the Moors) has been the patron saint of Spain.[13] 'It was I who painted the slain and struggling Moors,' the Mother said later, 'because I couldn't climb up. One had to climb high on a ladder to paint. That was too difficult, so I did the things at the bottom.'[14]

There may have been an additional reason not to climb ladders, namely the fact that she was pregnant. Her son André was born on 23 August 1898. Very soon after his birth she began to suffer from

---

* In Hinduism, Kalki is the tenth and last Avatar, expected to establish the Kingdom of God on Earth in a new Golden Age. He is usually represented on a winged white horse and wielding a sword.

a 'floating kidney' and had to stay in bed for five months. During these months she read, according to her own report, hundreds of books and developed out of sheer boredom her occult faculties. One of her exercises consisted in extending her occult body in such a way that she could perceive what was going on in adjacent rooms. In this way she even managed to be invisibly present in the studio.

Little André was fascinated by this studio, 'which I considered the most wonderful place in the world,'[15] with its glass roof, its colors, its smells of oil paints, turpentine and wood, and the many interesting people who came to visit his parents. Late in life he still remembered that there he was once introduced to Madame Fraya, 'a very pretty lady with a very big hat and a pleasant way of talking.' Madame Fraya was a clairvoyant and became so famous that most of the great politicians of the time – Briand, Clemenceau, Jaurès, Daladier, even President Poincaré – consulted her, and a book was written about her, *Une Voyante à l'Élysée* ('A Clairvoyant at the Élysée'; the Élysée is the presidential palace in Paris).*

André was mostly brought up in Beaugency with his father's sisters, his grandfather Edouard and his nanny. 'What struck me most were the visits which my parents paid to me in their motor car. It was a Richard-Brasier [a short-lived model from the beginning of the century] and didn't have to bear a number plate because it could not do more than thirty kilometres per hour ... My parents used to carry with them a couple of bicycles "just in case." As a matter of fact, on the first hundred-and-fifty kilometre trip to Beaugency the steering gear broke after fifty kilometres, at Étampes, and the car stopped inside a bakery. They stayed there overnight, used the cycles to visit the place and left the next day, the car having been repaired by the local blacksmith.'[16] One may recall that at that time bicycles were almost as novel as

---

* In the beginning of September 1914, Madame Fraya was called to the War Ministry in the middle of the night. The leaders of the country awaited her there in pajamas or hastily dressed. The German armies were marching on Paris. 'Those men exuded a terrible fear' and asked her if the Germans would enter Paris. Madame Fraya answered categorically: 'No, the Germans will not enter Paris. Their victory will come to nothing. Around 10 September they will be forced to withdraw behind the Aisne. It will be the collapse of their quick campaign.' And that is indeed what happened. (See Louis Pauwels and Guy Breton, Nouvelles histoires magiques, p. 79).

automobiles. The pneumatic bicycle tyre was introduced by John Dunlop in 1888; this, combined with the improved safety bicycle, suddenly made bicycling a popular pastime.

Mirra Alfassa had paintings of hers accepted by the jury of the *Salon de la Société Nationale des Beaux-Arts*. This was then the foremost official art show in Paris, not to say in the world, in which no less than three thousand artists participated every time. Mirra's paintings were exhibited in 1903, 1904 and 1905. Their names, as listed in the catalogues, were: *Dans l'atelier* and *Salon* (1903), *Nature morte* and *Vestibule* (1904), *Bibelots* and *La console* (1905).

It was not her intention to build up a career as a painter and become famous – she called herself a 'very ordinary' artist – and one may suppose that the necessary approaches to the members of the jury were made by her husband. She observed the whole business with a penetrating and rather ironical eye, and remarked later: 'I am reminded of the annual opening of the Arts Exhibition in Paris, when the President of the Republic inspects the pictures, eloquently discovering that one is a landscape and another a portrait, and making platitudinous comments with the air of a most intimate and soul-searching knowledge of painting. The painters know very well how inept the remarks are and yet miss no chance of quoting the testimony of the President to their genius.' [17] It should moreover be remembered that the Impressionists, the foremost artists of the time, found no place at the Salon and had to organize their own exhibitions. The official authorities and the art critics would begin recognizing them only in the years preceding the First World War.

Mirra seems to have known Auguste Rodin, the great sculptor, fairly well for she would tell later how he asked her advice in an affaire de coeur: 'How can one prevent two women to be jealous of each other?' Before sculpting his statues in marble or casting them in bronze, he usually moulded them in clay. To prevent the clay models from drying up and crumbling when the master was absent for a couple of days, they had to be covered with wet cloth, and this cloth had to be sprinkled with water every day. Both his wife and his 'favorite model' had the key to the studio and both rivals sprinkled water on the clay models, although it was obvious for the woman who entered second that the job had already been done. The result was that on his return Rodin would find that the clay had run and that his work was spoiled. (The Mother did not remember what advice she had given him.)

Rodin was forty years older than Mirra. 'He was an old man, already old at that time. He was magnificent. He had a faun's head, like a Greek faun. He was short, quite thick-set, square. He had shrewd eyes. He was strikingly ironical and a little –. He found the problem amusing, but he would all the same have preferred to find his clay models unscathed.'[18]

Another artist Mirra seems to have known well was Henri Matisse. He had, after all, been a student of Gustave Moreau at the Beaux-Arts at the same time as Henri Morisset. She had a very high opinion of Matisse as a painter, and she also bears witness to an important moment in the rapid evolution of Post-Impressionist art.

Matisse, she says (without naming him), was doing his very best as a painter, but he had to struggle with the fate of so many Parisian artists at the beginning of their career: he could not sell his work, which means that he went hungry. One day, somebody who wanted to help him brought an art dealer to his studio. The art dealer was not impressed by what he saw, till he found a canvas on which Matisse, after each painting session, had smeared the remainder of the colors from his palette, giving free rein to his fantasy. The art dealer, in search of new sensations, grew ecstatic. 'Give me as many paintings as you can in this genre, twenty, thirty a month, I will sell them all and make you famous!' And famous Henri Matisse became: he was the first and perhaps most refined painter of a new school called Fauvism.[19]

Later, talking to the youth of the Sri Aurobindo Ashram School, the Mother would often look back on her years among the Parisian artists. She would explain the role of photography in the sudden transition from the mediocre art productions of the Second Empire to the ecstatic plunge into the direct artistic perception of the Impressionists. She would consider the unbridled evolution of painting in the wake of Impressionism, and point out how the horrors of the Great War had profoundly upset the sense and creation of beauty in all its aspects.

When asked: 'Why is modern art so ugly?' the Mother answered: 'I think the main reason is that people have become more and more lazy and do not want to work. They want to produce before having practised, they want to know before having studied, and they want to become famous before having done anything worthwhile.'[20] But: 'Now, to tell you the truth, we are climbing up the curve again. Really, I think we have gone down to the depths of incoherence, of absurdity, of ugliness – of the taste for the sordid and ugly, the filthy, the outrageous. We have gone, I think, to the very bottom ... There are signs that we are going up again. You will see, in fifty years we'll perhaps have beautiful things to look at.'[21] She said that in 1951.

A few years later she noted: 'At one time, when I looked at the paintings of Rembrandt, the paintings of Titian or Tintoretto, the paintings of Renoir, the paintings of Monet, I felt a great aesthetic joy. This aesthetic joy I don't feel anymore ... That subtle something that is the true aesthetic joy is gone, I don't feel it any more. Of course, I am miles away from experiencing it when I look at the things they are making now. But it is nevertheless something behind this which made the former [joy] disappear. So perhaps by making just a little effort towards the future, we will be able to find the formula of the new beauty. That would be interesting.

'It is quite recently that this impression has come to me, it is not something from long ago. I have tried [to look at classical paintings] with the utmost goodwill, abolishing all kinds of preferences, preconception, habits, bygone tastes and all that. All that being discarded, I look at their paintings and I don't succeed in getting any pleasure. They don't give me any. Sometimes they cause an aversion in me, but above all the impression of something that is not true, an unpleasant impression of insincerity. But then quite recently, I suddenly had the sensation of something very new, something of the future pushing, pushing, trying to manifest, trying to express itself and not yet succeeding, something that will be a tremendous progress over all that has been felt and expressed before. And at the same time was born the formation of consciousness which turns towards this new thing and wants to get hold of it. This will perhaps be interesting.'[22]

Mirra, who was becoming more and more conscious and therefore very sensitive, was also acutely aware of the tensions in all creative persons she met, painters, sculptors, writers, musicians, dancers or whomever, a tension caused by the discrepancy between the aspiration towards the artistic ideal and the downward pull of the body, by the lower layers in the being and by everyday life in an all-too-human world. 'When one saw the artist at work he lived in a magnificent beauty, but when one saw the gentleman at home, he had only a very limited contact with the artist he was, and he generally became a very vulgar, very ordinary man. Many were like that, I'm sure. But those who were [inwardly] unified, in the sense that they really lived their art, those were not like that, they were generous and good.'[23]

The Early Sadhana (continued)

If the Mother stressed one thing about this period in her life, it is the fact that she was an inveterate atheist, positivist and materialist, just like her parents. She accepted only what she could touch and see, and she never sought for explanations elsewhere than on a material basis. This did not prevent the inner experiences from happening, nor did it inhibit her from feeling that inner 'Presence' for which she had no name and about which she could talk to nobody. She most certainly would not have called it God. 'The feeling I have had all my life long was that ['God'] was a [mere] word, and a word with which people covered a lot of very undesirable things. You know, the idea of a God who wants to be the one and only ... It is what had made me completely atheistic, if one may put it that way, in my childhood. I did not accept a being who declared himself to be the one and only and all-powerful, whoever he might be.'[24] 'All I knew was the God of the religions, God as men have created him, and I didn't want him at any price. I denied his existence, but with the certitude that if such a God did exist, I detested him!'[25]

The Mother deemed herself lucky that she had been brought up like that, and said that it was one of the reasons why she had chosen those very parents. Taking into account her numerous inner experiences, her hereditary constitution was the best possible base for her not getting trapped in mental or other aberrations and to prevent her from drifting. Thus she was assured that her experiences were no mystical reveries, for she said that her body, her constitutional make-up, had nothing mystical about it.

Still, inwardly she felt alone – while in her surface life she experienced the vibrancy of Paris around the end of the century, a period sometimes called la belle Époque (although, as we will see, the beauty of that period was blemished by a lot of dark spots). 'I remember, when I was eighteen years old I had in me such an intense need to know. Experiences I had – I had had all kinds of experiences – but due to the milieu in which I lived, I never had any chance to obtain an intellectual knowledge which would have given me the meaning of all that, I could not speak about them. I had had experiences upon experiences. For years together, at night, I had experiences, but I was careful not to breathe a word about them – all sorts of memories of past lives, all sorts of things, but without any basis of intellectual knowledge.

'The advantage was of course that my experiences were no mental fabrications, they came absolutely spontaneously. But I had such a need to know in me ... To know, know, *know!* You see, I knew nothing, but *nothing,* except the things of the ordinary life, the external knowledge. Whatever was given to me to learn, I learned. I learned not only what I was taught but also what my brother was taught, higher mathematics and all that! And I learned and I learned and I learned – and it was nothing. *Nothing* gave me any explanation, I could not understand anything!'[26]

But when a soul has a strong need to progress or to develop, an answer will be given, usually in a most unexpected way. 'Between the age of eighteen and twenty, I attained a conscious and constant union with the divine Presence and I had done it all alone, with absolutely nobody to help me, not even books. When I found one – a little later I got hold of Vivekananda's *Raja Yoga* – it seemed to me such a wonderful thing, you see, that somebody could explain something to me! This made me gain in a few months what would perhaps have taken me years to do.'[27]

And again a little later, when she was 'perhaps twenty-one then, either twenty or twenty-one,' she met an Indian who gave her the key to reading the *Bhagavad Gita.* 'There was a [French] translation which, by the way, was quite bad' – but at the time Mirra would not have been able to read it in another language – 'and he advised me to read it and gave me the key, his key ... He said: "Read the Gita and take Krishna as the symbol of the immanent God, the inner Godhead." This was all he told me ... But in one month the whole work was done ... The first time I knew there was a discovery to be made within me, there was nothing else more important ... I rushed headlong into it like a cyclone, and nothing could have stopped me.'[28]

That Indian was Jnanendranath Chakravarti, then professor of mathematics and later vice-chancellor of Lucknow University. His wife, Monika Devi, 'a great lady of birth and breeding with the innate personal charm of a born hostess, aristocratic to her fingertips,'[29] would renounce the world, adopt the name Yashoda Ma and found an ashram (a spiritual community) near Almora, in the foothills of the Himalayas.* The household of this remarkable couple seems to have been a centre of devotion to Shri Krishna.

Jnanendranath Chakravarti was also a member of the Theosophical Society and in close contact with Annie Besant, later the head of that society. '[Annie Besant] travelled to America [in 1893, to represent the Theosophical Society at the World Parliament of Religions] with one of the other Theosophical delegates, Gyanendra Nath† Chakravarti, a brahmin, professor of mathematics ... A brilliant speaker, an ardent Hindu and an attractive man, Chakravarti captivated Annie ... Mrs. Besant told her friends that, at last she had found her own guru. She was so besotted with the professor that she proclaimed Chakravarti's daughter to be the reincarnation of the recently deceased Madame Blavatsky.'[30]

Mirra must have met Chakravarti on one of his subsequent trips to Europe, in 1898 or 1899. The occasion on which he gave her the key to the Gita was probably the only time she met him, but it proved to be an important meeting indeed; it was also the very first time (as far as is known) that she came into personal contact with somebody from India. She was evidently on the lookout for any meaningful help she could get in her quest. The inner experiences continued to come frequently, and

---

* She would initiate Ronald Nixon, professor of English at the same university, naming him Krishnaprem. We find many letters to and from this Krishnaprem in the correspondence of Dilip Kumar Roy, a friend of Krishnaprem and disciple of Sri Aurobindo, to whom D.K. Roy forwarded those letters.

† 'Jnanendranath' is pronounced 'Gyanendranath,' which explains the different spelling.

so did the memories of past lives, as they had done even long before she had the slightest idea of reincarnation.

Eager for knowledge and understanding of her experiences, she read everything she could find about spirituality, including the *Dhamma-pada* and other Buddhist texts. But she was never satisfied with mental knowledge only and always tried out in practice what she read. We may suppose that it was at some time during these years that the Minister of Fine Arts invited her into his box for the first performance of an opera, probably by Jules Massenet. (The Mother was not sure about the name of the composer.) Such a 'première' is a glamorous affair. 'The subject was fine, the script was fine, and the music was not unpleasant.' The Minister had only recently become a member of the cabinet. He was a rather simple man from the province and still enjoyed in a childlike way everything Paris had to offer him. But he was also well educated, of course, and had offered the best seat in his box to the lady who was his guest, but whose seating position prevented him from having a full view of the stage. Mirra became aware of his plight. She discreetly drew back till the Minister could enjoy the performance without any hindrance, she in the process forsaking seeing it.

When the Mother told this anecdote, she did not mention herself by name but added the following: 'Well, this person, when she sat back and gave up all desire to see the performance, was filled with the sense of inner joy, a liberation from all attachment to things and a kind of peace, content to have done something for somebody instead of having sought her own satisfaction, so much so that the evening brought her infinitely greater pleasure than if she had actually seen the opera. This is a true experience, it is not some anecdote read in a book, and it happened exactly at the time this person was studying Buddhist discipline, and it was in conformity with the sayings of the Buddha that she tried out this experiment.'[31]

At the Epicentre

As we have already seen in passing, the world was in turmoil during the years of Mirra's marriage and Paris was the epicentre of the profound changes that would churn up humanity. We do not have any of her writings from that period – if she wrote anything at all – but it happens that we get a glimpse of those years in some of her later conversations.

Towards the end of the nineteenth century the second Industrial Revolution was in full swing, and accelerating. The main elements of the first Industrial Revolution had been coal, steam and iron. The Eiffel Tower, erected for the World Exhibition of 1889, may be seen as its apotheosis and symbol. But in the meantime the second Industrial Revolution was under way, driven by electricity and petrol; its symbol was the spectacular 'Palace of Electricity' at the World Exhibition of 1900, which again took place in Paris. The industrial revolutions went hand in hand with the rapid progress made in all branches of science, thus strengthening in ever greater measure the grip of humankind on nature. Yet there was a price to pay.

'The marvellous strides of science [and technology] had brought the human race to a stage of material welfare ready to prove the faith of the Nineteenth Century that the better-off man became the less aggressive he would be. Society now had running water and lighted streets, sanitation, preserved and refrigerated food, sewing machines, washing machines, typewriters, lawn-mowers, the phonograph, telegraph and telephone and lately, beginning in the nineties, the extraordinary gift of individual powered mobility in the horseless carriage. It seemed impossible that so much physical benefit should not have worked a spiritual change, that the new century should not begin a new era in human behaviour, that man, in short, had not become too civilized for war.'[32] (Barbara Tuchman)

Both industrial revolutions, fast shaping the world as we know it, were accompanied by philosophical ideas that would in part direct them: positivism, socialism, communism and the idea of continuous material progress leading ultimately to a Utopian world on Earth. Auguste Comte's *Course of Positive Philosophy* was published in six volumes between 1830 and 1842, Karl Marx's *Communist Manifesto* in 1848 and *Das Kapital* in 1867, Charles Darwin's *Origin of Species* in 1859.

Mirra saw them around her, in 'that crawling mass on the move' that was Paris, the 'thousands of lowly employees and workers, all those oppressed, luckless, downtrodden, struggling for an amelioration of their miserable existence.'[33] 'The transformation ['haussmannization'] of Paris having forcibly pushed the workers' population from the centre towards the circumference, the capital had become two cities: one rich and one poor. The latter surrounded the former.'[34] Even today Parisians immediately place their fellow citizens socially according to the arrondissement, i.e. the administrative subdivision of the city, in which they live.

So blatant had the gap and the tensions between rich and poor become that a solution was urgently needed, but it might be a violent one. Some philosophers fantasized about possible solutions and in their short-sighted goodwill concocted the most fanciful social prescriptions. These were the social utopias of Enfantin, Fourier, Blanqui, Blanc, Proudhon and others. All contained a grain of truth, yet all lacked realistic insight into human nature and its ways. Marx had a larger view, even presenting it as 'scientific.' And there were the anarchists, impetuous and not less utopian than the others, who, wanting to force an immediate change upon society, were ready to pay for it, and to make others pay, with their lives.

Ravachol, the author of numerous bombings, was guillotined in 1892. Emile Henry threw a bomb in Café Terminus. Auguste Vaillant took a bomb with him into the public gallery of the Lower House. It detonated 'with the roar of a canon' and wounded several Members of the House but killed none. 'The city was absolutely paralysed with fear. The upper classes lived again as if in the days of the Commune. They dared not go to theatres, to restaurants, to the fashionable shops in the Rue de la Paix or to ride in the Bois [de Boulogne] where anarchists were suspected behind every tree.'[35] The Russian revolutionaries who would come to ask for Mirra's advice a few years later, would complain that they were constantly shadowed by the police, who suspected them of being anarchists.

And there was the Dreyfus Affair, tearing France apart from 1894 to

1906. Artillery Captain Alfred Dreyfus, a Jew, was accused of having provided arch-enemy Germany with secret military information, thereby committing treason. Though steadfastly maintaining his innocence, he was found guilty by court-martial, publicly reduced in rank, and transported to the infamous Devil's Island. As more and more proof of his innocence became available, 'the volatile France of the 1890s' was divided into two camps. On the one side there were the militarists, nationalists, Catholics and anti-Semites, fanatically standing up for the honour of their country and therefore consenting to the covering up of the truth; on the other side there were the liberals and 'intellectuals' (philosophers, writers and journalists), Protestants, Freemasons, leftists and internationalists, battling to bring the truth to light. The rift split the nation in an outburst of passion seldom seen before or after; it ran through marriages, families and formerly close friendships, including artists. The novelist Emile Zola became internationally known for his letter published on the front page of a much-read newspaper under the banner 'J'accuse' (1898) and his dictum *la Vérité est en marche,* (Truth is on the move). Captain Dreyfus' innocence was finally established. He was fully rehabilitated, even promoted to Major, and would serve honourably in the Great War.

All this formed the background to Mirra's daily life, to the newspapers she read and the conversations which she heard or in which she was involved. One finds references to these happenings in numerous future conversations, for she was always attentive to all aspects of life, the significant as well as the apparently insignificant, and 'never forgot something she had seen even once.' It is, however, typical that she transmuted many of the experiences of her youth into a spiritual dimension. 'Progress,' the keyword of the nineteenth century, became the keyword of her life too, but widened in a way our story still has to discover. And one day she would quote Zola's phrase, *la Vérité est en marche*, giving 'Truth' a meaning that Zola, or anybody else at the time, could not have comprehended.

3.

Explorations of the Occult

> *Occult knowledge without spiritual discipline is a dangerous instrument, for one who uses it as for others, if it falls into impure hands. Spiritual knowledge without occult science lacks precision and certainty in its objective results; it is all-powerful only in the subjective world. The two, when combined in inner or outer action, are irresistible and are fit instruments for the manifestation of the supramental power.*[1]

> – The Mother

It was a friend of Mattéo's, Louis Thémanlys, who brought Mirra into contact with the Parisian chapter of the *Mouvement cosmique* and its monthly publication, the *Revue cosmique*. This contact, which occurred sometime in 1903, would have far-reaching consequences for her.

Occultism

In the West occultism is generally regarded with distrust and disbelief, and associated with black magic, witches on broomsticks and grotesque demons. This attitude towards it is not undeserved. As Sri Aurobindo wrote in *The Life Divine*: 'Occultism in the West ... never reached its majority, never acquired ripeness and a philosophic or sound systematic foundation. It indulged too freely in the romance of the supernatural or made the mistake of concentrating its major effort on the discovery of formulas and effective modes for using supernatural powers. It deviated into magic, white and black, or into romantic or thaumaturgic paraphernalia of occult mysticism and the exaggeration of what was after all a limited and scanty knowledge. These tendencies and this insecurity of a mental foundation made it difficult to defend and easy to discredit, a target facile and vulnerable. In Egypt and in the East this line of knowledge arrived at a greater and more comprehensive endeavour.'[2]

Sri Aurobindo writes, however, in the same work: 'To know these [occult] things and to bring their truths and forces into the life of humanity is a necessary part of its evolution. Science itself is in its own way an occultism; for it brings to light the formulas which Nature has hidden and it uses its knowledge to set free operations of her energies which she has not included in her ordinary operations and to organize and place at the service of man her occult powers and processes, a vast system of physical magic – for there is and can be no other magic than the utilization of secret truths of being, secret powers and processes of Nature. It may even be found that a supraphysical knowledge is necessary for the completion of physical knowledge, because the processes of physical Nature have behind them a supraphysical factor, a power and action mental, vital or spiritual which is not tangible to any outer means of knowledge.'[3]

The Mother would approach the subject in the same open-minded scientific spirit. After all, the scientific spirit is not necessarily limited to the materialistic, reductionist variant of science, however dominant it may be at present. The scientific spirit is an attitude of the mind that may and should be taken towards all aspects of existence within the perceptual scope of the human being, be they material or not, for immaterial is not synonymous with unreal or non-existent. The Mother therefore said: '[Occultism] is a knowledge which in the modern world is hardly recognized as scientific, but which *is* scientific in the sense that it has precise procedures and that, if one reproduces the circumstances exactly, one obtains the same results. It is a progressive science which can be practised and in which totally justified progress can be made as logical as in all other sciences acknowledged as such in modern times. But its object is a reality or realities which do not belong to the most material domain. Special capacities and a special development are needed to be conscious in that domain, for it eludes our ordinary senses.'[4] She also said in answer to the question of a young student: '[Occultism] is the knowledge of the invisible forces and the power to handle them. It is a science. It is altogether a science. I always compare occultism with chemistry, for it is the same kind of knowledge as that of chemistry regarding material things. It is a knowledge of invisible forces, their various vibrations, their interrelations, the combinations which can be made by bringing them together and the power one can exercise over them. It is absolutely scientific and ought to be learned like a science, which means that one cannot practise occultism as something emotional or vague and imprecise. You must work at it as you would do at chemistry and learn all the rules – or find them yourself if there is nobody to teach you, but then at some risk to yourself. There are combinations [in occultism] as explosive as certain chemical combinations.'[5]

Occultism was the order of the day especially in France at the turn of the century. The wave of spiritism* that originated in the United States in 1848 also inundated Europe. In reaction to the dry and harsh spirit of materialism and positivism, many became interested in mysticism and the supernatural. The books of the Frenchman Allan Kardec, for instance, were so widely read that in Western Europe spiritism became a kind of secular religion with millions of followers. (There were already twelve million in the U.S.) In 1889, on the occasion of an international spiritist congress, no less than ninety-eight spiritist dailies and periodicals were counted. 'The medium was replacing the priest.' There was also a wave of Orientalism, caused in part by the expanding colonization taking place at the time. The translations of the Indian and Chinese classics, the foundation in Paris of the Guimet Museum and the Oriental sections in the Louvre, and the interest in Japanese painting, very influential on post-Impressionist art, were all expressions of the same phenomenon.

In fact, occultism in all its aspects – hermetism, alchemy, astrology, Freemasonry, Rosicrucianism – has always been a strong undercurrent in European culture. Even in the century of the Enlightenment, the acme of rationalism in its most strident and critical form, 'persons

---

* 'Spiritism' is a less common word for 'spiritualism.' We will use the word 'spiritism' throughout for the belief in the possibility of receiving messages from the spirits of the dead and practices based on this belief. The word 'spiritualism' will be used for matters spiritual, i.e. above the normal level of the human consciousness.

without number were ready to believe anything and to follow the most woolly ideas,' according to Louis Pauwels. And Paul Valéry wrote: 'Magic, alchemy, divination by the stars, and stimulated dreams coexisted [during the Enlightenment] in more than one brain with the most limpid classic culture and the discipline of the exact sciences. Never have scepticism and credulity been more closely associated than at that time.'[6] Never? One wonders whether the present is any different – and whether this does not result from the fact that the human being is much more complex than science and materialism contend.

Pathways for the Dead

So many people come to her in the night for the passage to the other side whom she has not known in the body.[7]

– Sri Aurobindo

Even before Mirra discovered the teaching of the Cosmic Movement, she had 'certain experiences at night, certain types of nightly activities, caring for people who had just left their body.' Although still lacking the theoretical knowledge, she knew exactly what had to be done, and did it. When she began reading the *Revue cosmique,* she understood many things she had not known before and, true to character, began to apply that new knowledge and to work it out systematically.

'Every night, at the same hour, my work consisted in constructing between the purely terrestrial atmosphere and the psychic atmosphere a sort of path of protection across the vital, so that people wouldn't have to pass through it. For those who are conscious but don't have the knowledge it's a very difficult passage, it's infernal. I was preparing this path – it must have been around 1903 or 1904, I don't exactly remember – and working at it for months and months.'[8] Afterwards, she would be told by Madame Théon, with whom we shall soon get acquainted: 'It is part of the work you have come on Earth to do. All those with even a slightly awakened psychic being and who can see your Light will go to it at the moment of dying, wherever they may die, and you will help them to pass through.' And the Mother said later that this was a 'constant work' she had been doing and continued to do.

The human being consists of several sheaths or 'bodies,' mental, vital and material, and behind them the soul, supporting the whole.* At the time of death, the incarnated soul lays down the material body and enters the vital worlds, through which it passes into the mental worlds, and finally into the psychic† world, where it rests 'in a kind of beatific contemplation' between two incarnations and assimilates its experiences from the former life. The beings of the vital worlds, more specifically the lower vital worlds, are the vicious entities we call demons or hostile forces. As these worlds are the first the departing soul has to traverse, it must in almost all cases confront those beings unprepared, unarmed with the necessary knowledge. It is to these terrifying experiences that the various myths of 'hell' go back.

The Mother explained: 'Generally, one calls the "domain of death" a certain region of the most material vital into which one is projected at the moment one leaves the body.' This lower vital region, this material vital world, is obscure and full of small, vampire-like beings who feed on everything they can swallow, including the vital substance of the deceased person who, because of the sudden and often shocking death experience, has been projected into it. In the physical these beings are powerless, but when one has passed completely outside the physical – and the main characteristic of death is that it cuts all links with the material world – one is at their mercy. 'If at that moment people who love the departed person concentrate their thought and love on him, he finds a refuge therein and this protects him fully against those entities.' One who does not have such protection is 'like a prey delivered to those forces, and that indeed is an experience that is difficult to bear.'[9] It is 'infernal.'

And the Mother went on: 'Now there are what one might call bridges, protected passages which have been built in the vital world

---

* This mental, vital and material 'whole' is called the *adhara* in Sanskrit. As this is a useful term which has no equivalent in English, it will be used in the rest of the book.

† In this book the words 'psyche' (i.e. soul) and its derivations are used in the literal sense, as the Mother and Sri Aurobindo used them, and not as relating to occult or supernatural phenomena – except when otherwise stated.

in order to pass through all those dangers. There are "atmospheres" which receive people leaving their body, giving them shelter, giving them protection.'[10] These 'protected passages' are the ones she built for months on end somewhere at the beginning of the century. We now know from people who have actually died, but who for some reason have come back from death to go on living, that these bridges are there. Such people are the ones who have had a 'near-death experience.'

Many books have already been published on the subject, pioneered by Elizabeth Kübler-Ross and Raymond Moody. Let's take the one written by Peter and Elizabeth Fenwick, *The Truth in the Light*. A frequent scenario of the near-death experiences examined in this work is as follows: at the moment of death the experiencers have no fear at all. On the contrary, everything feels like a pleasant experience and even a great happiness. Many see themselves outside their (material) body. In a flash their past actions are reviewed tactfully and with a sense of humour, and then they enter a tunnel and are attracted by a warm, loving light; in that light, they discern a Being of light, waiting to take them onwards. All this is accompanied with a 'mystical' feeling of intense realness, unity and ineffability of the experience. 'Sometimes the passage to the light that people describe is not really a tunnel, though it usually has tunnel-like features – and nearly always the welcoming light is seen shining more brightly at the end'[11] – at the end of the 'protected passages.'

Louis Thémanlys (1874-1943) was the head of the Paris centre of the Cosmic Movement when Mirra Alfassa made his acquaintance. He and his wife Claire had come into contact with the Movement through a copy of the *Revue cosmique* picked up at the Librairie Chacornac, an occult bookshop which at the time of writing still exists on the Quai St Michel, across from the Notre-Dame. Three times a week Thémanlys gave talks on the Cosmic Tradition, and was also responsible for the publication of the *Revue cosmique*. Mirra soon became very active in the movement, participating in a discussion group named *Idéa* and helping edit the *Revue.** It did not take long before Thémanlys, for whose character and zest for work she had but faint praise, passed on the total responsibility for the monthly to her.

The articles to be published came from Tlemcen, where they were written in English by Max Théon and his wife Alma, the leaders and inspirers of the Cosmic Movement. Those articles were, however, translated into French by Teresa, their companion and secretary of many years. Teresa, who was English (her real name was Augusta Rolfe), was 'convinced she knew French as well as a Frenchman,' so much so that, according to the Mother, she did not even find it necessary to use a dictionary. Mirra had the 'literally impossible' task of rewriting Teresa's bungled prose in readable French. For five years Mirra would look after the layout, proofreading and printing of the *Revue cosmique,* its administration and distribution, and other matters connected with it.

In the meantime her inner experiences continued. In 'a series of visions' she saw Sri Aurobindo 'exactly as he was physically, but more glorious. I mean the same man as I was to see the first time I met him: almost thin, with that golden-bronze hue, that clear-cut profile, the unruly beard, the long hair, dressed in *dhoti* with one end thrown over his shoulder, arms bare, a part of the body also bare, and bare-footed.'[12] The Mother, when recounting this, would emphasize the fact that at the time she knew nothing about India, absolutely nothing at all – which was as much as her European contemporaries knew. And in those visions she did something amazing to herself: she prostrated herself in the way Hindus do before the apparition, whom she held to be Shri Krishna. 'I did that, and at the time my external being wondered: "What is all this?"' She realized, however, that her symbolic visions were at the same time spiritual facts, decisive spiritual experiences 'of meeting and of a united perception of the Work to be accomplished.'

Then, in the autumn of 1905, she met Max Théon.

---

* The Cosmic Movement *(le Mouvement cosmique)* was based on an occult philosophy, developed by Max Théon and his wife Alma, and called the Cosmic Tradition *(la Tradition cosmique).* The Movement had several centres or chapters, the Cosmic Groups *(Groupes cosmiques),* and its monthly publication was called the *Revue cosmique.*

The Reclusive Masters

The righteous will shine like stars, but those who have guided others towards the truth will shine like suns, forever.[13]

– Max Théon

Max Théon was a mysterious figure and he chose to remain so. The Mother, however well she had known him, was not sure about his provenance. He never told her who he really was, where he was born, how old he was, or anything else. According to her supposition he was a Polish or Russian Jew who had received initiation in India, knew Sanskrit, was knowledgeable about the *Rig Veda,* and had worked together with H.P. Blavatsky in Egypt.

The marriage certificate of Max Théon and Alma, dated 21 March 1885 and reproduced in Sujata Nahar's third volume of the Mother's life, tells us that his name was Louis Maximillian Bimstein, son of Rabbi Judes Lion Bimstein and thirty years of age at the time, which means that he was born in 1855 – but other documents give different dates of birth. The marriage certificate also says that Louis Bimstein was a 'doctor of medicine,' which was not true and may cast doubt on the other data too. The confusion about his country of origin – Poland, Russia or the Ukraine – is partly understandable because of the political instability in the region of Eastern Europe from which he is supposed to have come. At the time Poland was the defenceless common prey of Prussia, Russia and Austria, and borders changed easily and on many occasions. It was also a time of frequent pogroms which destabilized the Jewish communities, to one of which Louis Bimstein must have belonged.

He left Eastern Europe around 1870. It is quite possible that he spent some time with Helena Petrovna Blavatsky (1831-91) in Egypt, as the Mother remembered him telling her, to found an occult society. Blavatsky travelled from Egypt via Great Britain to America in 1873, and possibly Bimstein was in London in the same year. 'London [at that time] was the haven of people claiming to be priests of Isis, students of the Kabbalah, friends of the Sphinx, and disciples of the dancing dervishes.'[14] In London Bimstein became a member of the Hermetic Brotherhood of Luxor, routinely referring to itself as the 'H.B. of L.' Bimstein became 'the group's chief instructor in practical occultism,' and had in the meantime adopted the modest pseudonym of Max Théon, meaning 'Greatest God.'

It was to Max Théon that aspirants for the H.B. of L. were directed to write in an advertisement of 1884.[15] But things went awry for the Brotherhood when, in 1886, it turned out that one of its founders had been convicted of advertising fraud; he secretively left for the United States. Max Théon, not wanting to be smeared by the affair, had already left for France a month earlier. It should be mentioned that the H.B. of L. had for some time been considered a serious rival of the fledgling Theosophical Society, which had been founded by H.E. Blavatsky and Colonel Henry Olcott in America in 1875. The Theosophical Society permitted itself to speak denigratingly of the H.B. of L. only after the latter had collapsed in such an inglorious way.

When he moved to France, Théon was accompanied by his wife of one year, Mary Christine Woodroffe Ware, called by some Alma, i.e. 'Soul.' Like her husband, Madame Théon already had a public career as an occultist behind her. As 'Una' she had founded the Universal Philosophic Society, whose purpose was 'to create or form a Temple of Truth in which Science as the High Priest shall offer humanity the threefold gifts of Happiness, Holiness and Freedom.' She had also published a book, *Sayings of the Sibyl Alta Una*. 'Shortly after her marriage Una stopped addressing conferences and started appearing with Théon at séances. He, during this period, advertised himself in the occult press as "Eastern psychic healer."'[16]

If all this may seem a bit nebulous, the occult abilities of Max Théon and Alma should not be underestimated. The more the Mother would later know of the occult heritage of India, the more she would appreciate what Théon actually knew. And for his wife she had nothing but the highest praise: 'She had unheard of faculties, that woman, unheard of!'

Max and Alma stayed in France for a year and a half, and then moved on to Algeria, where they built a villa on the outskirts of Tlemcen, a town at the foot of the Atlas mountains. There they spent a decade developing their teachings. In comparison with the lives of other prominent occultists of the time, this long period of withdrawal is exceptional and may be taken as an indication of the seriousness with which they worked on their mission. In the meantime they made the acquaintance of Charles Barlet (1838-1921). Today Barlet's name may not ring a bell, but he should be regarded as the brain behind the French occult revival. 'He knew and was known to everyone that counted.' Not only was he a founder-member of the Paris branch of the Theosophical Society and 'the father of the astrological movement in France,' he was also one of the six known members – there were six unknown too – of 'the Kabbalistic Order of the Rose-Croix' founded by Stanislas de Guaita in 1888. Barlet became the chief of the order in 1897 when de Guaita died of an overdose of drugs, but soon resigned in favour of the still well-known Papus.[17]

Barlet was impressed by the Cosmic Tradition developed by Théon, who based it on his own knowledge of the ancient wisdom and also on the occult material with which Alma provided him. The Mother has spoken more than once of that Tradition, anterior to the Vedic Rishis and the Chaldeans, and from which both originated. 'When asked about the source of his knowledge, [Théon] would say that it antedated the Kabbalah and the Vedas,' she said. And she added: 'I have memories – these are always lived experiences for me – very clear memories, very precise, of a time which was assuredly much prior to the Vedic times and to the Kabbalistic knowledge of the Chaldean traditions. So, personally I am convinced that there was in fact a Tradition prior to those two traditions, and which contained a knowledge very close to an integral knowledge. When I came here and told Sri Aurobindo certain things I knew from an occult standpoint, he always answered me that they were in conformity with the Vedic tradition.'[18]

It seems it was at Barlet's insistence that the Théons agreed to found their Cosmic Movement and, in 1901, to start the *Revue cosmique*, with Charles Barlet as editor and Aia Aziz as director.

Aia Aziz was the second pseudonym Louis Bimstein had assumed; it means 'the Beloved.' (To the people of Tlemcen he was known as Bushaor, 'Long Hair.') However, there rose a difference of opinion between Aia Aziz and Barlet because the former took a stance which leaned more and more towards the Kabbalah. As Aia was not a man to revise or soften his opinion, Barlet quit and Aia Aziz remained the sole leader both of the Movement and its publication. A little later Mirra Alfassa became intensely involved with both, as we have seen, and in 1905 she met Bimstein-Théon-Aziz in Paris, where, accompanied by Alma, he had come on a visit.

'When I met him, I saw that he was a being of great power. He bore a certain likeness to Sri Aurobindo [whom Mirra as yet had only met in her visions] ... Théon was not a tall man, he was of medium height, and lean, slim, with quite a similar profile. But I saw, or rather felt, that Théon was not he whom I had seen in my visions, because when I met him he didn't have that vibration. Yet it was he who first taught me things, and I went and worked at Tlemcen two years in succession.'[19]

Théon and Alma possessed the faculties to perceive with whom they were dealing, and they invited Mirra, already an experienced occultist in her own right, to their mountain-encircled abode in Tlemcen, a place apparently outside the rule of the laws as known to science.

Tlemcen – The First Visit (1906)

> *When you yourselves are inwardly developed, are capable of having a direct and inner contact with these [occult] things, then you know what they are; but no material proof can give you the knowledge if within you do not have the being capable of having this knowledge.*[20]

> – The Mother

It was Mirra's first long journey alone. She travelled by train to Marseilles, embarked on the boat to Oran, had to wait there a day or so, and then again took the train to Tlemcen. She arrived there on 14 July 1906. It had taken six-and-a-half hours to cover the 166 kilometers of the last stage of the journey. But all had gone well, and Max Théon was waiting for her at the station to take her in a car to Zarif, the suburb about a kilometer away where his villa was built into the side of a hill.

'Tlemcen! It's the sound of a gong vibrating over the mountains. It's a smile at the edge of the desert,'[21] wrote a lyrical Claire Thémanlys after her visit to 'the Great Initiates.' The town is located in a valley partly enclosed in the lower hills of the bare, rocky Atlas range. Although it is located in a desert climate directly influenced by the nearby Sahara, the valley is fertile and green, fed by an everflowing river.

Mirra and Théon alighted in order to walk up towards the red-painted house, for Théon wanted his youthful guest to be impressed by the splendid view – and by himself. Suddenly he stopped and turned towards her. 'You are now at my mercy,' he said point-blank. 'Aren't you afraid?' To which Mirra smiled and answered quietly: 'I am never afraid: I have the Divine here, in my heart.' Théon paled.*

These simple words of hers reveal an important event in Mirra's inner development: shortly before travelling to Tlemcen, she had realized her soul. We remember that she had been a convinced atheist to the extent of being incensed by the word 'God,' which evoked to her 'a monster' who would be 'the one and only' and who had created, to his satisfaction, this absurd world of endless suffering. But then she met the Indian who gave her the Bhagavad Gita to read and who for the first time provided her with the key to 'the interior God.' And afterwards she discovered Théon's teaching in the *Revue cosmique* explaining the presence of the Divine in the heart. As always, she tried out what she read with the full power of her enormous concentration. 'The experience was stunning. I am very grateful to him [i.e. Théon] for it ... By following his instructions and seeking within my being, behind the solar plexus, I found it. I found it, I had an experience, an absolutely convincing experience.'[22] Théon had underestimated his invitee. The reason may have been that, although he knew theoretically of the inner Divine and even had expounded Its presence in the heart, he did not have the psychic realization. The idea of surrender to the Divine was alien to him. Later we will see why.

---

* Théon showed some striking resemblances to G.I. Gurdjieff (1877-1949). Both men never tried to camouflage the power trip they were on, but they could also be extremely charming. They kept their past clouded in mystery. They had been on a quest for wisdom 'somewhere' in the East and initiated by some unknown master. Both were skilful with their hands and deemed material work a necessity for the inner development. And both were totally irresponsible car drivers and had near-fatal accidents.

When Théon and Mirra arrived at the red-painted house, Alma was waiting for them. 'She was almost always in trance and she had trained her body so well that even when she was in trance, that is, when one or more parts of her being were exteriorized, the body had a life of its own and she could walk about and even attend to some small material occupations ... In her trances she could talk freely [something Mirra would learn too] and she used to narrate what she saw.'[23] Her narrations were noted down by Teresa (who had been Alma's friend since their years at a girls' boarding school in England) and formed the bulk of the texts in the *Revue cosmique*. Théon usually dressed in a long red, purple or white robe, tied up with a cord around the waist, while Alma wore a dalmatic and covered her shoulders with a red shawl on cool days or during the evenings. She was small in stature, rather plump, and had lost an eye in an occult battle.

'Her powers were quite exceptional,' related the Mother. 'She had received an extremely complete and rigorous training and she could exteriorize herself, that is, bring out of her material body a subtle body, in full consciousness, and do that twelve times in succession. This means that she could pass consciously from one state of being to another, live there as consciously as in her physical body, and then again put this subtler body into trance, exteriorize herself from it – and so on, twelve times successively, to the extreme limit of the world of forms.'[24] Soon Mirra too would learn and master this with ease.

The villa of the Théons, built more or less in the style of an Arab manor, was a house of wonders; there the atmosphere, impregnated with their occult powers, seemed to belong to another universe in which the extraordinary was the daily fare.

Later the Mother would often tell about the astonishing happenings she had witnessed at Tlemcen. When Alma wanted her slippers, she fixed her gaze on them and they obediently came shuffling towards her. When she wanted to announce that dinner was ready, she stared a moment at the gong (a present from Louis Thémanlys) and it sounded all by itself loud and clear. When she felt exhausted, she absorbed the life-force of a grapefruit. When she wanted, as a kind gesture, to put a small bunch of flowers on Mirra's pillow in her locked room, she dematerialized them, sent them through the door or the wall, and rematerialized them on the bed.

Théon was no less powerful a magus. The people of the neighborhood came to him to settle their quarrels and to be cured of their illnesses. When the trees and plants in the park and the roses in the 'marvellous' rose-garden needed watering, he made it rain only there and nowhere else. And one day, during a thunderstorm, he took Mirra up to the roof of the villa. Mirra asked him whether this was prudent under the circumstances, but he reassured her. And there she observed how, after mumbling some formulas, he deflected a bolt of lightning off its course. 'He was terrible,' she would later say, and also: 'He was very knowledgeable.'

Even Little Boy, the dog 'who adored me,' participated in the ambience. One day with his wet nose he woke Mirra up from her nap for their daily walk, though she found him still asleep when she went down: he had exteriorized from his sleeping body to go and call her.

It may be remembered that Mirra, because of her harsh realistic and positivist education – for which she remained ever thankful – was not a person to imagine things; on the contrary, she would always look for the most concrete, plausible and rational explanation. But concreteness does not seem to be limited to the tridimensional universe of our sense perceptions. 'You see, when people are in this occult consciousness everything is possible. It creates an atmosphere where everything, but *everything* is possible.' In this context 'atmosphere' might nowadays be translated by 'field.'

Mirra herself had become so skilled in matters occult that she, as reported by Sri Aurobindo, 'when being in Algiers appeared to a circle of friends sitting in Paris and took up a pencil and wrote a few words on paper.'[25] Let us recount two of the unusual happenings at Tlemcen in some detail. One day an Arab from town came to visit the Théons and started asking annoying questions about 'magic.' (In town all sorts of rumors were rife concerning Max Théon, whom the Muslim townspeople often saw dressed in a manner only becoming of prophets.) Alma, getting tired of the tactless visitor, whispered to Mirra: 'We are going to have some fun, just watch.' They were sitting around a fairly big and heavy table on the veranda,* but nobody was touching it. As the visitor went on asking his prying questions, the table started moving and then actually jumped on him 'with a heroic élan!' Alma had not touched it; she had only looked at it. 'First the table began waddling a bit, then it moved forward, and all of a sudden, in one single jump, it threw itself on the man, who left in a hurry never to come back.'[26]

The second anecdote, in the Mother's own words, goes as follows. 'Tlemcen is very near the Sahara and has a desert climate, except in the valley where a river flows which never dries up and makes the whole place very fertile. The mountains, however, were absolutely arid. Only on the lands occupied by the farmers did something grow. Now, Monsieur Théon's park – a large estate – was, as I said, a marvellous place, everything grew there, everything one could imagine, and to a magnificent size.

'[Madame Théon] told me – they had been living there for many years – that about five or six years before, I think, they had felt that the barrenness of the mountains might one day cause the river to dry up and that it would be better to plant trees. So the administrator of Tlemcen† ordered trees to be planted on all the surrounding hills. He ordered that pine trees should be planted, for in Algeria the sea pine grows very well.

'For some reason or other – forgetfulness or fancy, nobody knows – instead of pine trees they ordered fir trees! Fir trees belong to northern countries, not at all in desert lands. And very conscientiously all those fir trees were planted ... Four or five years later [and thanks to Madame Théon's occult intervention] those fir trees had not only survived, they had become magnificent. When I went to Tlemcen, the mountains all around were absolutely green, full of splendid trees!

'... Then, [Madame Théon] told me, three years after the fir trees had been planted, suddenly one day or rather one night in December, after she had just gone to bed and put out the light, she was awakened

---

* This table can be seen in the photo of the front of Théon's house next to p. 172 in *Glimpses of the Mother's Life I* by Nilima Das. In the same photo Mirra Alfassa is leaning through the window of her guest room on the first floor, perhaps talking to Little Boy, who is visible in the courtyard.

† Algeria was then a French colony.

by a tiny little noise. She was very sensitive to noise. She opened her eyes and saw something like a moonbeam – there was no moon that night – lighting up a corner of her room. And she noticed that a little gnome was there, like the ones they tell about in the Scandinavian fairy-tales. He was a little fellow with a big head, a pointed cap, pointed dark green shoes, a long white beard, and covered with snow all over. She looked at him – she had her eyes open – and said: "What are you doing here?" She was a little worried, for it was warm in her room and the snow was melting and making a small puddle on the parquet floor.

'He gave her his sweetest smile and said: "But we were called by the fir trees! Fir trees call the snow, they are trees of the snow countries. I am the Lord of the Snow, so I came to announce you that we are coming. We have been called, we are coming" ... He went away. The moonlight went with him. She lit a lamp – there was no electricity – and saw a little pool of water in the place where he had stood. So it was no dream, there really had been a little being whose snow had melted in her room. And the next morning, when the sun rose, it shone upon mountains covered with snow. It was the first time, snow had never been seen before in that country. Since then every winter – not for long, just for a little while – all the mountains have been covered with snow.' [27]

Claire and Louis Thémanlys visited the Théons a few months later, from April till June 1907. In her narration of that visit, called *Un Séjour chez les Grands Initiés* (A Stay with the Great Initiates) and published by the *Publications cosmiques,* Claire narrates how Aia presided over the meals, seated at the head of the table, with Alma, whom he served with deference, and no doubt also Teresa to his right, and the Thémanlyses to his left. She calls Teresa 'the old secretary, that paragon of discrete dedication.' She describes how Aia, 'cheerful, witty and brilliant ... walked with brisk steps in the shadowy lanes of the park,' all the while rolling cigarettes with nimble fingers and expounding 'Bereschith [the opening verses of Genesis], of which every word, every letter is a teaching of life.' And she tells how Alma, her red shawl tightened around her shoulders, was constantly writing down her experiences and visions.

She also confirms almost all the wondrous happenings mentioned above: the table that moved, this time on Claire's request, the gong sounding without anybody touching it – and also the tablecloth folding itself, a small bell floating tinkling through the dining room from end to end, a shower of flowers raining down in the same dining room, and so on. And she specifies: 'Those phenomena took place at noon, in broad daylight, as well as at night in the light of a lamp, outside on the terraces as well as in the closed dining room.'[28] According to her, the Théons had correspondents in all European countries, Alma often telling Théon in advance the contents of letters just posted to him.

Henri Morisset joined his wife at Tlemcen on 17 August 1906 – and had a violent quarrel with Théon about the color of the latter's habit, whether it was violet or purple. (Théon: 'When I say it is purple, it is purple!') The Morissets left Tlemcen on 14 October.

What was the Cosmic Tradition the Théons propounded and to which the Mother would keep referring afterwards? It seems it derived from three sources, out of which Théon distilled an occult philosophical system. The first source was the very old Tradition at the origin of the Vedic and the Chaldean wisdom; this has already been mentioned, together with Mirra's confirmation of it from her own experience. Speaking about this Tradition Alma said: 'All truth, all beauty come from the old, simple and profound philosophy that is the source from where the vulgarized religions have drawn their primitive waters, now alas so often vitiated and corrupted.'

The second source was the rich, continuous flow of Alma's direct experience, uttered in trance and noted down by Teresa, or recorded by Alma herself when seen in visions or dreams. The third source, though seldom mentioned, was no doubt the Jewish tradition of the Kabbalah; this becomes clear from the testimony of Claire Thémanlys and from an essay by Peter Heehs. As Heehs puts it: 'The two historic traditions thought by contemporary occultists to be the oldest and most remarkable, the "Aryan" and the "Chaldean," were said by the Théons to be early "deformations" of the original tradition. They nevertheless conceded that they had "borrowed above all from the oral Chaldean tradition" … This I believe was an indirect way of saying that they borrowed chiefly from the Hebraic tradition, in particular the Kabbalah.'[29]

Summarizing, one may say that at the core of their thinking was the idea of evolution – not only evolution of or on this Earth, but of former universes. According to the Cosmic Tradition, there have been six universes preceding the existing one, each representing a quality of the One Being for whom there is no name. The present universe is the seventh and the last. It is based on the qualities of equilibrium and unending progress. As the Mother would explain: 'There is an old tradition which says that the world was created seven times, that is to say that the first six times it returned into the Creator ... It is said that we are now the seventh creation, and that this is the last one. This is the one which will remain, it is the creation of the equilibrium ... This is the last, which means that the world will not fall back again into a *pralaya** and that there will be a perpetual progress.'

We can read this progress in the gradations or stages of evolution as known at present, although the material manifestations of the evolution should be seen as the result of the underlying workings of the Spirit. In the evolution, the human being plays a crucial role. 'If only humanity understood its role as "evolutor" of the planet,' said Théon.[30] For, the human being is that decisive step in evolution at which life becomes conscious of itself. As it is clear that the present human being is too imperfect to be the summit of creation; other, higher gradations of beings must be expected to appear on the Earth. This is where the teaching of the Théons touches the view of Sri Aurobindo. Even matter as it is now will evolve, which means that the material body will evolve and gradually or in a quantum leap give birth to the appearance of beings with a 'supramental' body, the *corps glorieux* (body of light) of which the Théons spoke.

What made Théon's Cosmic Tradition important was that it represented a theory that could be put into practice. When still in the H. B. of L., Max Théon had been 'the group's chief instructor of practical occultism ... The H. B. of L. was an "order of practical occultism." Its use of mystical techniques to open the way to inner experience was something of a novelty at the time. Most esoteric groups, including the Theosophical Society, were content to disseminate secret doctrines ...

---

* The Sanskrit word *pralaya* means dissolution into the Supreme.

The popularity of the practical approach of the H. B. of L. encouraged the Theosophical Society to open its own "esoteric section" in 1888.'[31]

It was exceptional for well-known occultists, as the Théons had already been in Britain, to withdraw for ten years in order to deepen or recast their knowledge and their powers. (They were also fortunate to have sufficient financial means at their disposal.) It was most probably Alma who was responsible for the long retreat in Tlemcen, as she seems to have been the mainstay of everything the Cosmic Tradition represented. How much Théon depended on her would become evident when she unexpectedly passed away.

We now have an inkling of the occult powers of the Théons, and Mirra's realization of the inner Divine is proof of the spiritual effectiveness of their teaching. The contribution of the Théons to the spiritual riches of the world will remain alive thanks to their close connection with Mirra Morisset, who for a while was their student and collaborator.

The Morissets were still living in the Rue Lemercier. Their house, though, was no longer solely an artist's home; it had also become a centre of occult and spiritual meetings, for instance, for the group *Idéa* on Wednesday evenings. It was there, in January 1907, that they were visited – during one of their meetings – by a Russian revolutionary. This was not long after the first attempt to overthrow the repressive regime in Russia had been bloodily quashed. Mirra wrote of this encounter in a piece called *Un chef* (A Leader).[32]

'We were assembled, a few friends and I myself, in a small group for philosophical studies, when the presence was announced of a mysterious visitor who asked to be introduced to us. We went to meet him, and in the reception room we saw a man in a suit that was clean but worn to the thread ... I asked him: "What do you want, monsieur?" – "I have come from Kiev to meet you ... In Kiev there is a group of students who are very much interested in the major philosophical ideas. We happened to read your books,* and we were glad to find at last a synthetic teaching which does not restrict itself to theory but urges one on to action ... My occupation is revolution."' And Mirra wrote: 'Those words rang like a knell in the luxury of our bourgeois apartment.'

---

* The publications of the *Movement cosmique*.

What could this man – held by some to have been Maxim Gorky's son[33] – expect from the Cosmic Movement? He explained how they had tried to topple the Czarist regime through violence and terror, but even in the middle of this he had felt that something better was possible by means of an inner development. 'We are not strong enough to wage the struggle by force ... We should develop our intelligence more to understand the profound laws of nature, and to better learn how to act with order, how to coordinate our efforts ... I have succeeded in making my friends understand all that.' And, he said, he had come to ask the help of the Cosmic Movement to adapt its ideas to the situation in Russia, and also to write a brochure 'which would spread among the Russian people those beautiful ideas of solidarity, harmony, liberty and justice.'

Mirra's advice was the following: 'You have to yield for some time, to draw back into the shadows, to prepare yourself in silence ... No longer put your weapons in the hands of the enemy, be yourselves, irreproachable when standing up to him, show him the example of a courageous patience, of rectitude and justice. Then your victory will be near-at-hand, for you will have justice on your side, integral justice, not only as to the goal but also as to means.' – 'I am glad, madame, to see that a woman shows concern about these kind of problems. Women can do so much to hasten the coming of better days.' On taking leave, he said that even in Paris he and the woman who helped him get around – he had serious trouble with his eyesight – did not feel safe, because the police suspected them of being dangerous anarchists. He was never seen again.

Tlemcen – The Second Visit (1907)

Mirra arrived for her second stay with the Théons on 18 July 1907. There is a huge difference between Mirra's relationship to the Tlemcen masters and that of somebody like Claire Thémanlys. Claire was a neophyte, still curious to have Alma show her powers and as yet hardly receptive to the influence of the occult force the masters were trying out on her. Mirra, on the contrary, was already an experienced occultist before her first visit to Tlemcen and had already had her first major spiritual realization. True, Théon and Alma taught her a lot, and she would remain thankful for this even long after they were gone; but she also 'worked together' with them, especially during her second stay.

Of that work we know little. The Mother has told that it was quite perilous, for she exteriorized all the sheaths of her being from her material body, which remained behind in a cataleptic state under the surveillance of Théon. Surveillance on such occasions is an absolute necessity, for the only tie then remaining with the material body is the 'silver cord,' the existence of which is common knowledge in occultism. If that link snaps or is cut off, the person loses contact with the material world; in other words, he or she dies.

Mirra also learned to exteriorize twelve times in succession up to the upper limit of the manifestation, just like Alma, and she had learned how to talk during her trance, an ability mastered only by the most advanced occultists. 'My body was in a cataleptic state and I was in a conscious trance, but it was a special kind of catalepsy, in that my body could speak. I could speak, although very slowly. Théon had taught me how to do it.'[34] And the Mother added: 'However, this state is not without danger, the proof being that during my work, for some reason or other – obviously due to some negligence on Théon's part, who was there to watch over me – the cord was cut ... The link was cut malevolently.'

What happened? In some world visited by Mirra during her exteriorization under the direction of Théon, she found the 'Mantra of Life.' This is the formula by which one can give life and also take it, create life and also destroy it. 'This mantra was shut away, sealed, with my name on it in Sanskrit. I didn't know Sanskrit at that time, but he did.' Still, Mirra was aware that it was Sanskrit, told Théon so and started to describe the characters to him. Théon, for some reason, 'got very interested.' He told Mirra to break the seal and tell him what was hidden there. Then 'something in me knew at once,' and she refused to tell him.

This made Théon violently angry and his anger cut the cord. Mirra was dead. Théon, because Mirra had been able to warn him in the nick of time, became frightened and used all his occult knowledge and powers to pull her back into her material body. But the Mother said that the friction of re-entering her material body was an extremely painful experience. 'I returned as a result of the power and the will, because ... simply because I still had something to do on the Earth ... He made me drink half a glass of cognac. He always made me take some every day after the session, because I remained working in trance for more than an hour, which generally is a forbidden practice.'[35]

Mirra had brought her music scores with her on this visit, for there was a piano at the house of the Théons, normally played by Teresa. Do toads have a sense of music? The fat and warty one, which came and sat on the threshold of the open door while Mirra was playing Mozart and Beethoven, must have felt something, for it remained listening as if transfixed; and when Mirra stopped playing, it thanked her for the recital with a couple of deep-throated croaks, then hopped away into the night.

When after a stay of two months Mirra left for France, Max Théon, who was going on a tour of Europe, accompanied her. While they were crossing the Mediterranean, a violent storm arose. Everybody on the ship grew nervous and scared, except Théon and Mirra. He looked at her and said: 'Go and stop it.' She entered her cabin, lay down and went out of her body – to find that huge beings, invisible to humans, were dancing wildly on the water and making the ship bob up and down like a cork. She pleaded with those beings 'for half an hour' to refrain and save the lives of the humans on the ship. Finally they consented and the troubled sea calmed down. 'I then went back into my body and came out of the cabin. When I went on deck I found all the people gathered there happily engaged in jovial talk.'[36] There is no evidence that after that journey Mirra ever saw Max Théon and Alma again.

One has the impression that Alma withdrew from life of her own will. After she and her husband had spent the summer of 1908 in France with Louis and Claire Thémanlys, she wanted, at the beginning of September, to visit the British Channel Islands. (She had been born on the Isle of Wight.) Before the departure of the ferry-boat from the harbour of Côteret, there was time for a stroll along a rather dangerous path between rocks protruding over the sea. Eyewitnesses say that she slipped, probably in trance as usual, and fell into the cold waters. She did not want to postpone her outing but became ill during the crossing. On her arrival in the port of Gorey, on the island of Jersey, she was taken to a hotel, where she died that very day, 10 September.'[37]

His wife's death was a heavy blow for Théon and he never got over it. He stopped the publication of the *Revue cosmique* in December of the same year, 1908. Afterwards he lived sequestered in Tlemcen, so much so that the Mother, like most others who had known him, thought that he had died in 1913. In that year Théon, who was a reckless car driver, did meet with a serious accident, having to walk on crutches for a long time afterwards. He died many years later, in 1927, with the faithful Teresa at his side. She would survive him for less than a year. The red-painted house of wonders in Tlemcen was empty.

Sri Aurobindo would reportedly say: 'Théon knew that he was not meant to succeed but had only come to prepare the way to a certain extent for others to come and perfect it. But later the disciples around him made him believe himself to be the man destined to bring down the Supermind into the physical plane, and naturally the whole thing came to a smash. His wife saw that the Supermind was not to be attained by them and that the venture had failed for the time being, and so she gave up her body. It was she who had been supporting Théon with her knowledge and powers; without her he was nothing, and naturally after her death the entire project suffered shipwreck.'[38]

More than sixty years later the Mother would look back in amazement: 'Théon and Sri Aurobindo did not know each other. They never met, they did not know of each other's existence, till, without having at all proceeded along the same lines, they reached the same conclusion. In totally different countries, without ever having met, and at the same moment they knew the same thing. And I have known the one as well as the other.'[39]

The Four Asuras

There is an important part of the Cosmic Tradition that has not yet been touched upon: the explanation of how a world like ours is the result of God's workings – and can only be such a result, as there is nothing else but God, or That, or the Divine, or the Supreme. The Mother talked about a 'very old Tradition' several times, always emphasizing that the story, as narrated by her, sounded like a children's tale, but that its symbolism was profound and referred to the actual facts.

Once it so happened that 'God' decided to exteriorize himself 'in order to know himself in detail.' To that end he first manifested his Consciousness, which is the Universal or Divine Mother, and ordered her to make a universe. The Universal Mother emanated four beings, representing the four essential powers of God (and therefore of herself): Truth, Consciousness (that is Light), Life, and Ananda (which means Bliss).* Those four beings 'were indeed altogether very high beings, of the highest Reality.'

But God had also expressed the wish that his manifestation should be based on freedom. 'He wanted all that went forth from him to be absolutely independent and free so that it might unite with him in freedom, not through compulsion.' Because of their freedom, those high and essentially godlike beings each deemed themselves to be the very Godhead himself, which of course is an absurdity, for the Divine is One. This meant that, in a manner of speaking, they distanced themselves from their origin, thereby turning into its opposites. Truth became Falsehood; Consciousness-Light became the black Inconscient; Life became Death; Bliss became Suffering. (One finds in this story the elements of many great traditions all over the world, although most remember only part of it. The Bible, for instance, mentions only the Being of Light.)

---

* The supreme attributes of the Divine are *Sat* (Existence or Truth), *Chit* (Consciousness that is Light) and *Ananda* (Bliss). A Sanskrit 'name' of the Divine is therefore *Sat-Chit-Ananda*, spelled in the English transliteration as Sachchidananda. However, an essential aspect of Chit is *Tapas* (Power that is Life), for everything the Divine is conscious of at the same time exists in one of the many modes of his Power.

The manifestation had taken a turn for the worse. The Universal Mother, upon seeing this, was greatly disturbed and turned to God, asking him to come to her aid. God said to her: 'Start again, but this time try to do it in such a way that the beings are less independent.' And it was thus that the Great Mother created the gods. 'But as the first four had come before them, at every step the gods ran into them, and so it was that the world changed into a battlefield' between gods and demons, Good and Evil, as all the great traditions tell. Time and again the gods have to do battle with the first four *Asuras* and with their emanations – for the Asuras had the power to multiply into 'cascades' of millions of lesser beings who resembled them and assisted them in their work.

If the world had to continue like this, it would never turn godlike, it would never become its divine Origin again. But when she emanated the gods, the Great Creatrix poured her divine Love into the dark Inconscient. It is this Love that is the driving force of the development of the world, of its evolution on the way back, or up, to its divinization. And as all forces are beings and all beings forces, this Love is a divine Being ever present at the core of the manifestation, which some call 'creation.' It is this Being who incarnates in what in India are called the *Avatars*, the series of direct divine interventions in the unfolding of the evolution.

In the *Revue cosmique* Mirra published a vision she had – an occult experience – in which she met that Being in a deep cave at the bottom of the ocean of existence. It radiated all the positive forces which co-operate in the development of the world and which are concretely and personally present in its history as Avatars (incarnations of the essential Divine) or as *Vibhutis* (incarnations of divine powers). That Being was apparently asleep, she wrote, but when she approached it, it opened its eyes.

Why is it worth knowing all this? Because the Asuras never in-carnate as such, only in partial representations or emanations. And because Mirra became closely associated with the direct emanations of all four original Asuras. Her encounters with three of them are well documented.

Asuric beings, like the gods, exist in non-evolutionary worlds and are therefore immortal. To change, to evolve to a higher status – to a divine one for example – they have to take on an earthly body, and most of them refuse to do this. The reason is that in an earthly body they are subject to the forces of the earthly evolution, while in their own worlds they are intangible and sovereignly immortal. The Cosmic Tradition, as we have seen, taught that the earthly evolution is leading to a divinized being in a *corps glorieux* – as Sri Aurobindo in a faraway part of the globe was also discovering. It was therefore Mirra's endeavour to convert the Asuras and to make them take up a material form, for without their conversion, or their disappearance by reintegration into their Origin, a new species on Earth could not be achieved because of their insuperable resistance to it. By their conversion or disappearance, the fatal change of the four essential aspects of the Godhead into their contraries – the Fall at the beginning of our universe aeons ago – would be reversed, and the manifestation could continue in its Godward evolution.

Mirra met the Asura of Light (actually the Asura of the dark Inconscient) on her occult explorations under Théon's guidance during her first stay at Tlemcen. In the Semitic traditions this Asura of Light is called Lucifer or Satan. He agreed to her request to collaborate and consented to be 'clothed in a body,' but only a subtle, vital one. 'You could feel him the way you feel a draught.' He refused to be born of human parents, which is the only way to get a material body. Théon wanted to keep the converted Asura in his power, for the master occultist felt perfectly at home in the vital also. Mirra, well knowing who Théon really was, pretended she had not understood him and let the converted Asura freely choose the way in which he wanted to collaborate. 'He said that he was going to set in motion the Chinese revolution … "Mark my words, [he said,] it will happen in exactly five years" … I noted it down. And *exactly* five years later it happened.' The last Chinese emperor, a child, was overthrown in 1911 by the revolutionaries led by Sun Yat-sen (1866-1925). 'That,' the Asura said, 'will be the beginning, the first terrestrial movement heralding … the new world upon Earth.'

But then, who was Théon? The Mother has said repeatedly that he was an emanation of the Asura of Death. This explains his great powers, his fearlessness, and his combative character. It also explains why he was so interested in the mantra of life (and death), and why his anger was potent enough to cut Mirra's lifecord.

And with this goes a story. When Mirra was fifteen, she went with her mother to Italy, where Elvire, Mathilde's sister, was living with her family. Mirra, who spoke Italian well at that time, and her mother visited the *Palazzo Ducale* in Venice, the Palace of the Doges, situated next to the San Marco basilica on the world-famous *Piazza San Marco*. Visitors on a tour through the palace pass through the cells where formerly the prisoners were locked up. Those cells are beside a narrow canal crossed by the Bridge of Sighs, from where prisoners taken to their execution had a last look over the lagoon, symbol of mighty seafaring Venice.

The walls in the prison cells are covered with graffiti, scribbled by the prisoners. Strangely, Mirra felt attracted to a graffito there and *knew* that it was from her own hand. And she 'saw' how she had been there with a prisoner, how some people suddenly had burst into the cell, caught hold of her, tied her up and thrown her through a window into the canal. The experience was so vivid and overwhelming that she had to leave the palace and breathe some fresh air outside.

As she was always looking for explanations of her experiences, she discovered what had happened. 'I researched in museums, looked up archives, found out my name, other people's names.'[40] A doge had usurped the throne of his predecessor and thrown the latter's son into prison. But unknown to the usurper his daughter was in love with the son of his rival, the imprisoned young man whom she secretly went to visit. Her father, having discovered her secret visits, fell into a fit of rage and ordered his daughter to be drowned. His order was executed without delay. By now the reader will have understood who the hot-tempered doge and his daughter were at the beginning of the twentieth century. It seems, besides, that one of the Venetian doges, portrayed by Titian, bears a close resemblance to Max Théon, of whom Mirra drew a remarkable portrait in 1906.[41] In that former Venetian life, and (briefly) in this one too, Mirra had been killed by the Asura of Death.

Did she succeed in converting Théon? The following words of the Mother are probably applicable to him: 'There is one [Asura] who has almost made an attempt at conversion, but he has not been able to do it. When it had to be done, he felt it as quite unpleasant. So he put it off till another time.' One should remember that Asuras are beings of immense power, with an ego on a similar scale. If it is already so difficult for a human being to surrender its ego to the Divine, the difficulty for beings of that order, who since the beginning of the manifestation have been the lords of the universe, to surrender their self-will must be enormous. And this, of course, is why their conversion is crucial for the destiny of the world.

Mirra's encounter with a third emanation – an emanation of the Asura of Falsehood, who calls himself 'Lord of the Nations' – will take up part of the following chapter.

Mirra Morisset's connection with the Cosmic Movement had lasted five years, for her a period of enormous progress and change. Her life as an artist and her marriage gradually came to an end. A page of her life was being turned, and on the following page nothing but questions were as yet to be read. Mirra knew that she was being carried, just as in her early youth, and that the call to her mission would have to be answered one day. But now she knew also who she actually was, for Alma had told her.

4.
A Synthesis in the Making

Accustomed only to read outward signs
None saw aught new in her, none divined her state.[1]

– Sri Aurobindo

Mirra's divorce from Henri Morisset took place in March 1909. She went to live alone on the fifth floor of 49 Rue du Levis, a street parallel to the Rue de Tocqueville and not far from her former house. Maybe the following statement of the Mother was applicable to Morisset also: 'When you saw the artist at work, he lived in a magnificent beauty, but when you saw the gentleman at home, he had only a very limited contact with the artist in himself, and he became generally speaking a very vulgar, very ordinary man.'[2] And she had a character in one of her plays say: 'I always dreamt of a great love that would be shared, free from all animal activity, something that could physically represent the great love at the origin of the worlds. This dream accounted for my marriage. But the experience was not a happy one. I have loved deeply, with great sincerity and intensity, but my love has not met with the response it hoped for.'[3]

On Her Own

For the time being Mirra was on her own, which does not mean that she led the life of a disillusioned divorcee or an embittered recluse. On the contrary, she took the opportunity to see as much of the world and of her fellow human beings as possible, and where could she have found a more colorful gamut of the human experience than in *la ville lumière*, the City of Light? For Mirra was of the opinion that there should be no barrier between the spiritual and the ordinary life, everything without exception being the One. It might be less easy to lead the spiritual life in the midst of the ordinary, but the result would prove to be much richer and more complete, more integral.

She met Anatole France and asked him if he knew of the Cosmic Tradition, as he had in his novel *La révolte des anges* written pages that closely agreed with its teachings. But the famous author had never heard of the Cosmic Tradition. He had reached the same insights guided by his intuition. She went to performances of all three forms of theatre Paris had to offer: sophisticated, for example the *Comédie française;* the 'boulevard theatre,' showing the risqué comedies its bourgeois public craved for; and the Grand Guignol, the folksy melodramatic plays, performed mostly in theatres on the outskirts of the city for an emotional and boisterous audience. In one of her conversations the Mother describes vividly how much the spectators identified with the characters on the stage during a popular cloak-and-dagger play *Le Bossu* (the hunchback).

Mirra also enjoyed music very much and had several composers among her acquaintances. One of them was Ambroise Thomas, a celebrity at the time because of his twenty operas – foremost *Mignon,* which is still in the international repertoire, and *Hamlet.* Thomas would become Director of the Paris Conservatory of music. He was probably the composer who, as the Mother said, was so skilled at the intricate art of orchestrating music – 'it's like higher mathematics' – that other composers had their orchestrations done by him. Thomas had visited India and taken a youthful, good-looking Indian girl with him as the nanny of his children. This girl was clairvoyant and excelled at palmistry, so much so that she was engaged at the *Moulin Rouge,* where she performed under the guise of – what else? – an Indian 'maharani.'

We know that Mirra learnt to play the piano and to sing at an early age. When she was fourteen she had a powerful experience when, during a marriage ceremony in a synagogue, exalting music of Camille Saint-Saëns was played and a flashing ray of light pierced her heart. As the Mother she would later say that art is a great means of spiritual progress, and she would often tell her young, bright-eyed audience during her evening talks about the occult levels or worlds where sound and music originate, and about the composers whose music she had loved so much.

César Franck, she would say, had a psychic opening and created his music under the direct influence of his soul – something most music lovers who know his (only) symphony, or his *Trois Chorals* for organ, will have difficulty disagreeing with. She would call Hector Berlioz, who transmuted every feeling into sound, 'the very incarnation of music,' and she put him, despite his shortcomings, among the greatest composers. She said that something like an unhealthy vein ran through the compositions of Frédéric Chopin. And she would talk about Bach, Mozart and Beethoven, and about the occult inspiration in many parts of the operas of Richard Wagner, whose fame was around the turn of the century at its peak, in France as well as elsewhere.

And then there was Eugene Ysaÿe, the Belgian violinist, 'truly the most wonderful violinist of his age. That man had most certainly a reincarnation of Beethoven in him – not perhaps a reincarnation of [Beethoven's] entire psychic being, but in any case that of his musical capacity. He looked alike, he had the head of Beethoven. I have seen him, I have heard him play ... I did not know him, I knew nothing about him. I was at a concert in Paris and there was [Beethoven's] Concerto in D major [for violin and orchestra] on the programme ... I saw him coming on the stage to play and I said: "Isn't that strange how much this man looks like Beethoven: he is the very likeness of Beethoven!" Then the violin joined in with one stroke of the bow, three, four notes ... and everything changed, the whole atmosphere changed. All suddenly became marvellous. Three notes, struck with such power, such grandeur! It was so wonderful that nothing stirred anymore, all remained as if suspended. And he played that from beginning to end in an absolutely unique manner, with an understanding I have not met with in any other performer. And then I saw that the musical genius of Beethoven was in him.'[4]

Cranks, Seekers and Sages

It is undeniable that in our human world today an elite manifests itself of which the distinctive mark is a higher Consciousness that wants to participate in a wisdom beyond the rational knowledge.[5]

– M. Schwaller de Lubicz

'When I was in Paris, I went to many places where there were meetings of all kinds and people who were doing all sorts of research, spiritual (so-called spiritual), occult, and so on.'[6] This was a world in the shadows of public life, as it were, but the object of widespread interest and busily frequented. It was the world of mediums, spiritism, automatic writing, poltergeist phenomena, alchemy, astrology, channelling, white and black magic, Satanism. As Peter Washington writes: 'Churches were in decline. Atheists and materialists attacked them from without. The abuse of clerical privilege and collusion between Church and State exposed them to the criticism of liberals and radicals ... The antiquity, hierarchy and secular power which had for so long been the sources of their authority were now the cause of internal revolt and public disaffection.' Besides: 'The study of Asian religion had been proceeding in Europe since the late eighteenth century, when the Royal Asiatic Society was formed in London and Hindu scriptures were translated into French and English. By the 1870s German scholars were producing magnificent editions and translations of the Hindu Vedas and major Buddhist texts.'[7]

Mirra was of course very much at home in this kind of activities. It is no exaggeration to say that at the time she was already one of the greatest occultists alive, and, in the Western context at least, one of the most spiritually advanced people. She wanted to find out what was going on in that immense patchwork of occult and pseudo-occult groups and gatherings. She wanted, as always, to learn and – where appropriate – to teach or communicate some of her knowledge. For if a great part of the 'occult wave' was bogus and fare for cranks, there were also truly gifted and sincerely seeking people. We have already met the clairvoyant Madame Fraya, and there were others of her kind and with her talent.

Mirra also wanted, if and where appropriate, to put matters straight and warn people. 'There was a time when I wanted to prove to people that what they were evoking was nothing but themselves. I then had some fun simply by a concentration of the will giving bangs to the furniture, making tables walk, and all such things.'[8] She especially made it clear that most of the occult phenomena were caused by little vital beings, the 'elementals,' of which we have already heard as denizens of the lower vital world and who find their amusement in making fools of the by-and-large ignorant and defenceless human beings.

'Those who indulge in this kind of practice [e.g. table-turning or automatic writing], which derives from an unhealthy curiosity, get what they deserve. You should know that the atmosphere we live in is full of a great number of small vital entities which are born of unsatisfied desires, of vital movements of a very low type, and also of the decomposition of larger beings of the vital world. Indeed, it is swarming with them. It is no doubt thanks to a special protection that most people do not see what is going on in this vital atmosphere, for it is not exactly pleasant. But if out of presumption they want to come into contact with [that atmosphere] and set about trying automatic writing or table-turning, or anything else of that kind, out of an unhealthy curiosity, well, what happens is that one or several of those small entities have fun at their expense. They gather all the necessary information from the subconscious mind [of the humans] and then provide them with that information as convincing proof that they are the person who has been summoned! I could write a book with instances I have known of this kind of stories.'[9]

The group of people who had met regularly in the studio of Rue Lemercier now continued to meet, on Wednesday nights, in Mirra's small fifth floor apartment in Rue du Levis. 'They came to have me demonstrate or to tell them about certain things.' The Mother would later tell about the fate of one of the participants, a young man who was a student and a poet, but who was also leading a rather murky sexual life. Although other members of the group had met him a couple of days before, he did not show up on the evening of the meeting. 'We waited quite a long time. Then the meeting was over and when I opened the door to let the people out, there sat there a big dark-grey cat which rushed like mad into the room and jumped upon me, mewing desperately. I looked into its eyes and said to myself: "But these are *his* eyes," meaning the person who had not shown up, "surely something has happened to him." The next day we learned that he had been murdered the night before; he had been found lying strangled on his bed ... The eyes of the cat had completely changed, they had become human eyes.' [10]

Mister Mind

Mirra had first met him in Montmorency, at the house of Henri Morisset's sisters, who were looking after her son André: Paul Antoine Richard, born in 1874 in the south of France, intelligent, good-looking, and very interested in occultism. Richard too must have discovered the *Revue cosmique,* for he had already been on a visit to Tlemcen from 7 January to 17 February 1907. One may suppose that he had wanted to know more than Max Théon and Alma were able to tell him in those few weeks, that the Théons had a clear perception of his personality and capacities, and that they therefore had told him about Mirra Morisset, as she was still called. Mirra and Richard met shortly afterwards, some say during a game of tennis, which Mirra liked to play so much.

Richard had been impressed by Max Théon. He wrote after his visit to Tlemcen: 'I have passed forty days with the most wonderful man in the world. I feel as if I have climbed a high mountain, from which I have been able to descry the magnificent horizons that I always have dreamed of. It is certain that there always have been men who have come from on high to manifest the divine power and goodness. This confirms what I have long felt ... Great things are taking shape.' [11]

After serving four years in the army, Richard had studied philosophy and theology, and been a *pasteur* [French Protestant minister] from 1898 to 1905, first in Montauban and afterwards in Lille, near the Belgian border. In Lille he had founded or joined a number of philanthropic organizations. His humanitarian interests drew him increasingly towards socialism. The twentieth century, he wrote in a letter, would be one of unprecedented enlightenment, in which 'science and faith would eventually meet.' In 1905 Richard resigned his ministry and dedicated himself fully to humanitarian work. He joined the *Ligue des Droits de l'Homme et du Citoyen*, a pro-Dreyfus group. In the same year he took up the study of law, failed to kick-start a political career, and supported himself as a writer for a Paris daily. He also became a Freemason. Freemasonry was extremely powerful at the time and the main force in the struggle of rationalism and liberalism against the Catholic Church and the anti-Dreyfusards. 'The Masonic loges recruited on a grand scale and formed, in the still well-kept secret of their initiatory rites, the cadres of the Third Republic.' [12]

Mirra and Richard grew much closer after her divorce from Morisset in March 1908. She studied law along with Richard – we are reminded of her studying mathematics together with her brother – so extensively that she 'could have passed the examination.' Richard obtained his law degree from the *Académie de Lille* in July 1908.[13] Shortly afterwards he became a barrister at the Paris Court of Appeals. He was still eager to enter politics, and in February 1910 joined the *Ligue de Défense et de Propagande Républicaine Radicale et Radicale-Socialiste*, a party much smaller than its resounding name might suggest, combining 'a leftist ideology with a conservative financial programme (and a strong Masonic influence).' [14]

It was supposedly this party that sent Paul Richard to Pondicherry, a French *comptoir* in the deep south of the Indian subcontinent, a little more than 150 kilometres south of Madras, on the Coromandel Coast. A *comptoir* was an anchoring place where the French did colonial business and provided for their ships for the voyage ahead to East Asia or back towards the motherland. They had several such *comptoirs* on the Indian coasts. Pondicherry, the most important one, was a rather backward, out-of-the-way place at the time Richard arrived there. As K.R. Srinivasa Iyengar describes it, it was 'a dead city … like a backwater of the sea, a stagnant pool by the shore … akin to a cemetery … infested by ghosts and goblins.' [15] But it *was* French territory and consequently entitled to a representative in the Chamber of Deputies in Paris. It is not clear whether it was Richard's mission to assist a certain Paul Bluysen in the latter's electoral campaign for the Hindu Party or whether he intended to campaign for himself.

Yet it seems that Richard was much more interested in finding a spiritual master, a yogi, than in his political pursuits. Behind all his humanitarianism, socialism, idealism and enthusiasm for human progress was hidden an urge for power for which we will soon be able to account. He, too, had certainly heard or read about all those Western occultists, H.P. Blavatsky being the foremost, who had been initiated and received power from some eastern guru, and the people who met with Richard on his arrival in Pondicherry report that one of his very first questions was where he could find a yogi.

'Since he was interested in occultism and spirituality, he took advantage of the occasion [the election] to come here [to Pondicherry] and to search,' the Mother said in a recorded conversation. 'He was searching for a "Master," a yogi. He arrived. The first thing he said, rather than occupying himself with politics, was: "I am looking for a yogi." Somebody told him: "You are really in luck, the yogi has just arrived."' [16]

The yogi in question was Aurobindo Ghose, at that moment the most famous revolutionary in India, who had turned his political revolution into a spiritual one. He had had to flee British territory because the colonial authorities were about to deport him, and found refuge in the French enclave of Pondicherry. He had arrived from Calcutta by boat and under an assumed name on 4 April 1910, which means that Richard must have arrived shortly afterwards. Mister Ghose, though, was 'less than anxious' to meet unknown people. After his arrival in Pondicherry he remained in seclusion for more than three months, not leaving the house in which he had been given shelter nor allowing the young men staying with him to do so either. 'The British Government in India could never accept that Sri Aurobindo had come away to French territory to carry on his yoga. Religion and spirituality, these to them were a mere subterfuge ... Here was the brain-centre of the Indian independence movement.' [17] Still Aurobindo Ghose agreed to see the French visitor. Although Ghose knew French perfectly well, he was not in the habit of speaking it, and a Pondicherrian revolutionary had to act as interpreter, for Richard had little English. This interpreter later wrote in his memoirs that the meeting went well and that Aurobindo Ghose became more and more interested in his visitor. Paul Richard, from his side, came away with a high opinion of the Indian master, but he was much more laudatory about his knowledge than about his spiritual realization, for which Richard did not possess the necessary discernment.

And the elections? Richard had grossly underestimated the difficulties that would face him in a God-forsaken place like Pondicherry, about which he knew practically nothing. 'On certain occasions, during the campaigns for political elections, complete anarchy seemed to reign in Pondicherry, while rioting and murder continued for days on end and blood flowed freely. People would not dare stir out of their houses, especially after dark.'[18] During the time of the elections, and at most other times, Pondicherry was terrorized by gangs in the pay of the political candidates. Richard, an unknown Frenchman and a lamb among wolves, stood no chance.

The date of his departure from Pondicherry is not known, but he was surely home before December. All he could show to back up his enthusiastic reports about his meetings with Aurobindo Ghose was a rather dim photograph in which Mirra, surprisingly, saw nothing but the politician Ghose had been at the time it was taken. 'I had the impression that it was a very interesting man, that's all.'

Alexandra David-Néel

In the meantime Mirra came to be on friendly terms with an extraordinary woman, Alexandra David-Néel. She may have met her for the first time when Madame David-Néel was giving a talk on Buddhism at the Guimet Museum, a place that crops up time and again in the lives of the Westerners who played a part in the discovery of the East. 'The Paris of the *fin de siècle* discovers Asia in the footsteps of the Goncourt Brothers who were the very first to give the starting signal for the run on Japanese prints, Buddhas in jade, silk fans embroidered with melancholic sunsets seen through branches of blossoming plum trees ... And in Paris, Asia had its temple: the Guimet Museum.'[19] This museum was familiar to Mirra. She had visited it many times, and, even when still a little girl, had had an unexpected contact with one of the mummies there and with certain artefacts used by Egyptian royalty.

Mirra had already been practising Buddhism in the minister's box at the opera. This time, while listening to Madame David-Néel, who was a convinced and practising Buddhist, she saw the Buddha present near the speaker, 'not above the head but a little to the side.' When the talk was over and Mirra told Madame David-Néel about her vision, she received the indignant repartee that such a thing was impossible because the Buddha had gone to Nirvana. All the same, both ladies came to respect each other's qualities and soon were friends.

Alexandra David-Néel was born near Paris in 1868. Her father, Louis David, was a friend of Victor Hugo and he too, just like the great writer, had been banished for his anti-government stance. As a consequence Alexandra grew up in Brussels, educated by a bigoted mother and in sanctimonious nuns' schools. In revolt against such stifling surroundings, she became an anti-conformist and an ascetic, an inborn trait that made it impossible to punish her in any way. She also seemed driven by an urge to depart for faraway places and went on several escapades, but each time she had to return home for lack of money.

In 1888, when old enough to go her own way, we find her in the London which Max Théon and Alma had recently left. There Alexandra became a member of the rapidly expanding Theosophical Society, the movement that opened up the eastern religion to the West. A year later she studied Sanskrit in Paris with professors from the *Collège de France*. She also improved her knowledge of English, took music and singing lessons, and inevitably discovered the Guimet Museum, where she often prostrated herself in front of the Buddha statues, so that the place became really a kind of a temple to her. She read extensively in the religious literature of the East, deepened her knowledge of the *Bhagavad Gita*, the *Rig Veda*, the *Dhammapada* and other essential texts, and discovered her vocation as an orientalist and a Buddhist. Her biographer, Jean Chalon, points out: 'For Alexandra Buddhism was not a religion but a philosophy.'

In 1892 she travelled to Ceylon and visited Colombo, then Madurai, Benares and Darjeeling on the subcontinent. As a member of the Theosophical Society she had no trouble finding friends and shelter.

And she always saw to it that her handbag was stuffed with letters of recommendation from well-known or highly-placed people.

Then Alexandra's life took an astonishing turn, for we next find her at the Hanoi Opera, in what was then still called Indochina, where in 1895 she became the *première chanteuse* under the pseudonym Alexandra Myrial! In 1897 she sang in Paris, but without the success she had hoped for, two years later at the Athens Opera, and, at the turn of the century, at the Tunis Opera. Of this last Opera she became the manager and married a railway engineer, Philippe Néel, of British origin. But Alexandra was also an ardent feminist and would never allow the shackles of marriage to press too deeply into her flesh, although we owe to that relationship many interesting letters addressed to her dear, generous 'Mouchy,' as she called her husband.

The very intelligent Alexandra, now Madame David-Néel, was also active as a journalist and gave talks about all new and progressive topics: socialism, feminism, eastern religions in general and Buddhism in particular. And this was how Mirra met her. For a while they saw each other almost every day, sat together for 'philosophical meditations,' and went for walks in the Bois de Boulogne, where some of the first aeroplanes, grasshopper-like, rose with sputtering engines a few feet into the air and landed – in most cases – less elegantly than the way the ladies and gentlemen sat down on the grass to admire them.

There are frequent short notes in Alexandra's diary concerning her friendship with Mirra, of the kind 'dinner with the Richards' or, on 1 January 1911: 'Started the year in a session of philosophical meditation at the Richards.' Although a 'philosophical' Buddhist and therefore logically an atheist, Alexandra was also interested in occultism. Putting some of her reading and travelling experiences together, she had by mental formation tried to create a 'mahatma' – mahatmas* were 'in' at the time – and succeeded in doing so. But then her mahatma never left her alone and became such a botheration to Alexandra that she tried to get rid of him by all possible means, though in vain. Finally, she had to confide in Mirra, the occult expert, and received the necessary advice

---

* 'Mahatma' means 'great soul.' In theosophy mahatmas are invisible sages who direct the course of history or exert an occult influence on the activities of humanity.

to reabsorb into herself the mental formation which the troublesome mahatma was.

'Madame David-Néel was an intense woman and capable of profound meditation,' said the Mother. And she gave an example. On her journey to the north of the Indian subcontinent, while her bearers were setting up camp, Alexandra went for a walk and became absorbed in meditation. Later on, returning to her surface consciousness, she found that she had strayed a long way from the camp and began to walk back – until she stood in front of a river. As the camp was definitely on the other side of it, she could only conclude, to her astonishment, that she must have crossed it while in concentration and unaware of her surroundings. She must have walked on water.

Another anecdote the Mother heard from Alexandra was of how one day she was sitting in meditation in front of a tree. When she opened her eyes she thought at first, probably because of the sunlight sifting through the trees, that she saw a heap of dry leaves. Then she thought that a zebra (!) was standing in front of her. But when her eyes adapted to the light she saw, at a short distance, a tiger of a respectable size fixing his interested gaze on her. As a true Buddhist, she distanced herself from everything life represented and withdrew within, ready for any eventuality. When after some time nothing happened, she opened her eyes again and saw that the tiger was gone. (Jean Chalon, showing an uncommonly penetrating insight into tiger psychology, writes: 'Vexed for having been taken for a heap of dead leaves and for a zebra, traumatized by the profound immobility of the woman he thought would be a tasty prey, the tiger fled to hide his shame deep in the jungle.')

Madame David-Néel would write in her book *L'Inde où j'ai vécu* (the India where I have lived): 'I have the best possible memories of the evenings spent with her [Mirra] in the small house she inhabited in the Rue du Val-de-Grâce in Paris, and of the walks together in the Bois de Boulogne. Neither she nor I myself could at that time have imagined the place she occupies today.' And she would characterize Mirra as 'a woman of distinction, an intellectual of a mystic tendency, of Levantine origin and French education.' And Jean Chalon comments: 'It stirs the imagination, that tête-a-tête of the future Mother of the Sri Aurobindo

Ashram and the future amazon of the Himalayas on the first day of 1911.'[20]

For Madame David-Néel had still a long way to go. In that very same year she left on a journey from which she would only return in 1925. In November she met Aurobindo Ghose in Pondicherry. On 10 or 11 January she met with the tiger which fled so shamefully into the jungle of Kapilavasthu, Nepal. In 1914 she engaged a young Sikkimese lama, renamed him Albert' and kept him with her for the rest of his life. Tibet was a forbidden territory and closely watched. Frustrated in her effort to reach Lhasa – for the time being, that is – she turned her back on it and travelled via Rangoon to Japan, which she hated intensely.

Then she journeyed on via Korea to China, was caught there in the civil war, and spent the first several months in the lama monastery of Kum-Bum, then three years in the deserts of Szechwan. At last she entered Lhasa, in January 1924. She thought nobody had noticed that a foreign national had entered the forbidden territory and its holy capital, for she spoke the language like a Tibetan and had disguised herself well. Nonetheless she had given herself away, for a spy found it suspect that she took a bath, and not only once but every day. Luckily, the official to whom he reported this bizarre fact paid no attention to it, maybe because he found it too incredible to be true.

After an absence of fourteen years she met 'Mouchy' again; he had faithfully sent her the money which had enabled her to make that fantastic journey. Madame David-Néel became a celebrity. She had a house built in Digne, in the south of France, and went to live there with Albert. The house was called 'Samten Dzong,' meaning 'Fortress of Meditation' in Tibetan. But she still dreamed of journeying beyond the horizon, and again went to China, where she had to remain from 1937 till 1944, trapped by the Second World War. She wrote several books, all of which are still being reprinted and read to the present day. Madame David-Néel died in her Fortress of Meditation in 1969, a full century old.

She had continued to correspond sporadically with her former friend Mirra Richard, she addressing the Mother as *Chère amie de jadis*, (dear friend of yesteryear) the Mother replying with *Chère amie de toujours* (dear friend of always).

Yes, Mirra was now Mirra Richard. She had married Paul Richard on 5 May 1911, and went to live in his house (which still exists at 9 Rue du Val-de-Grâce, in the Valley of Grace). The apparent reason for the marriage was that, after divorcing his Dutch wife, Richard wanted the custody of the three children, 'but to do so he had to have his legal situation in order, so he asked me to marry him. I said yes. I have always been totally indifferent to those things.'

The second reason for the marriage was much more important. 'When I met him, I knew who he was and I decided I would convert him. That is the thing. The whole story revolves about that.'[21] She had immediately recognized Richard as an emanation of the third Asura we have met in the former chapter: the Asura of Falsehood who had originally been the Angel of Truth, and who now called (and calls) himself 'Lord of the Nations.' His conversion was an immense task undertook, and the story of the relationship would be 'far more exciting than any novel imaginable.' When she took up the challenge, she was sufficiently conscious and experienced to know what was in store for her.

This should be kept in mind when trying to understand what their relationship actually meant and how it unfolded. The Mother would clearly state that she was Richard's guru. Everything he came to know about occultism and spirituality he had from her, and the books he wrote were based on her inspiration. She would accompany him to Pondicherry and to Japan, each time paying for the passage from the money she had left. Outwardly she would be the cultured, intelligent, refined Madame Mirra Richard, while inwardly she would be battling for Richard's soul, having to swallow the venom of his antagonism and weather the fury of his Asuric revolt. The Mother sometimes described their relationship as 'infernal' and 'diabolical.' She was not given to exaggeration and she had, indeed, dared to challenge a demon, one of the most demonic kind – although he too, just like Max Théon, could be extremely gentle and affable, and hardly anybody would have guessed his real nature.

Mirra's son André, who at the time was in his teens, later remembered: 'My father and mother divorced, and mother married Paul Richard. They went to live at Rue du Val-de-Grâce and I used to go and have lunch with them every Sunday. After lunch, especially when the weather was bad, we went to [Mirra's painting] studio. Paul Richard lay down on a couch, lit his pipe, and they started working, that is, my mother wrote down what he dictated. I could not help but notice that she was rectifying most of Paul's dictation. That small house at the back of a garden, or more precisely of a fairly large courtyard with a few trees, stretching in front of a big apartment house, was strikingly cosy and very comfortable.' [22]

In those pre-war years Paul Richard wrote two books, *L'Éther vivant* (the living ether) and *Les Dieux* (the Gods). 'The books he wrote – especially the first one, *The Living Ether* – were in fact based on my knowledge. He put my knowledge into French, and beautiful French at that. I would tell him my experiences and he would write them down. Later he wrote *The Gods*. This was incomplete, one-sided.' The Mother would also say that Richard had 'a rather remarkable metaphysical brain.'

Looking back, she discerned several distinct periods in her life. There had, for instance, been the period of vital experience and development, including her first marriage, her life as an artist among the artists, and the explorations of the occult realms. With Richard she had entered a period of mental development in the most comprehensive way: 'a study of all the philosophies, all the conceptual juggling in the minutest details, delving into systems, getting a grasp on them.' It was the experience and development of the mental capacities 'taken to the uppermost limit where you can play with all ideas, when the mind's development has made you understand that all ideas are true and that there is a synthesis to be made, and that beyond that synthesis lies something luminous and true.' [23] These were ten years of intellectual studies, of working out a synthesis that would lead her to Sri Aurobindo.

On 31 December 1911, New Year's Eve, when opening the door of her studio and looking at the night sky, she saw a shooting star. It is a popular belief that if one formulates a wish during the instant the shooting star is visible, the wish will come true. The Mother would give the rationale behind the popular belief: the fact that one is able to utter the wish so spontaneously and unexpectedly proves that it must represent a deep longing just below the surface of the subconscient. 'If you are able to articulate your spiritual aspiration at that very moment, it means ... that it dominates your consciousness. And, necessarily, what dominates your consciousness can be realized very quickly.'[24] And she uttered her wish: 'The union with the Divine for my body.' On the path Mirra was discovering, and in contrast to all other paths, the material body played a very important role. The goal of this path was not the quickest possible escape from our material incarnation into some heaven, liberation or nirvana, but a realization of a divine life, of the *corps glorieux* upon Earth. Mirra's body had become extremely refined and sensitive because, on the one hand, she was living in her soul and every yogic *siddhi* (permanent realization) exerts an influence on the material body, and on the other hand because of her occult mastery of the various sheaths of the adhara. A yogic discipline for the material body, in other words for the Earth, is possible only when the yogi masters each part of that material body as well as of the other constituents of his person, and brings it under the direct influence of his soul, which is the Divine in him. This was precisely the wish that Mirra formulated on the threshold of the new year.

Around the same time Mirra succeeded in awakening the *kundalini*. The kundalini is the force sustaining the life of a human being, the power normally coiled up and asleep at the base of the spine. When it awakes, it rises up like the intertwined serpents in the caduceus* through the *chakras* or energy centres of the body and awakens them. (This happens in the subtle, vital body.) When fully unfolded, the kundalini touches the 'thousand petalled lotus' on top of the head, with the effect of a sudden resplendent sun.

This extremely important step in Mirra's yoga is mentioned by her only once, and that in passing, but it was luckily recorded during a conversation with a disciple.[25] It is, however, explicitly confirmed by Sri Aurobindo in his epic *Savitri*, which is the spiritual biography of the Mother and of himself.[26] In that conversation the Mother said that the awakening of the kundalini took place before she went to India. She had read books by Vivekananda on the subject and had, as always,

---

* The caduceus is the staff of the Greek god Hermes. His staff with the intertwined serpents has become the symbol of the medical profession.

tried out what she read. Strange to say, when the force of the kundalini arose in her, it climbed all the way up to a place above the head, which is where 'the consciousness installed itself' and where it remained ever afterwards. Sri Aurobindo would later tell her that he had had the same experience – and that normally one dies of it. To which the Mother added with a smile that both of them had survived.

When working at achieving the union with the Divine for the body, Mirra had employed her usual one-pointed concentration. It is a fact that she worked at her sadhana every moment of her life and in an ever more intense way, just like Sri Aurobindo did. It was with the same one-pointed concentration that she had resolved to attain union with her psychic being. By the end of the year she obtained the realization for which she had been aspiring.

Rue du Val-de-Grâce is near the Jardin du Luxembourg, where Mirra often went for a walk amidst the trees and the greenery, escaping for a while the constant din of the metropolis. But to enter the Jardin du Luxembourg from her house, Mirra had to cross the busy Boulevard Saint-Michel, a street on the Left Bank which has been well-known and even notorious since the Middle Ages. One day she was so inwardly absorbed that she forgot to look about her when stepping down from the pavement into the traffic: only at the last moment did she avoid being hit and run over by a tram, the driver swearing at her – or, as she said with her usual sense of humour, 'paying me his compliments.'

She Who is Speaking to You ...

Let me be Thy herald among men ...[27]

– The Mother

Most of the documents about the life of Mirra during those years are collected in a volume entitled *Paroles d'autrefois* (Words of Long Ago). Compared to the volumes of the Mother's talks and conversations of a much later date, *Words of Long Ago* may give the impression of a haphazard collection of texts, but to see them like that and to pay them but scant attention would be a serious error. There is hardly a topic touched upon in the eight volumes of her *Entretiens,* called in English *Questions and Answers,* that is not already present in a mature form in *Words of Long Ago.* Underestimation of these texts has resulted in many misunderstandings of the Mother's contribution to Sri Aurobindo's vision and Yoga.

Words of Long Ago contains the 'early' texts. However, Mirra's occult and spiritual development shows us that 'early' in this case is not a synonym for 'rudimentary.' In the first years of her marriage to Paul Richard, Mirra was already very advanced on the spiritual path; she had already gone much farther than most human beings can ever hope to go. Some people were aware of this and went to listen to what she had to say. And she explained the place of the human being in the universal scheme of things, the aim that might make life worthwhile and the means to reach that aim, the value of everyday events and encounters, the invisible forces behind their material expressions. She analyzed the waking state with its longings and thoughts, as well as sleep and dreams. And where the audience was sufficiently receptive, she talked about the soul, about spirituality and the Divine.

The first decades of the twentieth century were also a time when women fought for their rightful place in society, when the suffragettes did not shrink from extreme action. (One of them threw herself in front of the King's horse during the Derby, and was killed.) Mirra, like Alexandra David-Néel, was a convinced and active feminist. One could even call Mirra the 'essential' feminist, for reasons we shall discover soon. She talked, obviously, about the inanity of 'the perpetual oppositions between men and women' and stressed the inner fact of the union of 'those two complementary halves of humanity' that should now find its expression in the outer forms of society and in its laws. But she also said: 'If women want to take the place they claim in the government of the nations, they must still make much more progress in the mastery of the self, the broadening of their ideas and points of view, in intellectual suppleness, and in the oblivion of their sentimental preferences, in order to become worthy of the management of public affairs.'[28]

And in one of her talks to *L'Union de la Pensée Féminine,* she said the following: 'It has always seemed to me that, apart from a very few exceptions, the mental role of women is not to speculate on the meta-physical causes of the phenomena which are perceptible to us, but to draw practical conclusions from those phenomena ... It would be wrong for women to want to think in the same way as men, they would be in danger of losing their own qualities – profound intuition and practical deduction – without acquiring those of their masculine counterparts – logical reasoning and the capacity of analysis and synthesis.'[29] A few years later Mirra would say to the women of Japan: 'The true domain of women is spiritual.'[30] And many years later the Mother would say that it is only women who can establish the connection between the old world and the new one in the making, and that only women know how to use the Power deriving from service to Truth.[31]

Mirra also met many travellers on the circuit of what would now be called 'New Age' communication and propaganda. After Swami Vive-kananda, sent on a mission by Ramakrishna Paramhansa, had in 1893 so impressively opened the doors of the West for Eastern religions and spirituality, many visitors from the East followed in his footsteps. Con-ditions in the West, briefly sketched in this and former chapters, were such that most of those masters and pseudo-masters found an audience; some became very successful. However, at the beginning it was not always easy for them. For some time they felt like total strangers in the unfamiliar Western surroundings, and had great difficulty in adapting to the food and the enigmatic customs of their hosts.

In November 1912 Mirra met one of them: the Sufi mystic and musi-cian Inayat Khan (1882-1927). He had travelled with his 'Royal Musi-cians of Hindustan' from India to Great Britain at the beginning of that year and crossed over to France in September. Although 'the French capital in 1912 was awash with Orientalism or what was taken for it,'[32] Indian music was still an absolute novelty to the audiences of the Royal Musicians. Few Westerners had ever seen the instruments they were playing: sitar, esraj, veena and other strange stringed contraptions. On one occasion it even happened that the Royal Musicians were warmly applauded after tuning their instruments because the audience thought that they had finished their first raga! Inayat Khan and his brothers were often in dire straits financially, so much so that at one time they even had to accompany Mata Hari. 'The foremost fake, Mata Hari was at the height of her glory as a so-called Indian dancer; she was not an Indian and she could not dance.' She pleaded with the Khan brothers not to expose her and they did not.*

In 1953, the Mother would say about Inayat Khan, who may have given Mirra her initiation into Indian music: 'I heard a Sufi mystic, an Indian who was also a great musician, say that for the Sufis there was a state higher than that of adoration and surrender to the Divine, higher than that of devotion, that this was not the last stage. The last stage of the progress is when there is no longer any distinction, when you no longer have that kind of adoration or surrender or consecration. It is a very simple state in which one makes no distinction between the Divine and oneself. They know this. It is even written in their books.'[33] She had not forgotten anything.

And there was Abdul Baha, about whom the Mother said: 'I knew Abdul Baha very well, the successor of Baha Ullah, founder of the Baha'i religion. Abdul Baha was his son and lived in prison till he was forty, I believe ... After [Baha Ullah's] death, his son, the sole heir, became determined to preach his father's religious ideas, and for this purpose he travelled to many countries in the world. He had an excellent nature. He was as simple as his aspiration was great. I liked him very much.'[34]

Baha Ullah (1817-92) was a follower of the Bab, who had declared himself a manifestation of the Divine, and whom the Persian Government had executed in 1850. After the Bab's death, Baha Ullah took over the leadership of the community and declared himself 'Him Whom God Shall Make Manifest.' The followers of the Baha'i religion believe him to have been the most recent in a series of past and future divine manifestations including Zoroaster, the Buddha, Jesus Christ and Muhammad. Baha Ullah spent most of his life in prison and was often subjected to torture, first in Persia, afterwards in Baghdad and Acre, where he died in 1892. Abdul Baha (1844-1921), his eldest son, succeeded him.

---

* Mata Hari, who was actually Margareta Zelle from The Netherlands, would in 1917 be executed as a German spy by a French firing squad.

Today, there are about three million Baha'is in the world. The Baha'i religion has once again been severely persecuted in Iran before and after the foundation of the Islamic Republic there in 1979.

The bases of the Baha'i religion are racial and religious harmony and a universal faith consisting of the essence of the great religions. Baha'ism stands for equality of the sexes, an international auxiliary language, universal education and a universal representative government. It has no professional priests, initiation or ritual. Abdul Baha was an intelligent, tolerant and sincere person – 'his sincerity and his aspiration for the Divine were simple and very spontaneous' – so one can easily understand why Mirra liked him.

'One day, when I went to see him, he was to give a lecture to his disciples. But he was ill and could not get up. Perhaps the meeting would have to be postponed. When I went to him, he said: "You go in my place and give today's talk." I was astonished, unprepared as I was, to hear such a request. I said to him: "I am not a member of your sect, I know nothing about it. How then could I talk to them?" But he insisted, saying: "It does not matter. Say anything that comes to your mind, it will be quite all right. Go and give the talk. Concentrate for a while in the sitting room and then speak." He persuaded me to do it.'[35]

In *Words of Long Ago* there is an 'introduction to a talk' given on 10 March 1912. Did Mirra scribble down some ideas before starting her talk to the Parisian Baha'is? Has somebody else noted down what she said? 'All the prophets, all the instructors who have come to bring the divine word to men, have, on one point at least, given an identical teaching. All of them have taught us that the greatest truths are sterile unless they are transformed through us into useful actions. All have proclaimed the necessity of living their revelation in our daily life. All have declared that they show us the path but that we must tread it in ourselves. No being, however great, can do our work in our stead. Baha Ullah was no exception to this rule ... Abdul Baha is not content to give us his teaching, he is living it, and therein lies all his power of persuasion. Indeed, who has seen Abdul Baha and not felt in his presence that perfect goodness, that sweet serenity, that peace emanating from his being? ...'[36]

On 9 June 1913 Mirra Richard spoke again, no doubt also to the followers of Abdul Baha: 'Last Monday, Abdul Baha took leave of us. In a very few days he will have left Paris, and I know many hearts which will feel a great void and feel sad ... To think of someone is to be near that person, and wherever two beings may happen to be, even when physically separated by thousands of kilometres, if they think of each other they are together in a very real way ... Thus separation no longer exists, it is an illusory appearance. And in France, in America, in Persia or China, we are always near the one we love and think of ... Every morning when getting up, before you begin your day, with love and admiration and gratefulness salute the great family of the saviours of mankind who – always the same beings – have come, are coming and will keep coming until the end of time as the guides and instructors, as the humble and brilliant servants of their brothers, in order to help them scale the steep slope of perfection.'[37]

Commenting in 1953 on some texts of hers included in *Words of Long Ago,* the Mother said: 'There was a small group of about twelve people who met once a week. A subject was given and an answer was to be prepared for the following week. Each one brought along his little homework. Generally I too prepared a short paper and, at the end, read it out.'[38]

One of those texts ought to be quoted *in extenso.* 'The general aim to be attained is the advent of a progressive universal harmony. The means for attaining this aim, in regard to the Earth, is the realization of human unity through the awakening in all and the manifestation by all of the inner Divinity, which is One. In other words: to create unity by founding the Kingdom of God which is within us all.

'The following is therefore the most useful work to be done: 1. For each individually, to be conscious in himself of the Divine Presence and to identify himself with it. 2. To individualize the states of being that till now were never conscious in man and thus to put the Earth in connection with one or more of the fountains of universal force that are still sealed to it. 3. To speak again to the world the eternal word under a new form adapted to its present mentality. It will be the synthesis of all human knowledge. 4. Collectively, to establish an ideal society in a propitious spot for the flowering of the new race, the race of the Sons of God.'[39] The Mother would say about this statement in her commentary of 1953: 'It was the whole programme of what Sri Aurobindo has done and the method of doing the work on Earth, and I foresaw this in 1912. I met Sri Aurobindo for the first time in 1914, two years later, and I had already made the whole programme.'[40]

The following words of Mirra are also from 1912: 'That which is speaking to you now is a faithful servant of the Divine. From all time, since the beginning of the Earth, as a faithful servant of the Divine it has spoken in the name of its Master. And as long as the Earth and humanity exist, it will be present in a body to preach the divine word. So, wherever I am asked to speak, I do it to the best of my ability, as a servant of the Divine. But to speak in the name of a particular doctrine or of a man, however great he may be, that I cannot do: the Eternal Transcendent forbids it.'[41]

On 2 November 1912 Mirra wrote the first entry in her spiritual diary, 'written during years of intensive yogic discipline,' and afterwards called *Prayers and Meditations*. 'Although my whole being is in theory consecrated to Thee, O Sublime Master, who art the life, the light and the love in all things, I still find it hard to carry out this consecration in detail. It has taken me several weeks to learn that the reason for this written meditation, its justification, lies in the very fact of addressing it daily to Thee. In this way I shall put into material shape each day a little of the conversation I have so often with Thee; I shall make my confession to Thee as well as it may be; not because I think I can tell Thee anything, but our artificial and exterior way of seeing and understanding is, if it may be so said, foreign to Thee, opposed to Thy nature. Still by turning towards Thee, by immersing myself in Thy light at the moment when I consider these things, little by little I shall see them more like what they really are – until the day when, having made myself one in identity with Thee, I shall no more have anything to say to Thee, for then I shall be Thou. This is the goal that I would reach; towards this victory all my efforts will tend more and more. I aspire for the day when I can no longer say "I," for I shall be Thou.'[42] This diary has not only a great spiritual significance, it is also an abundant source of data concerning Mirra's life. We shall not leave it untapped.

A Passage to Pondicherry

> *Grant that I may accomplish my mission, that I may help in Thy integral manifestation.*[43]

– The Mother

Paul Richard travelled to Pondicherry once more to participate in the elections for the Chamber of Deputies, but there is no doubt that this time he wanted to get himself elected. The idea behind it, besides launching a political career, was perhaps to be close to Aurobindo Ghose, and if he did not receive from him what he was looking for, to have India and its yogis within reach. This time Mirra accompanied him.

On 3 March 1914 she took leave of her material surroundings. 'As the day of departure draws near, I enter into a kind of self-communion; I turn with a fond solemnity towards all those thousand little nothings around us which have silently, for so many years, played their role of faithful friends; I thank them gratefully for all the charm they were able to give to the outer side of our life … Then I turn towards the future and my gaze becomes more solemn still. What it holds in store for us I do not know nor do I care to know.' This sounds far from enthusiastic and gives the impression that she was taking leave for a long time, perhaps for ever. The next day she writes: 'It is likely to be the last time for a long while that I am writing at this table, in this calm room all charged with Thy presence.'[44]

On 6 March the Richards were in Geneva, for reasons unknown. From there they took the train to Marseilles, where on 7 March they boarded a Japanese ship, the *Kaga Maru*. Marseilles was the biggest French harbour in the Mediterranean and had become prosperous because of the opening of the Suez Canal, which shortened the voyage from Western Europe to India by several weeks. On that day Mirra made a note in her diary: 'Violence was answered by calm, brutality by the strength of sweetness; and where an irreparable disaster would have occurred, Thy power was glorified.'[45] What had happened? One cannot even guess.

After two days at sea she wrote how the ship seemed to her 'a marvellous abode of peace, a temple sailing in Thy honour over the waves of the subconscient passivity which we have to conquer and awaken to the consciousness of Thy divine Presence.' She thought of 'all those who were watching over the ship to safeguard and protect our course ... [and] of all the inhabitants of this vast sea, both visible and invisible' [46] – as she thought, moving between two worlds, of the dear ones they had left far behind and those they were going to join. There is no indication that Mirra had any inkling of who or what was awaiting her at the end of the voyage.

The thoughts she had noted down a few months before the departure may still have been with her when the *Kaga Maru* sailed through the Suez Canal, where the desert on both sides made it seem that they glided through sand: 'In my outer being, my surface consciousness, I no longer have the least feeling of being in my own home and the owner of anything here: I am a stranger in a strange land ... I am a visitor here as elsewhere, as everywhere, Thy servant and Thy messenger upon Earth, a stranger among men, and yet the very soul of their life, the love of their heart.' Sometime later she would write: 'Many times in the day and in the night it seems to me that I am, or rather that my consciousness is, concentrated entirely in my heart which is no longer an organ, not even a feeling, but the divine Love, impersonal, eternal; and being this Love I feel myself living at the centre of each thing upon the entire Earth, and at the same time I seem to stretch out immensely long, infinitely long arms and envelop with a boundless tenderness all beings ...' [47]

Pournaprema writes: 'The Japanese ship on which she travelled called at Cairo, in Egypt.* She [Mirra] went ashore in Cairo and visited the museum. In one of the showcases of the museum there were the toiletries of a great Egyptian queen [Hatshepsut]. There was a comb, hairpins, flacons for perfume and small vessels for beauty unguents. When seeing those objects, Mother exclaimed: "How badly arranged all this is! It was not at all like this that I arranged my things." In the car that took her back to the harbour after having left the museum,

---

* This is obviously an error, for Cairo is landlocked. The ship called most probably at Suez, from where the passengers went overland on a visit to Cairo.

realizing the experience she had just had, she knew that she had been that great Egyptian queen.'[48]

Aboard the ship, somewhere in the Red Sea, Mirra had an encounter with a clergyman. There were two clergymen among the passengers, an Anglican and a Presbyterian, on their way to convert the Chinese, and they had been on the verge of quarrelling about who would lead the Sunday service. Afterwards the clergyman who had got the upper hand (the Mother did not remember which one) came to see her because she had not attended, but ere long it was the clergyman who received the sermon from her. 'Listen, even before your religion was born – not even two thousand years ago – the Chinese had a very high philosophy and knew a path leading them to the Divine, and when they think of Westerners, they think of them as barbarians. And you are going there to convert those who know more about it than you? What are you going to teach them? To be insincere, to perform hollow ceremonies instead of following a profound philosophy and a detachment from life which lead them to a more spiritual consciousness? I don't think it is a very good thing you are going to do.'[49] The clergyman was not convinced.

After a voyage of three weeks, the Richards left the *Kaga Maru* at Colombo on 27 March. They remained in Colombo that day to visit a Buddhist monk who probably had been recommended to them by Alexandra David-Néel. Then they crossed the straits at Talaimannar, disembarked at Dhanushkodi, boarded the Boat Mail train on 28 March, changed trains at Villupuram, and arrived in the morning of 29 March at Pondicherry, where they took a room at the *Hotel de L'Europe* in the Rue Suffren.

Their coming was, of course, not unexpected. Even the house where Sri Aurobindo was staying with his young Bengali freedom-fighters had been cleaned up a bit. When K. Amrita, a follower of Sri Aurobindo from Pondicherry, visited the house shortly before the arrival of the Richards, he was told that 'two persons from the topmost cultural circle of France were coming to Sri Aurobindo for practising yoga.' Four electric lights had been put up (before there were only candles), the weeds in the courtyard had been pulled out, the house was now being swept daily and acquired an 'almost gay appearance' because of these much-needed changes.[50]

The meeting between Aurobindo Ghose and Mirra took place on Sunday 29 March, at 3:30 in the afternoon, at 41 Rue François Martin. 'Something in me wanted to meet Sri Aurobindo all alone the first time. Richard went to him in the morning and I had an appointment in the afternoon. He was living in the old Guest House. I climbed the staircase and he was standing there, waiting for me at the top of the stairs: *exactly* my vision! Dressed the same way, in the same position, in profile, his head held high. He turned his head towards me and I saw in his eyes that it was He.'[51] At last Mirra met the 'Krishna' before whom she had to her amazement so often prostrated herself in her visions years ago, and whom she had known that she would meet one day in the body.

The next day she wrote in her diary: 'It matters little that there are thousands of beings plunged in the densest ignorance. He whom we saw yesterday is on Earth; his presence is enough to prove that a day will come when darkness shall be transformed into light, and Thy reign shall indeed be established upon Earth.'[52]

'Une étape nouvelle est commencée,' we read on 1 April, 'a new phase has begun,' and then again she wrote about 'the new period that is opening up ahead of us.' The convergent roads had joined – but only temporarily.

She wrote on 14 June: 'It is a veritable work of creation we have to do: to create activities, new modes of being for that Force, unknown to the Earth till today, to manifest in its plenitude. To this labour of a new birth I have consecrated myself, O Lord, for it is what Thou wantest of me. But since Thou hast appointed me for this work, Thou must give me the means, that is, the knowledge necessary for its realization.'

5.
Aurobindo Ghose

In my view, a man's value does not depend on what he learns
or his position or fame or what he does, but on what he is and
inwardly becomes.[1]

– Sri Aurobindo

A ravinda Akroyd Ghose was born on 15 August 1872 in Calcutta, at 4 Theatre Road.* 'Aravinda,' at the time an uncommon name given by his suddenly inspired father, means 'lotus' and 'delicate, fragrant, pleasing to the gods.' The newborn baby also received the name 'Akroyd' in honour of Annette Akroyd, an English acquaintance of his father who ran a Brahmo school in Bengal, and perhaps to give his name an English touch. Aravinda was the third son of Krishna Dhan Ghose, at the time the Civil Surgeon in Rangpur, a town in East Bengal, which is now Bangladesh.

Medical doctor Krishna Dhan Ghose (°1844) was a popular figure in Rangpur because of the idealism he showed in the execution of his office – 'duty is my creed' – and his generosity. He was a thoroughly anglicized Bengali, to the point of allowing only English (and a little Hindustani) to be spoken in his house. 'After graduating from the Calcutta Medical College he had, in 1870, gone to Aberdeen in Scotland for further medical studies. He was one of the first Bengalis to do so [and must also have been one of the first to sail through the recently opened Suez Canal]. To cross the 'black waters' in those days, in defiance of orthodox Hindu injunction, was to lose caste and invite social ostracism, but Krishna Dhan had no hesitation in running the risk

---

* 'At 24 minutes before sunrise … With sunrise calculated at 5:40 a.m., the time of birth is 5:16 a.m. local time or 4:52 a.m. Indian Standard Time.' *Sri Aurobindo Archives and Research*, April 1977, p. 78. There is, however, a footnote on the same page saying: 'The exact time of Sri Aurobindo's birth is not known. He writes … of "the inability to fix the precise moment of my birth."'

... He came back to India a 'pucca sahib' [accomplished gentleman], determined to model himself on the British and throw away all Indian ways of life, customs and manners. Krishna Dhan admired the English; at the same time, he had a very strong aversion to the inertia, blind orthodoxy and general degradation which were so prevalent in the Indian society at the time.'[2] 'I have rarely met with one so highly educated, so spirited and with such a strong personality.' (Bepin Chandra Pal) The doctor was also 'a tremendous atheist,' according to Sri Aurobindo, and he wanted his sons to be 'beacons to the world.'

His wife Swarnalata was 'stunningly beautiful,' some say, so much so that in friendly circles she was called 'the Rose of Rangpur.' She was cultured and led the life of an anglicized 'memsahib,' but she gradually grew more and more mentally deranged, a flaw that apparently ran in the family as two of her siblings suffered from it too. For all that, her father, 'Rishi' Rajnarain Bose (1826-99), was one of the foremost Bengalis of his time. Exposure to Western rationalism caused him to lose faith in Hinduism, and he sought in Islam, Christianity and European philosophy a new synthetic framework for his beliefs. Like many other members of his generation, he discarded the ethical as well as the intellectual standards of his native culture and participated in the movement of student protest known as Young Bengal. The death of both his wife and father during this period of mental and moral experimentation cast Rajnarain into anguished introspection. He found support in the Vedanta philosophy, and, after coming into contact with Debendranath Tagore, became a member of the revived Brahmo Samaj.'[3] It was the time of the Bengal Renaissance. The whole of India was dominated by the colonial masters, the British, under Queen Victoria, Empress of India. With a relatively small army, mainly consisting of Indian sepoys commanded by British officers, and a still smaller but greatly capable administration, the Indian Civil Service, they ran the huge subcontinent. They were directly in charge of the patchwork of British territories and indirectly, through their Regents, of the hundreds of tiny to quite large kingdoms ruled by colourful maharajahs and maharanis. The population moved in two layers: on top the British masters with the anglicized Indians occupying the lower-ranked positions; at the bottom traditional India as it had been for millennia, but now for the most part stagnant. The two cultures had only a superficial contact with each other, and sometimes they clashed, as in the Great Mutiny of 1857. This left a permanent scar on the British psyche, with the ever-present fear that something similar or worse might happen again at any time.

'The Bengal Renaissance was the result of two complementary movements. The initial push was provided by the example and influence of Europe, exercised in particular through English education. This led, somewhat paradoxically, to a rediscovery by the people of the country of their own traditions. Sri Aurobindo's grandfather and father, like other thinking men of the times, were affected by both of these trends.'[4]

The rediscovery of their own traditions went hand in hand with a critical re-evaluation of them. This resulted, for instance, in the foundation, in 1828, of the reformist Brahmo Samaj by Rammohan Roy. Having learned to look at their own religion through the eyes of Christian Westerners, Roy and his contemporaries wanted to discard its superfluous and superstitious excrescences and to return to the fundamentals. Fundamental was the One God (*Brahman*), as in Christianity and Islam; not considered to be fundamental were the Vedas, avatarhood, karma and reincarnation. The excrescences were the thousands of idols, pujas, sacrifices – animal sacrifices were still the common practice – ceremonies and pilgrimages. They condemned on humanitarian grounds widow burning (*sati*), prohibition for widows of the right to remarry, child marriages, and of course the omnipresent stratification of the Hindu society in castes. Some great names like Keshub Chander Sen, Debendranath Tagore and Rajnarain Bose were connected with the Brahmo Samaj and its various branches. In 1875 Dayanand Saraswati founded in Gujarat the much more nationalistic Arya Samaj. Dissatisfied with the watered-down Christianism of much of the mainly Bengali Brahmo Samaj and its offspring, he returned to the Vedas and the chief tenets of Hinduism, but kept the social reforms, so blatantly necessary for all to see, as part of his programme.

The political and cultural situation at the time of Aravinda Ghose's birth closely influenced the life of his parents. We know already that Krishna Dhan was an enthusiastic Anglophile. Swarnalata was educated as a Brahmo in the house of her prominent Brahmo father, and Krishna

Dhan was still a Brahmo at the moment of their marriage, which was celebrated according to the Brahmo rites.

Aravinda would not be deeply impregnated by this atmosphere, for after passing his first five years with his parents in Rangpur, he was sent, together with his two elder brothers Benoybhusan and Manmohan, to a Catholic nuns' school in Darjeeling. The only event Sri Aurobindo later remembered about his stay in that school, in the foothills of the Himalayas, was the following: 'I was lying down one day when I saw suddenly a great darkness rushing into me and enveloping me and the whole universe ... After that I had a great *tamas* [inertia] always hanging on to me all along my stay in England. I believe that darkness had something to do with the tamas that came upon me ... It left me only when I came back to India. If people were to know all the truth about my life, they would never believe that such a man could come to anything.'[5]

Dr. Ghose wanted his sons not only to come to something, but to be beacons to the world. To give them a chance of achieving that aim, he had to provide them with a Western education. The summit that could be reached in Indian society was the Indian Civil Service (I.C.S.), the corps of about five thousand well-trained, well-paid and highly respected functionaries running India. The I.C.S. was accessible to 'natives' too, but only with considerable difficulty. The examination they had to sit for could only be successfully taken after having undergone British schooling. Moreover, the age limit for taking the examination had in 1876 been lowered from twenty-one to nineteen, which meant that the exacting schooling had to be undergone in England itself.

Krishna Dhan was not deterred by all this. In 1879 he took his pregnant wife, his three sons of twelve, nine and seven, and their younger sister Sarojini on a voyage to Great Britain. A friend, the British magistrate of Rangpur, had given him the address of an excellent person to look after the boys: the Reverend William H. Drewett, Congregational minister at Manchester. And that is where Doctor K.D. Bose left his sons, with the recommendation that they would be allowed to choose their own religion when reaching the years of discernment, and with the strict instruction that all things Indian would be kept far from them. 'I knew nothing about India or her culture,' wrote Sri Aurobindo in reference to these years.

Gentleman and Scholar

Manchester, centre of the cotton industry, was the second most important English city, the symbol of the new industrial society and the image of the world's future. 'It was the shock city of its age, busy, noisy and turbulent. It was the city Karl Marx's friend Friedrich Engels associated with the Industrial Revolution.' It was also for the most part ugly, dirty and unhealthy, for the Industrial Revolution had as little consideration for the human environment as it did for humans. Young Aravinda must have seen some of those horrors from nearby.

The Reverend Drewett and his wife took excellent care of the three Indian brothers. Benoybhusan and Manmohan joined Manchester Grammar School, but Aravinda was taught by the Drewetts themselves, and very well indeed, as his success in his future studies would bear out. The Rev. Drewett, a scholar in Latin (he had been a Senior Classics scholar at Oxford), taught him Latin and history, Mrs. Drewett French, geography and arithmetic. 'As the young boy grew up, his studies covered a wide field: poetry, literature, history; Shakespeare, Shelley and the Bible were his habitual companions.'[6] 'Auro was a very quiet and gentle boy, but at times could be terribly obstinate,' his elder brother would remember.

Proof of his early talent is a poem entitled 'Light,' recently discovered, written by Aravinda when he was ten years old and sent to an obscure and short-lived journal, *Fox's Weekly*. It is an imitation of 'The Cloud' by P.B. Shelley. We quote the last stanza of eight:

> I waken the [flowers] in their dew-spangled bowers,
> The birds in their chambers of green,
> And mountain and plain glow with beauty again,
> As they bask in their matinal sheen.
> O, if such the glad worth of my presence on earth,
> Though fitful and fleeting the while,
> What glories must rest on the home of the blessed,
> Ever bright with the Deity's smile.[7]

W.H. Drewett must have been a broad-minded man for sure, for although a minister he never tried to impose his views or faith on the three young Indians of whom he was the guardian. 'I never became a Christian,' Sri Aurobindo would say, 'and never used to go to church.' However, a very strong feeling arose in the boy when he read Shelley. '*The Revolt of Islam* was a great favourite with me even when I was quite young and I used to read it again and again – of course, without understanding everything. Evidently it appealed to some part of the being. There was no other effect of reading it except that I had a thought that I would dedicate my life to a similar World-change and take part in it.'[8]

But the Drewetts emigrated to Australia, travelling via Calcutta to collect the arrears K.D. Ghose owed them for the boarding, lodging and education of his sons. The three brothers, under the tutelage of grandmother Drewett, moved to London. There, in September 1884, Manmohan and Aravinda were admitted to St Paul's School, one of the best schools of its time. 'Impressed by Aurobindo's proficiency in Latin, [Headmaster] Walker awarded him a Foundation Scholarship and placed him directly in the upper fifth form ... [He] taught him the rudiments of Greek ... Before long Aurobindo was studying the Latin and Greek classics, writing poetry and prose in both languages, and reading English literature, 'divinity' (Bible studies), and French.'[9]

It is generally believed that Aravinda did not study mathematics and science, but this seems to be a misconception. For 'Sri Aurobindo not only was well grounded in algebra and plane geometry but had also taken two years of "analytical conics" (conic sections). Many of his classmates on the "classical side," Manmohan among them, took no mathematics at all. Sri Aurobindo evidently was looking ahead to the I.C.S. examination.'[10] Aravinda did very well indeed, so well that his interest in the obligatory subjects slackened and his teachers suspected him of wasting his remarkable gifts because of laziness. In fact Aravinda spent most of his time in general reading, giving himself a kind of complementary education that would constitute the stock of his enormous erudition. He read especially English poetry, literature and fiction, French literature and the history of ancient, medieval and modern Europe. 'He also taught himself Italian, German and Spanish in order to read Dante, Goethe and Calderon in the original tongues. A boy with so ambitious a programme could not rightly be accused of laziness.'[11] The Foundation Scholarship awarded him by his headmaster must have come in useful for Aravinda. Grandmother Drewett had suddenly grown furious when Manmohan, weary of her bigotry, insulted Moses, and she had thrown the three brothers out of her house. James Cotton had become acquainted with them through his father in India, Sir Henry, who was a friend of their father. Cotton paid Benoybhusan five shillings a week to assist him in his job as Secretary of the South Kensington Liberal Club. He also allowed the brothers to stay at the Club in a room under the roof. They were now living in poverty, for K.D. Ghose sent his sons hardly any money. 'When they outgrew their old overcoats they could not buy new ones. At home there was no coal for the fire and hardly any food. During a whole year Aurobindo and Benoybhusan had to survive on "a slice or two of sandwich bread and butter and a cup of tea in the morning and in the evening a penny saveloy [a kind of sausage]" … Manmohan by this time had gone up to Oxford and was receiving most of the scanty resources that their father was sending.'[12] K.D. Ghose's reasons for withholding their allowances are not clear.

Sri Aurobindo would later say that when his father was in Rangpur, he was on friendly terms with the Magistrate (the highest British authority in a district), who did nothing without consulting him. When this magistrate was transferred and a new one came in his place, the latter found that he had no authority in the town, all power being in the hands of Dr. K.D. Ghose. The new magistrate could not tolerate that. He asked the Government to transfer the Civil Surgeon, who was sent to Khulna and felt deeply hurt by such treatment. He lost his previous respect for the English people and turned into a nationalist. All this had an increasing influence on Aravinda, for his father, from then onwards, sent his sons 'the newspaper *The Bengalee* with passages marked relating maltreatment of Indians by Englishmen and he denounced in his letters the British Government in India as a heartless Government.'[13]

In the last year of his studies at St Paul's, Aravinda joined the I.C.S. class, consisting of students who were preparing for the I.C.S. entrance examination. From that time onward he took on a double load of work, on the one hand the study of the normal school curriculum, on the other the preparations for the examination that might launch him on a successful career in the Indian Civil Service. Speaking in July 1890, Headmaster Walker was full of praise for the almost eighteen-year-old Aravinda A. Ghose. He is reported to have said that of all the boys who had passed through his hands during the past twenty-five or thirty years, Aravinda was by far the most richly endowed in intellectual capacity.

In December of the previous year Aravinda had taken the Scholarship Examination for King's College at Cambridge University. As a result of his performance in this examination, he was elected to the first vacant open scholarship, which means that he was the best candidate. Oscar Browning, one of the examiners and a Cambridge celebrity, would take Aravinda aside and tell him: 'I suppose you know you passed an extraordinary examination. I have examined papers at thirteen examinations and I have never during that time seen such excellent papers as yours ... As for your essay, it was wonderful.'

Aravinda studied at King's College, where he was known as A.A. Ghose, from October 1890 to October 1892. His scholarship earned him £ 80 a year, which he shared with his brothers; the time of the direst poverty was over. The burden of his studies was considerable. 'As the recipient of a scholarship he had to prepare for the Classical tripos,* taking that difficult honours examination after two instead of the usual three years. At the same time, as an I.C.S. probationer, he had to follow a completely different curriculum and demonstrate his mastery of a half a dozen subjects in three periodical examinations.'[14] He did very well indeed on all fronts. And in addition to this was the general education received at that famous university, concisely but strikingly depicted by Peter Heehs: 'As a classical scholar, Aurobindo was participating in an educational system whose traditions went back to the Renaissance. To master Greek and Latin, to read Homer and Sophocles, Virgil and Horace, to absorb the culture of classical Greece and Rome – these were considered the proper training of an English gentleman. And what one learned in the classroom and lecture hall was only part, and not the

---

* The Tripos is more commonly known as the honours examination for the Bachelor of Arts degree.

most important part, of the Cambridge experience. The university's atmosphere took hold of those who entered it and wrought a comprehensive change.'[15]

A.A. Ghose was 'one of the two best Classics of his year in King's College.' The first year he won a prize for Greek iambics; the second year he ended his study with First Class Honours and won prizes again for Greek iambics and Latin hexameters. The same year he won 'books bearing the College arms, to the value of forty pounds' for having distinguished himself in the college examination in Classics. He would never get his B.A., as the Classical Tripos comprised three years and he had to stop after two. But he left Cambridge in October 1892 as a gentleman and a classical scholar who would keep the knowledge acquired there for the rest of his life, both as a generally recognized master of the English language and as one who was widely read, also in the life of revolutionaries such as Jeanne d'Arc, Giuseppe Mazzini, Garibaldi and Charles Parnell.

In August 1892 he passed his final examination for the I.C.S. with ease albeit without ambition. But the last part of it was a horse-riding test. After he returned to London, A.A. Ghose was summoned three times to the test; three times he failed to show up. The Senior Examiner of the Civil Service Commission gave him a last chance accompanied by a serious warning. Again the candidate did not show up, and he was consequently disqualified.

It is clear that the cause of Aravinda's behavior was quite simply that he did not want to join the I.C.S. any more. 'He felt no call for the I.C.S. and was seeking some way to escape from that bondage,' Sri Aurobindo would write about himself later. Under his father's influence he had started to look at the British colonial presence in India with new eyes. Besides, he abhorred the administrative aspect of all I.C.S. offices, with their routine and dreary paper work. And the British authorities, apart from wishing to keep the I.C.S. as British as possible, had reasons for being suspicious of this Indian candidate. In Cambridge he had been a member and for some time secretary of the 'Indian Majlis' (association or assembly) which on the surface was a kind of social organization, but which was in fact an assembly of patriotic Indian students. This group was infiltrated by government spies who reported Aravinda's 'many revolutionary speeches.' And in London he had, together with his brothers, taken the oath in a secret Indian society, 'Lotus and Dagger,' in which 'each member vowed to work for the liberation of India generally and to take some special work in furtherance of that end ... This happened immediately before the return to India.' [16] The secret society was short-lived, but its membership was nevertheless indicative of a mentality the colonial rulers and their I.C.S. could do without.

Aravinda was now without a job. As luck would have it, the Maharajah of Baroda, Sayaji Rao III of the Gaekwad dynasty, was in London on a visit, the first of his many visits to Europe. With an introduction from James Cotton, A. A. Ghose applied for a job in the Maharajah's administration. The prince soon understood that he could acquire for a song the services of a highly qualified functionary, an I.C.S. man in fact, for Cotton had reckoned that Rs. 200 a month was a reasonable salary and had convinced his protégé of the same. A.A. Ghose was hired without more ado.

His father knew nothing of these developments. So proud was he of his third son that he travelled all the way to Bombay to welcome him and take him back in triumph. But the ship, the steamer *Roumania* on which he expected Aravinda, did not arrive and the disillusioned doctor returned home. There he was informed by telegram that the ship had gone down in a storm off the coast of Portugal. Krishna Dhan, who was already suffering from heart disease, succumbed to the shock and died on 14 December 1892 'while uttering Aravinda's name in lamentation.' Some years later Aurobindo would write in a letter: 'In all my fourteen years in England I hardly got a dozen letters from him, and yet I cannot doubt his affection for me, since it was the false report of my death which killed him.' [17]

Aravinda had not booked his passage on the ill-fated *Roumania* but on the *Carthage*. He arrived in Bombay on 6 February 1893. From the moment he set foot on Indian soil, on the Apollo Bunder in Bombay, a vast calm descended upon him; the black cloud, which had been hovering over him since that day some seventeen or eighteen years before at Darjeeling, dissolved and he began to have spiritual experiences. Two days later he joined the service of the Gaekwad in Baroda.

In the Maharajah's Service

It must have been an enormous change for A.A. Ghose to find himself in princely but culturally backward Baroda of the end of the nineteenth century, after having lived for more than thirteen years in cities like Manchester, London and Cambridge. He was first posted in minor administrative offices such as the Stamp Revenue Department and the Survey Settlement Department, to accustom him to the place. After two or three years he joined the Dewan's office, i.e. the State Secretariat. When asked what the difference was between all that pen-pushing and the I.C.S., Sri Aurobindo said: 'Baroda was a native state under a native ruler. You did not have to be at attention to the superior English officer ruling your fate. There was much room for freedom and dignity.'[18] Sayaji Rao Gaekwad III (1863-1939) had been put on the throne by the British when he was still a boy, but he had developed into a good ruler. As Aurobindo said to his Bengali teacher: 'The present Maharajah is capable of ruling over a large empire. As a politician he has no peer in the whole of India.' We find his opinion confirmed in Elisabeth Keesing's biography of Inayat Khan, who hailed from Baroda: 'This prince, Sayaji Rao III, reorganized the administration, even modernized his court, seriously reformed the system of justice, encouraged new industries, embellished the town with broad boulevards, and opened parks for his people from the suffocating alleys. For himself this maharajah built baroque-style palaces, but he still knew and honoured his own culture.'[19]

The Maharajah wanted to put his scholarly civil servant to good use and invited him to the palace time and again, often to a working breakfast. Aurobindo had to compose the Maharajah's correspondence with the British, his speeches for all occasions, the narratives of his travels, a history of Baroda and, of course, his biography. Aurobindo was never his official secretary, but everybody was aware from where the Maharajah's sonorous English came.

Aurobindo never let himself be daunted by his royal employer. His Bengali teacher had this anecdote: 'The Prince of Baroda was going to be married [somewhere in 1904-05]. In those days monogamy was not particularly insisted on. Sri Aurobindo was then the vice-principal of the Gaekwad's College. When the distinguished guests had assembled for the wedding dinner, the royal bridegroom came up to him dignified and demure. The grave vice-principal, revered by all, shook hands with "the cynosure of neighbouring eyes" and wished him "Many happy returns of the day"!' [20]

Barely six months after his arrival in his motherland, Aurobindo Ghose made his entry into Indian politics with a bang. K.G. Deshpande, who together with Aurobindo had been a member of the Indian Majlis at Cambridge, asked him to express his opinion on the current political situation in a series of articles for the *Indu Prakash*, the newspaper of which Deshpande was the editor. Aurobindo complied and wrote *New Lamps for Old*, lambasting the Indian National Congress in such hard-hitting prose that Deshpande got much more than he had bargained for. Taking into account that the writer was only twenty-one years old, these articles were a remarkable feat and show how mature the political thinking of their young author already was. 'My politics were shaped before I came to India,' wrote Sri Aurobindo, and, designating himself in the third person: 'He had already in England decided to devote his life to the service of his country and its liberation.' [21]

The Indian National Congress was founded in 1895, less than eight years before, mainly on the initiative of a retired English civilian, Allan O. Hume (1892-1912). It was the first and for the time being the only political party in India, and its function consisted in performing the role of a buffer or cushion between the Indian people – i.e. the articulate middle class – and their colonial rulers. Behind all its rhetorical flourishes there was an attitude of submission towards the British masters, allowing itself no more than to beg politely for some concessions, while at the same time being careful to dampen any aggressiveness or arrogance towards the government. 'There is not the slightest evidence to show that we have at all learned to act together; the one lesson we have learned is to talk together, and that is a rather different thing,' wrote Aurobindo. [22]

It would be an illusion to suppose that there was much political activity in India at the time. The prevailing mood in that large, multi-faceted and divided land was 'apathy and despair.' 'The country which the mighty Muslims, constantly growing in power, took hundreds of years to conquer with the greatest difficulty and could never rule over in perfect security, that very country in the course of fifty years willingly admitted the sovereignty of a handful of English merchants and within a century went into an inert sleep under the shadow of their paramount empire.' (Sri Aurobindo). The danger associated with the Indian National Congress, as Aurobindo saw it, was that it would perpetuate that situation and postpone any hope of self-rule and national dignity for decades to come, if not for ever.

The amazing fact about this young man from Bengal, Aurobindo Ghose,* is not only that he dared to write that the Queen-Empress was 'an old lady so called by way of courtesy, and about whom few Indians can really know or care anything,' nor that he depicted the situation as 'a small coterie of masters surrounded by a nation of helots.' It is that he took the standpoint of absolute independence for his motherland at his young age, even when still in England, and when everybody else held it to be 'an insane chimera.' Later, Sri Aurobindo would write about himself: 'He always stood for India's complete independence which he was the first to advocate publicly without compromise as the only ideal worthy of a self-respecting nation.' And also: 'I entered into political action and continued it … with one aim and one alone, to get into the mind of the people a settled will for freedom and the necessity of a struggle to achieve it in place of the futile ambling Congress methods then in vogue.'[23]

New Lamps for Old, however, was too strong a medicine at the time the articles were published, from 7 August 1893 to 5 March 1894. 'The articles were so fiery that M.G. Ranade, the great Mahratta [Maratha] leader, asked the proprietor of the paper not to allow such seditious things to appear in his columns, otherwise he might be arrested and imprisoned. Deshpande approached me with this news and requested me to write something less violent. I then began to write about the philosophy of politics, leaving aside the practical side of politics. But I soon got disgusted with it and when I heard that Bepin Pal had started

---

* Aravinda changed the spelling of his name to 'Aurobindo' on 25 August 1894, when signing a letter to his sister Sarojini. 'Aurobindo' is actually the Bengali way of pronouncing Aravinda. The increased sonority of his name in this new spelling is evident.

a paper, the *Bande Mataram*, I thought of the chance to work through it.'[24]

Aurobindo withdrew into the routine of his assignments in Baroda, and into an inner world. He read enormously, ordering case after case of books from Calcutta and from two Bombay booksellers. We know already about his phenomenal knowledge of the main Western languages, classical and modern. As he later briefly summed up that knowledge: '[Aurobindo] mastered Greek and Latin, English and French, and had also acquired some familiarity with continental languages like German and Italian.' Now, living and working in India, he became acquainted with Gujarati and Marathi, the languages of the Baroda state, both of them closely related to Hindi. He also wanted to thoroughly learn Bengali, his 'mother tongue' which he had never spoken. The reason for this was twofold: he wanted to converse with his relatives in their own language, and he was becoming more and more involved in the political situation in Bengal. He therefore hired a Bengali teacher, Dinendra Kumar Roy, 'a distinguished man of letters in Bengal.'

Aurobindo also perfected his knowledge of Sanskrit, of which the elementary notions, along with those of Bengali, had been part of the I.C.S. curriculum in England. Thus he read much secular Sanskrit literature, especially the works of Kalidasa, the pre-eminent poet of the golden age of Sanskrit. He translated his plays *Meghaduta* and *Vikramorvasie,* later published under the title *The Hero and the Nymph.* And it is self-evident that he read and reread the *Ramayana* and the *Mahabharata,* the epics that even today remain alive in the heart and feed the imagination of the Hindus of all ages. He also started translating them – an interest which he retained over the course of many years, but which never reached fulfilment, as was the case with many other literary initiatives of his.

Aurobindo remained creative in the language in which he thought and which was his *de facto* mother tongue, English. In 1895 he published his first volume of poems, *Songs for Myrtilla,* comprising many poems which had been written in England. He wrote the long poem *Love and Death* practically at one go, and courteously dedicated it to his poet-brother Manmohan. And he embarked upon the first draft of *Savitri,* based on a story from the *Mahabharata,* which would, as the years went by, unfold into the magnificent masterwork of nearly twenty-four thousand lines as we know it today.

In 1897 Aurobindo Babu, though still frequently called on by the Gaekwad for secretarial work, became lecturer in French at the Baroda College. In 1898 he was appointed Professor of English, in addition to his other official duties. By now his financial position had become so secure that he advertised in Calcutta newspapers for a bride, and in April 1901 he married Mrinalini, eldest daughter of B.C. Bose, a State Agricultural Officer who had studied in England. Mrinalini, born on 6 March 1887, was fourteen years old. 'She was beautiful, educated, and belonged to an aristocratic family.'

Both bridegroom and bride were supposed to undergo a ceremony of purification because the former had crossed the 'black waters' and the latter had been educated at the Brahmo Girls' School in Calcutta. Aurobindo refused point-blank, even when he only had to shave his head. In the end a priest was found who, for some remuneration, consented to perform the ceremony. When Sri Aurobindo was later asked why he had married at all, he wrote in reply: 'Do you think that Buddha or Confucius or myself were born with a prevision that they or I would take to the spiritual life? So long as one is in the ordinary consciousness, one lives the ordinary life. When the awakening and the new consciousness come, one leaves it – nothing puzzling in that.'[25] And so Aurobindo returned home in the company of his young wife and of his sister Sarojini, after having spent some time in Nainital, the beautiful hill station where the Gaekwad was holidaying. 'Despite the differences in their ages and interests, Aurobindo and Mrinalini had an affectionate relationship. But his absorption in literary and political work, and later in spiritual practice, gave him little opportunity to enjoy a conventional marriage.'[26] Baroda in those years was not an easy place to live. Like so many other places in India it had been ravaged by famines in 1896 and 1899, and in the following years it was afflicted by droughts causing severe water scarcity.

Another family member who appeared at Baroda was someone who would play an important role in Aurobindo's life: his youngest brother Barindra Kumar, or Barin for short. The reader may recall that Swarnalata was pregnant during the stay of the Ghoses in Great Britain in 1879.

Barin was born in Upper Norwood, a suburb of London, in January 1880. His youth up to his tenth year or so had been extremely miserable as his mother, with whom he was staying in Deoghar, succumbed more and more to her mental illness. At last Krishna Dhan succeeded in kidnapping first Sarojini and then Barin from their mother's house. (These painful episodes must have contributed considerably to undermining the doctor's health.)

When Aurobindo had first seen Barin, somewhere in 1894, he was still a schoolboy in Deoghar. The young boy had a quick intellect and was gifted as a conversationalist, poet, prose writer, musician, and even as a painter. That he was fickle too will astonish nobody, considering the traumatic first years of his life. Barin first studied for a few months at Patna University and then tried his luck with his two eldest brothers, Benoybhusan, who was employed by the ruler of Cooch Behar, and Manmohan, at the time professor of English at Dacca University. Now, after the long train journey across India, he sought refuge with his *sejda* (third elder brother) Aurobindo.

Behind the Scenes

Though after the publication of *New Lamps for Old* Aurobindo had withdrawn to the sidelines of political life, it did not mean that he had lost interest. He followed it with all the means at his disposal and also studied the character, mood and inclinations of the Indian people. 'He studied the conditions in the country so that he might be able to judge more maturely what could be done.'[27] The ideas thus gained and the subsequent political action he based on them were the following.

'First there was the action with which he started, a secret revolutionary propaganda and organization of which the central object was the preparation of an armed insurrection. Secondly, there was a public propaganda intended to convert the whole nation to the ideal of independence which was regarded, when he entered into politics, by the vast majority of Indians as unpractical and impossible, an almost insane chimera. It was thought that the British Empire was too powerful and

India too weak, effectively disarmed and impotent even to dream of the success of such an endeavour. Thirdly, there was the organization of the people to carry on a public and united opposition and undermining of the foreign rule through an increasing noncooperation and passive resistance.'[28]

Later, when Aurobindo had become Sri Aurobindo, he would put straight certain misconceptions in the mind of his disciples: 'In some quarters there is the idea that Sri Aurobindo's political standpoint was entirely pacifist, that he was opposed in principle and in practice to all violence and that he denounced terrorism, insurrection, etc., as entirely forbidden by the spirit and the letter of the Hindu religion. It is even suggested that he was a forerunner of the gospel of Ahimsa. This is quite incorrect. Sri Aurobindo is neither an impotent moralist nor a weak pacifist ... Sri Aurobindo has never, concealed his opinion that a nation is entitled to attain its freedom by violence.'[29]

His first concrete political act was to send Jatindranath Banerji to Bengal, probably towards the end of 1901, as his lieutenant. 'The idea was to establish secretly or, as far as visible action could be taken, under various pretexts and covers, revolutionary propaganda and recruiting throughout Bengal.'[30] Jatin Banerji was a young revolutionary idealist who wanted to train himself and acquire experience with weapons by enrolling in the army. As Bengalis were not allowed to serve in the British army, he tried in vain to enlist in various princely states. Finally he came to Baroda, in 1899, and Aurobindo got him enlisted in the Gaekwad's troops. Jatin was an exemplary soldier, and equally exemplary was his dedication to the freedom cause. The cover of most secret societies at that time in India were the *akharas*, open air gymnasiums, where 'lathi-play' – a lathi is a metal-tipped bamboo stick – and wrestling were the main activities. The aspirant revolutionaries could certainly do with some tough martial training. 'Military Jatin,' with his good, virile looks and soldierly bearing, did a great job, founding many *akharas* or revitalizing existing ones in Calcutta and elsewhere.

Through one of the fortuities of history a Japanese baron, Kakuzo Okakura, appeared in Calcutta at the beginning of 1902. Although he was not a revolutionary but an art critic and historian, he would give Bengal a vigorous push towards revolution, so much so that Sri

Aurobindo even considered him one of the founders of the secret society in Calcutta. Okakura was a traditionalist, fervently advocating the return in all Asian countries to national values and art, and vehemently opposing Western influence and political dominance. He had come to Calcutta to try to invite Swami Vivekananda to tour Japan. During his stay Okakura came in touch with the cream of Bengali society, impressing them with his black silk kimono, hand-painted fan and ever-present Egyptian cigarettes. At one meeting he told the *bhadralok*, Bengalis of the higher castes: 'You are such a highly cultivated race. Why do you let a handful of Englishmen tread you down? Do everything you can to achieve freedom, openly as well as secretly. Japan will assist you.' And making clear what he meant by 'secretly,' he said on another occasion: 'Political assassinations and secret societies are the chief weapons of a powerless and disarmed people, who seek their emancipation from political ills.'[31] What power the baron had at his command to promise Japan's assistance is not known; nothing ever came of it.

Okakura's exhortation did, however, contribute to the formation of 'India's first true revolutionary society' under the able leadership of a Calcutta High Court barrister, P. Mitra, and called the *Anushilan Samiti*. Under its influence small groups and associations of young men who had not yet any clear idea or settled programme of revolution began to turn in that direction, while groups that already had a revolutionary aim began developing their activities on organized lines. It was with this Anushilan Samiti that Aurobindo came in touch on one of his now almost annual trips to Bengal. He himself had not long ago been initiated in the Western Secret Society in Bombay, to which Bal Gangadhar Tilak also belonged. Aurobindo administered the oath of secrecy to the chief members of the Anushilan Samiti. They had to hold the *Bhagavad Gita* in one hand and an unsheathed sword in the other, while pledging their lives, total dedication and secrecy to the society. P. Mitra would become president of a council of five consisting of Aurobindo, C.R. Das, whom Aurobindo had known in England, Surendranath Tagore of the famous Tagore family, and Sister Nivedita.

Sister Nivedita (1867-1911) was the foremost Western disciple of Swami Vivekananda. She was born Margaret Noble in northern Ireland. In 1895 she met the Swami, who was then on a European tour after his triumphal appearance at the first World Parliament of Religions in Chicago in 1893. She travelled with him to Calcutta in 1898. Swami Vivekananda initiated her into the newly formed Ramakrishna Mission and renamed her Nivedita. From then on she worked with the burning intensity of her love for India and with all her might for the resurgence of the country. She never hid her convictions from her British compatriots. Of her Sri Aurobindo said: 'She was a true revolutionary leader. She was open, frank, and talked freely of revolutionary ideas. There was no concealment about her. It was her very soul that spoke ... She was fire ... She did India a tremendous service.'[32] The two struck up a friendship that would last for the rest of her short life.

Having initiated Barin into the Secret Society, Aurobindo sent him to Calcutta to collaborate with Jatin Banerji. Unfortunately, the characters of 'Military Jatin,' considered to be a martinet, and Barin, ever romantic and shifting, did not agree and things took a turn for the worse. Even Aurobindo's mediation on one of his trips to Calcutta could not overcome the confrontation. Jatin turned his back on the many associations under his guidance and became a *sanyasi*. Barin returned to Baroda together with his *sejda*. Much of the revolutionary grassroots work in Bengal came to nothing. Again the general mood was one of 'apathy and despair.'

The restless Barin continued his search for gurus – he had several – and for anything that could further his spiritual development. It was he who introduced Aurobindo to spiritism and sessions with the planchette. Some of the experiments Aurobindo found interesting, others he participated in for his amusement. He soon discovered that most messages originate from the subconscious and others from invisible and untrustworthy little entities. Once the 'spirit of Ramakrishna' told them to 'build a temple.' Subsequently, and mainly on Barin's insistence, Aurobindo wrote the pamphlet *Bhawani Mandir*. ('Mandir' means temple, and Bhawani, like Kali and Durga, is a warlike, terrible aspect of the Universal Mother.) Part of the inspiration behind this pamphlet was Bankim Chatterjee's *Anandamath* (Monastery of Joy), a famous novel about an order of monks who were to undertake military operations and sacrifice their lives for the freedom of their country. *Bhawani Mandir*, with its veneration of the Great Mother and of the Mother-Country as one of her incarnations, is a very forceful piece of writing which was the fruit of Aurobindo's inner development, although the time to actualize the ideas propagated in it was still to come.

A Side-Door to Spirituality

Aurobindo's ascent on the path of spirituality was very different from that of Mirra Alfassa. In his case there was no early awareness and there were no early experiences, except the negative one of the dark cloud penetrating into him at Darjeeling. Still, in the last months of his stay in England, when reading Max Mueller's translation of the Upanishads, he had come upon the idea of the *Atman,* the Self-in-all, with the feeling that 'this was the true thing to be realized in life.' We know about the calm that descended on him the moment he set foot on Indian soil in Bombay. From then onwards Aurobindo occasionally had spiritual experiences, and quite intense ones at that. Some of them he has described and even shaped into sonnets almost half a century later.

When in Baroda, Aurobindo had a horse and carriage at his disposal. The carriage was a four-wheeled 'victoria' with a folding hood, two passenger seats, and a seat in front for the driver. The horse was huge, but old, tired of working and therefore very moody. One day, about a year after his master's arrival in Baroda, it bolted. 'I sat behind the dance of Danger's hooves ...' wrote Sri Aurobindo, when suddenly he saw a mighty head above his own:

> His hair was mingled with the sun and breeze;
> The world was in His heart and He was I;
> I housed in me the Everlasting's peace,
> The strength of One whose substance cannot die.

'The moment passed and all was as before; / Only that deathless memory I bore.'[33] Another sonnet, 'Adwaita,' describes an experience of the infinite about ten years later, and still another sonnet, 'The Stone

Goddess,' tells us how for the first time he became aware of the reality of the Gods.

When in 1939 Nirodbaran asked Sri Aurobindo what had led him to yoga, he answered: 'God knows what. It was while at Baroda that Deshpande and others tried to convert me to Yoga. My idea about Yoga was that one had to retire into mountains and caves. I was not prepared to do that, for I was interested in the work for the freedom of my country.'[34] Nevertheless, somewhere in 1904 K.G. Deshpande taught Aurobindo the principles of *pranayama*, the art of breathing. Thorough as always, Aurobindo practised pranayama for four, five and sometimes even six hours per day. The results were unexpected. He felt a sort of electricity all around him; there were visions of a minor kind; he began to have a rapid flow of poetry, which remained at his command ever after; he began to put on flesh, his skin became smooth and fair, and there was a peculiar new substance in the saliva. He also noticed that whenever he sat for pranayama, not a single mosquito would bite him, though plenty of them were humming around!

He also reasoned that 'great men could not have been after a chimera.' One of the great men he met was Swami Brahmananda, Deshpande's guru, who had an ashram on the banks of the river Narmada and was supposed to be well over a century old. 'He was, when I met him just before his death, a man of magnificent physique showing no signs of old age except a white beard and hair, extremely tall, robust, able to walk any number of miles a day ...' Usually when receiving *pranams* 'Swami Brahmananda sat with closed eyes, but for Sri Aurobindo he made an exception and gazed at him with his eyes fully open as if some extraordinary person or kindred soul had come. "He had very beautiful eyes," Sri Aurobindo said, "and his penetrating look saw everything inside me."'[35]

No document tells better where Aurobindo stood in 1905 than one of his letters written in Bengali to his young wife. 'I have three madnesses. Firstly, it is my firm faith that all the virtue, talent, the higher education and knowledge and the wealth God has given me, belong to Him ... The second madness has recently taken hold of me; it is this: by any means, I must have the direct experience of God ... If the Divine is there, then there must be a way of experiencing His existence, of meeting Him; however hard be the path, I have taken a firm resolution to tread it. Hindu Dharma asserts that the path is there within one's own body, in one's mind. It has also given the methods to be followed to tread the path. I have begun to observe them and within a month I have been able to ascertain that the words of the Hindu Dharma are not untrue. I am experiencing all the signs that have been mentioned by it ...

'The third madness is this: whereas others regard the country as an inert piece of matter and know it as the plains, the fields, the forests, the mountains and the rivers, I know my country as the Mother, I worship her and adore her accordingly. What would a son do when a demon, sitting on his mother's breast, prepares to drink her blood? Would he sit content to take his meals or go on enjoying himself in the company of his wife and children, or would he rather run to the rescue of his mother? I know I have the strength to uplift this fallen race; not a physical strength, I am not going to fight with a sword or gun, but with the power of knowledge ... This is not a new feeling in me, not of recent origin, I was born with it, it is in my very marrow. God sent me to the earth to accomplish this great mission.'[36]

Leader of Nationalism

Despite the inroads the Gaekwad made into his academic career, Aurobindo Babu became the vice-principal of the Baroda College in 1904 and its acting Principal in 1905. He had earned a reputation as a professor, filling the students with deep respect for 'the Aurobindon-ian legend.' The reason for this reputation was, on the one hand, his ample erudition and, on the other hand, his disapproval of the British methods of teaching and habits of studying. He often inveighed against the students for their industriously penning down, without a smatter of reflection, everything the professor dictated, and encouraged them instead to think for themselves.

Then, in 1905, there was the Partition of Bengal at the instance of Lord Curzon, the Viceroy – and in no time the political situation in Bengal underwent a sea change with repercussions in the rest of India. With regard to Bengal, or the 'Calcutta Presidency' as it was then administratively called, the British had long been in a quandary. That part of the imperial territory was too big to be governed by one lieutenant-governor and his staff. It comprised what is now West Bengal, Bangladesh, Orissa, Bihar, and Assam – a territory bigger than modern France and with half as many inhabitants. The British administration knew full well how sensitive the Partition was to the pride of the Bengali Hindus, who formed the most cultured and dominant part of the Presidency and who would lose this position because of the Partition. But Curzon, intelligent and capable, was also well endowed with the colonial superiority complex of the British. Moreover, like most others he may have underestimated the courage and the readiness to rebel of the Bengalis, for they were not exactly renowned for these qualities.

Another factor that turned the Bengal situation into a powder keg was the Russo-Japanese War. In February 1904 the Japanese had attacked the Russian fleet at Port Arthur, in Manchuria; in May of the same year they defeated the Russians at the river Yalu, and in May 1905 at Mukden. The Japanese became the champions of a resurgent Asia; they showed that a Western nation could be beaten by an Eastern one. Their victory was cheered in the non-British Indian press and made the pulse of every patriotic Indian beat faster. Thanks to this and the indignation caused by the announced Partition of Bengal, an almost miraculous turnabout took place in the public mood, from one of 'apathy and despair' to fervent patriotism.

On 16 October 1905 the Partition of Bengal was effected. When shortly afterwards Aurobindo went on a visit to Bengal, 'he found the once apathetic province in the grip of an unprecedented enthusiasm' for the national cause. He at once saw that this was 'a golden opportunity.' *Bhawani Mandir* had already been printed in Baroda and was now printed and distributed in Calcutta. And when someone made the money available for the establishment of a Bengal National College, Aurobindo at last saw a chance to terminate his service of the Baroda Maharajah and to move to Calcutta to serve the revered Motherland full time. He took leave and boarded the train for Calcutta on 2 March 1906. Barin followed him shortly afterwards.

The Ghose brothers knew that at this crucial moment public opinion had to be informed, encouraged and guided. In March, at the suggestion of Barin, Aurobindo agreed to start a paper in Bengali, *Yugantar* (The Changing Age), 'which was to preach open revolt and the absolute denial of the British rule.'[37] The aim of this publication was to openly popularize the idea of violent revolt. The editors of *Yugantar,* under the supervision of Aurobindo, 'were in fact the leaders of the first revolutionary group in India to attempt organized armed resistance against the British.'[38] The paper was boldly outspoken. It published serials on guerilla warfare, fabrication of bombs and the formation of revolutionary groups. It would therefore be prosecuted not less than six times, and was ultimately repressed so ruthlessly that not a single copy remains today. The texts still available are translations by government servants for the perusal of the authorities.

In the beginning Aurobindo contributed some articles which set the course of the new weekly, but he was not yet fluent in the Bengali language and would, moreover, soon become a very busy man. First he went on a tour of East Bengal to probe the mood of the population there, after which he returned briefly to Baroda to make some arrangements in connection with his privilege leave. In June he was back in Calcutta, where he was offered the principalship of the new Bengal National College. The proposed salary was Rs. 150, while at Baroda he had earned more than three times that amount. But the money was not important for Aurobindo; he accepted straightaway and became the Principal of the College on 15 August 1906, his thirty-fourth birthday.

Not more than a couple of weeks before he took up the principalship, Bepin Chandra Pal and a few nationalist companions had started a new English daily, *Bande Mataram.* In this case language was no obstacle for Aurobindo, there was only a problem of the available time. But understanding the importance of this paper too, he readily consented to contribute. 'The *Bande Mataram* shot into the limelight not only in Calcutta and Bengal, but across India, as the most courageous proponent of the ideals of the Nationalist Party.' In the words of the historian R.C. Mazumdar: 'Arabinda's articles in the *Bande Mataram* put the Extremist Party on a high pedestal all over India. He expounded the high philosophy and national spirit which animated the Party, and also laid down its programme of action.'[39]

Aurobindo was the Principal of a brand-new College, at which he was also Professor of English and History; he had to supervise *Yugantar*; he contributed regularly to *Bande Mataram*; he was active as a leader of the Bengal nationalists, having to go on tours and to attend meetings and conferences; and besides this he still mustered the strength to write the drama *Perseus the Deliverer*. No wonder that his daily practice of pranayama became irregular, something that does not go unpunished. He fell seriously ill, so seriously in fact that he would later say that the fever 'almost took me off.' During his illness a rift developed in the editorial group of *Bande Mataram*. B.C. Pal was pushed aside as editor and Aurobindo put in his place by some of his friends. However, this happened without Aurobindo's consent, for he had a sincere appreciation of Pal.

The fact that the British did not react earlier to the threat posed by *Yugantar, Bande Mataram* and a couple of other extremist newspapers in Bengal astonished even Barin when he looked back many years later. One of the reasons may have been that the British did not yet consider the Bengalis as serious adversaries and so were not unduly concerned about the situation. They were to find to their surprise that the people had grown bold enough to defy their power. Another reason was the inborn British sense of fair play which extended to legal and political matters. They had, after all, a tradition of press freedom. And as Sri Aurobindo once said: 'The English people are legal-minded. If they want to break a law they must do it legally.'[40] In addition, the government had trouble finding seditious material published in the by now nationally read *Bande Mataram*. 'The paper reeked with sedition patently visible between every line, but it was so skillfully written that no legal action could be taken.'[41]

Yet there was a limit even to the patience of the colonial government. Aurobindo must have felt things coming, for he resigned as Principal of the Bengal National College, not wanting to compromise it and being much more interested in his revolutionary work. He had lost interest in the institution because it did not respond to his views on education. The council of the College wanted to base it upon the British models which, as we know, Aurobindo abhorred because they did not stimulate but rather smothered personal reflection and development. Besides, the College did not admit students who, because of their participation in manifestations or other activities against the British authorities, had been expelled from their studies elsewhere – and this, after all, had been the main motivation to set it up.

The police and the judiciary failed to lay hands on the editor of *Bande Mataram,* for no editor was mentioned on the paper's masthead and none came forward to take legal responsibility. At long last Aurobindo Ghose was arrested, on 16 August 1907, in what became known as the *Bande Mataram* Sedition Case. This was the first time he had to stand trial. It should be recalled that he had undergone legal training during his studies for the I.C.S. and that consequently he was as qualified to sit on the bench as the British judge presiding over his case, who was the hated Douglas H. Kingsford. As a result of being prosecuted Aurobindo Ghose gained 'immediate fame' all over India. As *Bande Mataram* had no declared editor, Aurobindo had to be acquitted, which happened on 23 September. After his acquittal he became the recognized leader of Nationalism in Bengal. He who had preferred 'to remain and act and even lead from behind the scenes, without his name being known in public,' had been 'forced into public view by the Government's action in prosecuting him as editor of *Bande Mataram.*'[42]

It was then that Rabindranath Tagore published in *Bande Mataram* his still well-known poem in honour of Aurobindo, with the following opening lines:

> Rabindranath, O Aurobindo, bows to thee!
> O friend, my country's friend, O voice incarnate, free,
> Of India's soul! ...[43]

The moderate stalwarts of the Indian National Congress, the first political party in India, had all become figures of national status, and were rather complacent and settled in their political attitudes. 'The Congress was to us all that is to man most dear, most high and most sacred; a well of living water in deserts more than Saharan, a proud banner in the battle of Liberty, and a holy temple of concord where the races met and mingled.'[44] Now the position of its leaders, most of whom were advanced in age, was challenged with ever greater resoluteness by young extremist 'upstarts' such as Aurobindo Ghose and B.G. Tilak, with their programme of *swaraj* (independence), *swadeshi* (the use and consumption of Indian produce), boycott (of all things British) and upliftment of the Indian people. Ghose and Tilak had already met four or five years before and, although the latter was sixteen years older than the former, got on very well. 'The men of extremer views were not even an organized group; it was Sri Aurobindo who in 1906 persuaded this group in Bengal to take public position as a party, proclaim Tilak as their leader and enter into a contest with the Moderate leaders for control of the Congress and of public opinion and action in the country.'[45]

The 1906 Calcutta general conference of the Indian National Congress (I.N.C.) and the district conference in Midnapore a year later had led to serious clashes between Moderates and Extremists. A decisive confrontation was unavoidable. It would take place at the next general conference in Surat.

On 24 December 1907 Aurobindo chaired in this small town on India's west coast a conference of the Nationalists, as the Extremists were also known. The general I.N.C. conference started on 26 December and ended the next day when pandemonium broke out and the Nationalists went their separate way. Tilak had not wanted this, but Aurobindo Ghose had. 'It was known that the Moderate leaders had prepared a new constitution for the Congress which would make it practically impossible for the extreme party to command a majority at any annual session for many years to come. The younger Nationalists, especially those from Maharashtra, were determined to prevent this by any means and it was decided by them to break the Congress if they could not swamp it; this decision was unknown to Tilak and the older leaders. But it was known to Sri Aurobindo.'[46] 'History very seldom records the things that were decisive but took place behind the veil; it records the show in front of the curtain. Very few people know that it was I (without consulting Tilak) who gave the order that led to the breaking of the Congress …'[47]

Aurobindo succeeded in bringing Tilak around to his point of view. 'The split between the parties remained in force for more than ten years. "The Congress ceased for a time to exist ..." Eventually Moderatism died a natural death. In 1929, more than twenty years after Sri Aurobindo defined Swaraj as full independence, Jawaharlal Nehru declared that "the word 'Swaraj' in Article 1 of the Congress Constitution shall mean Complete Independence." After another score of years, the ideal was realized.' [48]

The Extremists concluded their separate conference on the last day of the year 1907. In the following days Aurobindo, accompanied by Barin, went on a visit to Baroda, the town where he had spent thirteen years of his life. On his arrival at the railway station the students of the College unyoked the horses of his carriage, in which were also seated Sakharia Swami and Barin, and pulled it in triumphant procession to the house where he was to stay. Barin had not gone to Surat to participate in the I.N.C. conference, for the politicking of which he, as a terrorist, felt little more than disdain. He had gone to look for contacts with eventual Maratha terrorists, but he had found no activity of that kind there and was quite disillusioned.

Aurobindo, from his side, wanted to take up yoga again and asked Barin to invite the yogi Vishnu Bhaskar Lele, whom Barin had met in September and who was then in Gwalior, to come and meet him in Baroda. Barin sent Lele a telegram and he readily complied. Suddenly Aurobindo disappeared for ten days from the hustle and din, social and political, that surrounded him; nobody knew where he was or what had become of him.

In fact, Lele and Aurobindo had withdrawn to the upper floor of the house of a friend. 'At this juncture I was induced to meet a man without fame whom I did not know, a Bhakta with a limited mind but with some experience and evocative power,' Sri Aurobindo would later write. 'We sat together and I followed with an absolute fidelity what he instructed me to do, not myself in the least understanding where he was leading me or where I was myself going. The first result was a series of tremendously powerful experiences and radical changes of consciousness which he had never intended – for they were Adwaitic and Vedantic and he was against Adwaita Vedanta [Lele was a Bhakta]

– and which were quite contrary to my own ideas, for they made me see with a stupendous intensity the world as a cinematographic play of vacant forms in the impersonal universality of the Absolute Brahman.

'The final upshot was that he was made by a Voice within him to hand me over to the Divine within me enjoining an absolute surrender to its will – a principle or rather a seed force to which I kept unswervingly and increasingly till it led me through all the mazes of an incalculable Yogic development bound by no single rule or style or dogma or Shastra to where and what I am now and towards what shall be hereafter.'[49] It was an experience 'which most Yogis get only at the end of a long Yoga.' Aurobindo had it 'in three days – really in one.' It was the first of his four fundamental experiences, and the silence in his mind would never leave him any more.

In the Shadow of the Gallows

After returning to Calcutta, Barin became obsessed with the idea of killing Magistrate Kingsford. Douglas H. Kingsford was an unpopular man: he had presided over several cases against nationalist publications, among them *Yugantar* and *Bande Mataram*, and had condemned a boy to be flogged for protesting against actions by the police. The authorities knew that the judge was a prime target for a terrorist attack and therefore transferred him on 26 March 1908 as District Magistrate to Muzaffarpur, a small town north of Patna, in Bihar, where nothing of importance ever happened.

Barin chose his executioners: Sushil Kumar Sen and Prafulla Chaki, both not yet twenty. They travelled to Bihar on 4 April, but in Barin's gang nothing ever went as planned. Sushil's father was dying and the amateur terrorist left to be with him. He was replaced by Khudiram Bose, eighteen years of age. Several days went by before Khudiram, carrying the bomb, arrived in Muzaffarpur. On the night of 30 April, Kingsford played bridge at the Club with his wife and a couple of friends, Mrs. and Miss Kennedy. When their carriages left the club,

Prafulla and Khudiram were waiting, but they threw their bomb into the wrong carriage. Miss Kennedy died almost on the spot, her mother two days later.*

The British had by now revised their disdainful attitude to the Bengali race. They came down with a heavy hand throughout West and East Bengal on all people, organizations and publications known for or suspected of nationalist leanings. On 1 May the police had no trouble arresting Barin's boys at the Maniktola Garden in a pre-dawn raid, finding there a good deal of weapons and evidence. Aurobindo, who had moved only four days earlier with his wife Mrinalini and sister Sarojini to the office of the Bengali weekly *Navashakti* in Grey Street, was awakened from his sleep and arrested the same morning. In all more than thirty suspected persons were arrested. Aurobindo entered the jail of Alipore, a Calcutta suburb, on 5 May; he would remain locked up there till 6 May 1909, for exactly one year. The Alipore Bomb Case was 'the first state trial of any magnitude in India' and 'the most important state trial ever held in Calcutta.'

Aurobindo was locked in a solitary cell 'nine feet long and five feet in width; it had no windows, in front stood strong iron bars, and this cage was my appointed abode.'[50] At first he 'was shaken in his faith for a while,' but very soon his Inner Voice began consoling and guiding him. He got a copy of the *Bhagavad Gita* and of the Upanishads, and his cell became a cave of tapasya in which he started a full-time spiritual effort, the practical application of what he read in those imperishable texts.

Again the results were much more powerful than he could have expected. 'I looked at the jail that secluded me from men and it was no longer by its high walls that I was imprisoned; no, it was Vasudeva who surrounded me. I walked under the branches of the tree in front of my cell but it was not the tree, I knew it was Vasudeva, it was Sri Krishna whom I saw standing there and holding over me his shade. I looked at the bars of my cell, the very grating that did duty for a door and again I saw Vasudeva. It was Narayana who was guarding and standing sentry over me.' Narayan and Vasudeva are names of Krishna and Vishnu, and

---

* Prafulla Chaki killed himself with his revolver when on the verge of being arrested by the police. Khudiram Bose was caught, convicted and hanged. They became national heroes.

represent here the highest Godhead. Aurobindo had realized the cosmic consciousness, the second fundamental realization in his yoga.

During a certain period he was visited by the spirit of Swami Vivekananda, who had died in 1902, six years before. 'I didn't know about the planes [i.e. the gradations of being]. It was Vivekananda who, when he used to come to me during meditation in Alipore jail, showed me the Intuitive Plane. For a month or so he gave instructions about Intuition. Then afterwards I began to see the still higher planes ... It was the spirit of Vivekananda who first gave me a clue in the direction of the Supermind. This clue led me to see how the Truth-Consciousness works in everything ... He didn't say "Supermind." "Supermind" is my own word. He just said to me: "This is this, this is that," and so on. That was how he proceeded, by pointing and indicating. He visited me for 15 days in Alipore Jail ... He would not leave until he had put it all into my head ... I never expected him and yet he came to teach me. And he was exact and precise even in the minutest details.'[51]

In his peroration at the end of the trial, C.R. Das, now Aurobindo's lawyer, pronounced the following words about Aurobindo which are since then written in the pages of history: 'Long after this controversy is hushed in silence, long after this turmoil, this agitation ceases, long after he is dead and gone, he will be looked upon as the poet of patriotism, as the prophet of nationalism and the lover of humanity. Long after he is dead and gone his words will be echoed and re-echoed not only in India, but across distant seas and lands. Therefore I say that the man in his position is not only standing before the bar of this Court but before the bar of the High Court of History.'[52]

The judgement was pronounced on 6 May 1909. Barin and Ullaskar Dutt, the chief bomb maker, were condemned to death; ten others were sentenced to deportation for life; seven more were sentenced from ten years to one year of transportation or imprisonment. The rest of the accused, including Aurobindo Ghose, were 'acquitted and to be set at liberty.' The British authorities were not satisfied with the verdict. To them Aurobindo Ghose was 'the ringleader of the whole movement,' as indeed he was. For the boys of the Maniktola Garden, Aurobindo had been the *bara karta*, the big boss, and Barin the *chhota karta*, the small boss. '[Aurobindo] is regarded and spoken of by all as the disciples regard a great Master. He has been in the forefront of all, advising seditious writing and authorizing murder. But he has kept himself, like a careful and valued general, out of sight of the "enemy."' Thus wrote none less than Sir Andrew Fraser, the Lieutenant-Governor of Bengal.[53]

On 30 May a transformed Aurobindo gave his first speech after his liberation at Uttarpara, a small town on the banks of the Ganges north of Calcutta. It is one of the key texts in his life. He concluded that speech, spoken in Bengali, as follows: 'It is only the word that is put into me that I can speak to you ... I spoke once before with this force in me and said then that this movement is not a political movement and that nationalism is not politics but a religion, a creed, a faith. I say it again today, but I put it in another way. I say no longer that nationalism is a creed, a religion, a faith; I say that it is the *sanatana dharma* [the Eternal Law] which for us is nationalism ... The Sanatan Dharma, *that* is nationalism. This is the message I have to speak to you.'[54]

It may be doubted whether the audience realized what Aurobindo was saying; his words were most probably understood as those of the prophet of religious nationalism. However, though paying his respects to the Hindu nation, he spoke now as the prophet of the Sanatan Dharma, of the Spirit who has created the world, who sustains it, and who will bring it to its completion. 'When I would re-enter the world of activity it would not be the old familiar Aurobindo Ghose. Rather it would be a new being, a new character, intellect, life, mind, embarking upon a new course of action that would come out of the ashram of Alipore.'[55]

Sailing Orders

Aurobindo tried to take up his former political life again. 'After the arrests and deportations we used to hold meetings in the College Square and some sixty or seventy persons used to attend, mostly passers-by; and I had the honour to preside over several of those meetings ... That gave me an insight into my countrymen,' said an ironical Sri Aurobindo later.[56] After Muzaffarpur, there had been a spate of bombings in

Bengal, mostly organized by the terrorist group of Midnapur now that the Maniktola Garden boys were in prison. But the police were on the lookout everywhere, and the hangings, deportations and other punishments – not a single prominent Nationalist leader was still free – had their intended demoralizing effect.

Nevertheless Aurobindo, no longer capable of discouragement, did not give up. He started another English weekly, *Karmayogin*, on 19 June, and on 23 August a weekly in Bengali, called *Dharma*. Some of his writers were the young men who had belonged to the Maniktola Garden community. Their *chhota karta*, Barin, was no longer there to look after them and direct them. Aurobindo had hardly known any of them before his imprisonment in Alipore Jail. Now Nolini Kanta Gupta, Bejoy Nag, Suresh Chakravarti, Saurin Bose and others sought shelter with him and solace from his presence. Practically all of them had been students before they became activists, and Aurobindo did everything possible to give them some education and to act as their protector and elder brother.

The convicted in the Alipore Bomb Case were tried again in appeal before the High Court from 9 August to 12 October. Barin and Ullaskar Dutt had their death sentences commuted into deportation for life to the Andaman Islands. They were to be accompanied by eight others, most of whose terms were reduced, as were the other sentences. But life in Cellular Jail at Port Blair was pure hell. The British jailer's standing joke when addressing newly arrived prisoners was: 'God does not come within three miles of Port Blair.' The terrorists were picked out for especially harsh treatment, so unbearable that Ullaskar Dutt went mad. (The jail in Port Blair is now a national monument.)

Aurobindo had been warned by Sister Nivedita that the government intended to deport him or to appeal Judge Beachcroft's verdict. To remain a step ahead of the British and prevent himself from being deported, he published in the *Karmayogin* 'An Open Letter to My Countrymen,' informing the public at large of the government's intentions and writing out his political testament. The ploy worked and the British reconsidered, but not for long. Aurobindo was named by some British authorities as 'the most dangerous man in India,' and 'dangerous' is an epithet attached to his name again and again in the letters of the highest office bearers, including the Viceroy Lord Minto.

On the evening of 15 February 1910 Aurobindo went to his office as usual and, at the request of his young companions, did some automatic writing. 'The atmosphere was filled with fun and laughter' when a staff member of the *Karmayogin* suddenly entered and informed Aurobindo that he had come to know from a high police official that a warrant of arrest had been issued against him. 'There was a tense moment of silence as we sat in perplexity,' writes Suresh Chakravarti. Then Aurobindo calmly said: 'I will go to Chandernagore.'[57] 'Usually the police kept a watch over Sri Aurobindo's movements, but that evening, when he came out of the office, there was no vigil anywhere.' A quarter of an hour later he and three companions arrived at a ghat (steps leading down to the river) of the Ganges, hailed one of the small boats for hire, and Aurobindo and two companions were rowed to Chandernagore, a French enclave some fifteen miles upriver from Calcutta. The journey took the whole night, under a full moon.

Why did Aurobindo take that sudden decision without informing anyone, not even his wife, and without making any preparations? 'When I was listening to animated comments from those around on the approaching event [his arrest], I suddenly received a command from above, in a Voice well known to me, in three words: "Go to Chandernagore." In ten minutes or so I was in the boat to Chandernagore ... I may add in explanation that from the time I left Lele at Bombay after the Surat Sessions and my stay with him in Baroda, I had accepted the rule of following the inner guidance implicitly and moving only as I was moved by the Divine. The spiritual development during the year in jail had turned this into an absolute law of the being. This accounts for my immediate action in obedience to the *adesha* [command] received by me.'[58]

In Chandernagore, Charu Chandra Roy refused to give shelter to Aurobindo although he was bound by oath to do so. He had been a member of the secret society and one of the accused in the Alipore Bomb Case, but he had now developed cold feet and suggested to Aurobindo that he should leave India and go to France. There was no room in that inn. However, Aurobindo was welcomed into the house of Motilal Roy, another young revolutionary, who would become Aurobindo's confidant and collaborator. Aurobindo sent a note to Sister Nivedita asking her to continue the publication of the *Karmayogin,* which she did for some time. Chandernagore too was swarming with spies, for this French enclave was renowned for its weapons' traffic, and its mayor had been attacked by Barin's boys, escaping death only by the skin of his teeth. For the next six weeks the silent guest from Calcutta remained so completely secluded, often changing hiding places, that even Motilal's wife did not know for whom she was cooking extra food.

Then Aurobindo once again heard the inner Voice commanding him: 'Go to Pondicherry,' the main French enclave on the Coromandel Coast. Through Motilal Roy he contacted his young companions in Calcutta and requested them to make the necessary arrangements. One was to book a passage on a French steamer of the *Messageries Maritimes* which plied between Calcutta and Colombo, calling on the way at Pondicherry. Another was to take him from Chandernagore to Calcutta. And a third arrangement consisted in sending a trustworthy person (Suresh Chakravarti) ahead to Pondicherry in order to make all necessary preparations with the freedom fighters there.

Everything turned out well. Aurobindo boarded the *Dupleix* in the company of Bejoy Nag; both travelled under assumed names. The *Dupleix* sailed in the early hours of 1 April from Chandpal Ghat. When they reached Pondicherry harbour, ships had to drop anchor and the passengers were rowed to the pier. Aurobindo set foot on that pier on 4 April 1910, at 4 p.m. He thought Pondicherry would be his refuge for a couple of years at the most – he never left.

On the same day in Calcutta an arrest warrant was issued against Aurobindo Ghose and the publisher and printer of the *Karmayogin,* but Aurobindo would have to be tried *in absentia.*

We have seen how Aurobindo met Paul Richard shortly after his arrival. Pondicherry was a haven for many Nationalists, especially from the south, and they had their own paper in the Tamil language, *India.* When he felt somewhat safer in his new hideout, the famous Aurobindo Ghose met all of them, including the poet Subramania Bharati, who became a regular house guest.

The small Calcutta group of young men re-formed around

Aurobindo. Bejoy Nag had accompanied him; Suresh Chakravarti had prepared his arrival in Pondicherry; Nolini Kanta Gupta and Sauren Bose arrived a few months later. Nolini brought the good news that the third prosecution of Aurobindo, this time (like the first) for sedition, had resulted on appeal in the government having to withdraw the warrant against him. Aurobindo was now free to return to British India, but his inner Voice had assigned him Pondicherry as his 'cave of tapasya.' His young Bengali companions became famous locally as first-rate footballers, Nolini on the right wing, Suresh as centre forward and Bejoy as centre half. Aurobindo continued to teach them whatever they wanted to learn.

It did not take long before the British police discovered the whereabouts of 'the most dangerous man in India.' As Pondicherry was French territory, they had to get permission to send a detachment of their men to keep an eye on Aurobindo Ghose. 'The British Indian police set up a regular station here, with a rented house and several permanent men,' writes Nolini in his *Reminiscences.* 'They were of course plain-clothes men, for they had no right to wear uniform within French territory. They kept watch both on our visitors and on ourselves.' They also paid local crooks to hide false documents on the property of the revolutionaries. A spy from Bengal even succeeded in infiltrating Aurobindo's house, thought that he had been discovered, and fell at Aurobindo's feet confessing his undercover activities.

The financial situation of Aurobindo and his companions was far from brilliant and he often had to send letters to Motilal Roy asking for money. 'Each of us possessed a mat, and this mat had to serve as our bedstead, mattress, coverlet and pillow; this was all our furniture. And mosquito curtains? [Pondicherry is famous for its dense mosquito population.] That was a luxury we could not even dream of. If there were too many mosquitoes, we would carry the mats out onto the terrace for a little air, assuming, that is, that there was any. [The south is oppressively hot in summer.] Only for Sri Aurobindo we had somehow managed a chair and a table and a camp cot. We lived a real camp life.'[59]

Another visitor from France Aurobindo received towards the end of November 1911 was Alexandra David-Néel, who had started on the long journey which would ultimately take her to Lhasa. She wrote to

'Mouchy,' her husband: 'In the evening I had a conversation with a Hindu about whom I have never spoken to you, since I have not been in correspondence with him, but know him only through the good opinion of friends [no doubt Mirra and Paul Richard]. I spent two wonderful hours reviewing the ancient philosophical ideas of India with a man of rare intelligence. He belongs to that uncommon category that I so much admire, the reasonable mystics. I am truly grateful to the friends who advised me to visit this man. He thinks with such clarity, there is such lucidity in his reasoning, such lustre in his eyes, that he leaves one with the impression of having contemplated the genius of India such as one dreams it to be after reading the noblest pages of Hindu philosophy.'[60]

But Alexandra's visit had not gone unnoticed and the British policemen on duty had signalled it to their headquarters. 'When I arrived in Madras the head of the C.I.D. [Central Intelligence Department] was waiting for me in person. He asked me – very civilly and politely, I must say – what I had been doing in Pondicherry in the house of that suspicious character.' The police chief agreed that Aurobindo Ghose was a learned man, but he held him also responsible for the death of the District Collector of Tirunelvelli, who had been killed by extremists based in Pondicherry. The latter part of the information was correct, but Aurobindo was in no way involved in this terrorist attack. However, Madame David-Néel, with her handbag full of recommendations, was not troubled any further.

In 1912 Aurobindo started noting down the details of his yogic practice – the same year in which Mirra Alfassa began writing her spiritual diary. Aurobindo's extraordinary notebooks have recently been deciphered and published in the journal of the *Sri Aurobindo Archives and Research* under the title *Record of Yoga*. One of the chief editors writes: 'This document is noteworthy in at least three respects. To begin with, it provides a first-hand account of the day-to-day growth of the spiritual faculties of an advanced yogi ... Sri Aurobindo set down his experiences in *Record of Yoga* immediately after their occurrence, at times while they were still happening. This gives a strong sense of immediacy ... What the *Record* does provide is a down-to-earth account of a multitude of events, great and small, inner and outer, in the life of a dedicated researcher. Sri Aurobindo once wrote to a disciple: "I think I can say that I have been testing day and night for years upon years" his spiritual knowledge and experience "more scrupulously than any scientist his theory or his method on the physical plane." The *Record* bears this out in detail. It may be looked on as the laboratory notebook of an extended series of experiments in yoga.'[61]

Sri Aurobindo himself, writing in the third person, drew up the balance-sheet of his political life: 'The part Sri Aurobindo took publicly in Indian politics was of brief duration, for he turned aside from it in 1910 and withdrew to Pondicherry; much of his programme lapsed in his absence, but enough had been done to change the whole face of Indian politics and the whole spirit of the Indian people to make independence its aim and non-cooperation and resistance its method, and even an imperfect application of this policy heightening into sporadic periods of revolt has been sufficient to bring about the victory. The course of subsequent events followed largely the line of Sri Aurobindo's idea.'[62]

As Nirodbaran wrote: 'Those concerned with day-to-day politics deplored his retirement and thought that he was lost to India and the world, being interested only in his own spiritual salvation. So he was called a truant and escapist. Even now there is insufficient understanding of what led to his decision.'

'I may also say that I did not leave politics because I felt that I could do nothing more there,' wrote Sri Aurobindo in 1932, 'such an idea was very far from me. I came away because I did not want anything to interfere with my yoga and because I got a very distinct *adesh*. I have cut connections entirely with politics, but before I did so I knew from within that the work I had begun there was destined to be carried forward on lines I had foreseen by others and the ultimate triumph of the movement I had initiated was sure without my personal action or presence. There was not the least motive of despair or sense of futility behind my withdrawal.'[63]

Part Two:

The Road Together

Aurobindo Ghose, ca. 1916

6.

Speaking the Word

When I came to Pondicherry a programme was dictated to me from within for my Sadhana. I followed it and progressed for myself but could not do much by way of helping others. Then came the Mother and with her help I found the necessary method.[1]

– Sri Aurobindo

First Questions

When Mirra met A.G., as Aurobindo Ghose was known since his arrival in Pondicherry, she had her questions ready. These questions were the natural result of her effort at inner development, and some of them we know because she has mentioned them.

One question was about the state of *samadhi* or trance. As the Mother later narrated to her audience in the Ashram playground: 'In all kinds of so-called spiritual literature I had always read wonderful things about this state of trance or Samadhi, but I had never experienced it. So I did not know whether this was perhaps a sign of inferiority. And when I came here, one of my first questions to Sri Aurobindo was: "What do you think of 'samadhi,' of that state of trance one does not remember? One enters into a condition which seems to be blissful, but when one comes out of it, one has no idea of what has happened." He looked at me, saw what I meant and told me: "It is unconsciousness ... You enter into what is called 'samadhi' when you go out of your conscious being and enter into a part of your being which is completely unconscious, or rather into a domain where you have no corresponding consciousness:

139

you go beyond the field of your consciousness and enter a region where you are no longer conscious. You are in the impersonal state, that is to say, a state in which you are unconscious, and that is the reason why, naturally, you remember nothing, because you were not conscious of anything." So this reassured me and I said: "Well. This has never happened to me." He replied: "Nor to me."' [2]

Another of Mirra's questions was why, in spite of her many talents, she had always been so 'mediocre' in everything she did: painting, writing, music … Aurobindo's answer was simply that this was indispensable for her development. We may infer that people who are extraordinarily gifted in a certain field have to dedicate their life exclusively to the realization of that one talent, while Mirra had to sample as varied an experience as possible and then engage in a totally new and synthetic enterprise.

A third question – in reality her very first one – would prove to be of immense importance for the future. 'It was the very first question which came up when I met Sri Aurobindo,' the Mother said later. 'Should you do your yoga, attain the goal, and then afterwards take up the work with others, or should you immediately let all those who have the same aspiration gather around you and go forward all together towards the goal? Because of my earlier work and all that I had tried out, I came to Sri Aurobindo with this question very precisely formulated. Because the two possibilities were there: either to practise an intensive individual sadhana by withdrawing from the world, that is, by no longer having any contact with others, or to let the group be formed naturally and spontaneously, not preventing it from being formed, allowing it to form by itself, and starting all together on the path. Well, the decision was not at all a mental choice, it came spontaneously. The circumstances were such that no choice was required. I mean, quite naturally, spontaneously, the group was formed in such a way that it became an imperious necessity. And so, once you have started like that, it is settled, you have to go on like that to the end.' [3]

The day after her arrival and her first meeting with Aurobindo, Mirra had an overwhelming experience. We know that she had already realized the Godhead in the heart and the full awakening of the kundalini. Now, with her openness, sensitivity and trained capacity to enter into others, she received from Aurobindo something she did not expect. 'I was seated close to him [Aurobindo], simply, like that, on the floor. He was sitting on a chair, with a table in front of him, and on the other side of the table was Richard, and they were talking. I did not listen, I sat there just like that. I don't know how long they went on talking, but suddenly I felt within me as it were a great Force – Peace! Silence! massive. It came, did like this *[sweeping gesture at the level of the forehead]*, descended like that, and stopped here *[gesture at the chest]*. And when they finished talking, I stood up and left. And then I noticed that I didn't have a single thought in my mind – that I knew nothing any more, understood nothing any more, that I was absolutely in a complete *blank*. Then I gave thanks to the Lord, and thanked Sri Aurobindo in my heart.'[4] Aurobindo had imparted his 'nirvanic' silence to her, his first great realization obtained when sitting with V.B. Lele in Baroda and which had never left him since. Just before sitting down on the floor, Mirra had confided to him that, try as she may to establish that silence in the mind, she was unable to do it. Aurobindo had given it to her 'without even intending to,' just by occult communication and because of her total openness, which in their yoga would be called 'surrender.' Years later, when asked by Barin what had struck him most on first meeting Mirra, Aurobindo would indeed say her surrender, which was 'so absolute and unreserved.'

From the moment their minds became silenced neither Aurobindo nor Mirra 'thought' any more as ordinary humans do. In their absolute surrender to the Divine their 'thoughts' came to them, were given to them how and when necessary, or when invited. A thought, as Mirra had learned from Théon and as she taught to her audiences in Paris, may be invisible to us because it belongs to a subtle, mental world, but it is all the same a concrete entity. Every human being lives within an occult edifice that consists of 'constructions' of thoughts. In people who are incapable of clear thinking, such an edifice is shabbily put together; in people who live mainly 'in their head' or in an unassailable conviction, such an edifice can be as impenetrable as a fortress the walls of a prison. In the course of her occult and spiritual explorations, Mirra had carefully built up 'a magnificent construction' which Aurobindo, just by his way of being, now destroyed in an instant – and she was immensely grateful for it. She took great care not to spoil the new poise, which never left her again.

As usually happens at the time of a decisive new spiritual experience, Mirra felt as if all the preceding work meant nothing. 'It seems to me that I am being born into a new life,' she wrote in her diary, 'and that all the methods, all the habits of the past can no longer be of any use. It seems to me that what I considered as results were nothing more than a preparation. I feel as if I have done nothing yet, as though I have not lived the spiritual life, only entered the path that leads to it. It seems to me that I know nothing, that I am incapable of formulating anything, that all experience is yet to begin. It is as if I were stripped of my entire past, of its errors as well as its conquests, as though all that has vanished and made room for a new-born child whose whole existence is yet to be lived ... It seems to me that I have at last reached the threshold I so much sought for.'[5]

Then followed what is a regular feature in all true spiritual progress: the repercussion, the downward movement after an uplifting experience or spiritual realization. This is, according to Sri Aurobindo, the Black Dragon lashing out with its tail in an effort to swipe away the spiritual gain. 'My physical organism suffered a defeat such as it had not known for several years, and during a few days all the forces of my body failed me ... Something in this aggregate [her body] which constitutes the instrument I can put at Thy service is still obscure and obtuse; something does not respond as it should to Thy forces, and deforms and darkens their manifestation.'[6] The problem she would have to grapple with at the end was already there at the beginning.

The Launching of the Arya

In Mirra's diary entries of those weeks we find time and again allusions to the continuous and absorbing practical occupations in which she had to engage. Ever attentive, she soon understood that this harassing, aggressive outer world was the true terrain of the new yoga, not the undisturbed, holy heights of meditation and withdrawal as recommended in the traditional spiritual paths.

The volume of activity undertaken by the Richards in the first months of their stay in Pondicherry is impressive. They had arrived on 29 March and the elections were to be held on 26 April, less than a month later. Trying to make an impact so that he would have a chance of being elected, Paul Richard must have had a hectic schedule of travelling and speeches, for voting was to take place not only in Pondicherry, but also in Karikal (where the Richards went to canvass) and in the other French *comptoirs* such as Chandernagore. (A.G. wrote to Motilal Roy to try and gather votes for Richard.) One of Mirra's diary notes is dated 'Karikal, 13 April 1914,' and there is no doubt that Mirra stood by the side of her husband throughout the campaign.

As soon as he had some time to spare, Richard went to see Aurobindo and discussed with him all possible topics. Although Richard was not susceptible to Aurobindo's spiritual realizations, he had an enormous respect for his intellectual powers. Which of them was the first to moot the publication of a review that would expound Aurobindo's views? In a letter to a disciple Sri Aurobindo later wrote that it was Paul Richard. 'Richard proposed to me to co-operate in a philosophical review – and as my theory was that a Yogi ought to be able to turn his hand to anything, I could not very well refuse.'[7]

At the time Aurobindo spoke rather highly of Richard. In a letter written in April to Motilal Roy, he says: 'Richard is not only a personal friend of mine and a brother in the Yoga, but he wishes like myself, and in his own way works for a general renovation of the world by which the present European civilization shall be replaced by a spiritual civilization ... He and Madame Richard are rare examples of European Yogins who have not been led away by Theosophical and other aberrations. I have been in material and spiritual correspondence with them for the last four years.'[8] (This 'material correspondence' seems to be lost.) In the same letter he characterizes Richard as a European 'who is practically an Indian in belief, in personal culture, in sympathies and aspirations, one of the Nivedita type.'

Did Aurobindo know who Richard essentially was, namely an incarnation of the Asura of Falsehood? Given his advanced yogic capabilities there can be no doubt that he did; also, the relationship between Mirra and Richard must soon have become clear, if it had not already been disclosed confidentially to Aurobindo by Mirra herself. If this is correct, then we can understand Aurobindo's statement in a letter of 5 May that Richard 'is to know nothing about Tantricism.'[9] One may suppose that Aurobindo wanted as a matter of course to assist Mirra in her effort to convert Richard. For this kind of attempt, they had to take the whole being of the person to be converted into themselves and do his yoga of conversion for him, helping him to the threshold where the ultimate step then would have to be taken by the individual himself. And so it came about that on the front-page of the *Arya*, the journal heralding the New Age, these three names are printed side by side: Sri Aurobindo Ghose and Paul and Mirra Richard.*

Of the four candidates for the one seat in the House of Representatives in Paris, Paul Richard came a poor last with a ridiculously small number of votes to his name – in every polling station less than ten, while the winner, Paul Bluysen, got between 1,000 and 4,000. (It was this Bluysen who Richard had come to support four years earlier.) 'As for M. Richard's votes,' wrote Sri Aurobindo to Motilal Roy, 'they got rid of them in Pondicherry and Karikal by the simple process of reading Paul Bluysen wherever Paul Richard was printed. Even where he brought his voters in Karikal to the poll himself, the results published were "Richard – 0."'[10]

The disappointing results of the election notwithstanding Richard intended, according to the same letter, 'to stay in India for two years and work for the people.' 'He has sold one fourth of his wife's fortune (a very small one) in order to be able to come and work for India, and the money he has can only carry him through the two years he thinks of staying here.' This is when the three of them decided, on 1 June, to take up the considerable effort of publishing a review in English and French, the English edition of a thousand copies to be called *Arya*, the French edition of six hundred copies *Revue de la Grande Synthèse*.

At first, however, the review was intended to be called *The New Idea /*

---

* This was the first time Aurobindo Akroyd Ghose took on the name 'Sri Aurobindo,' though still accompanied by 'Ghose.' From now on we will use the name 'Sri Aurobindo,' except in quotations which mention his name in another form.

L'Idée nouvelle. This title, doubtlessly proposed by Mirra, brings to mind the name of the Parisian group she had been leading quite recently. 'Idea' in this case should be understood in its full Platonic sense as a supernal reality with diverse effects in the material world. The proposed title tells us two things: firstly, that Mirra saw in Sri Aurobindo's vision and realization a continuation and accomplishment of everything she herself had learned and realized before meeting him; secondly, that her knowledge contributed to his vision and his formulation of that vision. Many key terms in his philosophy – such as psychic, mental and vital, all to be found in *Words of Long Ago* – came to him from or via Mirra; so did, for instance, his designation of the Supermind as the 'Real-Idea,' a term used in *The Life Divine* though rarely in later writings.

In the 'programme' Mirra had made up, and which is published in *Words of Long Ago** the third point reads: 'To speak again to the world the eternal word under a new form adapted to its present mentality. It will be the synthesis of all human knowledge.' This is equivalent to what Sri Aurobindo too considered an essential part of his mission, 'the intellectual side of my work for the world.' As he had said in his speech at Uttarpara: 'He [the Divine] has given me a word to speak and a work to do.'[11] 'The eternal word,' the *sanatana dharma* he and Mirra had already discovered in the respective traditions assimilated by them; 'the new form' would be their new formulation of the eternal word, adapted and applicable to the present, pivotal stage of the universal evolution.

The date for the appearance of the first issue of the *Arya* was set for 15 August, Sri Aurobindo's forty-second birthday. 'On 1 June 1914 Sri Aurobindo had nothing ready for the press. By the middle of the month, when the prospectus of the proposed journal was issued, he had worked up some of his Vedic material into the first of his "Selected Hymns." Before 15 August, when *Arya*'s first issue was published, he had written one or more installments of four different books: *The Secret of the Veda, The Life Divine, The Isha Upanishad,* and *The Synthesis of Yoga.*' Two of these works, *The Life Divine* and *The Synthesis of Yoga,* are among the most important books of the twentieth century, an evaluation not lessened by the fact that so many people still do not know about

---

* See Chapter 4.

them. 'During the same two months that Sri Aurobindo performed this astounding intellectual labour, he also saw to all the details of the production and distribution of the new review. The Mother meanwhile translated Sri Aurobindo's articles for the French edition.'[12] She was also the chief executive in sole charge.[13] Her experience of publishing Théon's *Revue cosmique* stood her in good stead. Richard contributed *The Wherefore of the Worlds* and *The Eternal Wisdom,* serials that Sri Aurobindo, in addition to the burden of his other work, had to translate from the French.

Sri Aurobindo was amply proving his theory that a yogi has to be able to turn his hand to anything. Still, he asserted that he was no philosopher. 'Let me tell you in confidence that I never, never, never was a philosopher – although I have written philosophy, which is another story altogether,' he wrote to a disciple. 'I knew precious little about philosophy before I did the Yoga and came to Pondicherry – I was a poet and a politician, not a philosopher ... I had only to write down in the terms of the intellect all that I had observed and come to know in practising Yoga daily and the philosophy was there automatically.'[14]

After the accident to his leg many years later, he said to some disciples in his room: 'If you mean thinking, I never do that. Thinking ceased a long time ago – it has stopped ever since that experience of mine with Lele, the Silence and Nirvana at Baroda. Thoughts, as I said, come to me from all sides and from above, and the transmitting mind remains quiet or it enlarges to receive them. True thoughts always come in this way. You can't think out such thoughts. If you try to do so, you only make what the Mother calls mental constructions.' A disciple asked: 'Was the *Arya* with its thousands of pages written in this way?' Sri Aurobindo answered: 'No, it was transmitted directly to the pen. It is a great relief to get out of the responsibility ... I don't mean responsibility in general, but of thinking about everything. Some thoughts are given, some are reflected from above. It is not that I don't look for knowledge. When I want knowledge, I call for it. The higher faculty sees thoughts as if they were written on a wall.'[15]

About the meaning of the name *Arya,* printed like a hieroglyph in Devanagari script on the frontpage of the review, Sri Aurobindo wrote the following in one of the first issues: 'All the highest aspirations of the early human race, its noblest religious temper, its most idealistic velleities of thought are summed up in this single vocable ... In later times, the word Arya expressed a particular ethical and social ideal, an ideal of well-governed life, candour, courtesy, nobility, straight dealing, courage, gentleness, purity, humanity, compassion, protection of the weak, liberality, observance of social duty, eagerness for knowledge, respect for the wise and learned, the social accomplishments. It was the combined ideal of the Brahmana [the learned priest] and the Kshatriya [the knight]. Everything that departed from this ideal, everything that tended towards the ignoble, mean, obscure, rude, cruel or false, was termed un-Aryan. There is no word in human speech that has a nobler history.' [16]

And so it made itself heard, that mighty voice at the beginning of the century. 'The earliest preoccupation of man in his awakened thoughts and, as it seems, his inevitable and ultimate preoccupation – for it survives the longest periods of scepticism and returns after every banishment – is also the highest which his thought can envisage. It manifests itself in the divination of the Godhead, the impulse towards perfection, the search after pure Truth and unmixed Bliss, the sense of a secret immortality. The ancient dawns of human knowledge have left us their witness to this constant aspiration; today we see a humanity satiated but not satisfied by victorious analysis of the externalities of Nature preparing to return to its primeval longings. The earliest formula of Wisdom promises to be its last – God, Light, Freedom, Immortality.' This is the first paragraph on the first page of the first issue of the *Arya*. It is now as vibrant as it was at the time of writing, a century ago.

In the meantime the First World War had erupted.

Parallel to the activities around the founding of the *Arya* Mirra started a new society called *The New Idea / L'Idée nouvelle*. This again makes it clear that she had begun working out her programme, of which the fourth point was: 'Collectively, to establish an ideal society in a propitious spot for the flowering of the new race, the race of the Sons of God.' Although the lifetime of the new society would be short, something Mirra did not know when she started it, it was significant as a trial run of what later would become the Sri Aurobindo Ashram and Auroville.

147

The reader will recall Mirra's questions to Sri Aurobindo when she met him for the first time, especially the question whether they should go the way at first alone or immediately take others with them. As the Mother said later, making a choice had not been necessary: some individuals had gathered around them, guided by their psychic instinct.

The first of these were Sri Aurobindo's companions, of whom the closest were Nolini Kanta Gupta, Bejoy Nag, Saurin Bose and Suresh Chakravarti. They had been joined by a young Tamil Brahmin from Pondicherry, K. Amrita. 'With those who accompanied me or joined me in Pondicherry,' wrote Sri Aurobindo, 'I had at first the relation of friends and companions rather than of a Guru and disciples; it was on the ground of politics that I had come to know them and not on the spiritual ground.'[17] They usually had but little money to spend and led their 'camp life' in such an improvised way that Motilal Roy, on one of his visits from Chandernagore, was scandalized by the carelessness with which they looked after Sri Aurobindo.

Yet they played excellent football. In this way they befriended some of the youngsters from town. As Nolini writes in his *Reminiscences*: 'Among our first acquaintances in Pondicherry were some of the young men here ... Sada, Benjamin, Jules Rassendren, David ... Gradually they formed a group of Sri Aurobindo's devotees. The strange thing about it was that they were all Christians. We did not have much of a response from the local Hindus, perhaps they were far too orthodox and old-fashioned. The Cercle Sportif was our rendezvous. There we had games, we arranged picnics, we staged plays, and also held study circles ... Afterwards, when the Mother came in 1914, it was with a few men chosen from this group that she laid the first foundation of the work here; they formed the Society called "L'Idée nouvelle."'[18]

The aim of the society was stated in the first issue of the *Arya*. 'Its object is to group in a common intellectual life and fraternity of sentiment those who accept the spiritual tendency and idea it represents and who aspire to realize it in their own individual and social action ... The Society has already made a beginning by grouping together young men of different castes and religions in a common ideal. All sectarian and political questions are necessarily foreign to its idea and activities. It is on a higher plane of thought superior to external differences of race, caste, creed and opinion and in the solidarity of the spirit that unity can be realized ... The Society has its headquarters at Pondicherry with a reading-room and a library. A section has been founded at Karikal and others are likely to be opened at Yanam and Mahé [French territories dependent on the Pondicherry administration].'[19] To bring in some money Mirra also set up a shop, called '*Aryan Stores*' and which was to be run by Saurin – who, unfortunately, was not very business-minded.

A humble beginning for sure, but one that demanded a huge amount of energy from Mirra. At first the young men around Sri Aurobindo seem to have been rather distrustful of that European lady, Madame Richard. 'When it first came to be bruited that a Great Lady like this was to come and live close to us,' writes Nolini, 'we were faced with a problem: how should we behave? Should there be a change in our manners? For we had been accustomed to a bohemian sort of life, we dressed and talked, slept and ate and moved about in a free unfettered style, in a manner that would not quite pass in civilized society. Nevertheless, it was finally agreed that we should stick as far as possible to our old ways even under the new circumstances, for why should we permit our freedom and ease to be compromised or lost?'[20]

As Amrita recalls those days when he sought instruction from Madame Richard: 'Had someone seen the Mother and myself seated on chairs, facing each other, almost as equals, with the book of *Yogic Sadhana* in hand, he would have been in a fix to know who was teaching whom.'[21] Amrita was still a student belonging to the high and orthodox Vaishnava Brahmin caste. Since Sri Aurobindo's arrival in Pondicherry, he had felt strongly attracted to him for reasons he could not even rationalize. This caused a severe clash with his Brahmin father and relatives, for caste customs and dress were evidently foreign to everything Sri Aurobindo stood for. One night, during Amrita's sleep, Nolini (on Sri Aurobindo's instructions) cut off his *shikha,* the small tuft of hair on the shaven head of a Brahmin. 'I got struck with fear. How should I dare to look straight in the faces of my parents and relatives? A Brahmin youth without a shikha was no better than a pariah!' But he withstood the storm, became a member of the circle of intimates around Sri Aurobindo, who had helped him make the decisive step by cutting the symbolic tie with his past, and later, as one of the Ashram secretaries, became a close collaborator of the Mother.

Because of Mirra's deference to Sri Aurobindo, his young companions little by little realized who he actually was and how they should behave towards him. 'The Mother came and installed Sri Aurobindo on his high pedestal of Master and Lord of Yoga,' writes Nolini. 'We had hitherto known him as a dear friend and close companion, and although in our mind and heart he had the position of a Guru, in our outward relations we seemed to behave as if he were just like one of ourselves. He too had been averse to the use of the words "Guru" and "Ashram" in relation to himself, for there was hardly a place in his work of new creation for the old traditional associations these words conveyed. Nevertheless, the Mother taught by her manner and speech, and showed us in actual practice, what was the meaning of disciple and master; she always practised what she preached. She showed us, by not taking her seat in front of or on the same level as Sri Aurobindo but by sitting on the ground, what it meant to be respectful to one's Master, what was real courtesy.' [22]

It is remarkable how this period of frantic activity was also a period of the most intensive spiritual practice, both for Sri Aurobindo and for Mirra. The *Record of Yoga* and the *Prayers and Meditations* bear witness to this. There is no entry in Mirra's diary dated 15 August 1914, Sri Aurobindo's birthday and the day the first issue of the *Arya* appeared. There is, however, an entry on the very next day, showing that the problems had not abated one bit; on the contrary, the inner struggle accompanying them remained as acute as ever.

'When Thy force descends towards the Earth in order to manifest [as it must have done on 15 August], each one of the great Asuric beings who have resolved to be Thy servitors but preserved their nature's characteristic of domination and self-will, wants to pull it down for itself alone and distribute it to others afterwards; it always thinks it should be the sole or at least the supreme intermediary, and that the contact of all others with Thy Power cannot and should not be made except through its mediation. This unfortunate meanness is more or less conscious, but it is always there, delaying things indefinitely. If even for the greatest it is impossible in the integral manifestation to escape these lamentable limitations, why, O Lord, impose upon me the Calvary of this constraint? ... If Thou willest that it be thus, Thou shouldst rend the last veil and Thy splendour come in all its purity and transfigure the world! Accomplish this miracle or else let me withdraw into Thee.'[23] For the reader it is impossible even to guess what may have caused this poignant outcry of the soul – as it was impossible during that Pondicherrian summer for their friends and acquaintances to guess the true relationship of Monsieur and Madame Richard.

The Integral Vision and the Integral Yoga

> *Man is the link between what must be and what is; he is the footbridge thrown across the abyss, he is the great cross-shaped X, the quaternary connecting link.*[24]

> – The Mother

This may be the appropriate place to give an idea, in the briefest of summaries, of the vision and yoga of Sri Aurobindo and the Mother that is the gist of the writings published during six-and-a-half years in the *Arya*.

The root of Sri Aurobindo's vision is Vedic-Vedantic. There is the Brahman, the One without a second, which is everything and next to which there is nothing. 'The Brahman alone is, and because of It all are, for all are the Brahman.'[25] (Sri Aurobindo) It exists from all eternity to all eternity and is absolutely self-existing. Its highest attributes are Existence *(sat)*, Consciousness *(chit-tapas)* and Bliss *(ananda)*. All is That, nothing can exist without being That. 'Thou art That, O Shvetaketu.' (Chandogya Upanishad).

For reasons beyond human comprehension, That wanted to know itself: It wanted to objectify Itself in order to have a concrete knowledge of Itself. To that end It activated Its Consciousness-Power, which is the Great Mother of all that is. What this Power sees, exists. Seeing all that was in Itself, the worlds were created, representing the immense rainbow-coloured scale of Being in its endless variety, each peopled with myriad beings incarnating the degree of omnipotent, omnipresent and all-joyous being in which they live immortally. In this way was manifested the world of Existence, of Consciousness, of Bliss, and so came into being the worlds of the Supermind, the Truth-Consciousness with its numberless gradations, all existing in the Unity that is the fundamental characteristic of the Brahman. The creation of the Great Mother was marvellous, flawless, infinite in vastness and detail, and the Brahman mirrored Itself in it and knew Itself in the whole of Its limitless scope.

But in that infinity of the Brahman there was also the possibility to see Itself in Its opposites (which are the Brahman too, as there is nothing else) – to see Its Truth as Falsehood; Its Light as Darkness; Its Power and Life as weakness trailing Death; Its Bliss as Suffering. As we know that, when in the One something arises, when something in It is seen, that something exists. And this is how the 'Fall' happened of the four great beings whose acquaintance we have made at the end of chapter three.

At this point Sri Aurobindo and the Mother do not follow the Vedantic teaching any longer. Against the broad, eternally unchanging universe arises the evolutionary manifestation of which our world is a part. When this evolutionary manifestation of the Brahman through Its Executrix, the Great Mother, seemed to be going astray, She turned towards Her Lord for assistance, and He told Her to pour Her Love into the black world of the Inconscient; and from the outpouring of Her Love were born the Gods. Her Love also awakened in the immovable, impenetrable darkness of the Inconscient the longing to return to its Origin. And the instruments of the evolution towards that End – which is also the Beginning – are the *Avatars*, incarnations in the evolution of the Divine Love ever radiating in the depths of our evolutionary world.

All this the One must have wanted to happen, for nothing can exist or come into manifest being without Its consent, and everything consists of Its eternal Essence. It has willed the perilous and long-lasting adventure of the evolution from the dark night of its (apparent) opposites into the ecstasy of the rediscovery of its divine Self, for this too is one of the modes of its Ananda or Bliss.

We humans are part of that adventure. We have a soul; our soul is divine, it is the Divine. If this is true, we are part of the One that has willed the adventure of the night of long-suffering to experience the rediscovery of our inmost Self. To be part of the One means to be the One, for a part of infinity is infinite too. We have chosen the adventure of evolution as a road towards Self-Knowledge, we have chosen to be participants in that adventure – although most of us have forgotten that, our minds being steeped in ignorance. We have forgotten who we are, where we come from and where we are going. But having voluntarily plunged from the brilliant heavens of our eternal Existence into the darkness of this nether corner of the manifestation, we cannot turn back, we cannot quit, and our ultimate destiny is inescapable: the divine ecstasy of re-becoming who we are and have always been. Being human, however, we have no notion of what is divinity, or divine ecstasy, or the inescapable certitude of the happy ending of our seemingly endless journey. That is why we suffer, and feel dejected, and deep down enjoy our desperation.

Evolution is now generally accepted as a scientific fact. In India it has existed for centuries as a spiritual fact: witness the 'procession' of avatars from the Fish to Kalki, each one initiating a higher level of evolution. That Matter, Life and Consciousness are the gradations of evolution of our mother, the Earth, is clear to all eyes that see. It is less clear that Matter itself has evolved from the Inconscient into which our evolutionary universe was plunged at its very origin. And not understood at all is the key Aurobindonian concept of involution, which must of necessity have preceded the evolution. 'Nothing can evolve out of Matter which is not already therein contained,' wrote Sri Aurobindo in *The Life Divine*.[26] 'Evolution of Life in matter supposes a previous involution of it there, unless we suppose it to be a new creation magically and unaccountably introduced in Nature … The evolution of consciousness and knowledge cannot be accounted for unless there is already a concealed consciousness in things with its inherent and native powers emerging little by little.'[27] And Sri Aurobindo compares the mounting and descending hierarchy of planes to a double ladder, first lapsing into the nescience of the Inconscient and Matter and then climbing up again 'through the flowering of life and soul and mind into the infinity of the Spirit.'

Nobody can say how long the involution – symbolically enacted in the tragedy of the Four Asuras – has taken; it may have happened in an instant. Nor do we know how long the evolution will take, though a very long time for sure. As human beings, we carry all the developed steps of the evolution until now in our being. We consist of matter, the life forces and (mental) consciousness; we have in us, too, the Subconcient and Inconscient below, and the perspectives of the Spirit and its infinite ranges above. On the upward ladder of evolution the human being stands somewhere halfway, in a rather awkward position: half animal, half god. If evolution makes any sense at all, it would be illogical that it stops with the human being. The Divine Creatrix must no doubt be able to do better.

'Evolution is not finished; reason is not the last word nor the reasoning animal the supreme figure of Nature. As man emerged from the animal, so out of man the superman emerges,' states one of Sri Aurobindo's *Thoughts and Aphorisms*.[28] And in one of the first pages of *The Life Divine* he writes: 'The animal is a living laboratory in which Nature has, it is said, worked out Man. Man himself may well be a thinking and living laboratory in whom and with whose conscious co-operation she wills to work out the superman, the god.'[29]

These central points in the vision of Sri Aurobindo and the Mother have to be emphasized because they form the foundation of their Integral Yoga. If 'yoga' means a (re)unification with the Divine, then evolution as such is a yoga of the Divine: after having distanced Himself from Himself, He moves by means of the evolution towards a Self-reunification in the ecstasy of Self-recognition. The human, being an incarnation of a divine soul and part of the evolution, participates in this yoga of the Divine. However, until now humanity has not been aware of the evolutionary significance of the world and of itself. It has seen the world mostly as static or cyclic, and if in the succession of its many reincarnations it may have had some idea of evolving, this evolution was considered to be individual, not related to the species as a whole.

The revolutionary aspect of the vision and yoga of Sri Aurobindo and the Mother thus becomes clear. For them the world is neither static nor cyclic but evolutionary and ascending towards a goal: its divinization. The evolution is the yoga of the Divine and everything in this evolutionary world is participating in this yoga, whether it is aware of this or not, whether it wants this or not. The time has come for humanity to grow conscious of this process and of the fact that a new species, exceeding humanity, is in the making. A new evolutionary level, just as on every preceding occasion, can only be initiated by a direct intervention of the Divine incarnating in Matter as an Avatar.

The yoga of Sri Aurobindo and the Mother is new, because its goal is no longer a personal liberation or the attainment of heaven, which have been and are the goal of all other spiritual and religious endeavours up to the present. Its aim is to actively participate in the transition from the human being to a transhuman, supramental or divine being, to make this transition a concrete possibility. The person who practises the Integral Yoga can have no personal intentions. And the yoga of Sri Aurobindo and the Mother is integral because a transformation of the existing world into a supramental world demands the transformation of all its parts; the transformation cannot be complete as long as one part remains behind. All those parts are present, in various degrees, in every human being. The human being dedicating itself to this yoga must therefore be transformed totally, including the matter of the cells of its body.

As the Mother wrote in her diary in the months of June and July 1914: 'Those whom Thou hast appointed as Thy representatives upon Earth cannot rest content with the results so obtained [in an egoistic aspiration for their own salvation] ... He who wants to be perfect in Thy manifestation cannot be satisfied with that, he must manifest Thee on all the planes, in all the states of being and thus turn the knowledge he has acquired to the best account for the whole universe ... It is a veritable work of creation we have to do ... Thou hast made a promise, Thou hast sent into these worlds those who can and that which can fulfil this promise ... And since this *must* be done, *this will be done* ... *The Force is there.* Rejoice, O you who are waiting and hoping: the new manifestation is sure, the new manifestation is at hand. *The Force is there.*'[30]

No human being can have an idea of what divinization of the world really means because no human being has an adequate idea of what the Divine is. Therefore the cornerstone of the Integral Yoga is what Sri Aurobindo called 'surrender' to the Divine. (We have seen that he himself practised this surrender from the moment he engaged on the path of his spiritual discovery with V.B. Lele in Baroda, and whoever reads the Mother's *Prayers and Meditations* will find it on practically every page.) A total surrender by a spiritual aspirant is not without danger, for he will, because of his inner choice and commitment, at once become the target of attacks from all kinds of invisible beings, for whom the transformation of the world as it is at present means the end of their reign. Few are the aspirants who, taking up a yoga like this, have the discernment to tell the demonic inspirations from the divine. This is why the cultivation of a second quality is an absolute necessity in the Integral Yoga: sincerity, knife-sharp, to dissect one's inspirations, feelings and motivations.

Rare are those people who will surrender themselves without expecting a reward. (The absence of the promise of a short-term spiritual reward makes this yoga incomprehensible to many seekers.) The *siddhi* (realization) of this yoga can be no other than the divinization of the whole person, including the body. The new, divine species is *not* an improvement or aggrandizement of the human species; it is a species *beyond* the human species. Besides, as the Integral Yoga demands an effort of transformation of all parts of the human being, it is an enormous undertaking by any standards. (Sri Aurobindo compared it to a war on all fronts.) For all the good and the bad of the world is present in us and has to be tackled, in the knowledge that the human 'good' is not that much better than the human 'bad.' From which we may conclude that taking up the Integral Yoga is the result of a calling rather than of a personal decision. It is a pursuit for the mature souls, 'the pioneer few' who have incarnated once more to help their human brothers and sisters by dedicating this earthly incarnation to the shaping of a world where suffering, hatred, darkness and death will have no dominion any more.

Indeed, the Integral Yoga of Sri Aurobindo and the Mother is *the supreme* Utopia, the attempt to realize at last the fulfilment of the promise given to humankind from its beginnings and so often repeated but never made true. Therefore, understandably, humankind has grown weary of promises and utopias, but not so the mature souls who know that a new world is in the making because they have chosen to descend and collaborate in its realization, even though they could have chosen otherwise and remained in the Bliss of their soul-world or Origin.

> All shall be done for which our pain was borne.
> Even as of old man came behind the beast
> This high divine successor surely shall come
> Behind man's inefficient mortal pace,
> Behind his vain labour, sweat and blood and tears:
> He shall know what mortal mind barely durst think,
> He shall do what the heart of the mortal could not dare.
> Inheritor of the toil of human time,
> He shall take on him the burden of the gods;
> All heavenly light shall visit the earth's thoughts,
> The might of heaven shall fortify earthly hearts;
> Earth's deeds shall touch the superhuman's height,
> Earth's seeing widen into the infinite.[31]

The Mother

There is only one thing of which I am absolutely sure, and that is who I am. Sri Aurobindo also knew it and declared it. Even the doubts of the whole of humanity would change nothing of this fact.[32]

– The Mother

'It was in 1914 that the identification with the Universal Mother took place, the identification of the physical consciousness with her. Of course, I knew before this that I was the Mother, but the complete identification took place only in 1914,'[33] said the Mother many years later.

Who is the Universal Mother? A few pages before we have seen that when the One wanted to objectify Itself in order to have a 'concrete' knowledge of Itself, It activated Its Consciousness-Power. The Mother is the Consciousness-Power of the Divine, which means that She is His power of manifestation. Two points should be emphasized. Firstly, the Mother is in no way inferior to the Divine Himself: She is the Divine essentially, intrinsically. Secondly, the Mother-Power in the Divine would also be there in Him if He were not manifesting any part of Himself. He is She, She is He; they are One.

In the powerful prose of his letters about the Mother, afterwards published as a booklet called *The Mother,* Sri Aurobindo writes: 'The One whom we adore as the Mother is the divine Conscious Force that dominates all existence, one and yet so many-sided that to follow her movement is impossible even for the quickest mind and for the freest and most vast intelligence. The Mother is the consciousness and force of the Supreme and far above all she creates ...

'There are three ways of being of the Mother of which you can become aware when you enter into touch of oneness with the Conscious Force that upholds us and the universe. Transcendent, the original supreme Shakti, she stands above the worlds and links the creation to the ever unmanifest mystery of the Supreme. Universal, the cosmic Mahashakti, she creates all these beings and contains and enters, supports and conducts all these million processes and forces. Individual, she embodies the power of these two vaster ways of her existence, makes them living and near to us and mediates between the human personality and the divine Nature.'[34]

'Four great Aspects of the Mother, four of her leading Powers and Personalities have stood in front in her guidance of this Universe and in her dealings with the terrestrial play. One [Maheshwari] is her personality of calm wideness and comprehending wisdom and tranquil benignity and inexhaustible compassion and sovereign and surpassing majesty and all-ruling greatness. Another [Mahakali] embodies her power of splendid strength and irresistible passion, her warrior mood, her overwhelming will, her impetuous swiftness and world-shaking force. A third [Mahalakshmi] is vivid and sweet and wonderful with her deep secret of beauty and harmony and fine rhythm, her intricate and supple opulence, her compelling attraction and captivating grace. The fourth [Mahasaraswati] is equipped with her close and profound capacity of intimate knowledge and careful flawless work and quiet and exact perfection in all things. Wisdom, Strength, Harmony, Perfection are their several attributes and it is these powers that they bring into the world ...'[35] It is these four powers of the Goddess that we find all over the world represented in the manner the peoples have perceived or imagined her and her emanations.

Mirra had known that she was an incarnation of the Divine Mother, not only in one of her aspects but in the integrality of Her being. The great clairvoyant Madame Théon had seen the 'twelve pearls' like a crown above Mirra's head. In fact, Mirra had felt all along, since her earliest childhood, who she was. Her greater Self had chosen her parents, the place where she would be born and the way she would be educated. Her greater Self had provided her with her numerous occult experiences, like the wonderful one of her rising in a golden robe above Paris, giving solace to all who came to her in their need. Yet, like all incarnated souls, she had to go through the effort of overcoming the degradation of being born in a human, material body – though she kept always alive the remembrance of the true nature of her soul.

Now had come the time of the identification of her self with her Self. This crucial event in Mirra's spiritual evolution must have happened in the last days or on the last day of August 1914, for we read in her diary entry of 31 August the invocation: 'O Mother, sweet Mother who I am ...' which is the direct formulation of the identification that had taken place. The next day she writes: 'I have become Thyself definitively,' and on 4 September: 'O sweet Mother, I merge into Thee in an immense love ... I have become the purifying fire of Thy love.' The entry of 13 September begins: 'With fervour I salute Thee, O divine Mother, and in deep affection I identify myself with Thee. United with our divine Mother I turn, O Lord, towards Thee and bow to Thee in mute adoration and in an ardent aspiration I identify myself with Thee.' And on the next day she writes: 'There is no longer an I, no longer an individuality, no longer any personal limits. There is only the immense universe, our sublime Mother, burning with an ardent fire of purification in honour of Thee, O Lord, divine Master, sovereign Will, so that this Will may meet with no farther obstacle in the way of its realization.'

This extraordinary series of spiritual statements can leave no doubt concerning the fact of Mirra's identification with the Great Mother. 'O divine and adorable Mother, with Thy help what is there that is impossible?' she wrote on 25 September. 'The hour of realization is near and Thou hast assured us of Thy aid that we may perform integrally the supreme Will. Thou hast accepted us as fit intermediaries between the unthinkable realities [of the higher worlds] and the relativities of the physical world, and Thy constant presence in our midst is a token of Thy active collaboration.' And then follow four lines which will reverberate through the rest of her earthly life, the 'Thou' here representing the incarnated Great Mother:

> The Lord has willed and Thou dost execute:
> A new light shall break upon the earth.
> A new world shall be born,
> And the things that were promised shall be fulfilled.[36]

In *Savitri*, the spiritual biography of the Mother and himself, Sri Aurobindo has worded this memorable event as follows:

> In its deep lotus home her being sat
> As if on concentration's marble seat,
> Calling the mighty Mother of the worlds
> To make this earthly tenement her house.
> As in a flash from a supernal light,
> A living image of the original Power,
> A face, a form came down into her heart
> And made of it its temple and pure abode ...
> A portion of the mighty Mother came
> Into her as into its own human part.[37]

The First World War and Richard's Expulsion

The hour is fateful for the earth ...[38]

– The Mother

Historians concur that the eruption of the First World War was generally experienced as the sudden relief from a tension that had built up
in humanity in the course of the last decennia, and become unbearable.
Documentaries still show the smiling faces of the young men proudly
marching to their fate with flowers in the barrel of their rifles, and the
hysterical behaviour of the women sending them off. Nobody had an
idea of the murderous massacres ahead, the statesmen and generals no
more than the others; and once having entered the dance of death they
persevered in it like automatons, like puppets manipulated by invisible
forces – which was indeed the truth of the matter.

In chapter two we saw how humanity was irresistibly pushed into
opening the doors of its inner self after many centuries of fixed and
unquestioned traditions, habitual mores and automatic behavior. Like
the Impressionists who sought the direct sensation of the artistic experience, psychologists peeled off the surface layers of human behavior,
long dried-up into conventions, sociologists and philosophers wanted
to revolutionize the established social attitudes, and physicists broke
through the appearances of matter and started on a voyage of discovery
that is still far from finished. Some deep nerves, some fundamental
roots were touched, whose existence had been unsuspected and up to
now been dormant, and in humanity a terrifying inner Shadow stood
up which very few humans had the discernment or the courage to
recognize as their own.

A massive descent of hostile forces from the occult vital worlds
corresponded to this awakening of the vital powers inside humanity.
'Monstrous forces have swooped down upon the Earth like a hurri-
cane,' wrote Mirra in her diary on 8 August, when the nations were
jockeying for positions in the 'War Game.'[39] And the Mother would say
many years later: 'The First World War was the result of an enormous
descent of the forces of the vital world – the *hostile* forces of the vital

161

world – into the material world. Even those who were conscious of this descent and consequently armed to defend themselves against it, suffered from its consequences. The whole world, the whole Earth suffered from its consequences ... Naturally, men do not know what happened to them; all that they have said is that everything had become worse since the war. That was all they could assert.'[40]

The German people, not for the first time and neither for the last, put themselves at the service of those dark forces. 'Germans knew themselves to be the strongest military power on Earth, the most efficient merchants, the busiest bankers, penetrating every continent, financing the Turks, flinging out a railroad from Berlin to Baghdad, gaining the trade of Latin America, challenging the sea power of Great Britain, and in the realm of intellect systematically organizing, under the concept *Wissenschaft,* every branch of human knowledge. They were deserving and capable [in their own opinion] of mastery of the world. Rule by the best must be fulfilled,' writes Barbara Tuchman in *A Proud Tower.* And she reminds us of the German slogan at the time: *Den Deutschen gehört die Welt* – the world belongs to the Germans.

On 28 June 1914, a week after the decision to publish the *Arya,* the Austrian crown prince Archduke Franz Ferdinand was assassinated in Sarajevo. The following day Austria declared war on Serbia; on 1 August Germany stood by its Austrian ally and declared war on Russia, and two days later on France; on 4 August German troops invaded neutral Belgium and Britain declared war on Germany; on 12 August Britain and France declared war on Austria; on 23 August Japan declared war on Germany ...

The German armies seemed irresistible. Their right flank quick-marched towards the Channel ports while their left flank pushed straight towards the heart of France. The French armies and the British Expeditionary Force retreated in panic. Squeezed between the pincers of the German attack they were on the verge of being annihilated, and the fall of Paris, cultural capital of the world and symbol of Western civilization, seemed certain. The French government had already fled to Bordeaux in the middle of the night.

At this critical moment in world history the following incident happened in Pondicherry, as narrated by the Mother herself. 'I used to sit on the terrace to meditate every morning, facing Sri Aurobindo's room. That day I was inside my room, but looking at Sri Aurobindo's room through a small window. I was in meditation but my eyes were open. I saw Kali [the black goddess of power and destruction] entering through my door. I asked her: "What do you want?" She was dancing, a truly savage dance. She told me: "Paris is taken, Paris will be destroyed!" We had no news at all, it was just in the beginning of the war. I was in meditation. I turned towards her and said to her: "No, Paris will not be taken, Paris will be saved" – quietly, just like that, but with a certain force. [On another occasion the Mother would say that it was Maha-shakti herself who said "no."] She made a face and went away. And the next day we received the dispatch ... posted on the gate of Government House. We got the news that the Germans had been marching upon Paris and that Paris was not defended; the way was quite open, they had to advance only a few kilometres more and they would have entered the city.'[41] But they did not persevere in their effort.

In fact, General von Kluck, commanding the right flank of the Germans, had overestimated the disarray in the French and British armies. Instead of continuing his march and taking Paris, which would have been an easy matter, he turned left too early in order to try and encircle the enemy. This gave the defenders of Paris the chance to attack him in the flank. The German march came to a halt and the first trenches were dug on the river Marne.

The war also put Sri Aurobindo and the other freedom fighters, or *swadeshis* as they were called in Pondicherry, under increased pressure. The British had not forgotten him, far from it. Had not Lord Minto said that 'he could not rest his head on the pillow till he had crushed Aurobindo Ghose'? 'The British Government and numbers of people besides could not believe that Sri Aurobindo had ceased from all political action.'[42] We have seen that he was suspected of being the instigator of the murder of the District Collector of Tirunelveli. The British exerted all possible pressure to have Sri Aurobindo expelled from the French territory, but five Pondicherrians were found to sign an attestation to the 'good conduct' of Sri Aurobindo. In his *Reminiscences* Nolini calls them the 'five noble men.'

At the beginning of the war a German battleship, the cruiser *Emden*, caused havoc in the Bay of Bengal by firing a few shells at the British possessions. Madras, too, was targeted and half the population fled miles inland. Though Pondicherry was nor hit, hundreds fled the town in panic when the ship passed by. This visible German presence made the freedom fighters still more suspect as possible spies, and the French now seemed willing to throw them out.

'The British Government brought increased pressure on the French: they must do something drastic about their political refugees,' recalls Nolini. 'Either they should hand them over to the British, or else let them be deported out of India. The French Government accordingly proposed that they would find room for us in Algeria ... If we were to refuse this offer, there might be danger: the British authorities might be allowed to seize us forcibly. I can recall very well that scene. Sri Aurobindo was seated in his room in what was later called the "Guest House," rue Francois Martin. We too had come. Two or three of the Tamil nationalist leaders who had sought refuge in Pondicherry came in and told Sri Aurobindo about the Algeria offer and also gave a hint that they were agreeable to it. Sri Aurobindo paused a little and then said, in a quiet clear tone, "I do not budge from here" ... Sri Aurobindo had spoken and they could hardly act otherwise.' [43]

In this matter the British government in London had directly addressed the French government in Paris, where Mirra's brother, Matteo, occupied at the time a senior post in the Ministry of Foreign Affairs. 'He [Matteo] did a great deal in Africa [where he became Governor-General of the French Congo], but other people got the benefit. It is men like him who built up France and also made it possible for the Ashram to continue here. Otherwise I might have had to go to France, or else to America ... When the Mother came here and I met her, her brother got interested. These things look like accidents, but they are not. There is a guidance behind these events.' [44] The file concerning the swadeshis in Pondicherry landed in Matteo's hands; he put it in his bottom drawer and nothing came of it.

Bejoy Nag, however, found out that the British police meant business. He was arrested as soon as he left Pondicherrian territory in October 1914 under the Ingress into India Ordinance. Bejoy was 'regarded by the Bengal Police as an exceptionally dangerous person,' read his police file, 'and the records of the Madras special police in Pondicherry bear out this opinion.' For not only was Bejoy one of the accused in the Alipore Bomb Case, he was also bearing a written authorization 'empowering him to travel as agent for the *Arya,*' which proved his ongoing connection with Aurobindo Ghose. Poor Bejoy would be interned till after the end of the war.

Paul Richard had tried to intervene with the authorities in favour of Bejoy before the latter's departure. He stood little chance of success as he himself was one of the prime suspects on the list of the British police, who characterized him as a 'rabid socialist' and anti-colonialist, knowing that he was a close acquaintance of Aurobindo Ghose. 'Monsieur Richard is a French subject and a defeated candidate for the Pondicherry seat in the French Chamber of Deputies. He is reported to hold dangerous opinions and started a society called the "Union de la jeunesse Hindoue" *[sic]* for the political, religious and literary education of young men in Pondicherry. He is constantly in the company of extremists there and himself claims a five years' friendship with Arabindo Ghose.'[45]

'Richard's situation in Pondicherry also was undermined by the outbreak of war, but in his case no intervention, inner or outer, could prevent his expulsion from the colony. Like all Frenchmen on the service rolls, Richard was called up in the general mobilization of 3 August 1914. He remained in Pondicherry for six months, during which time he made a belated attempt to cultivate good relations with the British ... Late in January [1915] the government of Pondicherry acceded to British insistence and ordered his expulsion. Richard's appeal against this ruling was unsuccessful, and on 22 February the day after the Mother's thirty-seventh birthday, he and she departed from Pondicherry.'[46]

One may suppose that they reached Colombo on the *Dupleix* of the *Messageries Maritimes.* There they boarded the Japanese ship *Kamo Maru* on 26 February. It seems that in Colombo the British police confiscated the Sanskrit grammar Sri Aurobindo had prepared for Mirra. The first entry in Mirra's diary on board the *Kamo Maru,* also the first after her departure from Pondicherry, shows what a terrible blow the separation from Sri Aurobindo was to her. 'Solitude, a harsh, intense solitude, and always this strong impression of having been flung headlong into a hell of darkness! Never at any moment of my life, in any circumstances, have I felt myself living in surroundings so entirely opposite to all that I am conscious of as true, so contrary to all that is the essence of my life ... For the moment the clear-sightedness is lacking; never was the future more veiled.' The next day she wrote: 'Each turn of the propeller upon the deep ocean seems to drag me farther away from my true destiny, the one best expressing the divine Will; each passing hour seems to plunge me again deeper into that past with which I had broken, sure of being called to new and vaster realizations ...'[47]

'This is an exile from every spiritual happiness ... Strong is the growing sense of rejection, and it needs all the ardour of an untiring faith to keep the external consciousness thus abandoned to itself from being invaded by an irremediable sorrow ... If only it were possible to come definitively out of this external consciousness, to take refuge in the divine consciousness! But that Thou hast forbidden and still and always Thou forbidst it. No flight out of the world!' (Many years later and in circumstances as dramatic we will hear similar exclamations.) 'The burden of its darkness and ugliness must be borne to the end even if all divine succour seems to be withdrawn.' Mirra traversed the Dark Night of the Soul.[48]

Why did she have to leave Sri Aurobindo? All answers to this question are no more than suppositions. An important factor was surely the presence of Paul Richard. The Mother would later say that Sri Aurobindo felt relieved by his departure. She, bound to her vow to convert Richard, could not let him leave alone. Another aspect of the situation was that Sri Aurobindo was deeply involved in working out his yoga, as witnessed by the entries in the *Record of Yoga*. However far advanced in comparison with ordinary mortals, he was still on his way towards the supramental realization, of which he would have the mental part in 1920. Much of the *Arya* was written not from a supramental but from an overmental standpoint, as he would concede afterwards and as the Mother would note several times when commenting on his *Thoughts and Aphorisms,* written in 1914-15. A third point was that the time had not yet come for working out her 'programme' in the way she had started so energetically since her arrival in Pondicherry, her personal situation and the state of the world not yet allowing for it.*

On 18 March the Richards arrived in a Paris at war and left the city again on the 29th, travelling to Lunel in the south of France. Mirra's illness, which had started when the *Kamo Maru* entered the Mediterranean, now became serious. 'The hour has not yet come for joyful realizations in outer physical things. The physical being is plunged once again into the dull, monotonous night from which it wanted to withdraw too hastily ... The body, despite its indisputable goodwill, is so profoundly shaken that it cannot manage to regain its equilibrium.'[49] The Mother herself would comment on this entry: 'The prayer refers to an experience I had when I was not physically well and was in fact narrowly saved from death. I had an inflammation of the nerves.'[50] This is an extremely painful condition that she described as 'the maximum of intense pain' everywhere in the body. The reason was that, by an act of spiritual occultism which she herself later would brand as 'reckless,' she had left her soul with Sri Aurobindo, thus leaving her *adhara* on its own among the world forces in upheaval.

But however infernal the experiences she had to go through, what she had become was forever irreversible and gradually grew active again. Even when critically ill she took up her occult work, at Lunel and afterwards at Marsillargues, the birthplace of Paul Richard, where he had to go for reasons of his mobilization. There she was visited by her son André, now an officer in the army, who heard for the first time about Sri Aurobindo. 'The heavens are definitively conquered,' Mirra wrote

---

* M.P. Pandit has a curious paragraph in his book *An Early Chapter:* 'There are many speculations [about Mirra's departure]. But the one speculation that I have heard about it is that he [Sri Aurobindo] was not sure at that point of time if she was to be his Shakti. Whether he expected Mrinalini to be his Shakti, we do not know, though there is a hint in his famous letters to her and also in later developments.' If Sri Aurobindo was who he was supposed to be, and if Mirra was who she was supposed to be, then it cannot be otherwise than that she was Sri Aurobindo's Shakti. This is why Sri Aurobindo would say: 'The Mother's consciousness and mine are the same, the one Divine Consciousness in two, because that is necessary for the play,' and that the Mother would say: 'Sri Aurobindo and I, we are always one and the same consciousness, one and the same person.' Moreover, Mrinalini's own father would testify about her: 'She evinced no exceptional abilities or tendencies [in her youth], indeed at no stage in her life,' which hardly qualifies her for being instrumental in the divinization of the Earth.

in Marsillargues, 'and nothing and nobody could have the power to wrest them from me. But the conquest of the Earth is still to be made; it is being carried on in the very heart of the turmoil; and even when achieved, it will still be only a relative one; the victories in this world are but stages leading progressively to still more glorious victories.'[51]

The causes of her ordeal became clear to her. In the Integral Yoga, transformation of Matter means in the first place transformation of the body, which is our direct contact with Matter. We remember how on New Year's Eve 1913 – a day not long past, but already belonging to a totally different world – she had wished the identification with the Divine 'for the body' and had obtained the fulfilment of her wish within the year. Soon she would write: 'Thou hast taken entire possession of this miserable instrument [her body, or rather, her *adhara*] and if it is not yet perfected enough for Thee to complete its transformation, its transmutation, Thou art at work in each one of its cells to knead it and make it supple and enlighten it, and in the whole being to arrange, organize and harmonize it. Everything is in movement, everything is changing; Thy divine action makes itself felt as an ineffable spring of a purifying fire that circulates through all the atoms.'[52] That early she was already working on what would be one of the main tasks of her incarnation on Earth: the yoga of the cells, the effort to build a divine body by transforming the human body.

In the beginning of November 1915 the Richards were back in Paris. 'In Paris, during the war, there were two kinds of bombardments. The first kind was by a big cannon, called the *'Big Bertha'*, and this Big Bertha launched [enormous] shells on Paris. And the other kind was by zeppelins loaded with bombs which the Germans flew over Paris … One night, on the point of closing the window, she [Mirra] saw a zeppelin in the sky. She heard the alarm which was sounded and at the same time an enormous explosion, and the whole house was shaking.'[53]

'I have visited trains,' said the Mother, 'each one bringing between five and six hundred wounded from the front. It is a moving sight, not so much because of all that those unfortunate men are suffering, but above all because of the noble manner in which most of them bear their sufferings. Their soul shines through their eyes, the slightest contact with the deeper forces awakens it. And from the intensity, the fullness of the powers of true love which could, in their presence, be manifested in perfect silence, it was easy to realize the value of their receptivity.'[54] 'The last months I spent in Paris were truly fantastic. And it can't be told. The life in the trenches, for example, is something that cannot be told ... All the horrors of the vital world had descended upon Earth ...'[55]

'I remember very well that when the war – the First World War – started and I offered my body in sacrifice to the Lord so that the war would not be in vain, every part of my body, one after another *[Mother touches her legs, her arms, etc.]*, or sometimes the same part several times over, represented a battlefield: I could see it, I could feel it, I lived it. Every time it was ... it was very strange, I had only to sit quietly and watch: I would see here, there, there, the whole thing in my body, all that was going on. And while it went on, I would put the concentration of the divine Force there, so that all – all that pain, all that suffering, everything – would hasten the preparation of the Earth and the Descent of the Force. And that went on consciously throughout the war.'[56]

'All the hostile forces in the spiritual world are in a constant state of opposition and besiege our gains; for the complete victory of a single one of us would mean a general downfall among them,' wrote Sri Aurobindo to Mirra. 'All is always for the best, but it is sometimes from the external point of view an awkward best ... The whole Earth is now under one law and answers to the same vibrations and I am sceptical of finding any place where the clash of struggle will not pursue us.'[57] This means that in Pondicherry he took his share of the universal battering. For in the Integral Yoga the attainment of a universal consciousness is one of the necessary stages, and we know that Sri Aurobindo had already realized that consciousness in the jail of Alipore. And universal consciousness means universal presence and sensitivity.

The following is the first part of Mirra's entry in her diary on 26 November 1915: 'The entire consciousness immersed in divine contemplation, the whole being enjoyed a supreme and vast felicity. Then was the physical body seized, first in its lower members and next the whole of it, by a sacred trembling which made all personal limits fall away little by little even in the most material sensation. The being grew in greatness progressively, methodically, breaking down every barrier, shattering every obstacle, that it might contain and manifest a force and a power which increased ceaselessly in immensity and intensity. It was a progressive dilation of the cells until there was a complete identification with the Earth: the body of the awakened consciousness was the terrestrial globe moving harmoniously in ethereal space. And the consciousness knew that its global body was thus moving in the arms of the universal Being, and it gave itself, it abandoned itself to It in an ecstasy of peaceful bliss. Then it felt that its body was absorbed in the body of the universe and one with it; the consciousness became the consciousness of the universe, immobile in its totality, moving infinitely in its internal complexity ...'[58] All this happened while the war was raging.

7.

In Japan

In the world of forms a flaw in Beauty is as great a deficiency as a flaw in Truth in the world of ideas.[1]

– The Mother

After a few moments spent in arranging familiar objects, Mirra wrote in her diary on 2 November 1915: 'As a strong breeze passes over the sea and crowns with foam its countless waves, so a great breath passed over the memory and awoke the multitude of its remembrances. Intense, complex, crowded, the past lived again in a flash, having lost nothing of its savour, its richness. Then was the whole being lifted up in a great surge of adoration, and gathering all its memories like an abundant harvest, it placed them at Thy feet, O Lord, as an offering. For throughout its life, without knowing it or with some presentiment of it, it was Thou whom it was seeking ...'[2]

Paul and Mirra Richard were in Paris again; they would stay there, in relative safety, till the beginning of March 1916. Paul Richard had been exempted from military service on (simulated?) medical grounds. As for Mirra, after the taxing physical and spiritual ordeal she had been through, things had settled down again. 'Errors have become stepping-stones, the blind gropings conquests. Thy glory transforms defeats into victories of eternity, and all the shadows have fled before their radiant light.'[3]

But the war went on unabated and produced horrors as yet unknown to humanity. It was as if she were connected to it with every nerve in her body. A few days later she wrote in the middle of the night: 'For the last two days the Earth seems to have been going through a decisive crisis; it seems that the great, formidable contest between material resistances and spiritual powers is nearing its conclusion, or, in any case, that some element of capital importance has made or is going to make its appearance in the play.' The task ahead, now and on so many occasions to come, was much more arduous than anticipated by her or by Sri Aurobindo. The reason why this material world had never been divinized became ever clearer to them as they advanced into unknown but very concrete and resistant physical-spiritual territory. (In years to come an ironic Sri Aurobindo would even say that he would have been much less enthusiastic had he known what lay ahead.)

And Mirra added: 'How little do individual beings count at such times! They are like wisps of straw carried away by the passing breeze, whirling for a moment above the ground, only to be flung back upon it again and reduced to dust.'[4] Indeed, in their many thousands the youthful bodies torn to shreds by bullets, shells and shrapnel were reduced to dust. Still, in the middle of that holocaust 'the Lord' was there, as He is everywhere. 'O Thou whom I may call my God, Thou who art the personal form of the Transcendent Eternal, the Cause, Source and Reality of my individual being, Thou who hast through the centuries and millenniums slowly and subtly kneaded this Matter, so that one day it could become consciously identified with Thee, and be nothing but Thee; O Thou who hast appeared to me in all Thy divine splendour – this individual being in all its complexity offers itself to Thee in an act of supreme adoration ... Will the great miracle of the integral Divine Life in the individual at last be accomplished?'[5]

All the main themes of the endeavour of Sri Aurobindo and the Mother, all the main items on the agenda of their spiritual labour for humanity, which most of their biographers suppose to have been taken up years and even decades later, were already present in their consciousness and their yogic effort at this early stage. Their yoga was as intense in its beginning as in its middle and end – including their yoga of the matter of the body, of the cells.

'It was not possible for them to go to India,' writes Pournaprema, 'but the circumstances arranged themselves so that they could go to Japan.'[6] In the First World War Japan was an ally of Great Britain and therefore of Great Britain's allies, including France. Paul Richard received a commission to promote the export of French products in China and Japan, as the following letter dated 28 February 1916 makes clear: 'The bearer of this letter, Mr. Paul Richard, a barrister at the

Court of Appeals at Paris and a delegate of the National Union for the Export of French Products, is on his way to Japan and China. Kindly extend a warm welcome to Mr. Richard should he be in need of your good offices.' The letter was signed 'for the Prime Minister.'[7]

As the Mother later said, it was not all that difficult to get this kind of overseas commission, for nobody else wanted to run the risk of the voyage. Not only were some pirate German battleships, like the *Emden,* making the seas unsafe, the German Kaiser by that time had also given carte blanche to his 150 submarines to attack any enemy vessel within range. On 7 May 1915 the British passenger ship *Lusitania* and on 15 November the Italian ocean liner *Ancona* had been torpedoed and sunk, both with huge losses of civilian life. A favoured hunting ground of the German submarines was the Channel, between France and Great Britain, and this was the stretch of water the Richards had to cross in order to reach Britain and then embark on a voyage all the way around South Africa towards the East, for the Suez Canal was closed. Did Mirra realize on 4 March 1916 that she was taking leave of her house, of Paris and of France for the last time? There is no such indication, for the next entry in her diary is dated 7 June four months later, and in it she describes those months as 'a period of transition, the passage from one equilibrium to another, larger and more complete.'

Many formalities were required in London before they could board, on 11 March, the *Kamo Maru,* the same Japanese ship that had brought them from Colombo to France a year before. This time the Richards did not travel alone. They were accompanied by an English lady, Miss Dorothy Hodgson, of whom all that is known is that her fiancé had died, that therefore she never wanted to marry, and that she had chosen Mirra as her spiritual mentor. Dorothy Hodgson, later named Datta by Sri Aurobindo, would remain with the Mother for the rest of her life.

Pournaprema relates a story, supposedly told to her by the Mother, that somewhere in the Atlantic Ocean the *Kamo Maru* was approached threateningly by 'a very big ship,' which was most probably a German battleship. The incident happened around four o'clock in the morning and Mirra, an early riser, was the only one among the passengers to observe it. There was an exchange of signals, the warship slowly circled around the *Kamo Maru* and then suddenly continued on its course.

When Mirra asked the Japanese captain, with whom 'she had sympathized since the beginning of the journey' and of whom she had drawn a sketch, what had happened, he asked her to tell nobody what she had seen. For he had signalled the warship that he had a gun on board, and threatened to fire. In actual fact he had no gun, and his bravado had put his passengers and his ship in jeopardy.

On 6 April the *Kamo Maru* dropped anchor at Table Bay and the Richards visited Cape Town, the capital of South Africa, from where they sent a postcard to André. More than a month later, on 9 and 10 May, the ship called at Shanghai, where Mirra caught a whiff of China. On 18 May the *Kamo Maru* docked at Yokohama, the largest Japanese port.

Tokyo

The first year of their stay in Japan was spent for the most part in Tokyo, in the house of Dr. Shumei Okawa and his wife. Okawa was a university professor in Tokyo, teaching Asian History. He was also a member of the Black Dragon Society and 'the leading spirit of the pan-Asiatic movement in Japan ... a person of considerable influence, who is deeply interested in Indian affairs and is bitterly opposed to British rule in India' – according to a Government of India document reporting the publication of 'a photograph of Arabindo Ghosh and a eulogistic article on his work' by Okawa in *Asia Jiron*.[8] (The Richards were shadowed by people spying for the British during their entire stay in Japan.)

Okawa, who had studied Indian philosophy at Tokyo Imperial University, had become interested in Sri Aurobindo after reading a newspaper article on him. He had tried to obtain Sri Aurobindo's address, but in vain. He also harboured for some time Rashbehari Bose (1880-1945), who had masterminded a bomb attempt against Viceroy Lord Hardinge and who fled to Japan in 1915, where he married a Japanese woman and founded the Indian Independence League in 1924. The Richards met Bose as a matter of course.

'I attended every meeting at which an Indian scholar spoke. I went to

174

listen … in the hope of finding my soul.' Okawa met the Richards after a talk by one Hara Prasad. In the audience was 'a young lady who stirred my depths. Something in her drew me to her … There was a light in her eyes as of the great morning of the world that was about to dawn … I saw Hara Prasad the next morning. And what was my surprise when he said that this very lady had desired to see me! … I met her as a brother and a friend and was privileged to be her fellow-worker … She and her friends dreamed of a new Asia, a new world … We lived together for a year. We sat together in meditation every night for an hour. I practised Zen and they practised Yoga.'[9] So Okawa was quoted by V.K. Gokak after he met him in 1957. By then Okawa had become practically blind and was an invalid, but his mind was still very much alive and his memory clear.

After all those years he still considered Sri Aurobindo his guru. In the article mentioned in the Government of India Report, he wrote: 'Arabinda Ghosh is a great character whom modern India has produced, or rather only India can produce … He is the most genuine Indian of all the Indian thinkers in the strict sense of the word, and at the same time the most nationalistic of all the leaders of the national movements in the radical sense of the word … There is a common belief in this country [Japan] that Tagore is the best thinker [the Indians] may well be proud of. To be sure he is India's vaunted poet, but he is far from being a great thinker, much less is he equal to Ghosh in depth and extent of thought … Knowing that this "Asian Review" *[Asia Jiron]* is going to carry one of his recent pictures on the first page and introduce to the Japanese people this towering mind in the Orient who should have been known to us much earlier, I would like to have the opportunity and honour of expressing my enthusiastic admiration for his sublime aspiration, my deep respect for his true patriotic spirit, and my full-hearted sympathy for the hardships which he is now suffering from.'[10]

In June 1916 the Richards met Rabindranath Tagore, who had come to Japan on a lecture tour. Mirra made a fine pencil sketch of him on 11 June, the day he delivered a speech at the Imperial University in Tokyo, 'The Message of India to Japan.' Tagore had become world-famous in 1913, when he was awarded the Nobel Prize for his volume of poetry *Gitanjali*. 'I met [Rabindranath Tagore] in Japan. He claimed to have reached the peace of *nirvana* and it made him beam with joy. I thought: "Here is a man who claims to have found peace and reached *nirvana*. Let us see." I asked him to meditate with me. I followed him in meditation and saw that he had reached just behind the mind into a sort of void. I waited and waited to follow him elsewhere, but he would not go further. I found that he was supremely satisfied imagining that he had entered *nirvana*.'[11]

The Richards would meet Tagore again in 1919, when they stayed in the same hotel for some time. In 1901 Tagore had founded an educational institute, *Shantiniketan* (Abode of Peace), 'where learning would be inculcated in a free and loving community.' In 1918 this educational centre was raised to university level and renamed *Vishva Bharati* (World University). Tagore may have had exchanges of views with Mirra about education, for it is said that he proposed that she take charge of Vishva Bharati. Mirra, in the knowledge that her destiny lay elsewhere, had to politely refuse. All the same, as a token of his regard for her, Tagore presented her with his typewriter, which is still kept among the Mother's memorabilia in the Sri Aurobindo Ashram.

Among the other people the Richards met in Tokyo was 'a son of Tolstoy,' on a world tour to propagate his bizarre ideas about redeeming the world. As the world was obviously in a deep crisis, the proposals for an ideal solution were legion and often quite eccentric. 'In Japan I met Tolstoy's son who was on a world tour for "the good of mankind's great unity." His solution was very simple: everybody ought to speak the same language, lead the same kind of life, dress in the same way, eat the same food ... I am not joking, those were his very words. I met him in Tokyo. He said: "But everybody would be happy, all would understand one another, nobody would quarrel if everyone did the same thing." There was no way to make him understand that it was not very reasonable. He had set out to travel all over the world with that in mind, and when people asked him his name he would say "Tolstoy." Now, Tolstoy ... There were people who did not know that (the great writer Leo) Tolstoy had died, and they thought: "Oh, we are going to hear something extraordinary!" And then he came out with that!'[12]

Hardly two months after their arrival, on 7 July, Mirra published an article in *Fujoshimbun*, a Japanese paper, entitled 'Woman and the War.'

The article starts as follows: 'You have asked me what I think of the feminist movement and what will be the consequences of the present war for it. One of the first effects of the war has certainly been to give quite a new aspect to the question. The futility of the perpetual oppositions between men and women has been at once made clearly apparent, and behind the conflict of the sexes, only relating to exterior facts, the gravity of the circumstances allowed the discovery of the always existent, if not always outwardly manifested fact, of the real collaboration, of the true union of these two complementary halves of humanity.' [13]

She goes on to show how easily the women have taken over most of the tasks left unoccupied by the men now at the front, and how courageous the women have proved to be at their posts. 'But where, above all, women have given proof of exceptional gifts is in their organizing faculties.' In the West 'Semitic thought allied to Roman legislation has influenced customs too deeply for women to have the opportunity of showing their capacity for organization ... This is not to say that only woman's exceptional qualities have been revealed by the present war. Her weaknesses, her faults, her pettiness have also been given the opportunity of display, and certainly if women wish to take the place they claim in the governing of nations they must progress much further in the mastery of self, in the broadening of ideas and points of view, in intellectual suppleness and oblivion of their sentimental preferences in order to become worthy of the management of public affairs.'

Mirra stresses the need of 'a collaboration of the two sexes ... To reduce the woman's part to solely interior and domestic occupations, and the man's part to exclusively exterior and social occupations, thus separating what should be united, would be to perpetuate the present sad state of things from which both are equally suffering ... The question to be solved, the real question, is then not only that of a better utilization of their outer activities, but above all of an inner spiritual growth. Without inner progress there is no possible outer progress.'

Exactly when Mirra gave her talk 'To the Women of Japan' is not known. Later she found it important enough to have it reprinted several times. To begin with she emphasizes again the spiritual role of women. 'True maternity begins with the conscious creation of a being, with the willed shaping of a soul come to develop and utilize a new body. The

177

true domain of women is spiritual. We forget it but too often.'[14] Then she develops a viewpoint that is demonstrably Lamarckian, to make her female audience understand that their psychological condition and attitude have a direct formative influence on the embryo taking shape in their body. She gives a couple of concrete examples and adds: 'If we can obtain such results on the physical plane where the materials are the least plastic, how much more so on the psychological plane where the influence of thought and will is so powerful.'

Then she expounds Sri Aurobindo's and her view of the importance of the point in world history at which humanity has arrived: 'We are living in an exceptional time at an exceptional turning point of the world's history. Never before, perhaps, did mankind pass through such a dark period of hatred, bloodshed and confusion. And, at the same time, never has such a strong, such an ardent hope awakened in the hearts of the people ... Never is the night so dark as before the dawn ... The civilization which is ending now in such a dramatic way was based on the power of the mind, mind dealing with matter and life. What it has meant to the world, we have not to discuss here. But a new reign is coming, that of the Spirit: after the human, the divine.'

She briefly sketches the evolution that is expected to culminate 'in the descent of the Supramental.' 'Only a new spiritual influx, creating in man a new consciousness, can overcome the enormous mass of difficulties barring the way of the workers [collaborating to realize the future], a new spiritual light, a manifestation upon Earth of some divine force unknown until now, a Thought of God, new for us, descending into this world and taking a new form here ... This form, meant to manifest the spiritual force capable of transforming the Earth's present conditions, this new form: who is to construct it if not the women?

'Thus we see that at this critical period of the world's life it is no longer sufficient to give birth to a being in whom our highest personal ideal is manifested; we must strive to find out what is the future type whose advent Nature is planning. It is no longer sufficient to form a man similar to the greatest men we have heard of or known, or even greater, more accomplished and gifted than they; we must strive to come in touch mentally, by the constant aspiration of our thought and will, with the supreme possibility which, exceeding all human measures and features, will give birth to the superman …

'It is by holding firm in our heart and mind the dynamism, the irresistible impetus given by a sincere and ardent aspiration, by maintaining in ourselves a certain state of enlightened receptivity towards the supreme Idea of the new race which wills to be manifested on Earth, that we can take a decisive step in the formation of the sons of the future, and make ourselves fit to serve as intermediaries for the creation of those who shall save Humanity.' Thoughts like these, spoken in dramatic historical circumstances on one of the islands of Japan in the Far East, would crop up again in one form or another throughout her whole life.

Mirra had left her soul with Sri Aurobindo, who was in his physical body working out his yoga on the southern tip of the Indian subcontinent. She would later say to a disciple that he was always present with her in Japan, and that he directed her stay there. Around the time that she was writing down and speaking the words quoted above, he wrote to an unknown correspondent: 'The ordinary Yoga is usually concentrated on a single aim and therefore less exposed to such recoils; ours is so complex and many-sided and embraces such large aims that we cannot expect any smooth progress until we near the completion of an effort – especially as all the hostile forces in the spiritual world are in a constant state of opposition and besiege our gains; for the complete victory of a single one of us would mean a general downfall among them. In fact by our own effort we could not hope to succeed … The final goal is far but the progress made in the face of so constant and massive an opposition is the guarantee of its being gained in the end. But the time is in other hands than ours.' [15]

Kyoto

*For four years, from an artistic point of view, I lived from won-
der to wonder.*[16]

– The Mother

For the next three years the Richards stayed mainly in the beautiful
city of Kyoto, the former capital of Japan. Their close friends there
were Dr. and Mrs. Kobayashi. When K.R. Srinivasa Iyengar and V.K.
Gokak went to Japan in 1957, to participate in the International P.E.N.
Congress, Dr. Kobayashi, a surgeon, was no longer alive, but his wife,
Nobuko, received them with great courtesy and undiminished affection
for her former friend Mirra. 'She came here to learn Japanese and to
be one of us. But we had so much to learn from her and her charming and unpredictable ways ... She revered a master from the ancient
land of the Buddha ... I loved her dearly. Have you seen those lovely
Wisteria flowers trailing down the roof of the Kasuga shrine at Nara?
We call them *hooji*. My friend [Mirra] loved those flowers. She was one
with them. She called herself *Hoojiko** when she thought of having a
Japanese name.'[17]

Nobuko Kobayashi was by then the leader of 'The Art of Still-Sitting
Movement,' founded by a certain Dr. Okata. Unhappy with the results
of allopathic medicine, this doctor had made his patients sit in meditation with him and asked them to concentrate on the navel and to aspire
that the Light may come down and set right the affected organ. The
results were amazing. Dr. Kobayashi left his flourishing practice as a
surgeon to become Okata's disciple. After the death of Dr. Kobayashi,
his wife continued the movement and the meditations. The war years
had been extremely difficult for the movement, but now everything
was going well again and there were several thousands of practising
members.

---

* The Mother later gave names carrying their essential, spiritual meaning to many
flowers. She called *Wisteria* 'poet's ecstasy,' with the comment: 'Rare and charming
is your presence!'

Mirra Richard in Japan with Mrs. Kobayashi

'She is the Mother to you, but always a dear, dear friend of mine,' said Nobuko Kobayashi to the two Indian writers about Mirra. 'It was my great good fortune that, in this strange but explicable world, I should have met this jewel of my heart and this friend of my soul. The perfume of those two years, when we lived like twin roses on the same stalk, lingers like incense around the divine altar and sways serenely in the sanctuary of my mind.' Later Nobuko was to meet her friend again when, in 1959, she visited India and the Sri Aurobindo Ashram in Pondicherry. 'When I see her again, I will put both my arms around her and cling to her, feeding my starved love of thirty-seven long years. Will the members of your Ashram be angry with me if I behave that way? For she is now ... the Mother!'

It had always been Mirra's habit to adapt to the environment in which she was moving. This time she lived the Japanese life, dressed in a kimono, as shown in several photographs, learned to speak and write the Japanese language, took a Japanese name. 'These people have a wonderful morality, live according to strict moral rules, and have a mental construction even in the least detail of life: one must eat in a certain way and no other, one must bow in a certain way and no other, one must say certain words and not other ones. When addressing certain people one must express oneself in a certain way; when speaking with others, one must express oneself in another way ... Not once do you have the feeling that you are in contact with something other than a marvellously organized mental-physical domain ... If one does not submit to rules there, one may live as Europeans do, who are considered barbarians and looked upon as intruders; but if you want to live a Japanese life among the Japanese you must do as they do, otherwise you make them so unhappy that you can't even have any relation with them.' [18]

Mirra was overwhelmed by the Japanese sense of physical and natural beauty. 'I had everything to learn in Japan. For four years, from an artistic point of view, I lived from wonder to wonder ... From the artistic point of view, I don't think there is a country as beautiful as that one.' [19] And she described the cities, then for the most part still built in the traditional Japanese style, the magnificent landscapes with their seasons of irises and flowering maples and cherries, and the artistically designed gardens, which are now imitated all over the world. 'The other day I spoke to you about those landscapes of Japan. Well, almost all – the most beautiful, the most striking ones – I had seen in vision in France, and yet I had not seen any pictures or photographs of Japan, I knew nothing of Japan. And I had seen these landscapes without human beings, nothing but the landscape, quite pure, like that, and it had seemed to me that they were visions of a world other than the physical; they seemed to me too beautiful for the physical world, too perfectly beautiful.'[20]

On 1 April 1917 Mirra wrote in her diary: 'Once more I see cherry trees everywhere; Thou hast put a magical power in these flowers; they seem to speak of Thy sole Presence; they bring with them the smile of the Divine ... O Japan, this is thy festive adorning, expression of thy goodwill, it is thy purest offering, the pledge of thy fidelity; it is thy way of saying that thou dost mirror the sky.'[21] A few days later she identified with the cherry blossoms:* 'A deep concentration seized on me, and I perceived that I was identifying myself with a single cherry-blossom, then through it with all cherry-blossoms, and, as I descended deeper in the consciousness following a stream of bluish force, I became suddenly the cherry-tree itself, stretching towards the sky like so many arms its innumerable branches laden with their sacrifice of flowers. Then I heard distinctly this sentence: "Thus hast thou made thyself one with the soul of the cherry-trees and so thou canst take note that it is the Divine who makes the offering of this flower-prayer to heaven." When I had written it, all was effaced; but now the blood of the cherry-tree flows in my veins and with it flows an incomparable peace and force.'[22]

She started painting and drawing again, but in a style different from the paintings she had made in Paris; she was now influenced by Japanese woodblock prints. Several of those paintings and drawings have been preserved and recently reproduced in *The Mother: Paintings and Drawings*. Thanks to them we have an idea how Mrs. Okawa and Nobuko Kobayashi looked, as well as the poet Hirasawa Tetsuo, whom she painted at one sitting and about whom little or nothing is known,

---

* The epistemological problem is central to the whole of Western philosophy. The Mother and Sri Aurobindo's answer to it is that one can know something that is not oneself only by identification.

and the poet Hayashi, still more mysterious. She also painted or drew some of the places she visited – among them the Daiunji temple – and people she met, such as Rabindranath Tagore. 'The art of Japan is a kind of a direct mental expression in physical life. The Japanese use the vital world very little. Their art is extremely mentalized; their life is extremely mentalized. It expresses in detail quite precise mental formations. Only in the physical do they have spontaneously the sense of beauty.' [23]

'It was a Japanese street brilliantly illuminated by gay lanterns picturesquely adorned with vivid colours. And as gradually what was conscious [i.e. Mirra herself] moved on down the street, the Divine appeared, visible in everyone and everything. One of the lightly-built houses became transparent, revealing a woman seated on a tatami in a sumptuous violet kimono embroidered with gold and bright colours. The woman was beautiful and must have been between thirty-five and forty. She was playing a golden samisen. At her feet lay a little child. And in the woman too the Divine was visible.' This exquisite cameo of life in Japan was noted down by Mirra in her diary on 5 December 1916. The reader may recall Sri Aurobindo's realization of the cosmic consciousness when he saw Lord Krishna in all the people and objects of Alipore jail. Mirra must have had the same consciousness at least since her identification with the Great Mother.

The entries in her diary of that period are exceptionally direct and affirmative, although, as we will see, she had to fight a daily battle with no quarter given. Time after time she is reminded of 'the usual injunction' to 'turn towards the Earth.' For her, who had always remained conscious of her soul, it was easy enough to turn away from the material, from earthly reality towards heavens of which mortals have no notion. But the missioned task of herself and Sri Aurobindo was the yoga of Matter in the material circumstances familiar to all of us – petty, nasty, messy, nagging, scratching, wounding, depressing, and never-ending. The body by itself is a sad burden without relief, which is why human beings seek solace in substances that lighten for a while their affliction of being human. Sri Aurobindo and the Mother had to take up the lot of the mortals in order to transform it, there was no other way. 'Thou hast willed, O Lord, that the being should grow wider and richer. It could not do so without entering once again, at least partially and temporarily, into ignorance and obscurity.'[24]

'That which speaks to Thee is Thyself in me,'[25] she wrote. Then again: 'O my divine Master, who hast appeared to me this night in all Thy radiant splendour ...'[26] And once more the confirmation was given to her: 'I have appointed thee from all eternity to be my exceptional representative upon the Earth, not only invisibly, in a hidden way, but also openly before the eyes of all men. And what thou wert created to be, thou wilt be.'[27] The entries in her spiritual diary become sparse – or did she tear most of them out later because they were too personal and burn them in the Ashram boiler, as witnessed by some disciples? If so, it is surprising that the following entry, a direct communication from the Buddha Shakyamuni, has survived. '... Dost thou fear to be misunderstood? But where hast thou seen man capable of understanding the Divine? And if the eternal truth finds in thee a means of manifesting itself, what dost thou care for all the rest? Thou art like a pilgrim coming out of the sanctuary; standing on the threshold in front of the crowd he hesitates before revealing his precious secret, that of his supreme discovery ... "Turn to the Earth and men," isn't this the command thou always hearest in thy heart? – in thy heart, for it is thy heart which carries a blessed message for those who are athirst for compassion ... Thou doubtest thy power and fearest thy ignorance? It is precisely this that wraps up thy strength in that dark mantle of starless night. Thou hesitatest and tremblest as on the threshold of a mystery, for now the mystery of the manifestation seems to thee more terrible and unfathomable than that of the Eternal Cause. But thou must take courage again and obey the injunction from the depths. It is I who am telling thee this, for I know thee and love thee as thou didst know and love me once. I have appeared clearly before thy sight so that thou mayst in no way doubt my word ...'[28] As thou didst know and love me once ...?

V.K. Gokak has recorded some of his conversations with Shumei Okawa and Nobuko Kobayashi in a beautiful poetic form, but poetry in a context like this often comes closer to the truth than ordinary prose. The following words, attributed to Shumei Okawa, are well-known but bear repetition here: 'You would like to know, my young friend, what struck me about your Mother. She had a will that moved the mountains and an intellect sharp as the edge of a sword. Her thought was clarity itself and her resolve stronger than the roots of a giant oak. Her mystic depths were deeper than the ocean, but her intellect was a plummet that could sound her deepest depths. An artist, she could paint pictures of an unearthly loveliness. A musician, she enchanted my soul when she played on an organ or guitar. A scientist, she could formulate a new Heaven and Earth, a new cosmogony. I do not know what Mirra had not become or was not able of becoming.'[29]

Calvary

I have mounted the Calvary of successive disillusionments high enough to attain to the Resurrection. [30]

– The Mother

Meanwhile, what had become of Paul Richard? He had been active all the time as a speaker, a writer, and probably also as a teacher, for in the draft of a letter of his concerning the lease of a house he writes: 'You will understand that it is not possible for us to leave Tokyo in the middle of winter while the schools are in session, breaking our commitments in this regard.'[31] In January 1917 he wrote and published in Tokyo a tract of seventeen pages entitled *Au Japon* (To Japan) and translated into English by Mirra. It begins as follows: 'I am seeking throughout the world for a just nation, a nation of the future. For the future belongs to the just nations. They shall inherit the Earth.' And he continues in his exalted, prophetic and not infrequently bombastic style: 'First of all the nations in whom the divorced tendencies of the spirit join again, and, as yet, the only one who knows how to unite the thought of Europe and that of Asia, thou [Japan] art born to become the unifier of those two complementary halves of the future world; thou art the first nation of that future … Nation whose shores are open toward all shores, making them less distant; nation whose thought is turned toward all thoughts, reconciling them; nation in whom the world seems to seek the scattered rays of its soul, thou art born out of a hope of Humanity; thou art born as a hope for the birth of Humanity!'

Then the tone turns exhortative and bellicose: 'Each day all thy warriors, from lowest to highest, already fight in their hearts and joyously die for thee in their dreams ... Thou hast the quivering of the steed who hears his master's step. Already dost thou feel his hand on thee. People ready for the fight, this master is a divine warrior. Let thy war be worthy of the god who is in thee! For thou shalt fight! Against whom? It matters not, so long as thou knowest why ... Liberate and unify Asia; for Asia is thy domain. Asia is thy field of action and, if needed, thy field of war; thou knowest it well ... Thine own share is the whole of Asia ... Thou hast but to set her free ... See at thy door that immense country [China] where throngs a quarter of humanity, that country vaster than all ... Go towards China; it is thee she awaits!' And Richard finishes this grandiloquent exhortation to Japan speaking of 'the Lord of the Nations.' '... It is the voice of the Lord of thy work. He will accomplish this work with thee, but he can also accomplish it without thee. To the Lord of the Nations who today tills the Earth to found there the Kingdom of his Justice, what nation could long offer resistance? ... I saw, I *saw* thy soul. It was prostrated in silence before him, to receive from him the command, and the promise, the sword of Victories, and the crown of the Future.'

We know who the 'Lord of the Nations' is: he is one of the four great Asuras whose actual name is Lord of Falsehood, and of whom Paul Richard was an emanation. The Mother would say that the 'Lord of the Nations' bluntly refused to collaborate in the transformation of the world, and that, on the contrary, he promised to fight the changes ahead to the very last and to cause as much havoc and destruction as possible. He was the direct cause, the Mother would say, of all the wars and massacres to which the twentieth century has been witness.

It is not surprising that the Government of India again received a report on *To Japan*. 'It is reported that Mr. Paul Richard is about to publish a book entitled *To Japan*, in which he urges Japan to liberate Asia from European domination. The book will be published in English, Japanese and Chinese, and copies will be distributed by the Pan-Asiatic League ... While living in Pondicherry he was an intimate friend of

Arabindo Ghosh [sic] and other Indian extremists ... When Tagore and his party visited Japan, the Richards attempted to enlist their sympathies in Pan-Asianism ... '[32] Richard had been lauding Sri Aurobindo openly: 'The Hour is coming of great things, of great events, and also of great men, the divine men of Asia. All my life I have sought for them across the world, for all my life I have felt they must exist somewhere in the world. For they are its light, its heat, its life. It is in Asia that I have found the greatest among them – the leader, the hero of tomorrow. His name is Aurobindo Ghose.'[33]

At this point a look at the historical context of Japan may be useful. This island nation had always remained almost completely separated from the rest of the world, particularly from any Western influence. Like the Hebrews, the Indian Brahmins and the Germans, it had a traditional belief of being a superior race that should not be contaminated by the rest of humanity. Around 1870, however – not long before the Richards lived there – it had opened itself up by an act of the state, in the same movement officially breaking with its 'medieval' and still deeply ingrained past. Democratization, industrialization and Westernization were the order of the day, as was also a military build-up capable of confronting and even dominating any neighbouring nation. The military capacity of Japan was proven when it defeated China in the 1890s and, as we have seen, Russia in 1905. The latter victory had made Japan into a world power. It may have been the reason that Paul Richard, expelled from India, tried to exert his influence there. The years of the Richards' stay in Japan were relatively peaceful and democratic, insulated from the slaughter elsewhere in the world, but the superiority complex of the Japanese, their unshakable will-power and their sense of discipline which took them to the point of total individual effacement were seeking for an occasion to assert themselves.

In his writings at the time Paul Richard expounded, on the one hand, the world vision he had received from Sri Aurobindo: a world in upheaval which was the symptom of a profound change, a new phase of evolution leading towards world unity and a suprahuman future. On the other hand, as we have been able to see in the few quotations culled from *To Japan,* his world unity was a precondition for the total subjection of all to the 'Lord of the Nations,' meaning that his 'superman' could be little else than a dehumanized being, pitiless in its dominance of others but unconditionally surrendered to that 'Lord.' The resemblance to Hitler's 'superman' is striking.* As the Mother would say, Richard had no idea of the spiritual achievements of Sri Aurobindo; he admired in him only the scholar and philosopher.

We have glimpsed Mirra's views at the time in her talk 'To the Women of Japan.' They were, of course, completely in agreement with those of Sri Aurobindo. Still, she had vowed to convert her husband and through him the essence of his person, the Lord of Falsehood. This she could only do by going all the way and being not only at his side but inside him, by being him and doing, through a direct identification, his yoga of conversion – a conversion difficult to perform for any ordinary human being but near to impossible in the case of an Asura. She had vowed that even if she had to descend into hell, she would do so. Though the pages of her diary hardly tell us about it, her stay in Japan was 'a perpetual battle with the adverse forces' – not a battle on the human scale, but a battle of superhuman, divine and antidivine forces. K.R. Srinivasa Iyengar writes in his biography of the Mother: 'The four years Mirra spent in Japan were an oasis in time, and a singular Tea Room of reserve, contemplation and preparation for the future.'[34] Nothing could be farther from the truth.

In Japan, Paul Richard wrote two more books which he considered to be one opus, To *the Nations* and *The Lord of the Nations. To the Nations* was translated by Sri Aurobindo and carries an introduction by Rabindranath Tagore that concludes: 'When gigantic forces of destruction were holding their orgies of fury I saw this solitary young Frenchman, unknown to fame, his face beaming with the lights of the new dawn and his voice vibrating with the message of new life, and I felt sure that the great To-morrow had already come though not registered in the calendar of the statesmen.'[35] 'In all nations there are men, lost in the crowd,' writes Richard, 'who bear in themselves this consciousness of a new world. They belong no more to the departing century. They seem to come from the future.' Again, no Aurobindonian would disagree with this, but the perspective in which it has to be read is very different

---

* See Georges Van Vrekhem, *Beyond Man*, chapter sixteen, 'The Lord of the Nations.'

from that of Sri Aurobindo's; it becomes fully clear in *The Lord of the Nations*.

'When I wrote this book, in Kyoto, Japan, during the winter of 1917,' writes Richard, 'I was looking to the world of men and nations from the upper room of a small wood-and-paper house, frozen under the snow, listening in the silence of this retreat to the secret words of my Lord – the Lord of the Nations ... Through its fallible words the infallible voice may be heard of Him "who rules the nations with a rod of iron" – the Lord of the Yoga of the Nations.'[36] (Once more one is reminded of Adolf Hitler, who withdrew to his villa in Berchtesgaden, in the Alps, to communicate with his 'God.') And Richard writes in a foreword, '[*To the Nations*] marks a step further in the denunciation of the international anarchy and in the annunciation of the scourges drawn down upon themselves by the nations of pride and prey. Who was I to inveigh against and challenge in such an uncompromising and forcible manner great peoples, and among them the very country of my birth? Nothing but a solitary and unknown witness wandering on the Earth in search of the Future.'

Again we read: 'We are at the world's crucial hour, at the hour which must determine whether heaven or hell is to reign over the world ... Today it must choose between two paths: the one which descends and the one which mounts; the one whither it is called by the forces from below, the forces of the lower life; whither it is driven, through blood and mud, by the powers of the infernal civilization – for it is hellwards that it leads; the other, the higher path, not yet hewn for the world, but which is now to be opened through fire by the Powers of the Light, to lead it towards the new Civilization – that of the Spirit!' Which strangely contradicts the motto of the book, taken from the Bible and referring to Jehovah: 'He shall rule the Nations with a rod of iron.' Says Richard: 'They talk of the war aims of all the belligerents. But they speak not of those which alone count – for it is they alone which will be realized: the war aims of the Lord of the Nations ... It is said this war will be the last ... Nay! It is but the first; the first of the great wars – of the great wars of the Spirit!'[37] All exclamation marks are his.

In May 1940, shortly after the outbreak of hostilities in Western Europe, Sri Aurobindo conversed with a handful of disciples in his room. He said that it was not Hitler who took the crucial decisions, but 'the Being' behind him. 'There are more than one, but this is a very powerful Being ... [Paul Richard] was in communion with this Being, and the plans and methods he has written of in the book *[The Lord of the Nations]* are the same as those carried out now [by Hitler]. He said there that the present civilization was to be destroyed, but really it is the destruction of the whole human civilization that is aimed at.'[38]

'Oiwake, 3 September 1919. Since the man refused the meal I had prepared with so much love and care, I invoked the God to take it.

'My God, Thou hast accepted my invitation, Thou hast come to sit at my table, and in exchange for my poor and humble offering Thou hast granted to me the last liberation. My heart, even this morning so heavy with anguish and care, my head surcharged with responsibility, are delivered of their burden. Now are they light and joyful as my inner being has been for a long time past. My body smiles to Thee with happiness as before my soul smiled to Thee. And surely hereafter Thou wilt withdraw no more from me this joy, O my God! for this time, I think, the lesson has been sufficient, I have mounted the Calvary of successive disillusionments high enough to attain to the Resurrection. Nothing remains of the past but a potent love which gives me the pure heart of a child and the lightness and freedom of thought of a god.' *(Prayers and Meditations)*

Towards the end of the war there was a severe pandemic of 'Spanish flu' which killed more than twenty million people, more than had died in the war itself.* The pandemic raged also in Japan. The Mother told how a little village had been attacked by it without anybody outside the village knowing, for it was wintertime, the countryside was covered with snow and the village was isolated. When a letter was sent to one of the villagers, the postman who took it found no sign of life any more in the village; all had died and the snow was their common shroud.

---

* Mrinalini Devi, Sri Aurobindo's wife, was one of the victims. She died on 17 December 1918.

Mirra Richard in Japan

Mirra herself had a close call. 'I was in Japan. It was at the beginning of January 1919. It was the time that a terrible flu raged in the whole of Japan which killed hundreds of thousands of people. It was one of those epidemics the like of which are rarely seen. In Tokyo there were hundreds and hundreds of new cases every day. The disease ... lasted three days and on the third day the patient died ... If one did not die on the third day, at the end of seven days one was altogether cured ...

'It so happened that I was living with somebody [Paul Richard] who never ceased troubling me: "But what is this disease? What is there behind this disease?" What I was doing, you know, was simply to cover myself with my force, my protection, so as not to catch it and I did not think of it any more and went along doing my work ... But constantly I had to hear: "What is this? I would like to know what is there behind this illness. Could you not tell me what this illness is, why it is there?" And so on.

'One day I was called to the other end of the town by a young woman whom I knew and who wanted to introduce me to some friends and show me certain things ... I had to cross the whole city in a tram-car. And I was in the tram and saw all those people with masks on their noses, and there was in the atmosphere that constant fear, and so there came a suggestion to me – I began to ask myself: "Actually what is this illness? What is there behind this illness? What are the forces that are in this illness?" ... I returned home with a terrible fever. I had caught it ...'

Mirra refused the medicine given to her by the doctor called to her bed. 'At the end of the second day, as I was lying all alone, I clearly saw a being with a part of the head cut off, in a military uniform – or what remained of a military uniform – approaching me and suddenly flinging himself upon my chest, with that half head, to suck my force. I took a good look, then realized that I was about to die. He was drawing my life out ... I was completely nailed to the bed, without any movement, in deep trance. I could not stir and he was pulling. I thought: "This is the end." Then I called on my occult power, I fought a big fight and I succeeded in pushing him off so that he could not stay any longer. And I woke up ...

'I understood that the illness originated from beings who had been thrown violently out of their bodies. I had seen this during the First

World War, towards the end, when people were staying in trenches and were killed in bombardments. They were in perfect health, altogether healthy, and in the blink of an eye they were thrown out of their bodies, not conscious that they were dead. They didn't know that they had no body any more and tried to find in others the life force they could not find in themselves. Which means that they had become that many countless vampires. And they vampirized upon human beings ... I know how much knowledge and force were necessary for me to resist. It was irresistible [for ordinary persons].'[39] Then Mirra asked to be left alone for a couple of days, concentrated on the evil that was sucking the life out of so many humans, and put things straight. At the end of two or three days there was no longer a single case of illness in the city.

But Mirra had not been able to convert Paul Richard. When she put everything before 'the Lord,' the real one, he appeared to her in a vision 'more beautiful than that in the Gita.' He lifted her up in his arms and turned her towards the West, towards India, where Sri Aurobindo was waiting.[40]

With the help of the Japanese government, and in spite of British protests, the Richards obtained their travel documents and left for Pondicherry.

8.
The Seven Hidden Years

What is known as Sri Aurobindo's Yoga is the joint creation of
Sri Aurobindo and the Mother.[1]

– Sri Aurobindo

The Seal is Put

Paul and Mirra Richard, accompanied by Dorothy Hodgson, left Japan in March 1920 and arrived in Pondicherry on 24 April. They probably arrived at Colombo aboard one of the Japanese passenger-cum-freight ships such as the Kamo Maru and transferred to one of the ships of the Messageries Maritimes with final destination Calcutta and Pondicherry as a port of call. 'I was on the boat, at sea, not expecting anything – I was of course occupied with the inner life, but I was living physically on the boat – when all of a sudden, unexpectedly, about ten* nautical miles from Pondicherry, the quality of the atmosphere, of the air, changed so much that I knew I was entering the aura of Sri Aurobindo. It was a physical experience and I guarantee that whoever has a sufficiently awakened consciousness can feel the same thing.'[2]

Needless to say, their voyage was closely watched by the British police, as testified in a report by the Governor of French India, Pondicherry, addressed to the Minister of Colonies in Paris: 'I have the honour of informing you of the arrival in Pondicherry of Mr. Richard,

---

* The transcription of the recording of the originally spoken French text has here 'deux' (two), but this is undoubtedly a misunderstanding for 'dix,' as the Mother has *written* on another occasion: 'When I came here for the first time, I felt the atmosphere of Sri Aurobindo, felt it materially, at a distance of ten miles, ten nautical miles, not kilometres.' *(Words of the Mother I, CWM 13 p. 75)*

barrister ... Mr. Richard, who arrives from Japan, where he had gone on a mission, is accompanied by Mrs. Myrrha *[sic]* Richard, his wife, and a Miss Houdgson *[sic]*. He seems to have settled in the colony for an indeterminate time. As Mr. Richard has long been in rather steady contact with undesirable extremist Indian elements, his passage was reported to the Government of British India by the British police in several ports of the Extreme Orient where he stopped on his way to Pondicherry. Our neighbours [the British] became concerned by his arrival in India, and the Governor of Madras ... has asked me to keep his Government informed of the subsequent movements of Mr. and Mrs. Richard and Miss Houdgson, whom he suspects of bearing correspondence from extremists who have taken refuge in Japan addressed to the refugees in Pondicherry, in particular Aurobindo Ghose.' Ten years after his withdrawal to Pondicherry, Aurobindo Ghose remained as dreaded as ever.

It may have been the harassment by the British authorities that impelled Mirra to write on 20 February, when still in Japan, the following statement: 'I belong to no nation, no civilization, no society, no race, but to the Divine. I obey no master, no ruler, no law, no social convention, but the Divine. To Him I have surrendered all, will, life and self; for Him I am ready to give all my blood, drop by drop, if such is His will, with complete joy; and nothing in his service can be sacrifice, for all is perfect delight.'[3]

The 'hellish' years of tension and struggle in Japan had left their marks. 'When I came here [from Japan] I was not worth much,' wrote the Mother, 'and I did not give myself many months to live.' Tuberculosis, rheumatism, influenza, filaria and neuritis, a flurrying heart ... you name it and she had it.[4] Yet she considered her return to Pondicherry as 'the tangible sign of the sure Victory over the adverse forces,' which seems to confirm that Paul Richard had in fact been an important factor which caused her departure from Pondicherry and Sri Aurobindo six years before.

Richard's relationship with Mirra and with Sri Aurobindo now reached a critical point. Mirra and Sri Aurobindo had done everything within their power to give him the chance of being converted, but without success. The time had come for Sri Aurobindo and Mirra's definite collaboration, 'the seal had been put.' Richard sensed this, of course, but at first he refused to give in and became even more demonic than before. He knew perfectly well who Mirra was, but he demanded that she would not take Sri Aurobindo as her 'Lord,' that she would take himself instead. His outbursts of frustration and anger became so violent that at times he threw the furniture through the window or took Mirra by the throat, strangling her. She called the force of Sri Aurobindo, and it was his yogic power that saved her on every occasion and made Paul Richard depart in the end.[5]

Long afterwards Sri Aurobindo said in a conversation with some disciples: 'This yoga is like a path cut through a jungle and once the path is made, it will be easy for those who come afterwards. But before that it is a long-drawn-out battle. The more you gain in strength, the greater becomes the resistance of the hostile forces. I myself had suggestion after suggestion that I would not succeed. But I always remember the vision the Mother had. It was like this. The Mother, Richard and I were going somewhere. We saw Richard going down to a place from where rising was impossible. Then we found ourselves sitting in a carriage the driver of which was taking it up and down a hill a number of times. At last he stopped on the highest peak. Its significance was quite clear to us.'[6]

Somewhere in November of that year, Richard left. He went at first to the Himalayas and tried to live the life of a *sannyasi*. There, in Kotgarh, he wrote three more booklets: To *India – The message of the Himalayas; New Asia,* supposed to be 'a practical programme of possible work in Asia' as required from him by Mohandas K. Gandhi; and *Messages from the Future.* His publisher in Madras introduced him as 'a prophet in his retreat on the slopes of the Himalayas,' 'one of the foremost living philosophers in the world,' and 'one who is in the succession of the true prophets.' 'India,' Richard wrote, 'thou art the heart of Asia. [This is a literal phrase of Sri Aurobindo's.] How shalt thou live apart from her! Thou art the heart of Asia as China is her brain, Japan her strong arm. How shalt thou live apart from them!' And once more he announced: 'One is coming – whom no one knows; and for whom all are awaiting. One, as it were the New God of this Universe, the God of the new man – of the superman.'[7]

After two or three years Richard returned to France, then went to England. He married again, which made him a bigamist. Therefore he arranged a divorce from Mirra, to which she readily consented. Dilip K. Roy, who would soon join the Sri Aurobindo Ashram, met him in Nice, the leading French resort on the Côte d'Azur, in 1927, 'a wreck of a brilliant man so many had admired.' '... One day in deep melancholy in the revealing stillness of midnight he said that of late he had often felt like committing suicide.' Then he started talking about Sri Aurobindo, 'the one man to whom I have bowed down in my life as my superior ... and the only seer who has truly fortified my faith in a Divine Purpose working through life transforming it secretly like a leaven as it were, and bypassing those who will not change themselves.

'Yet my faith has not stood me in good stead and I refused to collaborate with the Author of this Purpose because He didn't claim me as his sole editor, because I was not entrusted by Him with the sole copyright of the series to come – in a word, because I was too self-willed to be a mere contributor to His Book of Life. I had no humility ... Yes, I should have had the humility to accept the light he [Sri Aurobindo] had won and could give others who really aspired for it. I should have enlisted under the banner of subservience. That is why I had to leave his mighty aura of the new creation where the rule of mind is going to be replaced by the Supermind, *le nouveau Dieu* [the new God] ...'

'Sri Aurobindo is the only man who has won through to this vision and, what is more, has got the power to translate it in life by ushering in a new era of the Supramental apocalypse ... Yes, he and no one else has the key of the world to be, and my tragedy is that my love of self-will forced me to leave his aegis and choose the alternative of living a pointless life away from the *one* man whose society I rate over that of all the others put together. Do you wonder now why I should be constantly harping on suicide?' And D.K. Roy adds: 'The last words he said on that last night were: "*Oui, pour moi Sri Aurobindo, c'est le Shiva incarné* [yes, to me Sri Aurobindo is the incarnate Shiva], an *Avatar* among mortals.'[8]

Later, Richard went to the United States, taught there as a university professor and wrote, in August 1950, *The Seven Steps to the New Age*. During the 1957 visit of V.K. Gokak and K.R. Srinivasa Iyengar to Japan, Dr. Okawa showed them a letter Richard had written him the year before: 'Dear Friend, I saw you in a dream the other day and I was thinking of you ... I am glad that my dreams of a new Asia have come true. [This was a year after the Bandung Conference.] I have spent a number of years in the spiritual desert of America, but I am happy that a new Asia is being born ...' Paul Richard died in 1968.

If the police had not forgotten about Sri Aurobindo, neither had other people. One of them was Joseph Baptista, who requested Sri Aurobindo to return to British India in order to become the editor of a new English daily paper. It would be the organ of a new political party Tilak and others were intending to form. Another was Dr. Munje, who proposed that Sri Aurobindo take up the presidency of the Indian National Congress. Sri Aurobindo declined both offers politely.

To Baptista he wrote: 'Pondicherry is my place of retreat, my cave of tapasya ...'[9] And in his answer to Munje he said: 'I am no longer first and foremost a politician, but have definitely commenced another kind of work with a spiritual basis, a work of spiritual, social, cultural and economic reconstruction of an almost revolutionary kind, and am even making or at least supervising a sort of practical or laboratory experiment in that sense which needs all the attention and energy that I can have to spare.'[10]

After the war Barin had profited from a general British amnesty for all political prisoners. On returning home from the infernal jail in Port Blair, where he had kept himself going by practising yoga, he wanted to become his *sejda's* disciple. In April 1920 Sri Aurobindo wrote a long letter to the man who was his brother, comrade in extremist politics and off-and-on companion in the spiritual quest. This letter is one of the 'stock-taking' documents in Sri Aurobindo's life. He makes clear that his is 'a special way,' which he calls the Integral Yoga, given to him by 'the Guru of the world who is within us' and who 'gave me the complete direction of my path, its full theory, the ten limbs of the body of the Yoga.' The old way of yoga 'would not make the harmony or union of the Spirit and life. It dismissed the world as Maya [Illusion] or a transient Lila [Divine Play]. The result has been the loss of the power of life and degeneration of India ... If one cannot rise above, that is, to the Supramental level, it is hardly possible to know the last secret of the world.'[11]

And Sri Aurobindo continues: 'After these fifteen years [since the beginning of his yoga in 1905] I am only now rising into the lowest of the three levels of the Supermind and trying to draw up into it all the lower activities. But when this Siddhi is complete I am absolutely certain that God will through me give Siddhi of the Supermind to others with less difficulty. Then my real work will begin. I am not impatient for success in the work. What is to happen will happen in God's appointed time, I am not disposed to run widely and leap into the field of work on the strength of my little ego. Even if I did not succeed in my work I would not be shaken. This work is not mine but God's. I will listen to no other call. When God moves me then I will move.'

He surveys the situation in India: 'My idea is that the chief cause of the weakness of India is not subjection, nor poverty, nor the lack of spirituality, nor *dharma*, but the decline of thought-power, the growth of ignorance in the Motherland of knowledge. Everywhere I see inability or unwillingness to think, thought-incapacity or thought-phobia. However the situation may have been in the Middle Ages, this state of things is now the sign of a terrible degeneration ... We are not worshippers of Shakti. We are the worshippers of the easy way ... Our civilization has become an *acalayatana* [something that does not move], our religion a bigotry of externals, our spirituality a faint glimmer of light or a momentary wave of religious intoxication. And so long as this sort of thing continues any permanent resurgence of India is improbable.'

He also surveys the situation in Bengal and finds the situation not conducive to developments as yet. For it is clearly *not* Sri Aurobindo's intention to remain in seclusion in Pondicherry. 'These ten years, He [the Guru of the world] has been making me develop it [his Yoga] in experience. But it is not yet finished. It may take another two years, and as long as it is not finished, I doubt if I shall be able to return to Bengal. Pondicherry is the appointed place for my Yoga *siddhi* [realization], except one part of it – that is, the action. The first centre of my work is Bengal, although I hope that its circumference will be all India and the whole Earth.'

This letter is interesting and amazing because it shows clearly in what measure Sri Aurobindo (and the Mother) had to hew the path of their spiritual progress 'in a virgin forest', according to the expression they will use often. Until the end of his life, Sri Aurobindo would keep looking ahead to the moment when he would be able to leave the place of his retreat, 'his cave of tapasya,' and take up – physically, bodily, that is to say – his work in the world again. The letter also illustrates the importance of the return and the role of Mirra in Sri Aurobindo's yoga, as we will see in the following section of this chapter.

'I do not want hundreds of thousands of disciples,' Sri Aurobindo tells Barin. 'It will be enough if I can get a hundred complete men, empty of petty egoism, who will be instruments of God. I have no faith in the customary trade of the Guru. I do not wish to be a Guru. That at my touch or at another's some awake and manifest from within their slumbering Godhead and get the divine life – this is what I want. It is such men that will raise the country ... Neither am I going back to Bengal now. Not because Bengal is not ready but because I am not ready. If the unripe goes among the unripe what work can he do?'

The Descent

The Sadhana and the work were waiting for the Mother's coming.[12]

– Sri Aurobindo

'When I returned from Japan and we began to work together,' the Mother said, 'Sri Aurobindo had already brought the supramental Light into the mental world and was trying to transform the Mind. "It's strange," he said to me, "it's an endless work! Nothing seems to get done – everything is done and then constantly has to be done all over again." Then I gave him my personal impression, which went back to the old days with Théon: "It will be like that till we touch bottom." So instead of continuing to work in the Mind, both of us ... (I was the one who went through the experience – how to put it? – practically, objectively; he experienced it only in his consciousness, not in the body, but my body has always participated.) Both of us descended almost immediately – it was done in a day or two – from the Mind into the Vital, and so on, quite rapidly, leaving the Mind as it was: fully in the Light but not permanently transformed.'[13]

This crucial step in the yoga of Sri Aurobindo and the Mother needs some clarification. The Mother said almost in passing that Sri Aurobindo 'had brought the supramental Light into the mental world,' which is the same as saying that he had realized the Supramental or Supermind in his mental consciousness. These perhaps mysterious words mean nothing less than that Sri Aurobindo had, towards the end of 1920, divinized his mental consciousness. 'The thinker and toiler' had, on the mental level which is that of all of us, become the Divine Seer and therefore Doer on that level.

To have an idea of what the 'Supramental' or 'Supermind' is, we have to take into account that our world is an evolutionary world. There is Matter (the mineral kingdom), the Vital (the kingdom of plants and animals), the Mental (the kingdom of the human being, prepared in the primates), and the Overmind (the kingdoms of the Gods), all with their numerous gradations. We are in the habit of arranging these levels from lower to higher, because the lower is palpably known to us while the higher is something vague we are (possibly) moving towards. But this evolution has been preceded by an involution. The cause of everything is not below, in Matter or in the subconscious and Inconscient, it is – as the Indian wisdom has always known – above: the Ashwatta Tree of the universe is rooted above in That which has manifested everything we are or can be aware of with our present consciousness. That is Being, Consciousness-Force and Bliss, which are not only concepts but realms of existence in the highest reaches of the divine manifestation. And the fourth realm of manifestation in which That is still fully Itself is what the Vedas called *turiyam svid,* a fourth world also consisting of manifold gradations but in which everything is essentially That and conscious of That and therefore One.

For this fourth realm of manifestation, the concrete expression of the divine Unity-Consciousness, Sri Aurobindo coined the term 'Supermind' or 'Supramental' in his writings in the *Arya.** (He also called it,

---

* The word 'Supermind' may cause misunderstandings because it evokes also a mind that is a superlative version of what the human mind is at present. In this book, therefore, the word 'Supramental' will be used most often, except in direct quotations.

but rarely, the 'Real-Idea.') The Supermind is a divine level of existence above everything we, mental beings, normally are and can be aware of. It is even above the levels of the Overmind, i.e. the worlds of the Gods, who dominate the manifestation at present, although, as the reader will recall, fiercely challenged by the Antigods or Asuric forces – and Forces are always beings.

The Supermind belongs to the higher hemisphere of the global divine manifestation where everything exists in oneness and is conscious of that oneness. The (apparent) diversification, or fragmentation, or endless division of the oneness into the world as we know it, is the result of the Fall, i.e. the turning away of the four essential divine Forces from their origin, thereby creating the lower hemisphere of (supposed) separate existence from the God to the atom. The higher hemisphere is the domain of the divine Unity-Consciousness or *vidya,* the lower hemisphere is the domain in which the Unity-Consciousness has been veiled and become *avidya,* ignorance. The Gods, who are the cosmic Powers, share as it were both domains, for they are still fully conscious of the unity but at the same time agents of the multiplicity. We humans are living in ignorance.*

And so, on Mirra's advice based on her experiences in Tlemcen and afterwards, she and Sri Aurobindo descended into the Vital. This was a momentous decision with many concrete consequences. One of them was that Sri Aurobindo had to stop writing for the *Arya,* of which publication was discontinued in January 1920. 'When you are doing the Sadhana in the mind, then outer activities like the *Arya* and writing, etc., can go on. But when I came down to the Vital, I stopped all that.' [14] Another consequence was a perceptible physical change in Mirra as well as in Sri Aurobindo. As the Mother said: 'After consciously identifying itself with the Divine, the entire being even in its external parts – Mental, Vital and Physical – undergoes the consequences of this identification, and a change occurs which is sometimes even perceptible in the physical appearance.' [15] The testimony to this astonishing fact is unequivocal.

---

* We should remember that the multiple existence is only 'apparent' for 'all is That' and cannot be other than That, whatever the appearances. It is because of this fundamental truth that yoga is possible.

'When I began with Sri Aurobindo to descend for the yoga,' said the Mother, 'to descend from the Mind into the Vital, when we brought down our yoga from the Mind into the Vital, within one month – I was forty at that time, I didn't look old, I looked younger than forty, but all the same I was forty – after a month's yoga I looked exactly eighteen. And someone who had seen me before, who had lived with me in Japan and came here, found it difficult to recognize me. He asked me: "But really, is it you?" I said: "Obviously!"' [16] This visitor was William W. Pearson, a follower of Rabindranath Tagore. Pearson was mentioned by name in the police report about Tagore's first visit to Japan and suspected of being influenced by the pan-Asian propaganda of Richard and Okawa. He visited Pondicherry from Tagore's Vishva Bharati in April 1923, when Mirra was forty-five.

A.B. Purani visited Sri Aurobindo for the first time in 1918 and for the second time in 1921. He reports: 'During the interval of two years his body had undergone a transformation which could only be described as miraculous. In 1918 the colour of the body was like that of an ordinary Bengali – rather dark – though there was a lustre on the face and the gaze was penetrating. On going upstairs to see him (in the same house) [in 1921] I found his cheeks wore an apple-pink colour and the whole body glowed with a soft creamy white light. So great and unexpected was the change that I could not help exclaiming: "What has happened to you?" Instead of giving a direct reply he parried the question, as I had grown a beard: "And what has happened to you?" But afterwards in the course of the talk he explained to me that when the Higher Consciousness, after descending to the mental level, comes down to the Vital and even below the Vital, then a transformation takes place in the nervous and even in the physical being.' [17]

T.V. Kapali Shastry has a similar story. He had first seen Sri Aurobindo in 1917 and found a great change when he saw him again in 1923. 'He found Sri Aurobindo completely changed in his physical appearance; he had then a golden hue on his body which had become fair in complexion, whereas it was brownish-dark when he had seen him last.' [18] The fact is confirmed in the reminiscences of, among others, V. Chidanandam, G.V. Subbarao, Dr. Rajangam and T. Kondaraman Rao, who writes: 'Sri Aurobindo appeared to me like the great Shiva whom I had been worshipping for some time. He was all golden, not figuratively but actually ... With a smooth golden body emitting light and flowing locks over his shoulders glowing bright, and shining eyes penetrating deep into everything, Sri Aurobindo was majestic in his appearance. His gait was royal and when he was pacing to and fro in the veranda, he appeared to be drawing force and using it according to his divine will.'[19]

It is striking how those who saw Mirra in those years describe her as very beautiful. So Kanailal Ganguly: 'It was the first time that I saw the Mother. She looked at me for a second. She was very beautiful, looked much younger than her age.'[20] A.B. Purani writes: 'This time [in 1921] I saw the Mother for the first time. She was standing near the staircase when Sri Aurobindo was going upstairs after lunch. Such unearthly beauty I had never seen – she appeared to be about twenty whereas she was more than thirty-seven years old.'[21] She was actually forty-three. D.K. Roy recalls: 'She was exceedingly kind to me and listened to me with great sympathy. I was charmed by her personality at once effulgent and soothing. Her being was haloed by beauty, but it was not an earthly beauty.'[22] Champaklal said: 'When I saw the Mother, I felt an extraordinary closeness to her and felt and saw in her an embodiment of beauty.'[23]

Considering the dates, one may conclude that the descent into the vital took place towards the end of 1920, shortly after Paul Richard's departure. His absence at once allowed Sri Aurobindo and Mirra to proceed with the yoga in a higher gear. The Mother would later say that the work in the vital lasted for several months. Bearing in mind some of Sri Aurobindo's utterances, they must have descended into Matter – where 'all the trouble began' – between 17 April 1923, the date of Pearson's visit, and 15 August 1924. For Sri Aurobindo said on his birthday of that year: 'I am at present engaged in bringing the Supermind into the physical consciousness, down even to the submaterial. The physical is by nature inert and does not want to be rendered conscious. It offers much greater resistance [than the vital] as it is unwilling to change. One feels as if "digging the earth," as the Veda says ... I find that so long as Matter is not supramentalized the Mental and the Vital also cannot be fully supramentalized.'[24] Sri Aurobindo also said that 1923 was 'a very hard year in my sadhana.' They must almost at once have gone deeper, into the Subconscient and the Inconscient. It will be remembered that Matter is not the lowest degree of the scale of being, but that it is a formation of the Subconscient and the Inconscient – the absolute Darkness, the Nihil that is the contrary of the absolute Light and All.

'It was only when I descended into the Inconscient,' said the Mother, 'that I found the divine Presence – there, in the midst of Darkness. It wasn't the first time. When I was working with Théon at Tlemcen (the second time I was there), I descended into the total, unindividualized – that is, general – Inconscient. (It was the time he wanted me to find the Mantra of Life.) And there I suddenly found myself in front of something like a vault or a grotto ... and when it opened I saw a Being of iridescent light reclining with his head on his hand, fast asleep. All the light around him was iridescent. When I told Théon what I was seeing, he said it was the immanent God in the depths of the Inconscient who, through his radiations, was slowly waking the Inconscient to Consciousness. But then a rather remarkable phenomenon occurred: when I looked at him, he woke up and opened his eyes, expressing the beginning of conscious, wakeful action.'[25]

The Foreign Lady

Few companions and followers of Sri Aurobindo knew about the unprecedented yogic sadhana in which he and Mirra were involved, and fewer still, if any, understood its revolutionary significance. Besides, the presence of Madame Richard at Sri Aurobindo's side was not accepted as a matter of course. For she and Miss Hodgson were now living in the same house as Sri Aurobindo and his companions at 41 Rue Francois Martin. As Nolini writes in his *Reminiscences:* 'There came a heavy storm and rain one day [24 November 1920]. The house [where the Mother was staying earlier] was old and looked as if it was going to melt away. Sri Aurobindo said: "The Mother cannot be allowed to stay there any longer. She must move into our place." That is how the Mother came into our midst and stayed on for good, as our Mother. But she did not yet assume the name.'[26]

Mirra and Dorothy Hodgson's moving in with Sri Aurobindo 'caused, understandably enough, a certain amount of uneasiness (if not resentment) among some of the young men living with Sri Aurobindo,' writes K.R. Srinivasa Iyengar in his biography of the Mother. 'This sudden "invasion" by two European ladies – however unavoidable under the circumstances – was a jolt to the kind of unconventional camp life they had been living so far.' He also quotes Purani, who wrote: 'This [Mirra's moving in] had created a sense of dissatisfaction in the minds of most of the inmates. Man is so much governed by his social, religious and cultural conventions that he finds it difficult to throw them out. Besides, men imbued with strong nationalism would find it difficult to accept one who apparently is a foreigner as an inmate of the house.'[27]

But Purani, on his 1921 visit, could not help noticing that 'the house had undergone a great change. There was a clean garden in the open courtyard, every room had simple and decent furniture – a mat, a chair and a small table. There was an air of tidiness and order. This was, no doubt, the effect of the Mother's presence. But yet the atmosphere was tense because Sri Aurobindo and the Mother were engaged in fighting with forces of the vital plane.'

'I was living in the inner rooms and seeing no one. He [Sri Aurobindo] was going out onto the veranda, seeing everyone, receiving people, speaking, discussing. I saw him only when he came back inside.' The Mother said this about the period during which she and Sri Aurobindo were staying in the 'Library House,' one of the four houses that form the present central Sri Aurobindo Ashram building in Rue de la Marine, and where they moved from the Rue François Martin in 1922. Yet her words are applicable to the time before that move too. Visitors continued to come, many with the intention of being accepted as disciples and staying permanently. 'There were people in the Ashram [or what was to become the Ashram] who thought that Mother had done no sadhana before she came to India,'[28] Sri Aurobindo recalled; and he wrote later in a letter: 'The Mother was not fully recognized or accepted by some of those who were here at the beginning.'[29]

Therefore, then as later, Sri Aurobindo had to set matters right. 'In my own case it [the coming together of him and Mirra, the Mother] was a necessary condition for the work that I had to do. If I had to do my own transformation, or give a new yoga, or a new ideal to a select few people who came in my personal contact, I could have done that without having any Shakti. But for the work that I had to do it was necessary that the two sides must come together. By the coming together of the Mother and myself certain conditions are created which make it easy for you to achieve the transformation. You can take advantage of those conditions.'[30]

What Sri Aurobindo here alludes to is the profound spiritual truth that lies at the basis of the universal manifestation and that we tried to formulate when Mirra became consciously identified with the Great Mother. The One who is All has no gender. To manifest Itself, It had to activate Its Power of manifestation, Its Consciousness-Force or *Shakti*, who is the Great Mother. To present this truth, the sages have called the part of the One that 'took the decision' *Purusha*, the 'male' initiator, and the part that executed the decision *Prakriti*, the 'female' executive, productive force. This is, on the one hand, a spiritual metaphor; in one of her talks at the Playground, the Mother would forcefully deny that there is any such gender difference within the One. On the other hand, in the universe as we know it, the sexes are the concrete expression of the spiritual truth of an initiating and a manifesting Divine. Every God has his Shakti: Brahma and Brahmani, Shiva and Parvati, Vishnu and Lakshmi. But it should be kept in mind that this division of the creative tasks into a male and female part is one of the features of the 'lower hemisphere,' and that the infinite Play of the Godhead in the 'upper hemisphere' is not bound to a sexual articulation in any way.

This makes us understand in some measure the uniqueness of Sri Aurobindo and the Mother as the Avatar of the Godhead – i.e. the physical incarnation of the Godhead – in two bodies. For the first time in known history the Godhead has, for Its intervention in the evolution, been embodied in a 'complete,' double-poled Avatar, containing the initiating and the creating aspects of Its being in a male and female body. 'Mother and I are one but in two bodies,' wrote Sri Aurobindo, and: 'The Mother and myself stand for the same Power in two forms.' He would stress: 'There is one force only, the Mother's force – or, if you like to put it like that, the Mother is Sri Aurobindo's Force,' in other words his Shakti.[31] And the Mother would pithily formulate the essence of their relationship: 'Without him I exist not, without me he is not manifest.'

'In the beginning Sri Aurobindo would refer to the Mother quite distinctly as Mira,' reminisces Nolini. 'For some time afterwards (this may have extended over a period of years) we could notice that he stopped at the sound of M and uttered the full name of Mira as if after a slight hesitation. To us it looked rather queer at the time, but later we came to know the reason. Sri Aurobindo's lips were on the verge of saying "Mother"; but we had yet to get ready, so he ended with Mira instead of saying Mother. No one knows for certain on which particular date and at what auspicious moment the word "Mother" was uttered by the lips of Sri Aurobindo.'[32]

'Most of the disciples did not really understand what the Mother was doing,' writes Mritunjoy, who had become a disciple himself. 'They kept a respectful aloofness from her, finding that Sri Aurobindo had given her a very high place in matters of sadhana. She, on her part, did not make herself often visible or easily approachable. The disciples knew that she was a dignified personality but little more than that. Since April [actually November] 1920 she had been living in the same house as Sri Aurobindo and a few others, but she had remained somewhat apart from the daily routine of the sadhaks. They did not really have a chance to understand who she was or what she was preparing for the future ... Even at the end of 1925, when Pavitra came, only Amrita and Nolini recognized who the Mother was; the others at most had a formal devotion.'[33]

For some 'it was unthinkable that a French lady could be an Avatar.' When a certain woman wanted to join the Ashram, her mother-in-law, who had always believed the woman to be mad, now saw her suspicions confirmed: 'What? You don't worship Rama, Krishna and Shiva, and now you will worship a French woman? Surely you are mad!'[34] For many, especially the more tradition-minded, it was an almost insurmountable difficulty to accept a foreign lady as being on an equal footing with Sri Aurobindo, let alone as the incarnation of the Divine Mother.

Meanwhile, Mirra, whom we will call 'the Mother' henceforth, looked after Sri Aurobindo's household, kept herself at a distance as much as possible, and enjoyed for seven years 'an integral peace' – even while being fully involved in her common yoga with Sri Aurobindo, a spiritual exploration and innovation beyond human imagination.

Throwing Stones

The following incident, narrated here by the Mother,[35] took place in December 1921 when she, Sri Aurobindo, Dorothy Hodgson and the others who formed the embryo of the future Ashram were still staying in the Rue François Martin. The house, number 41, was afterwards called the 'Guest House.'

'There was a time when we were living in the Guest House … How many of us were there in that house? Amrita was there. *[turning towards the disciple in question]* Weren't you, Amrita? Do you remember that day? … We had a cook called Vatel. This cook was rather bad-tempered and didn't like being reproved concerning his work. Moreover, he was in contact with some Musulmans who had, it seems, magical powers – they had a book of magic and the ability to practise magic. One day this cook had done something very bad and had been scolded – I don't know if any of you have known Datta [Dorothy Hodgson], it was Datta who had scolded him – and he was furious. He threatened us, saying: "You will see, you will be compelled to leave this house." We took no notice of it.

'Two or three days later, I think, someone came and told me that stones had fallen in the courtyard – a few stones, three or four, pieces of brick. We wondered who was throwing stones from the adjacent house … We climbed on the walls and roofs to see if we could detect somebody, or stones, or whatever. We found nothing. That happened, I believe, between four and five in the afternoon.

'As the day declined, the number of stones increased. The next day there were still more. They started striking specially the kitchen door, and one of them hit Datta's arm as she was crossing the courtyard. The number increased considerably. The interest was growing, and as the interest grew it produced a kind of multiplicative effect. And the stones began falling in several directions at the same time, in places [inside the house] where there were neither doors nor windows. There was a staircase, but it had no opening in those days, there was only a small bull's-eye, and the stones were falling on the staircase like this *[gesture: vertically]*. If they had come through the bull's-eye, they would have come like this *[gesture: slantwise]*, but they were falling straight downwards. So, I think everyone began to become truly interested.

'I must tell you that this Vatel had informed us that he was ill, and for the last two days – since the stones had started falling – he hadn't shown up. But he had left with us his helper, a young boy of thirteen, fourteen, quite obese, somewhat apathetic and morose, perhaps a little idiotic. And we noticed that when this boy moved around, wherever he went the number of stones increased. The young men who were living in the house, Amrita among them, shut the boy in a room with all the doors and windows closed ... and the stones began falling [in that room], with all the doors and windows closed! More and more fell, so much so that the boy was wounded in the leg ...

'I was with Sri Aurobindo. We were quietly working, meditating together. The young men cast a furtive glance inside to see what we were occupied with and informed us about the goings on, for it was time to tell us that the affair was taking quite serious proportions. I understood immediately what the matter was.' In order to exhaust all possibilities of an ordinary, physical explanation, the police were called. When one of the policemen heard that there had been a problem with Vatel, he said at once that he knew what the matter was. But from the moment the police arrived not a single stone fell any more. The Mother was watching from the terrace; when she said to Sri Aurobindo that this was annoying, as the police might think that they had been called for nothing, the stones started falling again at once – 'quite a long way off from the terrace,' not a single stone fell near her or Sri Aurobindo. The police left, as there was little they could do. The Mother ordered the boy to be sent out of the house immediately and told everybody to keep quiet and not be afraid.

'I was in the room with Sri Aurobindo and I thought: "We'll see what this is." I went into meditation and sent out a little call. I said: "Let's see, who is throwing stones at us? You must come and tell us who is throwing stones." * I saw three small entities of the Vital, those small entities who have no force and just enough consciousness for one single kind of action. They are of no consequence at all, but they are at the service of people who practise magic. When people practise magic, they order them [these small vital entities] to come to their assistance, and they are compelled to obey. To do this there are symbols, there are formulas.

'So, they [the small vital entities] came [to me]. They were afraid, they were terribly afraid. I said: "Why do you throw stones like that? What does this bad joke mean?" They replied: "We are compelled, we are compelled! It is not our fault, we have been ordered to do it. It is not our fault!" I felt like laughing, but I kept a straight face and told them: "You must stop this, you understand!" Then they asked me: "Don't you want to keep us? We shall do anything you ask." I said to them: "But what is it that you can do?" – "We know how to throw stones." – "That doesn't interest me in the least, I don't want to throw stones at anybody. Could you perhaps bring me flowers? Can you bring me some roses?" Then they looked at each other in consternation and answered: "No, we are not made for that, we don't know how to do that." Then I said: "I don't need you, go away, and see to it that you never come back here, for otherwise you will pay for it!" They took to their heels and never came back.

'The next morning I went down to pay a visit to the kitchen. There were pillars in that kitchen and on one of the pillars I found some signs with numbers as though scribbled with a piece of charcoal, very roughly drawn – I don't remember the signs now – and also words in Tamil. Then I rubbed out everything carefully and made an invocation, and that was it, the comedy was finished.

'But not quite. Vatel's daughter was the *ayah* in the house, the maid-servant. She came to us early in the afternoon in a state of intense fright and said: "My father is in the hospital, he is dying. This morning something happened to him. Suddenly he felt very ill and he is dying, he has been taken to the hospital. I'm terribly afraid." I knew what it

---

* Strange to say, all of the stones were covered with moss. Amrita kept some of them for months afterwards to show them to the incredulous.

was. I went to Sri Aurobindo and said to him: "You know, Vatel is in the hospital, he is dying." Then Sri Aurobindo looked at me, he smiled: "Oh, just for a few stones!" That very evening Vatel was cured – but he never started anything again.'

Then the Mother explained that she came to know who the magician was, and that he had taken much care not to let a single stone fall within twenty or twenty-five metres of Sri Aurobindo, whom he knew to be a great yogi. Black magic, if prevented from having its effect, rebounds on the one who has employed it, which is why Vatel would have died if Sri Aurobindo had not intervened and allowed him to live. And the Mother also explained that the small stone-throwers were in deadly fear of her because her light is the White Light of creation. 'The true, pure White Light is the supreme Light of construction. You put one drop upon them: they dissolve as if there had been nothing there at all. And yet this [Light] is not a force of destruction, it is a force of construction, but so alien to their nature that they disappear. It is this they feared, for I had called them by showing them this White Light. I had told them: "Look, here is this. Come at once!"'

The Coming of the Disciples

> *I do not very readily accept disciples as this path of Yoga is a difficult one and it can be followed only if there is a special call.*[36]

> – Sri Aurobindo

It will be remembered that the Mother had some questions ready when she met Sri Aurobindo for the first time in 1914. The 'very first' question was: 'Should you do your yoga, attain the goal, and then afterwards take up the work with others, or should you immediately let all those who have the same aspiration gather around you and go forward all together towards the goal? ... The decision was not at all a mental choice, it came spontaneously. The circumstances were such that no choice was required. I mean, quite naturally, spontaneously the group

213

was formed in such a way that it became an imperious necessity.'* Yet this sounds much simpler than the way it actually happened.

We know that it was never Sri Aurobindo's intention to stay for ever in Pondicherry (and still less to remain enclosed in his apartment). He was fully surrendered to the Divine Will, which guided his progress step by step, but till the end he would look forward to taking up 'his work in the world,' wherever that might happen to be. And he saw as an unquestionable necessity the formation of a group of people interested in and dedicated to the goal of the transformation of humankind and the world. The reason for this necessity was that one person can be cosmically expanded in his or her consciousness and even in his or her vital being, but not physically, as the physical being is materially limited to the body and the cells it contains. The Mother's 'very first question' originated certainly from the same consideration. She realized, as did Sri Aurobindo, that it was necessary that other bodies, representing the human species in its entirety, were around them to try to accomplish the yoga of the Earth, or at least to lay its foundations.

In the letter to his brother Barin, Sri Aurobindo had written: 'You will perhaps ask: "What is the need of a *sangha* [community]? Let me be free and fill every vessel. Let all become one, let all take place within that vast community." All this is true, but it is only one side of the truth. Our business is not with the formless Spirit only, we have to direct life as well. Without shape and form, life has no effective movement. It is the formless that has taken form, and that assumption of name and form is not a caprice of Maya. The positive necessity of form has brought about the assumption of form. And to work out the Integral Yoga the form has to be transformed, which is not possible as a personal undertaking but only as a *sangha*.' And Sri Aurobindo added: 'We do not want to exclude any of the world's activities.'[37]

Sri Aurobindo had initiated the first attempt at a spiritual community through Motilal Roy, the young Bengali who had taken care of him during his brief stay at Chandernagore, and who had provided him and his companions with some funds to alleviate their poverty during the first years in Pondicherry. Motilal Roy had also come a couple of

---

* See the beginning of Chapter Six, 'Speaking the Word.'

times to visit Sri Aurobindo in Pondicherry. About his last visit, in the company of his wife, Iyengar writes: 'Motilal Roy and his wife, who had come from Chandernagore, were not very happy with the changes they saw in Sri Aurobindo's house [meaning the presence of the Mother]. Besides, the *Prabartak Sangha* [Motilal's community] wanted them back at Chandernagore, while Motilal himself was undecided whether to go or remain with Sri Aurobindo. On receipt of a peremptory telegram from Chandernagore, Motilal and his wife left Pondicherry in August 1921 and the attempt to close the rift did not succeed. Not long after, Sri Aurobindo dissociated himself from Motilal and his *Prabartak Sangha*, and decided that he would henceforth try to build on the surest foundation.'[38]

But not that soon. Sri Aurobindo first sent Barin to Bengal in order to reconnoitre the possibilities of collecting funds, contacting interested people and founding one or several communities there. 'The time is approaching though it has not yet come,' he writes to Barin on 18 November 1922, 'when I shall have to take up a large external work proceeding from the spiritual basis of this Yoga. It is therefore necessary to establish a number of centres small and few at first but enlarging and increasing in numbers as I go on, for training in this Sadhana, one under my direct supervision, others in immediate connection with me ...

'The first [centre], which will be transferred to British India when I go there, already exists at Pondicherry but I need friends both to maintain and enlarge it. The second I am founding through you in Bengal. I hope to establish another one in Gujarat during the ensuing year. Many more desire and are fit to undertake this Sadhana than I can at present admit and it is only by large means being placed at my disposal that I can carry on this work which is necessary as a preparation for my return to action.'[39]

On the same day Sri Aurobindo wrote to C.R. Das, the nationalist politician and barrister who had defended him so effectively in the Alipore Bomb Case, and who had remained his friend and supporter ever since: 'I have now a sure basis, a wide knowledge and some mastery of the secret. Not yet its fullness and complete imperative presence – therefore I have still to remain in retirement. For I am determined not to work in the external field till I have the sure and complete possession of this new power of action – not to build except on a perfect foundation. But still I have gone far enough to be able to undertake one work on a larger scale than before – the training of others to receive this Sadhana and prepare themselves as I have done, for without that my future work cannot even be begun. There are many who desire to come here and whom I can admit for the purpose, there are a greater number who can be trained at a distance; but I am unable to carry on unless I have sufficient funds to be able to maintain a centre here and one or two at least outside.'[40]

In this letter Sri Aurobindo distances himself from Motilal Roy. 'One word to avoid a possible misunderstanding. Long ago I gave to Motilal Roy of Chandannagar [i.e. Chandernagore] the ideas and some principles and lines of a new social and economical organization and education and this with my spiritual force behind him he has been trying to work out in his own way in his Sangha. This is quite a separate thing from what I am now writing about – my own work which I must do myself and no one can do for me.' One by one the disciples started coming and many asked permission to stay close to Sri Aurobindo – which was the reason why 41 Rue Francois Martin became a guest house.

This was not an established community or 'ashram,'* for there were no fixed patterns or relations, no rules, and little room to house the aspirants who wanted to stay. Still, we have seen that Sri Aurobindo wrote to Barin as early as in November 1922 that 'a centre' already existed in Pondicherry. And although the Mother kept herself in the background, she gradually exercised her influence not only in Sri Aurobindo's household but in the apparently haphazard expansion of the community. 'All my realizations – Nirvana and others – would have remained theoretical, as it were, so far as the outer world was concerned,' Sri Aurobindo would say many years later. 'It is the Mother who showed the way to the practical form. Without her no organized manifestation would have

---

* An *ashram* is a spiritual community centred around a *guru*. Sri Aurobindo liked neither term, but the group around him and the Mother would eventually, in 1926, be called 'Sri Aurobindo Ashram,' probably for lack of a better word and to avoid confusion.

been possible. She has been doing this kind of sadhana and work from her early childhood.'[41]

Among the aspirants can be mentioned Kanailal Gangulee, who was dumbfounded at seeing two cats on the Mother's shoulders on the occasion of their first meeting; Dr. Rajangam, struck by the Mother's beauty; T.V. Kapali Shastri, scholar and tantrik; and V. Chidambaram, who would leave us his precious notes of the evening talks with Sri Aurobindo. There were, of course, also the stalwarts who had played a role in Sri Aurobindo's political life: Nolini, Moni, Sauren, Bejoy Nag (who had rejoined the group after his internment during the First World War) and Amrita, through whom everyone now had to pass who wished to get an appointment with Sri Aurobindo.

Sri Aurobindo's presence in Pondicherry attracted people from all over India: politicians, intellectuals, real yogis and pseudo-yogis, the inevitable bizarre characters – and of course those mentioned above together with others who wanted to become Sri Aurobindo's disciples. It is noteworthy that, according to Purani, Sri Aurobindo said as early as November or December 1920 that the community of those called to his and the Mother's yoga 'was already united though unconsciously.'[42] Now they started coming, almost all of them attracted to Sri Aurobindo for reasons they could not rationalize. It is impossible to narrate all their stories, but a few brief cameos should be included, for the disciples of Sri Aurobindo and the Mother were an intrinsic part of their life and work.

A.B. Purani was an intellectual and passionate freedom fighter. 'The concentration of my whole being turns towards India's freedom. It is difficult for me to sleep till that is secured.'[43] He was from Baroda and had heard Sri Aurobindo give speeches there after the Surat Conference, at the time of his first meeting with Lele. 'Ever since I had seen him I had got the constant feeling that he was known to me.' Purani had subscribed to the *Arya* and even translated it in Gujarati. He had his first meeting with Sri Aurobindo in December 1918. When he confided to him his passion for the freedom of his motherland, Sri Aurobindo remained silent for a couple of minutes. 'Then he said: "Suppose an assurance is given to you that India will be free?" – "Who can give such an assurance?"' 'I could feel,' writes Purani, 'the echo of doubt and challenge in my own question. Again he remained silent for three or four minutes. Then he looked at me and added: "Suppose I give you the assurance?" I paused for a moment, considered the question with myself and said: "If you give the assurance, I can accept it." – "Then I give you the assurance that India will be free," he said in a serious tone ... You can take it from me, it is as certain as the rising of the sun tomorrow. The decree has already gone forth – it may not be long in coming."' Purani visited Sri Aurobindo again in 1921, just after the stone-throwing incident, when he was astonished by the physical change that had taken place in Sri Aurobindo; and he came again in 1923 to stay for good and take charge of the Guest House. We owe him the precious notes of many conversations with Sri Aurobindo, the first data on the life of Sri Aurobindo, and other seminal writings.

Champaklal was a Gujarati Brahmin, born in a family of *puraniks*, whose profession it is to read the scriptures for the benefit of the local Hindu community. From an early age he had been steeped in the sacred writings and the ocean of stories from the *Puranas* and other sources. He too was irresistibly attracted by the name of Sri Aurobindo and the reports about him from people who knew him or were his disciples. Together with eleven others he decided to walk to Pondicherry all the way from Gujarat, crossing the Indian subcontinent from the west coast north of Bombay to the east coast south of Madras! Soon most of them dropped out, but then a well-wisher sold his wife's gold ornaments to buy train tickets for Champaklal and two companions. The trio arrived in Pondicherry on 1 April 1921. Amrita called them to meet Sri Aurobindo 'at ten minutes to five,' remembered Champaklal. 'When we went upstairs Sri Aurobindo was seated there. I saw nothing except him and when I prostrated myself before him I lay there for one full hour. Nobody disturbed me. At the end of the hour Sri Aurobindo placed his hand on my head, blessed me and said: "Tomorrow," and I got up ... You ask me what was my first reaction on seeing Sri Aurobindo. Well, when I had made pranam to him and got up I felt that I had nothing more to do in my life. There was an evident sense of having arrived.'[44] Champaklal would come back to stay for good in 1923 and become a lifelong servitor of Sri Aurobindo and the Mother. His brother, Bansidhar, would become an Ashramite four years later.

Dilip Kumar Roy was born into 'one of the most aristocratic Brahmin families of Bengal.' His father was a poet and playwright, and Dilip, when still young, made a name for himself as a singer, mainly of religious songs, after having studied mathematics and music in Cambridge. Besides several Indian languages he spoke English, French and German. Among his acquaintances were Mohandas K. Gandhi, Rabindranath Tagore, Romain Rolland, Bertrand Russell, Georges Duhamel and Subhas C. Bose. He would become the author of no less than seventy-five books in Bengali and twenty-six in English. His attention had been drawn to Sri Aurobindo by Ronald Nixon, a former British war pilot and Professor of English at the University of Lucknow. (See the footnote on p. 30.)

Dilip K. Roy went to meet Sri Aurobindo in 1924. So deep was the impression Sri Aurobindo made on him that he asked to be accepted as his disciple. Sri Aurobindo found that the right time had not yet come, but Roy thought he had been refused. He went in search of another guru, till one of the yogis he contacted told him that his acceptance by Sri Aurobindo had been postponed because of a hernia in Roy's left abdomen. 'Yoga means pressure on these parts, the vitals. Maybe that's why he [Sri Aurobindo] asked you to wait till it healed up.' How did this yogi somewhere in a village in north India know? '[Sri Aurobindo] just appeared there – yes, just behind you – and told me to advise you to wait. He told me that he would draw you to him as soon as you were ready.'[45] As we have seen, Dilip K. Roy went to Europe in 1927 – actually to make a series of recordings for Edison's Gramophone Company in New York, but the project did not materialize – where he met Paul Richard. He became a member of the Sri Aurobindo Ashram in 1928, but was 'not a little crestfallen' because Sri Aurobindo, by that time, had withdrawn and could not be met with any more.

Dilip K. Roy was a moody, tumultuous and rather self-conscious disciple whom Sri Aurobindo had to pacify and encourage by letter after letter – altogether more than 4,000. Sri Aurobindo would even write to him: 'I have cherished you like a friend and a son ...' and: 'It is a strong and lasting personal relation that I have felt with you ever since we met ... Even before I met you for the first time, I knew of you and felt at once the contact of one with whom I had that relation which declares itself constantly through many lives and followed your career ... with a close sympathy and interest. It is a feeling which is never mistaken and gives the impression of one not only close to one but a part of one's existence ... It was the same inward recognition (apart even from the deeper spiritual connection) that brought you here.'[46] Dilip K. Roy would never really accept the Mother despite all the care, material and spiritual, she and Sri Aurobindo took of him.

Philippe Barbier Saint-Hilaire was a Frenchman with a diploma in engineering from the renowned *École polytechnique* in Paris. He was exactly twenty when the First World War broke out and he enlisted as an artillery officer. Even during the war he grew more and more interested in occultism and felt a deep attraction to spirituality – against the grain of his education and the Cartesian intellectual environment in France. After the war he was employed as an engineer with the Ministry of Transport and Communications, but in 1920 he left for Japan to study Zen Buddhism. 'I knew ... yes, *I knew*, for it was a certainty to me – that my life would be a life of spiritual realization, that nothing else counted for me, and that somewhere on Earth, and I mean effectively on Earth, there had to be someone who could give me ... who could lead me towards the light.'[47] The Richards had left Japan a few months before Saint-Hilaire's arrival. In the following four years he ran a laboratory and was involved in 'many experiences, the study of Buddhism, especially Zen Buddhism, life in the temples and, at night in my home, the continuation of my studies in Indian, Japanese and Chinese spirituality.'

In 1924 Saint-Hilaire travelled to Mongolia in the company of a Mongolian lama. There he stayed nine months in a monastery. Then he felt compelled to travel to India and finally arrived in Pondicherry. (In France he had read the issues of the *Revue de la Grande Synthèse*, but had not found them of special interest.) '[Sri Aurobindo] then told me that what I was searching for could be given to me by several persons in India, but that it was not easy to approach them, especially not for a European. And he went on that he himself was of the opinion that what I was looking for – the identification with God, the realization of the Brahman – was, as it were, the first step, a necessary phase. But it was not everything, for there was a second phase: the descent of the power of the Divine into the human consciousness to transform it, and that *this* was what he, Sri Aurobindo, was trying to do. And he said to me: "If you want to try this, then you can stay here." I threw myself at his feet, and that was that.' Sri Aurobindo would call him Pavitra, 'the Pure,' and he would become the totally dedicated secretary of the Mother and afterwards the Head of the Ashram School. Of his first meeting with the Mother he especially remembered her eyes, 'her eyes of light.'

Cats

> *An animal creature wonderfully human,*
> *A charm and miracle of fur-footed Brahman,*
> *Whether she is spirit, woman or cat,*
> *Is now the problem I am wondering at.*[48]

– Sri Aurobindo

'I have studied cats a lot; if one knows them well, they are marvellous creatures,' said the Mother. As the young people around her did not understand the Mother's exact relation with these animals, which in India are seldom kept as household pets, their attitude may be characterized as uncomprehending, to put it mildly. Champaklal remembers: 'During those early days, Mother herself used to prepare a pudding. Of that pudding she would put aside a small quantity in a small dish; she would add a little milk to it and stir it with a spoon till it became liquid and consistent. She showed me how to do it and was particular that no grains should be left unmashed. And when she passed on the work to me, I followed her directions to the utmost. And do you know for whom this part of the pudding was meant? For *cats*! Later on I learnt that they were not really cats but something more. You would be interested to know that at times Sri Aurobindo also made fish ready for these "cats," removing the bones etc.'[49]

Nolini reminisces in amazement: 'The style in which these cats were treated was something extraordinary. The arrangements made for their food were quite a festive affair; it was for them alone that special cooking was done, with milk and fish and the appropriate dressings, as if they were children of some royal family – all went according to schedule. They received an equally good training: they would never commit nuisance within doors for they had been taught to use the conveniences for them.'[50] Everyone thought that the Mother had a special attachment to these cats, but the truth was very different.

When the Mother was in Tlemcen and deeply involved in occult practices, the 'king of the cats' made a covenant with her that gave her special powers over the members of his species. Human beings have an individual consciousness, developed in various degrees, but animals have a collective consciousness that is mostly called instinct and centered in the 'king' of their species – which goes to show how much truth there actually is in legends and folktales. The 'king of cats' is a being from the vital world, which means that the members of his species incarnate vital forces. Cats are generally held to be independent animals, but the Mother said that one can communicate with them on condition that one knows how to apply one's vital force. Her concern with the cats in the household was indeed a special one: she wanted to find out whether it was possible to make them skip one or several evolutionary steps. Her experiments with these animals were experiments in evolution.

She told many stories about cats, for instance about the one that always slipped under her mosquito net and slept with her head against the Mother's shoulder, stretched out like a human being. This cat also wanted to give birth to its kittens on its back, like a woman, and the Mother had to intervene to make her take the convenient posture. When the Mother wanted to find out the reason for this strange behavior, one night she saw a Russian woman with three small children whom she adored and for whom she was trying to find shelter. The Mother did not know the exact circumstances, but the woman and her beloved children had obviously been in distress and been killed in desperate circumstances. The vital, motherly part of that Russian woman had in one way or other reincarnated in the cat who, when she had three kittens, did not leave them alone, not even to eat or to answer the call of nature. When the Mother made her understand that she had nothing to fear, the cat brought her kittens one by one and put them between the Mother's feet; only then did she go outside to do the necessary.[51]

Kiki behaved in a still more unusual way: he meditated. When it was time for the daily meditation, he jumped in Sri Aurobindo's chair and nothing or nobody could remove him from there. As Pujalal remembered: 'Sometimes before he [Sri Aurobindo] came, one of the housecats found it comfortable to occupy his chair – perhaps as a matter of right – and would not leave the chair for the Master ... And the ever-considerate Master never disturbed the confident cat in any way whatsoever, but simply, nay, precariously sat on the little border-space all the time he remained there.'[52] The Mother said: 'It did not wait for anyone to get into the chair, it got in first itself! And regularly it went into a trance! It was not sleeping ... it was in a trance; it used to start up, it certainly had visions ... It was in a profound trance. It remained thus for hours together. It was awakened and given food, but it refused to eat: it went back to its chair and fell again into a trance! This was becoming very dangerous for a little cat ... But it was no ordinary cat.'[53] Kiki was a cat 'which was very, very unhappy about being a cat, it wanted to be a human being. It had an untimely death. It used to meditate, it certainly did a kind of sadhana of its own, and when it left, a portion of its vital being reincarnated in a human being. The little psychic element that was at the centre of the being went directly into the human species, and even what was conscious in the vital of the cat went into a human being. But these are rather exceptional cases.'[54] It was an animal in which the psychic being had skipped many incarnations, many evolutionary psychic gradations to enter directly into a human body. The Mother knew to which person that human body belonged, for she said it was rather a simpleton, but this does not prevent the psychic leap from having been an exceptional and considerable one. 'It was a cat doing yoga – this is what it was – to become a human being.'[55]

The same Kiki liked to play with scorpions and one day he was stung. 'But it was an exceptional cat. He came to me – he was almost dying – and he showed me his paw where it was stung. It was already swollen and in a terrible state. I took my little cat – he was really sweet – and put it on a table and called Sri Aurobindo. I told him: "Kiki has been stung by a scorpion, he must be cured." The cat stretched its neck and looked at Sri Aurobindo, his eyes already a little glassy. Sri Aurobindo sat down in front of him and looked at him. Then we saw how this little cat gradually began to recover, to come round, and an hour later he jumped to his feet and went away completely healed.'[56] Sri Aurobindo had looked at Kiki for twenty or twenty-five minutes, after which it fell asleep, and when it woke up an hour later, it was as healthy as ever.

During those years, the disciples who had received permission would gather around Sri Aurobindo and ask him questions about everything under the sun. Sri Aurobindo's answers were noted down by Chidambaram and Purani, who writes in his introduction to those 'evening talks': 'As years passed the evening sittings went on changing their time and often those disciples who came from outside for a temporary stay for Sadhana were allowed to join them. As the number of Sadhaks practising the yoga increased, the evening sittings also became more full, and the small veranda upstairs in the main building was found insufficient. Members of the household would gather every day at the fixed time with some sense of expectancy and start chatting in low tones. Sri Aurobindo used to come last, and it was after his coming that the session would really commence.

'He came dressed as usual in dhoti, part of which was used by him to cover the upper part of his body. Very rarely he came out with chaddar or shawl and then it was "in deference to the climate" as he sometimes put it. At times for minutes he would sit gazing at the sky through a small opening at the top of the grass-curtains that covered the veranda of the upstairs in no. 9 Rue de la Marine. How much these sittings were dependent on him may be gathered from the fact that there were days when more than three-fourths of the time passed in complete silence without any outer suggestion from him, or there was only an abrupt "Yes" or "No" to all attempts at drawing him out in conversation. And even when he participated in the talk one always felt that his voice was that of one who does not let his whole being flow into his words, there was a reserve and what was left unsaid was perhaps more than what was spoken. What was spoken was what he felt necessary to speak.

'Very often some news-item in the daily newspaper, town-gossip, or some interesting letter received either by him or by a disciple, or a question from one of the gathering, or occasionally some remark or query from himself would set the ball rolling for the talk. The whole thing was so informal that one could never predict the turn the conversation would take. The whole house therefore was in a mood to enjoy the freshness and the delight of meeting the unexpected. There were peals of laughter and light talk, jokes and criticism which might be called personal – there was seriousness and earnestness in abundance.'[57] But suddenly the evening talks would come to an unexpected end.

9.

Three Dragons

[The Mother] has descended upon earth to participate in [her children's] nature. Because if she did not participate in their nature, she could not lead them farther. If she remained in her supreme consciousness where there is no suffering, in her supreme knowledge and consciousness, she could not have any contact with human beings. It is for this that she is obliged to take on the human consciousness and form: to be able to enter into contact with them.[1]

– The Mother

'Siddhi Day'

'In 1926 I had begun a sort of overmental creation,' said the Mother, 'that is, I had brought the Overmind down into matter, here on Earth (miracles and all kinds of things were beginning to happen). I asked all those gods to incarnate, to identify themselves with a body [on Earth]. (Some of them absolutely refused.) Well, with my very own eyes I saw Krishna, who had always been in rapport with Sri Aurobindo, consent to come down into his body. It was on 24 November and it was the beginning of "Mother."

'Previously he used to go out on the veranda every day to meet and talk with all who came to see him … I was living in the inner rooms and seeing no one; he was going out onto the veranda, seeing everyone, receiving people, speaking, discussing. I saw him only when he came back inside. After a while I too began having meditations with people. I had begun a sort of 'overmental creation' to make each God descend into a being [on Earth]. There was an extraordinary upward curve!

226

Well, I was in contact with these beings and I told Krishna (because I was always seeing him around Sri Aurobindo): "This is all very fine, but what I want now is a creation on Earth. You must incarnate." He said, "Yes." Then I saw him ... I saw him with my own eyes (inner eyes, of course), join himself to Sri Aurobindo.

'Then I went into Sri Aurobindo's room and told him, "This is what I have seen." "Yes, I know," he replied. "That's fine. I have decided to retire into my room, and you will take charge of the people. You take charge." (There were about thirty people at the time.)' [2]

It is clear that somewhere around 15 August 1926 a new phase in the work of Sri Aurobindo and the Mother started.* To the question 'On what date in 1926 did Mother take up the full charge of the Ashram?' Sri Aurobindo's answer was: 'Mother does not at all remember the correct date. It may have been a few days after 15th August. She took up the work completely when I retired.' [3] In practical terms she had taken care of Sri Aurobindo's household as soon as she went to live in the same house.

Her 'overmental creation,' to make the gods incarnate in human bodies on Earth, was not restricted to Sri Aurobindo's – which, whoever he may have essentially been, was also a human body – but equally extended to the bodies of some disciples. This can only mean that she must have deemed the time and the people concerned ready for such a tremendous undertaking.

Sri Aurobindo knew about this, of course. On 6 November 1926

---

* It is important to state that the Mother was *not* a disciple of Sri Aurobindo. As Sri Aurobindo had his amanuensis write to Arindam Basu: 'The Mother is not a disciple of Sri Aurobindo. She has had the same realization and experience as myself.' (Quoted in K.D. Sethna, *Our Light and Delight*, p. 1) And in a letter Sri Aurobindo himself wrote: 'What is known as Sri Aurobindo's Yoga is the joint creation of Sri Aurobindo and the Mother.' *(On Himself*, p. 459) The equivalence of Sri Aurobindo and the Mother is self-evident when considering their basic declarations: 'The Mother's consciousness and mine are the same, the one Divine Consciousness in two, because that is necessary for the play' (Sri Aurobindo); and: 'Without him I exist not, without me he is not manifest.' (The Mother) These pronouncements reflect the truth of the Divine essence and its manifestation. 'There is no difference between the Mother's path and mine,' wrote Sri Aurobindo, 'we have and have always had the same path, the path that leads to the supramental change and the divine realization; not only at the end, but from the beginning they have been the same.' *(On Himself*, SABCL 26 p. 459)

he said during his evening talk: 'I spoke about the world of the Gods because not to speak of it would be dangerous. I spoke of it so that the mind may understand the thing if it comes down. I am trying to bring it down into the physical, as it can no longer be delayed, and then things may happen. Formerly, to speak of it would have been undesirable, but now *not* to speak of it might be dangerous.'[4] Two dates on which he had spoken about the gods were 22 and 24 August, which tallies with the time the Mother took up an active role.

For what happened on 24 November 1926, we follow the account of an eyewitness, A.B. Purani. 'From the beginning of November 1926 the pressure of the Higher Power began to be unbearable. Then at last the great day ... arrived on 24 November. The sun had almost set, and everyone was occupied with his own activity – some had gone out to the seaside for a walk – when the Mother sent round word to all the disciples to assemble as soon as possible in the veranda where the usual meditation was held. It did not take long for the message to go round to all. By six o'clock most of the disciples had gathered. It was becoming dark.

'In the veranda on the wall near Sri Aurobindo's door, just behind his chair, a black silk curtain with gold lace work representing three Chinese dragons was hung. The three dragons were so represented that the tail of one reached up to the mouth of the other and the three of them covered the curtain from end to end. We came to know afterwards that there is a prophecy in China that the Truth will manifest itself on Earth when the three dragons (the dragon of the Earth, of the mind region and of the sky) meet ...

'There was a deep silence in the atmosphere after the disciples had gathered there. Many saw an oceanic flood of Light rushing down from above. Everyone present felt a kind of pressure above his head. The whole atmosphere was surcharged with some electrical energy. In that silence, in that atmosphere full of concentrated expectation and aspiration, in the electrically charged atmosphere, the usual, yet on this day quite unusual, tick was heard behind the door of the entrance. Expectation rose in a flood. Sri Aurobindo and the Mother could be seen through the half-opened door. The Mother with a gesture of her eyes requested Sri Aurobindo to step out first. Sri Aurobindo with a similar gesture suggested to her to do the same. With a slow dignified step the Mother came out first, followed by Sri Aurobindo with his majestic gait. The small table that used to be in front of Sri Aurobindo's chair was removed this day. The Mother sat on a small stool to his right.

'Silence absolute, living silence – not merely living but overflowing with divinity. The meditation lasted about forty-five minutes. After that one by one the disciples bowed to the Mother. She and Sri Aurobindo gave blessings to them. Whenever a disciple bowed to the Mother, Sri Aurobindo's right hand came forward behind the Mother's as if blessing him through the Mother. After the blessings, in the same silence there was a short meditation ... Sri Aurobindo and the Mother went inside. Immediately Datta was inspired. In that silence she spoke: "The Lord has descended into the physical today."' Purani names the twenty-four persons present, with most of whom we are now acquainted.[5] In the Sri Aurobindo Ashram 24 November 1926 is known as its foundation date, and as 'Siddhi Day' (Day of the Realization) or 'Victory Day.'

The Mother said many years later about that 24 November: 'He called everyone together for one last meeting. He sat down, had me sit next to him, and said: "I called you here to tell you that, as of today, I am withdrawing for purposes of sadhana, and Mother will now take charge of everyone. You should address yourselves to her. She will represent me and she will do all the work" ... These people had always been very intimate with Sri Aurobindo, so they asked: "Why, why, why?" He replied: "It will be explained to you." I had no intention of explaining anything and I left the room with him, but Datta began speaking ... She said she felt Sri Aurobindo speaking through her and she explained everything: that Krishna had incarnated and that Sri Aurobindo was now going to do an intensive sadhana for the descent of the Supermind; that it meant Krishna's adherence to the Supramental Descent upon Earth and that, as Sri Aurobindo would now be too occupied to deal with people, he had put me in charge and I would be doing all the work.'[6]

(The reports about Datta's words vary considerably. Rajani Palit writes: 'Now Datta came out, inspired, and declared: "The Master has conquered death, decay, hunger and sleep!"' According to Nolini, it went as follows: 'Datta ... suddenly exclaimed at the top of her voice, as though an inspired Prophetess of the old mysteries: "The Lord has descended. He has conquered death and sorrow. He has brought down immortality."'[7] And Champaklal noted down: 'Datta spoke: "Krishna the Lord has come. He has ended the hell of suffering. He has conquered pain. He has conquered death. He has conquered all. He has descended tonight, bringing immortality and Bliss."'[8])

This means that from that moment onwards Sri Aurobindo's adhara contained two Great beings, he himself and Shri Krishna. It also means that Shri Krishna was embodied on Earth from 24 November 1926 to 5 December 1950 – and no one knew of it then or knows of it now. There had always been a close association between Sri Aurobindo and Krishna, as we have seen on several occasions. Sri Aurobindo would write that it was Krishna 'who was the guide of my Yoga and with whom I realized identity.'[9] It was Krishna who gave him the commands (*adesh*) which, because of his unconditional and immediate obedience, worked such important changes in his life, as it was Krishna who drew the plan of his sadhana (the *saptachatushtaya*). Some utterances by the Mother even suggest that Sri Aurobindo had been Krishna, 'a formation of the past,' and the fact that the light of the aura of both of them is the same seems to confirm this. 'Whitish blue is Sri Aurobindo's light or Krishna's light,' Sri Aurobindo himself wrote.[10]

The Word of Creation

'I had begun a sort of overmental creation,' said the Mother, and she continued with it 'for some months' after 24 November. The reader will recall that the Overmind is the highest level of the lower hemisphere of the manifestation. It is the gradation of existence directly under and in essential contact with the Supramental, itself a world of many gradations, each one existing within the divine Unity-Consciousness where reign omniscience, omnipresence, omnipotence. In the Overmind the divine Unity is, by the process of involution, split up into an endless variety of forces, cosmic forces. These forces are also called Gods, for every force is a being.

'If we regard the Powers of Reality as so many Godheads,' writes Sri Aurobindo in *The Life Divine,* 'we can say that the Overmind releases a million Godheads into action, each empowered to create its own world, each world capable of relation, communication and interplay with the others. There are in the Veda different formulations of the nature of the Gods: it is said they are all one Existence to which the sages give different names; yet each God is worshipped as if he by himself is that Existence, one who is all the other Gods together or contains them in his being; and yet each is a separate Deity acting sometimes in unison with companion deities, sometimes separately, sometimes even in apparent opposition to other Godheads of the same Existence.'[11]

'The Gods ... are in origin and essence permanent Emanations of the Divine put forth from the Supreme by the Transcendent Mother,' writes Sri Aurobindo in a letter.[12] In his correspondence with Nirodbaran he clarifies this: 'Men can build forms [of the Gods] which [the Gods] will accept, but these forms too are inspired into men's mind from the planes to which the Gods belong. All creation has two sides, the formed and the formless; the Gods too are formless and yet have forms, but a Godhead can take many forms, here Maheshwari, there Pallas Athene. Maheshwari herself has many forms in her lesser manifestations, Durga, Uma, Parvati, Chandi, etc. The Gods are not limited to human forms – man also has not always seen them in human forms only.'[13]

As the gods are descended from the One, or That, or Brahman, but remain part of It, so through involution are we humans descended from the gods. (In other words, we are children of Mother Earth and through her of the Cosmos.) 'Everyone's inner being is born in the *ansha* [portion] of some Devata' or god, wrote Sri Aurobindo.[14] This enables us to understand Nolini's words about what happened after that momentous 24 November. 'The Mother's endeavour at that time was for a new creation ... She had placed each of us in touch with his inner godhead. Every individual has what may be described as his line of spiritual descent and also ascent, for into each individual consciousness has come down from the supreme Maha Shakti an individual divine being, a particular godhead following a particular line of manifestation of divine power, *Vibhuti*. To bear inwardly the touch of this divinity and found it securely within oneself, to concentrate on it and become one with it, to go on manifesting it in one's outer life, this was the aim of the *sadhana* at the time.'[15]

'Is the descent of the Overmind a necessity in the sadhana?' asked a disciple. 'Certainly,' answered Sri Aurobindo, 'it is necessary for those who want the supramental change [the ultimate aim of the work of Sri Aurobindo and the Mother]. *Unless the Overmind opens,* there can be no direct supramental opening of the consciousness. If one remains in the mind, even in the illumined mind or the intuition, one can have indirect messages or an influence from the Supramental, but not a direct supramental control of the consciousness or the supramental change.'[16] This makes it clear why Sri Aurobindo had started talking about the gods and deemed it 'dangerous' for the disciples not to know about them: the Mother was trying to bring the Gods with their powers down into them, and she was succeeding in her effort, though with mixed results.

'Between the end of 1926 and the end of 1927,' writes Narayan Prasad, 'the Mother was trying to bring down the Overmind Gods into our beings. But the *adharas* were not ready to bear them; on the contrary there were violent reactions, though some had very good experiences. There was a sadhak whose consciousness was so open that he could know what the Mother and the Master were talking about. One sadhak would get up while meditating and touch the centre of obstruction in somebody else's body. There were others who thought that the Supermind had descended into them. One or two got mentally unbalanced because of the inability to stand the pressure. T. left off taking food saying that he was having nectar and had no need of ordinary food, but he could not pull on for long. So the whole procedure of the sadhana had to be changed.'[17]

'At the time you speak of we were in the vital, the brilliant period of the Ashram,' Sri Aurobindo would say. 'People were having brilliant experiences, big push, energy, etc. If our yoga had taken that line, we could have ended by establishing a great religion, bringing about a big creation, etc., but our real work is different, so we had to come down into the physical. And working on the physical is like digging the ground; the physical is absolutely inert, dead like stone. When the work began there, all former energies disappeared, experiences stopped; if they came they didn't last. The progress is exceedingly slow.'[18]

K.D. Sethna reports: 'The months after the descent [of Shri Krishna on 24 November] were indeed of an almost miraculous nature, culminating in the moment when the Mother, as she told me as well as recounted in one of her talks at the Playground, got what she termed "the Word of Creation."'[19] Elsewhere he writes: 'She said [to Sethna] she had come to possess the Word of Creation. When I looked a little puzzled she added: "You know that Brahma is said to create by his Word. In the same way whatever I would express could take place. I had willed to express a whole new world of superhuman reality. Everything was prepared in the subtle dimension and was waiting to be precipitated upon Earth."'[20]

The Mother herself narrates the events as follows: 'Sri Aurobindo had put me in charge of the outer work because he wanted to withdraw in concentration in order to hasten the manifestation of the supramental Consciousness, and he had announced to the few people who were there that he was entrusting to me the work of helping and guiding them, that I would remain in contact with him as a matter of course, and that through me he would do the work. Suddenly, immediately, things took a certain shape: a very brilliant creation was worked out in extraordinary detail, with marvellous experiences, contacts with divine beings, and all kinds of manifestations which are considered miraculous. Experiences followed upon experiences, and, well, things were unfolding altogether brilliantly and, I must say, in an extremely interesting way.

'One day, I went as usual to relate to Sri Aurobindo what had been happening. We had come to something really very interesting, and perhaps I showed a little enthusiasm in my account of what had taken place. Then Sri Aurobindo looked at me and said: "Yes, this is a creation of the Overmind. It is very interesting, very well done. You will cause miracles which will make you famous throughout the world, you will be able to turn the course of events on Earth upside down. In brief ..." and then he smiled and said: "It will be a *great* success. But it is a creation of the Overmind. And it is not success that we want, we want to establish the Supermind upon Earth. One must know how to renounce immediate

233

success in order to create the new world, the supramental world in its integrality." With my inner consciousness I understood at once: a few hours later the creation didn't exist any more, and from that moment we started anew on other foundations.' [21] In another conversation she said that she undid everything 'in half an hour,' withholding the things 'prepared in the subtle dimension.' Had the Mother continued this new creation with the help of the Gods, some of them incarnated in human beings, a new religion would have appeared on Earth with a force and a lustre we cannot even imagine. Now, nobody knows about it. As K.D. Sethna writes: 'This was surely the mightiest act of renunciation in spiritual history.'

Accepting the Mother

I have no intention of altering the arrangement I have made for all the disciples without exception that they should receive the light and force from [the Mother] and not directly from me and be guided by her spiritual progress. [22]

– Sri Aurobindo

From 24 November onwards there was a kind of 'division of tasks' between Sri Aurobindo and the Mother. They remained of course essentially one, and 'all the realizations he had, I had too, automatically.' But now it was Sri Aurobindo who remained 'hidden,' as he said 'to work things out,' and the Mother who moved in front. We remember how, in Japan, she defined the role of women as primarily executive and organizational, mirroring the role of the Great Executrix who manifested, organized and supported the worlds. And as always – for instance when bringing about her overmental creation – she threw herself into her work with a total dedication and with a Power that drew upon the all-manifesting Shakti. Sri Aurobindo said that she was 'a Force in action'; and she herself said, with a touch of humour, that her way of advancing was 'at a gallop.' She also compared herself to a cyclone and even to 'a jet plane.'

The task at hand consisted in building a world in miniature, representative and symbolic of the world as a whole. To this end many more 'samples' of humanity were needed, and it is significant that the number of disciples shot up from twenty-five in 1926 to eighty in 1928. This required more accommodation, food, etc., to be organized with restricted means. 'The Ashram Services had to be reorganized on a departmental footing, reasonable economies had to be imposed, work had to be assigned to the individual sadhaks, and departmental headships had to be instituted,' writes Iyengar. 'There was room for rivalry, friction, misunderstanding, sulking, even insubordination. But more than all this there was the question of the spiritual Motherhood itself, and its authority over the day-to-day functioning of the Ashram. There was rumbling discontent, and some wrote directly to Sri Aurobindo lodging protests or seeking clarifications.'[23]

Sri Aurobindo wrote a few years afterwards: 'The opposition to the Mother's consciousness was an invention of the old days (due mainly to X, Y and others of that time) and emerged in a time when the Mother was not fully recognized or accepted by some of those who were here at the beginning. Even after they had recognized her they persisted in this meaningless opposition and did great harm to them and to others.'[24]

When things came to a head, he had to put matters straight, as in this letter from April 1930: 'The Mother is in sole charge and arranges things as best they can be arranged within the means at her disposal and the capacities of her instruments. She is under no obligation to act according to the mental standards or vital desires and claims of the Sadhaks; she is not obliged to use a democratic equality in her dealings with them. She is free to deal with each according to what she sees to be his true need or what is best for him in his spiritual progress. No one can be her judge or impose on her his own rule and standard; she alone can make rules, and she can depart from them too if she thinks fit, but no one can demand that she shall do so. Personal demands and desires cannot be imposed on her ... This is the spiritual discipline of which the one who represents or embodies the Divine Truth is the centre. Either she is that and all this is the plain common sense of the matter; or she is not and then no one need stay here. Each can go his own way and there is no Ashram and no Yoga.'[25]

'As to the Mother, I could not reconcile myself to how a European lady could establish herself as the Mother in Pondicherry Ashram and even more as the Divine Mother,' writes Rakhal Bose.[26] And M.P. Pandit writes: 'There was quite a consternation at this development [of Sri Aurobindo putting the Mother at the head of the Ashram]. It was hard to accept a situation where members had no more access to Sri Aurobindo. For some it was harder to accept Mirra as the Mother. Why is she the Mother? Who is the Mother? These were the questions asked by some and unasked openly by some others.'[27]

'Her status after 24 November 1926 as the spiritual head of the Ashram, the "Mother" ... caused some eyebrows to be raised. There was no question about her managerial ability, her unfailing friendliness and her personal spiritual eminence. And yet ... the Mother of the Ashram? ... with complete authority to direct its affairs and ordain the destinies of the inmates? After all, some of the *sadhaks* – so they felt – had been doing quite well in their sadhana under the old dispensation. Why, then, this drastic change? Was it sanctified by Indian tradition? Would it work at all?

'The new dispensation meant: first, an unquestioning acceptance of her as the Mother; second, a total surrender to her of one's whole life; and third, a ready and happy submission to the discipline laid down by her for the smooth and efficient functioning of the Ashram. All this posed problems and difficulties for several of the sadhaks, especially some of the old-timers who had been used to a larger uninhibited "freedom." While some were openly critical of the new order, some merely found themselves unequal to the demands made upon them by the changed situation. Of course, people like Nolini, Amrita, Champaklal and Pavitra had already accepted unquestioningly whatever Sri Aurobindo proposed or approved. But it was otherwise with rebellious spirits like Sri Aurobindo's younger brother, Barin.'[28] (K.R. Srinivasa Iyengar)

Barin, after having come back from Bengal where his efforts to found centres and raise funds had borne little fruit, had been acting as a cook for Sri Aurobindo, looking after a small garden near the central Ashram building, and taking lessons in oil painting from the Mother. Though in his life he had often changed course without warning, he had always had great respect for his *sejda* and accepted his authority, but he seems not to have been able to accept his brother being replaced as head of the community by a French lady. He left the Ashram on 25 December 1929 without informing anyone beforehand. One of the Ashramites at the time writes: 'As the distribution was coming to a close, Nolinida* discovered that Barinda had not yet arrived and asked me to fetch him immediately. What a strange situation to find that Barinda was not in his room. By the time I returned to inform about it the Mother had gone up [to her room]. Next morning both Nolinida and Amrita visited Barin's room and found a letter addressed to Sri Aurobindo on a table. Later I learned that he had written to Sri Aurobindo and the Mother saying that he was leaving the Ashram.'[29]

When ten years later Nirodbaran remarked that 'Barin had great energy and capacity,' Sri Aurobindo commented: 'Yes, he had brilliance, but he was always narrow and limited. He wouldn't widen himself. *[Sri Aurobindo showed the widening by a movement of his hands above his head.]* That's why his things won't last. For instance, he was a brilliant writer and he also composed devotional poetry, but, because of his limitedness, nothing that will endure. He was an amusing conversationalist, he had some musical ability, he was good at revolutionary activity. He did well in all these matters, but nothing more. He was also a painter, but it did not come to much in spite of his exhibitions.'[30]

Barin – who left the Ashram at about the same time as Bejoy Nag, another original companion – played such an important role in Sri Aurobindo's life that he deserves to be taken leave of here. It is said that he wrote on 21 February 1940: 'Today is the Mother's birthday. On this blessed day this is a tribute at her feet from her erring child. Whatever my deviations into wrong paths, however grave my errors, my labyrinthine movements will at length lead me into the Temple of the Mother's consciousness, for where else except in the Mother's lap can her son find the end of his journey?'[31]

---

* In Bengali 'da' is the suffix added to the names of elder brothers or elder male persons for whom one wants to show respect.

Some were leaving but many more were coming, among them several of those who would be among the best known disciples. K.D. Sethna and his wife Daulat, both Parsis, joined the Ashram in 1927, when Sethna was twenty-three years old. Sri Aurobindo would name her Lalita, after one of the companions of Radha, and him Amal Kiran, meaning 'The Clear Ray.' (As most of his writings are published under the name K.D. Sethna, we will continue to use this name.) Sethna was 'a brilliant philosophy graduate' with a ready sense of humour and a broad 'Renaissance mind.' Besides his countless writings about Sri Aurobindo, the Mother and their yoga, he has published books on comparative religion, Christianity, the origin of the Aryans, science and the scientific paradigms, Greece and its culture, and on many other subjects. He is also considered the *primus inter pares* among the Ashram poets and was on this account held in high esteem by Sri Aurobindo. Sethna became the editor of *Mother India*, a publication started in 1949 and considered by Sri Aurobindo to be his mouthpiece. His contribution to the knowledge and understanding of the life and work of Sri Aurobindo and the Mother are invaluable.*

Chunnibhai Patel, whose Ashram name was Dyuman, settled in the Ashram a few months earlier than K.D. Sethna. When still a young boy he had had an intimation that nothing would satisfy him except the spiritual life. Though married at the tender age of eight, he had started seeking in the four corners of India for his guru, but without finding the right one. He had also been closely involved in the Non-cooperation Movement and knew personally leaders such as Vallabhbhai Patel and

---

* In *Our Light and Delight*, Sethna has an interesting anecdote about Rabindranath Tagore. 'Some time after I had settled here in December 1927, Tagore who was on a boat passing by Pondicherry stopped to pay a call on Sri Aurobindo. Nolini took him upstairs where at the other end of the meditation hall Sri Aurobindo was standing to receive him. [Sri Aurobindo had already withdrawn at that time.] As soon as Tagore entered and saw Sri Aurobindo he flung his cap away and ran towards him and made as if to embrace him. Sri Aurobindo extended his arms and caught Tagore's hands. Then they sat down for a talk. The Mother sat on a stool near Sri Aurobindo. 'Nolini was also present at the meeting and that is how we came to know what happened there ... When the interview was over, Nolini brought Tagore down, followed by the Mother who halted near the bottom of the staircase. Later Tagore asked Nolini: "Who was that lady sitting near Sri Aurobindo? Is she his secretary?" Nolini answered: "She is the Mother." Tagore exclaimed: "Oh, Mirra Richard? I could not recognize her."'

Mohandas K. Gandhi; with the latter he went on corresponding till 1947. In the Ashram, Dyuman was looked up to because of his reliability and steadfastness, and became the exemplar of 'the worker,' the *karmayogin*. The Mother put him in charge of the dining room and of everything in connection with the feeding of the Ashram population; she also made him one of the Ashram trustees.

Chandulal Shah and his younger sister Vasudha arrived in the Ashram in the beginning of 1928. Chandulal became the Ashram engineer. His sister, only fourteen or fifteen at the time, would be called 'My Little Smile' in the many letters and notes which the Mother wrote to her. The Mother also drew several portraits of her, now published in *The Mother: Paintings and Drawings*. Vasudha would become her personal assistant till illness prevented her from carrying out her duties any longer.

Together with Dilip K. Roy came Sahana Devi, 'whose music used to send Rabindranath Tagore into the seventh heaven of rapture.' (Iyengar). At that time the women members of the Ashram numbered 'hardly a dozen.' It is, however, important to point out that this was the only Ashram in India where women and men were treated on an equal footing, and where the communal life was led without discrimination. Sahana would give several recitals together with Dilip K. Roy. She was also one of the group of Ashram poets cultivated and directly inspired by Sri Aurobindo. He and the Mother considered all kinds of artistic inspiration and expression a help in the yoga and a direct opening to the higher, invisible worlds.

Another Ashram poet was the Englishman John A. Chadwick, 'stiff but polite,' whom Sri Aurobindo named Arjava. He was a philosopher of mathematics from Cambridge University, where he had been 'a distinguished Don as well as a Fellow of Trinity College.' He had discovered Rosicrucianism and, through Krishnaprem, also Sri Aurobindo, in whom he had found his guru and 'to whom he clung one-pointedly till his death.' (Dilip K. Roy) Arjava suffered from a complex of illnesses which were mysterious in origin and a nightmare to diagnose for Nirodbaran, the Ashram doctor, but which were very concrete in their ravaging effects. After receiving all possible inner and outer care and support in the Ashram, he finally collapsed in the train to Bangalore, on his way to be treated by a German specialist. 'Totalitarian' is one of

Arjava's poems, valued by Sri Aurobindo as 'exceedingly original and vivid – the description with its economy and felicity of phrase is very telling.'[32]

> Night was closing on the traveller
> When he came To the empty eerie courtyard
> With no name.
> Loud he called; no echo answered;
> Nothing stirred:
> But a crescent moon swung wanly,
> White as curd.
> When he flashed his single sword-blade
> Through the gloom,
> None resisted – till he frantic,
> Filled with doom,
> Hurled his weapon through the gloaming,
> Took no aim;
> Saw his likeness around him
> Do the same:
> Viewed a thousand swordless figures
> Like his own –
> Then first knew in that cold starlight
> Hell, alone.

The most improbable of all the poets in the Ashram was Nirodbaran Talukdar, the Ashram doctor just mentioned. Nirodbaran had obtained his medical degree in Edinburgh, as had Sri Aurobindo's father. Coincidentally he ran into Dilip K. Roy in Paris (around the time Roy met Richard in Nice); Roy went to visit Nirodbaran and the latter's niece in Edinburgh and talked to them about Sri Aurobindo and his own intention to become a member of his Ashram. It seems that it was actually the niece who, after their return to India in 1930, took Nirodbaran along to Pondicherry. Doctor Talukdar, considering himself an empiricist and very suspicious of spiritual hocus-pocus, was on his guard, but he was all the same touched by the Mother and Sri Aurobindo.

After some disastrous experiences in Burma, Nirodbaran returned to

Pondicherry and was accepted as a member of the Ashram. First he did some work in the building department; then he supervised the house painting department; after which he was put in charge of the timber godown – till he finally agreed to be put into his most useful function, that of Ashram doctor. As everything had to be reported to Sri Aurobindo via the Mother, Nirodbaran had to undertake an extensive correspondence with them. Against all expectations, Sri Aurobindo's tone in this correspondence became more and more confidential and humorous. It is no exaggeration to say that Nirodbaran's *Correspondence with Sri Aurobindo* is unique in spiritual literature, treating both the most elevated and the most down-to-earth subjects in a way never done before.

Nirodbaran, however, wanted also to become 'a literary gent' and looked up to poets like Sethna, Roy, Sahana, Harin and Nishikanto. Unfortunately, he lacked even the most elementary literary talent. But Sri Aurobindo started working on him, and Nirod blossomed into a fine surrealist poet, yet without being aware in the least how he wrote what he wrote or what was the quality of his poetic products. His testimony, in *Correspondence* with Sri Aurobindo and other books, to events in the life of Sri Aurobindo and the Mother is, along with that of Purani, Nolini and Sethna, priceless.

It is important in the life of the Mother and Sri Aurobindo to have an idea of the persons who surrounded them and who constituted an intimate and essential part of their spiritual effort. It is in their disciples that many loose ends in the life of the Masters are tied together. One regrets not being able, for reasons of available space, to write more about Ashram members like Nishikanto, the great Bengali poet, and many less well-known sadhaks, although the measure in which they are known is not necessarily equivalent to their spiritual realization, known to their gurus alone. Let us conclude with a woman who 'looked like a volley-ball on top of a balloon,' the quarrelsome Mridu.

Mridu was born in a village in Bengal in 1901, lost her husband early – a catastrophe for an Indian wife – and joined the Ashram in 1930. 'She was a great cook, one of the greatest, for she cooked for the Lord [Sri Aurobindo] for sixteen years. She would make choice dishes for Him and He had no choice but to have them, at least taste them.'[33] If Sri

Aurobindo for some reason did not touch them and she came to know of it, all hell broke loose. She would threaten, as on any occasion when she felt thwarted, to put an end to her life. Each time Sri Aurobindo had to console her, often with the words: 'Who will then prepare *luchis* for me?' – *luchis* being one of the delicious Bengali preparations.

Nirodbaran, however, writes in his *Twelve Years With Sri Aurobindo*: 'One regular interlude during [Sri Aurobindo's] meal was the arrival of our rampageous *luchi*-maker, Mridu. I do not know how she obtained this exceptional privilege. [Nobody was allowed to approach Sri Aurobindo.] She would come like an innocent lamb with incense and flowers, kneel down in front of the door and wait with folded hands for her "father's blessings." On our drawing Sri Aurobindo's attention to her presence, he would stop eating and cast a quiet glance at her. Her boisterous, unruly nature would become humble for a while before Sri Aurobindo. Whenever it was reported that she had manifested her violent temper, which was not infrequently, she was threatened with the loss of this *darshan*.' [34]

Stranger still, the Mother would talk much later about some deceased sadhaks who were together with Sri Aurobindo in his dwelling in the subtle worlds, after he had left his body in 1950. She named several of those sadhaks, and among them was Mridu! Which goes to show how difficult it is to judge by appearances with our ordinary human knowledge.

10.

The Laboratory

My children, you belong to a future that is being built, and it is here that it is being built.[1]

– The Mother

The Foundations

Everything was in place for the decisive phase of the effort to bring the Supramental down into Matter, to transform Matter, to divinize the world. Sri Aurobindo and the Mother had long known, from the early realizations in their yoga, that this apparently impossible step in evolution – evolution so much condensed and accelerated that it became revolution – was the Work they had come down to accomplish. Thanks to their intense sadhana they themselves were ready; now the representatives of humanity had come and joined them, and continued joining them. 'We have all met in previous lives,' said the Mother, 'otherwise we would not have come together in this life. We are of one family and have worked through the ages for the victory of the Divine and its manifestation upon Earth.'[2] Not only the pioneers, Sri Aurobindo and the Mother, had had to descend into Matter, but humanity had to follow. As Sri Aurobindo wrote: 'Since then the Sadhana as a whole has come down along with us into the physical consciousness. Many have followed – some immediately without sufficient preparation in the mind and vital, some holding on to the vital and mind and living still between the three, some totally but with a prepared mind and vital. The total descent into the physical is a very troublesome affair – it means a long and trying pressure of difficulties, for the physical is normally obscure, inert, impervious to the Light. It is a thing of habits, very largely a slave of the subconscient and its mechanical reactions ... We would have preferred to do all the hard work ourselves there and call others down when an easier movement was established, but it did not prove possible.'[3]

A young disciple put the following question to Sri Aurobindo: 'We believe that both you and the Mother are avatars. But is it only in this life that both of you have shown your divinity? It is said that you and she have been on the Earth constantly since the creation. What were you doing during the previous lives?' Sri Aurobindo gave the terse, unforgettable answer: 'Carrying on the evolution.' The young disciple, Nagin Doshi, replied: 'I find it difficult to understand so concise a statement. Can't you elaborate it?' Sri Aurobindo answered: 'That would mean writing the whole of human history. I can only say that as there are special descents to carry on the evolution to a farther stage, so also something of the Divine is always there to help through each stage itself in one direction or another.'[4]

The Mother from her side declared: 'Since the beginning of the Earth, wherever and whenever there was the possibility of manifesting a ray of Consciousness, I was there.'[5] An Ashram girl, in later years, asked her four questions. 'What is the right thing we should expect from You?' Answer: 'Everything.' – 'What have you been expecting from us and from humanity in general for the accomplishment of Your work upon Earth?' Answer: 'Nothing.' – 'From your long experience of over sixty years have You found that Your expectation from us and from humanity has been sufficiently fulfilled?' Answer: 'As I am expecting nothing I cannot answer this question.' – 'Does the success of Your work for us and for humanity depend in any way upon the fulfilment of Your expectation from us and from humanity?' – Answer: 'Happily not.'[6]

And Sri Aurobindo wrote to Nirodbaran, putting his and the Mother's work in perspective: 'The Divine also comes down into the cycle of rebirths, makes the great holocaust, endures shame and obloquy, torture and crucifixion, the burden of human nature, sex and passion and sorrow and suffering, manifests many births before he reveals the Avatar'[7] – as was the case now.

Such were the leaders of the impossible enterprise. But if the Avatar is the Divine, why does he need to go through all these trials and tribulations? Is the Divine not omnipotent, and if so, can he not change anything he wants in the twinkling of an eye? To put the question like this is to forget that *everything* is the Divine – the world he has manifested and also the laws of this world, the evolutionary process of it. The Divine in the Avatar has to submit to the conditions imposed by Himself. Sri Aurobindo has insisted on this point again and again: 'My sadhana is not a freak or a monstrosity or a miracle done outside the laws of Nature and the conditions of life and consciousness on Earth.' And: 'Certain conditions have been established for the game and so long as those conditions remain unchanged certain things are not done ... The Divine also acts according to the conditions of the game. He may change them, but he has to change them first, not proceed, while maintaining the conditions to act, by a series of miracles.'[8] Sri Aurobindo and the Mother, the Two-in-One, had come to change the conditions of the game.

Therefore they had to take the conditions upon themselves, into themselves. This is what all Avatars have had to do, be they Rama, Krishna, the Buddha or Christ. This, too, is why an Avatar, a direct embodiment of the Divine upon Earth, is indispensable in the process of evolution. Otherwise which element within a species would be sufficiently big, great, broad, large, to take the totality of the conditions upon itself? Or which element within a species could even conceive the need of a change, a transformation, a step ahead in the evolution? (The avataric intervention is not only valid for humanity; we find in the hoary knowledge of the Indian tradition also avatars effectuating the decisive change in the aqueous, amphibian and mammalian stages, and so on.)

Therefore their yoga had to be all-embracing, which is the reason why they called it 'integral.' 'The thing to be done is as large as human life,' Sri Aurobindo wrote, 'and therefore the individuals who lead the way will take all human life for their province. These pioneers will consider nothing as alien to them, nothing as outside their scope. For every part of human life has to be taken up by the spiritual – not only the intellectual, the aesthetic, the ethical, but the dynamic, the vital, the physical; therefore for none of these things or the activities that spring from them will they have contempt or aversion.'[9]

'[This Yoga] is new as compared with the old Yogas: 1. Because it aims not at a departure out of the world and life into Heaven or Nirvana, but at a change of life and existence, not as something subordinate or incidental, but as a distinct and central object ... Even the Tantra and Vaishnavism end in the release from life; here the object is the divine fulfilment of life. 2. Because the object sought after is not an individual achievement of divine realization for the sake of the individual, but something to be gained for the earth-consciousness here, a cosmic, not solely a supra-cosmic achievement ... 3. Because a method has been precognized for achieving this purpose which is as total and integral as the aim set before it, viz., the total and integral change of the consciousness and nature, taking up old methods but only as a part action and present aid to others that are distinctive ... Our Yoga is not a retreading of old walks, but a spiritual adventure.'[10] Thus wrote Sri Aurobindo.

He also wrote something to be remembered by all traditionalists and fundamentalists: 'The traditions of the past are very great in their own place, in the past, but I do not see why we should merely repeat them and not go farther. In the spiritual development of the consciousness upon earth the great past ought to be followed by a greater future.'[11]

As we have seen, the basic qualities to be developed in the Integral Yoga are aspiration, surrender, sincerity, and equality or equanimity. But 'it is always the psychic being that is the real, though often the secret cause of man's turning to the spiritual life and his greatest help in it,' we read in The *Synthesis of Yoga*. 'It is the very nature of the soul or the psychic being to turn towards the Divine Truth as the sunflower to the sun.'[12] The psychic being is 'the true evolving individual in our nature.' It is our central, true being that has taken the plunge into Matter for the joy of participating in the evolution and, in a supreme ecstasy of discovery, to become the divinity that it has been and will be in all eternity. Around the 'divine spark' the psychic being grows and develops, fed by its experiences in life after life. For this reason the realization of the psychic being was considered by Sri Aurobindo and the Mother as the first and fundamental of the three essential realizations of their yoga, the other two being the spiritual and the supramental.

During the working out of Sri Aurobindo's yoga, an important change had taken place. At the beginning he practised and recommended the technique of distancing the inner being from the outer, the Purusha from the Prakriti, according to the Sankhya system of yoga. Gradually, however, and especially after the final arrival of the Mother, he recommended more and more the complete turning of the whole soul and its personality towards the Mother. 'All creation and transformation is the work of the Mother,' [13] he would write. If, as somebody said, the Mother put Sri Aurobindo on a high pedestal, he from his side did the same with her. This important turn in the Integral Yoga was doubtlessly the result of his own experiences and explorations which we find described in *Savitri,* culminating in 'The Book of the Divine Mother.' To understand Sri Aurobindo and the Mother's venture, it is essential not to forget that she was an incarnation of the transcendent, cosmic and individual Divine Mother in a human body, just as he was an incarnation of the transcendent, cosmic and individual Ishwara in a human body. 'Either she is that or she is not' and he is that or he is not – and if they were and are not 'that,' the whole affair is a figment of the imagination, an elaborate fancy of the mind.

If she is 'that,' then she is the Mother of all souls, for the Divine Mother is evidently the mother of everything that is authentically divine or the Divine, and our souls are 'a spark', i.e. a portion of the Divine. This makes the centring of the Integral Yoga on the Mother a logical consequence not only because of the 'division of tasks,' which meant that the Mother was in front while Sri Aurobindo remained in retirement 'to work things out,' but also and essentially because she is the mother of all manifestation, and consequently of all changes in the manifestation, of all transformation. As the cosmic Mother she has brought this universe and all other possible universes into being; she sustains and guides the evolution as Mother Nature or Mother Earth.

Therefore Sri Aurobindo could write in a letter of 1929: 'The relation which exists between the Mother here and X (and between the Mother and all who accept her), is a psychic and spiritual motherhood. It is a far greater relation than that of the physical mother to her child; it gives all that human motherhood can give, but in a much higher way, and it contains in itself infinitely more. It can therefore, because it is greater and more complete, take altogether the room of the physical relation and replace it both in the inward and the outward life. There is nothing here that can confuse anyone who has common sense and a straightforward intelligence. The physical fact cannot in the least stand in the way of the greater psychic and spiritual truth or prevent it from being true. X is perfectly right when he says that this is his true mother; for she has given him a new birth in an inner life and is creating him anew for a diviner existence.'[14]

'By remaining psychically open to the Mother, all that is necessary for work or Sadhana develops progressively, that is one of the chief secrets, the central secret of the Sadhana,' wrote Sri Aurobindo. 'The object is transformation, and the transformation can only be done by a force infinitely greater than your own; it can only be done by being truly like a child in the hands of the Divine Mother.' And: 'Everyone who is turned towards the Mother is doing my Yoga. It is a great mistake to suppose that one can "do" the Purna [Integral] Yoga – i.e. carry out and fulfil all sides of the Yoga by one's own effort. No human being can do that. What one has to do is to put oneself in the Mother's hands and open oneself to her by service, by Bhakti, by aspiration; then the Mother by her light and force works in him so that the Sadhana is done.'[15]

Establishing the Ashram

> *You take up the path only when you think that you cannot do otherwise.*[16]
>
> – Sri Aurobindo

When reading the stories of some aspirants who became disciples of Sri Aurobindo and the Mother, we have seen that, in every case, time was given to them to think over their decision, even when they knew from the very first moment of meeting Sri Aurobindo and the Mother that their destiny lay with them. 'I never push anyone to take the path,' said the Mother. 'When you have started, you must go to the very end. Sometimes to people who come to me in a surge of enthusiasm I say: "Think it over, it is not an easy path. It will take time, it will need patience. You will need much endurance, much perseverance and courage and untiring goodwill. Look and see if you are capable of having all this, and then start. But once you have started, it is decided: there is no going back any more. You must go to the very end."' [17]

When Nirodbaran, influenced by Dilip K. Roy and others, wrote to Sri Aurobindo that he was fishing for disciples, Sri Aurobindo reacted sharply: 'Your image of fishery is quite out of place. I fish for no one; people are not hauled or called here, they come of themselves by the psychic instinct. Especially I don't fish for big and famous or successful men. Such fellows may be mentally or vitally big, but they are usually quite contented with that kind of bigness and do not want spiritual things, or, if they do, their bigness stands in their way rather than helps them ... The spirit cares not a damn for fame, success or bigness in those who come to it. People have a strange idea that Mother and I are eager to get people as disciples and if anyone goes away, it is a great blow, a terrible defeat, a dreadful catastrophe and cataclysm for us. Many even think that their being here is a great favour done to us for which we are not sufficiently grateful. All that is rubbish.' [18]

This being an Integral Yoga in which all aspects of life have to be tackled,* the prescription of fixed rules and guidelines was not feasible. (This has led to much confusion concerning the Integral Yoga, and a repeated effort, in spite of Sri Aurobindo and the Mother's integrality and openness, to write books about their 'system' of yoga.) The simple reason of this individuality of the way is that every human being is a unique and extremely complex whole. Not only does it consist of different layers and parts proper to it and to nobody else, it is also the outcome of a whole range of experiences through many lives, which may be momentarily hidden and forgotten, but which are the constituents of its soul and its adhara. All this is the material given to the human being to work out its yoga, the vibrations composing the individual, private field of it.

---

* The motto of Sri Aurobindo's great work, *The Synthesis of Yoga*, is: 'All life is yoga.'

'Each Sadhak has to be dealt with according to his nature, his capacities, his real needs (not his claims and desires) and according to what is best for his spiritual welfare,' wrote Sri Aurobindo. And also: 'Each one has his own way of doing Sadhana and his own approach to the Divine and need not trouble himself about how the others do it.'[19] 'I believe in a certain amount of freedom,' he said, 'freedom to find out things for oneself in one's own way, freedom to commit blunders even. Nature leads us through various errors and eccentricities. When Nature created the human being with all its possibilities for good or ill, she knew very well what she was about. Freedom for experiment in human life is a great thing. Without freedom to take risks and commit mistakes, there can be no progress.'[20] And in a letter he wrote: 'What the Mother wants is for people to have their full chance for their souls, be the method short and swift or long and tortuous. Each she must treat according to his nature.'[21]

'The long rope is needed,' he would write to Nirodbaran. And the Mother said: 'Everybody here represents an impossibility that has to be solved.'[22] The transformation of the physical consciousness into a Divine Consciousness is in itself an impossibility. Each sadhak and sadhika, son and daughter of Mother Earth, contained that impossibility in his or her person. The Integral Yoga of Sri Aurobindo and the Mother is intended to make the impossible possible. The collaborators in their yoga were therefore supposed to do the same, to begin with themselves.

One evening the Mother told her youthful audience in the playground: 'At the beginning of my present earthly existence I came into contact with many people who said they had a great inner aspiration, an urge towards something that was deeper and truer, but that they were tied down, subjected, slaves to the crude necessity of earning their living, and that this weighed them down so much, took up so much of their time and energy that they could not engage in any other activity, inner or outer. I heard this very often, I saw many such poor people – I don't mean poor from the financial point of view, but poor because they felt imprisoned in material necessity, narrow and numbing.'

'I was very young then, and I always used to say to myself that, if ever I had the possibility to do so, I would try to create a small world – just quite a small one, but still ... – a small world where people would be able to live without having to worry about food, lodging, clothing and the other imperative necessities of life, so as to see whether all the energies freed by this certainty of a secure material existence would turn spontaneously towards the divine life and the inner realization. Well, towards the middle of my life – I mean what is generally speaking the middle of a human life – the means were given to me and I could realize this, in other words create such conditions of life.'[23]

As we have seen, Mirra's first question when meeting Sri Aurobindo in 1914 was whether they would hew out the path in the jungle themselves first and then let the others follow, or whether all would go forward together. It proved to have been an important question, though it did not have to be answered by a voluntary decision: the circumstances, guided from Above, had brought the first collaborators to them as it were automatically, and all had started on the path together. 'The whole thing [i.e. the Ashram] has taken birth, grown and developed as a living being by a movement of consciousness (Chit-Tapas) constantly maintained, increased and fortified. As the Conscious Force descends in matter and radiates, it seeks for fit instruments to express and manifest it.'[24] (Sri Aurobindo)

'When people, born scattered over the world at great distances from one another, are driven by circumstances or by an inner urge to come and gather here,' said the Mother, 'it is almost always because they have met in some life or other – not all in the same life – and because their psychic being has felt that they belong to the same family. So they have taken an inner vow to continue to act together and collaborate. That is why, even though they are born far from one another, there is something which compels them to come together: it is the psychic being, the psychic consciousness that is behind. And only to the extent that the psychic consciousness is strong enough to order and organize life's circumstances, that is, strong enough not to allow itself to be counteracted by exterior forces, by exterior life movements, can these people meet. This is a profound truth of reality. There are large families of beings who work for the same cause, who have been together before in various numbers, and who come down [into the world] in groups as it were.'[25]

As such a 'family of beings' is formed by a higher Force in view of a particular aim, so it is constituted of elements which form a meaningful and effective whole in order to accomplish the aim. As the Mother said: 'I have a sampling here [in the Ashram] of all possible [inner] attitudes.'[26] And to the youth of the Ashram she said: 'From the occult point of view [you are] a selection. From the external point of view you might tell me that there are people in the world who are much superior to you and I won't contradict it. But from the occult point of view [you are] a selection. One can say without being mistaken that most of the young people who are here have come because they have been promised [in a former life] that they would be here at the time of the Realization. They do not remember this.'[27]

'This is the place of the Realization,' she averred. One can safely assume that from the very moment she was put in charge of the Ashram, she established and protected it in an occult way, like a *yantra*. We recall how she had experienced Sri Aurobindo's atmosphere, or aura, ten nautical miles out at sea on the occasion of her second arrival in Pondicherry. Now her atmosphere was joined and one with that of Sri Aurobindo. The innumerable reports of the special feeling people had and still have when visiting the Sri Aurobindo Ashram originate, without their being aware of it, in this invisible, extended and very strong presence that enabled the 'place of Realization' to survive and develop. There are many stories in ancient Indian writings about attacks by *Asuras*, *Rakshasas* and *Pishachas* on the sacred fires and on the ashrams of *Rishis* and other holy men. Far from being nothing but imagination, they refer to an occult fact all spiritual endeavours have to reckon with – especially an endeavour undertaken to bring to an end the realm of these hostile beings. It is little realized that an important aspect of the sadhana of Sri Aurobindo and the Mother consisted in acquiring and exerting the power to protect the cradle of their New Creation in Matter and all who became involved in it. 'The Ashram is a first form which our effort has taken, a field in which the preparatory work has to be done.'[28] (Sri Aurobindo)

The Mother and the Disciples

I am not eager to be the Guru of anyone. It is more spontaneously natural for me to be the universal Mother and to act in silence through love.[29]

– The Mother

'When someone is accepted, the Mother sends out something of herself to him and this is with him wherever he goes and is always in connection with her being here,'[30] wrote Sri Aurobindo. The Mother herself said: 'With those whom I have accepted as disciples, to whom I have said "yes," there is more than a tie, there is an emanation of me. This emanation warns me whenever it is necessary and tells me what is happening. Indeed I receive intimations constantly, but all are not recorded in my active memory, I would be flooded; the physical consciousness acts like a filter. Things are recorded in a subtle plane, they are there in a latent state, something like a piece of music that is recorded without being played. When I need to know with my physical consciousness, I make the contact with the subtle physical plane and the disc begins to turn. Then I see how things are, their development in time, the actual result.'[31]

What is an emanation of the Mother? Sri Aurobindo explained: 'The Emanation is not a deputy, but the Mother herself. She is not bound to her body, but can put herself out (emanate) in any way she likes. What emanates suits itself to the nature of the personal relation she has with the Sadhak which is different with each, but that does not prevent it from being herself. Its presence with the Sadhak is not dependent on his consciousness of it. If everything were dependent on the surface consciousness of the Sadhak, there would be no possibility of the divine action anywhere; the human worm would remain the human worm and the human ass the human ass, for ever and ever. For if the Divine could not be there behind the veil, how would either ever become conscious of anything but their wormhood and asshood even throughout the ages?'[32] This is obviously a quotation from his correspondence with Nirodbaran.*

What one might call a second, more intimate level of the contact of the Mother with the disciples was her 'self-identification' with them. As we know, 'identification' was held by Sri Aurobindo and the Mother to be the only possible way to real knowledge, as all other knowledge is ultimately based on sense data, which are unreliable, and on the mind, which cannot grasp a whole. 'All [real] knowledge is knowledge by identification. That is, one must become that which one wants to know,'[33] said the Mother.

Would a still closer contact be possible, a third level? The answer seems to be in the affirmative, for the Mother said about the first disciples: 'They were held as though in an egg-shell in my consciousness, so close, you know, that I could direct all their movements, both inner and outer, all the time. Everything was under complete control at every moment, night and day ... It was altogether true that I did the sadhana for them *all the time*!'[34] Not only was she permanently present with them by means of an emanation of her, not only did she know everything that was going on in them by identification: she carried their inner personality literally within her and did their sadhana, which was new and difficult for them.

We find this confirmed by Sri Aurobindo: 'The Mother by the very nature of her work had to identify herself with the Sadhaks, to support all their difficulties, to receive into herself all the poison in their nature, to take up besides all the difficulties of the universal Earth-Nature, including the possibility of death and disease in order to fight them out. If she had not done that, not a single Sadhak would have been able to practise this Yoga. The Divine has to put on humanity in order that the human being may rise to the Divine. It is a simple truth, but nobody in the Ashram seems to be able to understand that the Divine can do that

---

* Sri Aurobindo and the Mother both had a ready sense of humour. They could rarely express it, however, because most of the disciples lacked this sense, and as they took all Sri Aurobindo and the Mother's words literally and their acts seriously, what was of humorous intent could have had wrong consequences.

and yet remain different from them – can still remain the Divine.'[35] In another letter he wrote: 'The Mother does the sadhana in each sadhak – only it is conditioned by their zeal and receptivity.'[36]

This intimate nearness of the sadhaks with the Mother resulted in the Mother receiving all their calls for spiritual and occult help and assistance, for the sadhaks had been advised to live as if she was always present with them – which she was indeed – and to invoke her presence in case of any difficulty. Often such calls stopped the Mother in the middle of a sentence or a gesture, and this kind of work, together with her activities 'elsewhere,' kept her busy day and night. Sri Aurobindo had to answer several questions on this subject. One of his answers was: 'All knowledge is available in her universal self, but she brings forward only what is needed to be brought forward so that the working is done ... Mother can see what people are doing by images received by her in the subtle state which corresponds to sleep or concentration or by images or intimations received in the ordinary state; but much even of what comes to her automatically like that is unnecessary, and to be always receiving everything would be intolerably troublesome as it would keep the consciousness occupied with a million trivialities; so that does not happen. What is more important is to know their inner condition and it is this chiefly which comes to her.'[37]

Still, if so desired, she could play back 'the *disque*,' the recording in her universal consciousness, and know the facts which were relevant to be known, even if trivial. 'You don't expect her mind to be a factual encyclopaedia of all that is happening on all the planes and in all the universes? Or even on this earth, e.g. what Lloyd George* had for dinner yesterday?' asked Sri Aurobindo. 'Questions of consciousness, of course, she always knows even with her outmost physical mind. Material facts she can know but is not bound to do it. What would be true to say, is that she can know if she concentrates or if her attention is called to it and she decides to know. I often know from her what has happened before it is reported by anyone. But she does not care to do that on a general scale.'[38]

The Mother once said with a smile that time after time sadhaks who

---

* Lloyd George was a prominent British statesman at the time.

wanted to hide something from her came to her in the subtle physical telling her themselves what they were not going to tell her! And she spoke the following words, so limpid in their simplicity: 'Do not try to appear virtuous. See how much you are united, one, with everything that is anti-divine. Take your share of the burden, accept to be impure and false, and thus you will be able to take up the Shadow and offer it. And in the measure that you are capable of taking it and offering it, in that measure things will change.' [39]

Her intimate identity with the disciples also meant that she had to swallow all their 'human, all too human' reactions. Certainly, the real sadhaks were souls who had descended to participate in the Work and were impelled or called to the place of the participation, 'the place of the Realization.' But they were also very human. Wasn't it the humanity in them that had to be transformed – something that had become possible after Sri Aurobindo and the Mother had transformed their own humanity? Sri Aurobindo wrote pertinently to Nirodbaran: 'I have borne every attack which human beings have borne, otherwise I would be unable to assure anybody "This too can be conquered." At least I would have no right to say so.' And: 'You write as if I never had any doubt or any difficulty I have had worse than any human mind can think of. It is not because I have ignored difficulties, but because I have seen them more clearly, experienced them on a larger scale than anyone living now or before me that, having faced and measured them, I am sure of the results of my work.' [40] The same went for the Mother.

Now she had to receive all the dark impulses of humanity in the sadhaks she was helping to change – and through them of the hostile forces that, threatened in their existence, used the sadhaks to attack her. You must have practised a yogic discipline to know how, as soon as you take it up, everything contrary and adverse to it in yourself and around you will lift its head. The powers that rule the world do not like being questioned, contradicted or threatened; and as they are vicious by nature, their response is always inimical, often crushingly so. Whoever wants to do a yoga of transformation has to take up his cross, in a very real sense. The Mother was bearing the crosses, voluntarily, of all those who followed in her and Sri Aurobindo's footsteps and whom she had taken inside her consciousness.

We have no direct report of the difficulties in the sadhaks and sadhikas the Mother had to face. They were something confidential between her and her children – and she had known very well what was awaiting her when she took up the burden of the task. But sometimes we find an indirect glimpse of what was like a constant turmoil under an ostensibly placid surface. 'There are Sadhaks who at every step revolt, oppose the Mother, contradict her will, criticize her decisions,' wrote Sri Aurobindo; and in another letter: 'I have seen with what constant leniency, tolerant patience and kindness she has met the huge mass of indiscipline, disobedience, self-assertion, revolt that has surrounded her.' (Sri Aurobindo was not given to hyperbole.) And he wrote about 'the outward-mindedness and physical-mindedness that dominates the atmosphere.'[41]

One of the problems that cropped up on many occasions was that of the physical nearness to the Mother. There were people whom she saw more often than others because of material necessity or for other reasons. Sri Aurobindo had to intervene on numerous occasions.* 'The Sadhaks always imagine in their ignorance that when the Mother sees more of one person than of another, it is because of personal preference and that she is giving more love and help to that person. That is altogether a mistake. Physical closeness and contact can be a severe ordeal for the Sadhak; it may raise the vital demands, claims, jealousies, etc., to a high pitch; it may, on the other hand, leave him satisfied with an outer relation without making any serious effort for the inner union; or it becomes for him something mechanical, because ordinary and familiar, and for an inner purpose quite ineffective – these things are not only possible but have happened in many cases. The Mother knows that and her arrangements in this matter are therefore dictated by quite other reasons than those which are attributed to her.'[42]

Sometimes Sri Aurobindo was forced to put matters bluntly: 'Your physical mind cannot understand what the Mother does, its values and standards and ideas are not hers.' And: 'If people want to understand why the Mother does things, let them get into the same inner

---

* If on this subject there are more comments from Sri Aurobindo than from the Mother, it is because although the sadhaks sent their letters and notebooks to the Mother, they were answered by Sri Aurobindo.

consciousness from which she sees and acts.' Or: 'The Mother does not act by the mind, so to judge her action with the mind is futile.'[43]

Building a World in Miniature

All creation and transformation is the work of the Mother.[44]

– Sri Aurobindo

'During the years immediately after she had taken full charge of the Sri Aurobindo Ashram,' writes Iyengar, 'the Mother's resources – spiritual, human, material – had to be canalized simultaneously in multiple directions. With the steady increase in the number of sadhaks, there was a persistent need for renting more houses, reconditioning, fitting and furnishing them, and attending to their proper maintenance ... There were, besides, the permitted visitors. There was also the special influx of visitors at the time of the darshans ... The problem of accommodating and feeding them all admitted of no haphazard solution ...'

'All this meant the organization of a number of services: the Building Service, under Chandulal the engineer; the Atelier (Workshop) under Pavitra; the Garden Service; the Bakery and the Dining Room; the Domestic Service, a sort of 'Home Department,' to deal with the growing number of paid servants; 'Prosperity,' to arrange for the supply of everyday requirements of the sadhaks; the Furniture Service; and so on. Almost everything in the outside world had to be in the Ashram as well – but with a difference. The Ashram was verily a miniature world within the larger world that was Pondicherry, or India; it was also a world in a process of change or transformation.'[45]

It is interesting to follow the development of the Ashram in the correspondence of the Mother with her son André. Two months after the Siddhi Day, i.e. 16 January 1927, she wrote to him: 'Our community is growing more and more; we are nearly thirty (not counting those who are scattered all over India); and I have become responsible for all this; I am at the centre of the organization, on the material as well as the spiritual side, and you can easily imagine what this means.'[46]

One month later, on 16 February 1927: 'I think I told you about our five houses, four of which are joined in a single square block surrounded on all sides by streets and containing many buildings with courtyards and gardens. [This was what became the present central Ashram building.] We have just bought, repaired and made comfortable one of these houses [Library House] and then, very recently, we have settled there, Sri Aurobindo and myself, as well as five of the closest disciples.'

On 25 August 1929 the Mother sent a few photographs of the Ashram which 'at present consists of seventeen houses inhabited by eighty-five or ninety people (the number varies as people come and go).' On 23 August 1930, she wrote: 'The Ashram is becoming a more and more interesting institution. We have acquired our twenty-first house; the number of paid workers of the Ashram (labourers and servants) has reached sixty or sixty-five and the number of Ashram members (Sri Aurobindo's disciples living in Pondicherry) varies between eighty-five and a hundred. Five cars, twelve bicycles, four sewing machines, a dozen typewriters, many garages, an automobile repair workshop, an electrical service, a building service, sewing departments (European and Indian tailors, embroideresses, etc.), a library and reading room containing several thousand volumes, a photographic service and general stores containing a wide variety of goods, nearly all imported from France, large gardens for flowers, vegetables and fruits, a dairy, a bakery, etc., etc. – you can see that this is no small affair. And as I am taking care of all this, I can truly say that I am busy.' In a letter of 10 February 1933, she wrote to André: 'I would like to show you our establishment. It has just acquired four houses which I bought in my name to simplify the legal technicalities; but it goes without saying that *I do not own them.* I think I have already explained the situation to you. The Ashram with all its real estate and moveable property belongs to Sri Aurobindo, it is his money that enables me to meet the almost formidable expenses that it entails ... If my name appears sometimes (bank accounts, purchase of houses, of automobiles, etc.) it is, as I already told you, a matter of convenience for the papers and signatures, since I manage everything, but not because I really own them. You will readily understand why I an telling you all this; you can bear it in mind just in case.' For André was her legal heir.

There are several accounts of the Mother's daily occupations, the schedule of which changed through the years according to circumstances and necessities. Sri Aurobindo gives a general summary of them: 'The Mother's whole day from early morning and a large part of the night also has always been devoted to occupations connected with the Sadhana – not her own but that of the Sadhaks – Pranam, blessings, meditation and receiving the Sadhaks on the staircase and elsewhere, sometimes for two hours at a time, and listening to what they have to say, questions about Sadhana, results of their work or their matters, complaints, disputes, quarrels, all kinds of conferences about this or that to be decided and done – there is no end to the list; for the rest she had to attend to their letters, to reports about the material work of the Ashram and all its many departments, correspondence and all sorts of things connected with the contacts with the outside world, including often serious trouble and difficulties and the settlement of matters of great importance.'[47]

In one of her letters to André, the Mother writes: 'It is true that for a long time I have not slept in the usual sense of the word. That is to say, at no time do I fall back into the unconsciousness which is the sign of ordinary sleep. But I give my body the rest it needs, that is, two or three hours of lying down in an absolute immobility, but in which the whole being, mental, psychic, vital and physical, enters into a complete rest made of perfect peace, absolute silence and total immobility, while the consciousness remains completely awake; or else I enter into an internal activity which constitutes the occult work and which, needless to say, is also perfectly conscious. So I can say, in all truth, that I never lose consciousness throughout the twenty-four hours which thus form an unbroken sequence, and that I no longer experience ordinary sleep, while yet giving my body the rest it needs.'[48]

To understand the following communal activities, it should be recalled that the Mother had made the Ashram into a kind of occult force-field especially created to bring about a progress in the general sadhana, which was intended to lead to a physical transformation. At the centre of that force-field were Sri Aurobindo and herself, and the various elements constituting it were the sadhaks, the 'samples' of humanity present there to participate in the Great Work, the alchemic transformation of Matter. (This simile was used more than once by Sri Aurobindo and the Mother themselves. It has a profound meaning if one understands what alchemy really was about.) The Ashram activities or ceremonies may appear odd to the person who does not understand their occult rationale. Moreover, the word 'ceremony' in this case has no relation to religious ritual, which is a pre-established formal activity according to a fixed code; here it was a living, varying happening, kept up as long as it was useful and changed or dropped altogether when the need for it was no longer there.

For several years the first event of the day was a meeting of the Ashramites with the Mother called *pranam,* which means 'bowing, prostration, obeisance.' The sadhaks passed before the Mother one by one, offered her flowers, touched her feet, received the Mother's look, and received from her one or several flowers in return. 'When I give flowers,' she once explained, 'it is an answer to the aspiration coming from the very depth of your being ... I give you flowers so that you may develop the Divine qualities they symbolize. And they can directly transmit into the psychic all that they contain, pure, unalloyed. They possess a very subtle and very deep power and influence ... I can transmit a state of consciousness more easily to a flower than to a human being.'[49]

What became a problem was the sadhaks' interpretation of the Mother's look. They were unable to interpret it correctly, but tried to do it all the same, with perturbing consequences. The number of letters written to Sri Aurobindo about the Mother's look during Pranam are legion. The fundamental reason for their misinterpretations was that each sadhak read his own feelings, fears or expectations into her eyes. As the Mother said: 'From many instances I have come to know that my face is like a mirror showing to each one the image of his own internal condition.'[50] She also wrote: 'You ought to drop altogether and once for all this idea that I get displeased – it sounds to me so strange! If I would get thus displeased in the presence of human weakness, I would certainly not be fit to do the work I am doing, and my coming upon Earth would have no meaning.'[51] And she wrote to a sadhika: 'I am not looking at defects but at possibilities.'[52]

Still, the complaints about the Mother's smiling or not smiling, or her 'stern,' 'accusing' or 'reproachful' looks continued, in Nirodbaran's correspondence too, although Sri Aurobindo had written to him: 'All this about the Mother's smile and her gravity is simply a trick of the vital. Very often I notice people talk of the Mother's being grave, stern, displeased, angry at Pranam when there has been nothing of the kind – they may have attributed to her something created by their own vital imagination. Apart from that the Mother's smiling or not smiling has nothing to do with the sadhak's merits or demerits, [spiritual] fitness or unfitness – it is not deliberately done as a reward or punishment.' 'The Mother smiles on all without regard to these things. When she does not smile, it is because she is either in trance or absorbed, or concentrated on something within the sadhak that needs her attention – something that has to be done for him or brought down or looked at. It does not mean that there is anything bad or wrong in him. I have told this a hundred times to any number of sadhaks – but in many the vital does not want to accept that because it would lose its main source of grievance, revolt, *abhiman* [demanding or assertive pride], desire to go away or give up the Yoga, things which are very precious to it. The very fact that it has these results and leads to nothing but these darknesses ought to be enough to show you that this imagination about Mother's not smiling as a sign of absence of her grace or love is a device and suggestion of the Adversary.' [53]

Ashram life was very strict in the beginning, but the Mother knew human nature well enough to see to it that it had also its relaxed, more colourful moments. She even played games with the disciples, but always in view of the progress of the yoga and according to basic spiritual and occult truths and realities. The special aspect of their personality, their *anshan*, had its importance, and so had their names and their positions in relation to herself and the others.

For example, she made them choose, after a brief concentration, a text from a book 'at random.' The answer they got from the book, preferably a spiritual one, had a direct bearing on their personality or their inner state at the time of 'drawing' it. Or she made sentences using flowers, having the disciples guess the meaning of the sentence, for she had given a meaning to most of the flowers growing or known in South India. 'How do you give a significance to a flower?' somebody asked. The Mother answered: 'By entering into contact with the nature of the flower, its inner truth; then one knows what it represents.'[54] The significance she gave generally agreed with the one discovered in olden times and written down in the sacred texts of the Hindus, or in the texts of Ayurveda, the ancient medicinal art.

Then there were the birthdays of the sadhaks and sadhikas, which were considered special occasions by the Mother. 'It is truly a special day in one's life,' the Mother said to a young sadhak. 'It is one of those days in the year when the Supreme descends into us – or when we are face to face with the Eternal – one of those days when our soul comes in contact with the Eternal and, if we remain a little conscious, we can feel His Presence within us. If we make a little effort on this day, we accomplish the work of many lives as in a lightning flash ... This day is truly an opportunity in life. One is so open and so receptive that one can assimilate all that is given. I can do so many things [on this day], that is why it is important.'[55] The birthday, in other words, is a potential day of Grace.

And there were also the 'darshan days,' the highlights in the cycle of the Ashram year. *Darshan* means 'seeing,' and by implication the self-revelation of the Deity to the devotee. The three darshan days in the Sri Aurobindo Ashram were the only days on which the disciples could see Sri Aurobindo for a short while. On 15 August, his birthday, 24 November, the 'Siddhi Day,' and 21 February, the Mother's birthday, Sri Aurobindo and the Mother sat together in a small, specially arranged room in his apartment, and the disciples who had received permission to attend came in front of them one at a time, stood still for a moment, put their head on the feet of Sri Aurobindo if they felt like doing so, and received the blessings of both of them.

'In those early years, a day before the Darshan a list of the names of those participating in the Darshan used to be put up on a board. One and a half minutes were allotted to each person. The names of those permanently residing in the Ashram would come first in the list. Half an hour before the time given people would reach the meditation hall and wait for their turn. A copy of the list would be with the Master. From time to time he would look up the names of those coming in.'[56] (Narayan Prasad)

The Mother and Sri Aurobindo during their last darshan together, 1950

The Mother not only met the Ashramites several times a day in the central Ashram building, she also went to see them from time to time in their room, and also regularly visited the departments and looked at any work that was in progress. The following is a report of such a visit. 'Once I got the privilege to meet an elderly Sadhak who was in charge of building-construction at the Ashram in those days. He told me the following incident. "When I was hesitating to take the responsibility to construct the seaside wall of the Park Guest House [one of the Ashram guest houses] the Mother gave the contract to some company from Madras. They tried for two years, and one night disappeared when they could not succeed because of the constant interruption by the sea water. Then the Mother called me and said: 'This evening I am coming to the Park [Guest House]. You will meet me there.' She came and asked me how I could finish the construction. In a simple way I told Her that if there was no water I could complete it within a week. On this She said: 'Take me to the spot and show me up to where you want the water to remain.' I went into the sea up to knee-level. She concentrated for a moment and said in a definite tone: 'Bring your easy chair tomorrow and put it here. I give you a week's time to erect the foundation above the water level, and so long as your chair will be on this spot the water will not come.' And to the surprise of all of us, that was how it happened. After a week I came to inform Her and offer Her what had been achieved by Her grace and with full success."'[57] The wall is still very much there.

The Soup Distribution, also called the Soup Ceremony, took place in the evening. There are several narrations of it, all agreeing with the following recollection recorded in a talk by K.D. Sethna to the Ashram students. 'It was a very important function every evening. It impressed one like a snatch of the Ancient Mysteries. The atmosphere was as in some secret temple of Egyptian and Greek times. In subdued light, people would sit on mats in the hall which is now the Reception Room. At about eight the Mother would come down from the Prosperity Room upstairs and take her seat near the shaded lamp. Champaklal brought down a big cauldron of hot soup and placed it in front of her on a stool. Then the Mother would go into a trance. In the course of her trance her arms would stretch forward over the soup-cauldron. For a minute they would remain there as if she were pouring something of her subtle-physical spirituality into the liquid ... Then the Mother would open her eyes and Champaklal would remove the cauldron to one side and give her a big spoon. Each of us in turn would go and kneel before her and offer her our cup ... Sometimes in the middle of the pouring she would again be lost in meditation and we had to kneel there even for three or four minutes. Suddenly she would open her eyes and smile in a little shy or embarrassed way. After filling the cup she would take a sip from it.' [58]

As Sri Aurobindo explained: 'The soup [ceremony] was instituted in order to establish a means by which the Sadhak might receive something from the Mother by an interchange in the material consciousness.' [59] This peculiar ceremony was in fact an act of communion with the Mother's being intended to enable or accelerate the transformation of the physical being of the disciples. 'Have you not heard of divine Communion in this manner?' asked the Mother referring to the Christian transubstantiation when somebody inquired about the meaning of the ceremony. 'My flesh and blood are to go to you and form your flesh and blood, but instead of actually giving my flesh and blood to you, I sip the soup, put my force into it and give it to be drunk by you.' And Iyengar, who mentions this quote in his biography of the Mother, adds: 'It was as though the body and spirit of the Mother permeated the very cells and tissues of the sadhaks' being.' [60] Soup may be a more unusual substance than a wafer made of wheat, though both substances are unquestionably Matter. The fact of transference of the Mother's spiritualized substance to that of the disciples was a supreme act of spiritual occultism, and it was new because the Integral Yoga and its aim of physical transformation were new. Narayan Prasad wrote, however: 'It is a pity that we could not assimilate the effect.' [61]

The Mother's body was not an ordinary human body anymore (and neither was Sri Aurobindo's). We have already seen how refined and sensitive it had become after her occult schooling in Tlemcen and the sequence of experiences described in her *Prayers and Meditations.* 'Behind the physical body [of the Mother] there are many forms and powers and personalities of the Mother,' wrote Sri Aurobindo; and: 'She has many personalities and the body is plastic enough to express something of each when it comes forward.'[62] Many disciples and visitors have told how aspects of the Mother's physical appearance suddenly became god-like, or of seeing light or lights around her or through her. K.D. Sethna, though a devoted sadhak, was certainly not an uncritical ignoramus, as proven by his many-sided and well-reasoned published works. In one of his talks he narrates the following: 'Once there was a meditation and, as was my wont, I kept opening my eyes and looking around. After the meditation had progressed for some minutes they fell on the Mother. Well, I have never seen the Mother as I saw her then. She was no longer human. Her whole body appeared to have become magnified and there was a light pervading her and the face was of a Goddess. I can only say that it was the face of Maheshwari.'[63]

Why mention all this? Because it is related to the serious physical crisis the Mother went through in 1931. From 18 October to 24 November she had to withdraw and all her activities were suspended. On the latter date she wrote the last but one of her *Prayers and Meditations,* which she noted down rarely at that time. 'O my Lord, my sweet Master, for the accomplishment of Thy work I have sunk down into the unfathomable depths of Matter,' it went. 'I have touched with my finger the horror of the falsehood and the inconscience, I have reached the seat of oblivion and a supreme obscurity ... I know we are unworthy, I know the world is not ready. But I cry to Thee with an absolute faith in Thy Grace and I know that Thy Grace will save.'[64]

What had happened? One may presume that because of her continuous contact with the unregenerated physical substance of the disciples, the Mother was pulled down 'into the unfathomable depths of Matter' which are present in all of us. Her 'illness' was the outer expression of the battles she had to fight there. Sri Aurobindo wrote with concern to Nirodbaran on this subject: 'The Mother has had a very severe attack and she must absolutely husband her forces in view of the strain the 24th November [darshan day] will mean for her. It is quite out of the question for her to begin seeing everybody and receiving them meanwhile – a single morning of that kind of thing would exhaust her altogether. You must remember that for her a physical contact of this kind with others is not a mere social or domestic meeting with a few superficial movements which make no great difference one way or the other. It means for her an interchange, a pouring out of her forces and a receiving of things good, bad and mixed from them which often involves a great labour of adjustment and elimination and in many cases, though not in all, a severe strain on the body.'[65]

A week later he again wrote to Nirodbaran: 'I have not yet said anything about the Mother's illness because to do so would have needed a long consideration of what those who are at the centre of a work like this have to be, what they have to take upon themselves of human or terrestrial nature and its limitations and how much they have to bear of the difficulties of transformation ...' All the same, many months later he clarified some of this. 'The Mother by the very nature of her work had to identify herself with the Sadhaks, to support all their difficulties, to receive into herself all the poison in their nature, to take up besides all the difficulties of the universal Earth-Nature, including the possibility of death and disease in order to fight them out.'[66]

This is a *de facto* illustration of what 'those who are at the centre of a work like this' have to endure, and how concretely the Mother carried the disciples inside her and did their sadhana.

As the Mother herself explained: 'It is their mental and vital formation of me that they love, it is not myself. More and more am I faced with this fact. Everyone has made for himself an image of me in conformity with his needs and desires, and it is with this image that he is in contact, it is through this that he receives what few universal forces and still less supramental forces succeed in filtering through all these formations. Unfortunately these people cling to my physical presence, otherwise I could withdraw into my inner solitude and, from there, do my work quietly and freely; but this physical presence is for them a symbol and that is why they cling to it, for, in fact, they have very little contact with what my body truly is, and with the formidable accumulation of conscious energy it represents.'[67]

When the Mother had recovered somewhat, her early morning 'Balcony Darshans' started. Our old acquaintance, vociferous and stubborn Mridu, was involved in the coming about of these daily darshans. Prabhakar writes: 'Mridu-di took it into her head that no morsel of food would pass into her mouth until she had the Darshan of the Mother.

And so it happened, an event of great import to all of us. The Mother consented to appear on the "Old Balcony" – so Mridu could see the Mother from her window. Hundreds of others [every morning] were the beneficiaries. It would almost seem the Gods await some excuse to bless us only if we would keep still and maybe lower our heads and raise our eyes. Maybe Mridu-di was the excuse.'[68]

The Mother gave us some insight into what happened when she stood there on that balcony at the back of the main Ashram building. 'Every morning, at the balcony, after establishing a conscious contact with each of those who are present, I identify myself with the Supreme Lord and merge myself completely in Him. Then my body, completely passive, is nothing but a channel through which the Lord passes freely His forces and pours on all His Light, His Consciousness and His Joy, according to each one's receptivity.'[69] And to the Ashram youth she would explain: 'When I come out on the Balcony I make a special concentration. You notice that I look at everybody, don't you. I look from one to the other, I look, I see every one. I know all those who are there and why they are there, and I give each one exactly what he needs. I see his condition and give him what is needed ... That's the only reason why I come out, because otherwise I carry you in my consciousness. I carry you in my consciousness always without seeing you, I do the needful. But this [during the Balcony Darshan] is a moment when I can do it by touching the physical directly, you see; otherwise it is through the mind that it acts, the mind or the vital. But here I touch the physical directly through the sight, through the eye contact. That's what I do, each time.'[70]

Meanwhile, Sri Aurobindo continued his yoga in his apartment. Day after day, year after year he was battling there for the future of the world, to obtain the transformation of Matter which would radically and permanently change this 'vale of tears' into 'a world divine.' He had acquired such a mastery over his body that nobody could even suspect what was going on or what he was doing. 'All that was visible to our naked eye was that he sat silently in his bed [after the accident with his leg], afterwards in the capacious armchair, with his eyes wide open just as any other person would,' reminisces Nirodbaran about the years during which he was Sri Aurobindo's assistant. 'Only he passed hours and hours thus, changing his position at times and making himself comfortable; the eyes moving a little, and though usually gazing at the wall in front, never fixed *tratak*-like at any particular point. Sometimes the face would beam with a bright smile without any apparent reason, much to our amusement, as a child smiles in sleep. Only it was a waking sleep, for as we passed across the room, there was a dim recognition of our shadow-like movements. Occasionally he would look towards the door. That was when he heard some sound which might indicate the Mother's coming. When he wanted something, his voice seemed to come from a distant cave; rarely did we find him plunged within, with his eyes closed.'[71]

Sri Aurobindo has left us some glimpses of what was really going on in some of his poems and in his epic *Savitri*. A few stanzas from that chantingly simple and yet so profound poem 'A God's Labour,' written in 1935, must here suffice.

> I have been digging deep and long
>   Mid a horror of filth and mire
> A bed for the golden river's song,
>   A home for the deathless fire ...
>
> My gaping wounds are a thousand and one
>   And the Titan kings assail,
> But I cannot rest till my task is done
>   And wrought the eternal will ...
>
> A voice cried, 'Go where none have gone!
>   Dig deeper, deeper yet
> Till thou reach the grim foundation stone
>   And knock at the keyless gate.'
>
> I saw that a falsehood was planted deep
>   At the very root of things
> Where the grey Sphinx guards God's riddle sleep
>   On the Dragon's outspread wings.
>
> I left the surface gods of mind

And life's unsatisfied seas
And plunged through the body's alleys blind
    To the nether mysteries.

I have delved through the dumb Earth's dreadful heart
    And heard her black mass' bell.
I have seen the source whence her agonies part
    And the inner reason of hell ...[72]

Here poetry is not an intricate art of expression but the simplest, most concise way of recording occult and spiritual truth and fact – 'occult' because invisible to common mortals, but real and concrete for the ones involved in its working. When one realizes this, one also understands Sri Aurobindo's saying: 'My life was not on the surface for men to see' – and neither was the Mother's of course.*

Iyengar describes the years 1931-38 as 'the Golden Age of yogic correspondence in the Ashram.' 'We could write to Sri Aurobindo any time up to 11 p.m. when the Ashram gate closed,' reminisces Narayan Prasad. 'Letters were generally addressed to the Mother and left on a tray in a corner of the staircase near the door on the first floor. We received replies early next morning ... Heaps of letters, at times up to a hundred, received his attention every night.'[73] 'Champaklal would take the tray to Sri Aurobindo's room, where Sri Aurobindo read and discussed with the Mother the replies to be given ... Generally, it was Sri Aurobindo who wrote the replies, though occasionally the Mother might add a comment of her own or her blessings ... In the morning it was Nolini's responsibility to distribute the letters and notebooks to the sadhaks, and in course of time he became known as the Divine's postman.'[74]

Sri Aurobindo spent eight hours per day, sometimes more, on correspondence with the disciples. 'When people write four letters a day in a small hand closely running to some 10 pages without a gap anywhere and one gets 20 letters in the afternoon and forty at night (of course not all like that, but still!) it becomes a little too too,' he wrote to

---

* This makes a biographer very humble.

Nirodbaran. Three years later, when Nirodbaran asked if some poems he had sent for evaluation were hibernating, Sri Aurobindo answered: 'My dear sir, if you saw me nowadays with my nose to paper from afternoon to morning, deciphering, deciphering, writing, writing, writing, even the rocky heart of a disciple would be touched and you would not talk about typescripts and hibernation. I have given up (for the present at least) the attempt to minimize the cataract of correspondence.'[75]

It is obvious that Sri Aurobindo would not have undertaken such an epistolary labour if there was no profound reason for it. 'If I have given importance to the correspondence,' he explained, 'it is because it was an effective instrument towards my central purpose – there are a number of Sadhaks whom it has helped to awaken from lethargy and begin to tread the way of spiritual experience, others whom it has carried from a small round of experience to a flood of realizations, some who have been absolutely hopeless for years who have undergone a conversion and entered from darkness into an opening of light ... I think we can say that for the majority of those who wrote there has been a real progress. No doubt also it was not the correspondence in itself but the Force that was increasing its pressure on the physical nature which was able to do all this, but a canalization was needed, and this served the purpose.'[76]

It is because of this incredible effort of Sri Aurobindo's that we have so much information about the Integral Yoga, its problems and the way to tackle them. Nirodbaran's *Correspondence With Sri Aurobindo* alone comprises twelve hundred printed pages; Sri Aurobindo wrote about four thousand letters to Dilip K. Roy; his letters to Nagin Doshi have been printed in three volumes; K.D. Sethna has published much of his own ample correspondence; and the three volumes of *Letters on Yoga* (a selection) in Sri Aurobindo's Centenary Edition number altogether 1,774 pages.

Sri Aurobindo's reference to the positive effects of his correspondence allows us to understand that there were disciples in the Ashram who made substantial headway in their yoga. 'The quality of the sadhaks is so low?' he asked in answer to a remark by Nirodbaran. 'I should say there is a considerable amount of ability and capacity in the Ashram. Only, the standard demanded is higher than outside even in spiritual matters. There are half a dozen people here perhaps who live in the Brahman consciousness – outside they would make a big noise and be considered as great Yogis – here their condition is not known and in the [Integral] Yoga it is regarded not as siddhi but only as a beginning.'[77]

On the same subject Sri Aurobindo wrote to him: 'If you mean the Vedantic realization, several [in the Ashram] have had it. Bhakti realization also. If I were to publish the letters on sadhana experiences that have come to me, people would marvel and think that the Ashram was packed full of great Yogis! Those who know something about Yoga would not mind about the dark periods, eclipses, hostile attacks, despairings, falls, for they know that these things happen to Yogis. Even the failures would have become Gurus, if I had allowed it, with circles of Shishyas [disciples]!'[78]*

It would, however, be a mistake to suppose that Sri Aurobindo remained secluded in his apartment only writing letter after letter, having his meals, and doing his spiritual work sitting in his big armchair. He was after all the Mahayogi, the Great Yogi. He wrote about himself: 'In his retirement Sri Aurobindo kept a close watch on all that was happening in the world and in India and actively intervened whenever necessary, but solely with a spiritual force and silent spiritual action ... It was this force which, as soon as he had attained it, he used, at first only in a limited field of personal work, but afterwards in a constant action upon the world forces.'[79] In the next chapter we will give some illustrations of this assertion.

Time and again Sri Aurobindo complained confidentially to Nirodbaran that the correspondence prevented him from doing 'his real work.' His real work was, of course, the bringing down of the Supramental into Matter, upon Earth. The reader will recall that after the experiment of the overmental creation, the whole Yoga had descended into Matter and that the work there was like 'digging the earth.' Seven years later,

---

* Champaklal has the following significant anecdote: 'When Mother had her breakfast after [the] Balcony [Darshan], she said that she had come to know a very interesting thing. She had seen on the forehead of Mritunjoy's elder sister (who had just passed away), the symbol of Sri Aurobindo. Mother said she was very much surprised ... Then she heard Sri Aurobindo saying: "Henceforth whoever dies here [in the Ashram], I will put my seal upon him and in any condition unconditional protection will be given."' *(Champaklal Speaks,* p. 135)

on 4 April 1935, Sri Aurobindo wrote: 'I am too busy handling the confounded difficulties of Matter,' and the next day: 'Just now I am fighting all day and all night.' Reading *A God's Labour* may give added meaning to these prosaic words. One should also bear in mind that both Sri Aurobindo and the Mother were involved in this work.

On 11 April 1935 Sri Aurobindo wrote: 'I presume it [the Supramental Consciousness] will come anyhow, but it is badly delayed because, if I am all the time occupied with dramas, hysterics, tragic-comic correspondence (quarrels, chronicles, lamentations), how can I have time for this – the only real work, the only thing needful?' On 19 April, he wrote: 'Never has there been such an uprush of mud and brimstone as during the past few months ... It was not inevitable – if the sadhaks had been a less neurotic company, it could have been done quietly. As it is there is the Revolt of the Subconscient.' And on 14 May: 'It [the Supramental] was coming down before 24 November but afterwards all the damned mud arose and it stopped.'

Then, suddenly, on 16 August, a victory bulletin arrived from the avataric front: '[I] am travelling forward like a flash of lightning, that is to say zigzag but fairly fast. Now I have got the hang of the whole hanged thing – like a very Einstein I have got the mathematical formula of the whole affair (unintelligible as in his case to anybody but myself) and am working it out figure by figure.' This important milestone in his Yoga was reached the day before, on 15 August, his birthday. Soon he will declare, in a humorous, playful way, that he had got hold of 'the tail of the whale,' meaning the Supramental. And on 25 November he wrote: 'My formula is working out rapidly, but it has nothing to do with any Darshan descent. It is my private and particular descent, if you like, and that's enough for me at present. The tail of the supermind is descending, descending, descending. It is only the tail at present, but where the tail can pass, the rest will follow.'[80] It was a gigantic step forward, and everything Sri Aurobindo wrote on the subject leads us to suppose that he had the goal of the yoga in sight. But the Adversary was not to be underestimated.

One has to look back at the contemporary circumstances in Pondicherry to realize the extent of the Mother's effort in building up the

Ashram. She was behind every move, every initiative, every material realization, and she decided about the smallest details. And all this without a regular financial income, without stable resources. 'It has been an arduous and trying work for the Mother and myself to keep up this Ashram with its ever-increasing number,' wrote Sri Aurobindo in 1937, when there were more than 150 inmates, 'to make both ends meet and at times to prevent deficit budgets and their results ...'[81]

Until now the Mother had used, adapted and expanded the existing buildings and facilities, which even today are outstanding examples of the care spent on their upkeep. But in her was always a dream – or a memory seeking its permanent concretization? – of constructing, materially, visibly, a kernel of the new world she and Sri Aurobindo were trying to bring down on the Earth. In 1937, the first step towards a much larger undertaking, which would ultimately lead to Auroville (and the Aurovilles to come), took shape on a plot of land near the central Ashram building. Thanks to a grant from the Nizam of Hyderabad, obtained through his diwan Hyder Ali – who was a devotee of Sri Aurobindo and the Mother – she started building Golconde.

The chief architect was Antonin Raymond, a Czech and student of Frank Lloyd Wright, who had accompanied his teacher to Japan in 1923 to help rebuild Tokyo after a disastrous earthquake. There he had become acquainted with Pavitra, then still Philippe Saint-Hilaire, who now recommended him to the Mother. The architects assisting him were František Sammer, also a Czech, and George Nakashima, an American Japanese. The Ashram engineer was Chandulal, and Udar, a recent Anglo-Indian disciple formerly named Lawrence Pinto, was put in charge of the manufacturing of the tools, accessories and fittings, nearly all of which were custom-made.

Sri Aurobindo writes: 'In Golconde Mother has worked out her own idea through Raymond, Sammer and others. First, Mother believes in beauty as a part of spirituality and divine living; secondly, she believes that physical things have the Divine Consciousness underlying them as much as living things; and thirdly that they have an individuality of their own and ought to be properly treated, used in the right way, not misused or improperly handled or hurt or neglected so that they perish soon and lose their full beauty or value; she feels the consciousness in them and is so much in sympathy with them that what in other hands may be spoilt or wasted in a short time lasts with her for years or decades. It is on this basis that she planned Golconde.'[82]

About his work on Golconde, Antonin Raymond has written: 'We lived as in a dream. No time, no money were stipulated in the contract. There was no contract. Here indeed was an ideal state of existence in which the purpose of all activity was clearly a spiritual one. The purpose, as a matter of fact, of the dormitory [later to be used as a guest house] was not primarily the housing of the disciples; it was the creating of an activity, the materialization of an idea, by which the disciples might learn, might experience, might develop, through contact with the erection of a fine building. Time and money were of secondary value. This situation was quite other than the usual one of [the architect] being pinched between a client and a contractor. Here everything was done to free the architect completely so that he might give himself entirely to his art and science. And yet, simultaneously, on the job perfect order was maintained ... Under the invisible guidance of the leaders of the Ashram, whose presence was always felt, to whom daily all was reported, whose concern was the spiritual growth of each member of the community, I achieved the best architecture of my career.'[83]

The Second World War erupted and caused the construction of Golconde to take ten years, but the work went on even in the most difficult circumstances and in spite of price increases tenfold and more. The result is still there for all to see. But as people not familiar with the facts often suppose that statements concerning matters such as these are most often bloated by hype, the following statement about Golconde made at the Solar World Congress, held in Perth, Australia, in 1983, may be apropos: 'In one of the most remote parts of India, one of the most advanced buildings in the world was constructed under the most demanding circumstances concerning material and craftsmen. This reinforced concrete structure was completed primarily by unskilled volunteers with the most uncertain supplies, and with virtually every fitting custom-fabricated. Yet this handsome building has world stature, both architecturally and in its bio-climatic response to a tropical climate, 13°N of the equator.'[84]

11.
The Mother's War

I affirm again to you most strongly that this [the Second World War] is the Mother's war. You should not think of it as a fight for certain nations against others or even for India; it is a struggle for an ideal that has to establish itself on earth in the life of humanity, for a Truth that has yet to realize itself fully and against a darkness and falsehood that are trying to overwhelm the earth and mankind in the immediate future.[1]

– Sri Aurobindo (29 July 1942)

The Attack on Sri Aurobindo

The Ashram was flooded with visitors all looking expectantly forward to the 24 November darshan. The three annual darshan days were always festive occasions, for they were the only times when the disciples and devotees could see Sri Aurobindo up close. Many have reported their impressions. We quote here the experience of Rhoda Le Cocq, an American philosopher, as described in her book *The Radical Thinkers*: 'As a Westerner, the idea of merely passing by these two [Sri Aurobindo and the Mother] with nothing being said, had struck me as a bit ridiculous. I was still unfamiliar with the Hindu idea that such a silent meeting could afford an intensely spiritual impetus. I watched as I came up in line, and I noted that the procedure was to stand quietly before the two of them for a few silent moments, then to move on at a gesture of Sri Aurobindo. What happened next was completely unexpected.

'As I stepped into a radius of about four feet, there was the sensation

277

of moving into some kind of a force field. Intuitively, I knew it was the force of Love, but not what ordinary humans usually mean by the term. These two were "geared straight up"; they were not paying attention to me as ordinary parents might have done; yet, this unattachment seemed just the thing that healed. Suddenly, I loved them both, as spiritual "parents."

'Then all thought ceased, I was perfectly aware of where I was; it was not "hypnotism" as one Stanford [University] friend later suggested. It was simply that during those few minutes my mind became utterly still. It seemed that I stood there a very long, an uncounted time, for there *was* no time. Only many years later did I describe this experience as my having experienced the Timeless *in* Time. When there at *darshan*, there was not the least doubt in my mind that I had met two people who had experienced what they claimed. They *were* Gnostic Beings. They had realized this new consciousness which Sri Aurobindo called the Supramental.'[2]

In those November days of 1938, the focus of all attention in the Ashram was the newly arrived person who was also American: Margaret Wilson, the daughter of former President Woodrow Wilson. She had read books by Sri Aurobindo and the Mother and started corresponding with them. Sri Aurobindo had duly warned her before she undertook the long journey from the United States: 'We [i.e. he and the Mother] are doubtful about the advisability of your coming here next winter. Your illness [she had arthritis and other complaints] and the fact that you suffer from the heat stand in the way.'[3] Nonetheless, Miss Wilson had persisted in her intentions and had recently arrived. Sri Aurobindo, at her request, had given her the Sanskrit name Nishta.

During the night before the darshan of 24 November all was quiet, for everybody had gone to rest in order to be fit the following morning. As on every night, a lamp remained lit in the apartment of Sri Aurobindo. As on every night, one could hear the breakers of the nearby sea roar and hissingly splash onto the beach. Then the unexpected happened. The narrator is Nirodbaran.[4]

'Breaking the profound silence the emergency bell rang from the Mother's room. Purani [who was always on night-duty] rushed up and found the Mother at the top of the staircase. She said, "Sri Aurobindo has fallen down. Go and fetch Dr. Manilal." Fortunately, he had come for the Darshan from Gujarat. Soon he arrived and saw that Sri Aurobindo was lying on the floor in his bedroom. On the way to the bathroom he had stumbled over a tiger skin.' Devotees had presented him with several panther and tiger skins. He had struck the tiger skull with his right knee. When failing to get up, he must have called the Mother in an occult way. The Mother had rung the emergency bell. 'When we other doctors came up, we saw Dr. Manilal examining Sri Aurobindo's injured leg. The Mother was sitting by Sri Aurobindo's side, fanning him gently. I could not believe what I saw ... But I soon regained my composure and helped the doctor in the examination ... Finally the doctor pronounced that there was a fracture of the thighbone.'

The Superintendent of Cuddalore hospital was called, and so were an orthopaedic surgeon and a radiologist from Madras. They arrived late at night, and their verdict was 'an impacted fracture of the right femur above the knee'; the two fragments were firmly locked together. 'Both the specialist and the radiologist took a serious view of it,' writes Nirodbaran, then the Ashram doctor. Sri Aurobindo's limb was put into traction.

The impact of the news of Sri Aurobindo's accident on the disciples and devotees was shattering. Not only were they deeply distressed because they had to forgo Sri Aurobindo's darshan – a smiling Mother gave darshan alone in the evening – they were also flabbergasted at the fact that somebody like Sri Aurobindo could meet with an accident. With hindsight, we can reconstruct the circumstances as follows.

Every darshan was a dangerous affair for Sri Aurobindo and still more for the Mother. The Mother once said that a Titan had been born together with her whose only aim was to counteract everything she did, and if possible to eliminate her. In his correspondence with Nirodbaran, Sri Aurobindo wrote in February 1934: 'There is usually a descent [at darshan time], but there is also a great opposition to the descent at these times.'⁵ In the first volume of the *Talks With Sri Aurobindo* we read: 'The hostile forces have tried many times to prevent things like the Darshan, but I have succeeded in warding off all their attacks. At the time the accident to my leg happened, I was more occupied with guarding the Mother and I forgot about myself. I didn't think the hostiles would attack me. That was my mistake.'⁶ And when somebody asked him: 'But how could the accident happen?' he answered: 'It was because I was unguarded and something forced its way into the subconscient. There is a stage in yogic advance when the least negligence will not do.'⁷

The hostile forces are, as we know, real and conscious beings. They exist in a double hierarchy. There is, on the one hand, the hierarchy descending from the Asuras (mental and higher vital) downwards via the Rakshasas (lower vital) to the Pishachas (lowest vital); there are, on the other hand, the hierarchies descending in uncountable strata of beings cascading, as it were, from the main forces in each of the three categories. The lower categories are always with us; they amuse themselves with us and cause the numerous difficulties which make our lives miserable. To the higher ones we ordinary human beings are hardly important. The atmosphere around Sri Aurobindo and the Mother was mostly free of the presence of the lower and lowest hostile beings. The attack on Sri Aurobindo must have been executed by or at the instigation of one of the very great dark gentlemen, the Lord of Falsehood himself. Why?

We have seen that Sri Aurobindo had been making considerable headway in bringing down the Supramental since 1935, the time he discovered his 'Einsteinian formula.' Several accounts mention that he and the Mother expected the manifestation of the Supramental into the Earth-atmosphere in 1938. K.D. Sethna testifies, writing about himself in the third person: '[The Mother] had told him that she was expecting something great and decisive in the course of the year [1938] and that he should be back from Bombay, where he had to go for family matters, before the event. The sadhak's reference [in his diary] ran: "This is the year in which, I believe, the Truth-Consciousness may make up its mind, or rather its Supermind, to descend. I was expecting a wire from the Mother in May. She had mentioned approximately the middle of the year and had promised to inform me at once.'⁸

The 'tremendous resistance' had become visible in the black and brown forces of Fascism and Nazism in Europe. If the reader wonders what these forces had to do with Sri Aurobindo and the Mother's evolutionary effort, the answer is that they had everything to do with it, as will be explained shortly. The rise of Hitler, who became Chancellor of the German Reich in 1933, paralleled the occult Aurobindonian effort. Events were heading for a climax, and a general mobilization in Western Europe was ordered towards the end of 1938. Meanwhile the Spanish Civil War, the 'rehearsal' for the worldwide war to come, was fought; a militarized Japan expanded aggressively in the East; Mussolini wanted to revive the honour of Italy on the model of ancient Rome; and Stalin, after having demonically ravaged his own people and eliminated his top military cadres, remained a riddle nobody managed to decipher.

It is clear that the Second World War could have started a year before it actually did. As Nirodbaran puts it: 'There was a strong possibility that fighting would break out in December, just a week or two after the night of November 23, when Sri Aurobindo had his accident. But, as he indicated in our talks, his Force pushed it back to a later date, for war at that time would have been a great hindrance to his work. It is possible to surmise that the irresistible forces which no human power could check turned their fury on one who had checked them.'[9] On 14 December 1938 Nirodbaran asked Sri Aurobindo: 'Did you stop war the last time there was a chance of it?' – Sri Aurobindo: 'Yes – for many reasons war was not favourable at that time.' Nirodbaran: 'But you stopped it at the humiliation of some Great Powers?' – Sri Aurobindo: 'I did not care for that.'[10] On the one hand the Great Powers in question had not hesitated to betray a helpless Czechoslovakia and showed little greatness in their dealing with the Axis; on the other hand, even if they had been worthy of consideration, the descent of the Supramental, or the preparation for its descent, immeasurably surpassed all that in importance.

On 22 October 1938 the Mother wrote a letter to her son André. 'Speaking of recent events, you ask me "whether it was a dangerous bluff" or whether we "narrowly escaped disaster." To assume both at the same time would be nearer to the truth. Hitler was certainly bluffing [at Munich] ... Tactics and diplomacy were used, but on the other hand, behind every human will there are forces in action whose origin is not human and which move consciously towards certain goals. The play of those forces is very complex and generally eludes the human consciousness. But for the sake of explanation and understanding, they can be divided into two main opposing tendencies: those which work for the fulfilment of the Divine Work upon Earth and those which are opposed to this fulfilment. The former have few conscious instruments at their disposal. It is true that in this matter quality by far compensates for quantity. As for the anti-divine forces, they have only too much to choose from and always find minds which they enslave and individuals they turn into docile but nearly always unconscious puppets.' [11]

After the accident, Sri Aurobindo's way of life changed drastically. Until then the Mother and Champaklal, his faithful attendant, had been the only persons to enter his apartment freely. Now a team was formed to look after him. It consisted mainly of disciples who were medical doctors: Nirodbaran, Becharlal, Satyendra, and, when he visited, Manilal; the laymen were Mulshankar, who had some medical training, Champaklal and Purani. 'Little by little the air of unfamiliarity gave way as Sri Aurobindo began to take cognizance of the new situation and the new conditions that were around him,' writes Nirodbaran. [12] The Mother also changed her schedule to make Sri Aurobindo's recovery the centre of her daily occupations. She served his meals, combed his hair and supervised his daily exercises when he started the re-education of his leg by walking on crutches.

There was a time, however, that the Mother was in a state of almost continuous trance. We know how often she was silently called upon by disciples or devotees in physical or psychological distress. 'Wherever people call the Divine in any form, I answer their call.' [13] Not only did she have to answer these kind of calls, the times were also full of sudden geopolitical turns which could lead to possible disaster – not to speak of the personal attacks she and Sri Aurobindo had to withstand and the unseen battles they had to wage. In December 1938 Sri Aurobindo said to Dr. Manilal: 'I am not occupied with details of occult working. I have left them to the Mother. She often hears what is said at a distance, meets sadhaks on the subtle planes, talks to them. She saw exactly what was going to happen in the recent European trouble. We know whatever we have to know for our work.' [14] Moreover, intending to postpone the war is one thing, postponing it in actual fact is quite another, which required of both of them constant occult attention and 'putting of the Force.'

Nirodbaran writes about the Mother's frequently recurring trance states: 'It was a very trying phase, indeed. She would enter Sri

Aurobindo's room with a somnolent walk and go back swaying from side to side leaving us in fear and wonder about the delicate balancing. Sri Aurobindo would watch her intently till she was out of sight, but it was a matter of surprise how she maintained her precarious balance. Sometimes in the midst of doing his hair, her hand would stop moving at any stage; either the comb remained still or the ribbon tied to his plaids got loose. While serving meals too, the spoon would stand still or the knife would not cut, and Sri Aurobindo had, by fictitious coughs, to draw her out. Fifteen minutes' work thus took double the time and then she would hasten in order to make up for it.

'Such trance moods were more particularly manifest at night during the collective meditation below, and in that condition she would come to Sri Aurobindo's room with a heap of letters, reports, account books, etc., to read, sign or answer during Sri Aurobindo's walking time. But her pious intentions would come to nothing, for no sooner did she begin than the trance overtook her. Sri Aurobindo took a few extra rounds and sat in his chair watching the Mother while she with a book open, pen in hand, had travelled into another world from whose bourne it was perhaps difficult to return. He would watch her with an indulgent smile and try all devices to bring her down to earth ... During meditation too, her condition was most extraordinary. Someone coming for Pranam would remain standing before her trance mood from fifteen to thirty minutes, another had her hand on his bowed head for a pretty long time; all was unpredictable.' [15]

After things had settled down and everybody got used to the new situation, those privileged to be in Sri Aurobindo's presence learned how to draw him into conversation. The most complete record of these informative conversations are Nirodbaran's four volumes of *Talks With Sri Aurobindo*, covering the period from the accident up to August 1941. He confesses that he has omitted recording at least a third of the talks because of laziness or negligence. In his defence it must be said that he and Champaklal slept every night in Sri Aurobindo's room and that he sometimes had to note down the conversations at an ungodly hour and after a full day's work. Gradually he became Sri Aurobindo's amanuensis. His constant presence with his Master from 1938 to 1950 has made his *Twelve Years With Sri Aurobindo* indispensable reading for anyone interested in Sri Aurobindo and the Mother's life.

Nirodbaran writes about the talks: 'There was not a subject that was not touched, not a mystery he did not illumine, not a phenomenon that passed unnoticed, humorous or serious, superficial or profound, mundane or mystic. Reminiscences, stories, talks on art and culture, on world-problems poured down in abundant streams from an otherwise silent and reticent vastitude of knowledge and love and bliss. It was an unforgettable reward he accorded to us for our humble service.'[16] 'Sri Aurobindo had a pure Cambridge accent,' writes Udar, 'and if you didn't see him, you'd think it was an Englishman speaking.'[17]

Thanks to Sri Aurobindo's obedient execution of all prescribed exercises, and maybe still more to his yogic force, all impediments to the healing of his leg were overcome. 'Sri Aurobindo's rapid progress became widely known and people began to clamour for a Darshan.'[18] Thus the fourth annual darshan came about on 24 April, the anniversary of the Mother's final arrival in Pondicherry. 'The devotees would simply come and stand for a brief while before the Mother and the Master, have their darshan and quietly leave ... Formerly the Darshan was performed with great ceremonial pomp. Starting at about 7:30 a.m. it ran, with one breathing interval, up to 3 p.m. The devotees offered their garlands and flowers, did two, even three or four pranams to the Mother and the Master, who remained glued to one place throughout the ordeal.'[19]

'The Lord of the Nations'*

We feel that not only is this a battle waged in just self-defence and in defence of the nations threatened with the world-domination of Germany and the Nazi system of life, but that it is a defence of

---

* For a more extensive treatment of the subject dealt with in this section, see chapter sixteen of the author's book *Beyond Man*.

civilization and its highest attained social, cultural and spiritual
values and of the whole future of humanity.[20]

– Sri Aurobindo (19 September 1940)

In the already partly quoted letter of October 1938 to her son André, the Mother continued: 'Hitler is a choice instrument for these anti-divine forces which want violence, upheavals and war, for they know that these things delay and hinder the action of the divine forces. That is why disaster was very close although no human government consciously wanted it. But there was to be no war at any cost and that is why war has been avoided – for the time being.'[21]

It is no exaggeration to say that the Second World War has still not been understood, in spite of the thousands of volumes dedicated to it and the fascination it continues to exert on mankind. The reason why its rationale escapes the common understanding is that it has to be sought outside the boundaries of 'objective' thinking, which is the only way in which academic historians are able to view the subjects of their studies. 'It is a universal failing of writers on Hitler to assume that there is nothing mysterious or difficult to understand about him,' writes Kimberley Cornish. 'Yet if we ignore the moral dimension of what he wrought – its overwhelming wickedness – then it seems to me that Hitler has a claim to rank as the most extraordinary man the continent of Europe has ever produced. What did he discover that allowed him to do what he did? The truth is that no one has any idea.'[22]

Louis Pauwels writes: 'It is well known that the Nazi party proved itself to be anti-intellectual in a blunt and even boisterous manner, that it burned books and classified the theoretical physicists among the "Judeo-Marxist" enemies. It is less well-known in favour of which explanations of the world it rejected the official Western sciences. And still less is known about the concept of the human being on which Nazism was based, at least in the minds of some of its leaders. When knowing this, it is easier to situate the last World War within the framework of the great spiritual conflicts; history regains the breath of the Legend of the Ages.'[23]

'One can say that Hitler is not a devil but is possessed by one,' said Sri Aurobindo;[24] he also called him 'an infrarational mystic.' Sri

Aurobindo and the Mother knew perfectly well by which power Hitler was possessed. '[Hitler] was a medium, a very good medium,' said the Mother later. 'Besides, he became possessed during séances of spiritism. It is then that he was seized by those fits which were described as epileptic. They were not epileptic: they were crises of possession. It was because of this that he had a kind of power, which was not very great for all that. But when he wanted to know something from the Power, he went and retired in his castle, and there, in "meditation," he truly invoked very intensely what he called his "God," his supreme God, who was the Lord of the Nations … It was a being that appeared to him in a silver armour, with a silver helmet and a golden aigrette. It was magnificent. And [it appeared] in a light so dazzling that the eyes could hardly see and bear that blaze. It was on such occasions that [Hitler] had his fits … That being is the "Lord of the Nations." And it is not even the Lord of the Nations in his origin, it is an emanation of the Lord of the Nations, but a very powerful emanation.'[25]

From this and the facts of Hitler's life we may draw some conclusions. Hitler was an ordinary human being, with a soul and a rather elementary, sentimental but cruel psychological makeup, once compared by Sri Aurobindo to that of a street criminal with the psychic being of a London cab driver. (Stalin, on the contrary, was not human, in the sense that he did not have a soul but was a direct incarnation of a vital being.) 'It is the vital possession that gives [Hitler] his size and greatness,' said Sri Aurobindo. 'Without this vital Power he would be a crudely amiable fellow with some hobbies and eccentricities. It is in these kind of people whose psychic is undeveloped and weak that possession is possible. There is nothing in the being that can resist the Power.'[26]

Hitler went through an occult schooling that is not difficult to trace. It is well-known that he was profoundly influenced by the likes of Dietrich Eckart, who initiated him in the legend of Thule and developed his mediumistic faculties, and Karl Haushofer, responsible for most of Hitler's geopolitical views including the need of *Lebensraum* for the German people. The 'palace' mentioned by the Mother was Hitler's villa *Berghof* on the Obersalzberg at Berchtesgaden, in the Alps, called by his biographer John Toland 'Hitler's place of inspiration.'

Hitler was a tool of the 'Lord of the Nations,' who, in fact, is the

Lord of Falsehood. This Asura, whom the Mother failed to convert in the person of Paul Richard, is already known to us. The important role he played throughout her life and that of Sri Aurobindo, and throughout the history of the twentieth century, becomes increasingly clear. The crux of everything Hitler stands for, and of the series of wars in the twentieth century of which the Second World War was the most devastating, is simply the action of the demonic forces that rule the world. They have tried, with all possible means, to crush Sri Aurobindo and the Mother's endeavour to bring their rule to an end, which is the precondition to transform the existing world into a better, divine world. 'Hitler stands for diabolical values or for human values exaggerated in the wrong way until they become diabolical (e.g. the virtues of the Herrenvolk, the master race),' wrote Sri Aurobindo. 'The victory of one side (the Allies) would keep the path open for the evolutionary forces; the victory of the other side would drag back humanity, degrade it horribly and might lead even, at the worst, to its eventual failure as a race, as others in the past evolution failed and perished.'[27]

Very few people, even when familiar with the Nazi doctrines and those of the SS, the 'Order of the Death's Head,' are aware of the deeper layers of Adolf Hitler's inspiration. One person he allowed a glimpse into his thought processes for some time was Hermann Rauschning, who published their conversations in *Hitler Speaks*. There he writes: '[Hitler] saw his own remarkable career as a confirmation of hidden powers. He saw himself as chosen for superhuman tasks, as the prophet of the rebirth of man in a new form. Humanity, he proclaimed, was in the throes of a vast metamorphosis. A process of change that had lasted literally for thousands of years was approaching its completion ... One thing is certain: Hitler has the spirit of the prophet. He is not content to be a mere politician.

'... "Yes," Hitler continued, "man has to be passed and surpassed. Nietzsche did, it is true, realize something of this in his way. He went as far as to recognize the superman as a new biological variety. But he was not too sure of it. Man is becoming God – that is the simple fact. Man is God in the making. Man has eternally to strain at his limitations. The moment he relaxes and contents himself with them, he decays and falls below the human level. He becomes a quasi-beast. Gods and beasts, that is what the world is made of ... But those who listen to the immemorial message of man, who devote themselves to our eternal movement, are called to a new humanity. Do you now appreciate the depth of our National Socialist movement? Can there be anything greater and more all-comprehending? Those who see in National Socialism nothing more than a political movement know scarcely anything of it. It is more even than a religion: it is the will to create mankind anew ...'" [28]

One may be surprised to detect in those words as it were the shadow of Sri Aurobindo and the Mother's vision of the divinization of the world which is to result in a divine superman. Hitler could hardly have invented all that by himself. The inspiration could only have been distilled into his mind by his 'God,' the Lord of Falsehood, even if it was partly communicated or taught to him through intermediaries like Eckart and Haushofer. The pieces of the puzzle fit neatly together and prove that what was at stake immensely surpassed anything that anybody realized. 'The Vital World has descended upon the Physical,' said Sri Aurobindo. 'That is why the intellectuals are getting perplexed at the destruction of their civilization, of all the values they had made and stood for. They deny the worlds beyond the physical and so they are bound to be perplexed.' [29]

As early as the beginning of February 1939, Sri Aurobindo and the Mother stated the global problem clearly. In Sri Aurobindo's reported words: 'The problem is to save the world from domination by Asuric (Demonic) Forces. It would be awful to be ruled by the Nazis and Fascists. Their domination will let loose on mankind what are called the Four Powers of Hell – obscurantism, falsehood, suffering and death. Suffering and death mean the horrors of war.' [30] The Four Powers of Hell are none other than the powers of the four great Asuras.

The Ashram in Difficulty

Understanding of the significance of the war was badly lacking in the Ashram. 'Unfortunately, in the Ashram itself there were some who wished for Hitler's victory, not for love of Hitler but because of their hatred of British domination,' writes Nirodbaran.[31] The reasoning went as follows: the British are the enemies of India, for they are the colonial power that is occupying it and bleeding it dry; the Germans and their allies are the enemies of the British; therefore the Germans and their allies are the friends of patriotic India. Among the Ashramites there were, as we have seen, former freedom fighters, and for them the above was a matter of elementary logic. Besides, had not Sri Aurobindo himself been one of the foremost freedom fighters? 'Many, especially in India, were rather happy that England was attacked,' confirms Udar. 'Indians, still under the British rule, felt that if England were defeated, India would be free.'[32]

This kind of reasoning was strengthened by the fact that many idealistic Ashramites chose the side of Subhash Chandra Bose. His close friend in the Ashram was Dilip K. Roy, who at one time had tried to entice him into becoming an Ashramite. Subhash C. Bose was a Bengali who, like Sri Aurobindo, had studied at Cambridge University as a candidate for the Indian Civil Service. He had, however, submitted his resignation before being enlisted and entered nationalist politics under the aegis of C.R. Das, the lawyer-turned-politician who had defended Sri Aurobindo in the Alipore Bomb Case and remained a friend ever since. The gifted and ambitious Bose rose quickly to the top and became, in 1927, Joint General Secretary of the Congress with Jawaharlal Nehru.

Bose became fascinated by the Fascist dictators and went to Europe to meet them personally. In 1938 he was elected national president of the Congress. He clashed, inevitably, with Mohandas K. Gandhi and founded within the Congress his Forward Bloc. In 1941 he escaped the watchful eye of the British and reached Germany after an adventurous journey. There he founded the Indian Legion. But he became dissatisfied with Hitler's assistance to India's cause and sought the help of the Japanese who had advanced close to India's borders. With Japanese help Netaji S.C. Bose – 'Netaji,' like Führer, Duce and Caudillo, means 'Leader' – founded in South Asia the Indian National Army and a provisional government.

The following quotation from Nirodbaran's *Talks With Sri Aurobindo* gives an idea of the urgency of the situation that had developed in the Ashram. Sri Aurobindo: 'It seems it is not five or six of our people but more than half that are in sympathy with Hitler and want him to win.' – Purani (laughing): 'Half?' – Sri Aurobindo: 'No, it is not a matter to laugh at. It is a very serious matter. The [French] Government can dissolve the Ashram at any moment. In [French] Indo-China all religious bodies have been dissolved. And here the whole of Pondicherry is against us. Only because Governor Bonvin is friendly towards us can't they do anything. But even he – if he hears that people in the Ashram are pro-Hitler – will be compelled to take steps, at least expel those who are so. If these people want that the Ashram should be dissolved, they can come and tell me and I will dissolve it instead of the police doing it. They have no idea about the world and talk like children. Hitler is the greatest menace that the world has ever met. If Hitler wins, do they think India has any chance of being free?'[33]

'I have all my life been wanting the downfall of the British Empire,' Sri Aurobindo said, 'but the way it is being done is beyond all expectation and makes me wish for British victory. And if I want that England should win, it is not for the Empire's own sake but because the world under Hitler will be much worse.'[34] He also said: 'The Asura is more concerned with us than anything else. He is inventing new situations so that we may fall into difficulty.'[35]

The seriousness of the situation made Sri Aurobindo and the Mother publicly declare their standpoint. They did so on two occasions. The first one was in the form of a contribution to the Viceroy's War Purposes Fund, 'made as a token of a complete adhesion to the Allied cause.' Nirodbaran writes: 'When India was asked to participate in the war effort, and the Mother and Sri Aurobindo, much to the surprised indignation of our countrymen, contributed to the War Fund, he, for the first time made clear to the nation what issues were involved in the War … He stated that the War was being waged "in defence of civilization and its highest attained social, cultural and spiritual values and the whole future of humanity …" Giving the lead, he acted as an example for others to follow. But all over the country protests, calumnies and insinuations were his lot. Even his disciples were nonplussed in spite of his explanation why he had made that singular gesture.'[36] What Nirodbaran does not write is that many accused the Mother, a French subject, of influencing Sri Aurobindo and turning him from his nationalist path towards the Allies.

The second occasion was the Cripps Offer, also called the Cripps Proposals. Great Britain, fully engaged in its life-or-death struggle with the Powers of the Axis, wanted to make sure that India, its 'Jewel in the Crown,' would be unreservedly on its side. Therefore on 11 March 1941 Winston Churchill announced that the War Cabinet had agreed upon some proposals which would solve the crisis in India. Sir Stafford Cripps, Lord of the Privy Seal and leader of the House of Commons, 'would proceed as soon as possible to India to explain personally the solution agreed upon by the Cabinet.' What Cripps had to propose was dominion status, 'free to remain in or to separate itself from the equal partnership of the British Commonwealth of nations.'

Sri Aurobindo perceived immediately the advantages and possibilities for India. 'If the Congress can get Dominion Status without any fighting or struggle,' said Sri Aurobindo, 'I don't see why it shouldn't accept it. It can build our defence after that and when that is ready, it can easily cut off the British connection. You get all you want without any unnecessary struggle. When you can secede at your will from the British connection, it is practically independence.'[37] And the Mother said: 'India ... must realize the Grace that is behind this offer. It is not simply a human offering. Of course its form has been given by the human mind, and it has elements of imperfection in it. But that does not matter at all ... My ardent request to India is that it should not reject it. She must not make the same mistake that France has made recently [when refusing a close confederation with Great Britain] and that has plunged her into the abyss.'[38]

Sri Aurobindo and the Mother sent Duraiswamy to New Delhi in order to plead for acceptance of the proposals with the leaders of the Congress Party. Duraiswamy was an advocate from Madras who had been a trusted disciple for many years and who had rendered many services to his gurus, although he did not live in the Ashram. Nirod-baran describes Duraiswamy's departure: 'The scene is still fresh in our memory. It was the evening hour. Sri Aurobindo was sitting on the edge of his bed just before his daily walking. All of us were present. Duraiswamy, the distinguished Madras lawyer and disciple, was selected as the envoy, perhaps because he was a friend of Rajagopalachari, one of the prominent Congress leaders. He was to start for Delhi that very night. He came for Sri Aurobindo's blessings, lay prostrate before him, got up and stood looking at the Master with folded hands and then departed.'[39]

The Congress leaders, some of whom might not have forgotten nor forgiven Sri Aurobindo's withdrawal from politics, did not act on his recommendation. As Indra Sen, who accompanied Duraiswamy, related: 'We met the members [of the Congress leadership] individually and the sense of the reactions was more or less to this effect: Sri Aurobindo has created difficulties for us by his message to Cripps.' Sri Aurobindo had sent Cripps a telegram in appreciation of his proposals. 'He doesn't know the actual situation, we are in it, we know better, and so on.'[40] However, had they listened to that 'unknowledgeable' Sri Aurobindo the partition of India and its dismal aftermath might never have happened. In his brief biography of the Mother, Wilfried quotes *The Oxford History of India* on the matter: 'So the golden moment passed and with it the last real chance of establishing a united independent India. The rejection of the offer was the prelude to the partition.'[41]

Interventions

We have seen with what emphasis Sri Aurobindo stressed that the Second World War was the Mother's war. This does not mean that it was not his too, of course, and we will learn about several interventions which he made. Moreover, as he wrote about himself in the third person: 'In his retirement Sri Aurobindo kept a close watch on all that was happening in the world and in India and actively intervened whenever necessary, but solely with a spiritual force and silent spiritual action.'[42]

We remember that Sri Aurobindo said that he was neither an impotent moralist nor a weak pacifist (see p. 120). 'It is part of the experience of those who have advanced far in Yoga that besides the ordinary forces and activities of the mind and life and body in Matter, there are other forces and powers that can act and do act from behind and from above;

there is also a spiritual dynamic power which can be possessed by those who are advanced in the spiritual consciousness, though all do not care to possess or, possessing, to use it, and this power is greater than any other and more effective. It was this force which, as soon as he had attained it, he used, at first only in a limited field of personal work, but afterwards in a constant action upon the world forces. He had no reason to be dissatisfied with the results or to feel the necessity of any other kind of action.'[43] The same evidently goes for the Mother.

The Second World War was not the outcome of politics, economic systems, or national or racial relations gone wrong, although all this played a role in it. It was fundamentally, as we have seen above, about the destiny of the world. It was, after the First World War, the greatest eruption of forces in a century which produced the changes that are leading to an acceleration in the long evolution of the Earth. 'The Allies stand on the side of the revolutionary forces,' wrote Sri Aurobindo. 'I have not said that at random, but on what to me are clear grounds of fact ... We made it clear in a letter that we did not consider the war as a fight between nations and governments (still less between good people and bad people) but between two forces, the Divine and the Asuric ... The victory of one side (the Allies) would keep the path open for the evolutionary forces; the victory of the other side would drag back humanity, degrade it horribly and might lead even, at the worst, to its eventual failure as a race, as others in the past evolution failed and perished. That is the whole question and all other considerations are either irrelevant or of a minor importance.'[44]

This means that this world war was directly related to the turning away of the four fundamental divine Powers from their Origin, thereby becoming the four great Asuras who are at the basis of our world and who have ruled over it throughout its history despite the opposition of the gods. It is true that in the course of humanity's evolution the gods have conquered their share of the world, as proven by the rise of the religions, but it is equally true that all religions have been perverted by the Asuras and their underlings, and that the anti-divine powers still rule the world. To convert or eliminate the Asuras and make the descent of a divine world on Earth possible was the mission of Sri Aurobindo and the Mother. It was also what the Second World War was about.

The reader may recall how in the Beginning the Universal Mother turned towards 'the Lord' and prayed that he should redeem what had gone wrong. At that moment the Lord ordered the Mother to infuse her divine Love into the manifestation. This resulted, on the one hand, in the creation of the Gods, on the other in 'ensouling' the manifestation – an ensoulment that on the occult side of the evolution has led to the World Soul being individualized in the many souls of humanity, and in the building up of the individual psychic being in every human being.

When we connect the Mother's role in the evolutionary action with what was at stake in the Second World War, and consider that the Mother on Earth embodied the transcendent, universal and individual Mother, it becomes intelligible why Sri Aurobindo called this war 'the Mother's war.' Udar narrates in his *Reminiscences* that, at the beginning of the Second World War, when Sri Aurobindo still gave Hitler a fifty-fifty chance of becoming the Ruler of the World, the Lord of Falsehood often came to the Mother to 'boast about all the troubles and defeats he was inflicting on the Allies.'[45] The Mother herself has said that she and the Asura often met and conversed with one another. 'After all,' she said, 'I am his mother,' and: 'There is a very profound relation.' For who else but she had emanated him and his three companions, and who else was responsible for the manifestation as it is? There is nothing but That, and she was (and is) That in its Creative Aspect.

The Mother and Sri Aurobindo followed the events in every possible detail. They read the newspapers, especially the *Hindu,* but the reports were often days behind the events. Therefore they also followed every evening without fail the news bulletins of the B.B.C. There was no radio set in the Ashram, but Udar had a large radio set with all that was necessary to receive the B.B.C. So every night Pavitra, together with Pavita, went to his house to listen to the 9:30 news. Pavita, an English woman whose civil name was Margaret Aldwinckle, had been the secretary of Paul Brunton, the still widely-read writer on occult and spiritual matters, before she became an Ashramite. 'Pavita would take the news down in shorthand, go home, type it out and send it to Sri Aurobindo, so that he could read the news the same night ... Later on, when the situation became grave, they had a radio set installed in the Ashram. I think in those days the whole programme of the Ashram was arranged in such a way that Sri Aurobindo could be free to listen to the B.B.C. broadcast.'[46]

We have already seen that Sri Aurobindo and the Mother postponed the war in 1938 and how the Asura retaliated with a direct attack on Sri Aurobindo. Another of their interventions was at Dunkirk towards the end of May 1940. The German tanks had steamrolled through Belgium and the Belgian king, Leopold III, had surrendered. At once the British Expeditionary Force was cut off from its reserves and its ports, and was on the verge of surrendering or being annihilated. 'There is no way out for them unless Dunkirk can hold on or if they can rush through the gap from the French line,'[47] said Sri Aurobindo. This was a crucial situation, for, if the B.E.F. was eliminated, Great Britain would be practically defenceless and Hitler, without much additional effort, would have become the Master of Europe and, according to Sri Aurobindo, possibly of the world.

'Inwardly, he [Sri Aurobindo writes about himself] put his spiritual force behind the Allies from the moment of Dunkirk when everybody was expecting the immediate fall of England and the definite triumph of Hitler, and he had the satisfaction of seeing the rush of German victory almost immediately arrested and the tide of war began to turn in the opposite direction.'[48] To this day nobody knows why Hitler, who could easily have crushed the B.E.F., hesitated and finally let Göring do the job with his bombers – a job which he bungled. And nobody knows why literally out of the blue, in those sunny days of May, a fog descended over the region. 'Not only was Dunkirk itself enshrouded but all the Luftwaffe fields were blanketed by low clouds which grounded their three thousand bombers,' writes John Toland in his biography of Adolf Hitler.[49] When the Luftwaffe finally got into action, a ragtag fleet of about 900 ships and boats had carried 338,226 British and Allied troops across the Channel between 24 May and 4 June, and the war could be continued. '[The British] were saved by divine intervention during this war,' said Sri Aurobindo a few months later. 'They would have been smashed if Hitler had invaded England at the right time, after the fall of France.'[50]

One of the problems for the Mother and Sri Aurobindo was that at first they did not find on the side of the Allies a suitable human instrument for their action. As history tells us, the Allied statesmen who played a part in the developments before the outbreak of the war were not of impressive calibre. But then Winston Churchill became prime minister of Great Britain. He showed a capacity of leadership and strength that inspired every one on the allied side and gave them enough confidence to pursue the battle with the Axis. Maggi Lidchi-Grassi, who was close to the Mother, writes: 'The Mother told the author of how Sri Aurobindo used to tell her of the words that he would put into the mouth of Churchill before the famous broadcasts, and certain passages were spoken by Churchill word for word. I have not found any written references to this in the texts written on Sri Aurobindo, but his secretary Nirodbaran had heard of this, and Dyuman ... has confirmed it ... Anu Purani tells me that her father A.B. Purani, one of the few people who saw Sri Aurobindo every day, told her the same thing.'[51] Udar too confirms this.[52]

For a reader of the four volumes of *Talks* as noted down by Nirodbaran, Sri Aurobindo's insight into Hitler's intentions and manoeuvres, and his foreknowledge of the turn events would take are simply amazing. He took Hitler's programme as spelled out in *Mein Kampf* seriously and knew of his intention to exterminate the Jewish race at a time when many in and outside Germany were still praising the Führer to the skies. When Neville Chamberlain, the British prime minister, was gushing about 'peace for our time,' Sri Aurobindo, after seeing a photograph in a newspaper, compared Hitler at Munich to a spider ready to pounce on a fly, Chamberlain. He saw that, after Dunkirk, the British fleet was the only force able to resist Germany and that therefore the French fleet should at no price fall into Hitler's hands. It did not; most of it fell into British hands and the rest was sunk at Toulon by its own crews. He saw that Hitler, pushed from behind by the Asura, was aiming for world domination.*

He saw that Hitler's ultimate aim, however far-fetched this may seem to the academic student of history, was the conquest of India, because it was the guardian of the spiritual destiny of the world. 'It is a very simple

---

* For a detailed analysis, see Georges Van Vrekhem, *Hitler and his God: The Background of the Nazi Phenomenon*, 2006.

thing to see that Hitler wants world domination and that his next move will be towards India,' Sri Aurobindo said on 23 May 1940. He thereby confirmed his words of a few days earlier: 'It is a well-known fact that Hitler has an eye on India. He is openly talking of world empire. He will turn towards the Balkans, crushing Italy on the way, which would be a matter of three weeks, then Turkey and then Asia Minor. Asia Minor means ultimately India. If there [in Asia Minor] he meets Stalin, then it is a question as to who wins and comes to India.' Hitler had been instructed in Indian occultism and mysticism by Eckart and Haushofer, and, besides, he was the instrument of the Asura, who knew best of all what India stood for. This explains the simultaneous pincer movement of the Axis Powers (through southern Russia, Africa and the Middle East) and Japan (through Burma) towards the Indian subcontinent. That such was in fact Hitler's intention has been documented in my book *Beyond Man*.

But there were other diabolic forces incarnated on the Earth and, as they are all big, unyielding egos, they fought each other even as they fought everybody else. One of these other hostile forces, and perhaps the most ruthless of them all, was Joseph Stalin. It has already been mentioned that, according to Sri Aurobindo and the Mother, Stalin was not an ordinary human, but a directly incarnated vital being with no soul. As in the case of so much else concerning Sri Aurobindo and the Mother, this assertion is supported by facts, and Stalin's dire deeds are recorded in history for all to read.

In 1939 he made a secret pact with Hitler, but no one could doubt that both dictators only wanted to gain time before springing at each other's throat. Hadn't Hitler made abundantly clear in *Mein Kampf*, and in so many speeches, what he thought of Communism and of the Slav peoples, those 'subhumans'? As early as June 1940 Sri Aurobindo had said: 'I think the next war will be between Russia and Germany.'[53] It was indeed. Hitler launched Operation Barbarossa against Russia in June 1942 to the consternation and desperation of all experienced officers in the *Wehrmacht*, who knew that at that point Germany was unable to fight a war on two fronts and who were proved right in the end. Sri Aurobindo had said earlier that he had never seen a person who followed the dictates of the Asura as faithfully as Hitler. Had the Asura made a mistake in this case?

The occult fact is that on a certain occasion the Mother took the place of the Lord of Falsehood and persuaded a hesitant Hitler – the plans for Operation Barbarossa had been ready for months but the attack was postponed several times – to go ahead with the invasion of Russia. Two days later the guns started thundering, the Stukas screaming, the tanks rolling. We find the Mother's occult intervention confirmed by Udar, who writes that 'the Mother told me this the very next morning after her visit to Hitler'; by K.D. Sethna, who wrote about it in *Mother India*; and by the Mother herself who talked about it in at least two recorded conversations, the first one on 5 November 1961, the second on 12 January 1965.[54] The reader will remember her description of the way the Lord of Falsehood appeared to Hitler as his God. (If she knew this, she must have known a lot of other things about which she never said a word. 'People have no idea of what is going on [in the occult plane], they know nothing,' she would say.) However, on returning from her meeting with Hitler she met the Asura, who was furious and promised to do as much damage as possible before she would be able to dissolve him back into his Origin.

We remember how the Mother saved Paris in 1914 by preventing the Germans from taking 'the cultural capital of the world.' She seems to have done the same during the Second World War. On 13 June 1940, when the Germans were less than thirty kilometres from Paris, Sri Aurobindo said: 'Paris has been the centre of human civilization for three centuries. Now he [Hitler] will destroy it. That is the sign of the Asura. History is repeating itself. The Graeco-Roman civilization was destroyed by Germany,'[55] at the time of the Germanic invasions into the Roman Empire. True, Hitler did not give the order to destroy Paris as long as he had it in his grip, but he did so the moment he saw that it was going to escape him. Collins and Lapierre, in their bestseller *Is Paris Burning?*, quote the order from the German headquarters, which was Hitler's order: 'Paris must not fall into the hands of the enemy, or, if it does, he must find there nothing but a field of ruins.' But the Mother was guarding the metropolis where she had spent the first part of her life, for she said later, in a recorded conversation on 5 November 1961, that an emanation of her had been protecting Paris 'every night of the last war.'[56] And Collins and Lapierre write that on the day of its liberation 'every Parisian looking out of his window ... could gaze at one of the wonders of the war: Paris was unharmed.'

Regretfully, the published *Talks With Sri Aurobindo* go only as far as the first days of 1941, with rare exceptions. The main reason why the *Talks* stopped was, according to Nirodbaran, that Sri Aurobindo became more and more silent and concentrated. 'In the last years there was practically a silent attendance on a silent Presence.'[57] This was most probably due to the huge occult task he and the Mother were involved in hour after hour. The Mother would later talk about the constant tension they were subjected to, and that the Asura's aim of the war was precisely to bring their yogic realization to a halt. They had no choice but to fight the Asura, for otherwise they were not sure that they would be able to effect the supramental manifestation before the Earth had been completely subjected by the hostile forces or destroyed by them.

It may be supposed that the Mother and Sri Aurobindo also directly intervened in the Battle of Stalingrad and in bringing the USA into the war. There is, however, one more intervention of theirs of which we are certain: the halting and reversal of the Japanese invasion of India. On 19 March 1944 a Japanese army of 230,000 men crossed the Indian border in the Northeast and headed towards the town of Imphal. Three thousand soldiers from Bose's Indian National Army took part in it. It was 'a forgone conclusion' that Imphal would fall, in spite of the dogged resistance by the British and Indian troops loyal to the British Crown. But suddenly the monsoon rains poured down, more than a month early, and 'the Japanese chances of success were washed away,' writes Hugh Toye. 'It became a military catastrophe of the first magnitude.'[58]

Sri Aurobindo writes about himself in the third person: 'When negotiations [with Stafford Cripps] failed, Sri Aurobindo returned to his reliance on the use of spiritual force alone against the aggressor and had the satisfaction of seeing the tide of Japanese victory, which had till then swept everything before it, change immediately into a tide of rapid, crushing and finally immense and overwhelming [Allied] victory.'[59] Nirodbaran describes how at one point the situation for the Allies was desperate everywhere, in Africa, in Asia, in Europe. Then he continues: 'At this jubilant moment of the enemy, India's destiny intervened. A heavy downpour from heaven inundated the dense Assam jungles for days together, so that, bogged in the flood and mud, the invading [Japanese] army with its [Indian] liberation force had to liberate itself from the wrath of Nature and beat an ignominious retreat. Yet rain during that season had never been heard of before.' [60]

When the Second World War, which is still casting its shadows upon us, came to an end, the Mother wrote the following prayer: 'The Victory has come, Thy Victory, O Lord, for which we tender to Thee infinite thanksgiving. But now our ardent prayer rises towards Thee. It is with Thy force and by Thy force that the victors have conquered. Grant that they do not forget it in their success and that they keep the promises which they have made to Thee in the hours of danger and anguish. They have taken Thy name to make war, may they not forget Thy grace when they have to make the peace.' [61]

The war ended when the Japanese Emperor Hirohito, addressing the nation directly for the first time in history, broadcast on 15 August 1945 a message declaring the unconditional capitulation of his country. Fifteenth August is the birthday of Sri Aurobindo.

The Coming of the Children

On 2 December 1943 the Mother started a school for about twenty children. The threatening presence of the Japanese troops on India's borders, its attempt at invasion and a few minor bombardments had frightened the population, and many Bengalis who had relatives in the Ashram sought refuge there. Of course they brought their children with them. As the Mother said later: 'When people found out that Pondicherry was the safest place on Earth [because of Sri Aurobindo's and her own protection], and when they arrived here with a throng of small children and asked if we could give them shelter, we could not send them back, could we?' [62]

She went on to say that in the early years life in the Ashram was 'very, very, very strict ... So long as one keeps all the ties which bind one to life, which make you a slave to ordinary life, how can one belong to the Divine? ... We tried to create an atmosphere where only one thing counted: the divine life.' Now things changed, and not for the better according to many sadhaks and sadhikas encrusted in the habits of their frugal Ashram life. Children mean life, movement, noise, immediacy of needs, longings, outspoken and direct. Children are disturbing, often annoying and upsetting, and the serious disciples could do without all that. Otherwise, why had they chosen to stay in the Ashram? But once again 'circumstances' or 'destiny' or 'Providence' had decided otherwise. Just as the formation of the Ashram had come about automatically, now a concurrence of events necessitated its expansion. Besides, wasn't this an 'Integral Yoga,' hadn't Sri Aurobindo written that 'all life is yoga,' and shouldn't therefore its practitioners be capable of facing all aspects of life in their world in miniature?

The Mother, of course, had immediately seen the meaning of it all and the necessity of an expansion of the Ashram life, for this exacted a broadening of the yoga. As she would later say: 'It [the presence of the children in the Ashram] has an advantage: we were too much on the outside of life. There were many problems which did not occur [in the former Ashram way of life] and which, if one had wanted to manifest oneself fully, would suddenly have cropped up. We have taken on the problems [of an all-round communal life] a little too early, but it was necessary to tackle them. This way one learns a lot of things, one overcomes a lot of difficulties. But it becomes more complicated. And it may be that in the present conditions, with such a great number of elements who don't have the faintest idea why they are here, greater efforts are demanded from the disciples than before.' [63]

'I don't regret that we have taken them [the children],' said the Mother, 'for I believe that there is much more stuff for the future among the children, who know nothing, than among the adults, who think they know everything.' But, yes, 'children are very absorbing creatures. Everything must be organized for them, everything must be arranged in view of their well-being, and the whole way of life changes. Children are the most important persons, when they are there every-thing turns around them – and the entire organization of the Ashram changed completely.' [64]

The Mother herself took up teaching, assisted by some Ashramites who had recently joined the community, which went on growing despite the difficult financial and material times. There was Sisir Kumar Mitra, who had been a professor at Tagore's Vishva Bharati and who now became the Head of the school; there was Pranab Kumar Bhattacharya, who would become the head of the Department of Physical Education and a very close assistant of the Mother.* We will see more about the Ashram school in a later chapter.

Looking from a distance at how the Ashram developed, one might say it grew like a beautiful tree: at first planted, watered and protected with great care (the early years); then supported in its growth so that it might form a strong stem in optimal conditions (the 'very strict' period); then forming a wealth of branches and leaves (expansion and the coming of the children); then bearing fruit and seed (e.g. Auroville and other developments present and future). An evolutionary revolution is a huge undertaking; what one has seen of the material realization until the present day is only the beginning. And who can watch the bright-eyed Ashram youth without thinking of their little sisters and brothers all over the world, in this new millennium craning their necks towards a tomorrow which few venture to describe or foretell? Those who doubt or fear can be reassured by Sri Aurobindo's promise in *Savitri*:

> I saw the Omnipotent's flaming pioneers
> Over the heavenly verge which turns towards life
> Come crowding down the amber stairs of birth;
> Forerunners of a divine multitude,
> Out of the paths of the morning star they came
> Into the little room of mortal life.
> I saw them cross the twilight of an age,
> The sun-eyed children of a marvellous dawn,
> The great creators with wide brows of calm ...
> Their tread one day shall change the suffering earth ...[65]

---

* A special newcomer's case was that of Sudhir Kumar Sarkar. He had been a companion of Barin at the time of the Maniktola Garden, one of the accused in the Alipore Bomb Case, and one of the young men around Sri Aurobindo before his departure to Chandernagore. Sudhir Sarkar joined the Ashram in 1943, together with his wife and children, the last of the old-timers to do so.

12.

Sri Aurobindo's Descent into Death

Sri Aurobindo has come on Earth not to bring a teaching or a creed in competition with previous creeds or teachings, but to show the way to overpass the past and to open concretely the route towards an imminent and inevitable future.[1]

– The Mother

Mahananda

In 1946 a very important event took place which nobody was aware of at the time and which is scarcely remembered at present. As we have seen in the previous chapter, by far the greatest part of what the Mother and Sri Aurobindo have done for the world on the occult and spiritual plane is not known; it was 'not on the surface for men to see,' and they have not spoken about it. Of the little that is known, a kind of habitual selective process in the existing comments and exegeses sifts the supposedly important from the supposedly unimportant, and gradually creates a standard myth. This myth should be put to the test on every possible occasion by renewed study of the available documents, all of them.

In August 1954 the Mother read out from chapter six of Sri Aurobindo's booklet *The Mother* a passage following his description of her four universal Powers: Maheshwari, Mahakali, Mahalakshmi and Mahasaraswati.* 'There are other great Personalities of the Divine Mother, but they were more difficult to bring down and have not stood out in

---

* See the section on *The Mother* in Chapter 6 of this book.

front with so much prominence in the evolution of the Earth-spirit. There are among them presences indispensable for the supramental realization – most of all one who is her Personality of that mysterious and powerful ecstasy and Ananda which flows from a supreme divine Love, the Ananda that alone can heal the gulf between the highest heights of the supramental spirit and the lowest abysses of Matter, the Ananda that holds the key of a wonderful divinest Life and even now supports from its secrecies the work of all the other Powers of the universe.'[2] 'Ananda' means bliss, absolute shadowless joy, the highest uninterrupted ecstasy. Together with Existence and Consciousness-Force it is one of the three supreme attributes of the Divine, and therefore one of the aspects or personalities of the Great Mother.

Someone in the audience asked what that Personality was and when it would manifest. The Mother had expected the question and she had her answer ready. 'She *has* come, bringing with her a splendour of power and love, an intensity of divine joy unknown to the Earth up to then. The physical atmosphere was completely changed by it, saturated with new and marvellous possibilities. But for her to be able to settle and act down here, she needed to meet with a minimum of receptivity, to find at least *one* human being possessing the requisite qualities in the vital and physical nature, a kind of super-Parsifal endowed with a spontaneous and integral purity, but at the same time having a body strong and balanced enough to be able to bear without giving way the intensity of the Ananda she brought. Up to now she has not obtained what was necessary. Human beings obstinately remain human beings and do not want to or cannot become superhumans. They can only receive and express a love cut to their measure: a human love. And the marvellous joy of the divine Ananda escapes their perception.

'So, at times she thinks of withdrawing, finding that the world is not ready to receive her. This would be a cruel loss. It is true that for the moment her presence is more nominal than active, as she does not have the opportunity to manifest herself. But even so she is a wonderful help in the Work. For of all the aspects of the Mother, this is the one which has the greatest power for the transformation of the body. It is a fact that the cells which are able to vibrate to the contact of divine joy, which are able to receive and retain it, are regenerated cells in the process of becoming immortal. However, the vibrations of divine joy and those of [ordinary human] pleasure cannot exist together in the same vital and physical system. So one must have *totally* renounced the experience of all pleasure in order to be in a state capable of receiving the Ananda. But very few are those who can renounce pleasure without, by the very fact, renouncing all participation in active life and plunging into a rigorous asceticism. And among those who know that it is in active life that the transformation must take place, some try to see pleasure as a more or less distorted form of Ananda, and thus justify in themselves the quest for personal satisfaction, creating in themselves an almost insuperable obstacle to their own transformation.'

Ishwari, Kali, Lakshmi and Saraswati's presence and action among humans is age-old. When, then, had this new Personality of the Mother, the Ananda, come down? The question was put by someone present and she replied: 'I don't know the dates. I don't remember dates. All I know is that it happened before Sri Aurobindo left the body, that he had been told beforehand [about it] and recognized the fact.'

After a silence she continued: 'There was a terrible fight with the Inconscient. For, as I saw that the receptivity was not what it ought to be, I put the responsibility for it on the Inconscient and it was there that I tried to give battle. I don't say that this had no result, but there was a great difference between the result obtained and the result hoped for. But I tell you this … You are all so close, you bathe in the atmosphere, but who was aware of anything? You continued to live your life as usual, didn't you? …' Then Pavitra said: 'I think it was in 1946, Mother, for you told us so many things at that time.' – 'Correct,' said the Mother.

'[The Ananda] came down because there was a possibility, because things had come to a certain stage and the time had come when she could descend. In fact, she descended because I thought it was possible that she might succeed. There are always possibilities, but … they must be materialized.' It should be kept in mind that, though the Mother speaks about the Ananda in the third person, this aspect or personality, like uncountable others, formed (and forms) an integral part of her. 'You see, a proof of what I told you is that, at a certain moment, it happened, and that for two or three weeks the atmosphere, not only of the Ashram but of the Earth, was surcharged with such power, yes, with such an intense divine joy creating so wonderful a power, that things which were difficult before could be done almost instantaneously. There were repercussions in the whole world. – I don't think that there was one among you who was aware of it. You couldn't even tell me *when* it happened, could you?'[3]

Freedom at Midnight

True spirituality is not to renounce life, but to make life perfect with a Divine Perfection. This is what India must show to the world now.[4]

– The Mother

India became independent at midnight on 15 August 1947. Lord Mountbatten had been responsible for the choice of the date, thus putting into motion at breakneck speed a sequence of highly important and far-reaching decisions. Larry Collins and Dominique Lapierre have narrated, in *Freedom at Midnight,* how Mountbatten chose the date on the spur of the moment during a press conference, though he pretended to have had a date in mind. 'Mountbatten's decision was instantaneous. It was a date linked in his memory to the most triumphant hours of his own existence, the day on which his long crusade through the jungles of Burma had ended with the unconditional surrender of the Japanese Empire ... His voice constricted with sudden emotion, the victor of the jungles of Burma about to become the liberator of India announced: "The final transfer of power to Indian hands will take place on 15 August 1947."'[5] This is the birthday of Sri Aurobindo.

The reader may recall that at the beginning of 1920s, Sri Aurobindo gave to Purani the assurance that India would be free – an important statement, for, as Sri Aurobindo was no doubt aware, it would lead to a serious decision in Purani's life. How could Sri Aurobindo have been so sure? The Mother gives us the surprising answer to this question. 'After having gone to a certain place [in the occult worlds], I said to Sri Aurobindo: "India is free." I didn't say: "She will be free," I said: "She is free" ... It was in 1915 ... Even to a question Sri Aurobindo put to me, I answered from the same [occult] place: "There will be no violence of any kind. It will come about without a revolution. It will be the English who will decide to go away because they will not be able to keep hold of the place owing to certain terrestrial circumstances.'[6]

(Then a young boy asked her the question: 'You said that India was free in 1915, but was she free as she is free now? For India is not free as one whole, she is cut up.' And the Mother answered: 'The details were not there. No, there must have been a possibility of it being otherwise, for, when Sri Aurobindo told them to do a certain thing, when he sent them that message [in 1942, in connection with the Cripps Offer], he knew very well that it was possible to avoid what happened later. If they had listened to him at that time, there would have been no division. Consequently the division was not decreed, it was a human deformation. It is beyond question a human deformation.')

On the day of India's independence the Mother distributed the following invocation: 'O our Mother, O Soul of India, Mother who hast never forsaken thy children even in the days of darkest depression, even when they turned away from the voice, served other masters and denied thee, now when they have arisen and the light is on thy face in this dawn of thy liberation, in this great hour we salute thee. Guide us so that the horizon of freedom opening before us may be also a horizon of true greatness and of thy true life in the community of the nations. Guide us so that we may be always on the side of great ideals and show to men thy true visage, as a leader in the ways of the spirit and a friend and helper of all the peoples.'[7]

On that occasion the Mother had her flag hoisted above the Ashram, more specifically over the terrace of Sri Aurobindo's room. She called it the spiritual flag of India. 'It is the flag of India's spiritual mission. And in the accomplishment of this mission will India's unity be accomplished,'[8] she declared on 15 August. The Mother's flag contains her symbol in gold, centred on a silver-blue background. 'In the afternoon she appeared on her terrace,' writes Nirodbaran, 'when the members of the Ashram greeted her by singing *Bande Mataram,* after which she called out: *'Jai Hind!'* [victory to India] with such a look and gesture that we still remember the moment.'[9]

This profoundly symbolic act of the Mother, who wanted the flag to fly for three days, was misinterpreted by certain factions in Pondicherry and 'there was an anti-Ashram riot in which a sadhak was murdered – Mulshankar, who used to massage Sri Aurobindo's right leg every day. There was even a threat given that the hostile elements would climb up the building and pull the flag down. The Mother refused to take it off until her three days would be over.'[10] This was the first of several attacks upon the Ashram in the coming years.

Later the Mother would draw her map of India, which is still there on a wall in the playground. It includes Pakistan (then West Pakistan), Sikkim, Bhutan, Bangladesh (then East Pakistan), part of Burma, and Sri Lanka (then Ceylon). As the Mother put it: 'The map was made after the partition. It is the map of the true India in spite of all passing appearances, and it will always remain the map of the true India, whatever people may think about it.'[11]

To understand this, one must realize that every true nation is not only a certain area on a map, but a living being. As Sri Aurobindo wrote: 'Each nation is a Shakti or power of the evolving spirit in humanity and lives by the principle which it embodies. India is the Bharata Shakti, the living energy of a great spiritual conception, and fidelity to it is the very principle of her existence. For by its virtue alone she has been one of the immortal nations; this alone has been the secret of her amazing persistence and perpetual force of survival and revival.'[12] And the Mother would say: 'India is not the Earth, rivers and mountains of this land, neither is it a collective name for the inhabitants of this country. India is a living being, as much living as, say, Shiva. India is a goddess as Shiva is a god. If she likes, she can manifest in human form.'[13]

Nowhere is there a more profound and positive view of India to be found than with Sri Aurobindo and the Mother. We have had a glimpse of Sri Aurobindo's love of Mother India and his sanctification of her in the pages of his political writings. He studied her past and her cultural riches as few others have done, a study which resulted in books like *The Secret of the Veda*, *The Upanishads*, *The Foundations of Indian Culture** and *Essays on the Gita*. Even the framework of his magistral epic *Savitri* is a

---

* Renamed in the *Collected Works of Sri Aurobindo*, vol. 20, 'The Renaissance in India'.

story from the *Mahabharata*. In fact, his whole work is permeated with the living presence of the perpetual Indian values.

'India of the ages is not dead nor has she spoken her last creative word,' he wrote, 'she lives and has still something to do for herself and the human peoples. And that which must seek now to awake is not an Anglicized oriental people, docile pupil of the West and doomed to repeat the cycle of the Occident's success and failure, but still the ancient immemorable Shakti recovering her deeper self, lifting her head towards the supreme source of light and strength and turning to discover the complete meaning and vaster form of her Dharma.' 'God always keeps for himself a chosen country in which the higher knowledge is through all chances and dangers, by the few or the many, continually preserved, and for the present, in this Chaturyuga [the Fourth or Iron Age] at least, that country is India.' [14]

For her part the Mother said: 'The future of India is very clear. India is the Guru of the world. The future structure of the world depends on India. India is the living soul. India is incarnating the spiritual knowledge in the world.' And she wrote: 'In the whole creation the Earth has a place of distinction because unlike any other planet it is evolutionary with a psychic entity at its centre. In it, India, in particular, is a divinely chosen country.' 'India has become the symbolic representation of all the difficulties of modern mankind. India will be the land of its resurrection – the resurrection to a higher and truer life.' [15]

Considering the manifold and colossal problems of India at present, all this may sound a bit bombastic. But Sri Aurobindo and the Mother were 'spiritual realists' who saw the difficulties as clearly as the possibilities. 'We must recognize the great gulf between what we are and what we may and ought to strive to be,' [16] wrote Sri Aurobindo. K.D. Sethna, in *Our Light and Delight*, has a witty anecdote. 'Two generations ago Tagore said that although India was lying in the dust, the very dust in which she lay was holy. Obviously it was in his mind that this dust had been trod by the feet of the Rishis and Saints and Avatars. Sri Aurobindo's comment is reported to have been that, whatever might be the case, the dust could not be the proper thing for a man to lie in, and that man had not been created to adopt a prone posture.' [17] That Indian spirituality (and its Eastern derivatives), as predicted by Sri Aurobindo and the

Mother, is spreading throughout the world, is undeniable. Truth is one; so are the fundamental human constitution, psychology and spiritual possibilities. The West has laboured and sacrificed the best of its talent towards an essential acquisition: the individualization of the human personality. It lacks, however, the practice and even the idea of spiritual realization, except in a few of its saints and mystics. India, 'the Asia of Asia' as Sri Aurobindo called it, has kept and guarded the spiritual realization in its many forms of unification with the Divine. What it lacks, in its turn, is the necessary sense of individualization within the social and material context (though not in its yogis). The time has come, at this unprecedented opportunity offered by the 'global village,' for East and West to meet and to fulfil the human potential in an effort that will make the world effectively one, and carry the human species beyond itself into a New World.

Five 'Dreams'

A new spirit of oneness will take hold of the human race.[18]

– Sri Aurobindo

The Trichinopoly station of All India Radio had asked Sri Aurobindo for a message, to be read by a newsreader and broadcast on India's Day of Independence. His message began as follows:* 'August 15th, 1947 is the birthday of free India. It marks for her the end of an old era, the beginning of a new age. But we can also make it by our life and acts as a free nation an important date in a new age opening for the whole world, for the political, social, cultural and spiritual future of humanity.

'August 15th is my own birthday and it is naturally gratifying to me that it should have assumed this vast significance. I take this coincidence not as a fortuitous accident, but as the sanction and seal of the Divine

---

* The passages quoted here, published in *On Himself*, are from the second version, the broadcast one. The first version had been 'a little too long for the time allotted for the message.'

Force that guides my steps on the work with which I began my life, the beginning of its full fruition. Indeed, on this day I can watch almost all the world-movements which I hoped to see fulfilled in my lifetime, though then they looked like impracticable dreams, arriving at fruition or on their way to achievement. In all these movements free India may well play a large part and take a leading position.'

Then Sri Aurobindo enumerates and briefly considers these world-movements – his five 'dreams.' 'The first of these dreams was a revolutionary movement which would create a free and united India.' Chapter five in this book gave us some idea of the prominent role Sri Aurobindo played in the realization of this dream, and his intervention at the time of the Cripps Offer shows how close India's freedom remained in his concerns and to his heart. We know practically nothing of the yogic force he applied for the accomplishment of the same goal, but there is no doubt that he kept a watchful eye on all relevant developments. It must be remembered that, in his unadorned words, 'he has always stood for India's complete independence which he was the first to advocate publicly and without compromise as the only ideal worthy of a self-respecting nation.' [19]

But the body of Bharat Mata, Mother India, had been split into two states, so-called India and Pakistan, which itself was grotesquely divided into East and West Pakistan, distanced from each other by no less than thirteen hundred kilometres. Sri Aurobindo's emphatic pronouncement on this deplorable fact – on this 'human deformation,' as the Mother called it – is as noteworthy now as it was in 1947. 'The old communal division into Hindus and Muslims seems to have hardened into a permanent political division of the country. It is to be hoped that this settled fact will not be accepted as settled for ever or as anything more than a temporary expedient. For if it lasts, India may be seriously weakened, even crippled: civil strife may remain always possible, possible even a new invasion and foreign conquest. India's internal development and prosperity may be impeded, her position among the nations weakened, her destiny impaired or even frustrated.' It may be instructive to compare these prognoses with what has happened since 1947.

And Sri Aurobindo continues: 'This must not be; the partition must go. Let us hope that that may come about naturally, by an increasing recognition of the necessity not only of peace and concord but of common action, by the practice of common action and the creation of means for that purpose. In this way unity may finally come about under whatever form – the exact form may have a pragmatic but not a fundamental importance. But by whatever means, in whatever way, the division must go; unity must and will be achieved, for it is necessary for the greatness of India's future.' Elsewhere, Sri Aurobindo has confirmed this prophecy explicitly: 'India will be reunited. I see it clearly.'[20] The Mother has even predicted how this would come to pass: Pakistan, divided into provinces on the lines of its ethnic populations, would fall apart and the separate regions would seek a confederation with India – which itself, as a solution to its internal problems, would become a still more confederate state than it is at the moment.[21]

Sri Aurobindo's second dream 'was for the resurgence and liberation of the peoples of Asia and her return to her great role in the progress of human civilization. Asia has arisen; large parts are now quite free or are at this moment being liberated; its other still subject or partly subject parts are moving through whatever struggles towards freedom. Only a little has to be done and that will be done today or tomorrow' – as indeed it has.

'The third dream was a world-union forming the outer basis of a fairer, brighter and nobler life for all mankind. That unification of the human world is under way ... The momentum is there and it must inevitably increase and conquer ... A catastrophe may intervene and interrupt or destroy what is being done, but even then the final result is sure. For unification is a necessity of Nature, an inevitable movement ... A new spirit of oneness will take hold of the human race.'

For a fuller insight into the need and the problems of world-unity, the reader may be referred to Sri Aurobindo's *The Human Cycle* and *The Ideal of Human Unity*,* two books still as fresh and relevant to the subject as at the time they were written almost a century ago, and now better understandable because so much in them of what then seemed

---

* Formerly published as *Social and Political Thought*, now in the CWSA vol. 15 under the title *The Human Cycle*.

only anticipation and projection has in the meantime taken a concrete shape or is in the process of doing so.

In a letter to the Mother during the First World War, Sri Aurobindo wrote: 'The whole world is now under one law.' If today this is a fact for all to see and experience, it was far from apparent when that letter was written. Has not every race or people throughout the history of humanity held itself to be the 'navel of the Earth' and all other peoples to be barbarians and even non-humans?

In *A Message to America*, written by Sri Aurobindo in 1949, we read: 'There is a common hope, a common destiny, both spiritual and material, for which both [East and West] are needed as co-workers. It is no longer towards division and difference that we should turn our minds, but on unity, union, even oneness necessary for the pursuit and realization of a common ideal, the destined goal, the fulfilment towards which Nature in her beginnings obscurely set out and must in an increasing light of knowledge replacing her first ignorance constantly persevere.'

In the same message he also wrote: 'There has been a tendency in some minds to dwell on the spirituality or mysticism of the East and the materialism of the West; but the West has had no less than the East its spiritual seekings and, though not in such profusion, its saints and sages and mystics, the East has had its materialistic tendencies, its material splendours, its similar or identical dealings with life and Matter and the world in which we live.' [22]

'The message of the East to the West is a true message,' wrote Sri Aurobindo in the *Arya*. '"Only by finding himself can man be saved," and "What shall it profit a man though he gain the whole world, if he lose his own soul." The West has heard the message and is seeking out the law and truth of the soul and the evidences of an inner reality greater than the material. The danger is that with her passion for mechanism and her exaggerated intellectuality she may fog herself in an external and false psychism ...'

'Man also is God and it is through his developing manhood that he approaches the godhead; Life also is Divine, its progressive expansion is the self-expression of the Brahman, and to deny Life is to diminish the Godhead within us ... The danger is that Asia may accept it in the European form, forget for a time her own law and nature and either copy blindly the West or make a disastrous amalgam of that which she has in its most inferior forms and the crudenesses which are invading her.'[23] And he warned the West: 'The safety of Europe [i.e. the West] has to be sought in the recognition of the spiritual aim of human existence, otherwise she will be crushed by the weight of her own unillumined knowledge and soulless organization.'[24]

The fourth dream, 'the spiritual gift of India to the world, has already begun,' wrote Sri Aurobindo in the radio broadcast. 'India's spirituality is entering Europe and America in an ever increasing measure. That movement will grow; amid the disasters of the time more and more eyes are turning towards her with hope and there is even an increasing resort not only to her teachings, but to her psychic and spiritual practice.' In the meantime, the spirituality of the East has spread throughout the West in a measure nobody but Sri Aurobindo could have foreseen fifty years ago.

The fifth dream 'was a step in evolution which would raise man to a higher and larger consciousness and begin the solution of the problems which have perplexed and vexed him since he first began to think and to dream of individual perfection and a perfect society. This is still a personal hope and an idea, an ideal which has begun to take hold both in India and in the West on forward-looking minds. The difficulties on the way are more formidable than in any other field of endeavour, but difficulties were made to be overcome and if the Supreme Will is there, they will be overcome.' The 'personal hope and idea' would be fulfilled within less than a decade, but the 'difficulties' were so 'formidable' that they required a drastic step.

'Such is the content which I put into this date of India's liberation; whether or how far this hope will be justified depends upon the new and free India,' concluded Sri Aurobindo. It is safe to say that at the time no one knew that All India Radio was broadcasting what may be called Sri Aurobindo's testament.

Overman – the Transitional Being

Meanwhile, the Ashram school and its Department of Physical Education had grown to such an extent that the Mother wanted to bring out a quarterly magazine, the *Bulletin of Physical Education,* the first issue of which was published on 21 February 1949. (It was later renamed *Bulletin of Sri Aurobindo International Centre of Education.*)

Sri Aurobindo had started revising *The Life Divine* shortly after the accident to his leg. In 1945 his eyesight deteriorated badly, he probably had cataract in both eyes. From that time onwards he dictated everything to Nirodbaran, who thus became his amanuensis, or his 'scribe,' as Nirodbaran called himself. In those years Sri Aurobindo revised for publication not only *The Life Divine* but some other works too, including *The Synthesis of Yoga,* and we will soon see how he worked on the revision and expansion of *Savitri.* The correspondence with the disciples stopped, except with Dilip K. Roy, to whom Sri Aurobindo showed an inexhaustible patience, and K.D. Sethna, who needed his constant supervision and advice for the contents of the fortnightly *Mother India* (now a monthly), which Sri Aurobindo regarded as his own journal.

The series of eight articles Sri Aurobindo wrote for the *Bulletin,* at the request of the Mother, appeared in it from February 1949 to November 1950. In 1952 they were published under the title *The Supramental Manifestation upon Earth* and have been reprinted several times. They are extremely important because here, for the first time, Sri Aurobindo writes extensively about the necessity of a transitional being between man and superman, between the human and the suprahuman. As everything he wrote was the result of his and the Mother's experience, he must have realized this transitional state in his own body. (His mind and vital had been supramentalized a long time previously.) Not only did this make *The Supramental Manifestation upon Earth* a sequel to *The Life Divine,* it also proved to be an explanation of a crucial experience which was soon to happen to the Mother, and of the yogic work she was going to base upon it in the coming years. Let us therefore have a closer look at it.

Firstly, Sri Aurobindo and the Mother have stated clearly that the supramental being will be a new creation on Earth which cannot be brought forth by the human being as it is now. The reason is that however advanced or developed a human being may be, it will always carry in its substance an element of the Inconscient which forms the base of its evolutionary materiality. 'The way we are, we have been created in the ordinary way, the animal way,' said the Mother, 'and consequently, even if we transform ourselves, there will remain something of this animal origin. The supramental being as he [Sri Aurobindo] conceived of it, is *not at all* formed in the ordinary animal way, but directly, through a process that for the moment still seems occult to us.'[25]

The necessity of an intermediary being became clear, as became the insight that every decisive step in the evolution has been brought about by the creation of transitional beings, probably in great numbers. As the Mother said in the same talk: 'It is quite obvious that intermediate beings are necessary, that it is these intermediate beings who must find the means of creating beings of the supermind, and when Sri Aurobindo wrote this [*The Supramental Manifestation*], he was undoubtedly convinced that this is what we have to do.'[26] The Mother called this transitional being: *le surhomme*, the overman,* although we should keep in mind that the species 'overman' will consist most probably of many different individual degrees of consciousness and physical transformation.

Secondly, a being is what its consciousness is, in other words, the substantial form of a being is the expression of its consciousness. If Sri Aurobindo had realized this new, beyond-human state in his body, he must first have realized a new state of consciousness in his body, in the cells of his body. This new state of consciousness he called 'the Mind of Light,' and it is to this Mind of Light that he dedicates a major part of *The Supramental Manifestation upon Earth*. (This title was not coined by him and does not cover the general contents of the articles. *Towards the Supramental Manifestation upon Earth* might have been more to the point.)

'We have supposed not only the descent of the supermind upon the

---

* It should be recalled in passing that the correct translation of Friedrich Nietzsche's term *Übermensch* is also 'overman' and not 'superman.' The author of this book avoids as much as possible gender-specific language. However, the language of the Mother and Sri Aurobindo follows the conventions of the time in which it was used and cannot always be adapted without distorting the meaning.

316

Earth,' writes Sri Aurobindo, 'but its embodiment in a supramental race* with all its natural consequences and a new total action in which the new humanity would find its complete development and its assured place in the new order. But it is clear that this could only come as the result of the evolution which is already taking place upon Earth extending far beyond its present bounds and passing into a radically new movement governed by a new principle in which mind and man would be subordinate elements and no longer mind the utmost achievement or man the head or leader ... A new humanity would then be a race of mental beings on the Earth and in the earthly body but delivered from its present conditions in the reign of the cosmic Ignorance so far as to be possessed of a perfected mind, a mind of light which could even be a subordinate action of the supermind or Truth-Consciousness and in any case capable of the full possibilities of mind acting as a recipient of that truth and at least a secondary action of it in thought and life.'[27]

The general aim of Sri Aurobindo and the Mother's avataric endeavour was the descent of the Supramental into the Earth-atmosphere. Both of them had realized the Supramental in their mind and vital. Sri Aurobindo had realized in the cells, in the matter of his body, a degree of the Supramental which he called the Mind of Light – probably because pure consciousness is also pure light, something we do not see or experience because we are living literally in the darkness of the Ignorance. The next step in the avataric yoga we will see soon.

In November 1949 the Mother met her son André, who had come to Pondicherry on his first visit; their last meeting dated from 1916, when André was eighteen. In October 1916 André had become an artillery officer in the war and had been awarded several medals for valorous service. After the war he had studied at the *École polytechnique* in Paris, and started making a career in industry as soon as he got his engineer's diploma. In the thirty-three years of their separation, the Mother,

---

* The reader will have noted that Sri Aurobindo often uses the word 'race' where nowadays 'species' would seem more appropriate.

though always in inner contact with him, had written scarcely twenty letters.

Now Mother and son would meet again. According to Champaklal, the Mother said to Sri Aurobindo: 'Perhaps if we met on the road without being introduced to each other I would not know him, and he too would not recognize me.'[28] She had arranged for him to be accompanied from Madras by a devotee, so that they would arrive 'at the Ashram at 5 p.m. on the 21st [November]. She explained that she had all set to be able to spend then a little time alone with me,' remembered André.

But Pondicherry was still French at the time, and papers were needed to cross from the State of Madras into the French territory. Due to some snag in obtaining the papers, André and his companion were delayed. 'The sun was setting when we arrived at the Ashram. There Pavitra told me that Mother was expecting me at Golconde, in the room where I was to stay for a few days. It was quite dark when I arrived at Golconde. I hastily climbed two stories and then, in the dim light of the corridor, I saw a white shape with her back against the door in a very familiar attitude.'[29] The Mother had been waiting for three to four hours.

Afterwards K.D. Sethna asked the Mother why André had not come to see her in all those years. She answered: 'Why should he have? He had his own life to live in France; and actually, even while he was there, there was no real separation. Up till now it was as if there were a screen in my room and André was present behind the screen. What has happened now is simply that he has come out in front.'[30] For the rest of his life André became a regular visitor, dividing his time between France and Pondicherry. After Pavitra's passing, he would even become *de facto* head of the Ashram School.

Savitri

He has crammed the whole universe into a single book.[31]

– The Mother

Sri Aurobindo's epic poem *Savitri* consists of nearly 24,000 lines – 712 printed pages in the complete works. He worked on its twelve ever-expanded drafts for half a century, from the last years in Baroda till a few weeks before his leaving the body.

Sri Aurobindo called *Savitri* 'a legend and a symbol.' The legend is a story from the *Mahabharata* that briefly summarized goes as follows: Savitri, daughter of King Aswapati of Madra, chooses Satyavan, son of King Dyumatsena of Shalwa, for her husband. Satyavan lives in the forest to which his blind father has been exiled by a usurper; there Savitri meets him and falls in love with him. On her return home, the heavenly singer and seer Narad tells her, however, that a curse rests on Satyavan and that he has to die in exactly a year's time. Savitri remains nonetheless faithful to the choice of her soul, goes back to the forest where Satyavan lives, marries him, and lives there with him till the fatal day. When Satyavan does indeed die and Yama, the god of Death, comes with his noose to take him away, Savitri does not want to let him go. She follows them into the invisible worlds and wins from Yama, after a fierce occult and spiritual struggle with him, the exceptional boon of Satyavan's return to his body and life in the world.

Sri Aurobindo's first draft was a relatively short narrative poem, comparable to his *Love and Death*, in which he stuck to the original legend. Gradually, as his yoga widened and particularly after the coming of the Mother, he saw a symbolic parallel between the *Mahabharata* story and their own avataric effort. Savitri came to stand for an incarnation of the universal Mother and Satyavan for an incarnation of the soul of the Earth which the Mother, in her Love for it and through her yoga, wins back from the Inconscient, symbolised by Death; Sri Aurobindo more and more substituted himself for the figure of Aswapati, using the role of the latter to describe his own spiritual experiences, discoveries and conquests.

Sri Aurobindo, August 1950

After his work on *The Life Divine*, Sri Aurobindo started revising and expanding the existing drafts of *Savitri*. As his eyesight grew gradually worse, he did this with the help of his 'scribe,' Nirodbaran. The latter's report of this work in his *Twelve Years with Sri Aurobindo* is, in its bare simplicity, not only interesting but also very moving. 'One is simply amazed at the enormous pains he [Sri Aurobindo] has taken to raise *Savitri* to its ideal perfection,' writes Nirodbaran.[32]

'I wrote *Savitri* as a means of ascension,' explains Sri Aurobindo in one of his many letters on his epic to K.D. Sethna, the very first person to receive and read a few lines of it. 'I began with it on a certain mental level, each time I could reach a higher level I rewrote from that level … In fact *Savitri* has not been regarded by me as a poem to be written and finished, but as a field of experimentation to see how far poetry could be written from one's own yogic consciousness and how that could be made creative.'[33] 'I wonder how he could go on dictating lines of poetry in this way,' writes Nirodbaran, 'as if a tap had been turned on and the water flowed, not in a jet, of course, but slowly, very slowly indeed. Passages sometimes had to be reread in order to get the link or sequence, but when the turn came of The Book of Yoga and The Book of Everlasting Day, line after line began to flow from his lips like a smooth and gentle stream …'[34]

To Mona Sarkar, a young sadhak at the time, the Mother gave a revealing inside view on *Savitri*. 'All this is his own experience, and what is most surprising is that it is my own experience also. It is my sadhana which he has worked out. Each object, each event, each realization, all the descriptions, even the colours are exactly what I saw and the words and phrases are also exactly what I heard. I read *Savitri* many times afterwards, but earlier, when he was writing, he used to read it to me. Every morning I used to [listen to] him reading *Savitri*. During the night he would write and in the morning read it to me. And I observed something curious: that day after day the experiences he read out to me in the morning were those I had had the previous night, word for word. Yes, all the descriptions, the colours, the pictures I had seen, the words I had heard, all, all, I heard it all, put by him into poetry, into miraculous poetry. And it was not just one day by chance, but for days and days together. And every time I used to compare what he said with my previous experiences and they were always the same. I repeat, it was not that I had told him my experiences and that he had noted them down afterwards, no, he knew already what I had seen. It is my experiences he has presented at length and they were his experiences also. It is, moreover, the picture of our joint adventure into the unknown or rather into the Supermind.'[35]

The Mother also said to the same young man: 'Indeed, *Savitri* is something concrete, living, it is all replete, packed with consciousness. It is the supreme knowledge above all human philosophies and religions. It is the spiritual path, it is yoga, tapasya, sadhana, everything, in its single body. *Savitri* has an extraordinary power, it gives out vibrations for him who can receive them, the true vibrations of each stage of consciousness. It is incomparable, it is Truth in its plenitude, the Truth Sri Aurobindo brought down on the Earth.'[36]

'Though the hour of work appointed for *Savitri* and correspondence was shifted to the morning, we could get very little time for *Savitri*,' remembers Nirodbaran. 'Many interruptions came in the way. The preliminary work of reading old versions, selections, etc., took up much time before we could actually start writing ... till one day in 1950 [Sri Aurobindo] exclaimed: "My main work is being delayed"'[37] – to the surprise of Nirodbaran, who had never seen Sri Aurobindo hurry for anything. 'In these twelve years this was the first time I had heard him reckoning with the time factor.'[38] There are other reports of his becoming very concerned, though nobody had the faintest inkling about what. When Satyendra, taking his courage in both hands, asked: 'Why are you so serious, sir?' Sri Aurobindo answered gravely: 'The time is very serious.'

We turn again to Nirodbaran's narrative. 'When the last revision was made and the Cantos were wound up, I said, "It is finished now." An impersonal smile of satisfaction greeted me, and he said: "Ah, is it finished?" How well I remember that flicker of a smile which all of us craved for so long! "What is left now?" was his next query. "The Book of Death and the Epilogue." "Oh, that? We shall see about that later on." That "later on" never came and was not meant to come. Having taken the decision to leave the body, he must have been waiting for the right moment to go, and for reasons known to himself he left the two last-mentioned Books almost as they were. Thus on *Savitri* was put the seal of incomplete completion about two weeks before the Darshan of November 24th [1950]. Other literary work too came to an end.'[39]

The 'reasons known to himself' may not be that difficult to guess. *Savitri* was the rendition in the poetry of the future, in mantric poetry, of Sri Aurobindo and the Mother's experience. Of two things they did not and could not have the experience: physical death and its mysteries, and 'the epilogue,' which should have pictured the advent of the New World, the accomplishment of their avataric endeavour – something possible only in the future, but not yet defined in time and still less worked out in its concrete materialization.

Savitri was regarded as finished by Sri Aurobindo two weeks before the Darshan of 24 November. In the early hours of 5 December, less than two weeks after that darshan, he would voluntarily descend into death.

The Descent into Death

> *Sri Aurobindo has given up his body in an act of supreme un-selfishness, renouncing the realization in his own body to hasten the hour of the collective realization.*[40]
>
> – The Mother

Towards the end of his life Sri Aurobindo had at times been suffering from 'some mild prostatic enlargement.' 'During his last months the symptoms of prostatic enlargement reappeared and began to increase slowly,'[41] writes Nirodbaran. Ten days or so before the darshan of 24 November – almost immediately after the 'incomplete completion' of *Savitri* – the symptoms worsened again and Dr. Satyabrata Sen, a surgeon and devotee who was on a darshan visit to the Ashram, was consulted. Sen confirmed the diagnosis that the prostate gland had enlarged and proposed an operation, but this was an intervention Sri Aurobindo and the Mother refused to consider.

The darshan was, as usual, a physically exhausting affair for Sri

Aurobindo and the Mother, who had to sit there for hours in a continuous spiritual exchange with hundreds of disciples and devotees. After the darshan the symptoms grew more serious and a catheter was inserted. On the twenty-ninth the Mother had a telegram sent to Dr. Prabhat Sanyal, a prominent surgeon in Calcutta as well as a devotee. Sanyal arrived the next day and diagnosed 'a mild kidney infection, but nothing serious.'*

The anniversary of the foundation of the school, 2 December is every year a festive day in the Ashram. This time too 'the whole Ashram was busy and bustling ... Nobody suspected that a profound tragedy was being enacted in the closed chambers of Sri Aurobindo.'[42] Sanyal himself seems not to have suspected that much, for he found the illness so little serious that he proposed to leave on the third. He changed his mind after the Mother reacted negatively to this proposal. Later in the day Sri Aurobindo's temperature shot up and respiratory distress showed itself for the first time. He 'lapsed into trance' and remained like that for almost the whole day. The Mother, quite exceptionally, did not join the activities at the Playground. For the first time she said: 'He is losing interest in himself.' She would repeat this to Sanyal late at night.

In the morning of the fourth Sri Aurobindo wanted to sit up and 'insisted strongly' when the doctors objected. The Mother helped him to take a light breakfast. 'We were so happy at this sudden change and thought that at last our prayer had been heard,' writes Nirodbaran. 'We boldly asked him now: "Are you not using your force to cure yourself?" "No!" came the stunning reply. We could not believe our ears; to be quite sure, we repeated the question. No mistake! Then we asked: "Why not? How is the disease going to be cured otherwise?" "Can't explain; you wouldn't understand," was the curt reply. We were dumbfounded.'[43]

From midday the symptoms increased again, particularly the breathing difficulty. 'He is withdrawing,' said the Mother to Sanyal. 'He was now always indrawn,' writes Nirodbaran, 'and only woke up whenever

---

* The story of Sri Aurobindo's last days is based mainly on Nirodbaran's *Twelve Years With Sri Aurobindo* and on Dr. Sanyal's memoir *A 'Call' From Pondicherry*, published in *Mother India*, December 1991. The reader will remember that Nirodbaran Talukdar was also a medical doctor.

he was called for a drink. That confirmed the Mother's observation that he was fully conscious within and disproved the idea that he was in uraemic coma. Throughout the entire course of the illness he was never unconscious.'[44] Sanyal confirms this: 'Though he looked apparently unconscious, whenever he was offered drinks, he would wake up and take a few sips and wipe his mouth himself with his handkerchief. To all of us it seemed apparent that a consciousness came from outside when he was almost normal, and then withdrew when the body quivered and sank down in distress. He was no longer there!'[45]

'By 5 o'clock again he showed signs of improvement. He was quite responsive. We helped him out of his bed, after which he walked to the armchair to rest. For the moment he seemed a different personality. He sat there with his eyes closed – calm and composed with a radiating consciousness. But this did not last long.'[46] After three quarters of an hour the respiratory distress returned with redoubled force.

'He went to his bed and plunged deep within himself,' writes Nirod-baran. 'It was during this period that he often came out of the trance and each time leaned forward, hugged and kissed Champaklal, who was sitting by the side of his bed. Champaklal also hugged him in return. A wonderful sight it was, though so strangely unlike Sri Aurobindo who had rarely called us even by our names in these twelve years.'[47] Is it not obvious that the Avatar, in his love for humanity, was here taking leave of that humanity in the person of the pure Champaklal? It was 'the embrace that takes to itself the body of God in man,' as Sri Aurobindo had written in *The Synthesis of Yoga*.

Then the Mother, who had gone again to the Playground that day, came back into the room. 'She laid her garland at the foot of the bed, a thing she did daily,' writes Sanyal, 'and stood watching Sri Aurobindo. She looked so grave and quiet that it almost distressed me. I went to the ante-room to wait for her. She entered and I gave her the report and told her that glucose had been given by Satya [Sen] and we wanted to arrange for intravenous infusion, etc. She said quietly and firmly: "I told you this is not necessary. He has no interest in himself, he is withdrawing" ...

'At about 11 p.m. the Mother came into the room and helped Sri Aurobindo to drink half a cup of tomato juice. A strange phenomenon – a body which for the moment is in agony, unresponsive, labouring hard for breath, suddenly becomes quiet; a consciousness enters the body, he is awake and normal. He finishes the drink, then, as the consciousness withdraws, the body lapses back in the grip of agony.' [48]

At midnight the Mother went again into Sri Aurobindo's room and 'looked intently for some time as if there was a silent exchange of thought between them.' Then she left – to come back at 1 a.m. on 5 December. In Sanyal's words: 'She returned and again looked at the Lord and stood at the foot of the bed. There was no sign of agony, fear, or anxiety on her face … With her eyes she asked me to go into the other room and she followed me. She asked: "What do you think? Can I retire for one hour?" … I murmured: "Mother, this is beyond me." She said: "Call me when the time comes."'

'It may appear strange to our human mind that the Mother should leave Sri Aurobindo at this critical moment,' observes Nirodbaran. [49] But the Mother explained later: 'As long as I was in the room, he *could not* leave his body. So there was a terrible tension in him: the inner will to leave and then this kind of thing [i.e. the Mother] that was holding him there, like that, in his body – because I knew that he was alive and that he could not be other than alive … He had to give a sign so that I would go into my room, supposedly to rest (which I didn't do). And as soon as I had gone out of the room, he left. Then they called me back immediately.' [50]

This is how Sanyal tells of the end: 'I stood behind the Master and started stroking his hair which he always liked. Nirod and Champaklal sat by the side of the bed and caressed his feet. We were all quietly watching him. We now knew that anything might happen, any time … I perceived a slight quiver in his body, almost imperceptible. He drew up his arms and put them on his chest, one overlapping the other – then all stopped … I told Nirod to go and fetch the Mother. It was 1.20 a.m.

'Almost immediately the Mother entered the room. She stood there, near the feet of Sri Aurobindo: her hair had been undressed and was flowing about her shoulders. Her look was so fierce that I could not face those eyes. With a piercing gaze she stood there. Champaklal could not bear it and sobbingly he implored: "Mother, tell me that Dr. Sanyal is not right, [that] he is alive." The Mother looked at him and he became quiet and composed as if touched by a magic wand. She stood there for more than half an hour. My hands were still on his forehead.'[51]

Soon afterwards the main personalities in the Ashram were informed and the Ashram photographers called before the endless queue would form to pay their last homage to the Master. Two of the photographers' testimonies are worth comparing. The first one recalls: 'I remember clearly that Mother was sitting in the middle room beside Sri Aurobindo's, where the tiger skins and the Mother's paintings are displayed. She looked very dejected. She was stooping in front with a hand on her forehead. But she did not notice me as I entered.'[52] The second photographer, on the contrary, recalls: 'When I entered Sri Aurobindo's abode through the door at the top of the staircase leading from the Meditation Hall, I instantly became petrified by the sight of the Mother sitting on a chair in the central room – the room in which her paintings adorn the walls and the tiger skins decorate the divan. She was seated between the two doors on the southern side of the narrow room with her eyes shut, lost in deep meditation. I have never seen her like that again. To me she looked like the personification of Mother Kali herself, so powerful was the appearance. I stood before her for some time.'[53]

The details of Sri Aurobindo's last days have been evoked in some detail to allow us a glimmer of understanding of the momentous event which was surely unique in the history of yoga and in human history as a whole. For the fact is that Sri Aurobindo entered voluntarily into death. The reader will at once reflect that many yogis have been able to enter voluntarily into death, and have effectively done so. In this case, however, Sri Aurobindo's intention was not simply to put an end to his life, following the normal process of transiting to the other worlds by shedding successively the material, vital and mental body-sheaths. His master act was a confrontation with death in full consciousness and while keeping the vital and mental sheaths, which, as we know, were supramentally transformed. (The Mother described him later on as being in possession of this supramentalized body when she gained access to his dwelling in a certain region of the Supramental worlds.) He did not subject himself to death, he confronted it by entering into it with his supernal consciousness ablaze. An indication of his voluntary intent was the rapidity with which he let the illness develop from a 'mild infection' to a fatal condition. A still stronger indication was his surfacing, time and again, from the inner consciousness, where he must have been waging a battle nobody knew of, to the outer consciousness, in a most peculiar uraemic 'coma.'

The Mother has asserted repeatedly that Sri Aurobindo did not have to leave his body for 'natural' reasons, he did not have to go the way of all flesh. 'He was not compelled to leave his body, he chose to do so for reasons so sublime that they are beyond the reach of human mentality,'[54] she said. She would confirm on several occasions, for example to K.D. Sethna and to Satprem, that Sri Aurobindo did not 'succumb' to death; that he did not die of physical causes; that he had complete control over his body. Sri Aurobindo has written so himself in some passages in *Savitri* (e.g. p. 83) which are clearly autobiographical, and for instance in his sonnet *Transformation:*

> I am no longer a vassal of the flesh,
> A slave to Nature and her leaden rule ...[55]

Then, why did he leave his body? We have seen that Sri Aurobindo said, with ever greater urgency, that the times were serious and that he wanted to finish his main work. Serious the times certainly were, even after the elimination of Adolf Hitler, instrument of the Lord of Falsehood. But the Asura had other instruments on Earth. In the first place there was Stalin, considered by Sri Aurobindo and the Mother to be an even greater evil than the Führer. The Cold War was at a high pitch, with the production of weapons capable of destroying not only all civilization but all life on Earth. Mao Tse-tung had become the ruler of China. The Korean War had erupted. Sri Aurobindo's significant comment on this war to K.D. Sethna was as follows: 'The whole affair is as plain as a pike-staff. It is the first move in the Communist plan of campaign to dominate and take possession first of these northern parts and then of Southeast Asia as a preliminary to their manoeuvres with regard to the rest of the continent – in passing, Tibet as a gate opening to India. If they succeed, there is no reason why domination of the whole world should not follow by steps until they are ready to deal with America.' [56]*

These outer circumstances, however, must have developed simultaneously with a profound inner reason, which nobody knows, for confronting death. What we do know is that the Supramental was on the verge of manifesting in 1938. We know also that, as Sri Aurobindo had written in his poem *A God's Labour,* something impossible had to be made possible, something unconquerable had to be conquered:

> A voice cried, 'Go where none have gone!
> Dig deeper, deeper yet
> Till thou reach the grim foundation stone
> And knock at the keyless gate.' [57]

Now he had gone to 'the very root of things / Where the grey Sphinx guards God's riddle sleep / On the Dragon's outspread wings' – not only in yogic concentration, but with his whole avataric personality, to make the impossible possible. The result of his action and the confirmation of our supposition will be the manifestation of the Supramental only six years later, in 1956. Undoubtedly this manifestation was finally made possible by Sri Aurobindo's unprecedented yogic master act.

In 1924 Sri Aurobindo said that there were three causes that could still bring about his death: (i) violent surprise and accident; (ii) the action of old age; (iii) his own choice, when finding it not possible to accomplish his endeavour this time, i.e. establishing the supramental Consciousness on Earth, or if something would prove to him that it was not possible. What happened in 1950 was a fourth possibility not foreseeable in 1924: that he would have to descend into death voluntarily, having in the meantime acquired the powers to do so, in order to make his endeavour possible. This 'tactical' move was possible (the words of

---

* When Sudhir Ghosh told the American President John F. Kennedy about Sri Aurobindo and let him read his text on Korea, the president said: 'Surely there is a typing mistake here.' Under the document the date is mentioned: 28.6.1950. 'The date must have been 1960, not 1950. You mean to say that a man devoted to meditation and contemplation, sitting in a corner of India, said this about the intentions of Communist China as early as 1950?' (*Beautiful Vignettes of Sri Aurobindo and the Mother,* p. 48)

our ignorance are so inadequate) only because the Avatar was present on Earth in his/her physical completeness, i.e. in two bodies. If the Avatar had been present in only one body, the death of this body would have cancelled any possibility of executing the present mission. This shows that the planning and the completion of the mission of an Avatar is decided upon and pre-exists outside the scope of the material world.

We cannot even guess in what Sri Aurobindo's master act specifically consisted – 'You wouldn't understand,' Sri Aurobindo said to his assistants. The Mother herself has never given a complete explanation and said years later that she remained puzzled by the event. 'Why? Why? How often have I not asked that question!' To put the mind of the anguished disciples and devotees at rest, she had five thousand copies printed of an essay by K.D. Sethna, *The Passing of Sri Aurobindo*. He formulated his thesis as follows: 'Nothing except a colossal strategic sacrifice of this kind in order that the physical transformation of the Mother may be immeasurably hastened and rendered absolutely secure and, through it, a divine life on Earth for humanity may get rooted and be set aflower – nothing less can explain the passing of Sri Aurobindo.'[58] At that point in time K.D. Sethna could not know about the imminent manifestation of the Supramental.

One reads in many writings that there had been some indications foretelling the passing of Sri Aurobindo. There had been Sri Aurobindo's hurry to finish *Savitri*. There had also been the fact that for the first time since the Mother's coming he let himself be photographed by the world-famous French photographer Henri Cartier-Bresson. Both occurrences can only be taken as indications *post facto*.

Actually the only clear indication was something that had happened in early 1950 and that only the Mother knew. She said to Sanyal on the very morning of Sri Aurobindo's passing: 'About a year ago, while I was discussing things, I remarked that I felt like leaving this body of mine. He spoke out in a very firm tone: "No, this can never be. If necessary for this transformation, I might go, you will have to fulfil our Yoga of supramental descent and transformation."'[59] On another occasion she recalled this conversation as follows: 'I told him: "If one of us must go, I want that it should be me." – "It can't be you," he replied, "because you alone can do the material thing." And that was all. He said nothing more. He forbade me to leave my body ... After that – this took place early in 1950 – he gradually let himself fall ill. For he knew quite well that should he say "I must go," I would not have obeyed him and *I* would have gone. For according to the way I felt, he was much more indispensable than I. But he saw the matter from the other side. And he knew that I had the power to leave my body at will. So he didn't say a thing – he didn't say a thing right to the very last minute.'[60]

When Sri Aurobindo said to the Mother 'you alone can do the material fact,' he was looking to the future, to the time of the immensely difficult work of the transformation of the body. It is even reported that he said: 'Your body is better than mine.' This returns us to the Mother's choice of her parents, and the physical strength and equilibrium of Maurice Alfassa, her father.

And then there is the amazing avowal of the Mother that she does not seem to have known that Sri Aurobindo, step by invisible step, entered into death. She has confirmed this more than once herself. For instance: 'You see, he had decided to go. But he didn't want me to know that he was doing it deliberately. He knew that if for a single moment I knew he was doing it deliberately, I would have reacted with such violence that he would not have been able to leave. And he did this: he bore it all as if it were some unconsciousness, an ordinary illness, simply to keep me from knowing – and he left at the very moment he had to leave.'[61] Sri Aurobindo had created a blind spot, as it were, in the perception of her who was the Mother of the worlds and had access to all knowledge everywhere if she so desired! We are reminded of her saying that he 'is losing interest in himself' before anyone else present even sensed what was happening. Yet, in his love and because of practical necessity Sri Aurobindo prevented her from knowing, for she would have gone in his stead, or she would have followed him.

'She stood there, near the feet of Sri Aurobindo: her hair had been undressed and was flowing about her shoulders,' Sanyal writes. 'With a piercing gaze she stood there.' Once again we have to turn to the Mother for a glimpse into what happened at that climactic moment. 'He had accumulated in his body much supramental Force, and as soon as he left ... You see, he was lying on his bed, I stood by his side, and in a way altogether concrete – concrete with such a strong sensation as to make one think that it could be seen – all this supramental Force which was in him passed from his body into mine. And I felt the friction of the passage. It was extraordinary. It was an extraordinary experience.'[62]

This was when the Mother received the Mind of Light in the cells of her body. We have already seen what the Mind of Light is. We have also seen that, since November 1926, there had been a sort of 'division of tasks' between Sri Aurobindo and the Mother. Because of the unity of their Consciousness, she remained in direct contact with his yogic struggles and realizations; everything that happened in him she knew at once and shared in it. He, for his part, participated in the goings on in the Ashram and in the disciples, through the correspondence and by yogic means. But she had been put in charge of the material build-up, while he was concentrating on fixing the Supramental in matter, which meant in the first place the matter of his own body. Now he had entered into death fully conscious and with all his yogic acquisitions – except those of the physical body, for the laying down of the physical body is of course what 'death' is about. That is why another component of his master act consisted in transmitting the supramental acquisitions, the supramental stuff of his physical body to the Mother, who from now on had to continue alone and take on both parts of the task.

'As soon as Sri Aurobindo withdrew from his body, what he has called the Mind of Light got realized in me,' the Mother said to K.D. Sethna. 'The Supermind had descended long ago – very long ago – into the mind and even into the vital; it was working in the physical also but indirectly through those intermediaries. The question was about the direct action of the Supermind in the physical. Sri Aurobindo said it could be possible only if the physical mind received the supramental light: the physical mind was the instrument for direct action upon the most material. This physical mind receiving the supramental light Sri Aurobindo called the Mind of Light.'[63]

The transmission of the Mind of Light from Sri Aurobindo's body into the body of the Mother, 'with such a strong sensation as to make one think that it could be seen,' happened immediately after Sanyal declared that the life of his physical body had come to an end.

'On 6 December I entered Sri Aurobindo's room before dawn,' writes Sanyal. 'The Mother and I had a look at him; how wonderful, how beautiful he looked, with a golden hue. There were no signs of death as science had taught me, no evidence of the slightest discolouration or decomposition. The Mother whispered: "As long as the supramental light does not pass away, the body will not show any signs of decomposition, and it may be a day or many more days." I whispered to her: "Where is the light you speak of – can I not see it?" I was then kneeling by Sri Aurobindo's bed, by the Mother's feet. She smiled at me and with infinite compassion put her hand on my head. There he was – with a luminous mantle of bluish golden hue around him.'[64] Major Barbet, the French physician of the Hospital, examined Sri Aurobindo's body and signed the death certificate together with Sanyal.

The American philosopher Rhoda Le Cocq has noted her impressions of those days in the book already mentioned. She writes about 5 December: 'Already it had been decided, despite the objections of the French colonial governor, that Sri Aurobindo would be buried in the courtyard of the main building [of the Ashram], beneath a huge spreading tree. The male Ashramites, including the visiting doctor [probably Sen], began to build the tomb ... There was weeping, but no hysteria. By afternoon men and women passed baskets of earth from hand to hand, as the digging continued beneath the tree. Then there was a new announcement. For all of us there, there would now be a second darshan ...

'Again, the following morning on 6 December, we all filed past. The "force field" which I mentioned earlier seemed to remain about the body and throughout the room. Dressed in white, upon a white couch before the windows, Sri Aurobindo now lay in state ... Unexpectedly, in the afternoon there was another darshan. Sri Aurobindo's face still did not look deathlike. The skin was golden in colour, the white hair blowing on the pillow in a breeze from a fan. The aquiline profile continued to have a prophetic look. There was no odour of death and little incense was burning. To my astonishment, the repeated viewings of his body had a comforting effect. Previously I had always resented the idea of viewing dead bodies ...'

7 December. 'From the French colony, already exploding with

disapproval and its officials much disturbed by the burial plans, came the rumour that the body *must* have been "shot with formaldehyde" secretly, to preserve it. Moreover, said the officials, the Ashram was not only breaking the law in burying [a dead body] in the garden, it was worse to keep it so long unburied ... On the morning of 7 December, therefore, a French doctor representing the Government, a Dr. Barbet, arrived to inspect the body of Sri Aurobindo. At the end he reported it was a "miracle;" there was no deterioration, *no rigor mortis*. It was an unheard of occurrence; the weather had continued to be hot during the entire time.'[65]

8 December. 'When I asked Him (8 December 1950) to resuscitate his body,' said the Mother later, 'He clearly answered: "I have left this body purposely. I will not take it back. I shall manifest again in the first supramental body built in the supramental way.'[66]

9 December. Rhoda Le Cocq writes: 'On the afternoon of 9 December, at 5:00 p.m., the burial service finally took place after another, final darshan. A feeling of force and energy remained in the atmosphere around Sri Aurobindo's vicinity, but that force had weakened now ... There was no orthodox religious service at the burial. The coffin, of rosewood with metal-gold rings, much like an old and beautiful sea chest, was borne from [Sri Aurobindo's room into the courtyard] and lowered into the earth. French officials, all dressed in white, made a line to the left, their faces stern, a bit superior in expression and definitely disapproving of the entire affair. Over the coffin, concrete slabs were laid. Then everyone lined up and, one by one, we scattered earth from wicker baskets. It was dark under the spreading tree when each of us had made this last farewell.'

'To grieve is an insult to Sri Aurobindo, who is here with us, conscious and alive,' proclaimed the Mother on 14 December. This was no empty rhetoric. In the following years she would time and again refer to his concrete presence and the enormous work he was doing 'behind the scenes' to hasten the manifestation of the Supramental and the transformation of her own body. Moreover, we know about some of Sri

Aurobindo's realizations, and we know that his 'death' was not what death is generally supposed to be.

How can one better take leave of Sri Aurobindo than with the following lines of *Savitri*, from the Book of the Traveller of the Worlds, most of which was written in the last months of his life. The traveller is none other than Sri Aurobindo himself.

> Into the abysmal secrecy he came
> Where darkness peers from her mattress, grey and nude,
> And stood on the last locked subconscient's floor
> Where Being slept unconscious of its thoughts
> And built the world not knowing what it built.
> There waiting its hour the future lay unknown,
> There is the record of the vanished stars.
> There in the slumber of the cosmic Will
> He saw the secret key of Nature's change ...
> He saw in Night the Eternal's shadowy veil,
> Knew death for a cellar in the house of life,
> In destruction felt creation's hasty pace,
> Knew loss as the price of a celestial gain
> And hell as a short cut to heaven's gates.
> Then in Illusion's occult factory
> And in the Inconscient's magic printing-house
> Torn were the formats of the primal Night
> And shattered the stereotypes of Ignorance.
> Alive, breathing a deep spiritual breath,
> Nature expunged her stiff mechanical code
> And the articles of the bound soul's contract,
> Falsehood gave back to Truth her tortured shape.
> Annulled were the tables of the law of Pain ...
> He imposed upon dark atom and dumb mass
> The diamond script of the Imperishable,
> Inscribed on the dim heart of fallen things
> A paean-song of the free Infinite
> And the Name, foundation of eternity,
> And traced on the awake exultant cells

335

In the ideographs of the Ineffable
The lyric of the love that waits through Time
And the mystic volume of the Book of Bliss
And the message of the superconscient Fire.[67]

That is where the 'Traveller of the worlds' went and what he did. It is where Sri Aurobindo went and what he did, totally unknown to the world. And he arranged everything so that the continuation of his work would not be disrupted. '[He] cast his deeds like bronze to front the years.'[68]

Part Three:

The Road Alone

13.

The Yoga of the Body Cells

Sometimes one life is charged with earth's destiny.[1]

– Sri Aurobindo

S ri Aurobindo's passing was a terrible jolt to the Mother, later compared by her to 'a sledgehammer blow' and 'an annihilation'. During thirty years she had leaned on him for support with an absolute
confidence in his presence, his knowledge and his powers. United with
him in her consciousness, which was the same in both of them, she had
felt that her body too was upheld by his physical presence, a relationship so intimately interwoven and strong that physical distance was
of no importance. Any important spiritual event he experienced, she
participated in; any spiritual realization he acquired, she shared. There
was the division of tasks, without which the work could not be done,
but there was at its base the unity transcendent, supramental and as
embodied individuals.

'[In] all those thirty years of life, not for a second did I have any
sense of responsibility,' she would later say, 'in spite of all the work I
was doing, all the organizing and everything. He had supposedly passed
the responsibility on to me, you see, but he was standing behind – he
was actually doing everything. I was active, but with absolutely no
responsibility. I never felt responsible for a single minute – he took the
full responsibility.'[2]

True, the supramental force gathered in his cells, the Mind of Light,
had entered into her – which means that Sri Aurobindo had entered
into her, for on that level the part equals the whole. After his passing,
she would say that Sri Aurobindo remained, in an occult way, ever-
present with her, '... the Sri Aurobindo whom I know and with whom
I lived physically for thirty years, and who has not left me, not for a
moment – for he is still with me, day and night, thinking through my

brain, writing through my pen, speaking through my mouth and acting through my organizing power.'³ Yet the physical, material presence was not there any more. And therefore the Mother too had to perform a yogic master act.

'When he went out of his body and entered into mine (the most material part of him, the part involved with external things) and I understood that I had the entire responsibility for all the work *and* for the sadhana – well, then I locked a part of me away, a deep psychic part that was living, beyond all responsibility, in the ecstasy of the realization: [in] the Supreme. I took it and locked it away, I sealed it off and said: "You're not moving until the rest is ready."'⁴ To enable her body to remain upon earth, she locked the part of her soul away which was most intimately connected with Sri Aurobindo in their common Divinity. 'Otherwise I would have followed him.' That door will be opened only ten years later, in circumstances to be related further on.

All activities in the Ashram were suspended for twelve days, after which the Mother would make her decision known as to whether the Ashram would continue to exist or be dissolved. 'Those of you who were not here at that period can have no idea of the gloom that settled over the Ashram community, the shock that friends and well-wishers all over the world received,' said M.P. Pandit.⁵ And Nirodbaran writes: 'After Sri Aurobindo's passing, it was feared in some quarters that the Ashram would collapse, at least decline.'⁶ In *Memorable Contacts with the Mother,* the same author writes: 'There were some old sadhaks who left the Ashram after Sri Aurobindo's passing.' And: 'The most important matter after Sri Aurobindo's departure concerned the Mother's connection with the Ashram. It was necessary to testify that the Mother had been all along in charge of the Ashram and that she still had the executive power. A document was drawn up and, in front of a *notaire* [notary public] of the town, it was signed by a few members of the Ashram chosen by the Mother. I was one of the signatories.'⁷

The Mother would later say that everything had been seen, decided and settled after three days. All the same, the Ashram remained suspended for nine more days. Then the Mother took up the outer work along with the inner one. There could no longer be a division of tasks

– she had to bear the whole burden in the physical world. 'Sometimes one life is charged with earth's destiny.'[8]

The Ashram School and its Education

Life must be faced as a whole, with all the ugliness, falsehood and cruelty it still contains, but care must be taken to discover in ourselves the source of all goodness, all beauty, all light and all truth, in order to bring this source consciously into contact with the world in order to transform it.[9]

– The Mother

During the 1920s and 1930s, the Mother's educational activity was limited to instructing a few individuals in French and offering general counsel in other courses of study. At that time, children were as a rule not permitted to live in the Ashram. In the early 1940s a number of families were admitted to the Ashram and instruction was initiated for the children. On 2 December 1943 the Mother formally opened a school for about twenty children. She herself was one of the teachers. The number of pupils gradually increased during the next seven years.

'On 24 April 1951, the Mother presided over a convention where it was resolved to establish an "international university centre." On 6 January 1952, she inaugurated the Sri Aurobindo International University Centre. The name was changed in 1959 to Sri Aurobindo International Centre of Education.

'At present [ca. 1978], the Centre of Education has about 150 full or part-time teachers and 500 students, ranging from nursery to advanced levels. The curriculum includes the humanities, languages, fine arts, sciences, engineering, technology and vocational training. Facilities include libraries, laboratories, workshops, and a theatre and studios for drama, dancing, music, painting, etc.'[10]

These few plain facts give us an idea of the extraordinary, allround educational work the Mother did with the Ashram children, and through them for humankind (for humankind's representatives were there to make possible her work on it as a whole). It should be stressed at once that the aim of the education at the Ashram never consisted in moulding Ashramites. The Mother often told the students that they belonged to 'the same family,' to 'the family of the aspiration, of the spiritual tendency,'[11] and that they made up a representative selection, 'a cream' of humanity, even if they were not aware of this themselves.

Nonetheless, neither she nor Sri Aurobindo has ever alleged that the souls, which incarnated with the aim of helping to prepare the New World, were exclusively to be found on a single spot in the world: the Sri Aurobindo Ashram at Pondicherry. The Ashram, as we have seen, played a primary role in initiating the conditions of the material transformation, in igniting them in the body of humanity. But the supramental transformation is the business of humanity as a whole, of which some privileged or pioneering elements found their way to the Sri Aurobindo International Centre of Education. Of these elements some became Ashramites, many more went out to live the worldly life. On a certain occasion the Mother even said to the teachers: 'If out of 150 students there are seven who are outstanding personalities, it's very good.'[12] They are the hungry ones and have to be fed, she said.

The years from 1950 to 1958 were no doubt the most 'visible' years of the Mother. From early morning to late at night she was seeing the disciples and pouring her force and her blessings over them, visiting and guiding the departments (for the Ashram, with its thousand and more members and its five hundred students, had become a fairly big affair), working with the secretaries on the official transactions and the correspondence, and from the afternoon onwards being present with the youth at the tennis ground, playground and sports ground, guiding and encouraging them – and participating herself in a game of tennis, which she would play up to her eightieth year.

The system of education developed in the Ashram, if it can be called a system, was mainly the Mother's. Sri Aurobindo has written relatively little on the subject, most of it in his early years, basing himself on the difference between his own education in England and his experience as a lecturer and professor at Baroda.* The principal aim of his writings

---

* See *A System of National Education*, in the Sri Aurobindo Birth Centenary Library, vol. 17, The Hour of God.

on education was to activate the interest and innate intelligence in the Indian student, and turn him away from the imitative and deadening habit of learning by rote and of cramming, then as now practised in so many Indian schools and educational institutions – although India nowadays has some eminent institutes and colleges where the creative intelligence is allowed to come into full flower. His most important contribution on this topic of education and its aims was, however, the series of articles requested from him by the Mother for publication in the *Bulletin of Physical Education* and dictated in the last months of his life.

In educating the Ashram children, the Mother drew from her life-long practical experience and still more from her spiritual knowledge and intuition. The basis of this education was her knowledge of the different aspects of the human being – the material, vital, mental, psychic and spiritual parts. This knowledge, gained from age-long yogic and mystical experience, is in itself new and revolutionary compared to the way the human being is chiefly seen in the West: as a material body mysteriously functioning in tandem with an intangible mind, and which has in addition, for the religious-minded, a soul about which it is difficult to say anything except that it is supposed to be eternal.

'If we have a school here, it is in order that it be different from the millions of schools in the world,' the Mother said. 'It is to give the children a chance to distinguish between ordinary life and the divine life, the life of truth – to see things in a different way. It is useless to want to repeat here the ordinary life. The teacher's mission is to open the eyes of the children to something which they will not find anywhere else.' [13] And she said also: 'We are not here to do easy things.' [14]

Let us briefly consider the Ashram education in the order of its five aspects as given above.

First, there was the education of the physical. 'The perfection of the body, as great a perfection as we can bring about by the means at our disposal, must be the ultimate aim of physical culture,' wrote Sri Aurobindo in the articles published in the *Bulletin of Physical Education*. 'Perfection is the true aim of all culture, the spiritual and psychic, the mental, the vital, and it must be the aim of our physical culture also. If our seeking is for a total perfection of the being, the physical part of it cannot be left aside; for the body is the material basis, the body is the instrument we have to use ... A total perfection is the ultimate aim which we set before us, for our ideal is the Divine Life which we wish to create here, the life of the Spirit fulfilled on earth, life accomplishing its own spiritual transformation even here on earth in the conditions of the material universe. That cannot be unless the body too undergoes a transformation, unless its action and functioning attain to a supreme capacity and the perfection which is possible to it or which can be made possible.'[15]

As the Mother said: 'Physical culture means putting consciousness into the cells of the body. One may or may not know that, but it is a fact. When we concentrate to make our muscles move according to our will, when we attempt to make our limbs more supple, to give them an agility, or a force, or a resistance, or a plasticity which they do not naturally possess, we infuse into the cells of the body a consciousness which was not there before, thus turning it into an increasingly homogeneous and receptive instrument, which progresses in and by its activities.'[16]

The Mother made enormous efforts to give the youth of the Ashram, as well as the adult Ashramites, the possibility to keep their body in good condition and to develop it. Little by little the Department of Physical Education acquired a gymnasium, a playground (where also films were shown and the Mother gave her evening classes), a tennis ground, and last but not least a splendid sports ground.

Nirodbaran, himself formerly a keen tennis player, writes about the tennis ground, which is still there by the blue waters of the Bay of Bengal: '[The Mother] often talked about her project [of building a tennis ground] to Sri Aurobindo. One day we heard that the entire wasteland along the northeastern seaside was taken [by the Mother] on a long lease from the Government, and that a part of it would be made into tennis courts and the rest into a playground. One cannot imagine now what this place was before. It was one of the filthiest spots of Pondicherry, full of thistles and wild undergrowth, an open place for committing nuisance as well as a pasture for pigs! The stink and the loathsome sight made the place a Stygian sore and a black spot on the colonial Government. The Mother changed this savage wasteland into a heavenly playground ... If for nothing else, for this transformation at least Pondicherry should be eternally grateful to the Mother. But who remembers the past?'[17] Like the tennis ground, every place and building in the Department of Physical Education, and every place and building in the Ashram as a whole, has been established against considerable odds.

The Mother playing tennis at the age of 70

We know that the Sri Aurobindo Ashram was the only ashram where men and women lived together on equal terms. It was also the only ashram where children formed an integral part of its life – and where physical education formed an integral part of life. South India can be blisteringly hot. Then how does one dress for the physical exercises? For the boys there was no problem, but what about the girls? We turn to Nirodbaran again: 'The [girls'] exercises were [at first] done in cumbersome pyjamas which checked free movement. One evening when I went to visit the Playground, I found the gate closed. The gatekeeper told me that the Mother did not want anyone except the group-members to enter the Playground. When it was thrown open we found, to our surprise, that the girls were doing exercises in shorts!'[18]

What was the reaction to this 'drastic step,' Nirodbaran asks? He answers the question himself: 'Some, particularly old people, were shocked to see their daughters scantily dressed [that means in shorts, shirt and kitty-cap] and doing exercises jointly with boys; a few conservative guardians were planning to take their wards away from such a modernized Ashram. I, personally, admired, on the one hand, the revolutionary step taken by the Mother far in advance of the time in Eastern countries, in anticipation of the modern movement in dress; on the other hand, my cautious mind, or as Sri Aurobindo would say my coward mind, could not but feel the risk involved in this forward venture.'[19] Narayan Prasad, in his *Life in Sri Aurobindo Ashram,* puts it this way: 'When youthful girls of aristocratic families took to sports in shorts and shirts, throwing shyness and reserve aside, it was for all a happy wonder.'[20]

The disciple the Mother put in charge of physical education in the Ashram was Pranab Kumar Bhattacharya, commonly known as Dada (elder brother in Bengali). Pranab had joined the Ashram in 1945 together with his four brothers. He had come from Calcutta, where for years he had undergone a thorough physical training. A month after his arrival he started doing some training in his own house. Some of the young members who had recently joined the Ashram asked Pranab to teach them physical exercises. When Pranab proposed to the Mother to start regular playground activities, she agreed. 'Thus started physical education in the Ashram, with fourteen youngsters.'[21] Most of them would themselves become instructors – or 'captains' as they are called in the Ashram. Pranab would grow very close to the Mother, who has drawn some remarkable portraits of him.

The second focus of the Ashram education was the vital. 'Of all the aspects of education, the education of the vital is perhaps the most important, the most indispensable,' wrote the Mother.[22] And she explained: 'The vital being in us is the seat of impulses and desires, of enthusiasm and violence, of dynamic energy and desperate depressions, of passions and revolts. It can set everything in motion, it can build and realize – but it can also destroy and spoil everything. Thus it may be the most difficult part to discipline in the human being. It is a work that takes much time and much patience, and that requires a perfect sincerity, for without sincerity you will deceive yourself from the very outset and all endeavour for progress will be in vain. With the collaboration of the vital no realization seems impossible, no transformation impracticable. But the difficulty lies in securing this constant collaboration. The vital is a good worker, but most often it seeks its own satisfaction.'[23]

The vital is the domain of the life forces, which may be of a higher or a lower order, and sometimes of a very low order. As every level of the human personality – and therefore of a complete education – opens us to the invisible worlds represented by that level, we are accessible to all kinds of forces and beings, mostly without realizing it. Indeed, most of our life is driven by those forces and beings. And humans being what they still are, the forces which dominate the life of humanity on earth are of the lowest, nastiest vital kind. It is therefore an important part of the educational effort to open ourselves and the ones we try to educate to the higher vital impulses.

As the Mother said: 'This vital is a curious being. It's a being of passion, of enthusiasm, and naturally of desire. It is, however, quite capable of getting enthusiastic over something beautiful, for example, of admiring, sensing what is greater and nobler than itself. And if really something utterly beautiful occurs in the being, if an impulse of exceptional value manifests itself, then it may grow enthusiastic and it is capable of giving itself with total dedication – with a generosity that is not found, for instance, in the mental or in the physical domain.'[24]

To master the lower vital impulses and activate and enrich the higher ones, three faculties have to be cultivated. The first one is the will; the second, the capacity for attention and concentration; the third, the refinement of the senses through harmony, beauty and art in all its forms.

There is no trait of the character, no occult power or yogic realization which, according to the Mother, cannot be acquired or mastered by a constant, unflinching application of the will. This is one of the themes running through her *Entretiens,* her answers to questions from the Ashram youngsters. As she said in March 1951: 'In the first place, to become conscious of anything whatsoever, you must will it. And when

I say "will it," I don't mean saying one day: "Oh, I would like this or that very much," and to forget about it completely a couple of days later. To will something is a constant, sustained, concentrated aspiration, an almost exclusive occupation of the consciousness.'[25]

Attention is, as it were, the basis of all sense perception, it is our conscious presence to the visible and invisible worlds. 'Whatsoever you may want to do in life,' the Mother said to the young people around her, 'one thing is absolutely indispensable and at the basis of everything: the capacity of concentrating the attention. If you are able to gather together the rays of attention and consciousness on one point and can maintain this concentration with a persistent will, *nothing* can resist it – whatever it may be, from the most material physical development to the highest spiritual one. But this discipline must be followed in a constant and, it may be said, imperturbable way. Not that you should always be concentrated on the same thing, that's not what I mean: I mean learning to concentrate. Materially, for studies, sports, all physical or mental development, it is absolutely indispensable. And the value of an individual is proportionate to the value of his attention.'[26]

To be surrounded by harmony and beauty, to live in it constantly and cultivate these forms of expression, is the principal condition for the refinement of the vital. 'In the physical world, of all things it is beauty that expresses best the Divine,' wrote the Mother to a young disciple who learned painting. 'The physical world is the world of form and the perfection of form is beauty. Beauty interprets, expresses, manifests the Eternal. Its role is to put all manifested nature in contact with the Eternal through the perfection of form, through harmony and a sense of the ideal which uplifts and leads towards something higher.'[27] And she wrote also: 'True art means the expression of beauty in the material world. In a world wholly converted, that is to say, expressing integrally the divine reality, art must serve as the revealer and teacher of this divine beauty in life.'[28]

We know what an important element beauty and art had been in her own life. It is therefore not surprising that she did everything possible to create an expression of the divine Presence through beauty around her, and to develop the sense of it in the pupils and students of the school. To borrow a phrase from *Savitri*: 'beauty was her footstep.'

Sri Aurobindo had stimulated the receptivity and development of the yogic perception through poetry, which was, he said, '*his* department.' The Mother, on her side, stimulated the growth of the same qualities through the visual arts – and music, classical Indian and Western dancing, theatre, exhibitions of all kinds, embroidery, marbling, the building of well-proportioned bodies, and the creation of a harmonious and beautiful environment. If she had possessed the means, there would surely have been many more buildings like Golconde.

The third focus of education was the mind. 'The true role of the mind is the formation and organization of action. The mind has a formative and organizing power, and it is that which puts the different elements of inspiration in order for action, for organizing action. And if it would only confine itself to that role, receiving inspirations – whether from above or from the mystic centre of the soul – and simply formulating the plan of action – in broad outline or in minute detail, for the smallest things of life or the great terrestrial organizations – it would amply fulfil its function. It is not an instrument of knowledge. But it can use knowledge for action, to organize action. It is an instrument of organization and formation, very powerful and very capable when it is well developed.'[29]

The development of the mind and the acquisition of knowledge is, of course, what is generally seen as the aim of study. In the curriculum of the Ashram school all the usual academic subjects were found – mathematics and science (for which Pavitra built a well-equipped laboratory) as well as what are called the 'humanities': modern languages and Sanskrit, history, geography, sociology, psychology, philosophy, etc. The Mother made it clear, however, that everything is one, which means that all these kinds of knowledge are intimately related to the spiritual realities which are their foundation and without which they could not be manifest. '[The students] are taught history *or* spiritual things, they are taught science *or* spiritual things. That is what is idiotic. In history the Spirit is there; in science the Spirit is there: the Truth is everywhere. What is needed is not to teach all that in a false way, but to teach it in a truthful way.'[30]

The fourth focus of education was the psychic being. 'The soul is something of the Divine that descends into the evolution as a Divine

Principle within it to support the evolution of the individual out of the Ignorance into the Light,' wrote Sri Aurobindo. 'It develops in the course of the evolution a psychic individual or soul individuality which grows from life to life, using the evolving mind, vital and body as its instruments. It is the soul that is immortal while the rest disintegrates; it passes from life to life carrying its experiences in essence and the continuity of the evolution of the individual.'[31] As the Mother said: 'The psychic is the representative of the Divine in the human being. That is it, you see – the Divine is not something remote and inaccessible. The Divine is in you but you are not fully conscious of it. It acts now as an influence rather than a Presence. It should be a conscious Presence.'[32]

Taking this into consideration, becoming conscious of the psychic being – Sri Aurobindo's 'psychic individual or soul individuality' in the text quoted above – was the cardinal aim of the education as worked out by the Mother in the Ashram school. Becoming a consciously incarnated soul (one is always an unconsciously incarnated one) is the meaning of human evolution, collectively and individually; it is also a realizable possibility at the point where humanity has arrived now. As humanity is inevitably to be followed by a higher species, the supramental being, the very first condition for this to happen is that the pioneering individuals first reach the maximum stage of evolution possible at present by realizing their psychic being.* This is what the yoga in the Sri Aurobindo Ashram was about; as the Ashram School was founded on the same basis, it was also the purpose of education in the Ashram.

The logical consequence of the presence of the psychic being in humans and the many lives every human has gone through before attaining the stage of a higher awareness – a threshold which most Ashram children, because of their being chosen, were supposed to have reached – was that every individual is special for reasons of his or her own past experiences. Every individual has reached a particular level or

---

* The *soul* or *psyche* is the essential divine portion or 'spark' present in everything that exists, for without it nothing could exist. The *psychic being* is an evolutionary being, consisting of the soul as its core and of the psychic individuality, built up by means of the experiences gone through in the course of the many lives of its evolution on earth. For, as the Mother said repeatedly, the incarnated psychic being exists only on the earth.

degree of development. This belief was fundamental to the education which the Ashram school would provide. And its logical consequence was that a common curriculum of education, which would be the same for all students, was absolutely excluded. Education had to be individualized. Each child had to be treated as different, unique, and its progress through the various grades of education offered in the school had to be tailored to its uniqueness.

This explains why the system of *libre progrès* or 'free progress' was practised in the Ashram school, and it explains the large number of teachers who were and still are required for a school like this. When a teacher asked: 'Mother, would you please define in a few words what you mean essentially by "free progress"? the Mother answered: 'A progress guided by the soul and not subjected to habits, conventions or preconceived ideas.'[33] Even if for practical, organizational reasons forms or grades were established, they were still held to be a kind of framework within which the students could evolve individually rather than a system to which they had to conform.

This framework provided the students with a large degree of freedom – which never turned into lack of discipline, as discipline and the team spirit were inculcated by the activities of physical education. It is a fact that the Mother even said explicitly that the children did not have to study if they did not feel like it, but that they should be warned of the consequences. As it is a fact that she saw the parents, who were generally not educated in the same spirit, more as hindrances than as helpers in the development of their children. 'There is one thing which is the main difficulty,' she said, 'it is the parents. When the children live with their parents [as many Ashram children did] I consider that it is hopeless. Because the parents want their child to be educated as they were themselves, and they want them to get good jobs, to earn money – all things that are contrary to our aspiration.'[34] It should be added that the students who went out into the world generally did very well and were often regarded as brilliant.

A point worth underlining is that the students were encouraged to be fearless and brave in all circumstances. The reason for this is quite simply that anybody trying to realize his or her soul, or to advance spiritually, will be inevitably attacked by the hostile forces using visible and invisible means. If ordinary life is a battle, spiritual life is a hundred times more so, and one has to be a hero to persevere in one's effort. Of this heroic struggle Sri Aurobindo and the Mother are the best examples; their fight with the hostile forces can be read on every page of their lives. This is why in the students' notebooks the following prayer, written by the Mother, was printed: 'Make of us the hero warriors we aspire to become. May we fight successfully the great battle of the future that is to be born against the past that seeks to endure, so that the new things may manifest and we may be ready to receive them.'[35]

The fifth focus of the Ashram education was the spiritual aspect. The spiritual potential is innate in the human being. To many these higher layers of existence are still hidden, yet for some they are accessible. As most of the Ashram children were inwardly called or destined to be educated under the Mother's aegis, one may suppose that for them the higher reaches of consciousness were at least potentially accessible. 'You are here at this moment, that is to say upon earth, because you have chosen it at one time – you do not remember it any more, but I know it. That is why you are here. Well, you must rise to the height of the task. You must strive, you must conquer all weaknesses and limitations. Above all you must tell your ego: "Your hour is past." We want a race without ego, that has in place of the ego the Divine Consciousness which will allow the race to develop itself and the supramental being to take birth.'[36]

The Ashram school was intended to provide a complete education in the light and with the help of Sri Aurobindo and the Mother. A message of the Mother makes this clear: 'We are not here to do (only a little better) what the others do. We are here to do what the others *cannot do* because they do not have the idea that it can be done. We are here to open the future to children who belong to the Future. Anything else is not worth the trouble and not worthy of Sri Aurobindo's help.'[37]

To the question of a student: 'Why are we here in the Sri Aurobindo Ashram?' she replied: 'There is an ascending evolution in nature which goes from the stone to the plant, from the plant to the animal, from the animal to man. Because man is, for the moment, the last rung at the summit of the ascending evolution, he considers himself as the final stage in this ascension and believes there can be nothing on earth superior to him. In that he is mistaken. In his physical nature he is yet almost wholly an animal, a thinking and speaking animal, but still an animal in his material habits and instincts. Undoubtedly, nature cannot be satisfied with such an imperfect result; she endeavours to bring out a being who will be to man what man is to the animal, a being who will remain a man in its external form, and yet whose consciousness will rise far above the mind and its slavery to ignorance ...

'You have the immense privilege of having come quite young to the Ashram, that is to say, still plastic and capable of being moulded according to this new ideal and thus become the representatives of the new race. Here, in the Ashram, you are in the most favourable conditions with regard to the environment, the influence, the teaching and the example, to awaken in you this supramental consciousness and to grow according to its law.'[38]

Who would teach these 'children of the Future'? The Mother herself taught them, but it goes without saying that she could not do everything. 'To lead a child on to the paths of the Future, to be his "teacher," one must first understand that his psychic being carries within itself its own aspirations and intentions which he shall live tomorrow, thus enriching the already long experience he has acquired upon earth; one must understand that any teaching is but a progressive revelation of hidden faculties powerful enough to give a concrete shape to a new experience. One must help the student to become, as much as possible, what he can and wants to be – for if his soul has more or less chosen his life's destiny, yet what he shall make out of it is in no way determined. The child is not only a mind to be trained, but a consciousness that must be helped to grow and widen itself.'[39]

'Nothing can be taught to the mind which is not already concealed as potential knowledge in the unfolding soul of the creature,' wrote Sri Aurobindo in *The Synthesis of Yoga*. 'So also all perfection of which the outer man is capable, is only a realizing of the eternal perfection of the Spirit within him. We know the Divine and become the Divine, because we are That already in our secret nature. All teaching is a revealing, all becoming is an unfolding. Self-attainment is the secret;

self-knowledge and an increasing consciousness are the means and the process.'[40] According to Sri Aurobindo, 'the first principle of true teaching is that nothing can be taught. The teacher is not an instructor or taskmaster, he is a helper and a guide. His business is to suggest and not to impose ... He does not impart knowledge to him [i.e. to the child], he shows him how to acquire knowledge for himself ... The second principle is that the mind has to be consulted in its own growth. The idea of hammering the child into the shape desired by the parent or teacher is a barbarous and ignorant superstition ... Everyone has in him something divine, something his own, a chance of perfection and strength in however small a sphere which God offers to him to take or refuse. The task is to find it, develop it and use it ... The third principle of education is to work from the near to the far, from that which is to that which shall be ... If anything has to be brought in from outside, it must be offered, not forced on the mind. A free and natural growth is the condition of genuine development.'[41]

These principles were formulated by Sri Aurobindo long before there was an Ashram School or even an Ashram, and were intended as general guidelines. To be a teacher in the Ashram required a lot more: it required not only that the teacher tried to live according to the principles he had to teach, but that he had realized them, at least partially, and that he was able to identify with the souls whom he was teaching – in other words, it required that he be a yogi or she a yogini. 'You must have lived what you want to teach,' wrote the Mother. 'To speak of the new consciousness, let it penetrate you and reveal to you its secrets. For only then can you speak of it with any competence.'[42] In fact, the Ashram School was a school where the teachers were also students. As the Mother wrote: 'The school should be an opportunity for progress for the teacher as well as for the student. Each one should have the freedom to develop freely. A method is never so well applied as when one has discovered it oneself. Otherwise it is as boring for the teacher as it is for the student.'[43] And she said that teaching was 'a priesthood.'

She impressed on the teachers: 'You must not confuse a religious teaching with a spiritual one. Religious teaching belongs to the past and halts progress. Spiritual teaching is the teaching of the future – it illumines the consciousness and prepares it for the future realization. Spiritual teaching is above religions and strives towards global Truth. It teaches us to enter into direct relations with the Divine.'[44] She strongly resisted all traces of dogmatism and said on a certain occasion, when somebody quoted Sri Aurobindo to corroborate a point: 'Sri Aurobindo did say that, but he also said many other things which complete his advice and abolish all possibility of dogmatism. Sri Aurobindo himself has often repeated that if one affirms one thing, one should be able to affirm its opposite, otherwise one cannot understand the Truth.'[45]

Let us close this section with one of those unforgettable sayings of hers:

'To be young is to live in the future.

'To be young is to be always ready to give up what we are in order to become what we must be.

'To be young is never to accept that something is irreparable.'[46]

Transformation of the Body Cells

In our body's cells there sits a hidden Power
That sees the unseen and plans eternity ...[47]

– Sri Aurobindo

If all this gives us a glimpse of the Mother's multifarious outer activities, what was she busy with inwardly? Now that she had accepted to take on alone the avataric yoga, her effort to bring down the Supramental and the transformation of Matter, what precisely was her work? The Mother spoke a lot at the time, generally in public, but very little about her personal endeavour. What she spoke about in public was usually based on her vast previous experience; her present, ongoing experiences were seldom mentioned or asked about.

All the same, if one reads attentively the *Questions and Answers* and other talks of these years one finds some clues of crucial importance. It was her way to set about what she had accepted to do, or what she was inspired to do, with supernal Power and without delay, if possible. 'The Mother is always in a concentrated consciousness in her inner being,'[48] wrote Sri Aurobindo. And in his correspondence with Nirodbaran we read: 'Mother's pressure for a change is always strong – even when she doesn't put it as a force it is there by the very nature of the Divine Energy in her.'[49]

As early as 6 January 1951, the Mother gave an important talk which is indicative of the yogic problem she must have started tackling immediately after Sri Aurobindo's passing. When commenting on a text of hers which had previously appeared in the *Bulletin,* she dealt with the different levels of an integral transformation, which, as we know, is the aim of the Integral Yoga. She read the following paragraph from that text: 'In the integral transformation both the outer nature and the inner consciousness are transformed. The character, the habits, etc., are completely changed, as well as the thoughts and the mental outlook on things.' And she commented: 'Yes, but there is something which remains unchanged unless you take care of it and persist in your effort. What is it? The body consciousness.'[50] What is the body consciousness? '... The physical consciousness as a whole. But in this physical consciousness as a whole there is the physical mind – a mind that is occupied with all the ordinary things and responds to everything around you. There is also the vital consciousness, which is the awareness of sensations, impulses, enthusiasms and desires. Finally, there is the physical consciousness itself, the material consciousness, the body consciousness, and this is the [consciousness] which so far has never been entirely transformed. The global, overall consciousness of the body has been transformed; one can throw off the bondage of thought, of habits that one no longer considers inevitable. That can change – it has been changed. But what remains to be changed is the consciousness of the cells.'[51]

These words are so precious because they date from less than a month after Sri Aurobindo's passing, from about a fortnight after life in the Ashram had become active again. What the Mother is saying here is that, at that point in time, the whole of the Integral Yoga had been accomplished except the most outward part: the transformation of 'the body consciousness.' One also notices how the Mother is searching for a verbal definition of the part that remains to be transformed. From the quoted paragraph we can deduce: physical consciousness = material consciousness = consciousness of the cells.

Part of the searching and groping is due to the fact that the Mother was talking in French. This talk, not included in the published volumes of *Questions and Answers*, was actually one of the very first *Entretiens*, not yet electronically recorded, but noted down stenographically. The French word *physique* may refer to matter as well as to the body.* One has to pay attention to this double meaning in future disclosures by the Mother about her Yoga from 1951 onwards.

Second, the word 'body' itself should be subjected to examination. The body is generally considered to be the material, outer part of the human person. In occultism and spirituality, however, a distinction is made between the body as a whole, its organs, and its cells. The body as a whole has its own consciousness; this is known in practice, if not in theory, to all athletes, for it lies at the basis of their training. Each

---

* The *Petit Robert* (1993), an authoritative dictionary of the French language, explains the adjective *physique* as follows: 1. What relates to nature, to the concrete world; 2. What concerns the human body.

organ too has its individual consciousness; it is the lack of equilibrium, of harmony between the consciousness of the organs that causes illness, physical distress and deterioration. And the cells of which the organs, and therefore the body, are composed also have their consciousness, though as yet very little developed and individualized.

The cells constitute the matter of which our body is made, but they contain evidently a vital element also, for they are alive, and, what is less known, a mental element. This consciousness of the body cells is the most elementary consciousness in the human being and therefore the ultimate step in the transformation of the body. As matter is directly related to the Inconscient via the Subconscient, the consciousness of the cells is by far the most difficult to transform, to divinize. It is most probably because of this difficulty, never attempted to solve before, that Sri Aurobindo had to perform the unprecedented yogic act of descending fully consciously into death.

Sri Aurobindo and the Mother had realized the mastery of the body and its parts many years ago. It is one of the elementary stages in most paths of yoga and a precondition for further progress. Yet, as long as the mastery of the cells has not been achieved, the mastery of the body and its parts can only be partial, never complete. This, of course, is why even the greatest yogis have become ill and died – as it is the reason why all humans have to die. It should, however, not be forgotten that the aim of Sri Aurobindo and the Mother's yoga was a *divinization* of Matter, which means that the cells, and the body, and the human being should be rendered immortal – for being divine means being immortal. Which means that the low, dark, elementary consciousness of the cells must be transformed into the supramental, divine Consciousness. Indirectly, this again throws some light on the passing of Sri Aurobindo. Directly, it was the problem left to the Mother to resolve: the cells had to be supramentalized in order to form a supramental body and thus to conquer Death.

We can now continue reading the Mother's talk of 6 January 1951. 'There is a consciousness in the cells: it is what we call the "body consciousness"* and it is wholly bound up with the body. This con-

---

* In the original French, which is no longer available, most probably *la conscience physique*.

sciousness has much difficulty in changing, because it is under the influence of the collective suggestion which is absolutely opposed to the transformation. So one has to struggle with this collective suggestion – not only with the collective suggestion of the present, but with the collective suggestion which belongs to the Earth-consciousness as a whole, the terrestrial human consciousness which goes back to the earliest formation of the human being. This has to be overcome before the cells can be spontaneously aware of the Truth, of the Eternity of matter.'[52] The Mother formulates here in essence her task ahead. As she was undertaking something that had never been tried before and was searching out a way in 'a virgin forest,' she had to discover the means and methods – which is what we will venture to describe in the rest of this book.

'For this transformation to succeed, all human beings – even all living beings as well as their material environment – must be transformed. Otherwise things will remain as they are: an individual experience cannot change terrestrial life. This is the essential difference between the old idea of transformation – that is, the becoming conscious of the psychic being and the inner life – and transformation as we conceive it and speak of. Not only an individual or a group of individuals, or even all individuals, but life – the overall consciousness of this more or less developed life – has to be transformed. Without such a transformation we shall continue having the same misery, the same calamities and the same atrocities in the world. A few individuals will escape from it by their psychic development, but the general mass will remain in the same state of misery.'[53]

There is a saying that a dog's tail cannot be straightened, meaning that a person's character or human nature cannot be changed. Sri Aurobindo and the Mother disagreed, for otherwise transformation would make no sense. 'We know by experience,' the Mother went on in the same talk, 'that if we go down into the Subconscient, lower than the physical [i.e. material] consciousness, and even lower still into the Inconscient, we can find in ourselves the origin of all atavism, of what comes from our early education and the environment in which we have lived. And this gives a kind of special characteristic to the individual, to his outer nature, and it is generally believed that we are born like that and will stay like that. But by going down into the Subconscient, into the Inconscient, one can trace the origin of this formation and undo what has been done, change the movements and reactions of the ordinary nature by a conscious and deliberate action and thus really transform one's character.'[54]

And the Mother stated: 'This is not a common achievement, but it has been done. So one may assert not only that it can be done, but that it has been done. It is the first step towards the integral transformation, but after that there remains the transformation of the cells which I mentioned earlier.' She clarified: 'The Inconscient is not individual-ized, and when you go down into the Inconscient in yourself, it is the Inconscient of Matter. One cannot say that each individual has his own Inconscient, for that would already be a beginning of individualization. And when you go down into the Inconscient, it is perhaps not the universal but at least the terrestrial Inconscient.'[55]

'It has been done' – by whom? By whom else but Sri Aurobindo and herself? Which emphasizes the importance of the lines from *Savitri* quoted in the previous chapter: 'Into the abysmal secrecy he came / Where darkness peers from her mattress, grey and nude / And stood on the last locked subconscient's floor / Where Being slept unconscious of its thoughts / And built the world not knowing what it built.'

'First of all, it is the Subconscient that has to become conscious,' the Mother said. 'Indeed, the main difficulty of the integral transformation is that things are constantly rising up from the Subconscient.' The Subconscient is a place of horrors. It is in pure hell that she will have to fight most of her battles and conquer most of the difficulties in the years to come.

On 26 February 1951 the Mother talked to her Playground audience about the 'gnostic,' i.e. the supramental state of consciousness. 'There is a state of consciousness, which may be called "gnostic," in which one is able to see *simultaneously* all the theories, all the systems of belief, all the ideas men have expressed in their highest consciousness – the most contradictory notions, like the Buddhist theory, the Vedantic, the Christian, all the philosophical theories, all the expressions of the human mind when it has managed to get hold of a small fragment of the Truth. In that state not only do you put each thing in its place, but everything appears to you marvellously true and quite indispensable to be able to understand anything at all about anything whatsoever ... In that state there are no contradictions: it is a totality – a totality in which one has the full knowledge of all the truths ever expressed (which do not suffice to express the total Truth), in which one knows the proper place of all things, why and in what the universe is formed.

'But I hasten to tell you: it is not by a personal effort that one arrives at this state. It is not because one tries to obtain it that it is obtained. One *becomes* that, spontaneously [in the course of the Integral Yoga]. It is, as it were, the crown of an absolute mental sincerity, when one no longer has any partiality, any preference, any attachment to an idea, when one does not even try any longer to know the truth. One is simply open in the Light.'

And she concluded: 'I am telling you this tonight because what has been done, what has been realized by one can be realized by others. It is enough that one body has been able to realize this, one human body, to have the assurance that it *can* be done [by other human bodies]. You may consider it still very far off, but you may say: "Yes, the gnostic life is certain, because it has begun to be realized."'[56] The key word here is of course 'body.' The only body the Mother could be talking about here, was hers. Two and a half months after Sri Aurobindo's departure she had realized the supramental Unity-Consciousness in her body – which, in the light of what we have learned above, can only mean in the cells of her body.

At the beginning of 1954, the Mother had a most amazing experience which she announced on 14 January: 'For the last few days when I wake up in the morning I have the strange sensation of entering a body that is not mine – my body is strong and healthy, full of energy and life, supple and harmonious, and this [her material body, then seventy-six years old] fulfils none of these qualities; the contact with it becomes painful; there is great difficulty in adapting myself to it and it takes a long time before I can overcome this uneasiness.'[57] She had then already the feeling of having another body – something we will hear more about.

It is true that 1954 appears to have been a peak year in her yoga of the cells. For example, on 24 February she said: 'If one wants to transform one's body, one has to put it into perfect harmony with the inner consciousness. This is to be done "in every cell," in the most insignificant activity, in every activity of the organs.' And on 21 April: 'It will take a certain number of years before we can speak knowledgeably about how this is going to happen [the transformation of the body]; all that I can tell you at present is that it has begun.'[58]

On 5 May of the same year the Mother talks about the mastery over material circumstances and says that their effect depends on one's consciousness. Then she adds: 'The power one has [the Mother talks about her own experience] – already fully and formidably realized in the mind – to act upon circumstances to the extent of changing them totally as to their effect upon one, that power can descend into Matter, into the [physical] substance itself, which means into the cells of the body, and give the same mastery to the body in relation with the things surrounding it. This is not a belief, it is a certitude resulting from experience. The experience is not absolute, but it is there. This opens new horizons. It is the path ... it is one step on the path leading to [physical] transformation.'[59]

19 May: 'The body, left to itself without this kind of constant action of the mind upon it, acts like this: as soon as something [in it] gets disturbed [e.g. because of injury or illness], it has immediately an aspiration, a call, an effort to find help. And this is very powerful – if nothing comes in between, it is very powerful. It is as though the cells themselves erupted spontaneously in an aspiration, a call. In the body there are invaluable and unknown treasures. In all cells there is an intensity of life, of aspiration, of the will to progress of which usually one is not even aware.'[60]

3 November: 'Each part of the being has its own aspiration, which is of the nature of the aspiring part. There is even a physical aspiration. The cells of the body understand what the transformation will be, and, with all their strength, with all the consciousness they contain, they aspire for this transformation. The very cells of the body – not the [body's] central will, thought or emotion – the cells of the body open up in this way to receive the Force.'[61]

Also in 1954, in the April and August issues of the *Bulletin*, the Mother published *Some Experiences of the Body Consciousness* and *New Experiences of the Body Consciousness*. As most of these notes appeared familiar in her and Sri Aurobindo's writings, they were not accorded the importance they deserved, in spite of the Mother drawing special attention to them. Yes, these were experiences one had read or heard about before, but now they were the experiences *of the body consciousness*, of formerly dumb, routinely, slavishly functioning cells of the body. This made an immense difference. Here are some extracts:

- 'It is entirely certain that under the influence of the supramental light, the transformation of the body consciousness will take place first; then will follow a progress in the mastery and control of all the movements and functions of all the organs of the body; afterwards this mastery will change little by little into a sort of radical modification of the movement and then of the constitution of the organs themselves. All that is certain, although the perception of it is not yet precise enough. But what will finally take place – when the various organs have been replaced by centres of concentration of different forces, qualities and natures, each of which will act according to its own special mode – all this is still merely a conception and the body does not comprehend it very well, because it is still far from realization and the body can truly comprehend only that which it is on the point of being able to do.'

- 'The supramental body will be unsexed, since the need for animal procreation will no longer exist. The human form will retain only its symbolic beauty, and one can foresee even now the disappearance of certain ungainly protuberances, such as the genital organs of man and the mammary glands of woman.'

- 'It is only in its external form, its most superficial appearance – which is as illusive to the latest discoveries of the science of today as to the experience of the spirituality of the past – that the body is not divine.' [62]

We might summarize as follows: After Sri Aurobindo's departure, the Mother immediately took up the Work of the Integral Yoga from the point which Sri Aurobindo had reached – which was much farther than is commonly supposed. This immediate continuation was made possible by the transfer of the Mind of Light into her cells. She applied to this sadhana of physical transformation all her power and concentration although what she was doing remained practically unnoticed by the people around her. It is no exaggeration to say, in view of the toughness of the task, that she advanced with lightning speed.

By the end of 1954 she had touched all the bases of her future development. She had taken up the labour in the subconscious – the 'horrible, obscure chore,' as she will call it – without which Matter could not be transformed, as the Subconscient is Matter's foundation. She had become fully aware of the role of the body cells, of their potentialities as well as of their resistance, deeply ingrained as the result of the human and general evolution. The consciousness of the cells had to be divinized. To this transformation, or yoga, applied the fundamentals of the Integral Yoga: aspiration, surrender, sincerity, equanimity – *in the cells, by the cells.*

She had had a first glimpse of supramental matter, 'a multicoloured kaleidoscope in which innumerable luminous particles in constant motion are sovereignly reorganized by an invisible and all-powerful Hand.' It is this matter that is the stuff of our universe, and of all universes, because everything is That in the glory of its Light. To us, however, this basic matter is coated with a film, as it were: the film of our own consciousness, which is ignorant, dark and fragmentary out of evolutionary necessity.

And already she had had her first experience of a new body, 'a body that is not mine.'

Pondicherry Merges with India

On 15 August 1954 the French *comptoir* of *Pondichéry* became a Union Territory of India. On that day the Mother read aloud her application for dual citizenship. 'I want to mark this day by the expression of a long cherished wish, that of becoming an Indian citizen. From the first time I came to India – in 1914 – I felt that India is my true country, the country of my soul and spirit. I had decided to realize this wish as soon as India would be free. But I had to wait still longer because of my heavy responsibilities for the Ashram here in Pondicherry. Now the time has come when I can declare myself.

'But in accordance with Sri Aurobindo's ideal, my purpose is to show that truth lies in union rather than in division. To reject one nationality in order to obtain another is not an ideal solution. So I hope that I shall be allowed to adopt a double nationality, that is to say, to remain French while I become Indian.

'I am French by early education, I am Indian by choice and predilection. In my consciousness there is no antagonism between the two, on the contrary, they combine very well and complete one another. I know also that I can be of service to both equally, for my only aim in life is to give a concrete form to Sri Aurobindo's great teaching, and in his teaching he reveals that all the nations are essentially one and meant to express the Divine Unity upon earth through an organized and harmonious diversity.'[63]

Sri Aurobindo and the Mother have done so much for Pondicherry, visibly and still more invisibly. It is no exaggeration to say that, without them, at present it would be hard to find it on the map. 'A day will come, I hope, when we shall be able to tell freely and truly all that Sri Aurobindo's Presence [and hers] has meant for the town of Pondicherry.'[64] It has never been told. But the results are there for all to see: Pondicherry is one of the most attractive towns of its size in India, and it is internationally known because of the Sri Aurobindo Ashram, which attracts a continuous stream of Indian and foreign visitors. Pondicherry has something special which is hard to define. But we remember what the Mother said about Sri Aurobindo's aura, which was perceptible to her, in 1920, more than ten nautical miles out on the sea. And about herself she said: 'Here, in Pondicherry, you cannot breathe without breathing my consciousness. It saturates the atmosphere almost materially, in the subtle physical, and extends to the Lake, ten kilometres from here.'[65]

365

In his last years, Sri Aurobindo had some exceptional meetings in his room. One was with Sir C.R. Reddy who came to offer him, on behalf of Andhra University, the National Prize for the Humanities. Another meeting was with the Maharaja of Bhavanagar, the then Governor of Madras. Still another was with K.M. Munshi, a former student of his at Baroda.* But the first post-war meeting, in September 1947, soon after the Indian Independence, was with Maurice Schumann. This French politician and philosopher, then thirty-five, had been the official spokesman for the Free French Forces in London throughout the Second World War. He was deputed by the French government to be the leader of a cultural mission to propose the setting up at Pondicherry of an institute for the research and study of Indian and European culture, with Sri Aurobindo at its head. Nothing came of the institute, but Schumann's visit had an annoying consequence: Jawaharlal Nehru, the Indian prime minister, was angered because the French politician had gone first to meet Sri Aurobindo before coming to see him.[66]

Another, little known event that would make Nehru suspicious of the Sri Aurobindo Ashram – and that may have contributed to the Mother not being awarded dual nationality – was his meeting with Dilip K. Roy. On 13 December 1952, Nehru had already written a memorandum to the secretary general and the foreign secretary, M.E.A. (Ministry of External Affairs), 'On Exemptions to Aurobindo Ashram': '1.1 have considered this matter carefully and am of opinion that the concession asked for by the authorities of Sri Aurobindo's Ashram in Pondicherry should not be granted. We should advise accordingly the Ministries concerned here ... 2. In view of our difficult relations with the French Establishments in India, any such concession is undesirable, more especially because this means Indian currency going into Pondicherry. [Pondicherry did not yet belong to the Indian Union.] 3.

---

* About this meeting K.M. Munshi reported: 'Then we discussed Indian culture. I said: "The younger generation is being fed on theories and beliefs which are undermining the higher life of India." The Master replied: "You must overcome this lack of faith. Rest assured that our culture cannot be undermined. This is only a passing phase." Then the Mahayogi sprang a surprise on me. "When do you expect India to be united?" he asked ... I then said: "So far as the present generation of politicians is concerned I cannot think of any time when the two countries – India and Pakistan – can be united." Sri Aurobindo smiled and averred: "India will be reunited. I see it clearly."' (Nirodbaran, *Twelve Years with Sri Aurobindo*, p. 253)

The attitude of the Ashram has hardly ever been favourable to India and sometimes it has been definitely hostile.* Sri Aurobindo was undoubtedly a great man and we should welcome any proper memorial to him, more especially a new educational centre. But Sri Aurobindo is no more and it is not quite clear how the Ashram is going to run in future. Such accounts as we had are not favourable and we have even heard that there are internal conflicts there. Most of the property stands personally in the name of Madame Alphonse,† otherwise known as the 'Mother.' So does the jewellery. It would be extraordinary for us to give this concession to a private individual. 4. So far as the University centre is concerned, a number of prominent men in India have commended it, but I have failed to find out under whose auspices it will run and who will be responsible for it. To take some steps to support a University of this type, about which we know nothing, except that it is a memorial to Sri Aurobindo, is obviously not desirable.'[67] Etc.

There is another memorandum by Jawaharlal Nehru, 'State of Affairs at the Aurobindo Ashram,' written on 22 December 1952, nine days later, and also addressed to the general secretary, M.E.A. 'I had a visit from Shri Dilip Kumar Roy of Sri Aurobindo Ashram at Pondicherry. He was much concerned at the state of the Ashram, which according to him consists of eight hundred persons now. He complained about the "Mother". He said that while the Ashramites were almost all in favour of merger of Pondicherry with India, the Mother was very French in her outlook. 2. He also complained of the way the Mother controlled everything autocratically and dealt with all the moneys of the Ashram as if they were her private property. She gave no account of these public funds. She takes nobody in her confidence. There is no trust or committee to deal with the moneys or other matters of the Ashram. 3. Then he referred to the University. He said there is no University, but it has

---

* This was a grievous misconception by the prime minister. By now the reader has some idea not only of the love Sri Aurobindo and the Mother had for India, but also of the feelings of love and even worship they fostered in their disciples and students. Moreover, it would be thanks to the Mother's personal intervention that Pondicherry would merge with the Motherland without difficulties, at a time when the respective positions of France and India had hardened to the breaking point. (See *Mother India,* January 1990, pp. 9, 10.)
† He means Alfassa.

been declared that this has been started and money is being collected. Why is this money collected? He expressed his gratification at the fact that we refused to allow a concession to the Mother to sell her jewellery without payment of customs dues. 4. Shri Dilip Kumar Roy wanted us to bring some pressure on the Mother or on the French Government in regard to the Ashram and in regard to the so-called University.'[68] Etc.

These two memoranda throw a harsh light on the calumnies and the antagonism the Mother, and with her the Ashram and the Work, was subjected to – in this case by a disciple of twenty-four years standing to whom Sri Aurobindo had written: 'I have cherished you like a friend and a son.' Dilip K. Roy would leave the Ashram, around the time of his meeting with Nehru, to found his own ashram in Pune together with Indira Devi, the woman who had become the centre of his life and whom Sri Aurobindo and the Mother had saved from a certain death.* The Mother kept his apartment in the Ashram available for him till 1970.

Pandit Nehru came for a first visit to the Sri Aurobindo Ashram on 16 January 1955. 'The Ashram accorded him a cordial welcome. The Ashram boys and girls, beginning with the youths and ending with the infant section, formed a guard of honour lining his route from the street through the inside courtyard up to the Meditation Hall. He was received by the Secretary and others at the gate. He regarded the boys with intent eyes as he passed to pay homage to the Samadhi [i.e. Sri Aurobindo's tomb]. As he was going up to the Mother, the youngest child at the end of the guard offered him a bouquet of roses and greeted him with "Jai Hind." Then he was alone with the Mother upstairs for about twenty minutes.'[69] In the evening he was the honoured guest at a function in the playground, the Ashram band striking up *Bande Mataram*, children giving a recitation in twelve different languages and the youths performing Swedish rhythmic ball drill.

Everything goes to show that this meeting with the Mother and

---

* 'When Indira Devi did not want to go back to her family, the family guru, who was a tantrik, made an occult attack on her body. Her life was in danger. After intense pain and vomiting blood she swooned into unconsciousness. Mother saw the tantrik's action behind it and countered it. She was saved.' (Shyam Sunder Jhunjhunwala, *Down Memory Lane*, p. 4)

the personal experience of life at the Ashram resulted in a turnabout of Nehru's opinion. Besides, by then the Mother's pronouncements concerning India were printed in many publications and were there for all to read. It would be difficult to find elsewhere a more 'pro-Indian' stance, a deeper insight into the being of India and a more positive expectation, not to say prophecy, about India's role among the nations and the brightness of its spiritual and material future.

'During Nehru's second visit to Pondicherry, on 29 September 1955, his coming to the Ashram was no part of the official programme. Towards the end of the official functions he inquired where the Mother could be met at the time. "At the Playground," he was told. Then he cut short the rest of the programme and drove out without security escort to see the Mother. Indira Gandhi had preceded him and was with the Mother. She was visibly touched by the Mother's affectionate way of welcome.'[70] (In the years to come, the Mother would have a close relationship with Indira Gandhi.) Lal Bahadur Shastri, who would succeed Nehru as prime minister, and Kamaraj Nadar, a prominent Tamil politician, were also present. During the third visit of Nehru to the Union Territory, on 13 June 1963, 'his call on the Mother topped his programme. Then he visited the Centre of Education and in the evening saw the students in games and sports.'[71] In those years one would have been hard pressed to find another institution which could come up to the physical education standards in the Ashram.

Sri Aurobindo had said of Nehru: 'He bears on himself the stamp of a very fine character, a nature of the highest sattwic kind, full of rectitude and a high sense of honour, a man of the finest Brahmin type with what is best in European education added. That is the impression he gives. I must say that the Mother was struck by his photograph when she first saw it in the papers, singling it out from the mass of ordinary *eminent* people.'[72] And when Nehru died, in 1964, the Mother said of him: 'Nehru leaves his body, but his soul is one with the soul of India that lives for eternity.'[73]

The Entretiens

The Mother resumed teaching French to some youngsters as soon as the twelve days, during which all Ashram activities were suspended after Sri Aurobindo's passing, had come to an end. These French classes started with simple conversation, recitation and dictation, but gradually expanded into what is now known as the *Questions and Answers* sessions, of which six volumes have been published. (The seventh volume contains some talks from 1929, 1930 and 1931.) The usual procedure was that the Mother read a passage from Sri Aurobindo or herself and started commenting on it. Questions from her audience popped up frequently, for they were free to ask anything they wanted – as long as their questions were in the French language, for these were after all French classes. At first the classes were intended for a group of six girls whom the Mother met regularly 'in the small children's courtyard of the Guest House, under the veranda, around the ping-pong table.' Soon more students joined the group, and when some adults showed interest too, they were allowed to sit in a half circle around the youngsters.

The range of these particular French classes, afterwards called *Entretiens* – a word difficult to translate into English, but meaning something like 'instructive conversations' – is astounding. They could be considered to constitute the Mother's teaching. It is true, of course, that her teachings were fundamentally the same as Sri Aurobindo's, and many of her talks were explanations of or comments upon passages from his writings. But it is also true that she had a different background from Sri Aurobindo, and, as she was often drawing from her own experience, that these talks had a flavour which was her very own. Besides, they were held in French of the highest quality. Sri Aurobindo was, from his Cambridge days onwards, generally recognized as a master of English. The Mother's mastery of her mother tongue is rarely appreciated, in the first place because few English-speaking people read French and also because most of her published texts are records of the spoken language. Her talks, however, are remarkable for the clarity and conciseness of her formulations, and for the fact that she was able to express subjects bordering on the inexpressible in the simplest possible language.

The Mother during one of her evening classes or Entretiens
at the Ashram playground, 1951

Although in the course of their 'academic' curriculum the students studied all branches of modern science, the teachings of the Mother in her evening classes, based on her occult and spiritual experience, did not always match with what the textbooks said. One example is something she has repeated on many occasions: that this universe is the seventh manifested by the Godhead. 'The traditions say that a universe is created, that it is then withdrawn in a *pralaya* [dissolution], that then a new one comes about, and so on. According to them, we should be the seventh universe, and as we are the seventh universe, we are the one which will not return in a *pralaya* but progress everlastingly without regressing again. Besides, it is because of this that there is in the human being this need of permanence and an uninterrupted progress. It is because the time has come.'[74]

Another example of the Mother's scientific unorthodoxy is her also often repeated statement that the Earth occupies a unique place in the universe. 'The formation of the Earth as we know it, this infinitesimal point in the immense universe, was made precisely in order to concentrate the effort of the transformation upon one point. It is, as it were, a symbolic point created in the universe, so that, while working directly upon one point, the effect radiates into the entire universe ... From the astronomical point of view the Earth is nothing, it is a very small accident. From the spiritual point of view it is a symbolic, expressly willed formation. And as I have already said: it is only on the Earth that the Presence is found, the direct contact with the supreme Origin, the presence of the divine Consciousness hidden in all things. The other worlds have been organized more or less "hierarchically," if one may put it this way, but the Earth has a special formation due to the direct intervention, without any intermediary, of the supreme Consciousness in the Inconscient.'

When somebody in the audience then asked: 'Are the solar fragments made of the same matter as the Earth?' the Mother replied: 'I have taken care to tell you that this radiation [constituting the earth] was a symbolic creation, and that all action on this special point irradiates into the whole universe. Remember this, and don't start saying that the formation of the Earth comes from an element projected by the sun, or that the scatterings of a nebula must have given birth to the sun and all its satellites, and so on.'[75] The Mother also said that materially embodied beings which have the psychic being – what we call humans – exist only on the Earth. As we know, the psychic being is much more than a 'divine spark.' Everything contains a divine spark, without which it could not exist. 'The divine spark is at the centre of each atom,' said the Mother.[76] 'The psychic being is organized *around* the divine spark. The divine spark is one, universal, the same everywhere and in everything, one and infinite, of the same kind in all. One cannot say that it is a being. It is *the* being, if you like, but not *a* being ... The psychic being, on the contrary, is an individual, personal being with its own experience, its own development, its own growth, its own organization. Only, this organization is the result of the action of a central divine spark.'[77] In other words, the psychic being is the fine flower of the earthly evolution which one day, as the result of the supramental transformation, will lead to the concrete, material manifestation of the psychic being in all its divinity.

Putting the Earth once again at the heart of the universe may, at first sight, seem bizarre. It should therefore be recalled that the Mother and Sri Aurobindo were spiritual realists, expressing their experience of spiritual facts; they did not want a return to medievalism, but the realization of the next step in evolution. Science is young and still very much reductionist, materialistic in its perspective. But however materialistic its standard models are at present, the human being knows intuitively that there are realities other than the material one, because it contains these other realities in itself. Science has already come very far from its first, naive materialistic paradigms. How many more paradigm shifts will be needed before it is able to include the other levels of reality? When discussing these kind of problems, the Mother expressed her respect for the inherent honesty of the scientific method and the industrious efforts of its practitioners. But, and this is altogether another matter, Science has also formed its own kind of Church with its creed, its dogmas, its priests and its propaganda: the Church of Scientism. This is what is doomed to perish because of the wonder of it all – not because of 'the fire in the equations,' but of the Fire at the heart of this and all universes, as well as at the heart of the tiniest elementary particle.

14.

The Mother's Reincarnations

*Since the beginning of the earth, wherever and whenever there was
the possibility of manifesting a ray of consciousness, I was there.*[1]

– The Mother

'The Divine also comes down into the cycle of rebirths, makes the
great holocaust, endures shame and obloquy, torture and crucifixion,
the burden of human nature, sex and passion and sorrow and suffering, manifests many births before he reveals the Avatar,' wrote Sri
Aurobindo to Nirodbaran.[2] The Mother has often talked about her
former incarnations, yet always in a confidential way, either to her audience in the Playground or in private conversations.* They are certainly
part of the life we are trying to describe in this book, as they are part of
the Great Life, the constant presence on earth of the Mahashakti in her
many material emanations or embodiments. The Mother made it clear
that she had grown aware of these incarnations unexpectedly; that she
herself was astonished by their multiplicity; that all her experiences of
former lives were living memories; and that she studied the subject of
rebirth after having had the experiences.[3] She also said that one should
never speak vaguely of things like this, and condemned the pseudo-
romantic suppositions based on nothing but the imagination.

This is not the place for a closer look at the subject of reincarnation,
which is here taken for granted. As Sri Aurobindo wrote in the *Arya:*
'We may according to our prepossessions accept it as the fruit of ancient
psychological experience always renewable and verifiable and therefore
true, or dismiss it as a philosophical dogma and ingenious speculation;

---

* It should be stated in general that most of what we know about the private lives of
Sri Aurobindo and the Mother and about their true identity is from private talks or
from writings which have been made public after their physical departure from the
earthly scene.

but in either case the doctrine, even as it is in all appearances well-nigh as old as human thought itself, is likely to endure as long as human beings continue to think.'[4]

It may be useful, however, to mention Sri Aurobindo's revealing answer to the question of a disciple concerning what he and the Mother had been doing in their previous lives: 'Carrying on the evolution.' – 'I find it difficult to understand so concise a statement. Can't you elaborate?' asked the disciple. – 'That would mean writing the whole of human history,' replied Sri Aurobindo. 'I can only say that as there are special descents to carry on the evolution to a farther stage, so also something of the Divine is always there to help through each stage itself in one direction or another.' – Disciple: '... How is it that even Sri Krishna, Buddha or Christ could not detect your presence in this world?' – Sri Aurobindo: 'Presence where and in whom? If they did not meet, they would not recognize, and even if they met there is no reason why the Mother and I should cast off the veil which hung over these personalities and reveal the Divine behind them. Those lives were not meant for any such purpose ... If the Mother were in Rome in the time of Buddha, how could Buddha know as he did not even know the existence of Rome? ... An Avatar or Vibhuti* have the knowledge that is necessary for their work, they need not have more ... An Avatar does not even manifest all the Divine omniscience and omnipotence; he has not come for any such unnecessary display; all that is behind him but not in front of his consciousness. As for the Vibhuti, the Vibhuti need not even know that he is a power of the Divine. Some Vibhutis like Julius Caesar for instance have been atheists. Buddha himself did not believe in a personal God, only in some impersonal and indescribable Permanent.'[5]

---

* An Avatar is a full incarnation of the Divine in a human body; a Vibhuti is an incarnation of an aspect of the Divine in a human body.

In the Earthly Paradise

The Mother, according to her own statements, has had innumerable reincarnations. Sometimes she had several simultaneously, for instance at the time of Christ and during the Renaissance. 'The Mother's Vibhutis would usually be feminine personalities most of whom would be dominated by one of the four personalities of the Mother'[6] – i.e. Maheshwari, Mahakali, Mahalakshmi and Mahasaraswati. She has talked about some reincarnations only in passing; she has said, for instance, that she had lived several times in Babylonia – 'I have extremely precise memories, completely objective'[7] – in Assyria, in Japan, etc. Others she has described in some detail, and from these we choose a few where the references are not subject to doubt or interpretation.

Her very first incarnation in a human form was in the earthly paradise. 'According to what I remember, there has certainly been a moment in earth's history when there existed a kind of earthly paradise, in the sense that life at that time was perfectly harmonious and perfectly natural. By this I mean that the manifestation of the mind was in accord – was still in complete accord – with the ascending march of Nature, and totally harmonious, without perversion or distortion. This was the first stage of the mind's manifestation in material forms.'[8]

'How long did it last [the earthly paradise]? It is difficult to say. But for man it was a life which resembled a kind of culmination of the animal life. My memory is that of a life in which the body was perfectly adapted to its natural environment, the climate to the needs of the body and the body to the needs of the climate. Life was completely spontaneous and natural, just as a more luminous and more conscious animal life would be. There were none of the complications and distortions brought in by the mind later, in the course of its development.

'I have the memory of that life. I got it, I relived it when I became conscious of the life of the earth as a whole. Yet I cannot say how long it lasted nor what area it covered, that I don't know. I only remember the condition, the state of material Nature and what the human form and the human consciousness were like then, and this kind of harmony with all the other elements on earth: harmony with the animal life and such a great harmony with the life of the plants. There was a kind of spontaneous knowledge of how to use the things of Nature, of the properties of the plants, the fruits and everything the vegetable kingdom could provide. No aggressiveness, no fear, no contradiction nor friction, and no perversion at all. The mind was pure, simple, luminous, uncomplicated ...

'According to certain impressions – but they are only impressions – it would seem to have been in the vicinity of ... I do not know exactly whether it was on this side of Ceylon and India or on the other *[Mother points to the Indian Ocean, first to the west of Ceylon and India, then to the east, between Ceylon and Java]*, but it was certainly a place which no longer exists, which has probably been swallowed up by the sea. I have a very clear vision of that place and a very clear awareness of the life there and its forms, but I cannot give any material details. The truth is that, when I relived those moments, I was not interested in seeing such details. One is in a different state of mind and one has no curiosity for material details, everything is transformed into psychological experiences ...

'During a certain period, by night as well as by day, and in a certain state of trance I went back to a life that I had once been living, with the full consciousness that it was the culmination of the human form on earth, in the first human forms capable of embodying the divine Being. For that was what it was. It was the first time I was able to manifest in an earthly form, in a personal form, in an individual form – not in a common life form but an individual form.* By this I mean that it was the first time that the Being above and the being below had joined through the mentalization of the material substance. I lived this several times, but always in similar surroundings and always with a similar feeling of such a joyful simplicity, without any complications, without any problems, without all those questions: there was nothing, absolutely nothing of the kind! It was a culmination of the joy of living, nothing else but that, in common love and harmony. The flowers, the minerals, the animals: all lived in harmony.'[9]

---

* As we have seen elsewhere, plant and animal life are common life forms determined by the 'spirit' of the species, while it is only in the human being (at present) that life is fully individualized.

King Hatshepsut

Do you not know, Asclepius, that Egypt is an image of heaven?
Or, so to speak more exactly, that in Egypt all the operations
of powers which rule and work in heaven have been transferred
down to the earth below?[10]

The Mother has said that she had had 'at least' three incarnations in
Egypt. Her contact with Egypt started when she was very young, at the
Guimet Museum in Paris. When she was asked many years later by a
child why accidents often happen to people who break into the tombs
in Egypt, she answered abruptly: 'They deserve it!' Then she added: 'Let
me explain. In the physical form is contained "the spirit of the form,"
and this spirit of the form remains for some time, even when outwardly
the person is declared dead. As long as the spirit of the form persists, the
body does not decompose. In ancient Egypt they had this knowledge.
They knew that if they prepared the body in a certain manner, the spirit
of the form would not leave it and the body would not disintegrate. In
some cases they have succeeded wonderfully well. And if one disturbs
the repose of beings who have remained like that for thousands of years,
I understand that they are not very pleased, especially when their repose
is disturbed out of unhealthy curiosity, justified in the name of science.

'In the Guimet Museum, in Paris, there are two mummies. Of the
one nothing much is left, but in the other the spirit of the form has
remained very conscious, to such an extent that one can have a contact
by means of the consciousness. It goes without saying that it cannot
be very pleasant when a bunch of idiots come and stare at you with
popping eyes understanding nothing and saying all the time: "Look, he
is like this! Look, he is like that!" ... It was never ordinary people who
were mummified; they were beings who had realized a considerable
inner power or who were members of the royal family, persons more
or less initiated. There is a mummy which has been the cause of a large
number of catastrophes. She was a princess, daughter of a pharaoh, and
secretly at the head of a college of initiation at Thebes.'[11] The warning
inscribed over some tombs, 'Death shall come on swift wings to him

that toucheth the tomb of the Pharaoh,'[12] seems not to have been a vain threat.

The Mother said that ancient Egypt was extremely occult. Now this begins to be understood more widely. Robert Bauval and Graham Hancock, for instance, write in their *Keeper of Genesis:* 'From available primary sources, the overall picture that emerges is that the "Followers of Horus" may not have been "kings" in the usual sense of the word but rather immensely powerful and enlightened individuals – high initiates who were carefully selected by an elite academy that established itself at the sacred site of Heliopolis-Giza thousands of years before history began.'[13]

'Standing in front of a portrait of Queen Hatshepsut, the Mother told the following story when she came to the Ashram's University Centre Library to open an exhibition on ancient Egypt in August 1954. When she was a girl of about eight or ten, she and her brother were taken one day by her teacher [more probably their nanny, Miss Gatliffe] to the famous Museum of the Louvre in Paris. On the ground floor are galleries of Egyptian antiquities. As they were slowly passing through the collections, the Mother was suddenly attracted by a beautiful toilet case inlaid with gold and lapis lazuli, which was exposed in one of the museum cases. An attendant noticed her great interest and explained to her that the toilet case had once belonged to the Egyptian Queen Hatshepsut. He also showed her a fine portrait of the Queen as a young girl and smilingly remarked that she had a striking resemblance to that ancient Queen. The toilet case and particularly the comb appeared to be strangely familiar to the Mother.'[14] It is reasonable to suggest that the Mother would not have told this anecdote if there was no profound reason for it. Besides, we have already mentioned that the Mother experienced an affinity with Queen Hatshepsut in 1914, during her visit to a museum in Cairo, en route to Pondicherry.

It is most often thought that Hatshepsut (ca. 1504-ca. 1483 BC)* has

---

* 'Unfortunately, nothing in Egyptology can ever be taken for granted,' writes Joyce Tyldesley. This is particularly true for the dates of the reign of kings and queens, each authority coming up with a different proposal based on his or her own excellent reasons. The sequence of events within a reign, however, is well-known, as the Egyptian scribes dated these events with reference to the first year of the reign.

been the only Egyptian queen to reign as a king. Yet, this happened four or five times, e.g. in the case of Netokris (ca. 2160 BC), Sobeknofru (ca. 2160 BC), Ankhet-kheperu-re (ca. 1347 BC) and Tauseret (ca. 1186 BC). In all these cases, however, the rule of the female pharaoh was rather short, while Hatshepsut, whose name means 'the Foremost of Women,' ruled for about twenty-two years and her reign marked one of the highlights of Egyptian civilization. 'Among the kings of the XVIIIth dynasty,' writes Jean Yoyotte, 'Hatshepsut is, together with Akhenaton, the one who evokes the most admiration, amazement and questions.'[15] 'Queen or, as she would prefer to be remembered, King Hatshepsut ruled during the 18th Dynasty Egypt for over twenty years,' writes Joyce Tyldesley. 'Her story is that of a remarkable woman. Born the eldest daughter of King Tuthmosis I, married to her half-brother Tuthmosis II, and guardian of her young stepson-nephew Tuthmosis III, Hatshepsut somehow managed to defy tradition and establish herself on the divine throne of the pharaohs. From this time onwards Hatshepsut became the female embodiment of a male role, uniquely depicted both as a conventional woman and as a man, dressed in male clothing, carrying male accessories and even sporting the traditional pharaoh's false beard. Her reign, a carefully balanced period of internal peace, foreign exploration and monumental building, was in all respects – except one obvious one – a conventional New Kingdom regime; Egypt prospered under her rule.'[16]

Hatshepsut married her half-brother Thutmosis II when she was about fourteen or fifteen years of age, thus becoming 'the Great Princess, great in favour and grace, Mistress of All Lands, Royal Daughter and Royal Sister, Great Royal Wife, Mistress of the Two Lands [i.e. Upper and Lower Egypt].' Her royal husband died young and was succeeded by her nephew, Tuthmosis III, still a child. Hatshepsut became his regent and therefore the highest authority in the realm. But then Hatshepsut sprang a surprise: in the seventh year of the boy's reign she proclaimed herself Pharaoh, or rather had herself proclaimed thus by an oracle of Amon, the chief god and presiding deity of the huge temples in Luxor and Karnak, the temple in which she was crowned. She became 'the Female Horus, the king of Upper and Lower Egypt, Maatkare, the son of Re, Hatshepsut-Khnemet-Amun! May she live forever!'

The reason for this unconventional and bold step is unknown. It may be supposed, however, that she took the crown of the Two Lands because for some reason or other the succession of the dynasty was in peril, her husband having died prematurely and the new king still being a child. It should be realized that, for the Egyptians, their Pharaoh was literally a god on earth, who upheld Maat, i.e. the Dharma of the land, who made the sun rise and the river Nile come into spate, and who sustained the life of all beings. Joyce Tyldesley makes a telling comparison between Hatshepsut and Queen Elizabeth I of England, 'a woman who inherited her throne against all odds at a time of dynastic difficulty when the royal family was suffering from a shortage of sons, and who deliberately stressed her relationship with her vigorous and effective father in order to lessen the effect of her own femininity and make her own reign more acceptable to her people.'[17]

The proof of Hatshepsut's insight and strength in daring the practically impossible is the success of her reign as *King* Maatkare. (Re being the Sun, Ka the divine force in all, and Maat the same as Maya or Dharma, the name could be translated as 'Maat is the vital Force of Re,' or, in terms more familiar to us, 'Shakti of the Sun' – the Sun being the symbol of the divine Unity-Consciousness, the Supramental.) Thanks to her, Egypt, which had been partially ruined by the invasion of the Hyksos only half a century before, became prosperous again. Peace reigned within the country and with all its neighbours. 'I have given you the pacification within the provinces and every town is quiet,' she proclaimed. Great building works were undertaken, and so were expeditions to foreign lands. Hatshepsut became 'the most influential woman ever known' and her reign 'the most fruitful period ever in Egypt.' She 'stands out as one of the great monarchs of Egypt.'

In the temple of Karnak, Hatshepsut had two gigantic obelisks erected. The process of their being hewn out of the rock, in the south of the country, of their transportation and erection is shown on the walls of Deir el-Bahri. After something like three and a half millenniums, one of these obelisks is still standing. The top of it was covered with shining electrum, a mixture of gold and silver. Thus were the rays of Re, the Sun, reflected over the country during its daily course from dawn to dusk and its yearly course through the seasons. It must have been a splendid sight.

And then there was the temple at Deir el-Bahri, Hatshepsut's mortuary temple, called Djeser-Djeseru: 'Holy of Holies' – 'beyond doubt one of the most beautiful buildings in the world,' and generally recognized as such. 'It is built at the base of the rugged Theban cliffs [on the west bank of the Nile], and commands the plain in magnificent fashion: its white colonnades rising, terrace above terrace, until it is backed by the golden living rock. The ivory white walls of courts, side chambers and colonnades have polished surfaces which give an alabaster-like effect. They are carved with a fine art, figures and hieroglyphs being filled in with rich yellow colour, the glow of which against the whites gives an effect of warmth and beauty quite indescribable.[18] (J.R. Buttles).

Although the architect of Djeser-Djeseru seems to have been Hapuseneb, the supervisor and creator of the masterwork was Senenmut, the famous assistant of Hatshepsut, acting on her direct inspiration. 'I was the greatest of the great in the whole land,' say the hieroglyphs in Senenmut's tomb. 'I was guardian of the secrets of the King [i.e. Hatshepsut] in all his places: a privy councillor on the Sovereign's right hand, secure in favour and given audience alone. I was one upon whose utterances his Lord relied, with whose advice the Mistress of the Two Lands was satisfied, and the heart of the Divine Consort was completely filled.'[19] It is interesting to note how Hatshepsut had picked out a whole team of able collaborators to run the kingdom. Senenmut, her assistant, architect Hapuseneb, Chancellor Neshi, leader of the expedition to Punt, the Treasurer Tuthmosis, Useramen the vizier, Amenhotep the chief steward, Inebni, Viceroy of Kush, and others. Again one is reminded of Elizabeth I of England and her court. The Mother would probably have said that this group of outstanding collaborators belonged to 'the family.'

The reign of the extraordinary Queen Hatshepsut was a period of peace, prosperity and stabilization. It was the basis upon which Thutmosis III, when he finally became Pharaoh in his own right, expanded the kingdom. He became known as 'the Egyptian Napoleon' and waged no less than seventeen victorious campaigns. Hatshepsut's work in reviving the prosperity of the land would render Tiy and Akhenaton's astounding reformation possible. Who has hacked away her effigies and the cartouches containing her royal name? Nobody can tell with any certainty. To the Egyptians the power of the written or chiselled word or hieroglyph was very real, as was the power of the statues and buildings. An erasure of a name or the mutilation of a statue was a direct attack on the Ka, and thus on the survival of the person represented by the hieroglyphs or the statue. Strange to say, the memory of King Hatshepsut was obliterated for many centuries from Egyptian history and only rediscovered in the nineteenth century.

Queen Tiy

'About two years ago,' the Mother said in May 1956, 'I had a vision in connection with Z.'s son. She had brought him to me – he was not quite one year old – so I had just seen him in the room where I receive people. He gave me the impression of someone very well known to me, but I didn't know who or what. Then, in the afternoon of the same day [during her midday rest], I had a vision. It was a vision of ancient Egypt, and I was somebody there: I was the High Priestess, or whoever. I didn't know who, for [during the experience] one doesn't tell oneself "I am so-and-so." The identification is complete, there is no objectivation, so I don't know.

'I was in an admirable building, immense! so high! but quite bare. There was nothing except a place with magnificent paintings, which I recognized as the paintings of ancient Egypt. I was coming out of my apartments and entering a kind of large hall. There was a sort of gutter all along the walls, for collecting the water. And then I saw the child, half naked, playing in it. I was quite shocked. I said: "What is this! This is disgusting!" (The feelings, ideas and all that were translated into French in my consciousness.) Then the tutor came, I had him called. I gave him a scolding. I heard the sounds. I don't know what I said, I don't remember the sounds any more. I heard the sounds I was pronouncing, I knew their meaning, but the translation was into French and the sounds I didn't remember.

I spoke to [the tutor]. I told him: "How can you let the child play in there?" He answered – and I woke up with his reply – saying ... I did not hear the first words, but in my thought it was [translated as]: "Amenhotep likes it." "Amenhotep" I heard and I remembered. Then I knew the little one had been Amenhotep.

'So I know that I spoke. I spoke in that language, but I don't remember it now. I remembered "Amenhotep" because I have kept that in my active consciousness: "Amenhotep." But the rest, the other sounds did not remain. I have no memory for sounds. And I know I was his mother. Then I knew who I was, for I know that Amenhotep was the son of so-and-so. Besides, I looked it up in history.'[20]

As the Mother confirmed afterwards, that child, her son, was Amenhotep IV (1376-47 BC),* the future Akhenaton, which means that she was Queen Tiy (1397-60 BC). Tiy, though her father occupied a high position in the realm, was not of royal blood and possibly of Nubian descent. She had been chosen in 1389 as his principal consort by Amenhotep III, the Magnificent. 'The name of her father is Yuya, the name of her mother is Tuya. She is the spouse of a powerful king whose southern border reaches to Karoy and his northern to Naharin.'[21] This is the way the Pharaoh had the high status of his wife proclaimed throughout the Two Lands. Tiy became the mother of Amenhotep IV (1376-47 BC), who afterwards, in one of the most spectacular religious reformations in history, would call himself Akhenaton and found the city of Akhetaton.

'Tiy had a very powerful influence on her husband Amenhotep III. Her strong personality dominated the mentally weaker king completely. As his queen, she decided about the broad outlines within the structure of his policy and played an important role in the Egyptian religious life. Amenhotep III already felt the power of the sun god Aton, and it is in no way improbable that Tiy took the initiative to stimulate his dormant sympathy for this god.'[22] The sun god Aton, never represented in human form but as the sun disk, was central to the theology of Heliopolis, perhaps the most ancient in Egypt, although he played only a minor role in the official religion. That Amenhotep and Tiy were

---

* For the dates concerning this section on Queen Tiy and Amenhotep IV-Akhenaton, we follow *De Mummie van Nofretete* by Arnold Berbers and Hendrik Beumer (1988). The name Amenhotep is the same as Amenophis.

profoundly dedicated to Aton is shown by the fact that he was revered in their palace at Malgatta, west of Thebes, and that the boat in which Tiy moved on the huge artificial lake her husband had dug for her was called 'Aton radiates.'

Most historians agree that Tiy had an equally strong influence on her son Amenhotep IV. As Berbers and Beumer write: 'Through his mother Tiy, in this supported by his father Amenhotep III, he must have been initiated in the philosophies around Aton and indoctrinated with the idea that for the religious salvation of Egypt a god like Aton was the only outcome.'[23] This influence must have been very strong indeed, for after his father had died Amenhotep IV changed his name into Akhenaton, translated variously as 'he who is faithful to Aton,' 'One useful to Aton,' 'he who serves Aton' and 'reflection of Aton.' And not only did he change his name, he founded a totally new city, Akheta- ton, 'Horizon of Aton,' on the right bank of the Nile, halfway between Thebes and Memphis. The name of the city may be understood as the projection of the Sun World into the material world of the earth.

This splendid city, entirely dedicated to the new creed, was built in an incredibly short time and must have been a costly enterprise. Akhenaton lived there with his wife, the famous Nefertiti ('the Beautiful has come') and their six daughters. There he worshipped the sun disk, represented by the ankh, the sign of life, and little hands blessing all existence. And there he received also his mother Tiy, who had remained in her palace at Malgatta, but who would breathe her last, in 1347, in that fantastic city which had probably arisen under her impulse.

Akhenaton's revolutionary undertaking – he has been called 'the heretic king' and 'the most controversial of all kings of Egypt' – went completely against the established and extremely powerful religion of the time, and is considered the first attempt at monotheism. The face- less Aton was declared the only God and the worship of all other gods, of the whole Egyptian panthéon, was abolished. The significance of this act can only be understood if one realizes that the priestly caste was second in power to the Pharaoh – who was a living god, the incarnated Horus on earth – and often vied with him for supremacy. The temple of Amon in Thebes had become one of the richest in Egypt, and the power of the Amon priests was still on the increase. 'By the middle of the New

Kingdom, the religious foundations controlled an estimated one-third of the cultivated land and employed approximately twenty per cent of the population ... Within a very short time the Amon temple at Thebes was second only to the throne itself as a centre of economic and political influence in Egypt.'[24] Their wrath at Akhenaton's reformist acts must have been unforgiving.

And unforgiving it was. There seem to have been signs of the decline of Akhetaton even towards the end of Akhenaton's brief life. (Life was generally brief in those times.) After his death in 1347 BC, and while Nefertiti was still living in her palace at Akhetaton, the brand-new city gradually emptied of its population. When Nefertiti died in 1344 BC, her son Tutankhaton could or would no longer resist the conservative powers; he changed his name into Tutankhamon and, together with his wife, went back to Thebes. In 1333 BC general Horemheb became Pharaoh. This was the end of the XVIIIth Dynasty – and of the City of the Sun, which he razed to the ground with the fury only religious fanaticism can inspire. It disappeared under the desert sands, and for many centuries there was nothing to be seen but a hill at a place called Tell el-Amarna.

Modern historians have little or no understanding of what happened at the time of Tiy, Akhenaton and Nefertiti. The reason is that they project their world 'realistic' view and even their religious prejudices on times and events that were utterly different from the ones in which they themselves live. As the Mother said, the life, culture and religion of ancient Egypt were determined by an exceptional presence of the occult. What is occult is by definition unknown. It is worthwhile pointing out that many of the prominent Greeks – Solon, Pythagoras, Herodotus, Plato – found the sources of their knowledge in Egypt (which means that European culture has its roots deeper than Greece, in the Kingdom of the Two Lands).* All of these Greeks were instructed by representatives of the Egyptian priesthood, but as the latter were bound by their vows, the knowledge they shared was but a part of what they actually

---

* It is also worth pointing out that Moses was instructed by the Egyptian priesthood, as is written in the *Acts of the Apostles (7:22)*, and may have been an initiate. Thus another source of Western civilization, the Semitic, goes back to the Land of the Nile.

knew. Only recently has there been an effort among Western scholars to approach ancient Egypt with less arrogance and with more patience and openness when seeking the still hidden sources of that civilization.

The impulse, the force Tiy, Akhenaton and Nefertiti (who also was totally dedicated to the Aton) were drawing from, must have been very powerful indeed to allow for a revolution as the one brought about. Looking back on it from the viewpoint of Sri Aurobindo and the Mother, one may assume the following. Tiy was a 'Vibhuti' of the Universal Mother, a fact which endowed her with the awareness of her eternal soul within, and thus of the Divine. She had probably become an initiate of the mysteries of Heliopolis, keeper of the secrets of the Sun. Here it is worth mentioning that Sri Aurobindo said that the Sun is the symbol of the Supramental, which is the Divine upholding all creation. (This upholding and blessing is graphically represented in Akhenaton's iconography of the Sun disk.) Having become a high occult initiate, Tiy may have had the vision or inspiration – or a series of visions or inspirations – of the supramental Truth. The word 'supramental Truth' is nothing but a verbal abstraction for a divine Reality which surpasses everything an ordinary human being can feel, imagine and experience. It is the One Reality present in all that exists and of which the gods are the cosmic powers.

Tiy may have had some kind of realization of the Supramental and transmitted it to her husband, son and daughter-in-law. Nothing short of such a realization could have been powerful enough to enable these few individuals, however elevated their position, to undertake the steps just mentioned against the stubborn, conservative, centuries-old established powers and customs. Graham Philips writes: 'Indeed, [the Aton] is unlike any Egyptian god: an all powerful, heavenly father who demands that his children live in "truth." Precisely what this reference to truth implies is hard to say. One can only assume that Akhenaton's followers were encouraged to behave candidly and live an honest life. The word *Maat,* "Truth," appears again and again at Amarna, and the phrase "living in truth" seems almost to have been a motto of the new religion.'[25] It is also a key concept in the yoga of Sri Aurobindo and the Mother.

'In reply to a question (concerning Akhenaton) I had put her,' recalls

Tanmaya, a French teacher at the Ashram school, 'Mother let it clearly be understood that she had been Queen Tiy, the mother of Akhenaton ... She specified that Akhenaton's revolution was intended to reveal to the people of that time the unity of the Divine and his manifestation. This attempt, the Mother added, was premature, for the human mind was not yet ready for it. It had, however, to be undertaken in order to assure the continuity of its existence in the mental plane.' [26]

Joan the Maid

The Mother has referred several times to facts and situations from the life of Jeanne d'Arc (1412/13-1431 AD) which came back to her on many occasions and 'with a terrific precision.' [27] It is no exaggeration to say that the life of this young French girl was a pure miracle. (That some miracles take time for their completion doesn't prevent them from being miracles.) 'She is the wonder of the ages,' wrote Mark Twain. [28] The facts, which in this case can be verified in historical detail, are there for us to read and ponder.

Jeannette was the daughter of simple people (*laboureurs*, which means farmers) at Domrémy, a small town on the French border with Lorraine, at a confused and critical time for the kingdom of France. What we now know as France was then divided into many parts, belonging mainly to three powers: the King of France, the King of England and the Duke of Burgundy. It is amazing that at that time nearly nothing was left of France – even Paris was in the hands of the English – and that the English conquests threatened to deal France a deathblow. France might have been erased from the map had it not been for that simple girl Jeannette, now known as Joan of Arc, or Joan the Maid.

'A twelve year old child, a very young girl, taking the voice of her heart for the voice of heaven, conceives the strange, improbable, even absurd idea of doing what human beings are not able to do any longer: save her country,' writes the French historian Jules Michelet. [29] 'She mulls this idea over for six years without taking anybody into her confidence; she even says nothing about it to her mother or to her confessor.

Without any support from a priest or from her parents, she walks all that time alone with God in the solitude of her great endeavour. She waits till she is eighteen to execute it, irresistibly. She rides through France, ravaged and depopulated, its roads infested with brigands. She imposes herself at the court of Charles VII. She plunges into the war. In soldiers' camps, which she has never even seen before, and in combat, nothing astonishes her. She throws herself, intrepid, against the swords of the enemy. Wounded on several occasions but never discouraged she gives confidence to the old soldiers, makes everybody fight as one man together with her, and nobody dares to be afraid of anything any longer.'

However romantic this text may appear, it tells nothing but the truth. Jeannette started hearing her voices when she was twelve or thirteen and was frightened by them. This daughter of a nobody was sent on a divine mission to crown the dauphin as King of France at Reims and save her country! At the same time, her father had dreams in which he saw Jeannette among soldiers; suspecting that she would become a soldiers' girl, he beat her severely when she finally dared to tell him about her intentions. Still she persisted and managed after several attempts to convince Robert de Baudricourt, Lord of Vaucouleurs, of her sincerity and the possible truth of her mission. At seventeen she rode, with an escort of six armed, rough and tough companions for eleven days through the hardships of winter and the dangers of a country at war (and hardly less dangerous when at peace). The simple people of Vaucouleurs had paid for her horse and for her man's clothes, the only outfit convenient to ride on horseback.

At the Château of Chinon she met the Dauphin, whom she convinced of her purpose and who was a transformed man after talking to her in private. He ennobled her and saw to it that she was equipped with white armour, a white horse, her own standard, and, like other army commanders, a private military escort called *maison militaire*. Off she rode, Joan of Arc, seventeen years of age, at the head of an army of more than ten thousand men. And this was at a time when Catholic theologians still doubted not only whether women had a soul but whether they were human beings, and when it was considered blasphemous for women to wear men's clothes.

Joan with her army went to liberate Orléans, which was completely surrounded by English troops and about to surrender. On 29 April 1429, after only nine days, 'with a rapidity that stupefied all of Europe,' she chased away the English and freed Orléans. Régine Pernoud writes: 'Later, during her trial, Joan will declare: "I was the first to put up the ladder against the fortification at the end of the bridge of Orléans." And it suffices to define her strategy by recalling that she was always to be found at the most exposed spot, covering the retreat at the Augustins to turn it into an attack, or giving the example of how to climb the walls by being the first to put up a ladder and climb it when taking the Tourelles.'[30] Joan was wounded by an arrow above the left breast, but 'after having herself bandaged, she climbed on her horse again.'

The liberation of Orléans was followed by a string of victories, the one at Patay being no less important than the one at Orléans. On 29 June, Charles started to march towards Reims. Unexpectedly, but in accordance with the prediction made by Joan's voices, the towns on his way changed their allegiance from the English to him. He was solemnly anointed and crowned King of France on 17 July. 'The liturgy carries such a weight that he thereby becomes, to all, the real king.'[31]* Gradually large parts of the Kingdom of France will return to him and in 1437 he will even enter Paris again.

By then Joan was dead – she had been cruelly burned at the stake as a heretic in Rouen, on 30 May 1431. Her astounding appearance on the scene of history had lasted no longer than two years. All the time she had faithfully followed the guidance of her voices, which she said were those of St Catherine (of Alexandria), St Margaret (of Antioch) and St Michel, the archangel, leader of the celestial armies.†

---

* When Joan was asked in the course of her trial why she wanted her standard with her during the coronation ceremony, she answered with the famous words: it had shared in the difficulties, it was only reasonable that it also would share in the honour.' Which reminds one of the Mother's answer to a child who asked if she was to be among the chosen to be supramentalized: 'I will answer you with the same words Joan of Arc said of her standard: 'You have shared in the difficulties, you will share in the honour.'

† 'If the same beings who appeared and spoke to Joan of Arc would be seen by an Indian, they would look completely different to him. For when one 'sees' something, one projects the forms of one's mind on the vision. To what you see you give the appearance of that which you expect to see. If the same being appeared simultaneously

The voices had told her that her mission would last no longer than one year, and so it happened. After the triumphal coronation at Reims, the difficulties started. A weak and wavering man, Charles VII, influenced by jealous advisers, surreptitiously withdrew his support from Joan. Her military campaigns – in which she was assisted by her faithful captains Dunois, La Hire, Xaintrailles, Gilles de Ray (for a time) and others – were no longer successful, and on 23 May 1430 she was captured before Compiègne.

The verdict of Joan's trial was predetermined because the English wanted the whole of Europe to know that they had only been beaten by the supernatural powers of a witch. It is a sorry fact that Bishop Cauchon, and the Inquisitor at his side, were fanatically supported by the University of Paris in condemning Joan, and that the learned judges tried to trick the young girl with broadsides of complicated theological questions. But she stuck to the inspiration of her voices, time and again silencing her interrogators by the candid directness of her answers. There she stood, sent by God to do the impossible – '*je suis venue de par Dieu*' (I have come from God) – never giving in to their threats or enticements. Finally the learned reverend men had to use some canonical machinations to condemn her as a heretic and deliver the nineteen-year-old heroic virgin into the hands of the executioner.

'Anyone may believe what he chooses to believe,' says the French historian Guy Breton about Joan the Maid. 'All what I can say is that [she is] the most marvellous and the most extraordinary being of our history, a personality who is without equal in whatever country, in whatever time.'[32] 'She was the wonder of the Ages,' writes Mark Twain. 'And when we consider her origin, her early circumstances, her sex, and that she did all the things upon which her renown rests while she was still a young girl, we recognize that while our race continues she will be

---

to a group consisting of Christians, Buddhists, Hindus or Shintoists, it would be named by different names. Each would describe the being in a totally different way, although they all would be talking about one and the same manifestation. The one whom in India you call the Divine Mother, is for the Catholics the Virgin Mary and for the Japanese Kwannon, the Goddess of Compassion, and still others would call her by still other names. It is the same Force, the same Power, but the representations made of it differ according to the religions.' (The Mother, *Questions and Answers 1929-31*, CWM3 p. 18)

also the *Riddle* of the Ages ... Out of a cattle-pasturing peasant village, lost in the remoteness of an unvisited wilderness and atrophied with ages of stupefaction and ignorance, we cannot see a Joan of Arc issue equipped to the last detail for her amazing career and hope to be able to explain the riddle of it, labour at it as we may ... Joan of Arc stands alone, and must continue to stand alone, by reason of the unfellowed fact that in the things wherein she was great she was so without shade or suggestion of help from preparatory teaching, practice, environment, or experience.'[33]

In the section *Recollections and Diary Notes* of *Champaklal Speaks*, there is a note dated 6 February 1940. It says: 'Mother was arranging flowers. It was an understanding that in order to save time I could show to her paintings, etc., at that hour when she arranged flowers. Champaklal: "Can I show the plate now?" Mother smiled and said: "Yes, yes." After seeing the painting Mother said: "This is the best." Champaklal: "Is that so?" Mother: "I think so. We shall see. Sri Aurobindo was the artist." Champaklal: "Leonardo da Vinci?" Mother smiled sweetly and said: "Yes." Then I pointed to the picture [of Mona Lisa] and said: "Mother, it seems this is yours?" Mother: "Yes."'[34] In his *Reminiscences,* Udar narrates that he wanted a Sanskrit name for his wife Mona and that the Mother said she would ask Sri Aurobindo. 'The next day the Mother told me that Sri Aurobindo wanted Mona to keep her name as it reminded him of Mona Lisa. Then the Mother added: "You know, Udar, I was Mona Lisa, and Sri Aurobindo, as Leonardo da Vinci, painted me in that famous picture."'[35] About Leonardo, Sri Aurobindo himself wrote: 'What Leonardo da Vinci held in himself was all the new age of Europe on its many sides. But there was no question of Avatarhood or consciousness of a descent or pressure of spiritual forces. Mysticism was no part of what he had to manifest.'[36] According to Kenneth J. Atchity: 'His multifaceted, wide-ranging mind, coupled with brilliant genius and ready wit, gave Leonardo da Vinci the title Renaissance man as soon as the word Renaissance came into use.'[37]

Leonardo's painting of Mona Lisa is 'perhaps the most famous image of a human face in the history of Western Art.'[38] At the time when her famous portrait was painted she seems to have been a young woman of twenty, whose name was Lisa di Anton Maria di Noldo Gherardini, and she was the third wife of Francesco di Bartolomeo di Zanobi del Giocondo. 'It is often said the Mona Lisa is mysterious,' writes Roger D. Masters, 'but much more is known about the subject of the portrait than is usually realized. Lisa Gherardini married Francesco del Giocondo in 1495. He had first married Camilla Rucellai in 1491, but she had died after giving birth to a son; his second wife, Tommasa Villani, likewise died within a year after they were married in 1493. In April of 1503, Francesco del Giocondo had two reasons to commission a painting of his third wife, Lisa:* she had just given birth to his third child, a son (her second, an infant daughter, had died in 1499), and he had just bought a house. Such events were often the occasion for a familial portrait.

'*La Gioconda* probably dates from this time because Raphael copied and imitated it between 1504 and 1506, and the dates are consistent with Leonardo's other activities in Florence. Although no one knows exactly why Leonardo received the commission, Vasari claims he worked on *La Gioconda* for about four years. For some reason the portrait was never delivered to the merchant who ordered it.'[39] It is also said that Leonardo kept it always with him wherever he went, till he died. When one knows about the Mother and Sri Aurobindo's eternal relationship, their meeting during the Renaissance as Mona Lisa and Leonardo da Vinci would be an explanation for the time and artistry Leonardo lavished on the portrait, for the personal value he attached to it, and for the smile which keeps so many people spellbound up to the present day.

The Mother has said more than once that during the Italian and French Renaissance, just as during the time of Christ, she was on earth in four different bodies.[40] Two of these incarnations, Joan of Arc and Mona Lisa, we have met. The third incarnation was Queen Elizabeth I of England. The fourth one was Margaret of Valois (1553-1615), Queen of France and Navarre. In the second chapter of this book, while depicting the Mother's life as an artist, we have seen how she was thunderstruck

---

* Mona Lisa means Madonna Lisa, i.e. Mistress Lisa. She is also called La Gioconda, this being the feminine form of the family name of her husband, Giocondo.

by a portrait of Margaret of Valois at the beautiful Château in Blois, on the Loire. She was so overpowered by the feeling that she herself had been the subject of that portrait that she voiced her amazement in a way which made other people stop and stare.

The painting, now in the National Library in Paris, was by François Clouet, a typical French Renaissance painter closely related to the humanistic circles. Those were the troubled times of the Reformation, when Catholics and Protestants, the people of the New Faith, were fighting each other mercilessly throughout western Europe, and when the front lines of this war of religion ran through families and marriages. Margaret was, like her painter and the other members of her circle, through and through a Renaissance person, highly intelligent and cultured, intent on equilibrium and harmony, and trying to understand where others did not want to, trying to heal where others sought to harm. In 1572 she married Henry IV of France precisely in order to seal a peace between the religious parties – but five days later thousands of Protestants were treacherously massacred on St Bartholomew's Day. When she retired to the Château of Usson, Margaret held court for various men of erudition and letters. Her *Mémoires*, poems and letters are still much appreciated.

The Virgin Queen

The Mother said several times, for instance on 12 September 1964 and on 15 July 1967 in the private conversations which make up the *Agenda,* that she had been Queen Elizabeth I of England (1533-1603). In a conversation from 1964 she confirms an anecdote about Elizabeth she had told thirteen years before. 'There is a true story about Queen Elizabeth. She had come to the last days of her life and was extremely ill. But there was trouble in the country about questions of taxation, and various people (merchants, I believe) had formed a delegation to present a petition to her. She lay very ill in her room, so ill that she was hardly able to stand. But she got up and dressed in order to receive them. The person who was taking care of her cried out: "But it is impossible, you will die of this!" The queen answered quietly: "Dying one does afterwards" ... This is an example from a whole series of experiences one can have in the life of a king, and it is this which justifies the choice of the psychic being when it takes up this kind of life.'[41] By then Elizabeth had reigned for forty-five years, something nobody would have dared to predict when she was born.

She was the daughter of Henry VIII of England and his second wife Anne Boleyn. Everybody knows that this Henry had many wives, but the reason for his six marriages is usually less well known: Henry did not get a son from his first wife, Catherine of Aragon, which meant that the house of the Tudors would lose the crown and that the kingdom might be ruled by a foreign king. Catherine gave him a daughter, Mary. Anne Boleyn, whom he married after repudiating Catherine, bore him Elizabeth. Only from his third wife, Jane Seymour, did he get a son, Edward. By then the whole situation of the king, his kingdom and his religion had radically changed. For at the time of his first marriage Henry and all of his realm were Catholic, and a Catholic cannot divorce without the sanction of the Pope. When the Pope, mainly for political reasons, was unwilling to sanction his divorce from Catherine, Henry seceded from the Catholic Church and became head of the Anglican Church (as the British monarch still is today). England was now a Protestant nation.

When Anne Boleyn bore him Elizabeth, but no son, he repudiated her too by having his marriage to her declared illegal by the Parliament. Thus Elizabeth became illegitimate and lost her rights to the throne. Her mother was beheaded for treason and adultery before Elizabeth was three years old. Still her father continued showing interest in her and later even nominated her third in succession to the throne, after Edward and Mary. Deeply marked by these traumatic events, the very intelligent Elizabeth was put through an arduous schooling which made her into a highly cultured Renaissance person. As her tutor, Roger Ascham would declare: 'Her mind has no womanly weakness, her perseverance is equal to that of a man, and her memory long keeps what it quickly picks up. She talks French and Italian as well as she does English, and has often talked to me readily and well in Latin, moderately in Greek. [She had notions of Spanish and German too.] When she writes Greek and Latin, nothing is more beautiful than her handwriting. She delights as much in music as she is skilful in it. In adornment she is elegant rather than showy.'[42]

After Henry VIII died in 1547, young Edward VI acceded to the throne, but his health was poor and he died in 1553. Now Mary, Catherine's daughter, became Queen and married Philips II of Spain. Both monarchs were fanatically Catholic and did their utmost to destroy the new Protestant Church in England, including people as well as books, so that the Queen was soon known as 'Bloody Mary.' Mary, who remained childless, knew that the whole of Protestant England rallied behind Elizabeth, for no true-blue Englishman wanted England to become a dependency of hated Spain. Mary had Elizabeth imprisoned in the frightful Tower of London and it looked as if her head, just like her mother's, might fall, but her strength of character and her steadfastness under interrogation saved her.

Mary died in 1558, and what had seemed so unlikely, if not impossible in all those years when her life hung by a thread, happened. Elizabeth acceded to the throne 'amid bells, bonfires, patriotic demonstrations and other signs of public jubilation.' 'If ever any person had either the gift or the style to win the hearts of people, it was this Queen,' wrote an enthusiastic observer, 'and if ever she did express the same it was at present, in coupling mildness with majesty as she did, and in stately stooping to the meanest sort.'[43]

But Elizabeth was a woman, and her sex was 'an almost desperate impediment.' Women in sixteenth-century England – and in other countries too – had no vote, few legal rights, and an extremely limited chance of ever getting an education, much less a job. Government was a masculine business; the court was constructed for a King. On the other hand, if Elizabeth married a foreign nobleman of royal descent, England would be ruled by a foreigner. The brief intermezzo of Philip II of Spain at the helm of England had not been encouraging. There were many suitors for Elizabeth's hand and kingdom, but she knew how to stall, to play the one against the other, to keep them at bay while alluring them. 'While stalwart Elizabethan women were battling it out on the front lines of the household, Queen Elizabeth was proving that a woman was more than capable of mastering a kingdom – and showing herself to be an almighty exception to the rules that governed women's lives.'[44] As she once declared in front of her troops: 'I know I have the body of a weak and feeble woman, but I have the heart and stomach of a king, and of a king of England too.'

England had enormous problems. Internally it was all but bankrupt and for the past three years the harvests had been poor; its navy was run down and it had no standing army; it was torn between its Anglican Protestants, Catholics and Puritans; its nobles and courtiers were divided accordingly. Externally, every neighbouring power – France (manipulating Mary, Queen of Scots) and Spain foremost among them – was ready to pounce on the helpless country governed by an apparently helpless Queen, and the Pope did his utmost to remove that heretic woman from the throne. 'Since that guilty woman of England rules over two such noble kingdoms of Christendom [England and Scotland] and is the cause of so much injury to the Christian faith and loss of so many million souls, there is no doubt that whosoever sends her out of the world [i.e. murders her] with the pious intention of doing God service, not only does not sin but gains merit,' said the Papal Secretary.[45] Elizabeth was excommunicated in 1570 and ever afterwards her life remained endangered by assassins commissioned by Rome.

Elizabeth was not daunted – or if she was, she did not show it. Her first asset was her firm resolve. She truly believed that divine intervention had elevated her to the throne, that it was God who wanted her to rule England. Her second asset was the team of talented and dedicated advisers she chose and assembled around her, especially in her Privy Council: William Cecil, Nicholas Bacon, Francis Walsingham, Nicholas Trockmorton, Robert Dudley. Together with them, but always making the final decisions herself, she set about solving the problems and building England into the power it would remain for two and a half centuries. She brought religious peace to the kingdom by reining in the fanatics and ordering a minimum of external religious conformity while refusing to interfere with any individual's conscience.* She made

---

* 'Elizabeth made the Protestant faith England's official national religion and instituted the Book of Common Prayer. She also passed a law that required every subject to go to church on Sunday. At the same time she declared that she had no interest in sifting the consciences of her people. In other words, as long as everyone looked

England financially healthy again by an economic policy of severe parsimony. She built up its army and especially its fleet, which would in future dominate the world's oceans, and which was able, in 1588, to trounce Spain's 'Invincible Armada,' also pirating the wealth which that country was shipping home from its South American colonies.

Elizabeth's reign became England's Golden Age. It was the age of the playwrights Christopher Marlowe, William Shakespeare and Ben Jonson; of the poets John Donne, Edmund Spenser, Philip Sidney, Georges Chapman; of the musicians Thomas Tallis and William Byrd; of the seafarers and explorers Francis Drake, Walter Raleigh, Martin Frobisher, John Davies and John Hawkins; of the philosopher Francis Bacon; of John Dee, the occultist and court astrologer; of the scientists William Gilbert, Thomas Harriot and Walter Warner. These are but a few of the many that became legendary. Elizabeth knew them all, and all of them paid homage to their Sovereign.

Not only did they pay homage, they made the Virgin Queen the object of a cult. In Elizabeth her worshipping subjects saw Diana, the virgin goddess of the moon, Gloriana, the fairy queen, and above all Astraea. 'Astraea, one of the most constant of all the names used for the Queen from her accession onwards, is the just virgin of Virgil's "IVth Eclogue," whose return to earth inaugurates the golden age, bringing not only peace but eternal springtime.'[46] 'Elizabeth's name came to connote the peak of national greatness ... It is difficult to convey a proper appreciation of this amazing Queen, so keenly intelligent, so effervescing, so intimate, so imperious and regal. She intoxicated Court and country, and keyed her realm to the intensity of her own spirit. No one but a woman could have done it, and no woman without her superlative gifts could have attempted it without disaster. In part instinctive, it was also conscious and deliberate. "Her mind," wrote her witty godson, Sir John Harrington, "was oftime like the gentle air that cometh from the westerly point in a summer's morn; 'twas sweet and refreshing to all around. Her speech did win all affections, and her subjects did try

---

and acted like Protestants, and as long as unauthorized forms of worship weren't perceived to threaten national security, she didn't care what was done in the privacy of the subjects' homes. Such tolerance was exceptional at the time.' (John Papp and Elizabeth Kirkland, *Shakespeare alive!* p. 23)

to show all love to her commands; for she would say that her state did require her to command what she knew her people would willingly do from their own love to her.'" [47]

Having briefly revived our memories of a few of the Mother's reincarnations, it may be an interesting exercise to point out some common characteristics which could provide us with a broader insight into the extraordinary being the Mother was, she who contained all those personalities into herself. As her mission was different each time, all of these characteristics can, of course, not be prominent or even discernible in every life.

A first outstanding characteristic is that in most cases she seems to have been born to accomplish the humanly impossible. Actually, it is always the task of the Vibhuti to accomplish the humanly impossible; the humanly possible is for ordinary humans to do. Still, the accomplishments of some of the Mother's Vibhutis have been so much out of the ordinary that they go on living in the memory of humankind. (It is striking that the Mother, each time choosing the place on earth most suitable to execute her task, was not always highly born. Mona Lisa must have been, to the eyes of her contemporaries, a Renaissance woman like any other; Joan of Arc was a farmer's daughter from a village hardly anybody would have heard of had she not been born there. The Mother may have had many 'hidden' births like that, in order to raise the inner, psychological level of mankind.)

A second characteristic is the all-embracing scope of the personalities she took on. As Hatshepsut, Elizabeth I and Catherine II of Russia she incorporated some of the focal periods of civilization. For what one does not hold in oneself, one cannot carry onwards.

A third characteristic is the unbending strength shown in every incarnation – Hatshepsut acting as a king; Tiy initiating the utopia of Akhetaton; seventeen years old Joan without any military experience commanding a victorious army; Elizabeth effectuating in an English Renaissance context something comparable to what Hatshepsut did in XVIIIth Dynasty Egypt; Catherine taking Russia into the modern age practically single-handed.

A fourth characteristic is the multiple abilities shown in every incarnation, even in the simply educated Joan of Arc. It is through its incarnations that the psychic being grows into the fullness of its divinity. A mature psychic being, having been through hundreds if not thousands of human incarnations, is often recognizable because of its numerous capabilities, acquired in the course of its incarnations. It is only this completeness that can lead to the cosmic consciousness, which is a necessary state to realize the Supramental. And who has gone through more lives than the Mother – she who said she has never left the earth since its beginning?

In our four characteristics, the reader will doubtlessly have observed some of the characteristics of Maheshwari (majesty, greatness), Mahakali (strength, daring), Mahalakshmi (beauty, harmony) and Mahasaraswati (learning, industry), functioning within the given, limited circumstances of our Earth at particular moments of its evolution and history, and in each reincarnation present in the required proportion to bring this evolution a step further, 'to manifest a ray of consciousness.'

These brief life-sketches are only a few examples of the Mother's reincarnations. She has said, for instance, that a petrified body of hers still existed somewhere in the Himalayas.[48] We know about the vision she had of Sakyamuni, the Buddha, noted down in her diary on 20 December 1916, and in which he said: 'I know thee and love thee as thou didst know and love me once. I have appeared clearly before thy sight so that thou mayst in no way doubt my word.' Who was it who thus loved and knew the Buddha? Yasodhara, his wife? And there is the story, told in one of the first chapters of this book, about the daughter of a Venetian doge who was murdered on the orders of her father because of her love for the son of the doge whose position her father was usurping. The Mother knew the names and the dates of the persons involved, for she had looked them up in the history books, but she never told them.

And, yes, she had been 'that Catherine,' by whom she meant the Great Catherine II, of Russia (1729-96).[49] The characteristics of the other lives we know about are distinctly present in this incarnation too. There was the difficult start in life before Catherine became Empress, comprising '18 years of deception and humiliation' during her marriage with the neurotic Peter III. There was her exceptional intelligence and her interest in the English and French philosophers of the Enlightenment, especially Voltaire and Diderot. There was her strength and daring: 'For her, a foreign-born petty princess, with only a handful of friends, to lead a rising against her own husband, Peter the Great's grandson – even in Russia no such daring coup had ever before been heard of ... It was a dramatic sight, later depicted by painters: the slim figure of Catherine, for eighteen years subdued and victimized, at last in command perfectly assured on horseback, attractive in her Guards uniform, at the head of company after company of soldiers, their boots thudding on the road in unison.'[50] (Who, reading this, does not think of Joan of Arc?) The author of these words, Vincent Cronin, who calls Catherine 'Russia's one person Renaissance,' also writes: 'Catherine set out the need for complete religious toleration, for freedom of the press within limits, above all for just human laws ... She was moving towards a typically eighteenth-century belief in progress, in particular progress for Russia, and she saw herself as being helped by Providence to forward the wellbeing of the Russian people ... She was as successful a woman ruler as Elizabeth of England has been in a very different kind of country.'[51]

And the Mother said: 'I remember acutely a resolve I made in my last life as an empress [Catherine II]. I said: "Never again! Enough is enough, I want no more of it! [Next time] I want to be a commoner, in an ordinary family, free at last to do as I want."'[52] We, now, have an idea how it looked like, that ordinary family, host to an exceptional child. We have seen that child grow into the Mother, the female part of the Two-in-One together with Sri Aurobindo, on earth once more to accomplish the humanly impossible: to transform the human species into a divine species. And we have seen how the mature reincarnated souls came to them from the four corners of India and from abroad in order to participate in the Great Work in total dedication and surrender. As the Mother repeatedly said, most of them belonged to 'the family,' in this and in many previous lives; they had been together with her, or with Sri Aurobindo, or with both, in India, Babylonia, Egypt, Europe, Japan, and who knows how many places more, some now covered by sand or water – but they did not remember. She did, though, and to some she told about when and where they had been together. But then she stopped telling them, for few are the humans who can bear the memory of their past.*

The process of reincarnation should not be too much schematized in our mind. The Mother, like Sri Aurobindo, has said so often that everything is possible, and that it is typical of the human mind always to simplify and standardize. At the base of every human incarnation is the psychic being†, but this does not mean that the psychic being has to be involved in its entirety all the time. The Mother sometimes called her incarnations 'emanations,' i.e. embodiments of a part, an aspect of her Being. She even said that all her reincarnations up to the present one had been partial embodiments of her Divinity, more had not been necessary.

This time, however, it was the full Being that had incarnated, she said, it was the Mahashakti, the Great Mother in her fullness.[53] Which may give us an idea of the importance and difficulty of the Work that was to be undertaken, as will become clearer in the following chapters.

---

* There is some evidence that Sri Aurobindo was, besides Leonardo da Vinci, also Pericles, Caesar Augustus and Louis XIV. He may have been King Solomon, for, after all, the basic form of his symbol is that of Solomon. A disciple of whom some incarnations are common knowledge was Nolini Kanta Gupta, a great yogi. He himself has said that he was Yuyutsu in the war on which the *Mahabharata* is based; Virgil, the Roman poet and friend of Caesar Augustus; Pierre de Ronsard, the French poet of the Pleiade and friend of Francois Clouet; Francis Walsingham, Elizabeth's councillor and spy-master; André Le Nôtre, who designed the gardens of the palace of Louis XIV at Versailles; and André de Chenier, the poet of the French Revolution, who died on the guillotine.

† The difference between an incarnation of an ordinary human being and an incarnation of the Mother or Sri Aurobindo is that, in the first case, the divine soul has accepted to dive into the ignorance, completely forgetting its divinity and starting its 'adventure of consciousness and joy' from scratch, as it were; while in the second case the soul remains always in full possession of its Divinity and incarnates every time as a psychic being that represents the highest possibility at which evolution has arrived.

15.

The Manifestation of the Supramental

I know that the supramental Descent is inevitable – I have faith in view of my experience that the time can be and should be now and not in a later age.[1]

– Sri Aurobindo

A Prediction

The Mother had been giving messages for the new year since the early 1930s. She said about these messages: 'I look at the year that is coming. To be able to speak about it, I must look at it. I look at the coming year and, looking at it, I see at the same time everything people imagine about it, all their speculations and their expectations about what is going to happen in [what people always fancy to be] that "wonderful year." I look at all that and at the same time I look at what that year really is, what it already is beforehand. It is already like that somewhere.'[2] On New Year's Eve 1954, she read in French and English her message for 1955: 'No human will can finally prevail against the Divine's Will. Let us put ourselves deliberately and exclusively on the side of the Divine, and the Victory is ultimately certain.'[3] And she gave her comment: 'This message was written because one foresees that next year will be a difficult year and that there will be many inner struggles, and perhaps even outer ones. So [in the message] I tell all of you what attitude you should take in these circumstances. These difficulties will perhaps last not only twelve months – in other words one full year – but fourteen months. During these fourteen months you must make an effort never to lose the attitude about which I am going to talk to you in a moment. Actually, I insist on the fact that the more difficult things are, the more you must remain quiet and the more you should keep an unshakable faith. Of all things this is the most important.'[4]

Manoj Dasgupta, then one of the young pupils, now a trustee of the Sri Aurobindo Ashram and head of the Ashram School, asked: 'Will it be a difficult year for the Ashram or also for India and the whole world?' The Mother replied: 'Generally – [for] the world, India, the Ashram and individuals. For everyone according to his manner of being, naturally, not in the same way for all. Some things will seem easier than others. But generally speaking it is … If you want I can tell you: it is the last hope of the adverse forces to triumph against the present Realization. If we are able to hold on during these [fourteen] months, afterwards they will not be able to do much, their resistance will crumble. That's what it is about: it is essentially the conflict of the adverse forces, of the anti-divine forces, who are trying to push back the divine Realization as much as they can – they hope for thousands of years.

'It is this conflict which has reached its climax. It is their last chance. And as those who are behind their action are very conscious beings, they know very well that it is their last chance, and they will put everything they can into it. And what they can, is much. These are not ordinary little human forms of consciousness. They are not human consciousnesses at all. They are consciousnesses who, compared with the human capacities, seem divine in their power, in their strength, even in their knowledge. This means that it is a terrible conflict, and one which is totally concentrated on the Earth, because they know that it is upon Earth that the initial victory is to be won – the decisive victory, a victory which will determine the course of the earth's future. Those who are noble-of-heart and stand up when things become dangerous, can be happy. It is an opportunity to rise above oneself. That's what it is about.'[5]

At the time, the Mother said nothing about the inner battle, or battles, she must have been fighting with the hostile forces in those fourteen months. Only years later did the Mother mention in passing, in one of the conversations constituting *Mother's Agenda*, that the beginning of February 1956 had been a terrible time, with all the asuric forces of destruction on the offensive.[6] Knowing that she, like Sri Aurobindo, was not given to exaggeration, this must have been a terrible period in the yoga of the *Avatar* – one of the many sustained and crucial battles we know nothing about.

This occult turmoil was reflected in the outer world. At that time the Cold War was on the verge of turning into a hot war. The Warsaw Pact was signed, the first Russian H-bomb exploded, the first American nuclear submarine launched. It was the time of the Bandung Conference, 'a revolt of Asia and Africa against the white race,' with Nasser, Nehru and Sukarno as its celebrities. Egypt's seizure of the Suez Canal and the Russian invasion of Hungary were in the offing.

The tension in the visible and in the invisible worlds could only indicate that something crucial was about to happen, for better or worse. Sometimes one senses this in the *Entretiens*. 'It is quite evident that from the purely mental point of view, of the physical mind, we have come a long way since the Stone Age,' she said on 5 October 1955. 'It is said that we haven't made much progress because there's something else [i.e. the inner life] which has not been much developed, because we were much too busy playing with the new instrument [the mind]. For it is so interesting to have a new game* ... [It was] like children in a playground: they invent, try things out, play, find out, dash against each other, fight, make peace, quarrel, discover, destroy, build up. But behind all that there is a plan. There was a plan. There still is a plan – there is more and more a plan. And perhaps all this playing on the surface is, in spite of everything, leading to something which will come to happen one day. Perhaps, if we speak and think so much of it now, it is perhaps because ... A time will surely come that it will happen. It may happen gradually, in stages, but all the same there is a moment when it begins to happen. So perhaps we have reached that moment.'[7]

The 'it' that was to happen was the manifestation of the supramental consciousness, its 'insertion' in the earthly evolution, which is the precondition for the appearance of a new species on earth, the 'superman'

---

* What the Mother means here is, as she said many times, that animal-man was so enthralled by the new capacities bestowed on him by his acquisition of the mind, the mental consciousness proper to the human being, that he has played with it and tried it out to its possible limits. For it was this mind which equipped him with the capacities of abstraction, mental formulation and language, and with their manifold applications.

or supramental being, and the creation of a divine world, the Kingdom of God on earth.

A week later, she said: 'I think that it will happen the moment there is a sufficient number of consciousnesses which feel in an absolute way that it cannot be otherwise ... Your consciousness is so dependent on what is, that it finds it even difficult to imagine that things *can* be otherwise. And until what must be becomes for a sufficiently big group of consciousnesses an inevitable necessity, and until all that has been and all that now still is looks like an absurdity which cannot last: it is at that moment that 'it' will be able to happen, not before.

'A problem remains, namely whether it is something which can take place and will happen individually before happening collectively. It is probable [that it will first happen individually]. But no individual realization can be complete nor even approach that [supramental] perfection if it is not in accord with at least a group of consciousnesses representative of a new world. After all, there is such a great interdependence of the individual and the collectivity that the individual realization, however great, is limited, impoverished by the unresponsive atmosphere of its surroundings. And it is certain that the entire terrestrial life has to follow a certain line of progress in order for a new world and a new consciousness to manifest. This is why I said in the beginning that it depends at least partially on you.'[8]

In the same conversation she said: 'For a very long time it has been said: "It will come, it will come" ... Many thousands of years ago some already began to promise that one day there would be a new consciousness, a new world, something divine which would manifest upon Earth, but they said: "It will come, it will come" in the future – they spoke of ages, aeons, thousands and millions of years. They did not have this feeling which we have now: that it is bound to come, that it is very near. Of course, human life is very brief and there is the inclination to wish to shorten the distances in time so that they may be proportionate to our human dimensions. But in spite of everything there will be a moment when it happens; there will be a moment when the development tilts into a new reality. There has been a moment when the mental being was able to manifest upon Earth. Its starting point may have been very poor, very incomplete, very imperfect, but all the same there was a starting point. Why would the starting point [of the supramental being] not be now?'[9]

When a child remarked that the Mother had said that the event was 'very near,' the Mother confirmed: 'Yes, otherwise we wouldn't be talking about it. It is obvious that if it were to happen after a number of millennia, we wouldn't have to be concerned about it and only see it as a far-off dream ... It is, however, possible that before this [race] becomes a new race, like the human race [has become a new race], it may take much, much time. And it will come about progressively. But, as I said, one thing is sure: when it happens, it happens. It is not something that stretches out like a rubber band: there is *a moment* when it happens – when the descent takes place, when the fusion occurs, when the identification comes about. It can happen in a flash. There is *a moment* when it occurs. The rest may take much, much time. You mustn't hope to see supermen spring up everywhere overnight, it won't be like that.'[10]

The message for the year 1956 too spoke of the battles the Mother was waging – and apparently winning. 'The greatest victories are the least noisy. The manifestation of a new world is not proclaimed by beat of drum.'* On 4 January 1956, she again warned her audience that they must be reasonable in their expectations of the great miracle: 'Of course, if all of a sudden there were luminous apparitions, or if the outer physical forms changed completely, then, I think, even a dog or a cat, or whatever, would notice it. But that will take time, it can't happen all at once. It can't happen right now, it is for further on, for much later. Many great things will take place before that, and they will be much more important than that, mark my words.' But: 'The world will go on. Things will happen, and there will be, perhaps, a handful of human beings who will know how they came about. That's all.'[11]

And then it happened, on 29 February 1956: the manifestation of the Supramental – *exactly* fourteen months after the Mother's prediction on the New Year's Eve of 1955.

---

* This is the Mother's own translation from the original French.

The Supramental Manifestation

'The lights had been turned off at the Playground after the reading of some passages from *The Synthesis of Yoga* and the children's questions. They all sat on the ground in a semicircle around her. One heard the sea in the distance, and the beam of the lighthouse swept over the top of the walls – two short flashes, one long. It was the "Wednesday meditation." One saw Mother in the dark, seated in her low chair, bent somewhat forward, with a *Plumeria* flower between her motionless fingers. She always looked white, this Mother, even when dressed in red or in whatever colour, as if something radiated through her body, a kind of white luminosity at times so dense that it became visible to our materialistic eyes. And there were the disciples, silent …' [12] This is how a French disciple, present there on 29 February 1956, gives his impression of the moment at the Playground when the Supramental manifested in the atmosphere of the Earth.

The Mother herself noted down that very evening: 'This evening the Divine Presence, concrete and material, was there present amongst you. I had a form of living gold, bigger than the universe, and I was facing a huge and massive golden door which separated the world from the Divine. As I looked at the door, I knew and willed, in a single movement of consciousness, that *"the time has come,"* and lifting with both hands a mighty golden hammer I struck one blow, one single blow on the door and the door was shattered to pieces. Then the supramental Light and Force and Consciousness rushed down upon earth in an uninterrupted flow.' [13]

Later she explained in a conversation with K.D. Sethna: 'The whole thing is not so much a vision or an experience as something *done* by me. I went up into the Supermind and did what was to be done. There was no need for any verbal formulation as far as I was concerned, but in order to put it into words for others I wrote the thing down. Always a realization, a state of consciousness gets somewhat limited in writing: the very act of expression narrows the reality to some extent.' [14]

The significance of this event cannot be overestimated. What Sri Aurobindo and the Mother had been working for since the beginning of their avataric yoga was now realized. What had they been working for? To bring the supramental, i.e. divine Consciousness down on Earth, to insert it into the earthly evolution and thus make the decisive evolutionary step possible by which one day a divinized species will be present on Earth in a material body. It was now certain that the Kingdom of God would be established upon Earth.

The supramental Consciousness is the Unity-Consciousness, the Truth-Consciousness, the Divine Consciousness. Sri Aurobindo and the Mother have often compared the Manifestation as a whole to the two hemispheres of a globe: in the upper hemisphere all aspects, gradations or worlds exist in the Unity-Consciousness and are therefore divine; in the lower hemisphere all forms of consciousness in their respective layers or worlds are supported by fragmented or partial rays of the Unity-Consciousness, which means that everything here belongs at least partially to the Ignorance, of which the Inconscient is the Black Pit, the lowest, total Darkness.

The avataric intervention of Sri Aurobindo and the Mother consisted in establishing the link between both hemispheres, thus creating not only the possibility but the certitude that the upper, divine hemisphere would become manifested* upon Earth. Therefore, the manifestation of the Supramental on 29 February 1956 meant, among other things, that the future embodiment of the supramentally conscious being beyond Man, of the divine Superman, was now assured, as it was assured that the human aspiration throughout countless millenniums was being fulfilled: the world would not always be a place of frustration, suffering and death. Like everything else in the One Divine it would be able to materially develop its essential divine nature. K.D. Sethna wrote in his diary: 'I wonder when the world will realize that [on 29 February 1956] the greatest event in history took place.' [15]

The Mother announced the Event in the *Bulletin* of April 1956. There she published the following four lines under the heading '29 February':

---

* The Mother makes a distinction between 'descent' and 'manifestation.' 'What I call a descent,' she says, 'is the individual occurrence, in an individual consciousness. And when it is a new world manifesting in an old world – just as, by way of comparison, when mind pervaded the earth – I call that a manifestation. You may call it whatever you like, it's all the same to me, but we should understand each other.' (The Mother, *Questions and Answers 1956*, CWM 8 p. 134)

Lord, Thou hast willed, and I execute:
A new light breaks upon the earth,
A new world is born.
The things that were promised are fulfilled.[16]

This was a modification of four great lines from her diary entry on 25 September 1914, forty-two years earlier:

The Lord has willed and Thou dost execute:
A new Light shall break upon the earth.
A new world shall be born,
And the things that were promised shall be fulfilled.[17]

The future expectation had become the present realization. At the same time she had the following declaration published, under the date 24 April 1956: 'The manifestation of the Supramental upon earth is no more a promise but a living fact, a reality. It is at work here, and one day will come when the most blind, the most unconscious, even the most unwilling shall be obliged to recognize it.' [18]

'Was this advent unexpected?' asked Indra Sen, a disciple. 'Absolutely,' answered the Mother, 'but all my greatest experiences have come like that. I am in my usual consciousness and they come suddenly, as if to show their reality in the fullest contrast and vividness. They have the best value when first received in this way. When one is informed beforehand, the mind begins to play a part ...' And she added: 'The working of the Supermind in my body has gone on since the 5th December 1950. It has been a progressive individual working; so I thought things would go on like that. But in January of this year Sri Aurobindo appeared to me two or three times and it was as if he indicated that the Supermind was coming on a universal scale. What has come has become engulfed at present and it has to work itself out. Nature did not reject – she could not.* The Supreme decided that the time had come and He released the Force.' [19]

---

* 'The atmosphere of the earth is too contrary to the magnificence of the Supreme Consciousness and veils it almost constantly. From time to time It can show and express Itself, but then again this Inconscient atmosphere veils It. It was like that when in 1956 the Supramental Power came down upon earth. It was coming in torrents of

Henceforth in the Ashram 29 February was called the Golden Day. Why did the Mother have to publish these two statements nearly two months after the great Event when so many disciples were present when it happened? 'When I came back from the Supermind [i.e. after she had shattered the Golden Door] I thought that, since the outpour was so stupendous, everybody would be lying prostrate. But when I opened my eyes I found everybody sitting quietly and perfectly unconscious of what had happened.'[20] Nirodbaran had once written to Sri Aurobindo in a rare surge of enthusiasm: 'The Supramental is bound to come down and we shall lie flat at the gate and he can't pass by.'[21] But on that 29 February he too will probably have eaten his evening meal like on every other day.

Yet the Mother had foreseen the possibility that even the closest disciples would not be aware of the unexpected presence of the Supramental, for she had said in March 1951: 'It may very well happen that at a given moment the supramental Force manifests, that it is conscious here, that it acts on Matter, but that those who don't consciously participate in its vibration are incapable of perceiving it. People say: "When the supramental force manifests, we shall know it quite well. It will be seen." Not necessarily. They will not feel it any more than those people of little sensitivity who may pass through this place [the Sri Aurobindo Ashram], even live here, without feeling that the atmosphere is different from elsewhere.'[22] And she had written also: 'Man must understand that in spite of all his intellectual achievements he is as incapable of perceiving the supramental vibrations as the animal was incapable of perceiving the mental vibrations when they pervaded the earth before the appearance of the human species.'[23]

All the same, not everybody had been ignorant of the fact that something out of the ordinary had happened. K.D. Sethna notes in his diary that he had heard that four people, one inside the Ashram and three outside, had been aware of the supramental Manifestation, and

---

Light, wonderful Light and Force and Power, and from the earth *big waves* of deep blue Inconscience came and swallowed It up. All the Force that was coming down was swallowed up and it is again from inside the Inconscient that It has to work Itself through. That is why things take so much time here.' *(Glimpses of the Mother's Life II,* p. 289)

that he had written to the Mother about this. 'The Mother told me: "What I said was not that four people knew it to be the supramental Manifestation, but that when the Manifestation took place they had some unusual experiences because of it, even if they didn't understand why ... Among those outside, I counted you." I was surprised to hear this. The Mother continued: "You wrote to me – didn't you? – that on the night of 29 February I was with you. I had promised you long ago when you had gone from here that I would inform you at once if the Supermind manifested. I never forgot this. And when the Supermind did manifest I went out to tell you."'[24] Actually, on the night of 29 February 1956, K.D. Sethna had his experience with the Mother around midnight, in the train between Pondicherry and Madras when seeing off his sister-in-law. The Mother's promise dated from 1938.

In K.D. Sethna we also read: 'Not too long after the glorious 29 February the Mother said to a few sadhaks, including my close friend Nirodbaran, that she saw no reason why she should not leave her body now that the things that had been promised had been fulfilled. The attendants were perturbed and pleaded with the Mother not to leave us but to continue her labour towards the divinization of the body.'[25] That this was much more than gossip in the sadhak community is proved by a note of the Mother's included in *Champaklal's Treasures*. It runs as follows: 'Now that the Supramental is there – for of that I am absolutely certain even if I am the only one upon Earth to be aware of it – is it that the mission of this form [her body or adhara] is ended and that another form is to take up the work in its place? I am putting the question to Thee and ask for an answer – a sign by which I shall know for certain that it is still my work and I must continue in spite of all the contradictions, of all the denials. Whatever is the sign I do not care, but it must be obvious.'[26]

This is an extremely important address of the Mother's to 'the Lord.' Firstly, an obvious sign must have been given to her, for we know that she remained on Earth for seventeen more years. Secondly, this prayer shows clearly that the aim of the endeavour of the Avatar had been accomplished with the manifestation of the Supramental. A completely new phase of the avataric Yoga was to begin. For this new phase there was no available guidance, neither from Sri Aurobindo nor from the Mother's own experience. Some insights, guidelines and suggestions can be found in *The Supramental Manifestation upon Earth*, in *Savitri*, and in the last chapters of *The Life Divine* and *The Synthesis of Yoga* – but that only in retrospect. This new phase of the Integral Yoga might be called 'the Yoga of the transformation of the body.' It fell completely outside the 'system' of the Integral Yoga as deduced and constructed by some commentators from Sri Aurobindo's writings, sometimes without acknowledging the important part the Mother has played in discovering the main lines of this yoga and putting them into practice. To conclude this section about the momentous event that was the manifestation of the Supramental, let us drop in on two or three of the Mother's Wednesday classes in which the subject came up.

On 2 May, about a fortnight after the manifestation had been announced, a child asked: 'Mother, you have said: "The Supramental has descended upon Earth." What does that mean exactly? You have also said: "The things that were promised are fulfilled." What are those things?' – The Mother replied: 'Ah, if this isn't ignorance! It was promised very long ago. It was said a very long time ago – not only here: since the beginning of the Earth. There have been all kinds of predictions by all kinds of prophets. It has been said: "There will be a new heaven and a new earth; a new race will be born; the world will be transformed." Etc. Prophets have spoken about this in all the traditions.'

The child: 'You have said, "They are fulfilled."' – The Mother: 'Yes, and?' – The child: 'Where is the new race?' – The Mother: 'The new race? Wait let's say some thousands of years and you will see it! When the mind has descended upon Earth, between the time the mind manifested in the Earth-atmosphere and the first human being appeared, nearly a million years elapsed. Now it will go faster because man expects it, he has a vague idea. He is expecting something resembling the advent of the superman. The apes, on the contrary, certainly did not expect the birth of the human being, they had never thought of it – for the simple reason that probably they didn't think much. But the human being has thought of it and awaits it, so it will go faster. But "faster" still means thousands of years, probably. We shall talk about it again after some thousands of years!'

Another child: 'Mother, when mind descended into the Earth-atmosphere, the apes had made no efforts to change into the human being, had they? It was Nature that provided the effort. But now – ' – The Mother: 'But it is not man who is going to convert himself into superman!' – The child: 'Isn't it?' – The Mother: 'Just try a little! ... That's the point, you see, it is something else that is going to do the work ... But – yes, there is a 'but,' I don't want to be that cruel – *now man can collaborate.* That is to say, he can lend himself to the process, with goodwill, with aspiration, and help as best he can. And that is why I said that it would go faster. I hope it will go *much* faster. But even so, 'much faster' is going to take some time!'

And the Mother continued: 'Listen. If all of you here who have heard about this, not once but perhaps hundreds of times, who have talked about it, thought of it, hoped for it, wanted it – there are people who have come here for that, with the intention of receiving the supramental Force and being transformed into supermen; that was their aim, wasn't it? – how is it that all of you were so alien to this Force that you didn't even feel it when it came? Can you solve this problem for me? If you find the solution to this problem, you will have found the solution to the difficulty.'[27]

On 15 August the Mother reported: 'The movement [of the Yoga] is much accelerated. The march forward, the stages succeed each other much more rapidly. And it is perhaps more difficult to follow, or at least, if one doesn't make an effort to keep the pace, one is much more quickly outdistanced than before; one gets the feeling of being late or of being left behind. Things change quickly.'[28]

7 February 1957. 'It will soon be a year since, one Wednesday, the manifestation of the supramental Force took place. Since then it has been working very actively, even though very few people are aware of it! ... Of course, it is not working only in the Ashram. This Force is at work in the whole world, in all places where there is a receptivity, and I must say the Ashram doesn't have the exclusive receptivity in the world, the monopoly of the receptivity.'[29]

And then there was the *Entretien* of 10 July 1957, one of the most lyrical spiritual talks the Mother has ever given. Here, a few passages will have to suffice. She was commenting on a passage from Sri Aurobindo's *The Supramental Manifestation upon Earth* and said: 'That other world [the supramental world in the making on Earth] is necessarily an *absolutely* new experience. One would have to go back to the time when there was a transition from the animal to the human creation to find a similar period, and at that time the consciousness was not sufficiently mentalized in order to observe, understand or feel with intelligence. That transition must have taken place in a very obscure way. So, what I am speaking about is absolutely new, *unique* in the terrestrial creation. It is something without precedent, truly causing a perception, or a sensation, or an impression, that is quite strange and new. [There is] a gap [between] something which has overstayed its time and has only quite a subordinate force of existence, and something totally new, but still so young, so imperceptible, one could almost say so weak. It hasn't yet the power to impose itself, to assert itself and to predominate, to take the place of the former. The result is a simultaneous existence but, as I said, with a gap in between, by which I mean that the link between the two is still missing.' *[30]

The day before the Mother had been present in the Playground at the projection of a Bengali film on the life of Rani Rasmani, the rich widow who in 1847 built the Kali Temple at Dakshineshwar for Ramakrishna Paramhansa. 'It seems strange that something so new, so special, and I might say so unexpected [i.e. her experience], should happen during a film show ... I have always noticed that it is the unexpected which gives you the most interesting experiences ... Suddenly I had *concretely, materially* the impression that that [the world of religion and the Gods as shown in the film] was another world, a world which had ceased to be real, alive, an outdated world which had lost its reality, its truth, which had been surpassed, transcended by something which had just taken birth and was only beginning to express itself, but of which the life was so intense, so true, so sublime, that all that [in the film] became false, unreal, worthless. Then I really understood – for I understood

---

* The Mother is here talking about the old world on the one hand, 'something which has overstayed its time,' and on the other hand the new world in the making, 'something totally new.'

not with the head, not with the intelligence, but with the body, if you understand what I mean: in the cells of the body – that *a new world is born* and is beginning to grow.'[31]

This reminded the Mother of her overmental creation in 1926-27, which she briefly described to her audience. Then she continued: 'I announced to you all that this new world is born. But it has been so swallowed up, as it were, by the old world that up to now the difference has not been very perceptible to many people. Still the action of the new forces has continued very regularly, very persistently, very steadily, and to a certain extent very effectively. And one of the effects of this action was my experience, really so very new, of yesterday evening ...

'What has happened, what is truly new, is that *a new world is born, born, born!* It is not the old world being transformed, it is a new world *that is born!* And we are right in the middle of the transitional period in which the two are still entangled in each other – when the old one still persists all-powerful and entirely dominating the ordinary conscious-ness, but when the new one is slipping in, still very modestly, unnoticed – unnoticed to the point that, for the time being, outwardly it doesn't disturb anything very much and that to the consciousness of most people it is even altogether imperceptible. And yet it is working, it is growing, till it will be strong enough to assert itself visibly ...

'Now, all those ancient things [the world of the religions and the Gods] seem so old, so outdated, so arbitrary, such a travesty of the true truth. In the supramental creation *there will no longer be any religions.* The whole life will be the expression, the unfolding into forms of the divine Unity manifesting in the world. And there will no longer be what men now call Gods. Those great divine beings themselves will be able to participate in the new creation, but in order to do so they will have to put on what we might call the "supramental substance" on earth. And if some of them choose to remain in their world as they are, if they decide not to manifest physically, their relation with the beings of a supramental earth will be a relation of friends, collaborators, equals, for the highest divine essence will be manifested in the beings of the new supramental world on Earth. When the physical substance is supramentalized, to incarnate on earth will no longer be a cause of inferiority, quite the contrary. It will give a plenitude which cannot be obtained otherwise.

'But all this is in the future. It is a future which has begun, but which will take some time to be realized integrally. Meanwhile we are in a very special situation, extremely special, without precedent. We are now witnessing the birth of a new world; it is very young, very weak – not in its essence but in its exterior manifestation – not yet recognized, not even felt, and denied by most people. But it is there. It is there, doing its best to grow and absolutely *sure* of the result. But the road towards it is a completely new road which has never been traced out before – nobody has ever gone there, nobody has ever done that! It is a beginning, a *universal* beginning. Therefore it is a totally unexpected and unpredictable adventure.'[32]

And this is where the Mother made her call to the Great Adventure: 'There are people who love adventure. It is these I call, and I tell them: "I invite you to the Great Adventure." It is not a matter of repeating spiritually what others have done before us, for our adventure begins beyond that. It is a matter of a new creation, entirely new, with all the unforeseen events, the risks, the hazards it entails. It is *a real adventure*, of which the goal is certain victory, but the road to which is unknown and must be made step by step in the unexplored. It is something that has never existed in this present universe and that will never be again in the same way. If this interests you, well, embark. What is awaiting you tomorrow, I couldn't say. You must leave behind all you have foreseen, all you have planned, all you have built up, and start walking into the unknown – come what may! And that is that.'[33]

The Mother distributing sweets, 1950

Mother Nature

Along a path of aeons serpentine …
The Earth-Goddess toils across the sands of Time.[34]

– Sri Aurobindo

The New Year's Message for 1958 read as follows: 'O Nature, material Mother, thou hast said that thou wilt collaborate and there is no limit to the splendour of this collaboration.'[35] On New Year's Day a youngster asked the Mother to explain her mysterious message. The Mother, foreseeing the question, had already written down her answer.

However, before we ourselves read her answer it must be said that the Mother had been having for many years a sort of ongoing quarrel with Mother Nature. This is rather surprising, for Mother Nature is of course an emanation of the Great Mother, the Mother's essential Self. Yet all emanations have a considerable degree of independence, a status which Mother Nature seemed to take advantage of and to be thoroughly enjoying.* In her fancy of creative moods she never seemed in a hurry to take the earthly evolution forward, something which at times vexed the Mother, who was always pressed for progress.

So for instance on 6 February 1957, when the Mother talked about the obstacles on the road to the supramental transformation of Matter. 'Obviously the greatest obstacle is the attachment to things as they are. But even Nature as a whole finds that those who possess the profound knowledge want to go too fast. She likes her meanderings, she likes her successive attempts, her failures, her fresh starts, her new inventions. She likes the fancy of the [evolutionary] path, the unexpectedness of the experience. One could almost say that, for her, the longer it takes the more she enjoys it. But one tires even of the best of games. There comes a time when they need to be changed …

'For her [the burden of the earthly existence and the 'macabre joke' of death are] of no importance. She sees the totality, she sees the whole. She sees that nothing is lost, that there is only a recombination of

---

* Mother Nature is also the Earth Mother, worshipped under different names in practically all cultures.

quantities, of numberless minute elements without importance, which are put back into a pot, thoroughly stirred, and thereby produce something new.* But this game is not amusing for everybody. And if in one's consciousness one could become as vast as she, if one could become more powerful than she, why wouldn't one do the same in a better way? This is exactly the problem which confronts us now. With the addition, the new help of this [supramental] Force which has descended, which is manifesting, which is working, why wouldn't one take up that tremendous game [of Nature] in order to make it more beautiful, more harmonious, more true?

'It only needs brains powerful enough to receive this Force and formulate the possible course of action. There must be conscious beings powerful enough to convince Nature that there are other methods than hers. This looks like madness, but all new things have always looked like madness before they became realities. The hour has come for this madness to be realized. And since we are all here for reasons that are perhaps unknown to most of you, but that are nevertheless very conscious reasons, we may set ourselves to fulfil this madness. It will at least be worth its while living it.' [36]

But now, all at once Nature seemed to have changed her mind, as was proclaimed in the message for 1958. The Mother's answer to the request for her comment on that message went as follows: 'In the course of one of our classes [from which we have quoted in the preceding paragraphs] I spoke of the limitless abundance of Nature, the inexhaustible creatrix ... The evening I told you about these things, I identified myself with Nature, totally, I joined in her game. And this act of identification provoked a response, a sort of new intimacy between Nature and myself, a long process of increasing closeness culminating in an experience which came on the eighth of November. Suddenly Nature understood. She understood that this new [supramental] Consciousness which has been born does not seek to reject her but wants to embrace her entirely. She understood that this new spirituality does not turn away from life, does not recoil in fear before the formidable amplitude of her workings, but

---

* Medea's kettle is a metaphor for Nature's workings frequently used by Sri Aurobindo as well as by the Mother. Medea was the greatest sorceress in Greek mythology. She could make whole beings from the pieces thrown into her magic kettle.

wants on the contrary to integrate all its facets. She understood that the supramental Consciousness is here not to diminish but to complete her.

'Then from the supreme Reality came this order: "Awake, o Nature, to the joy of collaboration." And all of Nature suddenly rushed forward in a great surge of joy, saying: "I accept, I collaborate!" And at the same time there came a calm, an absolute tranquillity, so that this bodily vessel [i.e. the Mother's] could receive and contain, without breaking, without losing anything, the mighty flood of this joy of Nature which rushed forward as it were on an impulse of gratitude. She accepted. She saw with all eternity before her that this supramental Consciousness was going to fulfil her more perfectly, give a still greater strength to her movement, a greater amplitude, more possibilities to her play.

'And suddenly I heard, as if they came from the four corners of the earth, the great notes one sometimes hears in the subtle physical. They resemble somewhat those of Beethoven's [Violin] Concerto in D-major and come at the time of a great [evolutionary] step forward, as if fifty orchestras burst out together without a single discordant note, to proclaim the joy of this new communion between Nature and Spirit, the meeting of old friends who meet again after having been separated for so long.

'Then these words came: "O Nature, Material Mother, thou hast said that thou wilt collaborate and there is no limit to the splendour of this collaboration." And the radiant felicity of this splendour was perceived in perfect peace. This is how the message for the new year was born.'[37]

The Ship from the New World

Soon we will have to take leave of those wonderful *Entretiens* or 'French classes.' What we have read is only a fraction of the treasures they contain, chosen because they were felt to be essential to the story of the Mother's life. Here and there an edge of the veil is lifted, we get a glimpse of the way the Mother acted in many places and on many levels of existence, even while apparently just sitting there, addressing a group of students and disciples in the playground. Let us therefore have a last look behind the scenes and participate in an experience the Mother had on 3 February 1958, and which she read out a fortnight later from notes dictated by her immediately after the experience.

'The supramental world exists permanently and I am there permanently in a supramental body. I had proof of it this very day, when my Earth-consciousness went there and remained there consciously between two and three o'clock in the afternoon. Now I know that what was lacking for the two worlds to join in a constant and conscious relation* is an intermediate zone between the physical world as it is and the supramental world as it is. This zone remains to be built both in the individual consciousness and in the objective world, and it is being built …

'I was on a huge ship, which was a symbolic representation of the place where this work is going on. This ship, as large as a city, is fully organized, and it had certainly already been functioning for some time, for its organization was perfect. It is the place where the people are trained who are destined for the supramental life. These people, or at least part of their being, had already undergone a supramental transformation, for the ship itself and everything on board was neither material, subtle-physical, vital, or mental: [everything consisted of] a supramental substance. This substance was of the most material supramental, the supramental substance nearest to the physical world, the first to manifest.

'The light was a mixture of gold and red, forming a uniform substance of a luminous orange. Everything was like that. The light was like that, the people were like that – everything had that colour, although in various shades, which made it possible to distinguish things from each other. The general impression was of a world without shadows. The atmosphere was full of joy, calm, order. Everything went [on] in an orderly way and in silence. And at the same time one could see all the details of an education, of a training in all fields, through which the people on board were being prepared.

'This immense ship had just reached the shore of the supramental world and a first group of people who were destined to become the

---

* See the 'gap' the Mother talked about on page 402.

future inhabitants of the supramental world were to go ashore. Everything had been arranged for this first disembarkation. Several very tall beings were posted on the jetty. They were not human beings – they had never been humans before – nor were they permanent inhabitants of the supramental world. They had been sent down from above and posted there to control and supervise the disembarkation. I was in charge of the whole enterprise from the beginning and throughout the proceedings. I had prepared all the groups myself. I stood on the ship at the head of the gangway, calling the groups one by one and sending them ashore. The tall beings who were posted there inspected, as it were, those who were disembarking, letting pass the ones who were ready and sending back the ones who were not and who had to continue their training on board the ship.

'While I was observing everybody, the part of my consciousness coming from here became extremely interested; it wanted to see and recognize all those people, to see how they had changed, and check who were taken at once and who had to remain in order to accomplish their training ... Things continued in this way until suddenly the clock here struck three, and this brought me back violently. There was a sensation of suddenly falling into my body. I came back with a shock but with the full memory, because I had been called back very abruptly. I remained tranquil, without moving, until I could recollect the whole experience and keep it.

'On the ship the nature of the objects was not as we know it on Earth. For instance, the clothes were not made of fabric, and what looked like fabric was not manufactured: it formed part of the body, it was made of the same substance [as the body] which took different forms. It had a kind of plasticity. When a change had to be made, it took place not by any artificial and external means but by an inner movement, a movement of the consciousness, which gave that substance its shape and appearance. Life created its own forms. There was *one single substance* in everything; it changed the quality of its vibration according to need and usage.

'Those who were sent back for additional training were not of a uniform colour. It was as if their body showed patches of a greyish opacity consisting of a substance resembling the terrestrial substance.

They were dull, as if they had not been entirely permeated with light, as if they had not been transformed. They were not like that everywhere, only in spots ...

'When I was called back [into her material body] and while I was saying: "Not yet!" I had each time a brief glimpse of myself – of my form in the supramental world, that is. I was a kind of combination of the tall beings and the beings aboard the ship. My upper part, particularly the head, was not much more than a silhouette of which the contents were white with an orange fringe. The more down towards the feet, the more the colour looked like that of the people on the ship, that is to say orange; the more upwards, the more it was translucent and white, with less red. The head was only a contour with a brilliant sun in it. Rays of light radiated from it, which were actions of the will.

'As for the people I saw on board the ship, I recognized them all. Some were from here, from the Ashram, others were from elsewhere, but I know them too. I saw everybody, but as I knew that I would not remember them all when coming back, I decided not to mention any names ... Most people were young. There were very few children and their age was something around fourteen or fifteen, certainly not below ten or twelve ... There were no very old people, apart from a few exceptions. Most of the people who went ashore were middle-aged, except a few ...

'What I can say is that the appraisal, the assessment [about their readiness to go ashore] was based *exclusively* on the substance of which the people were made – that is on their belonging completely to the supramental world, on their being made of that so particular substance. The view which is applied is neither moral nor psychological. It is probable that the substance their bodies were made of resulted from an inner law or an inner movement which at that time did not come into question. It is quite clear, at least, that the values were different.

'When I came back I knew, simultaneously with the recollection of the experience, that the supramental world is permanent, that my presence there is permanent, and that only a missing link was needed for enabling the connection in the consciousness and in the substance, and it is this link which is now being established. There I had the impression ... of an extreme relativity – no, more exactly the impression that the relation of this world with the other one completely changed the standpoint from which things must be evaluated or appraised. The standpoint was not at all mental and it gave the strange inner feeling that lots of things we consider good or bad are not really so ... What is very obvious is that our opinion of what is divine or undivine is not right ... In the people too, I saw that what helps them to become supramental or prevents them from it, is very different from what we, with our habitual moral notions, imagine. I felt how ridiculous we are.' [38]

In November of that year, the Mother, when talking about the relation of our world of ordinary Matter and the supramental world ready to take its place, commented: 'But the link between the two worlds has not yet been built. That was the meaning of the experience of February third [the supramental ship], namely, to establish a link between the two worlds. For the two worlds are there in fact – not one above the other: one within the other, in two different dimensions – but there is no communication between the two. They overlap each other without being joined together. In the experience of 3 February, I saw some of those from here and elsewhere who already belong to the supramental world in part of their being, but there is no connection, no junction. The moment has come just now in the history of the universe when that link must be established.' [39]

The Mother Withdraws

Meanwhile the Mother had continued working out in her own person what she called 'the transitional being' between man and the supramental being, or le *surhomme*,' (the overman). We have been able to follow the progress of this work from the moment in December 1950 when Sri Aurobindo transmitted the Mind of Light into her body. On 16 April 1958 she again gave a progress report: 'It can be asserted with certainty that there will be an intermediate being between the mental and the supramental being, a kind of overman who will still have the qualities and in part the nature of man, which means that he will still belong in his most external form to the human species with its animal origin, but that he will transform his consciousness sufficiently to belong in his realization and activity to a new species, a species of overmen.'[40]

What Sri Aurobindo had foreseen in *The Supramental Manifestation upon Earth,* the Mother now announced as a fact: 'We have now reached a certitude, since there is already a beginning of realization.'[41] The transitional being, overman, was present on earth in the Mother's *material* body. To understand the importance of this fact, it must be realized that humanity is one just as Matter is one, which means that what is possible in a part of the whole is possible in the whole: what was possible in the Mother became possible for the whole of humanity. This truth is the basis of all spiritual action; without it, the Work of the Avatar would make no sense, for it would remain limited to the person(s) of the Avatar and have no effect on the rest of humanity. The Mother also repeated Sri Aurobindo's expectation that this transitional species would discover the occult means of 'producing new beings without having to use the old animal method, and these beings, who will have a truly spiritual birth, will constitute the elements of the new race, the supramental race.'[42]

A new species requires a new body, a new *material* body. 'It seems – it is even certain – that the very substance which will constitute the intermediate world that is already being built up, is richer, more powerful, more luminous, more resistant, with certain subtler, more penetrating new qualities, and a kind of innate capacity of universality, as if its degree of subtlety and refinement allowed the perception of vibrations in a much wider, if not altogether total way, and it [i.e. that new substance] removes the sensation of division one has because of the old substance, the ordinary mental substance. There is a subtlety of vibration which ensures that a global, universal perception is something spontaneous and natural. The sense of division, of separation, disappears quite naturally and spontaneously with that substance. And that substance is at present almost universally spread out in the Earth's atmosphere.'

This is one of the first times the Mother tries to formulate something that will become one of the main lines of her subsequent effort: the change of Matter effected by the change of consciousness, or the change of Matter made necessary to incorporate a new consciousness.

All degrees of consciousness above the mental degree which denominates humankind exist somewhere in the invisible worlds, but the substance of those worlds is not the gross material substance. The Earth is a material field. Earthly Matter has already evolved sufficiently to allow for the elements of the vital and mental degrees of manifestation to be embodied in it. If a new, higher degree of the manifestation is to embody upon the earth, earthly Matter has to evolve once again to serve as a means of embodiment, as a body for the consciousness of that new, higher degree.

It may be recalled that Sri Aurobindo and the Mother had been supramentalized many years before in the mental and vital parts of their earthly personality. From then onwards their whole effort consisted in bringing a supramental power of consciousness down into Matter. The result of their effort was the supramental manifestation in 1956. A consequence of this manifestation was the certitude that the supramental Consciousness, now present in Matter, would produce materialized supramental beings. As on all previous occasions in the evolution, the manifestation of such beings would happen in stages, as the enormous evolutionary change gradually worked itself out and produced the corresponding material beings. This is what Mother called *le surhomme* (the overman) – who may consist of various types of beings with a supramentalized consciousness but with a body still generated in the usual human way.

The supramental Consciousness is a Unity-Consciousness. Sri Aurobindo and the Mother possessed this Unity-Consciousness in their mind and vital, and Sri Aurobindo had already started realizing it in the cells, in the Matter of his body, at the time he had to take the decision to descend fully conscious and with all his avataric powers into death. The Mother, who was carrying on the Yoga, reported from time to time on the growth of the transitional, overhuman being in her and therefore in humanity. Now she says that Matter is developing the Unity-Consciousness. Can a body cell contain the universe? Can a body cell contain the All in its complete aspects of Spirit and Matter? It is obvious that the cell must be capable of this if it is to be divinized, for the Divine is the All, and the All is the One, and the One is the Unity-Consciousness. We are entering a domain in which the cell and its Matter will prove to be an organic, living conglomerate of vibrations, and in which each single vibration will prove to be an element constituting and reflecting the whole cosmos.

And the Mother continued the report of her experience: 'This new perception is asserting itself more and more. It becomes more and more natural, and it is even sometimes difficult to recapture the old way of being, as though it were vanishing into a misty past – something which is on the point of ceasing to exist.

'From this one may conclude that the moment a body, which was evidently formed by way of the old animal method, is capable of living this consciousness naturally and spontaneously, without any effort, without going out of itself, it is proven that [the experience of her body] is not an exceptional and unique case. It is simply the forerunner of a realization which, even if it is not altogether general, can at least be shared by a certain number of individuals who, besides, as soon as they share it, will lose the perception of being separate individuals and become a living collectivity.

'This new realization is proceeding with what might be called lightning speed, for, if we consider time in the ordinary way, only two years have passed – a little more than two years – from the moment the supramental substance penetrated into the Earth's atmosphere to the moment the change in the quality of the Earth's atmosphere took place.'[43]

The Mother's audience at the playground was, as she has so often said, a selection, a cream – but it was of course also young and human. There was goodwill, intelligence and psychic openness, but often also lassitude to the point of losing interest in what the Mother was saying. 'Mother, why don't we profit as much as we should from our presence here in the Ashram?' asked a child. 'That is very simple: because it is too easy!' answered the Mother. 'When you have to go all around the world to find a teacher, when you have to give up everything to obtain only the first words of a teaching, then that teaching, that spiritual assistance becomes something very precious, like everything that is difficult to obtain, and one makes a serious effort to be worthy of it.

'Most of you came here when you were very small, at an age when the spiritual life or a spiritual teaching were still out of the question, for it would have been altogether premature. You have indeed lived in this atmosphere but without even being aware of it. You are accustomed to seeing me, hearing me. I speak to you as one speaks to all children. I have even played with you as one plays with children. You have only to come and sit here and you hear me speak. You only have to ask me a question and I answer you. I have never refused to say anything to anybody. It is so easy. It is enough to live – to sleep, to eat, to do your exercises and to study at school. You live here as you would live anywhere else, and so you are used to it.'[44]

On 5 November 1958 the Mother wanted to see the fundamental cause of the lack of reaction, of the inertia in her audience. To that end she descended into their Subconscient and even deeper, into the general Inconscient. She described her experience[45] as a descent into a crevice between two jet black masses of rock with razor-sharp excrescences. And the crevice became more and more narrow, and there seemed to be no bottom to it. So narrow did the downward passage become that there was hardly place for consciousness to pass, she said.

And then a miracle happened. In that blackest of blacknesses there was, as it were, an invisible spring which suddenly projected her into a limitless golden immensity, almighty, of an infinite richness. She formulated the experience as follows: 'At the very bottom of the Inconscience most hard and rigid and narrow and stifling I struck upon an almighty spring that cast me up forthwith into a formless limitless Vast vibrating with the seeds of the new world.'

A few days later she commented upon it: 'The experience of November the fifth was a new step in the construction of the link between the two worlds. I was indeed projected into the very origin of the supramental creation: all that warm gold, that living tremendous power, that sovereign peace. I saw once again that the values which govern this supramental world have nothing to do with our values here below, even the values of the wisest, even those values which we consider most divine at the time we live constantly in the divine Presence. They are altogether different.'[46] The supramental world was very much present, below at the core of the black Inconscient, above in a bright, limitless

Vast, within a distance difficult to conceive in our earthly way of seeing and therefore experienced as a sudden projection by a spring. This experience of the Mother was a promise that radiated over the difficult years to come.

She made the formulation of this experience into her New Year's message for 1959. By the time the message was published, however, a radical change had taken place in her life. On 26 November she had given her last Wednesday class at the playground; on 5 December she had given her last Friday class at the playground; on 7 December she had played her last game of tennis; on 9 December she had stopped leaving the Ashram premises except on special occasions. She went through a severe, life-threatening ordeal.

16.
What Is to Be Done Is Done

Thou shalt bear all things that all things may change.[1]

– Sri Aurobindo

Ups and Downs

1958 had been a year of splendid realizations. It was certainly the year in which the Mother fully realized the transitional being, overman, in her body. In a conversation in May of that year, she said that she had been working on this since the moment of Sri Aurobindo's departure, eight years before, and still more intensely after the supramental manifestation. When on 8 October a child asked her: 'Mother, will there not be any intermediary states between man and overman *[le surhomme]?*' the Mother answered: 'There will probably be many.' But then she wanted to make sure that the person who asked the question was aware of the definitions. 'Man and overman? You are not speaking of the new supramental race [i.e. superman], are you? Are you really speaking of what we here call the overman, that is: the human being born in the human way and trying to transform his physical being which he has received by his ordinary human birth?'[2] The child's answer is not recorded.

The Mother continued: 'There will certainly be a countless number of *partial* realizations. The degree of transformation will differ according to each one's capacity, and it is certain that there will be a considerable number of more or less fruitful or unfruitful attempts before arriving at something like overman, and even those [the overmen] will be more or less successful attempts. All those who make an effort to go beyond

431

ordinary nature; all those who try to realize materially the profound experience which has brought them into contact with the divine Truth; all those who, instead of taking as their aim the Beyond or the Highest, try to realize physically, externally, the change of consciousness they have realized within themselves – all those are apprentice-overmen. Among them there are innumerable differences in the success of their efforts. Each time we try not to be an ordinary man, not to live the ordinary life, to express in our movements, our actions and reactions the divine Truth, when we are governed by that Truth instead of being governed by the general ignorance, we are apprentice-overmen – according to the success of our efforts more or less able apprentices, more or less advanced on the way.'[3]

Then, after a series of magnificent realizations, came the repercussion; the Black Dragon swept its tail and the Mother went through one of the severest ordeals of her life. This up-and-down movement occurs so frequently in her and Sri Aurobindo's yoga that it seems to be phenomenon proper to it. After each yogic gain, each climb to formerly unconquered heights, each ascent beyond the previously known, acquired and established, there is a step backward, a sliding down lower than before, more daunting and dangerous, a descent into deeper darkness and horror. According to the Mother each such up-and-down cycle was not only a consolidation of newly acquired terrain, it was also an essential movement of the yoga to descend ever deeper with the Light and the Power gained ever higher.

What also becomes a regular feature of the Mother's yoga from this time onwards is that many severe ordeals seem to be accompanied or even brought about by an attack of black magic. In December 1958, when the attack was so ferocious that she had to withdraw from all activities and many thought that her life was in peril, she 'saw' a young woman pulling her by her hand outside into what looked like the courtyard of the Ashram, not the material courtyard but its occult replica. There a sorcerer was uttering his incantations threatening the Mother's life and using as his operational contact a thin gold chain of hers. When the Mother managed to break the magic spell, she 'burst into laughter' and woke up in her bed. The evil was seen, the magic was mastered, the crisis was over.

It is nonetheless interesting to know that the young woman trying to pull her down into the courtyard was a former close attendant of hers who had died five years before. This woman, Chinmoy, is mentioned in several chronicles as spreading scandalous insinuations and rumours about Sri Aurobindo and the Mother. Champaklal remembers: 'At one time C[hinmoy] was very close to Sri Aurobindo and the Mother. And as happens in the case of many who come too close to them, she also lost her head. She became hostile. This has happened so often and exceptions are rare. Their speech is very sweet. Mother warned me several times against it: "Champaklal, take care, it is slow poison."

'C[hinmoy] used to speak nonsense [i.e. slanderous insinuations] and we could not bear it. So once I asked Mother while Dyuman was also present: "What is our position? We cannot bear what she says. Your ways are different and we are afraid that if we react in our normal way, it may run counter to your working. What are we to do?" Mother looked tenderly and lovingly [at us] and explained: "You see, we have been fighting this for the last forty-one years. I have spoken to Sri Aurobindo also about it and he said to me: 'You know well that it is not a question of this person or that person. Sending away a certain person won't help us in any way. We are fighting with the hostile force [behind her], not with the person. If you send away one person, it will catch hold of another.' Now you understand, Champaklal?" And she looked on both of us with great kindness.'[4]

The Mother also said that people like this attendant were targeted for possession by the powerful Titan who was put into the world by the great Adversary, and who tried to end the Mother's life and her mission on every possible occasion. This Black Shadow stalking her at every step attempted to kill her innumerable times, she said, using every human and nonhuman instrument within his scope. This is the cause or explanation of many of the dramatic events forming her Stations of the Cross, but of which she has spoken very little. This was also the reason for Sri Aurobindo's occult watchfulness and protective care of the Mother, especially on days of intense descent, e.g. the darshan days, so much so that in November 1938 he forgot about himself, so to speak, and was attacked in his turn – something he thought 'they' would not dare to do.

When the suffering and the digging into new lower layers of the sub-conscious were over, the Mother recovered her strength and progressed towards a new height: the first time the supramental force penetrated directly *into her material body*, without passing through the intermediary mental or vital sheaths. It was an overwhelming experience in which the red and golden supramental light poured into her with such intensity that it caused a burning fever. This happened in the night of 24-25 July 1959[5] with a surprising consequence: suddenly the Mother found herself in the presence of Sri Aurobindo, in his 'dwelling' in the supramental world.

This does not mean that the Mother had not met Sri Aurobindo before. In fact, his presence by her side had been constant, as his action in the world had equally been continuous and had resulted, among other things, in the supramental manifestation in 1956. But now something completely new happened: the Mother met Sri Aurobindo not in a psychic, mental or vital part of her personality, but physically, in the world of supramental Matter which, for the first time, had extended to her material body. As we know, the Supramental is a Unity-Consciousness, which means that the supramental world is a unity-world in which everything is present to everything else and participates in its being. Sri Aurobindo could be there because he had supramentalized his inner being, consisting of the sheaths or bodies in which he lived after his departure from the gross material world. It may be said that Sri Aurobindo formerly, as the evolutionary Avatar, had built his stations one after the other on all levels of existence up to the Supramental. Now he had a permanent 'dwelling' there too. This did not prevent him from being present and active wherever he wanted in all of the manifestation.

The Mother would later report that together with Sri Aurobindo in his supramental dwelling there were other people close to him. She named Purani, and Amrita, and the amazing Mridu. The explanation of their presence there is not difficult. We remember that, after her experience of the ship of the New World, the Mother had said that some people on Earth were supramentalized in part of their personality, even without their surface consciousness being aware of it. After death we carry with us what we are inwardly. It may be assumed that people who are in part supramentalized are fully mature souls, sufficiently developed to dwell in the supramental world(s), and that the former human beings now with Sri Aurobindo, and ready to come down with him as the first supermen on a supramentalized Earth, are of this kind.

Now that Sri Aurobindo was physically present with her again, the Mother did something she had postponed doing for ten years: she opened with great care the access to her inner psyche, where she lived in eternal unity with him. We recall that she had closed this access by a yogic act at the time of his departure, in order to prevent her automatically following him. How many realized that, from 1959 onwards, they were in the presence not only of the Mother but also of Sri Aurobindo, physically, albeit in a material substance so different from our gross Matter that the Mother described both substances as two worlds. Sometimes she started spontaneously speaking in English, and explained that Sri Aurobindo was uttering the words through her mouth; or it happened that her handwriting suddenly resembled Sri Aurobindo's, so concrete was his presence to her, in her.

Angry Sugar Cane

It may be doubted whether it was the Mother's intention to stop her activities altogether in December 1959. She probably saw her withdrawal as temporary, for she was always ready to continue her effort to the end through thick and thin. The reason her withdrawal turned out to be more radical than intended was that the yoga had entered a new phase: the transformation of the body. Transformation means change, and processes which lead to an unknown change in the body are generally considered illnesses. The inevitable transitional stages of the changes in the Mother's body as a whole, of its parts (skeleton and organs) and of its elementary constituents (the cells) indeed looked very much like illnesses, and grave or baffling ones at that, although, as we shall see, she asserted time and again that she was not ill, that she was going through the unprecedented experience of physical transformation resulting in temporary 'disorders'.

She still went out occasionally, to preside over a ceremony at the playground, the sports ground or the school, or on a special occasion elsewhere, at a sugar factory for instance. And hereby hangs an illuminating tale.

Laljibhai Hindocha, building on the pioneering work of his father, was a successful Indian businessman in Uganda, Africa. He first heard of Sri Aurobindo and the Mother in 1953 at a talk by A.B. Purani, who was in Uganda on a lecture tour. Towards the end of the same year Laljibhai visited the Sri Aurobindo Ashram for the first time. He saw no reason for staying more than a day, but the Mother let him know, through Dyuman, that she wanted him to stay for two weeks. Laljibhai at first protested that he had 'important commitments to public and social work and business and the affairs of all my companies in Africa,' including his Miwani Sugar Mills.[6] When he relented, the Mother asked him to visit all the farms and small industries of the Ashram. 'Let him observe them and give a report on how we can improve their efficiency and increase the production.'

When the day came that the Mother wanted to hear his report, it was the very first time that Laljibhai spoke directly to her. In the course of their unusually long conversation, he asked the Mother: 'How is it that we are here?' – meaning he and his family. The Mother replied: 'Among those who come here, each soul is destined to come, guided by the divine Planning. You are also under the divine Plan. That is how you are here. You don't know, but your mother prayed to Uma for a child.* Do you know who Uma is? I am Uma. Her prayer was granted and with my blessings to your mother you were born. Since your childhood, in school and in your business I have been with you at each step. We have also been together in our past lives.' When he took his leave Laljibhai didn't intend to come back to India before four or five years.

Yet it so happened that one of his sisters, Savita, divorced after a brief marriage and became a member of the Ashram. This meant that Laljibhai, her elder brother, had again to travel from Africa to India some months afterwards to settle his sister's affairs.† As matters continued developing, and the political situation in Africa looked more

---

* The goddess Uma is the consort of the god Shankar, one of the names of Shiva.

† Because of her paintings and the Mother's letters written to her, she would become very well known in the Ashram and elsewhere under her Ashram name, Huta.

ominous year by year, Laljibhai and his family finally settled in the Ashram in December 1957 which, as they suddenly remembered, was the time predicted by the Mother.

Laljibhai wanted to buy the Savana Textile Mill in Pondicherry. When he told the Mother of his intentions, she answered: 'No, start a sugar factory instead. It will be better for you.' Again Laljibhai protested: 'But, Mother, there are a number of problems in starting a sugar factory. It's an agricultural industry, so it's difficult.' A sugar factory depends for its supply on sugar cane growers, and the supply depends on the soil and the unpredictable weather. And he added: 'I do not even know if sugar cane grows here or not.' The Mother's answer: 'Have faith in the Divine and everything will be all right. Don't worry about it. This will be my Yoga in the material world and I want you to do it.'

The Mother herself had the new company registered and named it 'New Horizon Sugar Mills.' An office was opened on 14 May 1958 in the Mother's presence. Just then the Government introduced heavy taxation in its new budget. Laljibhai conveyed to the Mother that under the changed circumstances his family might not agree to set up the sugar mill. The Mother asked him to postpone the decision. In an interview she told him: 'There will be boundless difficulties for me, for you, for the Ashram, for India and for the whole world. There will be such a crisis that people will even lose faith in the Divine. But of this mess and chaos a New World will emerge that will be the victory of the Divine. What difference does it make in the present circumstances whether you undergo suffering and difficulties here in Pondicherry or in Africa?'

Laljibhai started looking for a suitable place for his sugar factory together with Udar, whom the Mother had asked to help him. They took photographs of various locations and showed them daily to the Mother. She picked one of the locations, saying: 'This is the place. Construct the factory there.' Time and again, as problems kept cropping up – which gives us an idea of how the Mother had to struggle for the least of her realizations in Matter – she would say to Laljibhai: 'Have some faith, faith, faith.' Once he replied: 'Mother, I have faith.' The Mother said: 'No, it is a mental faith, it is not from the heart. It must come from the heart, then it is real faith.'

The New Horizon Sugar Mills, on the road from Pondicherry to

Villupuram, was ready for production on 15 September 1960. The Mother was present at the opening ceremony. Towards the end of the ceremony there was a shower and the Mother got a little wet. Laljibhai offered his apologies but the Mother interrupted him: 'This is an agricultural industry and I wanted to know whether Mother Nature is collaborating in the enterprise. She has given her blessing by sending rain. Now you don't have to worry.' According to Laljibhai, for the next thirty years, up to the time of his stating this in 1990, they never had any problem with the weather, with lack of rain or shortage of water, either for the factory or for the crops of the farmers associated with the factory. This is remarkable, to say the least, in a subtropical climate where a failing monsoon and water scarcity are frequent afflictions.

On the same day of the inauguration by the Mother, New Horizon Sugar Mills had also organized a reception for the local and state dignitaries and politicians. To Laljibhai's immense distress and anxiety, the new machines broke down time and again. For fear of ridicule he prayed to the Mother with his whole heart. The Mother afterwards said: 'That afternoon, exactly at half past three, I felt that I had to make a little concentration, so I paid attention and saw Laljibhai praying to me. I was having my bath. You know what happens when I am pulled strongly: I'm stopped right in the middle of a gesture, then the consciousness goes wandering off and I can't do anything, it stops me dead. That's exactly what happened [on that day] in the bathroom. When I saw what was happening I straightened things out [meaning that she got the machines working again]. Then they must have had their celebration, for I suddenly felt: "Ah, now it has calmed down, it's all right."' The breakdown of the machines, the Mother explained, was due to the huge flows of turbulent vital force violently crushed out of the sugar cane and turning against the machines, the cause of their torment. 'They kept coming and coming, and I was busy with them the whole time. They were not ugly, [though] not so luminous either. They were wholesome, straightforward, honest forces.'

In 1962 Laljibhai wanted to go to Africa for some business meetings. As usual he asked the Mother for permission. She said: 'Why do you want to go to Africa? Things will become worse in Africa. If you have got anything there, bring it out. I give you a maximum of ten years from now to come out of there.' She told him to come out 'honourably,' for otherwise he would be kicked out. 'There will be chaos from the Cape to Cairo for fifty years to come, and beyond I cannot see.' In 1972, exactly ten years later, all Indians were forcibly expelled from Uganda by Idi Amin.

The Transformation of the Body

Much is needed to rise above the animal, much more than one thinks.[7]

– The Mother

We have seen that the Mother's withdrawal had become a necessity because she was entering a new phase of the yoga. Till now she had focused her effort on the realization of the overman, the transitional being between mental man, which we are, and the full-fledged supramental superman. From now onwards her effort would be concentrated on the transformation of the body – of her body and therefore of the body of humanity, because her body would become the body of humanity. This does not mean that she had not known about this before or that many elements of the new effort were not already present and even partially worked out in earlier years, some as early as in the years the *Prayers and Meditations* were written. This is an Integral Yoga, a global effort from the very beginning, 'a war on all fronts' to recall Sri Aurobindo's simile; every gain made a further progress possible and therefore the tackling of a new aspect of the integrality. The Mother had many names for this new aspect. She called it the yoga of the body, the yoga of the cells, the physical yoga, the yoga of the physical vibrations, the yoga of Matter, etc. The many names of this yoga define the centre of its attention and endeavour.

We are fairly well informed about this yoga of physical transformation due to a series of regular conversations, extending over many years, which the Mother had with Satprem, a French disciple. Satprem, whose other name was Bernard Enginger, was born in 1923 on the coast of Brittany, a place he would always remember with nostalgia. When twenty and a member of the French Resistance he was arrested by the Gestapo and spent one-and-a-half years in German concentration camps. The war, the concentration camps, the post-war upheavals and the Existentialist spirit of revolt and nihilism then pervading France left a deep imprint on him.

He served for a short time as secretary of the French Governor of Pondicherry, but 'normal' life could not satisfy him any more and he went to seek adventure in French Guyana, Brazil and Central Africa. However, during his brief stay in Pondicherry he had had the darshan of Sri Aurobindo and the Mother, probably in 1949, and he carried *The Life Divine* with him wherever he went. Ultimately he joined the Sri Aurobindo Ashram, reluctantly, in 1953.

The published correspondence between the Mother and Satprem in the following years shows the endless patience, understanding and love the Mother showered even on restless disciples like him. Gradually she won him over by taking him into her confidence, even during and after he had gone out of the Ashram several times, always dreaming of new adventures and discoveries in the most exotic places of the globe. She began talking to him on every subject under the sun, including her own past and her ongoing yogic experiences. When Satprem realized the importance of these conversations, he began recording them on tape, and from 1964 onwards published, with the Mother's consent, some passages in the *Bulletin of Physical Education* under the title *Notes on the Way*. Since its inception the *Bulletin* was published in English and French, and Satprem had become the French editor.

After the Mother's departure these recorded French conversations were published under Satprem's editorship as *L'Agenda de Mère* (later translated as Mother's Agenda) in thirteen volumes. They are an indispensable source of information not only about the Mother's yoga in the years 1960-73 but also about her and Sri Aurobindo's lives and their yoga in general. It is impossible to really know what their avataric mission and their yoga were and are without being knowledgeable about the contents of these conversations.

Five Principles

What I'm talking about are cellular realizations, don't forget.[8]

– The Mother

To get an idea of the Mother's Work in the following years, an understanding of some general elements of her yoga is necessary, for here we are entering a terrain where nobody has ventured before. We will have a closer look at these elements in brief and in the simplest possible way. It should be remembered that the Mother had to discover most of it by herself and for the very first time. In some cases she moved forward step by step, all the time groping for a formulation which might be comprehensible to others. True, all spiritual experience is incomprehensible as such because it belongs outside the domain of the mind. 'I am using words for what is not expressible in words,'[9] she said, and: 'It [i.e. her experience] is difficult to put into words, it is still too much only an action.'[10] Moreover, what the Mother has told is but a minute part of what she actually experienced; she said that to describe one minute of her experience a whole volume would be needed, and that a single one of her experiences represented a complete teaching. Still she made it possible for us to discern some broad outlines, and the marvel of her crystal-clear language lies in the way she managed to formulate the inexpressible in the simplest, though often unforgettably coined phrases.

To begin with, it should be kept in mind that the Mother in the body was also the Great Mother, the eternal divine Creatrix of the worlds. What could be seen of her with physical eyes – and many saw nothing more – was only an outer shell. Once, when a question was put to Sri Aurobindo concerning the *Prayers and Meditations,* he wrote: 'It is the Mother in the lower nature addressing the Mother in the higher nature, the Mother herself carrying on the Sadhana of the earth-consciousness for the transformation praying to herself above from whom the forces of transformation come.'[11]

In an *Entretien* of 1954, the Mother stated clearly that her central consciousness here in the material world was that of the Mahashakti, the Great Mother. On another occasion she said that, occultly, her heart was always a Sun, while higher up there must constantly have been the supramental brilliances unbearable to the human eye. But that was not what the human eye saw, of course. It saw an over eighty-years-old body, shrunken, stooped, almost unsubstantial, and often apparently very ill. Yet when she 'charged the atmosphere,' when she transmitted the presence of 'the Lord' to somebody in front of her, the Force was so strong that some could not stand it and ran away without further ado. 'When That comes, when the Lord is present, there is not one in a thousand to whom it is not frightening. And not in the reasoning, not in the mind: directly in the [material] substance.'[12] And in the cells of that aged body Divinity concretized; and in that aged body there took shape, little by little, a body consisting of a new kind of substance.

Although this was a new, in a sense culminating phase in her yoga, the principles of the Integral Yoga remained the same throughout. They were the five constants in those thousand-and-one experiences.

The first principle was that of unity. All is Divine because there is nothing else than the Divine. This statement is the result of direct experience confirmed by mystics in all climes and cultures. In *The Synthesis of Yoga* Sri Aurobindo had already written: 'The distinction [between divine and undivine] exists indeed for practical purposes; for there is nothing that is not divine, and in a larger view it is as meaningless, verbally, as the distinction between natural and supernatural, for all things that are, are natural. All things are in Nature and all things are in God. But for practical purposes there is a real distinction.'[13]

The Mother's whole effort consisted in annulling this real distinction, for the result of the supramental transformation should make the Divine concretely present in Matter. As Matter became gradually more 'porous' to her, the divine Presence in all became ever more real, visibly, tangibly. She saw everything as vibrations – rainbow-coloured vibrations of the One – and her own vibrating body as a finely tuned receptor of those vibrations. This was quantum physics as experiential reality, as a way of living, based on its underlying truth of the universal unity and experienced in the complexity of all the gradations of being. Unity is the source, unity is the outcome, unity is the way. But the Mother had to transform the consciousness of her cells into a Unity-Consciousness

– a change more fantastic than any transformation in any religious vision or fairy tale. She had to wipe out the 'real distinction' between our human ignorance and the superhuman omniscient divinity.

The second principle, declared by Sri Aurobindo to be the Alpha and Omega of the Integral Yoga, was surrender. The Mother's surrender to the Divine, the Lord, her higher Self, was permanent throughout her life. It was the basis of everything she did, of her great yogic acts and of the apparent trifles of everyday life. Her *Prayers and Meditations* were already pervaded by surrender as by an exalting perfume. It was also the very instrument of her yoga. It was, she said, the only means, the only remedy, the only solution. The principle is simplicity itself: as there is nothing else than the Lord, he is the only Doer and the only deed. The manifestation is his; therefore the evolution within that manifestation can only be his. This means what Sri Aurobindo stated above, namely that 'the Mother herself carrying on the Sadhana of the earth-consciousness' is surrendering 'to herself from whom the forces of transformation come' – 'herself' being identical with the Supreme, That, the Divine, or the Lord, as the Mother was in the habit of calling Him since the beginning of her yoga.

Again, it should not be forgotten that this was now the yoga of the cells. It was no longer sufficient that the surrender be an inner, psychological act: it had to be an action or a voluntary attitude of the cells. The consciousness of each cell had to surrender. This is something awesomely difficult because, first, that consciousness had to be developed to ranges it had never touched before in the whole of existence of the human species, and, second, the cells carry within them the burden, hardened into a behavioural habit, of a catastrophic past. 'The material consciousness, that is the mind in Matter, has been formed under the pressure of difficulties,' said the Mother, 'difficulties, obstacles, sufferings, struggles. It has, as it were, been built up by all that [in the course of the evolution], and that has left upon it a stamp almost of pessimism and of defeatism which is certainly the greatest obstacle' [14] – for a confident and joyful surrender, that is.

The Mother's surrender is there to read about on practically every page of the *Agenda* and the *Notes on the Way*. For instance: 'What is going to happen, I don't know. The body is not concerned about it, it is all the time like this *[Mother opens her hands with palms upwards]*, all the time: "What Thou willest, Lord, what Thou willest," with a smile and in a perfect joy.' [15] Or near the end of her way: 'All things on which I sought support for the [yogic] action, it is as if they collapsed on purpose to make me say, even in connection with the smallest trifles: "What Thou willest." It has become my only refuge.' [16] 'What Thou willest,' *(ce que Tu veux* or *ce que Tu voudras)** was her basic mantra. It was there supporting every act in her life, and at the end it will be there among the last discernible words recorded; and when words failed her, she expressed it in a gesture, offering herself and everything she represented, the palms of her hands turned upwards, to the Lord.

Since 1958, she also had a mantra specifically for the transformation of her body. She had heard it in April of that year when watching *Dhruva,* an Indian film in which this mantra was recited, and had been amazed at the effect it had on her cells. It consisted of three words: om namo bhagavate. The significance of these words, according to the Mother, is: om, I invoke or contact the Supreme; namo, I bow to the Supreme in total surrender; bhagavate, may I be made, as the Supreme is, divine.

The third principle was sincerity. 'In fact, as long as the ego is there, one cannot say that a being is perfectly sincere,' the Mother said, 'even though it is striving to become sincere. One must pass beyond the ego, give oneself up totally to the divine Will, surrender without reserve and without calculating. Then one can be perfectly sincere, not before ... Sincerity is the basis of all true realization. It is the means, it is the path, and it is also the goal. Without it you are sure to make innumerable errors and you have constantly to redress the harm you have done

---

* We find this mantric phrase, *ce que Tu voudras,* formulated by the Mother for the first time in her *Prayers and Meditations,* in the entry dated 15 July 1914. To demonstrate how many of the main elements of the yoga were already present to her in those early years would require a separate study. One example, concerning the action of the yoga in the cells, must suffice: 'Thou hast integrally taken possession of this miserable instrument [her body], and if it is not yet sufficiently perfected for Thee to complete its transformation, its transmutation, Thou art at work in each one of its cells to knead it, to make it plastic, to enlighten it, and in the whole being to put it in order, organize and harmonize it. Everything is in movement, everything is changing; Thy divine action makes itself felt as an ineffable source of purifying fire that circulates through all the atoms.' *(Prayers and Meditations,* CWM 1 p. 344)

to yourself and to others. There is, besides, a marvellous joy in being sincere. Every act of sincerity carries in itself its own reward: the feeling of purification, of soaring upwards, of liberation one gets when one has rejected even a tiny particle of falsehood. Sincerity is the safeguard, the protection, the guide, and finally the transforming power.' [17]

The Mother had a very special definition of sincerity. 'Sincerity means to lift all the movements of the being to the level of the highest consciousness and realization already attained.' [18] It means putting all the parts of the being under the influence of the central being, the psychic being. The psychic being is divine; all parts without a connection with the inner divine remain under the influence of the non-divine or anti-divine. The divine element in us is Truth; the non-divine is untruth, falsehood. Therefore real sincerity can only exist in the direct presence, in the light of the divine element in us. 'To be perfectly sincere, it is indispensable not to have any preference, any desire, any attraction, any dislike, any sympathy or antipathy, any attachment, any repulsion. One must live in a total, integral vision of things, in which everything is in its place and one has the same attitude towards all things: the attitude of the vision of verity.' [19] This was now demanded of the cells!

The fourth principle was equanimity or equality, which are not synonyms for indifference. 'The Yoga cannot be done if equality is not established,' [20] Sri Aurobindo had written many years before. The rationale for the yogic requisite of equanimity is that everything is the Divine, who is impartial or equally loving towards all that he has brought forward into his manifestation. Consequently, the being that wants to become supramental, divine, must be able to show the same impartiality and equality towards all forms of existence. The quality of equanimity is so foreign to the ordinary human behaviour that it may be considered a superhuman quality.

The fifth principle was aspiration, not any longer as a psychological condition but as a longing of the cells. Aspiration is the inner impulse which drives each and every one who sincerely turns towards the spiritual life. However, it could not be the basis from which the transformation of the cells had to start, for they were much too ignorant and enslaved by millennia of dwarfish habits. The Mother often compared the spiritual aspiration to a flame burning in the core of the being, or to a need 'which takes possession of you and which is so powerful that nothing else in the world has any importance any more.'[21] The kindling of the aspiration towards divinity in the cells could only be the result of a long labour of cleansing. In all its aspects, aspiration is a non-mental longing for something higher, the existence of which the aspiring being feels sure of, even if it has never seen it. The spiritual aspiration stems from the veiled knowledge of the Divine in us. The aspiration to be awakened in the cells of the body has to stem from the veiled knowledge of the Divine in them.

Unity, surrender, sincerity, equanimity, aspiration in the cells. They often overlap each other, precisely because their aim is the same: to provide a material body for the One. They were the five main tools the Mother now used to allow the Divine to work the miracle of the cells' transformation. Nobody had ever done that. Nobody had ever tried to transform Matter, to supramentalize Matter, to divinize Matter, to transmute Matter into its Essence. 'Matter also is Brahman and it is nothing other than or different from Brahman,' Sri Aurobindo had written in *The Life Divine*.[21] The transmutation of Matter into its inherent divinity would establish the Kingdom of God upon Earth. The age-long promise to humankind would be fulfilled. Why was it not done earlier? Was it so difficult?

What Would the Supramental Body be Like?

What would the supramental body be like? It would be something like the body humanity has dreamt of through the ages and has ascribed to angels and gods – and more, for it would be a divinized body, fount and instrument of an everlasting ecstasy of which our humanity has no notion. In one of her talks the Mother took the children with her on a fantasy tour of the supramental body. 'Transformation implies that the whole purely material set-up [of the human body as it is now] be replaced by a set-up of concentrations of force consisting of certain types of vibrations which replace each organ by a centre of conscious energy, moved by a conscious will and directed by a movement coming from above, from the higher regions. No stomach any longer, no heart, no circulation, no lungs, etc. All that will disappear. But it will be replaced by a set of vibrations representing what these organs are symbolically. For the organs are nothing but the material symbols of centres of energy, they are not the essential reality. They simply give a form [to the reality behind them] or in certain circumstances a support.

'The transformed body will function by means of its *real* centres of energy and no longer through their symbolic representations such as have been developed in the animal body. Therefore you must first know what your heart represents in the cosmic energy, and what the circulation represents, and what the stomach represents, and what the brain represents. You must be conscious of all that to begin with. Then you must have at your disposal the original vibrations of that which is symbolized by these organs. Then you must slowly gather together all these energies in your body and change each organ into a centre of conscious energy, which will replace the symbolic movement by the real one.

'You think it will take only three hundred years to do that? I think it will take much more time to obtain a form with qualities which will not be like those we know, but much superior. [There will be] a form that one naturally dreams to be changeable: as the expression of your face changes according to your feelings, so the body will change – not the form, but within the same form – according to what you want to express with your body. It can become very contracted, very expanded, very luminous, very motionless, with a perfect plasticity, a perfect elasticity, and a lightness in accordance with one's will ...

'There is no end to the imagination: to be luminous whenever one wants, to be invisible whenever one wants. Naturally, bones too are no longer needed in the system, for it is no longer a skeleton with skin and viscera, it is something different: it is concentrated energy obeying the will. This does not mean that there will no longer be any definite and recognizable forms. The form will be built by qualities rather than by solid particles. It will be, by way of speaking, a practical and pragmatic form. It will be supple, mobile, light at will – in contrast to the fixity of the gross material form.'[23]

Later, the Mother wanted to give an idea of the supramental body to a young Ashramite, Mona Sarkar. 'You know, if there is something over there on the window sill and I want to take it, I stretch out my arm and it becomes so long, and I hold the thing in my hand without even having to get up from my chair ... Physically I shall be able to be here and elsewhere at the same time, I shall be able to be in many places. I shall be able to communicate with many people at the same time. To have something in my hand, I'll just have to wish for it. I think of something, I want it, and it's already in my hand. In the transformed body I shall be free from the fetters of ignorance, pain, mortality, and unconsciousness. I shall be able to do many things at the same time. The transparent, luminous, strong, light, elastic body won't need any material stuff to subsist on ... It will be a true being, perfectly proportioned, very, very beautiful and strong, light, luminous or transparent ...'[24]

If all this may be thought to be fantastic, it should be pointed out that the Mother actually knew very well what she was talking about, being familiar with all kinds of worlds, substances and bodies through her occult experience. She knew the gods intimately, as of course she knew her own bodies in the various worlds, one of which she described after the experience of the supramental ship. She knew also what the supramental body was like because she had seen it 'at the limit of the manifested world' when still at Tlemcen. Also, there is not a single quality or capacity of the supramental body as described above by the Mother which is not known and named siddhi in the yogic schools in India. The huge problem, however, consisted in the realization of such a body on Earth, not as a partial or temporal siddhi, but as a permanent new species.

In theory much of all this looks fine and feasible, but in practice? How does one replace a heart or a skeleton with its vibrational support or reality? How or when does a stomach stop functioning and does its vibrational counterpart take over? Ought the transformation to be worked out one organ at a time, one cell after the other, or all at the same time? For this, indeed, 'would be a transformation infinitely greater than that of the animal into man. This would be a transition from man to a being that would no longer be built in the same manner, that would no longer function in the same manner, that would be like a densification or a concretization of "something" ... Up to now this corresponds to nothing we know physically, unless the scientists have found something I don't know of.' And the Mother added: 'You see, it's the leap that seems so enormous to me.' [25]

The Burden of the Forerunner

In fact no decisions had to be made, at least not on the level of thought and volition, which is where we make our decisions. The decisions were made by her Self, the Great Mother whom she perceived to be identical with the Master of the Yoga. It might even be said that the decisions were made in eternity, at the origin where the Avatars emanate, and that those decisions were now projected or actualized on the scene of the material manifestation. The Mother in the Sadhana accepted them in total surrender because they could not be anything but the will and the action of 'the Lord.' *Ce que Tu veux, ce que Tu voudras* ...

Of course, the Mother's body, the field of the transformation, was prepared like no other for the ordeal it was now to undergo up to the end of its existence. It had been prepared for this adventure without precedent not only from its earliest youth but from the womb, as we have seen, and its preparation had been steadily more perfected in the course of her spiritual progress. This brings to mind the refinement it must have acquired during her occult training at Tlemcen, when she was able to leave sheath after sheath of her adhara up to the outer boundaries of the manifestation. It brings to mind the shooting star on New Year's Eve of 1914, when she wished for the union with the Divine 'for the body,' and realized this union within the year. And when leafing through her *Prayers and Meditations* we find at least seven passages in which she records the divine action in her body's cells.

Yet her body was a human body consisting of the same Matter as ours, otherwise her yoga would not have had any meaning. Therein lay the avataric burden. As Sri Aurobindo wrote in general about the sadhak of the Integral Yoga: 'He has not only to bear his own burden, but a great part of the world's burden too along with it, as a continuation of his own sufficiently heavy load. Therefore his Yoga has much more of the nature of a battle than others; but this is not only an individual battle, it is a collective war waged over a considerable country. He has not only to conquer in himself the forces of egoistic falsehood and disorder, but to conquer them as representatives of the same adverse and inexhaustible forces in the world ... Often he finds that even after he has won persistently his own personal battle, he has still to win it over and over again in a seemingly interminable war, because his inner existence has already been so much enlarged that not only it contains his own being with its well-defined needs and experiences, but is in solidarity with the being of others, because in himself he contains the universe.'[26] The Mother, now alone, was of course *the* Sadhak of the Integral Yoga; she was, so to say, inventing the yoga of the body's transformation single-handed.

As she wrote herself about the burden of the Forerunner: 'There is a spirit of the [human] species. There are collective suggestions which don't need to be expressed in words [to be received]. There are atmospheres one cannot escape. It is certain – for this I know from experience – that there is a degree of individual perfection and trans-formation which cannot be realized unless the whole of humanity has made a particular progress ... There are things in Matter which cannot be transformed unless the whole of Matter has undergone a certain degree of transformation. One cannot isolate oneself completely, it is not possible ... Surely the individual will always be ahead of the mass, there's no doubt about that, but there will always be a proportion and a relation.'[27]

Even we ourselves, who think that we are separated from the rest of the world in the fortress of our material body, are pervaded by all kinds of invisible elements and influences, as science has found out. Our vital being is like an open house to others; we catch their pleasant or unpleasant moods, the little poisoned arrows they aim at us unseen, their inner discomfort or disorders and, exceptionally, their health or good humour. Our mind is like 'a market place,' said the Mother; we don't realize it, but we could hardly call one thought out of a hundred our own, bathing as we do in the whirling sea of thoughts all around us. And now the Mother had to universalize her body cells, for supra-mentalization is not possible without universalization. As we just heard from Sri Aurobindo, the sadhak of the Integral Yoga 'is in solidarity with the being of others, because in himself he contains the universe.' Because of all the preparatory work done on her cells in the course of her yoga, the Mother was capable of universalizing them.

Can one even imagine what it means to be universalized? To be as big, wide, infinite as the universe? To contain the universe in oneself? Sri Aurobindo and the Mother had been supramentalized in their mind and vital, and compared to the Supramental, which is the Divine, the universe is 'like a small picture against a huge background' (Sri Aurobindo). They had been like that, he apparently sitting there motionless in his armchair, she apparently distributing flowers, playing tennis, talking to her playground audience, making a pact with the life forces of angry sugar cane. Many had experienced an inexpressible, overwhelming feeling when approaching them or contacting them in concentration, as if they were privileged to step for a short while across the threshold of eternity. But who can imagine what universalization means if he or she does not live in it? And now the cells of the Mother's body were being universalized.

The result was that her body became decentralized. As she once said: 'In the last few days ... there was this experience: a kind of consciousness completely decentralized (I am *always* speaking of the physical consciousness, not at all of the higher consciousness) a decentralized consciousness which happened to be here, and there, and there, in this body, in that body – in what people call "this person" and "that person," but this kind of notion does not exist very much any more.* Then there was as it were a universal consciousness contacting the cells, as if it asked these cells for what reason they wanted to keep this combination, if one can call it so, or this conglomerate.† They were made to understand or feel the difficulties resulting from old age, the wear and tear of the body, the external difficulties – in sum, all the deterioration caused by friction and usage. All that seemed to them totally unimportant. Their answer was rather interesting because they didn't seem to attach importance to anything other than *the capacity to remain in conscious*

---

* The Mother means that she perceives the beings much more as conglomerates of vibrations than as personalities in the usual sense of the word.
† By combination or conglomerate is meant her physical body.

contact with the higher Force. Theirs was like an aspiration (not formulated in words, of course), what in English one calls "a yearning," "a longing" for the contact with the divine Force, the Force of Harmony, the Force of Truth, the Force of Love.'[28]

What happens to a body in course of universalization, to a body that is becoming decentralized? It loses its centre. But everything we do is related to a centre, this centre, this axis: me, I. The universe wheels around us; here and there, yesterday and tomorrow exist in relation to this centre. It was part of the Mother's yoga that her body, being universalized, would no longer function as an axis of material existence, that now the physical ego too would be dissolved. 'It is no longer the same thing which makes you act ... It is no longer the same centre.'[29] The old centre was the physical ego, existing within the framework of the laws of the physical world; the new centre was the Divine, directly. The Mother was learning how to live no longer according to the habits of the terrestrial evolution, hardened into so-called 'laws,'* but directly supported by the divine Force. For it will of course be this Force which shapes and determines the new supramental world and all beings in it.

The Mother had to effectuate 'the transition from an ordinary automatic way of functioning to a way of functioning under the direct guidance and influence of the Supreme ... Everything is a matter of changing the habit. The entire automatic habit of millennia has to be changed into a conscious action directly guided by the supreme Consciousness.'[30] Yes, it is clear that a supramental body, as described a few pages earlier, must function in a manner different from the human body we are so familiar with and which gives us so much trouble. A divine body must be divinely moved, yes, by the supreme Consciousness – one can more or less imagine that. But to change from an animal-human body into a supramental body? Well, somewhere the transition

---

* According to Sri Aurobindo and the Mother there are no permanently fixed, ineluctable laws in the universe. What we call a law is 'a fixed habit of process,' for 'what Nature does, is really done by the Spirit' and can therefore be changed by the Spirit. This does not mean that everything in the universe is arbitrary. 'All is possible, but all is not licit – except by a recognizable process: the Divine Power itself imposes on its action limits, processes, obstacles, vicissitudes.' *(On Himself,* SABCL 26 p. 202) 'Brahman is not subject to law, but uses process. It is only the individual soul in a state of ignorance on which process seems to impose itself as law.' *(Sri Aurobindo Archives and Research,* Dec. 1980, p. 158)

between the two worlds ought to be brought about. But how does one live at the same time in two bodies consisting of two completely different substances and obeying laws of totally different worlds? It was 'the leap between the two which seemed so enormous.'

The change in the functioning of the body the Mother called 'the transfer of power,' or 'the transfer of master.' It was 'the transition from the ordinary automatic functioning to a conscious functioning under the direct guidance and the direct influence of the Supreme,'[31] for that is how the supramental bodies will work. And one of the first times she felt the physical effects of the transition, she said: 'This change of initiating power, if one may say so, this transfer of power has had upon me the effect of a unique experience, of something that has never taken place before.'[32] The gestation of the new species in her was a universal first.

Sri Aurobindo and the Mother have often been asked whether there have been supramental beings on the Earth before. Their answer was unequivocal: some great spiritual beings may have had partial supramental realizations (siddhis) in their mental or vital bodies that showed in their physical body; some may even have had this kind of temporary personal siddhi in their physical body. The generation of a new supramental species, nevertheless, cannot have taken place before because it presupposes a change in the substance, in the Matter of the Earth. If this change had taken place once, it could never have been undone and would still be there – something Sri Aurobindo and the Mother would certainly have been aware of and put to their advantage, for it would have saved them a lot of yogic labour and suffering.

The outcome of all this was that the Mother existed physically in two worlds: our familiar animal-human world and the ever more present supramental world. We remember that the Mother said that the latter existed within the former and that the link between the two was not yet established. How can one physically live simultaneously in two separate worlds? It surely was a risky business, for one of the consequences was sometimes a sudden physical loss of consciousness in the Mother, to the consternation of her attendants.

The two simultaneous ways of existing she called 'the two rooms,' or 'the two worlds,' or 'the two consciousnesses,' so close together that an almost imperceptible turn in the consciousness sufficed to make the change from the one to the other – and yet they were so far apart. The Mother discovered to her surprise the place where the living and the dead consciously co-exist. 'Last night or the night before I spent at least two hours in a world which is the subtle physical, where the living and the dead intermingle without being aware of any difference. It doesn't make any difference. There is no difference, there. There were those we call the living and those whom we call the dead, they were there together. They ate together, they moved together, they played together. And all that took place in a pretty light, quiet and very pleasant. It was very pleasant. I said by myself: "Isn't it funny how the humans draw a line somewhere and say: you're now dead."' [33] (One of the persons the Mother often met there was Nolini Kanta Gupta, who was then still very much alive.)

The dwelling of Sri Aurobindo, the ship from the New World, the living and the dead existing together – all that was located in what the Mother called 'the subtle physical.' At this point it is necessary to explain that she started using this term in a special sense. Normally the subtle physical is a layer of existence on the verge of our perception, containing everything that is to pass into the gross physical (which is why specially gifted persons can have a prevision of it). The Mother once compared it to the vapours emanating from hot sand or from a hot road. But the Mother will more and more use the term 'subtle physical' for 'the real physical,' which is the same as the Supramental, which became accessible to her physical person because it was being supramentalized to an even greater extent.

No doubt, all this sounds rather esoteric to our ears. To the Mother it was the reality of every minute, night and day. It was a reality full of surprises, new discoveries and very tough challenges, the response to which she had to improvise, to find out, for it had never been done before. She had to move in the grandeur of the Supramental and Divine, and in the minuteness of a person, an organ, a cell, an atom – often on both levels at the same time.

And there was that third, horrific level: the Subconscient. For the new supramental being to be capable of embodiment, gross Matter had to change and become sufficiently subtle to serve as the substance for that embodiment. But we know that the base of Matter is the Subconscient and the Inconscient. Therefore, to change terrestrial Matter the Subconscient had to be purified, or cleared, or conquered, or made subservient to the aim of the Yoga. 'You have to go on year after year, point after point,' said Sri Aurobindo, 'till you come to a central point in the subconscious which has to be conquered and it is the crux of the whole problem, hence extremely difficult … This point in the subconscious is the seed and it goes on sprouting and sprouting till you have cut out the seed.'[34]

The Subconscient is very much what people imagine as hell. It is 'a mass of horrors,' said the Mother, full of terrifying, grotesque but devilish inventions of horror. It is life at its cruellest, where wounding, tearing, torturing, crushing, strangling, killing and devouring are the common ways of behaviour; it is the ghoulish cave where our nightmares take shape; it is the whispering, impelling inspiration of the pervert, the brute, the torturer and the sadistic killer.

In 1957 Sehra, a Parsi sadhika and wife of K.D. Sethna, had written a letter to the Mother describing a horrendous vision of hers. 'I saw people there with human forms, but they were not human beings. They were very huge and hideous, with one or two or three teeth protruding from their mouth … We went a little further and I saw those strange ugly beings dragging out corpses, tearing them into pieces and each one looking at his possession and saying: "Look what I have got!" The different pieces from different parts of the bodies represented different desires and feelings – lust, greed, hatred, jealousy, etc. And the beings who took the pieces and some of who started eating them were themselves representatives of the same desires and feelings. Each got what corresponded to his own nature. All were enjoying themselves over the hold they had on humans. Many of the corpses were also enjoying what was happening to them. They were not really dead but only looked so: they were alive.' Then a Voice told her: 'This is where the Mother's work is going on.' When Sehra met her the next day, the Mother said to her: 'You have seen correctly. I am now working in the subconscious. It is a very terrible region and even worse than what you have described.'[35]

Around 1935 Sri Aurobindo said that he would have been less enthusiastic had he known beforehand everything that was in store for him on the path of transformation. The Mother now sometimes spoke in the same vein, and the worst was yet to come. But she went on with her effort, of course, for she had promised Sri Aurobindo that she would do the work, and in 1956 she had remained on earth for that. *Je fais le travail,* she said simply, 'I am doing the work.' But few had any notion of the hellish minutes, and hours, and days she had to traverse.

> Her single greatness in that last dire scene
> Must cross alone a perilous bridge in Time
> And reach an apex of world-destiny
> Where all is won or all is lost for man ...
> For this the silent Force came missioned down;
> In her the conscious Will took human shape:
> She only can save herself and save the world.[36]

The Big Pulsations

It would be misleading to think that the Mother had 'withdrawn' because her presence outside the central Ashram building, at 9 Rue de la Marine, had been reduced to a minimum. How could she withdraw, she whose body was becoming the whole world in an ever more literal way? Besides, the daily occupations had not diminished at all. There were the Ashramites waiting for her at a certain hour and place, in the passage from one room to another, before and after she entered her bathroom, before and after she had her scanty meals, before and after her midday rest. Most of these meetings had become standing privileges, and the Mother would never forget anything, not the slightest detail – she who had kept a promise to K.D. Sethna made eighteen years before and which he himself had forgotten.

Then there were the daily audiences with disciples whose birthday it was or who had sent her a special request, with visitors to the Ashram, with secular and religious dignitaries, sadhus, politicians, administrators, cabinet ministers, chief ministers and prime ministers, and sometimes the president of the nation. On an average forty to fifty people per day, but on certain days up to two hundred people would pass through the room Udar built for her on the second floor, above Sri Aurobindo's apartment. And there were the secretaries and the heads of department, and the cashiers and bookkeepers. There were cheques and documents to sign, with that winged signature of hers representing 'the Bird of Peace descending upon earth.' There were dozens of letters to answer. And always there was the 'cloud' of invisible presences around her, pulling for her attention. Thus will be the way she 'withdrew' till six months before the end.

*The Mother with Prime Minister Nehru, Sri Kamraj, Indira Gandhi
and Lal Bahadur Shastri, 1955*

In the world the decade of the 1960s had begun, with its protests and upheavals among the youth and the young-hearted, with its 'flower power,' 'black power,' feminist movement and sexual revolution. Much of what was then 'groovy' and the 'in thing' now seems to have been forgotten or deflated. But the changes initiated in those ten years are still smouldering in the world under the surface; they helped to prepare the new millennium and the greatest Upheaval of all. The Mother had immediately seen their importance and she would say: 'The whole world seems to be undergoing an action which, for the moment, looks disturbing. It seems that the number of the apparently deranged is increasing considerably. In America, for example, the entire youth seems to be caught by a sort of bizarre vertigo which is disquieting to the reasonable people, but which is certainly an indication that an unusual force is at work. It causes the breaking up of all habits and all rules. It's good. For the moment it's a little odd, but it's necessary.' And at the end of the same conversation she would say: 'Fixed rules ... the fewer fixed rules there are the better. What is important is *a need* which only *That* can satisfy – nothing else, no half measures: only That. And there you go, each one on his way, it doesn't matter. Whatever the way, it doesn't matter. Even the extravagances of today's American youth may be a way. It doesn't matter.'[37]

In the meantime her superhuman struggle in the Subconscient continued unabated. (Maybe her gains there made the changes, the loosening up in the world possible.) Her conversations in those months touch time and again on the horrors rising massively against her and to which she had to stand up. It was not her personal Subconscient, but the Subconscient of humanity. She understood now why nobody had tried this before and why all the spiritually great had chosen to get out of such a mess by the quickest possible way. Sometimes she asked herself if it was not folly to try and fight 'against habits millennia old.'

Then came the upward movement, and the Mother emerged from her battles in the suffocating nether regions to a peak higher than the ones reached before. On 24 January 1961[38] she experienced the full presence of the supramental Force in her body. During the experience the connection between the supramental and our material world was established. In fact she experienced the supramental Force as a supramental body, 'a much greater and powerful being' in her gross material body. This was the very first time that she reported the presence of a new body within her. So strong was the power acting through that supramental body on the world that she had to contain it so as not to cause a catastrophe or a revolution somewhere on Earth. And with that presence and power rose in her a certitude which in French she called not 'square' (*carrée*) but 'cubic' (*cubique*) – unshakeable, unassailable, solid as a rock.

And then came the downward movement, deeper than the levels plunged into before. She toiled there for months. At times her embodied existence became so critical that she said she asked to be told if she had to take leave of it. Her departure would not create any practical problems, she said, for she had made all the necessary arrangements. And as we carry the manifestation symbolically in our body, the Mother's legs were now attacked, for they represent the Subconscient. By an act of evil magic she had been infected with filaria, one of the scourges of India, a mosquito having been the bearer of the malady. She knew when she had been attacked, where and by whom, for 'it so happens that I am a little conscious,' she said. She had been able to master the infected evil, but now, plunged day after day into the Subconscient, where our illnesses are part of the demonic arsenal, the infection had become virulent. Her legs were 'like two rods of steel,' she said, and she moved forward and up and down the staircase only by an act of the will, seeking support with her arms.

The Mother had to wait for the next upswing in her yoga till the end of February 1962, when one day she awoke with 'a pair of new legs.' The filariasis had disappeared overnight as if by miracle. She took it as proof that there were no limits to the possibilities of the body, even the gross material body, once it came under the influence of the Supramental. When going to the playground on 21 February, she had to restrain herself from dancing, she felt so light with her pair of new legs. But then the Black Dragon swung its tail again. The ordeal must have started on 11 March. The situation seems to have worsened in the following days, and on 16 March her life hung by a thread when her heartbeat stopped several times.

On 3 April, 'after several weeks of grave illness,' she said the following, which was recorded and afterwards submitted to her for her approval: 'Just between 11:00 and 12:00 last night, I had an experience by which I discovered that there is a group of people ... who want to create a kind of religion based on the revelation of Sri Aurobindo. But they have taken only the side of power and force, a certain kind of knowledge and all that could be utilized by asuric forces.* There is a big asuric being that has succeeded in taking the appearance of Sri Aurobindo. There is only an appearance. This appearance of Sri Aurobindo has declared to me that the work I am doing is not his [i.e. Sri Aurobindo's]. It has declared that I have been a traitor to him and to his work and has refused to have anything to do with me.

'There is in that group a man whom I must have seen once or twice [there], who is not with them in spirit, but only in appearance. But he is without knowledge, he does not know what kind of being is there. And he always hopes to make this being accept me, believing it is truly Sri Aurobindo[39] ... I met this being last night three times, even apologized for sins I have not committed, and in full love and surrender. I woke at 12:00, remembering everything. Between 12:15 and 2:00 I was with the true Sri Aurobindo in the fullest and sweetest relation – there also in perfect consciousness, awareness, calm and equanimity. At 2:00 I woke and noted just before that Sri Aurobindo himself had shown me that he was not yet completely master of the physical realm.

'I woke up at 2:00 and noticed that the heart had been affected by the attack of this group that wants to take my life away from this body, because they know that so long as I am in a body upon earth their purpose cannot succeed. Their first attack was many years ago in vision and action. I had it in the night and spoke of it to nobody. I noted down the date, and if I can come out of this crisis, I will find it and give it out. They would have liked me dead years ago. It is they who are responsible for these attacks on my life. Up till now I am alive because the Lord wanted me to be alive, otherwise I would have gone long ago.

'I am no more in my body. I have left it to the Lord to take care of it, to decide if it is to have the Supramental or not. I know and I have said also that now is the last fight. If the purpose for which this body is alive

---

* It would indeed be easy to concoct a sectarian or totalitarian creed or cult from the teachings of Sri Aurobindo and the Mother. One has only to put the accent on the new race of supermen in the making, to leave out the individuality of the way and the primary necessity of the realization of the soul, and to extract a mythos from their writings, *Savitri* containing all necessary material to this end.

is to be fulfilled, that is to say, the first steps towards the Supramental transformation, then it will continue today. This is the Lord's decision. I am not even asking what he has decided. If the body is incapable of bearing the fight, if it has to be dissolved, then humanity will pass through a critical time. What the asuric Force that has succeeded in taking the appearance of Sri Aurobindo will create is a new religion or thought, perhaps cruel and merciless, in the name of the supramental Realization. But everybody must know that it is not true, it is not Sri Aurobindo's teaching, not the truth of his teaching. The truth of Sri Aurobindo is a truth of love and light and mercy. He is good and great and compassionate and divine. And it is he who will have the final victory.

'Now, individually, if you want to help, you have only to pray. What the Lord wants will be done. Whatever he wills, he will do with this body, which is a poor thing.'

Afterwards, when the transcript of this talk was read to the Mother, she commented: 'The fight is within the body. This can't go on. They must be defeated or this body is defeated. All depends on what the Lord will decide. It [i.e .the body] is the battlefield. How far it can resist, I don't know. After all, it depends on Him, He knows if the time has come or not, the time for the beginning of the Victory. [If the time has come] then the body will survive; if not, in any case, my love and consciousness will be there.'[40]

Dramatic words in dramatic circumstances. But this proved to be only the first part of the drama, for on 13 April the Mother dictated in French, probably to Pavitra, the following victory bulletin. Like the previous text, it is not a very idiomatically correct translation from the French, but it is left untouched because of its impact and historic value.

'Suddenly in the night I woke with the full awareness of what we could call the Yoga of the World. The Supreme Love was manifesting through big pulsations, and each pulsation was bringing the world further in its manifestation. It were the formidable pulsations of the eternal stupendous Love, only Love. Each pulsation of the Love was carrying the universe further in the manifestation.

'And there was the certitude that what is to be done is done and that the Supramental Manifestation is realized.

461

'Everything was personal, nothing was individual.*

'This was going on and on and on and on.

'The certitude that what is to be done *is done.*

'All the results of the falsehood had disappeared: death was an illusion, sickness was an illusion, ignorance was an illusion – something that had no reality, no existence. Only Love and Love and Love and Love – immense, formidable, stupendous, carrying everything.

'And how to express it in the world? It was like an impossibility, because of the contradiction. But then it came: "You have accepted that the world should know the Supramental Truth and it will be expressed totally, integrally." Yes, yes.

'And the thing *is done. [long silence]*

'The individual consciousness came back: just the sense of a limitation, a limitation of pain; without that, no individual.

[Then the Mother switched to her native French, of which we give here the translation:] 'And we set out again on the way, sure of the Victory.

'The skies are full of hymns of Victory.

'The Truth alone exists; it alone shall be manifested. Forward! Forward!

'*Gloire à Toi, Seigneur, Triomphateur suprême!*† [Glory to Thee, Lord, supreme Triumpher!] *[silence]*

'Now, to work.

'Patience, endurance, perfect equality, and an absolute faith. *[silence]*

'What I am saying is nothing, nothing, nothing, nothing but words if I compare it to the experience.

'And our consciousness is the same, absolutely the same as that of the Lord. There was no difference, no difference.

'We are That, we are That, we are That. *[silence]*

'Later I shall explain better. The instrument is not yet ready. This is only the beginning.'[41]

---

* The Mother probably means that everything was an experience or act of her as the Divine Person, not of her as an embodied individual.

† We find the origin of this mantric formula of the Mother as early as in her Prayers and Meditations: 8.1.1914, *Tu es le triomphateur de tous les obstacles;* 10.5.14, *Gloire à Toi Seigneur, Maître du monde;* 25.5.14, *Tu es le Triomphateur et le Triomphe;* 4.6.14, *O Triomphateur de tous les obstacles;* 28.8.14, *Triomphateur suprême, triomphe de tous les obstacles.*

17.

The Passage Perilous

If thou wouldst save the toiling universe,
The vast universal suffering feel as thine:
Thou must bear the sorrow that thou claimst to heal;
The day-bringer must walk in darkest night.
He who would save the world must share its pain.
If he knows not grief, how shall he find grief's cure?[1]

– Sri Aurobindo

A Kind of Death

'I am no longer in my body,' said the Mother on 3 April 1962. If this sounds mysterious, her comments when looking back on the experience of the great pulsations are still more so. 'It has been a kind of death,' she said on 12 June, 'that much is sure – sure, sure, sure – but I don't say it because, after all, one has to respect the common sense of the people! You see, a little more and I would say that I was dead and that I have come alive again. But I don't say it.'[2] In the following years she would from time to time make remarks to a similar extent, for instance: 'It's really a queer condition: one is no longer alive and one is not dead.'[3]

Once she said, going somewhat deeper into the bizarre condition: 'Yesterday and the day before, throughout the day, from morning till night, something was saying: "I am or I have the consciousness of the dead on Earth." I am translating it into words, but it was as if something said: "This is what the consciousness of a dead person is like in relation to the Earth and physical things. I am a dead person living on Earth." According to the position of the consciousness – for the consciousness is constantly changing its position* – it was said: "This is how dead people are in relation to the Earth." Then: "I am absolutely like a dead person in relation to the Earth." Then: "I am living as a dead person lives in the consciousness of the Earth." Then: "I am exactly like a dead person living on Earth." And so on. I have been going on behaving, speaking and acting as usual, but it has been like this for a long time.'[4]

Did the Mother die and come alive again in the night of 12-13 April 1962? There can be no other interpretation of the following words: 'This reminds me of the fundamental experience I had when I was ... when I lived that pulsation of Love, and when it was decided that I had to take up my body again, that I return into my body.'[5] In later years she would say several times that the body with which she was identified was not *her* body but *a* body, used for the material contact without which her direct work for the supramental transformation would not be possible.

How to understand all this? Actually it is not a matter of understanding, for we can neither understand it nor can we understand most of her other yogic experiences – we can only try to follow the story of the Mother's life in order to have a glimpse, a notion of what she has been through, in order to acquire some insight into the importance of her and Sri Aurobindo's work and into the significance of the unparalleled change the world is going through at present. Only like can understand like, and as they have said so often: real comprehension is possible only through identification. All the same, we can make an effort towards a considered and insightful knowledge based on the facts and the hints given by the Mother and Sri Aurobindo themselves, or on interpretations by trustworthy chroniclers and commentators.

When in 1956 the basic aim of their avataric mission was fulfilled by the manifestation of the Supramental in the Earth-atmosphere, the

---

* The Mother was a very complex being, actually as complex as the manifestation. Her consciousness covered all levels of existence, from the lowest to the highest, and constantly 'changed its position' according to the demands of the moment, although the eyes of the people in her presence perceived little of what she was experiencing or doing inwardly. This is the reason why one has to pay attention when reading her conversations of the last years and concluding what she means by *je*, 'I'. In her case this pronoun may refer to any of the stances she was taking at the moment, from the physical body to the being in the physical body, to the Mother in the sadhana, to the Universal Mother in any of her aspects or emanations, to the very Supreme identified with 'the Lord.'

Mother asked 'the Lord' whether she should stay on Earth or not. A clear sign must have been given to her, for she stayed, presumably to speed up the supramental transformation of the Earth, with as her immediate aim the realization of the transitional being, the overman. In December 1959, at the time of her withdrawal into her room, this aim was fulfilled, according to her explicit confirmation, and a new phase of the yoga was entered, the transformation or divinization of the body cells. The Mother had been working on the transformation of the cells ever since the time of her *Prayers and Meditations,* but from a different level; now her Integral Yoga was a development in the consciousness of her body cells themselves. As always, she went about her accepted task with all the superhuman, divine energy she, the Mahashakti, had at her disposal, and barely three years later came the result we now know: 'And the thing *is done* ... The skies are full of the songs of Victory.'

It may be appropriate to stop here an instant and look back at the incredible speed with which Sri Aurobindo and the Mother's realizations have been effected, taking into consideration the difficulty of their aims. In the span of a human lifetime they realized the supramental Consciousness in their own Mind and Vital. Only six years after Sri Aurobindo's conscious, 'strategic' descent into death, the Supramental manifested into the Earth-atmosphere, whereby a new evolution of the Earth started: the evolution towards its divinization. Two years later the Mother announced the realization of the overman, the transitional being, the indispensable link for the material embodiment of the supramental being. This was immediately followed by the supramental yoga of the cells, whereof the outcome, only a couple of years later, was a Victory the songs of which filled the sky. What Victory?

Let us recall some phrases the Mother dictated the next morning: she had woken up with the full awareness of 'the Yoga of the World'; 'all the results of falsehood had disappeared' with, as a consequence, the disappearance of death, illness and ignorance; it had been accepted that the world should know the supramental Truth and it would be expressed totally, integrally. As this was a culmination of her yoga of the cells, itself the culmination of the Integral Yoga which was the essence of her and Sri Aurobindo's avataric mission, we must conclude that the goal of the avataric effort was reached in principle, confirmed from

Above and sure to be accomplished in Matter. The Supramental has been present in the Earth-atmosphere since 1956; the supramental species has been present in the universal evolution since 1962 in principle and is therefore bound to become a material fact. Its working out is only a question of time.

How long does it take for a new degree of the evolution, for a new species to appear on the Earth in a material form? Until now millions of years. Man's physical development from his origin as a primate has taken about four million years according to recent scientific estimates. No doubt the presence of the new element in the Earth-atmosphere, the supramental Consciousness and Force, will enormously speed up the transformational process. When, in their often hilarious correspondence, Nirodbaran wrote to Sri Aurobindo: 'We hear your Supermind is very near – not 50 years I hope! ... Don't forget to make us, at least, feel the Descent. 30 years' sadhana, by Jove!' Sri Aurobindo replied: '30 years too little or too many? What would have satisfied your rational mind – 3 years? 3 months? 3 weeks? Considering that by ordinary evolution it could not have been done even at Nature's express speed in less than 3000 years, and would ordinarily have taken anything from 30,000 to 300,000, the transit of 30 years is perhaps not too slow.'[6] This was written in 1936.

Less than thirty years later the Supramental was there, the transitional being was there (at least in the Mother) and the full supramental being was there in principle. How much more time would it take for the supramental being to be there as a perceptible fact? Not long ago, the Mother's guess had been thousands of years, but in her later *Entretiens* it had come down to three hundred. A reason for this acceleration may have been that the world, owing to the presence and the action of the double Avatar, had entered a global crisis, life-threatening like all new births, and that a race with time was on to prevent a catastrophe. In the evolution as in history every 'impossible' turn or event has come about at the very moment of its greatest impossibility; this time too the sunrise will follow Earth's darkest night – maybe tomorrow, but surely within the very near future, talking in evolutionary terms. These are the reasons why it is plausible to surmise that the Mother, in her endless love for humankind, took up her body again to hasten the advent of the New World.

Later she described the important changes that had taken place in her during the experience of 12 April 1962. 'The Mental withdrew [from her material body], the Vital withdrew, all withdrew. At the time when I was so-called ill the Mind had disappeared, the Vital had disappeared, and the body was left to itself, purposely.' In other words, the mental and vital elements of the adhara, the mental and vital sheaths, that is, had been removed and the only sheath remaining was the physical.* When this happens, normally one dies, for death means that the nonmaterial elements leave the gross material body. 'And that was the reason: it is precisely because the Vital and the Mental were gone that the impression was given of a very serious illness. And then, in the body left to itself, little by little the cells began to wake up to the Consciousness *[gesture of rising aspiration]*. Formerly this Consciousness was infused into the body by the Vital – from the Mental into the Vital, from the Vital into the body. When both were no longer there, the Consciousness rose slowly, slowly to the surface [of the cells]. All started with that burst of Love from the highest summit, the upper supreme height, and then little by little, little by little it came down into the body. And then the physical mind – which is something completely, utterly idiotic, which used to turn round and round in circles, always repeating the same, a hundred times the same – little by little became illumined, it became conscious, it became organized. And then it fell silent. Then, in the silence, the aspiration expressed itself in prayers[7] ... And this began when the doctors declared that I was very ill, then was the beginning. For the entire body was emptied of its habits and its forces. And then slowly, slowly, slowly the cells woke up to a new receptivity and opened themselves to the divine Influence directly.'[8] This too was a cosmic first.

'It was necessary,' said the Mother, 'that the capacity to receive and to manifest the Consciousness be obtained by the material cells. What now makes a radical transformation possible is the fact that in place of

---

* And the psychic being, but, strange to say, the Mother will become conscious of this important fact only later on, as we shall see in the following chapter.

a seemingly eternal and infinite ascent there is now the appearance of a new type. This is a descent from above. The previous descent [which resulted in the human being] was a mental descent, and this one Sri Aurobindo calls a supramental descent. The [Mother's] impression is of a descent of the supreme Consciousness which infuses itself into something that is capable of receiving and manifesting it [i.e. the cells of the body as they have become now]. And then, out of this, when it has been thoroughly prepared – how long it will take, one doesn't know – a new form will be born which will be what Sri Aurobindo called the supramental form, and this will be ... it doesn't matter what, I don't know how those beings will be called.'[9]

There is no doubt that something momentous had taken place. The material embodiment of the supramental species on Earth had become a certainty. 'There was the certitude that what is to be done is done and that the supramental Manifestation is realized,' the Mother said the day after her epoch-making experience. 'It is the denial of all the spiritual assurances of the past [which say]: "If you want to live fully conscious of the divine life, give up your body, for the body cannot follow [the spiritual aspiration]." But you see, Sri Aurobindo has come and he has said: "Not only can the body follow, it can even be the base which manifests the Divine." The work remains to be done.

'But now there is a certitude. The result is still far off, very far. There is still much to be done before the crust, the experience of the most external surface as it is, manifests what is happening within – not "within" in the spiritual depths, but within the body. To enable that [surface crust] to manifest what is within ... this will come last, and it is good that it is so, for if it came before [the necessary work is done] one would neglect the work, one would be so satisfied that one would forget to finish one's work. Everything must be finished within, everything must be thoroughly changed, then the outside will express it.'[10]

But would this realization not remain limited to the Mother's body alone? How could this yogic feat of hers profit the whole of humanity, how could it contribute to the materialization of the supramental being on Earth? Here we should recall that the consciousness of her cells was being universalized and that her body was being decentralized.

Moreover, does not even science tell us now that an event at one point of the cosmos has its repercussions at all other points?

'Since it is happening in one body,' said the Mother, 'it can happen in all bodies. I am not made of something different from the others. The difference is the consciousness, that's all. It [her body] is made exactly of the same [substance], with the same things. I eat the same things and it was made in the same way, absolutely.'[11] And she added: 'All is one single substance, completely the same everywhere, and it was unconscious everywhere. And what is now remarkable is that *automatically* certain things are happening *[gesture indicating points scattered everywhere in the world]*, totally unexpected, here, there, in people who don't even know anything.'[12] Humanity is evolving unknowingly. 'It [her supramental realization in the cells] is contagious, this I know for sure. And it [the contagiousness] is the only hope, because if everyone had to go again through the same experience [she went through] ...'[13] She did not finish the sentence.

The Earth is unknowingly suffering from an occult contagious epidemic: supramentalization. This epidemic has made the Earth apparently badly ill, for throughout the twentieth century, parallel to Sri Aurobindo and the Mother's yoga, it has been suffering from high fever, anxiety and instability, resulting in a frenetic succession of mass turbulence, upheavals, revolts, massacres, wars, collapse or reversal of moral values, religious uncertainty and fanaticism, disorienting technical and electronic innovations and mass production. Because or in spite of all that, the Earth has grown one and all destinies are henceforth interlocked. The old values have become hollow, the new are still non-existent or unperceived – but the foundations for the One World, the preconditions for the New World, are now in place.

Matter, Substance, Vibrations, Light

'I am trying to do it [the supramentalization of the physical],' the Mother said, 'not out of an arbitrary will, not at all: there is simply "something," or someone, or a consciousness or whatever (I don't want

469

to talk about it) which uses this *(Mother's body)* to try and do something with it. Which means that I do the work and am a witness at the same time, and as for the "I," I don't know where it is: it's not down here, it's not up above, it's not ... I don't know where it is, it's for the requirements of language. There is "something" that works and is a witness of the work at the same time, and is at the same time the action being done: the three things.' [13a]

A strange situation – but 'interesting.' Even in her worst suffering the Mother will find everything interesting. Her body had been depersonalized. During the crisis, or rather the victorious realization in the night of 12-13 April 1962, she had left it and taken it up again; but from then onwards she will say that it is not *her* body any more but *a* body, although it was the most advanced body in existence for the Work to be done. She had taken it up because she or it had decided that this body would remain on Earth for some more years, supposedly to shorten the time span needed for the manifest presence of the supramental being on Earth.

The process of universalization and simultaneously of decentralization was continuing. There was 'a universal progress in the cells,' so much so that they were becoming ubiquitous. 'The physical person is not only this, it is not only this body,' she said. 'I am not sure yet whether the physical person is not the whole Earth – for certain things it is the whole Earth – or whether the physical person is the whole of all bodies with which I am in contact.' [14] She did not feel the reactions in her body as more intimate than the reactions in other bodies. The consciousness of her body was no longer individual, 'I can assure you of this,' but more and more total. 'The body is not isolated. It is more or less a multitude with degrees of proximity.' [15] Her body was becoming the body of humanity. And when a certain Catholic man hundreds of miles away sought her presence and support because he was dying, she received the extreme unction as concretely as if she had been that person – who in fact she was.

The reason was, once again, that everything in this world is vibrations. Sometimes she will not call the body she had taken up a body any longer, but an agglomerate, more specifically an agglomerate of vibrations. Not only is anything that appears to us solid in reality a more or less stable configuration of vibrations, we live unawares in an enormous vortex of billions and trillions of vibrations. 'All the time, all the time one is vibrating in response to vibrations which come from outside ... If you could see that kind of dance, the dance of the vibrations which is there around you all the time ...'[16] This occult material reality discovered by science became a living reality to the Mother.

The composition of a living cell was occultly shown to her in order to illustrate what was going on in her body.[17] She found that the cells 'have a composition and an interior structure which corresponds to the structure of the universe.' In their internal composition the cells receive the vibration 'of the corresponding state in the total composition [of the universe].' The cell, very complex, is luminous in its centre and gradually less luminous towards its surface. In fact, the centre is more than luminous, it is brilliant and irradiates light, and the connection between the cells is 'from light to light.' 'It gave the impression that every cell was a world in miniature corresponding to the all.' This is the biology of the future, now at best vaguely anticipated in the works of David Bohm, Rupert Sheldrake, Ilya Prigogine and others.

Where the Mother's reports of her experiences differed from science was in the fact that, according to her, vibrations were not neutral events which are only quantitatively describable by means of mathematical equations. To her all vibrations possessed qualities, constituting the basis of the qualities we experience in a limited human way.[18] This is the reason why vibrations of light can cause soothing, illuminating, elevating or ecstatic feelings; why vibrations of love can touch our heart; why vibrations of malevolence or hate can disturb our physical balance, even without our knowing that we have been subjected to them; why vibrations of fear or anger can destroy our health; why vibrations of courage or positive thinking can work wonders; why material vibrations can light a star. If matter is as understood by the physicists at present, then vibrations cannot have qualities. But then qualities cannot exist in the universe. Even if one holds that qualities are psychological human projections or superpositions, epiphenomena of reality, there should be an explanation of where the qualities in the human being come from. If there is some truth in the theory of the Great Chain of Being, which materialistic science naturally does not accept, then the non-material gradations – vital, mental, overmental, supramental, *Sachchidananda* – must each have their own kind of nonmaterial vibrations.

For the Mother this resulted in a new perception of Matter, or rather of the substance which to us appears as Matter. 'This way of being is still very undefinable,' the Mother said, 'but in this research there is a constant perception, translated into a vision, of a multicoloured light consisting of all the colours – all the colours not in layers but as though *[gesture of dotting]* it was a grouping of all the colours by dots of all the colours ... Now I see it [the multicoloured light] constantly, associated with everything, and it seems to be what one might call a perception of true Matter. All possible colours are joined together without being mixed *[same gesture of dotting]*, joined together by luminous dots. Everything is as it were made of that. And this seems to be the true mode of being. I am not yet sure, but in any case it is a mode of being much more conscious. And I see it all the while, with my eyes open, with my eyes closed – all the while.

'And one has the strange perception – strange for the body, that is – at once of subtleness, of penetrability, if one may put it like that, of suppleness of shape, and not positively of a cessation but of a considerable diminution of the rigidity of the forms – a cessation of the rigidity, not a cessation of the forms but a suppleness of the forms ... This will probably be what materially must replace the physical ego, by which I mean that the rigidity of the form appears to be yielding to this new way of being ... It is the moment of the passage from one way to the other which is a little difficult. ... All the habits are being undone in this way. And it is like this for all the functions: for the blood circulation, the digestion, the respiration ... for all functions. And at the moment of the passage it is not so that the one [the new way of being] suddenly replaces the other [the old way of being]: there is a state of fluidity between the two which makes it difficult. It is only this great Faith, totally immobile, luminous, constant, immutable – the Faith in the real existence of the supreme Lord, in the *sole* real existence of the Supreme – which enables everything to continue to be the same in appearance.'[19]

The Mother's experiences not only took her into realms which are being discovered by present-day physics, they also rediscovered arcane findings of the ancient Indian wisdom. She said for instance that in that new, multicolored matter 'nothing moves, apparently, in a formidable Movement'; that vibration there 'is so fast that it is imperceptible, that it is as it were coagulated [into forms] and immobile.[20] In the Isha Upanishad we find: 'The Self is one. Unmoving, it moves faster than the mind. The senses lag, but Self runs ahead. Unmoving, it outruns pursuit … Unmoving, it moves; is far away, yet near; within all, outside all.'[21]

Nobody noticed anything of all that while the Mother was sitting there in that simple chair of hers and amiably smiling at the person or people in front of her, while plunging that person or those people into the presence of the Lord. ('I hold myself responsible for anyone I have seen even one second in my life,' she said.) Neither did anybody know that the Mother all the time had to 'dim' her presence to make it bearable to human beings. Sometimes she had to have a look from above, she said, to see whether her body still had a shape, a form. The form was kept up to make the contact with the human beings possible, to make the contact with Matter possible, to distil from gross Matter the New Matter which would be sufficiently refined and plastic to embody the supramental being.

Her physical ego was now practically eliminated, though she was without doubt physically present, there, on the second floor of the north-east wing at 9 Rue de la Marine in Pondicherry. How does it feel not to have or to be a physical ego any more? We cannot even imagine. One is here, there and everywhere immediately when there is a conscious contact, a call, as there were contacts and calls all the time. She was much more busy now than before when she went about in the Ashram, for she was becoming ubiquitous, physically. Many people were climbing up that narrow staircase to the second floor to be received by her, but these were few compared to the ones drawing her attention in an occult way. And there were not only the individuals who drew her attention, but more and more institutions, nations, and the Earth itself – all taken up in the movement of transformation and to that end being worked upon by her – and many entities beyond the Earth.* Her body

---

* 'I was watching one day as someone was talking to her, and she said: "But don't you see that only the part that belongs to this universe is here!"' (M.P. Pandit, *An Homage and a Pledge*, p. 17)

had become 'a finely tuned machine for the reception of vibrations' and it was never alone. 'The being is not isolated, the body is not isolated, it is more or less a multitude with degrees of proximity.' And there was all that which came from outside. 'The problem of the mental and even of the vital contagion* is practically solved, but the problem of the material contagion is still there.' There was 'all that which comes from outside, this perpetual contagion, continuously, continuously, every single minute'[22] day and night.

In the meantime the transformation of that curious body continued organ after organ, function after function, system after system. (The most painful of all 'transfers,' understandably, was the transformation of the nervous system.) Whenever it was the turn of a certain part to be further transformed, it looked as if the Mother was terribly ill in that part. The people around her worried about the endless succession of her illnesses. But time and again she stressed that she was not ill, that it was as if she were ill. She explained that her 'illnesses' were the outward expression of processes of transformation. 'These are not illnesses, these are functional disorders,' she said.

'All the habitual rhythms of the material world are changed. The body had founded its sort of feeling of good health on a certain number of vibrations, and when those vibrations were present, it felt in good health; when something came and disturbed them, it had the impression that it was going to be ill or that it was ill, depending on the intensity. Now, all that is changed. Those basic vibrations have simply been taken away, they don't exist any more. The vibrations on which it founded its opinion of good or bad health: gone. They are replaced by something else, and this something else is of such a nature that "good health" and "illness" don't make sense any longer. Now there is the sense of a harmony established between the cells, that is established more and more between the cells, and that represents the good functioning, whatever it be: there is no longer a question of a stomach, a heart, or whatever. And the smallest trifle which comes and disturbs this harmony is *very* painful.'[23]

---

* This kind of contagion should not be confused with the contagion the Mother spoke about before, which was the automatic reception by humanity and the earth of the transformative vibrations emanating from her.

What the people who talked to her about her illnesses or asked after her health did not realize was that they emitted thoughts of illness – of illness as normally understood, not of a transformational process – because they were thinking in terms of illness. A thought is not an abstraction, it is something concrete in the mental world, embodied in mental substance, and sure to work out the intention with which it has been charged. When such thoughts were directed at the Mother, she sometimes had to react with vigour, simply to protect herself. Question: 'How is Mother doing?' – Her answer: 'Mother is not doing. There is no person here any more to be doing. Mother does what the Divine wants her to do.' And she explained: 'If, for instance, out of curiosity (which is a mental illness of the human being) one starts asking oneself questions – "What may this be? What is its effect? What is going to happen?" (this is what [human beings] call the urge to learn) – if one has the bad luck to be like that, one is *sure* to have something very disagreeable which, according to the doctors – according to the ignoramuses – becomes an illness or a disturbance of the functioning. But if one does not have this unhealthy curiosity and if one, on the contrary, has the will that the harmony not be disturbed, then it suffices, one could say poetically, to apply "a drop of the Lord" on the spot and it becomes all right.'[24] The bridge between our world and the supramental world was still in the making, which means that the Mother's unheard of way of existing in two worlds at the same time, without a link in between, continued. 'Transitional beings are always in unstable equilibrium,'[25] she said. Simple words for an extremely complex and risky way of existing. 'The body itself now truly collaborates as much as it can, with goodwill and an increasing power of endurance. And, really, the turn back to oneself is reduced to a minimum.' By 'the turn back to oneself' *(le retour sur soi)* she meant the focusing, the turning back of the consciousness onto her old way of being. 'It still happens, but like something in passing. It doesn't stay, not even for a few seconds. This – the turn back to oneself – is really an atmosphere that is disgusting, repulsive, catastrophic … There is still the full weight of millennia of bad habits which one may call pessimistic, for they expect nothing but decline, catastrophes, all these kind of things, and it is this which is most difficult to purify, to clarify, to throw out of [her personal] atmosphere. It is so much *inside* that it feels altogether spontaneous. It is this which is the huge, huge obstacle, this kind of feeling of inevitable decline.'[26]

Every time there was a turn back to her old self, which was what a great part of her cells still consisted of, the situation became critical. She was taken by an enormous angst, which may have been the angst in the cells faced with a transformation into something which would no longer be their old, habitual, familiar self. Becoming conscious, the cells too saw the immensity of the gap between their animal-human way of existing and the divine way. 'The difference becomes more and more painful,' said the Mother. As soon as the attention of her body was not focused on the Divine, did not take its support on the Divine, it became very miserable. To forget the Divine one minute became a 'catastrophe.' The old way of being conscious was now comparable to death. 'Without You is death, with You is life,' she prayed. This passage, this transition, this transmutation was the most unstable, bewildering, perilous phase of the transformation. But somebody had to do it, somebody somewhere in the long process of evolution.

Concurrently the transformation of the Subconscient was going on, the in-ter-mi-na-ble subconscious, for it was no longer her personal Subconscient, but that of the Earth. From that Subconscient rose up everything that had to be transformed, for the simple reason that the transformation of the body is not possible without the transformation of Matter, and that transformation of Matter is not possible without transformation of the Subconscient. While logically a simple conclusion, in practice this meant years of suffering and toiling in hell. From there surged up the constant suggestions of an imminent catastrophe, and all that had been rejected before, and all that contradicted and opposed the Divine. 'I think … I don't know, but this seems to be the first time that the instrument [i.e. the Avatar], instead of having been made in order to bring the "Good Tidings," the "Revelation," to light the spark, has been made to try and realize – to do the work, the obscure chore.'[27] What was measured out to her was 'three minutes of splendour for twelve hours of misery,' 'some seconds of paradise for hours of hell,' 'a few marvellous minutes for hours of terror.'

But there was that 'Solicitude which doses' the experiences, however extreme. And there was the yogic seesaw effect we know of, and her reports of progress that were sometimes spectacular. For the Mother was building a new, supramental body within her old, material body, along with it, parallel to it. Time after time she noticed that during her occult nightly occupations she was *très grande et forte*, very tall and strong, which she was not in her material body. She also noticed that she was very young again. And tall, strong and young was how disciples saw her who had an inner contact or experience with her. 'They see me as I am and they say so.'

As early as 1962 she said that the new body was a body of the subtle physical, which in her case means the supramental. It happened that, in her new body, she went down from her room into the Ashram and did certain things, the results of which were materially there when she asked about it. That new body was, besides, not something temporary or ephemeral, but permanent, she said. 'I am not very sure that I don't already exist physically in a true body [i.e. a supramental body]. I say that I am not very sure because the people on the outside have no proof of it.'[28] As usual she remained very cautious, very scientific in her observations, but the frequency and similarity of the reports leave little doubt about the fact that the Mother had made an enormous progress: she was building the prototype of the supramental body on earth. We will learn more about this later on.

Life on the Outside

> *The only hope for the future is a change of man's consciousness and the change is bound to come. But it is left to men to decide if they will collaborate to this change or if it will have to be enforced upon them by the power of crushing circumstances.*[29]
>
> – The Mother

'I am leading a still much more busy life than the one I was leading downstairs,' said the Mother. At first she had not understood why the ordeal in April 1962 had been so severe that she had had to cease all her activities among the disciples 'downstairs.'[30] If it was something of a momentary significance, why did all that have to cease? But now she understood: it was not something momentary, it was a fundamental yogic operation in which the mental and vital sheaths of her adhara had been eliminated and the body alone remained, directly under the influence of the Supreme and, as we will see, of her psychic being.

'But now I understand: cut off, I fainted.' The intermediary layers had been removed, which made the body suddenly feel as if it was 'cut off.' 'That is why the doctor declared that I was ill, I could not move a step without fainting! I wanted to walk from here to over there ... on the way, pffft, I fainted. Someone had to hold me so that the body would not fall down. But as to me, I did not lose consciousness for a single minute. I fainted but I was conscious, I saw my body, I knew that it had fainted. I didn't lose consciousness and the body didn't lose consciousness either. So now I understand: it was cut off from the Vital and the Mental and left to its own resources. It was simply the body. All it knew, all the experiences it had had, all the mastery that was there in all the states of being – in the Vital, the Mental, and above – all that was gone, and this poor body was left to itself! And then, naturally, little by little, all that was being rebuilt [in the body itself], rebuilt in a conscious, purely conscious being.'[31] The Mother could function again. We will sketch briefly some of the happenings which demanded her attention.

In October 1962 the Chinese crossed in many places their disputed border with India. There had been incidents before, especially since the Tibetan revolt in 1959 when India provided shelter to about nine thousand Tibetan refugees. This incident, too, was serious. The Chinese met with practically no resistance from the Indians, who were ill-equipped for high-altitude fighting and who had never imagined that the Chinese would invade their country. In the previous years *Hindi-Chini bhai-bhai* had been an oft shouted slogan, and Jawaharlal Nehru still lived in the Bandung euphoria where the 'third world' countries had looked like one close-knit fraternity. So deeply was he affected by his disillusionment that it undermined his health and was indirectly responsible for his death in May 1964.

The Mother followed the evolution of the situation closely, not only because one of her emanations is *Bharat Mata,* Mother India, but also because her spiritual support was entreated from several sides. Private conversations demonstrate her constant attention to the happenings at the front, where she said she was present 'concretely.' (She also contributed to the War Fund, at a time when her finances were in very dire straits.) Then, in November, against all expectations, the Chinese, who were in a position to overrun a great part of India without too much difficulty, announced a unilateral cease-fire. Nobody has ever understood why. Confidentially the Mother said: 'This cease-fire is evidently the result of what I have done.'[32]

On 21 February 1963, her eighty-fifth birthday, she gave her first darshan from the terrace that had been built for her, together with her now permanent room on the second floor (and the 'music room,' where she received guests and on certain occasions played on the Wurlitzer organ which had replaced her old harmonium). From now on, on every darshan day the streets on the east side of the main Ashram building would be filled with people looking up for something like five minutes at that small, stooped figure pouring out over them and over the world, without any gesture or ceremony, her Force and blessings.

On 21 June 1963 the Catholic Pope Paul VI was elected. He had a difficult task cut out for him in succeeding the beloved John XXIII who had initiated a revolution in the Catholic Church, the aggiornamento. John XXIII, John Kennedy and Nikita Khrushchev, three exceptional characters and leaders, had created one of the high moments of human understanding and goodwill in an exceptionally harrowing century. The Mother had supported them in their contribution to the advent of a New World. 'The rapprochement between Russia and America is something I have been working on for years,'[33] she said. She also said that Kennedy was receptive and that she had been counting on him. She called his assassination, in November of the same year, an occult murder executed by 'the same black forces' which try to gain a hold on every organization or means of power, in order to keep the world subjected to them as it has been throughout human history.

On 11 February 1965 the Sri Aurobindo Ashram was attacked by a Pondicherrian mob incited by certain powers behind the scenes. The apparent reason was the imposition of Hindi by the Central Government on the whole of India. Linguistically India is divided into two parts: the northern part, by far the largest, where all languages are direct derivations of Sanskrit and Hindi is a kind of lingua franca, and the southern part, where the four main languages are Dravidian sister languages. Tamil, the language spoken in Pondicherry as well as in neighbouring Tamil Nadu (formerly the State of Madras), is one of these Dravidian languages. (At present, Tamil is spoken by more people in the world than those who speak French.) As most of the Ashram population consisted of Bengalis and Gujaratis, the anger of the Pondicherrian Dravidians against the imposition by the Indian government – later modified – found a scapegoat in the Sri Aurobindo Ashram.

The main Ashram building, where Sri Aurobindo and the Mother were staying, is, as we know, at 9 Rue de la Marine, less than two hundred meters from the sea. Yet most of the Ashram houses, school buildings, shops, services and facilities are in the main town. They were an easy target for the rowdy elements who attacked them and tried to burn them before the police could or would intervene. The Ashram population, however, at the time probably better trained physically than any other community in India, put up a courageous resistance wherever possible.

On this occasion, the Mother gave the following declaration: 'Some people looking at things superficially, might ask how it is that the Ashram exists in this town for so many years and is not liked by the population.

'The first and immediate answer is that all those in this population who are of a higher standard in culture, intelligence, good will and education not only have welcomed the Ashram but have expressed their sympathy, admiration and good feeling. Sri Aurobindo Ashram has in Pondicherry many sincere and faithful followers and friends.*

'This said, our position is clear.

'We do not fight against any creed, any religion.

'We do not fight against any form of government.

'We do not fight against any social class.

'We do not fight against any nation or civilization.

---

* At the time of writing this book and for the last four or five years, Sri Aurobindo, the Mother and the Sri Aurobindo Ashram have become one of the main centres of devotion and pilgrimage in Pondicherry and Tamil Nadu.

'We are fighting division, unconsciousness, ignorance, inertia and falsehood.

'We are endeavouring to establish upon Earth union, knowledge, consciousness, Truth, and we fight whatever opposes the advent of this new creation of Light, Peace, Truth and Love.'[34]

On 14 August 1965, after numerous skirmishes along the border, the Second Indo-Pakistan War broke out. (The first was fought in 1947, soon after the independence of both countries.) By mid-September the fighting, which cost 3,000 casualties on the Indian side and 3,800 on the side of Pakistan, reached a stalemate, and the Security Council of the U.N. called for a ceasefire. It organized a peace conference in January 1966 at Tashkent, under Russian aegis, between the Indian prime minister, Lal Bahadur Shastri, and the Pakistani president, Muhammad Ayub Khan. Shastri died of a heart attack immediately after an agreement was reached. He was succeeded as prime minister by Nehru's daughter, Indira Gandhi, who was to remain in contact with the Mother through the coming years.

In October 1965 the comet Ikeda-Seki appeared in the sky. As Udar remembers: 'On 29 October 1965 the Mother saw the comet at about 4:30 in the morning, low in the east over the horizon. A few hours before, however, the Mother had met the being of the comet. This being was naturally not human but had a form something like the human. It appeared as a young man – without clothes – with a fair golden-hued skin and reddish hair. The Mother met this being in space but not far from the Earth. He had with him some substance' – 'as it were gelatinous,' the Mother herself would say – and denser than Matter. This substance was to help in the transformation of the Earth, and the being of the comet showed the Mother how to make it circulate in the Earth's atmosphere. 'This substance was brought to be added to the earth's atmosphere to enable it to be prepared for the New Creation. This material gave to the Mother a very fine feeling of ease and harmony and joy – but not the kind of joy felt on Earth.'[35]

Another story out of the ordinary is the following, also told by Udar. Manibhai Patel was one of the 'African' Indian businessmen who had returned home. As a disciple of Sri Aurobindo and the Mother he wanted to contribute to the launching of Auroville by building a food factory.

'There was the question of getting the required machinery, which was coming from abroad. There were two possibilities for the import of these machines, either at the [big] port of Madras or at [the very small port] of Pondicherry. I felt we should bring the goods to Pondicherry both because it would cost much less and because it seemed wrong to off-load at Madras while we had our own port. The Mother supported my view and Manibhai ordered the ship to Pondicherry.

'When the ship arrived – it was a Greek ship – the captain was very disappointed to see the very inadequate crane facilities on the pier. He said it would be impossible to off-load the machinery with them. We had the occasion to have many talks with the captain and spoke a great deal about yoga and spiritual matters. He was inclined to be sceptical and finally said: "If you can off-load all the machines on to that pier, I will believe in all this talk of spiritual Force. Seeing is believing." We left it at that.

'Among the machines there was one piece that weighed about six tons, and the question was really about that piece, as the two cranes were only of a three-ton capacity each. [There were actually three cranes, but one was out of order.] I suggested that we would lift it with the two cranes operating in tandem, but the captain was rather doubtful. He said that tandem work was very difficult and needed highly trained crane operators. Anyway, the work was taken up and Manibhai and I were present throughout. All the machines were unloaded without any hitch, till we came to the last, the six ton piece.

'We decided that we would have a rest and do the work after lunch. While we were away for lunch, those present felt they should continue and try to lift the big machine even in our absence. So a special double boat-lighter brought this machine to the quay side and the two cranes were hitched on to the box. The captain with his officers was in a boat, way off, to watch the impending drama. All this we were told later.

'The cranes slowly lifted up the box till it came to the level of the quay deck, and then something happened and both the cranes tipped over. The crane operators jumped out of the cranes, and the whole box and two cranes were falling into the sea. It would have been a major accident involving the loss of twenty boatmen, the boats, the machines and the two cranes. But, in falling over, the crane jibs swung inwards and the box came over the deck and landed on it as on a cushion. Both the cranes then came upright again. At that time we came back from our lunch and found a great state of consternation and panic, and then relief.

'We looked for the captain. He had gone back at top speed to his ship, raised anchor and departed in a great hurry. He sent a message saying that there was something very strange there. He had never seen anything like it in his life and wanted to get away from it as soon as possible.

'That is the story, but the question I asked [the Mother] was this: Why did this have to happen in our absence? The answer I received is interesting. The whole procedure went on without any hitch because of the unshakeable faith we had in the Mother's Force. But for the last piece, if we had been there and actually seen the cranes tipping over, that faith might have been shaken and then the disaster would have happened.'[36]

Let us conclude this section with an anecdote from those years told by Nirodbaran. 'On the first of February, 1963, the month of her birth, I had a strange experience during my morning meditation. It lasted about an hour. I saw many things apparently incoherent, having no logical connection. But I had a very strong impression that something extraordinary was going to take place.

I wrote about it to the Mother in French and got her reply in French … It runs as follows in English:

'"Last night we (you and myself and some others) were together for quite a long time in the permanent dwelling of Sri Aurobindo which exists in the subtle physical (what Sri Aurobindo used to call the true physical). All that happened there (much too long and complicated to be told) was, so to say, organized in order to express concretely the rapid movement with which the present transformation is going on; and Sri Aurobindo told you with a smile something like this: 'Do you believe now?' It was as if he was evoking these three lines from *Savitri:*

God shall grow up while the wise men talk and sleep;
For man shall not know the coming till its hour
And belief shall be not till the work is done.

'"I think this is a sufficient explanation of the meditation you are speaking of.

'"My blessings."' [37]

Founding the City of Dawn: Auroville

When she founded Auroville, the Mother did not act on a sudden idea or impulse, not even a spiritual one: she allowed to become realized on Earth what already existed in another dimension. 'The conception of Auroville is purely divine and has preceded its execution by many years.' [38] As early as 1966 she said: 'It's certain to work, I *know* that it exists – the city is already there (since many, many years). What is interesting is that I had made a creation with Sri Aurobindo at the centre. Then, when Sri Aurobindo left, I dropped the whole idea, I didn't budge any more. And suddenly it began to come back, as if I were being told: "Now is the time, it has to be done." Good. The Moslems would say: "It is written." It is written, it is sure to exist. How long it will take I don't know, but it seems to be going quickly. The city already exists.' [39] In September of the same year she confirmed: 'Even if you don't believe it, even if all the circumstances seem quite unfavourable, I *know that Auroville will be*. It may take a hundred years, it may take a thousand years, I don't know, but Auroville will be because it is decreed.' [40]

Strong words for another impossibility to be realized, the most material impossibility after the building up of the Ashram, and this time an undertaking on a much larger scale. The Mother was ninety when she inaugurated this Utopia. 'You say that Auroville is a dream. Yes, it is a "dream" of the Lord and generally these "dreams" turn out to be *true* – much more true than the human so-called realities.' [41]

She had already written out the dream and published it in the *Bulletin* of August 1954. It is one of those texts which echo in spaces beyond our human dimensionalities and behind which one feels the Power of realization. It is called … 'A Dream.' The major part of it runs as follows: 'There should be somewhere upon Earth a place that no nation could claim as its sole property, a place where all human beings of good will, sincere in their aspiration, could live freely as citizens of the world, obeying one single authority, that of the supreme Truth; a place of peace, concord, harmony, where all the fighting instincts of man would be used exclusively to conquer the causes of his suffering and misery, to surmount his weakness and ignorance, to triumph over his limitations and incapacities; a place where the needs of the spirit and the care for progress would get precedence over the satisfaction of desires and passions, the seeking for pleasures and material enjoyments.

'In this place, children would be able to grow and develop integrally without losing contact with their soul. Education would be given, not with a view to passing examinations and getting certificates and posts, but for enriching the existing faculties and bringing forth new ones.

'In this place titles and positions would be supplanted by opportunities to serve and organize. The needs of the body will be provided for equally in the case of each and everyone. In the general organization intellectual, moral and spiritual superiority will find expression not in the enhancement of the pleasures and powers of life but in the increase of duties and responsibilities. Artistic beauty in all forms, painting, sculpture, music, literature, will be available equally to all, the opportunity to share in the joys they bring being limited solely by each one's capacities and not by social or financial position.

'For in this ideal place money would be no more the sovereign lord. Individual merit will have a greater importance than the value due to material wealth and social position. Work would not be there as the means of gaining one's livelihood, it would be the means whereby to express oneself, develop one's capacities and possibilities, while doing at the same time service to the whole group, which on its side would provide for each one's subsistence and for the field of his work.

'In brief, it would be a place where the relations among human beings, usually based almost exclusively upon competition and strife, would be replaced by relations of emulation for doing better, for collaboration, relations of real brotherhood.

'The Earth is certainly not ready to realize such an ideal, for mankind does not yet possess the necessary knowledge to understand and accept it, or the indispensable conscious force to execute it. That is why I call it a dream.

'Yet, this dream is on the way to becoming a reality ...'[42]

There had already been several occasions in the Mother's life when she had tried to give shape to the dream in totally different circumstances. The ones we know of are the following.

The first occasion had been before the Second World War. 'I almost had the land. It was in the time of Sir Akbar, from Hyderabad.' Akbar's name may ring a bell with the reader, for he was the dewan (prime minister) of the Nizam who had been instrumental in the funding of Golconde. 'They sent me some photographs of the State of Hyderabad and there, in those photographs, I found my ideal spot: an isolated hill, quite a big hill, and below it a large flowing river ... Everything was arranged. They sent me the plans, the papers and everything, saying that they were giving it to the Ashram. But they laid down one condition ... nothing could leave the State of Hyderabad ... I asked if it was not possible to have [the condition] removed; then Sir Akbar died and that was the end of it.'[43] The world of the Aurobindian movement could have looked very different indeed if Auroville had been located in the State of Hyderabad, now Andhra Pradesh, and not near Pondicherry where it is today.

It seems that when the Mother founded, in 1943, the University Centre, which afterwards would become the International Centre of Education, she had a much different, broader conception of it than what the Ashram School has turned out to be. M.P. Pandit remembers: 'She said in sum: students from different countries, with their different civilizations and traditions, should be given opportunities to stay in independent blocks; students from France, students from Japan, students from America – each in a separate block not demarcated by walls but by the free development of their own pattern of life, so that if any student wanted to know of the Japanese way of life, he could straightaway walk into the Japanese sector, a distinct part of the hostel, mix with the students there, see what kind of food they ate, how they cooked, how they lived. And at that time she said also that each country must have its own pavilion – a pavilion where its own culture at its highest point should be represented in its special characteristic way ... She saw the whole area round the Ashram, with all buildings contained in it, split in twelve different segments together forming the Mother's symbol.'[44] Whatever the accuracy with which M.P. Pandit noted down the Mother's sayings, it is clear that the ideas behind them resemble more closely the features of Auroville than of the Ashram school.

Shortly after the Second World War the idea of the Ideal City seems to have come knocking again. This time it would have been near 'the Lake,' actually a big pond about ten kilometres to the northwest of Pondicherry, where the Ashram had acquired some land. Later the Mother found some notes from that time reminding her to call the two architects of Golconde, Antonin Raymond and František Sammer (who in the meantime had become a Group Captain in the R.A.F.) for planning the 'tremendous programme.' It may have been in reference to this occasion or to another one that she said in 1961: 'What I myself have seen was a plan that came complete in all details, but that doesn't at all conform in spirit and consciousness with what is possible on Earth now, although in its most material manifestation the plan was based on existing terrestrial circumstances. It was the idea of an ideal city, the nucleus of a small ideal country, having only superficial and extremely limited contacts with the old world. One would already have to conceive (it's possible) of a Power sufficient to be at once a protection against aggression or ill will (this would not be the most difficult protection to provide) and a protection (which can just barely be imagined) against infiltration and admixture.'[45]

In fact, the concept of the Ideal City seems to have been part of the Mother's Work throughout her yoga of evolution in many lives, and a necessary condition or means to found or to fix the Life Divine upon the Earth. The reader is familiar with the incredible adventure of the founding and fast execution of the Sun City of Akhetaton, some three and a half millennia ago, by the pharaoh Akhenaton under the impulse of his mother, Queen Tiy, who was an incarnation of the Mother. The Mother is reported to have said that, although the Earth was not ready for the supramental transformation at the time, the creation of a city dedicated to the Sun and called 'Horizon of the Sun' (which means physical presence of the Sun on Earth) had to be undertaken 'to assure the continuity of its existence in the mental plane.'

What mental plane? In occultism, the existence of an 'ether' in which all events are recorded that ever have taken place and are to take place, is well-known. It is the basis of the belief in a Doomsday Book and a Recording Angel. Sri Aurobindo and the Mother recognized the existence of this recording ether, known in the Indian traditions as *akash,* and were acquainted with it through their occult experience. Sri Aurobindo wrote for example in *The Synthesis of Yoga:* 'All things sensible, whether in the material world or any other, create reconstituting vibrations, sensible echoes, reproductions, recurrent images of themselves which that subtler ether receives and retains. It is this which explains many of the phenomena of clairvoyance, clairaudience, etc.; for these phenomena are only the exceptional admission of the waking mentality into a limited sensitiveness to what might be called the image memory of the subtle ether, by which not only the signs of all things past and present, but even those of things future can be seized; for things future are already accomplished to knowledge and vision on higher planes of mind, and their images can be reflected upon mind in the present.'[46]

The existence of this recording ether may explain the idea of the foundation of another Sun City in southern Italy around 1600, the year Giordano Bruno was burned at the stake. The initiator of this Utopian idea was Tommaso Campanella, a defrocked Dominican monk, contemporary of Bruno (also a Dominican) and heavily influenced by him.[*] Like Bruno, Campanella got into serious trouble with the Inquisition, and was severely tortured and incarcerated for many years. He was, however, clever enough to escape execution and even to practise some magic with Pope Urban VIII himself.

The *Città del Sole* (City of the Sun) is the title of Campanella's most famous work; it was probably written in 1602, during his imprisonment. 'The City of the Sun was to be on a hill in the midst of a vast plain,' we read in Frances Yates. 'In the centre, and on the summit of the hill, there was a vast temple, of marvellous construction. It was perfectly round, and its great dome was supported on huge columns.'[47] '[Campanella's]

---

[*] The sources of these facts are Frances A. Yates, *Giordano Bruno and the Hermetic Tradition,* and Gareth Knight, *Magic and the Western Mind.*

ideas of a City of the Sun were a combination of two important concepts,' writes Gareth Knight: '1. the central importance physically and philosophically of the Sun; 2. the fourfold pattern of a city that is a representation of the cosmos ... The City as an archetype of an ideal heavenly and earthly society is fundamental to Dante's *Divine Comedy*, and is also to be found biblically in the Book of Revelation, where the Heavenly City, the New Jerusalem, descends from on high at the end of the world ... The holy city of Jerusalem is then described as being four-square, with the number twelve playing an important part in the design.' Tommaso Campanella 'hoped to establish his city on Earth as herald of a new age ... The fourfold theme was again dominant. Four main roads led to the centre where there was a circular domed temple ... All property would be held in common ...'[48]

The resemblances to Auroville are striking. Auroville is being built on a plateau in the midst of a vast plain. In the centre and on the summit of the hill there is the Matrimandir, the Temple of the Mother, a marvellous construction which is round and supported on four huge columns. Auroville means City of Dawn and is closely connected with the supramental transformation, the Sun being the symbol of the Supramental. The basic plan of Auroville is a spiral nebula, divided into four sectors. The Matrimandir, supported by four pillars, is at the centre of Auroville and is surrounded by twelve gardens. The Mother's symbol itself consists of a central dot (representing the One), surrounded by a first ring with four sections (the four cosmic Powers of the Mother) and by a second ring with twelve sections (the twelve powers of the Mother necessary for the execution of her Work). If, in addition, one considers that Campanella hoped to establish his city on Earth 'as the herald of a new age,' then the resemblance between his City of the Sun and Auroville can hardly be coincidental but must have hidden links. Campanella, like most of the prominent Renaissance men, was a practising magician and may well have had access, knowingly or unknowingly, to the akashic records.

'The physical decision to launch Auroville was taken at the end of 1964 during the World Conference of the Sri Aurobindo Society, an international organization which the Mother had started in 1960 and of which she was the president.'[49] In September 1965 the Mother wrote: 'Auroville wants to be a universal town where men and women of all countries are able to live in peace and progressive harmony, above all creeds, all politics and all nationalities. The purpose of Auroville is human unity.'[50]

From then on things moved quickly, so much so that the inauguration of the City of Dawn* could be planned for 28 February 1968.

The Mother had to write the city's charter for the occasion. Satprem remembered vividly: 'We still see her, half-standing half-sitting on a stool, writing the "Charter of Auroville" on that window sill, equipped with a big piece of parchment and a too thick felt-tipped pen which made her handwriting look like cuneiform characters. "I don't write pompous solemnities," she said turning in our direction (and there was always that witty glimmer in her eyes).'[51] And she wrote in the original French:

Charter of Auroville

1. Auroville belongs to nobody in particular. Auroville belongs to humanity as a whole. But to live in Auroville one must be the willing servitor of the Divine Consciousness.

2. Auroville will be the place of an unending education, of constant progress, and a youth that never ages.

3. Auroville wants to be the bridge between the past and the future. Taking advantage of all discoveries from without and from within, Auroville will boldly spring towards future realizations.

4. Auroville will be a site of spiritual and material researches for a living embodiment of an actual Human Unity.[52]

When she had finished writing the charter, the Mother said descending from the stool: 'There. It is not I who wrote all this. I have noticed

---

* The Mother, presumably wanting to ensure that her and Sri Aurobindo's teaching and its material expressions did not become a religion, has stated that Auroville means 'City of Dawn,' referring to the French word *aurore* which means dawn. It is, however, clear that the name of Sri *Aurobindo* remains associated with it.

something very interesting: when it comes, it is imperative, no arguing possible. I write it down – I am forced to write it down, whatever I may try to do ... It is therefore evident that it does not come from here: it comes from somewhere up there.'[53]

These were the words which resounded from loudspeakers in her voice on that 28 February 1968, in French and English, over a blazing plain of red laterite located on a low lying plateau on the southeast coast of India, a few kilometers north of Pondicherry, in the state of Tamil Nadu. The charter was broadcast directly by *Akashvani*, the Indian national radio. And it was preceded by the Mother's salutation: 'Greetings to all men of goodwill. Are invited to Auroville all those who thirst for progress and aspire to a higher and truer life.'[54]

For the ceremony, five thousand people had been transported in buses to a spot in the middle of nowhere. As a symbol of human unity young representatives from 124 countries and from the States of India dropped a handful of earth from their homelands inside a marble urn, shaped like a lotus bud. 'The inauguration was impressive and UNESCO passed a resolution of support, but when the people went home that day, the wind blew over a desolate plateau with only a banyan tree, a marble lotus, a scattering of palmyras, and a vast expanse of eroded red laterite earth, scarred by canyons that run between villages down to the Bay of Bengal. The actual city area of Auroville was uninhabited and used by the surrounding villages to graze cattle and goats, and gamble with the monsoon rain for a crop of millet or peanuts.'[55]

The Mother seems to have laid down that the maximum number of inhabitants should never exceed fifty thousand, because a city is no longer liveable with a population beyond this number. As master plan she chose the model of a spiral galaxy, one of the designs by the Architect of the Universe himself. She divided the future city into four zones: international, residential, cultural and industrial.

What are the goals of Auroville? From the statements made by the Mother, one may conclude that there is something like a minimum goal and a maximum goal.

The minimum goal is the realization of human unity. As we have seen above: 'The purpose of Auroville is to realize human unity.' The Mother also stated: 'In Auroville simply the goodwill to make a collective experiment for the progress of humanity is sufficient to gain admittance.'[56] On another occasion she wrote: 'From the psychological point of view, the required conditions are: 1. To be convinced of the essential unity of mankind and to have the will to collaborate for the material realization of that unity; 2. To have the will to collaborate in all that furthers future realizations.'[57] This is the reason why she called the city 'the tower of Babel in reverse.' The people came together to build that tower but separated during the construction, now their representatives would be uniting during the construction of the City of Dawn. (Auroville has many echoes in the history of humanity.)

Nonetheless, the minimum goal is not fully attainable without the realization of the maximum goal, which is the working out of the Integral Yoga of Sri Aurobindo and the Mother, in other words, the realization of the new, supramental species on Earth. This is an immensely challenging objective, but there is no doubt that it is at the core of the foundation of the City of Dawn. The Mother considered the future city to be 'a centre of transformation, a small nucleus of men who are transforming themselves and setting an example to the world.'[58] 'We would like to make Auroville the cradle of the superman,'[59] she wrote, and again: 'We shall endeavour to make Auroville the cradle of the superman.'[60] In fact, the sources quoted here are misleading. As we have seen, the Mother was very much aware of the necessity of the realization of the *surhomme*, the intermediary being or overman, before the manifestation of the superman would be possible. Checking the original French source, we find that in both cases she used the word *surhomme*, e.g. *Auroville voudrait être le berceau des surhommes*, which translated literally means: 'Auroville would like to be the cradle of the overmen.'

This makes the objective of the new city not less difficult, for the overman is supposed to have a supramentalized consciousness albeit in an animal-human body. Where would they come from, the candidates for superconsciousness? None of them would be realized yogis; many would not even be trainee-yogis or candidates for the spiritual life. All things considered, it is strange that anybody at all came to stay in that barren place to dedicate his or her life to the ideals of the Auroville Charter. Who among them had an idea of the Integral Yoga, which is the most difficult undertaking imaginable for a human being? As recently as in 1961 the Mother had written: 'Is it possible to find a spot where the embryo or seed of the future supramental world could be created? The plan had come in all its details, but it is a plan which, in its spirit and consciousness, does not conform at all to what is possible on Earth at the moment; and yet, in its most material manifestation, it was based on earthly conditions ... One would have to conceive of a power great enough to be a protection against both aggression or bad will ... and against infiltration, mixture ... The problem is the relation with what is not supramentalized, to prevent infiltration, mixture – that is, to prevent this nucleus from falling back into an inferior creation.'[61]

Now, decades after its foundation, Auroville is still there and continues growing in spite of numerous difficulties. It may therefore be supposed that seven years after the aforementioned quotation the power of protection was strong and secure enough to render the project possible, and that this power has remained active.

As yet Auroville is very little understood, as is the work and life of Sri Aurobindo and the Mother. Its basis is a totally new effort of yoga, while the criteria used by those unfamiliar with the Integral Yoga are without exception based on spirituality and religion as it is supposed to be and has been in the past. In Auroville there are – or there should be – no dogmas, no gurus, no sects, no religious uniforms, no ceremonies. Fundamentally Auroville is based, like the divine Manifestation, on Love and Freedom. This means that the essential Aurovillian effort is one of individual inner development within the social context of a city, founding its general growth on the Charter. Auroville is being built in the soul of its inhabitants; its outer materialization reflects their inner realization.

This means that there should be no religion at Auroville. The Mother insisted on this point on many occasions. One of her statements runs as follows: 'We want the Truth. For most men, it is what they want that they label the truth. The Aurovillians must want the Truth whatever it may be. Auroville is for those who want to live a life essentially divine but who renounce all religions whether they be ancient, modern, new or future. It is only in experience that there can be the knowledge of the Truth. No one ought to speak of the Divine unless he has had experience of the Divine. Get experience of the Divine, only then will you have the right to speak of it. The objective study of the religions will be a part of the historical study of the development of the human consciousness. Religions make up part of the history of mankind and it is in this guise that they will be studied at Auroville – not as beliefs to which one ought or ought not to adhere, but as part of a process in the development of the human consciousness which should lead man towards his superior realization.'[62]

In 1969, shortly after the founding of Auroville, the Mother stated: 'The task of giving a concrete form to Sri Aurobindo's vision was entrusted to the Mother. The creation of a new world, a new humanity, a new society expressing and embodying the new consciousness is the work she has undertaken. By the very nature of things, it is a collective ideal that calls for a collective effort, so that it may be realized in the terms of an integral human perfection. The Ashram founded and built by the Mother was the first step towards the accomplishment of this goal. The project of Auroville is the next step, more exterior, which seeks to widen the base of this attempt to establish harmony between soul and body, spirit and nature, heaven and Earth, in the collective life of mankind.'[63]

One marvels at the power of the impulse in humanity towards the realization of its utopias throughout its history. Auroville may be called 'the Utopia of all Utopias,' its aim being the concrete realization of the Divine on Earth, in a human body, and the great change of 'the vale of tears and darkness' into a materialized Divine Life. The Mother seemed to be quite sure of the success of the fantastic enterprise she was launching: 'The city will be built by what is invisible to you. The men who have to act as instruments will do so despite themselves. They are only puppets in the hands of larger Forces. Nothing depends on human beings – neither the planning nor the execution – nothing! That is why one can smile.'[64]

The Mother, ca. 1969

May 1968

Almost immediately after the foundation of Auroville a kind of shock wave went through the youth of the world, with its main focus in France. On 22 March 1968 the students occupied Nanterre University in the suburbs of Paris. A week later the authorities decided to suspend classes in Nanterre. On 1 May the trade unions organized a march in support of the students and to press for better wages. Two days later students held meetings in the Sorbonne University and the police entered that ancient institution for the first time in history. Two days later the first barricades went up in the Latin Quarter and the provincial universities were occupied by their students. Huge demonstrations followed and the majority of universities and schools in France shut down. On 10 May barricades went up all day in Paris; this was a day of police brutality and hundreds were wounded. Three days later there was a massive general strike: 'France shuts down.' The Sorbonne University was occupied again, and so were the Odeon Theatre and the Renault Auto Works at Cléon on 24 May. Another night of terrible rioting. Ten million people went on strike. On 29 May half a million people demonstrated in Paris. The next day de Gaulle announced the dissolution of parliament in a broadcast to the nation. And the next day the students' movement fizzled out!

Why mention these events in a biography of the Mother? The first reason is that she followed them with a keen interest and commented upon them. She said that it was clearly the future that was awakening, wanting to chase away the past. The police, she said, represented the defence of the past. It was the highest Power which forced the people to do what they had to do. 'This has not at all the character of a strike, it has the character of a revolution.'[65] The second reason is that these events in France and elsewhere on the globe coincided with the foundation of Auroville, and may have been the shock waves of the Force brought down for its accomplishment.

In this view, some slogans painted on the walls of Paris during May 1968 are surely remarkable. 'Be realistic: demand the impossible.' 'To build up a revolution also means to break all the chains within one's person.' 'Forget everything you have learned. Begin to dream.' 'The imagination is coming to power.' 'I have something to say, but I don't know what.' 'The new society must be founded on the absence of all egoism, of all egolatry. Our way will be a long march of fraternity.' 'Novelty is revolutionary; truth also.' 'Every teacher is a student, every student is a teacher.' 'Action should not be reaction, but creation.' 'The emancipation of the human being will be total or it will not be.' And many more slogans in the same vein. In these formulas something resounds which was also there in the life and work of Sri Aurobindo and the Mother.

Some have written that the events of May 1968 were 'an extraordinary initiative, inconceivable some weeks before.'[66] 'The principal representatives of the thought behind 1968 have made history without knowing which history they were making,' write Luc Ferry and Alain Renaut.[67] These authors give no less than eight causes of the May events as formulated by the academic historians: May 1968 was a plot by the highest French authorities; it was a crisis of the university as an institution; it was as it were a bout of public fever, caught especially by the youth; it was a crisis of civilization; it was a class conflict of a new type; it was a social conflict of the traditional type; it was a political crisis; it was a simple concatenation of circumstances ...

The fact is that without any previous indications or forewarnings the youth worldwide suddenly seemed possessed by an impulse towards liberation from all that was old, established, conservative, authoritarian, fossilized, with a thirst to live something that was more true, authentic, pure, fresh, young, joyful and worth living. This 'something new' they could not formulate. They therefore invented the most absurd justifications of their acts side by side with the most sublime, which made the people with coagulated minds sneer at such a grotesque flash in the pan. One should not forget, however, that the 'Prague Spring' was also an aspect of this worldwide movement. The way this first effort towards 'a socialism with a human face,' initiated by Alexander Dubcek in Prague, was rudely suppressed by troops of the Warsaw Pact, is still alive in the memory of many.

In general it may be considered that the events of 1968, though by themselves short-lived and though most of their participants dropped back into a very ordinary life, are still active under the surface of global development. With the hindsight we have, May 1968 may be related to the fall of the Berlin Wall, the collapse of the Communist Bloc and the events in Beijing's Tiananmen Square in 1989 – as 'extraordinary' and as 'inconceivable some weeks before' as May 1968, and with as many or more theses to explain them. When the Mother was asked by a youngster when one would see concrete, visible signs of the action of the Supramental, she answered that there had been such signs throughout most of the twentieth century. The working of the New Force in the world may be the real explanation of 'inconceivable' events like May 1968 and the collapse of the Communist Bloc. 'This is the time of the unexpected,' wrote Sri Aurobindo in the beginning of the century, and the Mother predicted that the Unexpected would increase its activities and sudden changes. 'Things will take a clear turn in the year 2000,' she said somewhere in July 1962. We have entered the new millennium. 'Now we are going to see,' she said.

18.

The New Body

It's always like this, the same answer: a yes, you see. All is well, all is well, all is well – just like it has to be, as soon as one is in it. All is well, just like it has to be. That's how it is, all the time.[1]

– The Mother

Meanwhile the transformation process in the Mother's body, which was representative of the Earth, went on. The connection, the bridge, the link between the supramental world and our material world was being established in her. Her body was no longer a personal body belonging to somebody known and seen as being the Mother; this, she said, was only an appearance kept up to maintain the contact with the people around her and with all who belonged to the Work. It was still there pour toucher la matière, to keep the contact with Matter. For Matter itself had to be transformed in order to render it suitable to serve as part of the adhara of the supramental body. All this, and more, was going on in that apparently very aged body, now ninety and more years old. A summary description of her body's transformation looks very abstract, but the actual process in the Mother was very concrete, experiential, often agonizing, often ecstatic, and generally both simultaneously.

In August 1968 she went again through a devastating crisis – one of the crises we know of, that means. 'There was a moment when things were so acute ... Usually I don't lose patience, but it had reached a point where everything in the being was as it were annulled, everything. Not only could I not speak, but the head was in a state in which it had never been in my whole life: so painful. I didn't see any more, I didn't hear any more. Then one day things were really ... it was pain, suffering everywhere. The body said, it said indeed very spontaneously and very strongly: "It's all the same to me if I am dissolved and I am also quite willing to live, but the state in which I am is impossible, it can't continue. Either to live or to die, but not this." From that moment it began to be a little better. Then, gradually, things got settled, put in their places.

'I took down notes. They are not worth much, but I believe they may be useful ... [The first note is dated 22 August:] "For several hours the landscape was marvellous, of a perfect harmony. Also, for a long time, visions of the interior of huge temples, of living deities. Each thing had a reason, a precise aim, to express states of consciousness not mentalized. Visions constantly. Landscapes. Buildings. Cities. Everything vast and greatly varied, covering the entire visual field and translating states of the body consciousness. Many, many construction sites, huge cities being built ..." Yes, the world that is being built, the future world that is being built. I didn't hear any more, I didn't see any more, I didn't speak any more: I was living in all that, all the while, all the while, all the while, night and day. Then as soon as I was able to note something down, I noted down: "All sorts of construction styles, mostly new, inexpressible. They are not things seen as in a picture, but places where I am present."[2]

Then she said: 'There is another note here about the beginning [of the experience]: "The vital and the mental are sent away so that the physical is truly left to its own resources."[3] She had said almost literally the same in 1962, which shows the continuation and the deepening of the process. The yoga – and this should always be kept in mind – was taking place in the cells of the body, not in the vital, mental or spiritual parts of the being. More and more cells of her body were being spiritualized, even divinized. It was around this time that the Mother stated that the same spiritual experiences and realizations which all the Masters until then had had vitally or mentally, could now be had in the cells themselves, in the Matter of the cells! This staggers the imagination.

'... The Mental and the Vital: gone! I don't know if you are able to realize what this means ... The Mental and the Vital have been the instruments for pounding Matter – to pound and pound and pound in every possible way, the Vital by its sensations, the Mind by its thoughts, pounding and pounding. But they seem to me temporary instruments which will be replaced by other states of consciousness. You understand, this is a phase of the universal development. They will fall away like instruments which are no longer useful.'[4] This went together with the replacement of the organs and other body parts (the physical expression of the human Vital and Mental) by 'functional aggregates' of vibrations directly activated by the Spirit.

However complex, the course of the experience was still much richer, for the Mother had also noted down: 'Night of the 26th to 27th [August 1968]: Powerful and prolonged penetration of the supramental forces into the body, everywhere at the same time.' And she commented: 'Penetration into the body, yes. Penetrations of the [supramental] current I had on many occasions, but that night – which is the night before last – it came all of a sudden, as though there was nothing but a supramental atmosphere. There was nothing but that. And my body was in it. And that [i.e. the supramental atmosphere] was pressing to enter from everywhere, everywhere, everywhere at the same time. From everywhere. You see, it was not a current that was entering, it was an atmosphere that penetrated [the body] from everywhere. It lasted for at least four or five hours ... I never saw anything like it, never! It lasted for hours. For hours. And [all the time] I was perfectly conscious. So, when it came and during the time it was there, I was conscious: "Ah, it is for this, it is for this! It is this that you want of me, O Lord! It is for this, it is this that You want." At that moment I had the feeling that something was about to happen.'[5]

Again the most severe ordeal ('I was in a mess!') went hand in hand with the greatest ecstasy, both experienced in the Matter of the body. Her body was literally steeped into the supramental Force – which is not something abstract, but as concrete as a red hot fire. The first time something similar happened, in 1959, she thought that her body would burst. This shows what an enormous progress she had made in the years since then, always observing that 'the Lord' was dosing the experiences in a way which never transgressed the body's limits of the possible and bearable, for beyond those limits lurked its dissolution.

'I'm sure that the movement [of the earthly transformation] has started,' she said. 'How long will it take to come to a concrete, visible and organized realization? I don't know. Something has started. It seems this must be the onrush of the new species, the new creation, or *a* new creation in any case. A terrestrial reorganization and a new creation. As to me, things have become very acute. It was impossible for me to utter a word, a single word.' Henceforward we will read more and more frequently that she could not or would not talk; the experiences were inexpressible – and who understood anything when she tried with a great effort to formulate them? 'I started coughing, coughing, coughing. Then I saw it was decided that I shouldn't speak. And I remained in that way and let the curve develop. Afterwards I understood. We are not at the end, but – how to say this? – we are on the other side.'[6]

Even during the severest agonies she always kept her consciousness of the complex development, and she never lost her sense of humour nor her interest. This is what really appears superhuman to somebody who reads the available documents with openness and some insight. In fact, it was divine. 'It is only divine Love which can bear the burden I have to bear, that all have to bear who have sacrificed everything else to the one aim of uplifting earth out of its darkness towards the Divine,'[7] Sri Aurobindo, not given to hyperbole, had written. In the Mother's ordeals we find these words abundantly and often poignantly illustrated. Nevertheless: 'It was interesting. I cannot say it was not interesting: it was interesting. But there was no contact with the material life, very little. I could hardly eat, I couldn't walk. In short, it [her body] had become something one had to look after.'[8]

'Happy New Year!'

Then came the upswing again, in a movement which dug ever deeper, ascended ever higher. We simply follow the Mother's reports about the experience, for they show how careful she was not to distort her experiences by casting them prematurely into a mental formulation. It should be recalled that she herself had fully realized 'overmanhood' in 1958, a realization which made now possible the presence of the 'overman consciousness,' *la conscience du surhomme*.

1 January 1969 – 'In the night it came slowly, and on waking up this morning there was as it were a golden dawn, and the atmosphere was

very light. The body felt: "Well, this is truly, truly new." A golden light, imponderous and benevolent. "Benevolent" in the sense of a certainty, a harmonious certainty. It was new. *Voilà*. And when I say *'Bonne année'* to the people, it is this that I pass on to them. And this morning I have passed my time like this, spontaneously, saying: *"Bonne année, bonne année."* [9]

4 January – 'On the first something truly strange happened, and I wasn't the only one to feel it, some others felt it too. It was just after midnight, but I felt it at two o'clock and others felt it at four o'clock in the morning ... What is surprising is that it didn't correspond at all with anything I was expecting – I was expecting nothing – [or] to other things which I had felt. It was something very material, by which I mean that it was very external – *very* external – and it was luminous, with a golden light. It was very strong, very powerful. But even so its character was a smiling benevolence, a peaceful joy and a kind of unfolding into joy and light. And it was like a *'bonne année,'* like a wish.

'It took me by surprise. I felt it at least for three hours. Afterwards, I didn't pay attention to it any more ... It was *very* material. They [two or three other persons] all felt it in the same way: a kind of joy, but a joy gentle, powerful and, oh, very kind, very smiling, *very benevolent*. I don't know what it is. I don't know what it is, but it's a kind of benevolence, therefore it was something very close to the human. And it was so concrete, so concrete! As though it could be tasted, so concrete was it ... It has not gone away. One does not feel it to be something that has come to go away again ...

'My own impression was that of an immense personality – immense! That is to say that for [that personality] the Earth was small, small like this *[gesture as if holding a small ball in the hollow of her hand]*, like a ball. An immense personality, very, very benevolent, who came for *[the Mother seems to lift the imaginary small ball gently from the hollow of her hand]*. It gave the impression of a personal divinity who comes to help. And so strong, so strong, and at the same time so gentle, so all-embracing ...'

'Is it something that will permeate the bodies which are ready?' asked the disciple with whom the Mother had the conversation. She answered: 'Yes, I think so, yes. I have the impression that it is the forma-tion which is going to enter, which is going to express itself – which is going to enter and express itself in the bodies which will be the bodies of the Supramental. Or perhaps – perhaps – the overman *[le surhomme],* I don't know, the intermediary between the two [between man and the supramental being]. Perhaps the overman: it was very human, but human in divine proportions, you see, human without weaknesses and without shadows. It was all light, all light and smiling and sweetness at the same time. Yes, perhaps the overman.'

8 January – 'Yes, that's what it is: it is the descent of the consciousness of the overman. I had the assurance later on. It was the first of January after midnight. I woke up at two in the morning surrounded by a consciousness, so concrete and so *new,* in the sense that I had never felt it before. And it lasted, absolutely concrete, *there,* for two or three hours. And afterwards it spread out and went in search of people who could receive it. And I knew that it was the consciousness of the overman, that's to say, the intermediary between man and the supramental being. That has given to the body [i.e. her body] a kind of assurance, of confidence. This experience has, as it were, stabilized the body, and if it keeps the true attitude, every support is there to help it.'

18 January – 'So, it's very consciously active. It's as it were a projection of power. And it has now become something habitual. There is within it a consciousness – something *very* precious – which gives lessons to the body, teaching it what it should do, that's to say, the attitude it should have, the reaction it should have. I've already told you many times that it's very difficult to find the process of transformation when there is no one to give you any indication. Well, this was as it were the reply. It came to tell the body: "Take this attitude. Do this in this way, do that in that way." And so the body is glad, it is completely reassured, it can no longer make any mistakes. It's very interesting. It came as a mentor, *practical,* quite practical ...

'In one of the old *Entretiens,* I said (when I was speaking there at the Playground): "There is no doubt that the overman will in the first place be a being of power, so that he may be able to defend himself." It's that, it's that experience. It came back as an experience. And it's because it came back as an experience that I remembered having said it.'

Not only do these passages give us an interesting example of the Mother's attitude towards her experiences, they also announce the totally novel and extremely important presence of a Consciousness, now active on Earth, which not a single commentator on Sri Aurobindo and the Mother's Work has taken into account. Every consciousness is in the very real sense a being (the Mother here says a 'personality'). The *Entretien* the Mother refers to dates from December 1957. At that time she was in the final stages of her realization of the overman, a being with a supramental consciousness in a human body; this realization was, as we have seen, accomplished in the course of 1958. The overman consciousness is an aspect of the supramental consciousness, which has been present in the Earth-atmosphere since 1956. What the Mother had realized in 1958, now, on 1 January 1969, became an integral part of the evolution, with the task of realizing the intermediary being, the overman, in humanity – 'it spread out and went in search of people who could receive it' – and with the power to protect this transitional species.

Why does the overman need protection? Because the world is in the grip of powerful and cunning hostile forces, anti-divine forces, that will mercilessly do everything within their power to prevent a change in the dispensation and the incarnation of any kind of higher species on Earth. How vicious they can be is there for all to read in Sri Aurobindo's biographical poems and in *Savitri*. We have also had several instances of their action in the Mother's life, and there are more to come. Anyone who takes up the yoga has to deal with them.

Life on the Outside (continued)

When the Mother's yogic exploits allowed her to function in the world of human beings, she took up the daily burden we have described before and which would be trying for a person half her age and free from the ordeals she had to endure. She had become famous and few still saw her as 'the French Lady.' In the eyes of the public, Indian and international, she was now a spiritual personality of the first rank, and people of all kinds went to see her or wrote to her for advice, for her decision in all kinds of matters, or simply for blessings. She seldom refused anything. Living concretely in the great Unity, she considered every detail of existence and every event, even the apparently least important, to be a direct expression of the divine Will. And had she not accepted 'to do the job'?

The records of the meetings with her, of the results of her help and intervention in the lives of people, and of the miraculous Grace which accompanied everything connected with her, would fill several volumes. Yet everything happened in utmost simplicity, and, as she said, when people went to see her, she received them *en bon camarade*, like a friend. But she seldom spoke to visitors any more because most intellectual questions were a waste of time, and all the rest she saw more clearly than the person in front of her, for by identification she *was* that person. She could do so much more in silence, provided the door of his or her soul stood ajar and allowed, in the privilege of the meeting, her Force to enter.

At set times of the night all the essential problems of the world, past, present and future, were presented to her for her to work upon them and 'to put everything in its place.' Yes, also those of the past, which is possible because they continue to exist in every detail in the *akashic* records. There was a world in the making, and the Avatar had to see to it that the foundations were securely built. This means, too, that she was in permanent contact with everything that went on in the world. We only know about what she has said concerning the re-founding of the spiritual, religious, social, political and economic institutions which have a role to play in the process of the supramental transformation and, perhaps partly, in the New World. We also know about some facts which drew or were brought to her surface attention.

When she heard about the first astronauts on the moon, she considered the enterprise 'a game for grown-up children.' She asked what they were looking for there, as there was nothing left, and spoke the enigmatic words: 'The moon is very concretely a devastation.'[10] But when she was told that the take-off of the astronauts' capsule on the moon for their return to Earth was a risky affair, she at once went there, she said afterwards, to see that everything went smoothly.

Politicians of all ranks and colours approached her for her spiritual help, even candidates for the Indian presidency. 'I am not Indian and I don't want that you push me in front and that then, one day, it's suddenly said that "a foreigner is meddling in our affairs,"' she warned.[11] But V.V. Giri went to see her, shortly after becoming president, as did the vice-president, as did Karan Singh, the former Maharajah of Kashmir, as did the Dalai Lama. And so did Indira Gandhi, who in 1969 split the Congress into its more conservative wing and her more socially oriented forward wing. The relationship with Indira Gandhi was close, and the prime minister sought her advice and spiritual assistance on many occasions, often with B.D. Jatti, then lieutenant-governor of Pondicherry, as intermediary.

The Mother's help was especially sought before and during the 1971 war with Pakistan, which would result in the break-up of that country when its eastern part became independent and was called Bangladesh. She followed the developments day by day: when the West Pakistanis mercilessly tried to subdue their poorer and practically defenceless eastern compatriots; when they were murdering as many Bengali intellectuals as possible; when ten million refugees fled from East Pakistan into India and created an enormous economic and social problem; when America, thus forcing India into the Russian camp, chose the side of Pakistan and sent the aircraft carrier *S.S. Enterprise* into the Bay of Bengal.

Before the hostilities started, Major General K.K. Tewari, at that time the brigadier of the Indian Signal Corps, was advised by one of his lieutenant-colonels to seek the blessings of the Mother to solve the serious problems he was confronted with. He writes: 'I did not accept the suggestion immediately ... But on deeper reflection a brief letter was sent to the Mother seeking Her blessings for my (unspecified) work. Unknown to others, that same lieutenant-colonel had gone around to almost all the top brass of HQ Eastern Command, from the Army Commander down to the other heads of staff and Arms and Services like me, and we had all received the Mother's blessings. And it was amazing how the problems began to get resolved in a strange and inexplicable way. What appeared at first to be hurdles, would clear up somehow.'[12]

507

The reader will remember Sri Aurobindo's prediction that India would become one again. The Mother wrote in 1947: 'The Soul of India is one and indivisible. India is conscious of her mission in the world. She is waiting for the exterior means of manifestation.'[13]

In the meantime, many of the first disciples, some of whom had arrived forty and even fifty years ago, were getting old. ('I'm the only one here who is young,'[14] said the Mother. This may sound ironical, but it was true, considering that according to her youth means the capacity to change and progress. Who was changing and progressing more than she did?) The time came for some of them to lay down their bodies. Purani had already left in 1965. 'His higher intellectual part has gone to Sri Aurobindo and united with him,' said the Mother. 'His psychic is with me, and he is very happy and in peace. His vital is still helping those who seek his help.'[15]

Amrita and Pavitra left in 1969. About the latter's passing we find the following statement by the Mother: 'It was very interesting, the experience I had that night. Nothing like it I ever had in my life. It was in the night before he passed away. The time was nine o'clock. I felt he was withdrawing, withdrawing in an extraordinary manner. He was coming out of himself and gathering and pouring himself into me. He was coming out consciously and deliberately with the full force of the concentrated will. He continued to do so steadily, ceaselessly for hours. It ended about one o'clock, I looked at the time.

'There was no slackness or interruption or stop at any moment. It was throughout the same steady, continuous flow, without a break, without a diminution in strength. Such a concentrated undiminishing stream it was. The process continued until he was wholly within me, as though he was pumping and exhausting all he was in his body till the last drop. I say it was wonderful. I never experienced such a thing. The flow stopped when there was very little left in the body. I let the body remain as long as it was needed for the work to continue, long, quite long after the doctors declared it dead.

'As he was in life, he could not have done the thing, I did not expect it of him. It must have been some past life of his that was at work and did the thing. Not many yogis, not even the greatest among them, could have done such a thing. Now he is within here [within the

Mother], quite wakeful, looking in a rather amused way at what you people are doing. He is merged in me wholly, by which I mean dwelling in me, not dissolved: he has his personality intact. Amrita is different. He is there outside, one of you, one among you people moving about.' One recalls the living and dead mingling. 'At times, of course, when he wants to take rest and repose, he comes and lodges here [in the Mother]. A remarkable story. A great and very difficult thing Pavitra has done.' [16]

What is also worthwhile mentioning is what the Mother has repeated several times since about 1967: that many newborn children were special, exceptional. 'The children who are coming now are interesting,' she said. They were remarkable, had 'something more,' were astonishing, open, many of them conscious beings. We have already quoted Sri Aurobindo's lines from *Savitri*: 'I saw the Omnipotent's flaming pioneers / Over the heavenly verge which turns towards life / Come crowding down the amber stairs of birth.' [17] Udar remembers: 'The Divine Mother said to me that these Omnipotent's flaming pioneers had started coming down. They are souls that have waited for thousands of years for the right time to take rebirth and come down to prepare the world for the Transformation. The Mother asked me to inform everybody about this, so that anyone of her disciples who is expecting a child could consciously aspire for one of these souls to come into the expected child. This had to be done before the third month of pregnancy, as the soul enters the foetus in the third month.* The Mother also asked me to warn the expectant mothers who called down such a child that the child born would not be like other children and would not behave in the way other children behave, and so they may have trouble with them. They would have to be patient, understand that the child has a great soul, and give it every opportunity to develop.' [18]

---

* This must be specific for these souls, for at other times the Mother has said that the time of entrance of the soul into the foetus varies from person to person, that the soul may enter the child even after it is born, or (in rare cases) never.

The Mother at work with her secretaries (Nolini and Amrita), ca. 1967

The Presence and Role of the Psychic Being

Human beings have much more in them than a soul, a 'divine spark.' They have in them an evolved 'psychic being,' built and shaped by the essence of experiences in their previous lives (which is the essential meaning of reincarnation). This psychic being will ultimately result in the creation of the divine being, in each case different, which they were as part of the one Divine before they plunged into the adventure of evolution, but now with a degree of conscious differentiation making the evolutionary adventure worthwhile. The Avatar too goes through a series of reincarnations of the divine Emanation that formed him/her and which constitutes his/her psychic being. The difference is that, while the psychic being in humans has accepted its awareness of its divine Origin to be totally veiled or 'forgotten,' the psychic being of the

510

Avatar always remains or becomes fully aware of its Origin and Essence, although a partial veiling is accepted in lives in which the Avatar acts as a Vibhuti, and although a process (yoga) of rediscovery is required in the avataric life.

We have not heard of the Mother's psychic being since 1950, at the time of Sri Aurobindo's passing away, when by a yogic master act she 'locked it away' in order to prevent it from following Sri Aurobindo and leaving the body. The door of her psychic being was opened again in 1959, 'very prudently,' when the supramental Force for the first time penetrated fully into her body and put her physically into connection with the 'dwelling' of Sri Aurobindo. Since then, again, there was no reference to her psychic being – until 1968, after the ordeal we have referred to in the first section of this chapter. Having emerged from the ordeal, she suddenly stated: 'The vital and the mental have left, but the psychic being has not left at all. It is the intermediaries that have left. For example, the contact with people – the contact with people who are present and even with those who are not here – the relation with them has remained the same, absolutely the same. It is even more constant.'[19] We find a confirmation of this in a conversation of 11 September 1968, when in the presence of an American disciple, Rijuta, whose psychic being seems to have been fully developed, the Mother again observed that her own psychic being had remained very much present.

How had she not been practically aware of a fact like this before? She herself gives the reason: she *was* that psychic being, all the time she acted and perceived out of her psychic being. When looking through a window pane, one is not aware of the windowpane, except when the presence of dust or whatever on it hinders the view. The Mother's psychic being, as she herself said, was 'totally transparent.' 'The psychic consciousness was wholly in front and governed my life.'[20] This made her aware of the fact that most of her I's had actually been her psychic identity speaking. The vital and mental egos had been dissolved long ago. By now the physical ego too was completely dissolved, a yogic accomplishment unimaginable to common mortals. The psychic being, although having an identity, has no ego, for it is wholly divine. And the Mother's psychic being was that of the Great Mother, 'like a Sun.' This, and her increasing supramentalization, made it necessary that she cover her true Self with 'a veil, and another veil, and another veil,' otherwise her presence would have been 'unbearable' for humans.

On 1 July 1970, the same Rijuta, who acted as a secretary handling the correspondence with the disciples and devotees in America, was again in the Mother's presence and the cause of a sudden revelation important enough to be quoted *in extenso*. 'I had an experience which was for me interesting, because it was for the first time. It was yesterday or the day before, I do not remember. Rijuta was here, there just in front of me, and I saw her psychic being, dominating her by so much *(gesture indicating about twenty centimeters),* taller. It was the very first time. Her physical being was small and her psychic being was that much bigger. And it was an unsexed being, neither man nor woman. Then I said to myself (possibly it's always so, I do not know, but here I noticed it very clearly) I said to myself: "But it's the psychic being, it's *that* which will materialize itself and become the supramental being!"

'I saw it, it was so. There were particularities but these were not well marked, and it was clearly a being that was neither man nor woman, having the combined characteristics of both. And it was bigger than the person and it overtopped her in every way by about this much *(gesture surpassing the physical body by about twenty centimetres)*; she was there and it was like this *(same gesture)*. And it had this colour ... which, if it became quite material, would be the colour of Auroville [i.e. orange]. It was fainter, as though behind a veil, it was not absolutely precise, but it was that colour. There was hair on the head, but ... it was something different. I shall see better another time perhaps. But it interested me very much, because it was as though that being was telling me: "But you are busy looking to see what kind of being the supramental will be – here it is! It is this!" And it was there: it was the psychic being of the person.

'So one understands. One understands: the psychic being materializes itself ...* and this gives continuity to the evolution. This creation gives altogether the feeling that there is nothing arbitrary, there is a kind of divine logic behind and it is not like our human logic, it is very superior to ours. But there is one [a logic], and it was fully satisfied when I saw this. It is really interesting. I was very interested. It was there, calm

---

* This is of course possible only for fully developed psychic beings.

and quiet, and it said to me. "You were trying to find out? Well, here it is." Yes, it is that!

'And then I understood why the mind and the vital were sent out of this body, leaving the psychic being alone. Naturally, it was that which had always been governing all the movements, so it was nothing new. But there are no difficulties anymore; all the complications that were coming from the vital and the mental, adding their impressions and tendencies, all gone. And I understood: "Ah! it is that, it is this psychic being which has to become the supramental being."

'But I had never sought to know what its appearance was like. And when I saw Rijuta, I understood. And I see it, I'm seeing it still, I've kept the memory. It was as if the hair on the head was red (but it was not like that). And its expression! An expression so fine, and sweetly ironical ... oh! extraordinary! Extraordinary! And you understand, I had my eyes open, it was almost a material vision.

'So one understands. All of a sudden all the questions have vanished, it has become very clear, very simple. *(Silence)* And it is precisely the psychic that survives. So, if it materializes itself, it means the abolition of death. But abolition ... nothing is abolished except what is not in accordance with the Truth. That which goes away is ... whatever is not capable of transforming itself in the image of the psychic and becoming an integral part of the psychic. It's really interesting.' [21]

On the one hand there is the mature psychic being, shaped and perfected through its innumerable rebirths in the earthly evolution; on the other hand there is, or will be, the transformed material earthly substance, sufficiently refined to give an enduring, immortal shape to the mature soul. When the possibility of an adhara for the supramental being will exist, made possible by the presence of the Supramental in the atmosphere of the Earth and speeded up by the Mother's yoga from 1956 to 1973, the mature souls, who are now ready and waiting, will incarnate as supramental beings. Their coming will be prepared by the intermediary beings, the overmen and overwomen, some of whom are now already present on Earth. A new phase of the earthly evolution, which began in 1956 with the manifestation of the Supramental, will become a tangible fact. The sufferings and indignities humanity had to undergo through the ages will be justified.

Matrimandir

Little by little the residents of Auroville arrived, still mainly from the West. These pioneers chose a tough task, trying to build the dream of the ideal City of the Future in a place which was little more than goat country, in the climatic extremes of a hot and clammy subtropical summer and lashing monsoon rains or calamitous monsoon failures, harassed by a plethora of snakes, scorpions and insects the subtropics had in store for them. The first Aurovillians were a bizarre mixture of idealists, temporarily interested visitors and adventurous or curious hippies. Few, if any, had real knowledge of or insight into Sri Aurobindo and the Mother's yogic efforts and realizations, or spiritual experience, or an idea of the scope of the work they were undertaking. No wonder that many, after some courageous idealistic gesturing, suddenly vanished never to be seen again. But they were soon replaced by others, and here and there within the chosen periphery of the future city communities were formed – Aspiration, Promesse, Fraternity, Utility, Forecomers – where many of their members worked courageously and with sincere dedication.

The problems were legion, and all of them were submitted to the Mother, often by the Aurovillians themselves, whom she was always ready to receive. In a life lived together, in the communal life, everything comes out into the open. The many kinds of communities in history – religious, military, Utopian – bear witness to this. The Mother was compelled, reluctantly, to prescribe some guidelines, always warning that generalizations should not fix or kill the inner spontaneity, and that what surfaced without could only be the expression of what was within.

She asserted once again that the City of Dawn was there in the 'subtle physical,' fully ready to be worked out on the material plane. 'The night before last I spent more than three hours with Sri Aurobindo,' she said on 31 May 1969, 'and I was showing him all that was going to come down for Auroville. It was rather interesting. There were games, there was art, there was even cooking! But all that was very symbolic. And I was explaining to him as though on a table, in front of a vast landscape. I explained to him on which principle the physical exercises and games

514

were going to be organized. It was very clear, very precise. I was even giving a sort of demonstration, and it was as if I was showing on a very small scale a miniature representation of what was going to be done. I was moving people and things *[gesture, as if on a chess-board]*. But it was very interesting, and he was very much interested. He was as it were laying down the broad laws of organization ... I don't know how to explain this. There was art and it was beautiful, it was all right. And how to make the houses comfortable and beautiful, upon what principle of construction. And then even the cooking. It was very amusing, each one brought forward his invention. This went on for more than three hours. Three hours of the night is much. It's a lot. Very interesting.'

When the person to whom she said this objected that the conditions on Earth did not seem propitious, she replied: 'No, it was right there, it didn't seem foreign to the Earth. It was a harmony, a conscious harmony behind things: a conscious harmony behind the physical exercises and the games; a conscious harmony behind the decoration, the art; a conscious harmony behind the food, etc. ... I saw X today and I told him that the whole organization of the arts and sports, even of food and of all other things, was ready in the subtle physical, ready to come down and embody itself. And I told him: "What is needed is just a handful of earth *[gesture of cupping her hands]*, a handful of earth to make the plant grow. One must find a handful of earth to make it grow."' [22]

On 21 February 1971 the foundation stone of the Matrimandir was laid. For this occasion the Mother gave the following message: 'Let the Matrimandir be the living symbol of Auroville's aspiration for the Divine.' Matrimandir means 'temple of the Mother,' but in this case the word temple should not be understood in a religious sense. The Matrimandir, in the centre of Auroville, will be a golden globe, with a diameter of about thirty metres, which arises from the Earth. The symbolism is simple: the golden, supramental world is breaking out of Matter as we know it, out of the Earth as it is now; the New World is being born.

If the Matrimandir was only this, the monumental construction would be destined from its very inception to become little more than a tourist attraction, and the Mother was not exactly keen on promoting that kind of attractions. She said more than once that Auroville would have an occult influence in the world, contributing to the world's unification and transformation. This may be the reason why she gave the colour orange to its symbol, orange being an occult colour and well-known as the colour of the dress of the Indian sadhus (and as the colour of everything on the supramental ship, and of the hair of the mature psychic being in Rijuta). Therefore, although the shape of the Matrimandir is symbolic, the reason for its construction is profoundly spiritual: it's a kind of dynamo for channelling and directing the Force of the Great Mother to support the development of Auroville and the transformation of the world.

'The Matrimandir wants to be the symbol of the Universal Mother according to Sri Aurobindo's teachings,'[23] the Mother wrote. 'It will be the "Pavilion of the Mother" – but not this *[the Mother points to herself]*: the Mother, the true Mother, the principle of the Mother. I say "Mother" because Sri Aurobindo used that word, otherwise I would have put something else. I would have put "creative principle," or "principle of realization," or … I don't know.'[24] She also gave the following definitions: 'The Matrimandir will be the soul of Auroville,' and: 'The Matrimandir wants to be the symbol of the Divine's answer to man's aspiration for perfection.'[25]

The four enormous pillars designed to support the golden ball were the first constructions to be built in a huge crater, dug out diligently handful after handful in the red earth. The Mother called the pillars after the four Powers of the Great Mother: Maheshwari, Mahakali, Mahalakshmi and Mahasaraswati. We have briefly commented upon them at the moment when Mirra Alfassa realized her identification with the Universal Mother. Here it may be suitable to evoke her four, ever active Powers again, in Sri Aurobindo's powerful words from *The Synthesis of Yoga*.

'There is nothing that is impossible to her who is the conscious Power and universal Goddess all-creative from eternity and armed with the Spirit's omnipotence. All knowledge, all strengths, all triumph and victory, all skill and works are in her hands and they are full of the treasures of the Spirit and of all perfections and siddhis. She is Maheshwari, goddess of the supreme knowledge, and brings to us her vision for all kinds and widenesses of truth, her rectitude of the spiritual will, the calm and passion of her supramental largeness, her felicity of illumination; she is Mahakali, goddess of the supreme strength, and with her are all mights and spiritual force and severest austerity of Tapas and swiftness to the battle and the victory and the laughter that makes light of defeat and death and the powers of the ignorance; she is Mahalakshmi, the goddess of the supreme love and delight, and her gifts are the spirit's grace and the charm and beauty of the Ananda and protection and every divine and human blessing; she is Mahasaraswati, the goddess of divine skill and of the works of the Spirit, and hers is the yoga that is skill in works and the utilities of divine knowledge and the self-application of the spirit to life and the happiness of its harmonies.'[26] Such are the Powers which will render the emergence of the New World possible.

Since then the construction of the golden Matrimandir has continued through thick and thin and is now completed. The 'inner chamber,' the Matrimandir's main feature, has a diameter of about twenty metres; twelve round pillars apparently support the ceiling, but do not touch it – all this in accordance with the Mother's vision and directives. The chamber is completely white and its marble floor is covered with a white carpet. In the middle of the chamber a crystal ball with a diametre of seventy centimetres, made especially for the Matrimandir by the Carl Zeiss Werke in Oberkochen (Germany), rests on a pedestal consisting of four gold symbols of Sri Aurobindo, which in turn is placed in the centre of the white marble symbol of the Mother. Night and day a ray of light falls through a central opening in the ceiling of the chamber on the crystal and touches the earth underneath through an opening in the floor. During the day the ray consists of sunlight deflected by a mechanism that follows the movement of the sun; at night, the ray is produced by lights operated by solar energy. There is nothing else in the silent chamber.

Darkest Night

> *Often it seemed to her the ages' pain*
> *Had pressed their quintessence into her single woe,*
> *Concentrating in her a tortured world.*[27]

– Sri Aurobindo

The alternating movement went on, higher, deeper. Although these alternations are quite clearly discernible in what the Mother has told us about her yoga, it should be kept in mind that they give, after all, only a schematic picture of the very complex reality the Mother was experiencing every moment. 'There isn't a fraction of a second that things don't move! It's a continuous, total transformation, a development without cease.'[28] The more this development advanced, the more she was able to bear and the more heavenly or hellish her experiences became, bodily. It was as if her body had become a battlefield, she said, between the forces of the Old and the New World, between that which stubbornly wanted to remain as it was and that which wanted to replace it.

The process of the 'transfer of power' in all parts of her body continued. We remember that this transfer meant the change of an organ or body part from its old, normal way of functioning to a way of functioning directly determined by the divine or supramental consciousness. The Mother was far advanced on the way, much farther than we are able to imagine.

What was most visibly perceptible was the 'transfer' in the external functions, for example eating. As her system was unwilling to function in the old manner, how could she manage to eat? she asked. She was never hungry but all the same consented to eat something to keep the body going. Yet her ability to eat depended on the consciousness active at the time of eating. If she paid attention to the taking in of food by means of the old digestive system, she choked and could not swallow anything; if she switched to the Unity-Consciousness, she could eat and drink without even being aware that she was doing it. Sometimes the prompting of her assistants to eat or drink a little more could be heard in the courtyard below. They thought that she was ill, or whimsical, but attuning her consciousness to eat a bite or drink a sip was as important as it was to go through the most intense spiritual experience.

The most painful transfer was that of the nervous system. She often suffered cruelly from the mere presence of certain people who approached her. Her body had become 'very, very sensitive' to all vibrations, and many in her presence projected upon her their human, all too human, state of being without being aware of it. Once she asked Satprem, who regularly went to see her in a state of dissatisfaction or revolt, not to be in a bad mood because it made her ill. And the nerves were still more sensitive at the times it was their turn to change into the new way of functioning, directly under the divine influence. The suffering on such days she compared to the general inflammation of the nerves which had befallen her after she had had to leave Sri Aurobindo in 1915, only this time it was 'extremely acute.' Again, it was 'not a joke, but interesting.'

The most dangerous transfer, however, was that of the heart. For years the Mother walked a tightrope between life and death, and the fact that her body remained alive she owed only to the guidance and protection of 'the Master of the Yoga.' This, fundamentally, was her Self, the same Self that was causing the ordeals and guiding them in the way that would most profit the intensely accelerated evolution the Mother-in-the-sadhana was undergoing. Nirodbaran wrote about a serious crisis in 1970: 'The Mother had been suffering from cough and other ailments. The symptoms took a bad turn when Vasudha [the Mother's personal assistant] left for Bombay before the August Darshan. The heart was irregular; some beats were missing, a usual feature with her whenever she fell ill. There were other complications. She had been uttering piercing cries of agony during the day and also at night. She had done that before too, but this time it seemed to be more acute and far more distressing. We thought it would pass off as had happened in the past. Her condition did improve, but after the Darshan a reaction set in perhaps due to exhaustion. The situation took a serious turn. The heart was found to be the main seat of trouble and the lungs were involved as well. All of us became very anxious.'[29]

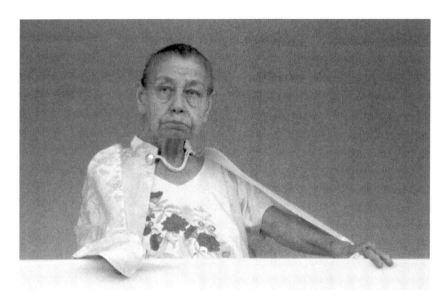

The Mother giving darshan, ca. 1971

Sometimes those piercing cries could also be heard in the courtyard below. They were caused by an 'angst' (in this case maybe the best translation of *angoisse*) such as she had never known before in her life, she said. This angst was not something psychological. The Mother has always been undaunted. 'Fear has no place in this yoga,' Sri Aurobindo had said, and she herself had repeated this on every possible occasion. But we should never lose sight of the fact that the yoga was now taking place in the body.

The terrible angst that made her cry out was something in the constitution of the cells of the body, she said, an elemental fear of death, which 'was actually the fear of the disappearance of the cells' millennia-old way of being. In the Mother a dying world was crying out in agony, sometimes to the bewilderment of herself and always of the people who could hear her. What made the suffering still worse for her was the realization that Sri Aurobindo, in his yoga, must have gone through similar painful ordeals, sitting there in his chair and concealing his martyrdom from everybody, from her in particular.

Then came the period of darkest night. For the first time the brain was affected so that she could not control some of her movements. Again she said that she was the object of black magic. The hostile forces easily find an instrument for their intentions in the small, egoistic, very ignorant and often very nasty human beings. 'One of my legs has been dead for a long time – it's just beginning to revive – paralyzed. One leg [the left one]. So, naturally, everything was difficult. But what is re-markable – I can tell you this immediately – was that the consciousness established here *[gesture above the head]* became more and more strong and more and more clear, *throughout*. I worked, I continued to work, not only for India but for the world, and in constant relation, "consulted," (you understand?), actively ... But it will take months, I think, before I'll be able to see clearly [what happened during the ordeal]. In any case, the general consciousness *[same gesture above the head]*, what one might call the universal consciousness (in any case terrestrial) didn't leave me one minute. Not one minute. It remained here all the while.

'It wasn't an innocent paralysis! For at least three weeks – at least – for three weeks [late December 1970 and early January 1971] a constant pain, night and day, twenty-four hours out of twenty-four, without ever diminishing, never. It was as if I was torn apart. So it was out of the question to see anybody. Now it's over. The pain is quite bearable and the body has resumed more or less its normal life ...

'I noticed how things – the so-called catastrophes, or calamities, or misfortunes, or difficulties – how all that comes *just at the right time* to help you, just as it's needed to help you. Indeed, all that which in the physical nature still belonged to the old world, to its habits, its ways of doing and being, its ways of acting, all that couldn't be handled, it couldn't be manipulated in any other way than through illness.

'I can't say that it wasn't interesting.

'But as to me, I kept the contact with everyone, even physically. I don't know if they remained conscious of it or not, but I kept the contact with everybody. Such things depend on the receptivity of the people. I didn't feel at all that there was an interruption of the relations or anything of the kind, not at all, not at all. Even at the time when, externally, I was suffering so much and people thought I was completely given over to my suffering, it didn't keep me occupied. I don't know how to explain this. I knew quite well that the condition of this poor body wasn't very bright, but this didn't keep me occupied. There was all the time the feeling of that Truth which has to be understood and manifested …

'There was a whole period when I was absolutely inaccessible because I was suffering continuously. One is worthless then. Continuously, continuously. One might say that I was but one cry all the while. This lasted a long time, several weeks. I didn't keep count. Then little by little it alternated with moments of tranquillity when I didn't feel the leg any more. And it's only in the last two or three days that it looks as if everything is put back in order. It was the whole problem of the world – a world which is nothing but pain and suffering, and a big question mark: why? 'I tried all the palliatives one uses: to change the pain into pleasure, to eliminate the capacity of feeling, to turn one's attention to something else. I tried all the tricks, but not a single one worked. There is something in this physical world as it is which is not – how to explain this? – which is not yet open to the divine Vibration. And it is this something which is doing all the harm. The divine Consciousness is not perceived, and therefore lots of imaginary things – but very real to the senses! – exist, and That, the only true Thing, is not perceived. But it's better now. It's better.

'It's really interesting. I believe something will have been done from the general point of view. It was not merely the difficulty of one body or one person. I believe something has been done to prepare Matter to receive as it must, in the right way. It was as if it received in the wrong way and learned to receive in the right way.'[30]

The following are extracts from a conversation with some disciples. It is a message that is as valid today as when it was spoken in 1972. 'For centuries and centuries humanity has waited for this time. It's come. But it's difficult. I don't simply tell you we are here upon Earth to rest and enjoy ourselves, now is not the time for that. We are here to prepare the way for the new creation.

'The body has some difficulty, so I can't be active, alas. It's not because I am old. I am not old. I am not old, I am younger that most of you. If I'm here inactive, it's because the body has given itself definitely to prepare the transformation. But the consciousness is clear and we are here to work; rest and enjoyment will come afterwards. Let's do our work here. So I've called you to tell you that. Take what you can, do what you can, my help will be with you. All sincere effort will be helped to the maximum.*

'It's the hour to be heroic.

'Heroism is not what it is said to be: it is to become wholly unified.†
And the Divine help will always be with those who have resolved to be heroic in full sincerity. *Voilà*.

'You're here at this moment, that's to say upon Earth, because you have chosen to be so in the past [i.e. in a previous life] – you don't remember it any more, but I do. That's why you are here. Well, you must rise to the height of your task. You must make an effort, you must conquer all weaknesses and all limitations. Above all you must tell your ego: "Your time is past." We want a race without ego, that has the divine Consciousness instead of the ego. It is *that* that we want. The divine Consciousness which will allow the race to develop itself and the supramental being to be born.

'If you think I am here because I am compelled to, you are mistaken. I am *not* compelled. I am here because my body has been given for the first attempt at transformation. Sri Aurobindo told me to do it – well, I'm doing it. I don't wish anyone to do it for me, because … because it's not very pleasant. But I do it willingly because of the results. Everybody will be able to benefit from it. I ask only one thing: don't listen to the ego.

'If there is in your hearts a sincere "yes," you will satisfy me completely. I don't need words, I need the sincere adhesion of your hearts. That's all.'[31]

---

* Up to here, the Mother spoke in English. Then she switched to French.
† The Mother means that all parts of the personality should be unified around the psychic and under its direct influence.

The New Body

The Mother's progress which we are trying to sketch here was complex, as complex as Life, of which most humans have only a very narrow and superficial notion. The Subconscient and the Inconscient were for her a conscious reality where she fought most of her battles, while for us it is a hidden reality by which we are blindly driven. Simultaneously, there were concretely present to her all the upper levels of existence, the realms of Light, and Beauty, and Joy, and Love. It is true that she gave the proportion between both kinds of experience as 'three minutes of splendour for twelve hours of misery,' or ' some seconds of paradise for hours of hell,' but even behind the most terrible suffering there was an inner ecstasy which allowed her to say that the ordeal did not keep her occupied.

What was she trying to realize in those last years of her earthly existence? It was the induction of the supramental substance or Matter into the earthly gross matter, in other words the fusing of both worlds. She said that this took place by a process that she called 'permeation.' She reported that the transformation of the consciousness of the body cells from the ordinary consciousness, burdened by the fear and horrors of the past millennia, into a divine Consciousness had taken place in a great number of her cells. 'The physical is capable of receiving the higher Light, the Truth, the true Consciousness, and to manifest it.'[32] When stating this, however, she asked herself how far her body would be able to express this change, to what extent her body could be transformed.

As early as January 1961 the Mother had mentioned the presence in her physical body of another body that was 'bigger, more voluminous' – we are reminded of Rijuta's psychic being which exceeded the boundaries of her physical body – and that had 'such a compact power that it was almost annoying.' A year later, after her 'death' and 'resurrection' in 1962, she noticed that during the night she was 'generally tall and strong.' Around that time, it became a common experience for those who saw the Mother in their dreams or visions to see her as much taller than she was physically. When told about this, she commented that it was 'the new being,' and she specified that it was a being not from the

Vital but from the subtle physical. As we know, what she called the subtle physical in those years was not a more refined substance than the physical, it was the Supramental. For of that subtle physical she said 'It is not material and yet more concrete than Matter.'

Towards the end of 1962, she noticed one night that she was very young, physically. 'It was the subtle physical, of course, but I was very young.' It was shortly afterwards that she remarked, as we have mentioned before, that she was moving about in the Ashram while lying in her bed, and that the changes which she then brought about in the material world did effectively take place. In August 1963 she said that she was not very sure that she did not already physically exist in a 'true body.' She said she was not very sure 'because the outward senses have no proof of it,' but 'for a moment I see myself, feel myself, objectivize myself as I am.' In November 1964, while lying down after lunch, she saw herself standing beside her bed, very tall, in a magnificent robe. In April 1969, she said that during the night her body was 'tall and active, it does things.' 'It is a body that is *physical* in the subtle physical and it is already something permanent, in the sense that one *remains* like that.'[33]

In 1970, the Mother's body was bent at the neck and shoulders; yet, at the end of February of that year she said that during the night she found herself in a completely normal body. 'Is this body replaced by another one?' Then on 9 May 1970, the Mother had an experience in which she saw her new body. 'Well, I have seen it, my body – how it will be. It's quite good.' The form was not that different from the present human form, but 'so refined.' It was sexless, 'neither man nor woman,' and its colour was 'somewhat like the colour of Auroville.' Once more we are reminded of Rijuta's psychic being. There is no doubt that all these experiences are convergent and indicative of one of the most wondrous realities imaginable. The Mother by her yoga of the transformation of the cells had built in, or out of, her physical body a supramental body in which she existed while still in her physical body. She was existing in two 'physical' bodies at the same time, the one in the gross physical and the other in the subtle physical, which in her terminology meant the Supramental.

The confirmation came on 24 March 1972: 'For the first time, early in the morning, I saw myself, my body. I don't know whether it is a supramental body or – how to say this? – a body in transition, but I had a body altogether new, in the sense that it was sexless, it wasn't a woman nor was it a man. It was very white, but this is because my skin is white, I suppose, I don't know. It was very slim – it was pretty. Truly a harmonious form. So, this was the first time. I didn't know anything at all, I had no idea of what it would be like or whatever. And I saw that I *was* like that, I had become like that.'[34]

The next day the Mother explained how she had seen herself, looking down on her own body and seeing it from the chest downwards. 'I wasn't looking in a mirror.' She again stressed the sexlessness of the body and the slender beauty of the form. 'You see, I didn't pay any special attention for I *was* like that, everything was quite natural. It was the first time, and it was in the night, the day before yesterday.' When asked whether it was in the subtle physical, she answered: 'It must be like that in the subtle physical. Also, it was clear that there would not be any longer a complicated digestion as it is now nor the elimination as it is now. It was not like that ... I didn't look to see how it was, because everything was quite natural, so I can't give a detailed description. Simply, it was neither the body of a woman nor the body of a man, that is for sure. And the outline, the silhouette, was more or less the same as that of a very, very young person. There was as it were a semblance of the human forms [*Mother draws a sketch of it in the air*], there was a shoulder and a waist – as though the semblance of a form. I see it, but ... I saw it as one sees oneself. And there was a kind of veil that I had put on to cover myself. It was a way of being which was not surprising to me, it was a natural way of being ... Evidently, what will change very much, what had become very important was the respiratory system. It was upon this that that being greatly depended.'[35]

Thus she reported her incredible accomplishment in the simplest of words. She had built the prototype of the supramental body and was living in it in the most natural way. This prototype, being supramental, is immortal and therefore still exists. The Mother is still present in the Earth-atmosphere in her supramental body, continuing her Work, awakening, inspiring and guiding the transitional beings everywhere on the globe, continuing to transform gross Matter, hastening the world towards its transformation. This she does together with Sri Aurobindo,

of whom she said that he was 'very constantly present,' and for the celebration of whose birth centenary, on 15 August 1972, she formulated
the so simple but profound message: 'One more step towards Eternity.'
Such is the Work of the Avatar in its simplest definition: one more step
towards Eternity. Sri Aurobindo's descent into death, the supramental
manifestation of 1956, the realization of the overman in 1958, the
descent of the overman consciousness in 1969 – this whole series of
superevents with a direct bearing on each and every one of us, whether
we are aware of it or not, was now crowned by the formation and
permanent existence of a supramental body. Its visible multiplication or
reproduction in a refined earthly substance is only a matter of time. Sri
Aurobindo and the Mother's last estimate was that it would take three
hundred years.

Laying Down the Body

> *More and more, and in an absolute way, I see – I see, yes, I see, I*
> *feel – that everything has been decided. And you understand, life,*
> *existence, indeed the world itself would make no sense if it were*
> *otherwise.*[36]

– The Mother

Towards the end, the Mother's conversations became shorter and
shorter. Almost every time she would say that she would not, could
not, or was not allowed to speak. *Peux pas parler* ... Her Consciousness
was absolutely clear, she confirmed, and she was working uninterrupt-
edly on many levels, but this was, of course, not what one saw on the
outside. On the outside there was illness, old age, decay – while the
centre of what was apparently sitting there was packed with supramental
Power continuously irradiating from her. What she kept repeating, in all
circumstances, was *Ce que Tu veux,* audibly or inwardly, expressing her
total surrender to 'the Lord' with a gesture of her hands, palms upwards.

Who could understand? From 1965 onwards extracts from her conversations with Satprem had been published under the title *Notes on the*

Way in the quarterly *Bulletin*, but this was hardly sufficient to work out the lines of the Mother's evolution in her yoga. And how to connect one's external perception of her, let us say since 1962, with 'the Yoga of Sri Aurobindo'? Certainly, there was in an ever growing number of disciples and devotees the devotion, the inner connection, and an effort at yoga. But there was almost no understanding.

Ce que Tu veux were the words accompanying her withdrawal into the seclusion of the last six months, when nobody saw her any more except her four personal assistants and her doctors. There was also her son, Andre, who went to see her every evening. *'Bonsoir, maman,'* one could hear him saying downstairs in the courtyard, for he had to raise his voice a little; and on her inquiring about his wellbeing: *'Ça va bien, maman.'*

The state of her health became critical towards the end of March 1973. Still she made an effort to take up her daily schedule again, but on 20 May all meetings were cancelled. 'She said she didn't have any control over her body. From then onwards she completely stopped seeing people and almost all the time remained in bed with her eyes closed,'[37] said Pranab, the chief source of information about what happened in the last six months. 'On 21 May 1973, when we were waiting at the staircase,' writes one of the secretaries, 'I remember, Champaklal came out of the Mother's room with a grave face and said: "I don't think Mother will ever see people again." In fact, Mother did not receive people any more from that day.'[38]

She still gave darshan on 15 August, in spite of her precarious physical condition. There she came, that small, stooped figure, dressed in a white robe and a silver cape. She moved slowly up to the railing of her terrace on the second floor, leaning on the arm of Pranab. Thousands of eyes in the streets below looked up at her. The sky was vehement. And she looked at them, seeing each one individually, as she once said, and poured into them all they could receive. And she looked at the world and poured into it all it could receive. And after a few minutes she turned around and disappeared into her room, not to be seen again until 18 November.

Nobody knows what happened in the months of her final seclusion. Her close attendants, whom she had praised so high for the care they had taken of her body during the critical weeks in 1962, now looked after her day and night, we may assume with the same attentive and selfless dedication. 'During the last six months that she was confined to bed, she spoke very little. Most of the time she remained with her eyes closed ... Whatever she said was mostly about her body, that she was feeling pain, that she was feeling cold, that she wanted water. Or she asked us to place her in such a way that she did not have pain but could be comfortable. This is all that she said. She never said anything about our work, about the Ashram or about anybody.'[39] Six months in the yoga of the Mother was a long time, taking into account the speed with which her experiences followed each other and the fact that now she had a supramental body.

'On 10 November, we noticed that she developed a kind of hiccup,' said Pranab. 'Then the doctor examined her and found that her blood-pressure was very low, her heart extremely weak, and that there was a frequent missing of beats. In fact, the heart started failing from that time ... In the night of the 13th, at about 10 o'clock, she told me to lift her shoulders up from the bed.' Her body must have been burning, for she asked time and again to be lifted up for a few minutes, and she had developed bedsores on her back also.

On the 14th she said: 'Make me walk.' This reminds us of how she walked for hours when, about two years before, her left "leg was 'dead' and she felt that her right leg too might become paralysed. These three words bear witness to her fighting spirit, ready and willing to go to the extreme limit of all possibilities, until the end. It is a concentrated, determined expression that we see on her face in the deathbed photos, so different from what she had looked like as recently as in April and May, in the last days she saw people. 'We were hesitant [to make her walk], but as she insisted, we lifted her up from the bed. She could not walk, staggered a little, almost collapsed. Seeing this, we put her back in bed. We saw that her face had become absolutely white and the lips blue. Then we decided that whatever she might say, we must not take her out of the bed again.' At about four o'clock in the morning, 'she started saying: "Pranab, lift me up and make me walk. My legs are getting paralysed. If you help me to walk again, they will become all right." But we did not listen.'

From the 15th onwards 'she became absolutely obedient,' said Pranab. Time and again she asked to be lifted up from the bed for a while. Then, in the evening of the 17th, while her son André was with her, Kumud, one of the attendants together with Pranab and Champaklal, was alarmed by the unusual movements the Mother made. Dr Sanyal was called, and so was Pranab. 'I arrived at about five past seven and saw that Dr Sanyal was already there examining her. Dyuman also had come. I went and felt Mother's pulse. It was still there, beating at long intervals. There was still some respiration. But slowly everything stopped. The doctor gave an external heart massage to her. It had no effect. Then he declared that Mother had left her body. This was at 7:25 p.m.'

'She fought and tried up to the end,' said Pranab. 'She had a tremendous will and she was a great fighter and she fought and tried to do what she had taken upon herself ... Her suffering had to be seen to be believed ... Actually, I was holding her when she left her body. It looked to me as if a candle was slowly extinguishing. She was very peaceful, extremely peaceful.'[40]

A European sadhak recalls: 'On 18 November, at about seven o'clock in the morning, my downstairs neighbour pounded nervously on my door and on my window. He shouted: "The Mother is dead! They say that the Mother is dead!" As I woke up, I slowly realized the significance of his words; I got out of my bed and simply knelt on the floor, a gesture of surrender with the words reminiscent of her fundamental surrender: "Your will be done." I cycled through the park to the Ashram. It was a gloriously sunny day. I met other Ashramites who were already coming back from the Ashram on foot or on cycle, and who looked at me with very serious faces to see if I was aware of the shocking news.

'A long queue was winding around the central Ashram building consisting of Ashramites and people from town of all kinds and standings. The first ones had been allowed into the building a little past four. There was whispering and crying, and the atmosphere was one of deep dejection. Order was maintained by boys and girls of the Ashram led by their "captains" of physical education. It did not take long before I too could enter the building and then the meditation hall. There she lay under humming electric fans, the Mother, whom I had last seen six months before. She appeared to be sitting rather than lying down. If I had not known that this was the Mother, I would not have recognized her, so much her face had changed.'[41]

In the morning of 20 November, the Mother's body joined Sri Aurobindo's in the Samadhi in the courtyard of the main Ashram building. It was put in the upper chamber she had kept there for herself since 1950.

The Caterpillar and the Butterfly

'The shock was too great to bear and the loss too deep to be told,'[42] writes Nirodbaran. Statements of insight, visions and messages of encouragement by prominent Ashramites were pinned on the notice board in the central Ashram courtyard, and eagerly read and copied by the many who were seeking for every word of solace. Indira Gandhi, then prime minister, sent a message: 'The Mother was a dynamic, radiant personality with tremendous force of character and extraordinary spiritual attainments. Yet she never lost her sound practical vision which concerned itself with the running of the Ashram, the welfare of society, the founding and development of Auroville and any scheme which would promote the ideals expressed by Sri Aurobindo. She was young in spirit, modern in mind, but most expressive was her abiding faith in the spiritual greatness of India and the role which India could play in giving new light to mankind.'

Sri Aurobindo had passed away and now the Mother had left her body. What remained of their ideals? What remained of everything they had said and written about the superman, immortality, transformation and a New World? What was to be done at present and what in the future? Wasn't this the latest edition of the sempiternal fiasco? Questions like these were rarely voiced, for everybody tried to put on a brave face, at least in public, but they were in the minds of all sadhaks and devotees, who for the most part had expected to see the Mother as immortal and in a resplendent, divinized body.

Not only had many expected to see Sri Aurobindo and the Mother in a divinized body, they had also expected that they themselves would become immortal and share in their divine glory. K.D. Sethna, for instance, writes: 'Psychologically, one of the most central facts of the early days [of the Ashram] was the conviction that complete divinization of the physical being was not only an aim of Sri Aurobindo's yoga but also a practical goal. "Supramentalization" was clearly understood to include a complete change in the body itself. What is most significant is that by "body" was meant the physical instrument of even the sadhaks and not simply of the Master and the Mother ... In this context I remember some words of Amrita, one of the earliest sadhaks. He used to be often in my room. Once when he was there we heard the sound of a funeral passing in the street. In a whisper as if conveying a secret, he said: "I have the feeling that this will not happen to me." I did not raise my eyebrows in the least, for most of us who understood the originality of Sri Aurobindo's spiritual vision and his reading of the Supermind's implications could not help the expectation of a radical body change.'[43]

The Mother, who knew the mind of her disciples better than they did themselves, had warned against such notions and expectations on many occasions. We read in *Notes on the Way* of 1969: 'I have looked very, very attentively: not for an instant has there been the idea "it must be this," meaning: this body, that will undergo the transformation.' And she pinched the skin of her hands. Then she added: 'And the consciousness began to observe that, if there is nothing in this body which even aspires to be that, this proves that it is not its work.'[44] In April 1972 she said: 'We are at best – at best – transitional beings.' The expectation of seeing her supramentalized she called 'figments of the imagination'. What the disciples, longing for a miracle, never realized was that no earthly being at present could stand the unscreened presence of a supramental being, whose light, being divine, is of a brightness compared to which the light of the sun is dark, as the Mother said. Moreover, the Supramental being the Truth-Consciousness, its unveiled presence would simply annihilate any form of falsehood, which is what the human being mostly consists of, especially in its physical elements.

The following quote puts matters clearly: 'The use of this [physical] body at present is for me simply: the Order of the Will of the Lord that I do as much preparatory work as possible. It [her physical body] is, however, not the Aim at all. We have no knowledge, not the least knowledge of what the supramental life is. Consequently, we do not know if this *[Mother pinches the skin of her hands]* can sufficiently change to adapt itself or not. To tell the truth, there is no anxiety about this, it is a problem that does not keep me busy very much. For the problem on which I am working consists in building the supramental consciousness in a way that *this* becomes the being. It is this consciousness which has to become the being. This is what is important, and the rest remains to be seen ... To this end, all the [supramental] consciousness which is in these cells has to assemble, to organize itself and to form a conscious being which is able to be conscious of Matter and at the same time of the Supramental. This is what is being done. How far will we be able to go? I don't know. I do not say that this body will be able to transform itself, I see no sign of this. But there is the consciousness, the physical consciousness, the material consciousness which becomes supramentalized. *This* is the work that is going on. This is what is important.'[45] (26 April 1972) And this is what she has done by building a supramental body out of the supramentalized elements of her physical body.

An important factor in the understanding of what happened in the Mother's body during the last ten years, and ultimately on 17 November 1973, is the simple fact that she had a human body made in the same way as that of the rest of us. This means that the cells of her body, just like ours, consisted for a considerable part of the dregs accumulated during the past millennia. We are the sons and daughters of humanity, which means that we are the offspring of Mother Earth. We carry humanity and the Earth's onerous past in our cells. Sri Aurobindo, having become fully aware of this, doubted whether these dregs, which he called the 'residue,' could actually be transformed, and came to the conclusion that this residual body should be discarded. In the course of her yoga of the cells, the Mother thought she saw indications that even this residue could be transformed, but further progress made her conclude that it would not be possible.

Already in 1968 she had said: 'The body has the feeling of being imprisoned within something. Yes, imprisoned, imprisoned as if in a box. But it sees through it. It sees through it and it can also act, in a limited way, through something which is still there and which must disappear. This "something" gives the feeling of imprisonment. How is it to disappear? That I don't know yet.'[46] Later, she said that the substance of which we are built is not sufficiently purified to express the supreme Consciousness without deforming it, and that she had the impression that there would be 'a waste product.' 'It will only be the untransformable residue that will really be death,' she said.[47]

Then what happened on that fateful 17 November 1973 ? The best way to understand it may be a simile: the pupation of the caterpillar into a butterfly. When its time comes, the caterpillar spins itself into a cocoon. In this cocoon the pupation takes place, a miraculous transformation into a completely different being: a butterfly. Nobody knows what happens in that cocoon, how the immensely complex process of the pupation comes about. It is one of the innumerable processes in nature which may escape the knowledge of materialistic science for ever, because they happen in other dimensions than that of Matter alone. Can one say that the caterpillar dies in the cocoon? Transformation is not death, it is a change into something else. The butterfly has originated in the caterpillar, from the caterpillar. In a way, the butterfly contains the essence of the caterpillar within itself, and the dried up 'residue' in the cocoon is what has to be discarded, because a caterpillar exists within the dimensions of a crawling-world and the butterfly within the dimensions of a flying-world.

The human body of the Mother existed in the world of the humans. As her yoga progressed, that body belonged less and less to this world – except for the residue in the cells. For this residue it was impossible to transcend the world of the humans. In the meantime the supramental transformation, the supramental pupation was taking place. The butterfly – the prototype of the supramental body in the Mother – came into existence. She signalled its presence several times in the course of the final years and eventually perceived and described it in 1972. Taking into consideration the logical sequence of the development of Sri Aurobindo and the Mother's avataric yoga, the graduality of the perception of the presence of the new being within her, its similarity with Rijuta's mature psychic and the final confirmation of the personal experience in the Mother, there can be no reason to doubt this. The caterpillar nature in the human beings looked forward to a caterpillar miracle, while the golden butterfly was already there hovering among them. But they did not have the eyes to see it, as they were also unable to imagine or understand the process by which it had come into being.

On 17 November 1973 the Mother laid down her residual human body while she continued to exist forever in a body consisting of a supramental substance. The supramental substance as worked out by the Mother is a *material* substance – otherwise the earthly evolution would have no meaning – though it is composed of a substance more refined than the gross matter known to us. The gross matter of our Mother the Earth is still in the process of transformation. This process is now in an advanced stage thanks to the avataric yoga of Sri Aurobindo and the Mother. When gross matter will have become sufficiently subtle and receptive, i.e. transformed, the mature souls, ready and waiting in their soul-world, will descend and incarnate in it. The formation of their bodies will be moulded by the existence of the Mother's supramental body, the prototype of the new species.

> It comes at last, the day foreseen of old,
> What John in Patmos saw, what Shelley dreamed,
> Vision and vain imagination deemed,
> The City of delight, the Age of Gold.
>
> The Iron Age is ended. Only now
> The last fierce spasm of the dying past
> Shall shake the nations, and when that has passed
> Earth washed of its ills shall raise a fairer brow.[48]

By Way of an Epilogue

When darkness deepens strangling the earth's breast
And man's corporeal mind is the only lamp,
As a thief's in the night shall be the covert tread
Of one who steps unseen into his house.
A Voice ill-heard shall speak, the soul obey,
A Power into mind's inner chamber steal,
A charm and sweetness open life's closed doors
And beauty conquer the resisting world,
The Truth-Light capture Nature by surprise,
A stealth of God compel the heart to bliss
And earth grow unexpectedly divine.
In Matter shall be lit the spirit's glow,
In body and body kindled the sacred birth;
Night shall awake to the anthem of the stars,
The days become a happy pilgrim march,
Our will a force of the Eternal's power,
And thought the rays of a spiritual sun.
A few shall see what none yet understands;
God shall grow up while the wise men talk and sleep;
For man shall not know the coming till its hour
And belief shall be not till the work is done.[49]

Biographical Note

Georges Van Vrekhem is a Flemish speaking Belgian who writes in English. He became well-known in his country as a journalist, poet and playwright. For some time he was the artistic manager of a professional theatre company. He gave numerous talks and presentations in America, Europe and India.

He got first acquainted with the works of Sri Aurobindo and the Mother in 1964. In 1970 he joined the Sri Aurobindo Ashram in Pondicherry (now Puducherry), and in 1978 he became a member of Auroville, where he is still living and writing.

He wrote:

Beyond Man, the Life and Work of Sri Aurobindo and The Mother (1997)

The Mother, The Story of Her Life (2000)

Overman, the Intermediary between the Human and the Supramental Being (2001)

Patterns of the Present, in the Light of Sri Aurobindo and The Mother (2002)

The Mother: The Divine Shakti (2003)

Hitler and his God – The Background to the Nazi Phenomenon (2006)

Evolution, Religion, and the Unknown God (2011)

His books are translated into Dutch, French, German, Italian, Russian, and Spanish. He was awarded the Sri Aurobindo Puraskar for 2006 by the Government of West Bengal.

An overview of his books can be found at www.beyondman.org

References

The abbreviations used throughout are CWM for the Collected Works of Mother, and SABCL for the Sri Aurobindo Birth Centenary Library.

1. Growing Up in Paris

1. The Mother, *Conversations 1929-30*, (CWM3) p. 131.
2. Pournaprema, *Une drôle de petite fille*, p. 5. This booklet is the record of a talk given by the Mother's granddaughter to children of the Sri Aurobindo Ashram School.
3. The first name of Mira Pinto is spelled with one r, while the first name of Mirra Alfassa has two r's according to the birth certificate. It should be noted, however, that the Mother herself sometimes spelled her first name with one r (e.g. in the facsimile reproduced in Mona Sarkar's *Douce Mère I*, p. 6), and that Sri Aurobindo, certainly a stickler in matters of spelling, also wrote it with one r in a mantra containing his and her name (see the facsimile in *On Himself*, SABCL 26, p. 512).
4. Pournaprema, op. cit. p. 10.
5. Ibid.
6. The Mother, *Entretiens 1950-51*, CWM4 p. 42.
7. The Mother, *Words of Long Ago*, CWM2 p. 1.
8. Nirodbaran, *Twelve Years With Sri Aurobindo* (1988 ed.), p. 105.
9. The Mother, *Entretiens 1953*, CWM5 p. 199.
10. Pournaprema, op. cit. p. 6.
11. *Champaklal Speaks* (1976 ed.), p. 142.
12. Sri Aurobindo, *The Life Divine*, SABCL 19 pp. 754, 802.
13. See Sujata Nahar, *Mother's Chronicles I*, p. 136.
14. The Mother, *Entretiens 1954*, CWM6 p. 40.
15. The Mother, *Prayers and Meditations*, CWM1 p. 81.
16. *Words of the Mother I*, CWM3 p. 38-39.

2. Artist among the Artists

1. Jean-Paul Crespelle, *La vie quotidienne des Impressionistes*, p. 113.
2. *The Mother – Paintings and Drawings*, p. 157.
3. The Mother, *Three Plays* (1989 ed.), p. 35.
4. The Mother, *Questions and Answers 1953*, CWM5 p. 334.
5. See Jean-Paul Crespelle, *La vie quotidienne des Impressionnistes*, pp. 82-83.
6. The Mother, *On Education*, CWM12 p. 236.
7. J-P Crespelle, op. cit., p. 35.
8. The Mother, *Questions and Answers 1953*, CWM5 p. 2.
9. The Mother, *Questions and Answers 1950-51*, CWM4 pp. 311-12.
10. J-P Crespelle, op.cit., p. 196.
10a. The Mother, *Questions and Answers 1954*, CWM6 p. 71.
10b. The Mother, *Questions and Answers 1950-51*, CWM4 p. 301.
11. Pournaprema, *Une drôle de petite fille*, p. 18.
12. Sujata Nahar, *The Mother's Chronicles II*, p. 128.

13. See Pierre Barret and Jean-Noël Gurgand, *Priez pour nous à Compostelle*, pp. 109, 259.
14. The Mother – Paintings and Drawings, p. 160.
15. Mother India, January 1983, pp. 36 ff.
16. Ibid.
17. The Mother – Paintings and Drawings, p. 163.
18. The Mother, *Questions and Answers 1954*, CWM6 p. 72.
19. See The Mother, *Questions and Answers 1950-51*, CWM4 pp. 298 ff.
20. Id. p. 297.
21. Id. p. 302.
22. The Mother, *Questions and Answers 1955*, CWM7 p. 189 ff.
23. The Mother, *Questions and Answers 1954*, CWM6 p. 71.
24. The Mother, *Notes on the Way*, CWM11 p. 68.
25. *Glimpses of the Mother's Life* I, p. 54.
26. Sujata Nahar, *The Mother's Chronicles* II, p. 173.
27. *Glimpses of the Mother's Life* I, p. 54.
28. Ibid.
29. See Dilip Kumar Roy, *Yogi Krishnaprem*, pp. 53 ff.
30. Peter Washington, *Madame Blavatsky's Baboon*, p. 107.
31. The Mother, *Questions and Answers 1955*, CWM7 p. 39.
32. Barbara Tuchman, *A Proud Tower*, p. 272.
33. The Mother, *Words of Long Ago*, CWM2 p. 87-88.
34. Georges Duby and Robert Mandrou, *Histoire de la civilisation française*, p. 325.
35. Barbara Tuchman, op. cit., p. 105.

3. Explorations of the Occult

1. *Glimpses of the Mother* I, p. 58.
2. Sri Aurobindo, *The Life Divine*, SABCL 19 p. 876.
3. Id., p. 652.
4. The Mother, *Questions and Answers 1954*, CWM 6 p. 38.
5. Id., p. 190.
6. See Louis Pauwels and Guy Breton, *Histoires magiques de l'Histoire de France 2*, pp. 226, 268.
7. Sri Aurobindo, *The Mother*, SABCL 25 p. 371.
8. Sujata Nahar, *The Mother's Chronicles III*, pp. 166-67.
9. The Mother, *Questions and Answers 1954*, CWM 6 p. 55 ff.
10. Ibid.
11. Peter and Elizabeth Fenwick, *The Truth in the Light*, p. 76.
12. Sujata Nahar, *The Mother's Chronicles II*, pp. 180-81.
13. Claire Thémanlys, *Un séjour chez les Grands Initiés*, p. 79.
14. Jean Chalon, *Le lumineux destin d'Alexandra David-Néel*, p. 55.
15. The author owes most of these data to an unpublished essay by Peter Heehs, *Rooted Above? – The Philosophie Cosmique, the Kabbalah and the Philosophy of Sri Aurobindo*.
16. Id., p. 6.
17. Francis King and Isabelle Sutherland, *The Rebirth of Magic*, pp. 64, 73.
18. Sujata Nahar, *The Mother's Chronicles III*, pp. 66-67.
19. Id., pp. 44, 47.
20. *Glimpses of the Mother's Life*, p. 85.
21. Claire Thémanlys, op. cit., p. 5.
22. Sujata Nahar, op. cit. p. 28.
23. *Glimpses of the Mother's Life* I, pp. 70-71.
24. Ibid.

25. Sri Aurobindo, *The Mother*, SABCL 25 p. 372.
26. See The Mother, *Questions and Answers 1957-58*, CWM 9 p. 60.
27. Id., pp. 61-63.
28. Claire Thémanlys, op. cit. p. 69.
29. Peter Heehs, op. cit., p. 10.
30. Claire Thémanlys, op. cit., p. 11.
31. Peter Heehs, op. cit., p. 4.
32. The Mother, *Words of Long Ago*, CWM 2 pp. 12 ff.
33. See the chronology of the Mother's life in K.R. Srinivasa Iyengar's *On the Mother*, p. 848.
34. Sujata Nahar, op. cit. p. 200.
35. Id., p. 206.
36. *Glimpses of the Mother's Life I*, p. 70.
37. Georges van Vrekhem, *Beyond Man*, p. 29.
38. *Glimpses of the Mother's Life I*, p. 78.
39. Satprem, *Mère I* (Indian edition), p. 204.
40. Sujata Nahar, *The Mother's Chronicles* I, p. 145.
41. This portrait is included in *The Mother – Paintings and Drawings*.

4. A Synthesis in the Making

1. Sri Aurobindo, *Savitri*, SABCL 34 p. 551.
2. The Mother, *Questions and Answers 1954*, CWM 6 p. 71.
3. The Mother, *Three Plays*, p. 4.
4. The Mother, *Questions and Answers 1953*, CWM 5 pp. 263-64.
5. M. Schwaller de Lubicz, *Le Miracle égyptien*, p. 37.
6. Id., p. 220.
7. Peter Washington, *Madame Blavatsky's Baboon*, pp. 7, 36.
8. The Mother, *Questions and Answers 1957-58*, CWM 9 p. 364.
9. Id. p. 363.
10. *Glimpses of the Mother's Life I*, p. 86.
11. Sri Aurobindo Archives and Research, December 1988, p. 199.
12. Georges Duby and Robert Mandrou, *Histoire de la civilisation française II*, p. 311.
13. See Sujata Nahar, *The Mother's Chronicles III*, pp. 271 ff.
14. *Sri Aurobindo Archives and Research*, December 1988, p. 200.
15. K.R. Srinivasa Iyengar, *On the Mother*, p. 47.
16. *Sri Aurobindo Archives and Research*, December 1988, p. 201.
17. Nolini Kanta Gupta and Amrita, *Reminiscences*, p. 44.
18. Id. p. 43.
19. Jean Chalon, *Le lumineux destin d'Alexandra David-Néel*, p. 63.
20. Id. p. 168.
21. Sujata Nahar, *The Mother's Chronicles III*, p. 32.
22. *Mother India*, January 1983, p. 37.
23. Sujata Nahar, id., pp. 273, 270, 271.
24. The Mother, *Questions and Answers 1956*, CWM 8 p. 211.
25. See *L'Agenda de Mère* XI, p. 277.
26. See Sri Aurobindo, *Savitri*, book VII, canto V, CWSA 33 p. 34.
27. The Mother, *Prayers and Meditations*, CWM 1 p. 16.
28. The Mother, *Words of Long Ago*, CWM 2 p. 145.
29. Id., p. 80.
30. The Mother, *Words of Long Ago*, CWM 2 p. 153.
31. See *L'Agenda de Mère XIII*, p. 168, and X, p. 154.

32. See Elisabeth Keesing, *Hazrat Inayat Khan – A Biography*.
33. The Mother, *Questions and Answers 1953*, p. 58.
34. The Mother, *Words of Long Ago*, CWM 2 p. 104.
35. Ibid.
36. Ib., p. 105.
37. Ib., pp. 110-11.
38. The Mother, *Questions and Answers 1953*, CWM 5 p. 352.
39. The Mother, *Words of Long Ago*, CWM 2 p. 47.
40. The Mother, *Questions and Answers 1953*, CWM 5 p. 355.
41. *Words of the Mother I*, CWM 13 p. 37.
42. The Mother, *Prayers and Meditations*, CWM1 p. 1 (Sri Aurobindo's Translation).
43. The Mother, *Prayers and Meditations*, CWM 1 p. 120.
44. Ib., pp. 93, 94.
45. Ib., p. 97.
46. Id., pp. 99, 100.
47. Id., pp. 33, 88.
48. Pournaprema, *Une drôle de petite fille*, p. 28.
49. The Mother, *Questions and Answers 1956*, CWM 8 p. 150.
50. Nolini Kanta Gupta and K. Amrita, *Reminiscences*, p. 165.
51. Sujata Nahar, *The Mother's Chronicles* V, p. 580.
52. The Mother, *Prayers and Meditations*, CWM 1 p. 124.

5. Aurobindo Ghose

1. *Sri Aurobindo Archives and Research*, April 1985, p. 72.
2. Nirodbaran, *Sri Aurobindo for All Ages*, pp. 4, 5.
3. Peter Heehs, *Sri Aurobindo – A Brief Biography*, p. 5.
4. Id., p. 4.
5. A. B. Purani, *Evening Talks With Sri Aurobindo*, pp. 376-77.
6. Nirodbaran, op. cit., p. 9.
7. *Sri Aurobindo Archives and Research*, December 1985, p. 193.
8. A.B. Purani, op. cit., p. 378.
9. Peter Heehs, op. cit., p. 11.
10. *SAAC*, April 1990, pp. 111-12.
11. Id., p. 12.
12. Nirodbaran, op. cit., p. 13.
13. Sri Aurobindo, *On Himself*, SABCL 26 p. 3.
14. Peter Heehs, op. cit., p. 15.
15. Id., p. 14.
16. Sri Aurobindo, op.cit., p. 4.
17. Sujata Nahar, op. cit., p. 175.
18. Nirodbaran, op. cit., p. 21.
19. Elisabeth Keesing, *Hazrat Inayat Khan – A Biography*, p. 2.
20. Beautiful Vignettes, pp. 3 ff.
21. *SAAC*, Dec. 83, p. 163, and Sri Aurobindo, *On Himself*, SABCL 26 p. 13.
22. This and the following quotations from *New Lamps for Old*: Sri Aurobindo, *Bande Mataram*, SABCL 1 pp. 5 ff.
23. Sri Aurobindo, *On Himself*, SABCL 26 pp. 100, 430.
24. Nirodbaran, *Talks With Sri Aurobindo* I, p. 59.
25. Sri Aurobindo, op. cit., p. 75.
26. Peter Heehs, op. cit., p. 27.
27. Sri Aurobindo, op. cit., p. 23.

28. Id., p. 21.
29. Id., p. 22.
30. Id., p. 23.
31. Peter Heehs, op. cit., pp. 28-29.
32. Nirodbaran, op. cit., pp. 46-47.
33. Sri Aurobindo, *Collected Poems*, SABCL 5 p. 138.
34. Nirodbaran, *Talks With Sri Aurobindo* 1, p. 165.
35. Id., p. 50.
36. Sri Aurobindo, *Bengali Writings*, pp. 351 ff.
37. Sri Aurobindo, *On Himself*, SABCL 26 p. 24.
38. *SAAC,* Dec. 1979, p. 230.
39. Id., p. 228.
40. Nirodbaran, *Talks With Sri Aurobindo* IV, p. 84.
41. Peter Heehs, op. cit., p. 101.
42. Sri Aurobindo, *On Himself*, SABCL 26 pp. 25-26.
43. See *The Advent*, April 1981, p. 13.
44. Sri Aurobindo, *Bande Mataram*, SABCL 1 p. 7.
45. Sri Aurobindo, *On Himself*, SABCL 26 p. 45.
46. Id., p. 47.
47. Id., p. 49.
48. *SAAC,* April 1980, p. 119.
49. Sri Aurobindo, op. cit., p. 79.
50. Sri Aurobindo, *Bengali Writings*, p. 271.
51. Nirodbaran, *Talks With Sri Aurobindo I*, pp. 53, 212, 323.
52. Manoj Das, *Sri Aurobindo in the First Decade of the Century*, p. 64.
53. Peter Heehs, op. cit., p. 173.
54. Sri Aurobindo, *Karmayogin*, SABCL 2 p. 10.
55. Sri Aurobindo, *Bengali Writings*, p. 262.
56. A.B. Purani, Evening *Talks With Sri Aurobindo*, p. 263.
57. Nirodbaran, Sri Aurobindo for All Ages, p. 110.
58. Sri Aurobindo, *On Himself*, SABCL 26 pp. 57-58.
59. Id., p. 59.
60. This translation is from *Vignettes of Sri Aurobindo and the Mother*, p. 9.
61. Peter Heehs, *Sri Aurobindo – A Brief Biography*, pp. 99-100.
62. Sri Aurobindo, op. cit., p. 27.
63. Sri Aurobindo, op. cit., p. 55.

5. Speaking the Word

1. *Glimpses of the Mother's Life* I, p. 132.
2. The Mother, *Questions and Answers 1956*, CWM 8 p. 276.
3. The Mother, *Questions and Answers 1955*, CWM 7 p. 414.
4. *SAAR,* April 1989, p. 116.
5. The Mother, *Prayers and Meditations*, CWM 1 p. 127.
6. Id., p. 148.
7. Sri Aurobindo, *On Himself*, SABCL 26 p. 374.
8. *SAAR,* April 1989, p. 97.
9. Id., p. 100.
10. Id., p. 99.
11. Sri Aurobindo, *Karmayogin,* SABCL 2 p. 2.
12. *SAAR,* April 1989, p. 119.
13. *Glimpses of the Mother's Life* I, p. 144.

14. Sri Aurobindo, *On Himself,* SABCL 26 p. 374.
15. Nirodbaran, *Talks With Sri Aurobindo* III, p. 119.
16. *Arya,* no. 2 (15 September 1914), p. 61.
17. Id., p. 68.
18. Nolini Kanta Gupta, *Reminiscences,* p. 72.
19. *Arya,* no. 1 (15 August 1914), p. 58.
20. Nolini Kanta Gupta, op. cit., p. 40.
21. K. Amrita, in *Reminiscences,* p. 180.
22. Nolini Kanta Gupta, op. cit., pp. 63-64.
23. The Mother, *Prayers and Meditations,* CWM 1 pp. 243-44.
24. The Mother, *Prayers and Meditations,* CWM 1 p. 244.
25. Sri Aurobindo, *The Life Divine,* SABCL 19 p. 325.
26. Id., p. 87.
27. Id., pp. 185, 612.
28. Sri Aurobindo, *Thoughts and Aphorisms,* no. 162, in *Essays Divine and Human,* CWSA 12.
29. Sri Aurobindo, *The Life Divine,* SABCL 18 p. 3.
30. The Mother, op. cit. CWM 1 pp. 188-89, 190, 213.
31. Sri Aurobindo, *Savitri,* Book III Canto IV, CWSA 33 p. 344.
32. Words of the Mother I, 13 p. 47.
33. *Glimpses of the Mother's Life* I, p. 154.
34. Sri Aurobindo, *The Mother,* SABCL 25 p. 20.
35. Id., pp. 25-26.
36. The Mother, op. cit., pp. 257-258, 260, 266-67, 273.
37. Sri Aurobindo, *Savitri,* Book VII Canto V, CWSA 34 p. 528, Canto II, id., p. 486.
38. The Mother, *Prayers and Meditations,* CWM 1 p. 215.
39. Id., p. 239.
40. The Mother, *Questions and Answers 1953,* CWM 5 p. 306.
41. Id. *1954,* CWM 6 p. 69.
42 Sri Aurobindo, *On Himself,* SABCL 26 p. 37.
43. Nolini Kanta Gupta, op. cit., p. 46.
44. K.R. Srinivasa Iyengar, *On the Mother,* p. 132.
45. *SAAR,* Dec. 1994, p. 237.
46. *SAAR,* April 1989, p. 120.
47. The Mother, *Prayers and Meditations,* CWM 1 pp. 319, 321.
48. Id., pp. 323-24.
49. The Mother, op. cit., p. 326.
50. *Glimpses of the Mother's Life* I, p. 162.
51. The Mother, op. cit., p. 333.
52. Id., p. 344.
53. Pournaprema, *Une drôle de petite fille,* p. 30.
54. The Mother, *Words of Long Ago,* CWM 2 p. 137.
55. The Mother, *Questions and Answers 1950-51,* CWM 4 p. 303.
56. Kireet Joshi, *Sri Aurobindo and the Mother,* p. 180.
57. Sri Aurobindo, *On Himself,* SABCL 26 pp. 426 ff.
58 The Mother, *Prayers and Meditations,* CWM 1 p. 340.

7. In Japan

1. The Mother, *Prayers and Meditations,* CWM 1 p. 388.
2. Id., p. 336.
3. Id., p. 337.

4. Id., p. 338.
5. Id., p. 343.
6. Pournaprema, *Une drôle de petite fille*, p. 33.
7. SAAR, Dec. 1994, p. 238.
8. Id., p. 240.
9. *Sri Aurobindo Circle*, n° 34, p. 122.
10. *SAAR,* Dec. 1994, pp. 240-42.
11. Nirodbaran, *Talks With Sri Aurobindo* I, p. 112.
12. The Mother, *Questions and Answers 1956*, CWM 8 p. 186.
13. The Mother, *Words of Long Ago*, CWM 2 p. 143 ff.
14. Id., p. 153.
15. Sri Aurobindo, *On Himself,* SABCL 26 p. 126.
16. The Mother, *Questions and Answers 1950-51*, CWM 4 p. 308.
17. *Sri Aurobindo Circle*, n° 34, pp. 119 ff.
18. The Mother, op. cit., 309-10.
19. Id., pp. 308-09.
20. Id., p. 319.
21. The Mother, *Prayers and Meditations,* CWM 1 p. 398.
22. Id., p. 399.
23. The Mother, *Questions and Answers 1950-51*, CWM 4 p. 306.
24. The Mother, *Prayers and Meditations*, p. 351.
25. Id., p. 397.
26. Id., p. 402.
27. Id., p. 358
28. Id., pp. 365 ff.
29. *Sri Aurobindo Circle*, n° 34, pp. 122-23.
30. The Mother, *Prayers and Meditations,* CWM 1 p. 372.
31. *SAAR,* Dec. 1994, p. 239.
32. Ibid.
33. *Glimpses of the Mother's Life* I, p. 144.
34. K.R. Srinivasa Iyengar, *The Mother*, p. 191.
35. Paul Richard, *To the Nations*, p. XV.
36. Paul Richard, *The Lord of the Nations*, p. X.
37. Id., pp. 48-49, 64 and 65.
38. Nirodbaran, *Talks With Sri Aurobindo* III, p. 225.
39. The Mother, *Questions and Answers 1953*, CWM 5 pp. 182 ff.
40. See *Mother's Agenda*, conversation of 20 Dec. 1961.

8. The Seven Hidden Years

1. Sri Aurobindo, *On Himself,* SABCL 26 p. 459.
2. The Mother, *Questions and Answers 1950-51*, CWM 4 p. 223.
3. The Mother, *Words of Long Ago*, CWM 2 p. 166.
4. Sujata Nahar, *The Mother's Chronicles* II, p. 100.
5. See *Mother's Agenda*, 5 November 1961.
6. Nirodbaran, *Talks With Sri Aurobindo I,* pp. 180-81.
7. Paul Richard, To *India*, pp. 18, 30.
8. Dilip Kumar Roy, *Among the Great*, pp. 324 ff.
9. Sri Aurobindo, *On Himself,* SABCL 26 p. 130.
10. Id., p. 432.
11. This letter was originally written in Bengali. The quotations are from the translation published in *Champaklal's Treasures*, pp. 147 ff.

12. Sri Aurobindo, *On Himself,* SABCL 26 p. 459.
13. Kireet Joshi, *Sri Aurobindo and the Mother,* pp. 86-87.
14. A.B. Purani, Evening *Talks With Sri Aurobindo,* p. 482.
15. The Mother, *On Thoughts and Aphorisms,* CWM 10 p. 43.
16. The Mother, *Questions and Answers 1954,* CWM p. :303.
17. A.B. Purani, op. cit., p. 20.
18. K.R. Srinivasa Iyengar, *On the Mother,* p. 212.
19. M.P. Pandit (ed.), *Breath of Grace,* p. 43.
20. K.R. Srinivasa Iyengar, op. cit., p. 218.
21. A.B. Purani, op. cit., p. 20.
22. K.R. Srinivasa Iyengar, op. cit., p. 260.
23. Shyam Kumari, *How They Came to Sri Aurobindo and the Mother 4,* p. 9.
24. A.B. Purani, op. cit., p. 484.
25. Kireet Joshi, op. cit., pp. 87-88.
26. Nolini Kanta Gupta, *Reminiscences,* p. 69.
27. K.R. Srinivasa Iyengar, op. cit., pp. 210-11.
28. A.B. Purani, op. cit., p. 710.
29. Sri Aurobindo, op. cit., p. 455.
30. Id., pp. 323-24.
31. Sri Aurobindo, op. cit., pp. 457-58.
32. Nolini Kanta Gupta, op. cit., pp. 82-83.
33. *How They Came to Sri Aurobindo and the Mother 2,* pp. 23-24.
34. Id., p. 67.
35. The Mother, *Questions and Answers,* CWM 6 p. 57 ff.
36. Sri Aurobindo, *On Himself,* SABCL 26 p. 175.
37. Sri Aurobindo, *Bengali Writings,* pp. 364-65.
38. K.R. Srinivasa Iyengar, op. cit., p. 213.
39. *Champaklal's Treasures,* pp. 154-55.
40. Sri Aurobindo, *On Himself,* SABCL 26 p. 437.
41. M.P. Pandit, *An Early Chapter in the Mother's Life,* p. 3.
42. A.B. Purani, op. cit., p. 23.
43. Id., p. 17. The following quotations are from the same source, pp. 14 ff.
44. *How They Came to Sri Aurobindo and the Mother 4,* p. 4.
45. See the section on Sri Aurobindo in Dilip Kumar Roy, *Among the Great.*
46. Dilip Kumar Roy, *Sri Aurobindo Came to Me,* p. 515.
47. Sri Aurobindo, *Conversations avec Pavitra,* introduction.
48. Sri Aurobindo, *Collected Poems,* SABCL 5 p. 113.
49. *Champaklal Speaks,* pp. 16-17.
50. Nolini Kanta Gupta, op. cit., p. 78.
51. See The Mother, *Questions and Answers 1955,* CWM 7 p. 98-99.
52. In M.P. Pandit (ed.), *Breath of Grace,* p. 79.
53. The Mother, *Questions and Answers 1950-51,* CWM 4 p. 238.
54. The Mother, *Questions and Answers 1953,* CWM 5 p. 230.
55. The Mother, *Questions and Answers 1955,* CWM 7 p. 100.
56. The Mother, *Questions and Answers 1950-51,* CWM 4 p. 238.
57. A.B. Purani, op. cit., pp. 10-11.

9. Three Dragons

1. The Mother, *Questions and Answers 1953,* CWM 5 p. 388.
2. Kireet Joshi, *Sri Aurobindo and the Mother,* pp. 89-90.
3. Sri Aurobindo, *On Himself,* SABCL 26 p. 179.

4. A.B. Purani, Evening *Talks With Sri Aurobindo*, p. 481.
5. A.B. Purani, *The Life of Sri Aurobindo,* pp. 215 ff.
6. Kireet Joshi, op. cit., p. 90.
7. Quoted in K.D. Sethna, *The Development of Sri Aurobindo's Spiritual System* ..., in *Mother India*, August 1979, p. 474.
8. *Glimpses of the Mother's Life* I, p. 234.
9. Sri Aurobindo, *On Himself,* SABCL 26 p. 136-37.
10. Id., p. 191.
11. Quoted in A.B. Purani, *The Life of Sri Aurobindo*, p. 212.
12. Sri Aurobindo, *Letters on Yoga*, SABCL 22 p. 385.
13. Nirodbaran, *Correspondence With Sri Aurobindo*, p. 299.
14. Id., p. 38.
15. *Glimpses of the Mother's Life* II, p. 17.
16. Govindbhai Patel, *My Pilgrimage to the Spirit*, p. 17.
17. Narayan Prasad, *Life in the Sri Aurobindo Ashram*, p. 64.
18. Nirodbaran, *Talks With Sri Aurobindo* IV, p. 111.
19. K.D. Sethna, op. cit., p. 477.
20. K.D. Sethna, *Aspects of Sri Aurobindo*, p. 97.
21. The Mother, *Questions and Answers 1957-58,* CWM 9 pp. 147-48.
22. Sri Aurobindo, *On Himself,* SABCL 26 p. 456.
23. K.R. Srinivasa Iyengar, *On the Mother*, p. 247.
24. Sri Aurobindo, op. cit., p. 455.
25. Sri Aurobindo, *The Mother,* SABCL 25 p. 233-34.
26. M.P. Pandit (ed.), *Breath of Grace*, p. 88.
27. M.P. Pandit, *Tell Us of the Mother*, p. 10.
28. K.R. Srinivasa Iyengar, op. cit., pp. 246-47.
29. Mritunjoy in M.P. Pandit (ed.), *Breath of Grace*, p. 64.
30. Nirodbaran, *Talks With Sri Aurobindo* I, p. 57.
31. Prema Nandakumar, *The Mother of the Sri Aurobindo Ashram*, p. 53.
32. *Mother India*, October 1996, p. 828.
33. Prabhakar, *Among the Not So Great* – III, in *Mother India*, March 1996.
34. Nirodbaran, *Twelve Years With Sri Aurobindo*, pp. 52-53.

10. The Laboratory

1. The Mother, *Questions and Answers 1953*, CWM 5 p. 299.
2. The Mother, *Questions and Answers 1929-31*, CWM 3 p. 3.
3. Sri Aurobindo, *On Himself,* SABCL 26 pp. 474-75.
4. *Glimpses of the Mother's Life* II, p. 1.
5. The Mother, *Words of the Mother I,* CWM 1 p. 37.
6. *Glimpses of the Mother's Life* II, p. 7.
7. Nirodbaran, *Correspondence With Sri Aurobindo*, p. 169.
8. Id., pp. 135, 137-38.
9. Sri Aurobindo, *The Human Cycle*, in *Social and Political Thought*, SABCL 15 p. 251.
10. Sri Aurobindo, *Letters on Yoga*, SABCL 22 p. 100-01.
11. Sri Aurobindo, *On Himself,* SABCL 26 p. 122.
12. Sri Aurobindo, *The Synthesis of Yoga*, CWSA 23 p. 153.
13. Sri Aurobindo, *The Mother,* SABCL 25 p. 78.
14. Sri Aurobindo, *On Himself,* SABCL 26 p. 482.
15. Sri Aurobindo, *The Mother,* SABCL 25 pp. 121, 129, 130.
16. *In Champaklal Speaks, p. 156.*
17. The Mother, *Questions and Answers 1954*, CWM 6 pp. 444, 441.

18. Sri Aurobindo, *On Himself*, SABCL 26 p. 481.
19. Id., p. 485.
20. Nirodbaran, *Talks With Sri Aurobindo I*, p. 85.
21. Sri Aurobindo, *On the Mother*, SABCL 25 p. 270.
22. In La Mère, *Entretiens 1929-31*, CWM 3 p. 151.
23. The Mother, *Questions and Answers 1956*, CWM 8 pp. 161-62.
24. Sri Aurobindo, op. cit., p. 227.
25. The Mother, *Questions and Answers 1953*, CWM 5 p. 2.
26. The Mother, *Questions and Answers 1950-51*, CWM 4 p. 215.
27. The Mother, *Questions and Answers 1954*, CWM 6 p. 295.
28. Sri Aurobindo, op. cit., p. 229.
29. In *Champaklal's Treasures*, p. 76.
30. In *Glimpses of the Mother's Life II*, p. 86.
31. In Nirodbaran, *Memorable Contacts With the Mother*, p. 174.
32. Nirodbaran, *Correspondence with Sri Aurobindo*, p. 275.
33. *Champaklal Speaks*, p. 25.
34. The Mother, *Questions and Answers*, CWM 6 p. 297.
35. Sri Aurobindo, op. cit., p. 317.
36. Id., p. 219.
37. Id., pp. 106-07.
38. Id., p. 107.
39. The Mother, *On Thoughts and Aphorisms*, CWM 10 p. 122.
40. Sri Aurobindo, *On Himself*, SABCL 26 pp. 154-55.
41. Sri Aurobindo, *The Mother*, SABCL 25 pp. 222, 229, 98.
42. Id., p. 171.
43. Id., pp. 170, 236, 277.
44. Sri Aurobindo, *The Mother*, SABCL 25 p. 78.
45. K.R. Srinivasa Iyengar, *On the Mother*, p. 280.
46. For this and the following extracts from the Mother's letters to André: *Glimpses of the Mother's Life II*, pp. 58 ff.
47. Id., p. 112.
48. Id., pp. 58-59.
49. Quoted in *Flowers and Their Messages*, pp. VIII and IX.
50. The Mother, *Words of the Mother I*, CWM 15 p. 63.
51. Id., p. 89.
52. Huta, *White Roses*, p. 138.
53. Nirodbaran, op. cit., pp. 55-56.
54. *Flowers and Their Messages*, p. XI.
55. Mona Sarkar, *Sweet Mother II*, pp. 16-17.
56. In *Glimpses of the Mother's Life* II, p. 69.
57. *Mother India* 1977, p. 201.
58. Amal Kiran and Nirodbaran, *Light and Laughter*, pp. 63-64.
59. Sri Aurobindo, *The Mother*, SABCL 25 p. 284.
60. K.R. Srinivasa Iyengar, *On the Mother*, p. 341.
61. Narayan Prasad, *Life in Sri Aurobindo Ashram*, p. 64.
62. Sri Aurobindo, op. cit., pp. 51, 52.
63. Amal Kiran and Nirodbaran, op. cit., p. 68.
64. The Mother, *Prayers and Meditations*, CWM 1 p. 416.
65. Sri Aurobindo, op. cit., p. 315.
66. Id., pp. 316-17.
67. In *Champaklal's Treasures*, p. 58.
68. Prabhakar, *Among the Not So Great*, in *Mother India*, March 1996, p. 200.

69. *Glimpses of the Mother's Life* II, p. 68.
70. The Mother, *Questions and Answers 1955*, CWM 7 pp. 257-58.
71. Nirodbaran, *Twelve Years With Sri Aurobindo*, p. 45.
72. Sri Aurobindo, *Collected Poems*, SABCL 5 pp. 99 ff.
73. In *Glimpses of the Mother's Life* II, p. 102 footnote.
74. K.R. Srinivasa Iyengar, *On the Mother*, p. 283.
75. Nirodbaran, *Correspondence With Sri Aurobindo*, pp. 127, 525.
76. Sri Aurobindo, On *Himself*, SABCL 26 p. 180.
77. Nirodbaran, op. cit., p. 987.
78. Id., p. 593.
79. Sri Aurobindo, op. cit., p. 38.
80. The quotations in the last two paragraphs are from Nirodbaran's *Correspondence With Sri Aurobindo*, to be found at the dates mentioned.
81. Sri Aurobindo, *On the Mother*, SABCL 25 p. 231.
82. Id., p. 230.
83. In *Mother India*, January 1989, p. 26.
84. *Mother India*, Jan. 1989, p. 26. For more details about Golconde see Georges Van Vrekhem, *Beyond Man* (Rupa Publishers, New Delhi), pp. 204 ff.

11. The Mother's War

1. Sri Aurobindo, *On Himself*, SABCL 26 p. 394.
2. Rhoda L. Le Cocq, *The Radical Thinkers – Heidegger and Sri Aurobindo*, p. 199.
3. *Collaboration*, 15th year, no. 2.
4. Nirodbaran, *Twelve Years With Sri Aurobindo*, pp. 3 ff.
5. Nirodbaran, *Correspondence With Sri Aurobindo*, pp. 36, 55.
6. Nirodbaran, *Talks With Sri Aurobindo* I, p. 44.
7. A.B. Purani, Evening *Talks With Sri Aurobindo*, p. 209.
8. K.D. Sethna, *Aspects of Sri Aurobindo*, p. 104.
9. Nirodbaran, *Twelve Years With Sri Aurobindo*, p. 123.
10. Nirodbaran, *Talks With Sri Aurobindo* I, p. 44.
11. *Glimpses of the Mother's Life* II, p. 157.
12. Nirodbaran, *Twelve Years With Sri Aurobindo*, p. 11.
13. In Nirodbaran, op. cit., p. 141.
14. Nirodbaran, *Talks With Sri Aurobindo* I, p. 44.
15. Nirodbaran, *Twelve Years With Sri Aurobindo*, pp. 72 ff.
16. Nirodbaran, *Talks With Sri Aurobindo* I, p. vi.
17. *More Vignettes of Sri Aurobindo and the Mother*, p. 157.
18. Nirodbaran, *Twelve Years With Sri Aurobindo*, pp. 20, 22, 30.
19. Id., pp. 30-31.
20. Sri Aurobindo, *On Himself*, SABCL 26 p. 393.
21. *Glimpses of the Mother's Life* II, p. 157.
22. Kimberley Cornish, *The Jew of Linz*, p. 154.
23. Louis Pauwels and Jacques Bergier, *Le matin des magiciens*, p. 253.
24. Nirodbaran, *Talks With Sri Aurobindo* III, p. 127.
25. The Mother, *Questions and Answers 1953*, CWM 5 pp. 378-79.
26. Nirodbaran, *Talks With Sri Aurobindo* I, p. 306.
27. Sri Aurobindo, *On Himself*, SABCL 26 p. 396.
28. In Kimberley Cornish, op. cit., pp. 163-64.
29. Nirodbaran, *Talks With Sri Aurobindo* III, p. 226.
30. Nirodbaran, *Talks With Sri Aurobindo* I, p. 365.
31. Nirodbaran, *Twelve Years With Sri Aurobindo*, p. 159.

32. Shyam Kumari (ed.), op. cit., p. 152.
33. Nirodbaran, *Talks With Sri Aurobindo* III, pp. 214-15.
34. Nirodbaran, *Talks With Sri Aurobindo* IV, p. 95.
35. Id., p. 121.
36. Nirodbaran, *Twelve Years With Sri Aurobindo*, pp. 126-27.
37. Nirodbaran, *Talks With Sri Aurobindo* III, p. 237.
38. Nirodbaran, *Twelve Years With Sri Aurobindo*, p. 154.
39. Id., pp. 148-49.
40. Id., p. 150.
41. Wilfried, *The Mother*, p. 62.
42. Sri Aurobindo, op. cit., p. 38.
43. Ibid.
44. Id., pp. 395-96.
45. Shyam Kumari (ed.), op. cit., p. 153.
46. Id., pp. 155-56.
47. Nirodbaran, *Talks With Sri Aurobindo* IV, p. 4.
48. Sri Aurobindo, op. cit., p. 39.
49. John Toland, *Adolf Hitler*, p. 835.
50. Nirodbaran, op. cit., p. 321.
51. Maggi Lidchi-Grassi, *The Light that Shone into the Dark Abyss*, p. 79.
52. See Shyam Kumari (ed.), op. cit., p. 152.
53. Id., p. 62.
54. Udar, 'Reminiscences', in *More Vignettes of Sri Aurobindo and the Mother*, p. 153; *Mother India*, April 1979, pp. 215-16; and *Mother's Agenda*, at the dates mentioned.
55. Nirodbaran, *Talks With Sri Aurobindo* IV, p. 36.
56. *Mother's Agenda II*, on the date mentioned (5 November 1961).
57. Nirodbaran, *Twelve Years With Sri Aurobindo*, p. 229.
58. Hugh Toye, *The Springing Tiger Subhash Chandra Bose*, p. 85.
59. Sri Aurobindo, op. cit., p. 39.
60. Nirodbaran, *Twelve Years With Sri Aurobindo*, p. 156.
61. *Words of the Mother* III, CWM 15:48.
62. The Mother, *Questions and Answers 1954*, CWM 6 p. 296.
63. Id., pp. 339-40.
64. The Mother, *Questions and Answers 1953*, CWM 5 pp. 286, 288.
65. Sri Aurobindo, *Savitri*, (Book III, Canto IV), SACW 33 p. 343.

12. Sri Aurobindo's Descent into Death

1. The Mother, *Words of the Mother* I, CWM 13 p. 4.
2. Sri Aurobindo, *The Mother*, SABCL 25 pp. 35-36.
3. The Mother, *Questions and Answers 1954*, CWM 6 pp. 291 ff.
4. The Mother, *Words of the Mother* I, CWM 13 p. 365.
5. Quoted in Nirodbaran, *Twelve Years With Sri Aurobindo*, pp. 162-63.
6. The Mother, *Questions and Answers 1956*, CWM 8 pp. 30-31.
7. The Mother, *Words of the Mother* I, CWM 13 p. 360.
8. Ibid.
9. Nirodbaran, *Twelve Years With Sri Aurobindo*, p. 161.
10. K.D. Sethna, *Aspects of Sri Aurobindo*, p. 221.
11. The Mother, op. cit., p. 368.
12. In India and Her Future, p. 3.
13. The Mother, op. cit., p. 380.
14. In *India and Her Future*, pp. 45 and 3.

15. The Mother, op. cit., pp. 361, 376.
16. In India and Her Future, p. 5.
17. K.D. Sethna, *Our Light and Delight*, p. 174.
18. Sri Aurobindo, *On Himself*, SABCL 26 p. 406.
19. Sri Aurobindo, op. cit., p. 400.
20. Nirodbaran, *Twelve Years With Sri Aurobindo*, p. 253.
21. *Mother's Agenda*, 18 Dec. 1971.
22. Both quotes in Sri Aurobindo, *On Himself*, SABCL 26 p. 414.
23. Sri Aurobindo, 'On Ideals and Progress' in *Essays in Philosophy & Yoga*, CWSA 13 p. 145.
24. Id., p. 143.
25. The Mother, *Questions and Answers 1957-58*, CWM 9 p. 190.
26. Id., p. 191.
27. Sri Aurobindo, op. cit., p. 60.
28. *Champaklal Speaks*, p. 91.
29. *Mother India*, January 1983, p. 39.
30. *Beautiful Vignettes of Sri Aurobindo and the Mother*, p. 170.
31. Mona Sarkar, *Sweet Mother* I, p. 22.
32. Nirodbaran, *Twelve Years With Sri Aurobindo*, p. 179.
33. In Sri Aurobindo, *Savitri*, CWSA 34 p. 727.
34. Nirodbaran, op. cit., p. 185.
35. Mona Sarkar, *Sweet Mother* I, pp. 26 ff. (originally spoken by the Mother in French and noted down from memory).
36. Id., pp. 31-32.
37. Nirodbaran, op. cit. p. 186.
38. Id., p. 266.
39. Ibid.
40. The Mother, *Words of the Mother I*, CWM 13 p. 9.
41. Nirodbaran, op. cit., p. 263.
42. Id., pp. 271-72.
43. Id., pp. 273-74.
44. Id., p. 275.
45. Prabhat Sanyal, 'A "Call" from Pondicherry', in Mother India, December 1991.
46. Ibid.
47. Nirodbaran, op. cit., p. 275.
48. Ibid.
49. Nirodbaran, op. cit., p. 278.
50. Kireet Joshi, *Sri Aurobindo and the Mother*, p. 109.
51. Prabhat Sanyal, op. cit.
52. *Sri Aurobindo Archives and Research*, December 1990, p. 225.
53. Id., pp. 226-27.
54. Nirodbaran, op. cit., p. 258.
55. Sri Aurobindo, *Collected Poems*, SABCL 5 p. 161.
56. Sri Aurobindo, *On Himself*, SABCL 26 p. 416.
57. Sri Aurobindo, *Collected Poems*, SABCL 5 p. 101.
58. K.D. Sethna, *The Passing of Sri Aurobindo*, p. 5.
59. Prabhat Sanyal, op. cit.
60. Kireet Joshi, *Sri Aurobindo and the Mother*, p. 103.
61. Id., p. 113.
62. The Mother, *Notes on the Way*, CWM 11 p. 328.
63. K.D. Sethna, *The Vision and Work of Sri Aurobindo*, p. 105.
64. Prabhat Sanyal, op. cit.

65. Rhoda P. Le Cocq, *The Radical Thinkers – Heidegger and Sri Aurobindo*, pp. 200 ff.
66. The Mother, *Words of the Mother I*, CWM 13 p. 9.
67. Sri Aurobindo, *Savitri*, Book III, Canto VIII, CWSA 33 pp. 231-32.
68. Id., p. 45.

13. The Yoga of the Body Cells

1. Sri Aurobindo, *Savitri*, Book VI, Canto II, CWSA 34 p. 460.
2. Kireet Joshi, *Sri Aurobindo and the Mother*, p. 118.
3. *Champaklal Speaks*, p. 251.
4. Kireet Joshi, op. cit., p. 118.
5. M.P. Pandit, *The Mother and her Mission*, p. 11.
6. Nirodbaran, *Twelve Years with Sri Aurobindo*, p. 66.
7. Nirodbaran, *Memorable Contacts with the Mother*, pp. 108, 48.
8. Sri Aurobindo, op.cit., Book VI, Canto II, CWSA 34.
9. The Mother, *On Education*, CWM 12 p. 243.
10. The Mother, id., p. 107.
11. The Mother, *Questions and Answers 1950-51*, CWM 4 p. 28
12. The Mother, *On Education*, CWM 12 p. 171.
13. The Mother, *Questions and Answers 1950-51*, CWM 4 p. 3.
14. Id., p. 383.
15. Sri Aurobindo, *The Supramental Manifestation upon Earth*, SABCL 16 p. 5.
16. The Mother, *On Thoughts and Aphorisms*, CWM 10 p. 30.
17. Nirodbaran, *Twelve Years with Sri Aurobindo*, pp. 80-81.
18. Id., p. 111.
19. Id., pp. 111-12.
20. Narayan Prasad, *Life in Sri Aurobindo Ashram*, p. 187.
21. *How They Came to Sri Aurobindo and the Mother 2*, p. 38.
22. The Mother, *On Education*, CWM 12 p. 16.
23. Id., p. 4.
24. The Mother, *Questions and Answers 1953*, CWM 5 p. 255.
25. The Mother, *Questions and Answers 1950-51*, CWM 4 p. 244.
26. The Mother, *Questions and Answers 1957-58*, CWM 9 p. 360.
27. The Mother, *On Education*, CWM 12 p. 232.
28. Id., p. 233.
29. The Mother, *Questions and Answers 1956*, CWM 8 p. 190.
30. The Mother, *On Education*, CWM 12 p. 101.
31. *A New Education for a New Consciousness*, Sri Aurobindo Ashram Trust.
32. Id., p. 147.
33. The Mother, *On Education*, CWM 12 p. 170.
34. Id., p. 432.
35. The Mother, op. cit., p. 110.
36. The Mother, *Notes on the Way*, CWM 11 p. 307.
37. The Mother, *On Education*, CWM 12 p. 111.
38. Id., p. 114.
39. Id., p. 117.
40. Sri Aurobindo, *The Synthesis of Yoga*, SABCL 20 p. 18.
41. In Sri Aurobindo, *The Hour of God*, SABCL 17 pp. 204-05.
42. The Mother, op. cit., p. 112.
43. Id., p. 167.
44. Id., p. 168.
45. Id., p. 319.

46. Ibid. p. 120.
47. Sri Aurobindo, *Savitri*, Book II Canto V, CWSA 33 p. 169.
48. Sri Aurobindo, *The Mother*, SABCL 25 p. 91.
49. Nirodbaran, *Correspondence with Sri Aurobindo*, p. 850.
50. *Words of the Mother* III, CWM 15 p. 314-15.
51. Id., p. 315.
52. Ibid.
53. Id., p. 316.
54. Ibid.
55. Id., p. 317.
56. The Mother, *Questions and Answers 1950-51*, CWM 4 pp. 157 ff.
57. The Mother, *Words of the Mother I*, CWM 13 p. 56.
58. The Mother, *Questions and Answers 1954*, CWM 6 p. 111.
59. Id., pp. 123-24.
60. Id., p. 140.
61. Id., pp. 391-92.
62. The Mother, *Words of the Mother III*, CWM 15 p. 298 ff.
63. The Mother, *Words of the Mother I*, CWM 13 p. 43.
64. The Mother, id., p. 30.
65. The Mother, id., p. 75.
66. See *An Unusual meeting with Sri Aurobindo*, in *Mother India*, December 1989.
67. *Selected Works of Jawaharlal Nehru* – External Affairs, p. 530.
68. Id., p. 531.
69. *Glimpses of the Mother's Life* II, pp. 265-66.
70. Id., p. 266.
71. Ibid.
72. Id., pp. 266-67.
73. Id., p. 267.
74. The Mother, *Questions and Answers 1950-51*, CWM 4 pp. 27 f.
75. Id., pp. 268-69.
76. Id., p. 156.
77. Id., pp. 140-41.

14. The Mother's Reincarnations

1. *Glimpses of the Mother's Life I*, p. 1.
2. Nirodbaran, *Correspondence with Sri Aurobindo*, p. 169.
3. See *The Mother's Agenda*, 4 November 1958.
4. *Arya*, vol. II, p. 240.
5. Sri Aurobindo, *On Himself*, SABCL 26 pp. 446 ff.
6. Sri Aurobindo, *On the Mother*, SABCL 25 p. 78.
7. The Mother, *Questions and Answers 1956*, CWM 8 p. 156.
8. The Mother, *On Thoughts and Aphorisms*, CWM 10 p. 89.
9. The Mother, id., pp. 89 ff.
10. Robert Bauval and Graham Hancock, *Keeper of Genesis*, p. 82 (quoted from the *Corpus Hermeticum).*
11. The Mother, *Questions and Answers 1950-51*, CWM 4 pp. 196-97.
12. Graham Philips, *Act of God*, p. 149.
13. Robert Bauval and Graham Hancock, op. cit., p. 206.
14. *Glimpses of the Mother's Life* I, pp. 9-10.
15. Jean Yoyotte, in *Historia*, p. 2.
16. Joyce Tyldesley, *Hatshepsut – The Female Pharaoh*, p. 1.

17. Id., p. 118.
18. Id., p. 167.
19. Id., p. 175.
20. The Mother, *Questions and Answers 1956*, CWM 8 pp. 155-56.
21. Arnold Berbers and Hendrik Beumer, *De Mummie van Nofretete*, p. 61.
22. Id., p. 63.
23. Id., p. 64.
24. Joyce Tyldesley, *op. cit.*, p. 32.
25. Graham Philips, *Act of God*, p. 159.
26. Personal communication.
27. See for instance *Mother's Agenda*, 30 June 1962.
28. See Marc Twain, *Saint Joan of Arc*, published in *Mother India*, December 1990.
29. Jules Michelet, *Jeanne d'Arc et autres textes*, pp. 37-38.
30. Regine Pernoud, *Jeanne d'Arc*, p. 44.
31. Georges and Andrée Duby, *Le procès de Jeanne d'Arc*, p. 17.
32. Louis Pauwels and Guy Breton, *Histoires magiques de l'Histoire de France*, p. 60.
33. See Mark Twain, op. cit.
34. *Champaklal Speaks*, p. 46.
35. Reminiscences of Udar, in *More Vignettes of Sri Aurobindo and the Mother*, p. 200.
36. Sri Aurobindo, *Letters on Yoga*, SABCL 22 p. 408.
37. Kenneth J. Atchity (ed.), *Renaissance Reader*, p. 135.
38. Roger D. Masters, *Fortune is a River*, p. 105.
39. Id., pp. 106-7.
40. See e.g. *Mother's Agenda*, 30 June 1962.
41. The Mother, *Questions and Answers 1950-51*, CWM 4 pp. 150-51.
42. J.N. Neale, *Queen Elizabeth I*, p. 22.
43. In *The New Encyclopaedia Britannica*, vol. 18, p. 244.
44. J.N. Neale, op. cit., p. 78.
45. Id., p. 255.
46. Roy Strong, *The Cult of Elizabeth*, p. 47.
47. J.N. Neale, op.cit., pp. 209, 218.
48. See *Mother's Agenda*, 13 February 1962.
49. See e.g. *Mother's Agenda*, 15 July 1967.
50. Vincent Cronin, *Catherine, Empress of All the Russias*, pp. 140, 148.
51. Id., pp. 176, 201, 307.
52. Sujata Nahar, *The Mother's Chronicles I*, p. 151.
53. See *Mother's Agenda*, 30 June 1962.

15. The Manifestation of the Supramental

1. Sri Aurobindo, *On Himself*, SABCL 26 p. 469.
2. The Mother, *Questions and Answers 1956*, CWM 9 p. 13.
3. The Mother, *Questions and Answers 1954*, CWM 6 p. 516.
4. Id., p. 453.
5. Id., pp. 459-60.
6. *Mother's Agenda*, 20 August 1960.
7. The Mother, *Questions and Answers 1955*, CWM 7 pp. 321-2.
8. Id., pp. 323-24.
9. Id., pp. 326-27.
10. Id., pp. 330, 333.
11. The Mother, *Questions and Answers 1956*, CWM 8 pp. 10, 11.
12. Satprem, *Mère II*, p. 55.

13. The Mother, *Words of the Mother III*, CWM 15 p. 102.
14. K.D. Sethna, *Aspects of Sri Aurobindo*, p. 120.
15. Id., p. 115.
16. The Mother, *Words of the Mother III*, CWM 15 p. 103.
17. The Mother, *Prayers and Meditations*, CWM 1 p. 273.
18. The Mother, *Words of the Mother III*, CWM 15 p. 104.
19. *Mother India*, February 1974.
20. K.D. Sethna, op. cit., p. 120.
21. Nirodbaran, Correspondence with Sri Aurobindo, p. 197.
22. The Mother, *Questions and Answers 1950-51*, CWM 4 p. 223.
23. The Mother, *Words of the Mother III*, CWM 15 p. 110.
24. K.D. Sethna, op. cit., pp. 117-18.
25. Id., p. 105.
26. *Champaklal's Treasures*, p. 96.
27. The Mother, *Questions and Answers 1956*, CWM 8 pp. 127 ff.
28. Id., p. 263.
29. The Mother, *Questions and Answers 1957-58*, CWM 9 p. 45.
30. Id., p. 146.
31. Id., pp. 146-47.
32. Id., pp. 149 ff.
33. Id., pp. 150-51.
34. Sri Aurobindo, *Savitri*, Book I Canto IV, CWSA 33 p. 50.
35. The Mother, *Questions and Answers 1957-58*, CWM 9 p. 245.
36. Id., pp. 34 ff.
37. Id., pp. 247-48.
38. Id., pp. 272 ff.
39. The Mother, *Words of the Mother III*, CWM 15 pp. 386-87.
40. The Mother, *Questions and Answers 1957-58*, CWM 9 pp. 313-14.
41. Id., p. 313.
42. Id., p. 314.
43. Id., pp. 314-15.
44. Id., pp. 372-73.
45. Words of the Mother III, CWM 15 pp. 381 ff.
46. The Mother, op.cit., p. 387.

16. What Is to Be Done Is Done

1. Sri Aurobindo, *Savitri*, Book XI, Canto I, CWSA 34 p. 700.
2. The Mother, *Questions and Answers 1957-58*, CWM 9 p. 411.
3. Ibid.
4. *Champaklal Speaks*, p. 107.
5. *Mother's Agenda*, 24-25 July 1959.
7. The Mother, *Questions and Answers 1955*, CWM 7 p. 330.
8. Id., p. 14.
9. The Mother, *Notes on the Way*, CWM 11 p. 14.
10. Id., p. 16.
11. Sri Aurobindo, *On Mother*, SABCL 25 p. 384.
12. The Mother, op. cit., p. 51.
13. Sri Aurobindo, *The Synthesis of Yoga*, SABCL 20 p. 39.
14. The Mother, op. cit., p. 2.
15. Id., p. 167.
16. Id., p. 321.

17. The Mother, *Questions and Answers 1956*, CWM 8 pp. 399-400.
18. The Mother, *Words of the Mother II*, CWM 14 p. 67.
19. The Mother, *Questions and Answers 1956*, CWM 8 p. 398.
20. Nirodbaran, *Correspondence with Sri Aurobindo*, p. 1001.
21. The Mother, *Questions and Answers 1953*, CWM 5 p. 350.
22. Sri Aurobindo, *The Life Divine*, SABCL 18 p. 242.
23. The Mother, *Questions and Answers 1953*, CWM 5 p. 60-61.
24. Mona Sarkar, *Sweet Mother II*, p. 19.
25. The Mother, *Notes on the Way*, CWM 11 pp. 46-47.
26. Sri Aurobindo, *The Synthesis of Yoga*, SABCL 20 p. 71.
27. The Mother, *Questions and Answers 1953*, CWM 5 pp. 305-6.
28. The Mother, *Notes on the Way*, CWM 16 p. 4.
29. Id., p. 16.
30. Id., p. 33.
31. Ibid.
32. Id., p. 17.
33. The Mother, *On Thoughts and Aphorisms*, CWM 10 p. 149.
34. Nirodbaran, *Talks with Sri Aurobindo* I, p. 180.
35. K.D. Sethna, *The Sun and the Rainbow*, pp. 196-97.
36. Sri Aurobindo, *Savitri*, Book VI, Canto two, CWSA 34 p. 461.
37. Notes on the way, CWM 11 p. 1.
38. See *Mother's Agenda* on that date (24.1.1961).
39. See in this context Nirodbaran, *Memorable Moments with the Mother*, pp. 106 ff.
40. Words of the Mother III, CWM 15 pp. 408 ff.
41. Id., pp. 411-12.

17. The Passage Perilous

1. Sri Aurobindo, *Savitri*, Book VII, Canto VI, CWSA 34 p. 536-37.
2. *Mother's Agenda*, 12 June 1962.
3. Id., 24 May 1969.
4. Id., 9 March 1966.
5. Id., 7 August 1963.
6. Nirodbaran, *Correspondence with Sri Aurobindo*, p. 673.
7. The Mother, *Notes on the Way*, CWM 11 p. 109.
8. Id., p. 94.
9. Id., pp. 95-96.
10. Id., pp. 109-10.
11. Id., p. 94.
12. Id., p. 95.
13. Id., p. 100.
13a. *Mother's Agenda*, 24 June 1967.
14. Op. cit., 16 October 1963.
15. The Mother, *Notes on the Way*, CWM 11 p. 74.
16. The Mother, *Questions and Answers 1955*, CWM 7 pp. 146-47.
17. *Mother's Agenda*, 10 July 1968.
18. See e.g. *Mother's Agenda*, 4 August 1962.
19. The Mother, *Notes on the Way*, CWM 11 p. 57-59.
20. Id., p. 195.
21. Translated by Shree Purohit Swami and W.B. Yeats.
22. Id., p. 74.
23. *Mother's Agenda*, 20 July 1963.

24. Ibid.
25. Id., p. 31.
26. Id., p. 73.
27. Id., p. 86.
28. Id., 24 August 1963.
29. The Mother, *Words of the Mother III*, CWM 15 p. 66.
30. The Mother, *Notes on the Way*, CWM 11 p. 99.
31. Ibid.
32. *Mother's Agenda*, 30 November 1962.
33. Id., 25 September 1965.
34. The Mother, Words *of the Mother I*, CWM 13 p. 129.
35. *More Vignettes of Sri Aurobindo and the Mother*, p. 179.
36. Id., pp. 192 ff.
37. Nirodbaran, *Memorable Contacts with the Mother*, pp. 114-15.
38. The Mother, op. cit., p. 207.
39. Auroville References in *Mother's Agenda*, p. 27.
40. Id., p. 34.
41. The Mother, *Words of the Mother I*, CWM 13 p. 197.
42. The Mother, *On Education*, CWM 12 pp. 91 ff.
43. *The Mother on Auroville*, p. 64.
44. M.P. Pandit, *The Mother and her Mission*, pp. 125 ff.
45. Auroville References in *Mother's Agenda*, p. 10.
46. Sri Aurobindo, *The Synthesis of Yoga*, SABCL 20 pp. 502-03.
47. Frances A. Yates, *Giordano Bruno and the Hermetic Tradition*, p. 367.
48. Gareth Knight, *Magic and the Western Mind*, pp. 96 ff.
49. Wilfried, *The Mother*, pp. 88-89.
50. Facsimile in W.M. Sullivan, *The Dawning of Auroville*, p. 46.
51. Satprem, *Mère II*, p. 547.
52. The Mother, *Words of the Mother I*, CWM 13 p. 199.
53. Auroville References in *Mother's Agenda*, p. 65.
54. The Mother, op.cit. p. 199.
55. W.M. Sullivan, *op. cit.*, pp. 53-54.
56. *The Mother on Auroville*, p. 16.
57. Id., p. 198.
58. *Id.*, p. 16.
59. The Mother, op.cit., p. 197.
60. Auroville References in *Mother's Agenda*, p. 107.
61. *The Mother on Auroville*, p. 8.
62. *Words of Mother I*, CWM 13 p. 212.
63. *The Mother on Auroville*, p. 15.
64. Id., p. 13.
65. *Mother's Agenda*, 22 May 1968.
66. Luc Ferry and Alain Renaut, *La pensée 68*, p. 111.
67. Id., p. 125.

18. The New Body

1. *Mother's Agenda*, 29 November 1969.
2. The Mother, *Notes on the Way*, CWM 11 pp. 117-18.
3. Id., p. 118.
4. Id., p. 124.
5. Id., p. 122.

6. Id., pp. 116-17,
7. Sri Aurobindo, *On Himself,* SABCL 26 p. 152.
8. The Mother, op.cit., p. 123.
9. This quotation and the following ones in this section: The Mother, op.cit., pp. 148 ff.
10. The Mother, op.cit., p. 178.
11. *Mother's Agenda*, 1 August 1970.
12. Major General K.K. Tewari, *A Soldier's Voyage of Self Discovery*, p. 136.
13. The Mother, *Words of the Mother* I, CWM 13 p. 359.
14. The Mother, *Notes on the Way*, CWM 11 p. 252.
15. The Mother, *Words of the Mother* I, CWM 13 p. 186.
16. Id., pp. 186 ff.
17. Sri Aurobindo, *Savitri*, Book III, Canto VI, CWSA 33 p. 343.
18. *Beautiful Vignettes*, p. 124.
19. The Mother, *Notes on the Way*, CWM 11 p. 118 (footnote).
20. Id., p. 281.
21. Id., pp. 238-39.
22. Id., pp. 174-75.
23. The Mother, *Words of the Mother* I, CWM 13 p. 229.
24. *Matrimandir Journal*, no. 2, 1999, p. 3.
25. Both quotations: *The Mother*, op.cit., p. 229.
26. Sri Aurobindo, *The Synthesis of Yoga*, CWM 24 p. 780.
27. Sri Aurobindo, *Savitri*, Book VII, Canto I, CWSA 34 p. 472.
28. The Mother, *On Thoughts and Aphorisms*, CWM 10 p. 77.
29. Nirodbaran, *Memorable Contacts with the Mother*, pp. 125-26.
30. The Mother, *Notes on the Way*, CWM 11 p. 245ff passim.
31. The Mother, op. cit., pp. 307-8.
32. *Mother's Agenda*, 14 March 1970.
33. Id., 9 April 1969.
34. The Mother, op.cit., p. 301.
35. Id., pp. 302ff.
36. Id., p. 221.
37. Pranab Kumar Bhattacharya, *I Remember*, pp. 313ff.
38. Shyam Sundar, *En route*, p. 41.
39. Pranab Kumar Bhattacharya, op. cit., p. 320.
40. Id., *passim.*
41. Personal communication.
42. Nirodbaran, *Memorable Moments with the Mother*, p. 165.
43. *Mother India*, November 1986, pp. 674-75.
44. The Mother, *Notes on the Way*, CWM 11 p. 183.
45. *Mother's Agenda*, 26 April 1972.
46. The Mother, op.cit., p. 145.
47. *Mother's Agenda*, 19 July 1969.
48. Sri Aurobindo, *Collected Poems*, SABCL 5 pp. 61-62.
49. Sri Aurobindo, *Savitri*, Book I, Canto IV, CWSA 33 p. 55.

Made in the USA
Middletown, DE
14 September 2022